EDITORS

Allan G. Bogue   UNIVERSITY OF WISCONSIN

Thomas D. Phillips   UNIVERSITY OF WISCONSIN

James E. Wright   DARTMOUTH COLLEGE

The WEST of the

AMERICAN PEOPLE

F. E. PEACOCK PUBLISHERS, INC.
ITASCA, ILLINOIS

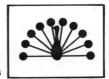

CONTENTS

INTRODUCTION

Y EARS BEFORE that cheerful publicist Captain John Smith and his companions began the successful occupation of Virginia, Richard Hakluyt presented the case for colonizing the New World in *The Discourse on the Western Planting*. Enthused by the findings of seafaring adventurers, he argued that Englishmen could find or grow raw materials there, discover precious minerals perhaps, provide a market for English goods, and furnish work for a growing merchant marine. Here too were Indians to be christianized and lands to be saved from the Roman Catholics. Later Hakluyt was a member of that London Company which sent Smith to the New World in 1606. So, if brave men sailed westward after 1450 and began a new era in the history of western civilization, their voyages influenced the speculations and writings of scholars and were in turn influenced by them. From the new colonies of England along the eastern coast of North America, men continued "westering"; exploring, trading with the natives, and colonizing the interior of the great continent. The tradition of the westward movement in American history, therefore, is as old as the original settlements and the written exegesis even older. Despite the importance of the colonial heritage, limitations of space have led the editors to restrict the readings and commentary in this volume to the national experience.

During much of the history of the United States a great reservoir of natural resources lay beyond the edge of the organized settlements, challenging an industrious and acquisitive people to explore it and to locate the most attractive and valuable features. Thereafter development involved settlement of greater or lesser density. But settlement and development in themselves posed problems or challenges to the Anglo-Americans. Their representatives in government must perfect a system of removing the title to the lands of the original inhabitants so that the newcomers could use them in relative peace. Such cross-cultural diplomacy was most effective, the Anglo-Americans discovered, if they maintained troops to reinforce it. The peculiar requirements of military duty on the Indian frontier placed their stamp upon the American military establishment, but this role was not the army's only function. It was used in many other ways as well to aid in the conquest of the West.

Not only must the western lands be delivered from Indian title, believed the new Americans, they must be managed so as to contribute most effectively to the development of the nation. Until the end of the nineteenth century most of our citizens approved of a system of land disposal in which the government transferred ownership of the public lands rapidly and cheaply to individuals and corporations. But if those who acquired title to western resources were to remain satisfied citizens, they must have a voice in their own government. So the Founding Fathers created the territorial system and later generations of politicians modified it to meet the changing circumstances of the nineteenth century. They were not completely successful; the territorial system almost shattered in eastern Kansas and the nation with it. But nationalism prevailed and since the Civil War, Americans have brought almost half of the nation's land area successfully through the territorial stage of government.

If settlers were to push deeper and deeper into the interior of North America, Americans must improve their lines of communication and use industrial technology to better transportation. Road, canal, steamboat and railroad all contributed to that end, while individual competed with individual in exploiting the opportunities of the new regions, town strove with town, and city fought with city, as their businessmen tried to win the lion's share of local and interregional trade. In shaping western economic growth, Americans faced the greatest and most perplexing challenge of all.

In response to the challenges of western space and raw resources and out of the Anglo-American value systems and technological sophistication, there emerged solutions. Whatever the human suffering involved, and there was much, the Indian policy achieved its goals, much of the western land was distributed to the people of the nation, the territorial system did provide a framework of government in the new regions and Americans did successfully apply the technology of the time to the raw riches of the West. The results were entered on census rolls which showed the growth of population beyond the Appalachians, in the registers of the patent office, on the statute books of territorial, state and federal government and in districts filled with productive farms and profitable industries.

If we change focus and examine the initial utilization of the West's resources, we discover various patterns of exploitation—the fur trade, the mining frontier, the lumber industry, the grazing empire and the extension of intensive agriculture, among others. The Americans involved in these processes of exploitation confronted their challenges, or problems, as well. The history of each pattern of exploitation is studded with innovation, either institutional or technological in nature, although frontier Americans built upon the heritage of their past, as did residents of longer settled regions. And western developments ultimately contributed to the modern industries that replaced the frontier patterns. They were part of the seamless web of change which produced modern America.

There was another dimension to the frontier process as well. It was a region of community building, of social process, where people came and established institutions of government, schools, colleges, churches and a great variety of less formal systems of social relationship. In the West community and social structure developed under the guidance of leaders recruited in diverse ways: some, sent to the frontier by the federal government; some, representing the economic interests that supplied or financed the dominant industry; others, selected from the population that had come of its own accord to seek fortune in the new communities.

By most definitions the United States is no longer a frontier nation. Yet evidence of the frontier process remains. The North American Indian, the "Vanishing American," did not in the end disappear but remains in numbers that approach those of his ancestors in the age of Columbus. Nor did the government divest itself completely of the public domain. Millions of acres of public lands remain under the administration of federal agencies and their future is no less interesting to large numbers of Americans than was the case in 1800. And the West perhaps lives on in more subtle ways in American life and culture. Some believe that our institutions of government, school, church and home, our approach to the problems of business and social life, and our value systems still reflect to some extent the fact that we have been a frontier nation. But the analytical tools of the historian have been unequal to the task of proving the proposition irrefutably. Scraps of corroborative evidence abound; the argument rings true to us intuitively. Historians push beyond firm footing, however, when they suggest that the frontier was the only major influence shaping American development, institutions and character until very recently in our national existence. And historians who disregard the frontier in explaining the American nation are as wrong, we believe, as they who consider it alone. In this reader we have tried to present the frontier theme in broad perspective, to show it as its better historians have seen it, not dominant in American history perhaps, but interwoven as it was in the personal and institutional life of the nation, as truly the West of the American People.

In order to include as many exciting ideas as possible, we have reluctantly abridged many of the selections printed in this volume. None is more keenly aware than are we that the impact of writing may be changed when supporting material is removed. We have, however, worked conscientiously to preserve the authors' central ideas and we have read each selection at least three times with this in mind. Excisions are marked by ellipses. We do, however, urge all who use this book to read the originals of those readings that seem useful or interesting to them.

This reader developed directly from the teaching needs of one of the editors, who has found it increasingly difficult to provide readings for his class in History of the American West that combine a judicious selection of enduring old and interesting new viewpoints. Two young men who were teaching the undergraduate discussion sections in the course were willing to bring their knowledge of undergraduate needs into the enterprise. Should any reader be curious concerning the division of labor among the editors, Thomas Phillips prepared the initial drafts of the introductory materials in Chapters IV and XII, James E. Wright wrote the editorial continuity in Chapters XI and XIV and Allan G. Bogue wrote the remaining introductions. The editors shared the other duties involved in the preparation of this book. All three are deeply grateful to the many individuals who helped in its preparation.

PART ONE

Challenges for
a Free Land Nation

CHAPTER I

Some Theories
of Frontier Influence

T HE COURSES in the History of the American West which are taught
in a large number of colleges and universities are rooted in the teachings
of Frederick Jackson Turner, although they appear today under various
descriptive titles and differ greatly in organization and emphasis. When
the disarming young Wisconsin historian announced at the meeting of
the American Historical Association in 1893 that, "The existence of an
area of free land, its continuous recession, and the advance of American
settlement westward, explain American development," he proclaimed a
doctrine that his students and other followers subsequently made the best
known of all theories of the development of American political, economic
and social institutions. Had not Turner pictured the impact of the westward movement on America so vividly and so poetically, historians might
have paid much less attention to a theory that has inspired a great deal
of interesting and useful history as well as sterile antiquarianism.

The idea that the West was a major factor in American development
was not original, of course, with Turner; indeed we may never identify
all of the early disseminators of the doctrine. English Conservatives enun-
ciated a version of the frontier hypothesis while they fought against extension of the suffrage during the mid-nineteenth century. They argued
that free land in the United States allowed the discontented and oppressed
of the older settlements to flee their troubles and shed their grievances
while developing a new farm on the frontier. Free land in the United
States, they argued, produced a nation of property holders and this in
turn was reflected in political equality. Popular rule therefore was not
the gamble in America that it would be in England. Publishing his
famous tract, *Progress and Poverty*, 14 years before Turner's address
of 1893, Henry George argued, in rhetoric very similar to that of the
young academic, "This public domain . . . the enormous common to
which the faces of the energetic were always turned, has been the great

fact that, since the days when the first settlements began to fringe the Atlantic Coast, has formed our national character and colored our national thought." Turner, we now believe, found the free land or frontier hypothesis in the work of the Italian political economist, Achille Loria. Even as he presented his version of the doctrine to academia, pressure groups in the country were arguing that the disappearance of the frontier justified the restriction of immigration, and also made it unnecessary for the government to assist the depressed farmers of the nation, since the number of farms in the United States would not greatly increase in the future and the surging industry of the nation would guarantee larger markets and higher prices for agricultural goods.

Such facts should not diminish our respect for Turner, because it was he who fitted the theory to our history with an imagination and richness previously unknown and it was he and his students who gave the theory academic respectability in America. Unfortunately many of his followers presented the history of the West inflexibly in Turnerian terms. When critics of the frontier hypothesis became common during the 1920's and 1930's, they often stressed the omissions, inconsistencies and contradictions in Turner's writing and seemed to suggest that to refute Turner's interpretation of western America was to refute the importance of the West in American history. Although many who raised the war whoop tried for a bang and settled for a whimper, it became clear that of itself the frontier did not explain America, even in those periods when the movement to the frontier was greatest. And increasingly was this true as America became more and more an industrial nation.

During this last generation some historians have been trying to rethink the role of the frontier in American history. Just as Turner was influenced by the social science theories of his time, these scholars have tried to bring new perspectives to the study of the American West. In this first chapter we present selections from some work of this sort following Turner's classic statement and Walter Prescott Webb's environmental analysis of the frontier process on the Great Plains. These will, we hope, serve as useful background for the chapters to follow.

·1·

FREDERICK JACKSON TURNER

The Significance of the
Frontier in American History

Perhaps no work of comparable length by an American historian has influenced so many scholars and students as the
paper from which this reading is taken. Emphasizing the importance of the frontier in American development, it also
stressed the significance of sectionalism, a concept which
continues to be of great utility in understanding our political
and economic life. Like all historical writing, the article reflected its era, and Turner's use of the theories of social
evolution current in the late nineteenth century is particularly
striking.

... Up to our own day American history has been in a large degree the
history of the colonization of the Great West. The existence of an area of
free land, its continuous recession, and the advance of American settlement westward, explain American development.

Behind institutions, behind constitutional forms and modifications, lie
the vital forces that call these organs into life and shape them to meet
changing conditions. The peculiarity of American institutions is, the fact
that they have been compelled to adapt themselves to the changes of an
expanding people—to the changes involved in crossing a continent, in
winning a wilderness, and in developing at each area of this progress out
of the primitive economic and political conditions of the frontier into
the complexity of city life. . . .

All peoples show development; the germ theory of politics has been
sufficiently emphasized. In the case of most nations, however, the development has occurred in a limited area; and if the nation has expanded, it
has met other growing peoples whom it has conquered. But in the case
of the United States we have a different phenomenon. Limiting our attention to the Atlantic coast, we have the familiar phenomenon of the evolu-

SOURCE: Abridged from Frederick J. Turner, "The Significance of the Frontier in
American History," *Report of the American Historical Association* (Washington,
D. C., 1894), 199-227.

tion of institutions in a limited area, such as the rise of representative government; the differentiation of simple colonial governments into complex organs; the progress from primitive industrial society, without division of labor, up to manufacturing civilization. But we have in addition to this a recurrence of the process of evolution in each western area reached in the process of expansion. Thus American development has exhibited not merely advance along a single line, but a return to primitive conditions on a continually advancing frontier line, and a new development for that area. American social development has been continually beginning over again on the frontier. This perennial rebirth, this fluidity of American life, this expansion westward with its new opportunities, its continuous touch with the simplicity of primitive society, furnish the forces dominating American character. The true point of view in the history of this nation is not the Atlantic coast, it is the great West. . . .

In this advance, the frontier is the outer edge of the wave—the meeting point between savagery and civilization. . . . The American frontier is sharply distinguished from the European frontier—a fortified boundary line running through dense populations. The most significant thing about the American frontier is, that it lies at the hither edge of free land. In the census reports it is treated as the margin of that settlement which has a density of two or more to the square mile. The term is an elastic one, and for our purposes does not need sharp definition. We shall consider the whole frontier belt, including the Indian country and the outer margin of the "settled area" of the census reports. . . .

In the settlement of America we have to observe how European life entered the continent, and how America modified and developed that life and reacted on Europe. Our early history is the study of European germs developing in an American environment. Too exclusive attention has been paid by institutional students to the Germanic origins, too little to the American factors. The frontier is the line of most rapid and effective Americanization. The wilderness masters the colonist. It finds him a European in dress, industries, tools, modes of travel, and thought. It takes him from the railroad car and puts him in the birch canoe. It strips off the garments of civilization and arrays him in the hunting shirt and the moccasin. It puts him in the log cabin of the Cherokee and Iroquois and runs an Indian palisade around him. Before long he has gone to planting Indian corn and plowing with a sharp stick; he shouts the war cry and takes the scalp in orthodox Indian fashion. In short, at the frontier the environment is at first too strong for the man. He must accept the conditions which it furnishes, or perish, and so he fits himself into the Indian clearings and follows the Indian trails. Little by little he transforms the wilderness, but the outcome is not the old Europe, not simply the development of Germanic germs, any more than the first phenomenon was a case of reversion to the Germanic mark. The fact is, that here is a new product that is American. At first, the frontier was the Atlantic coast. It was the frontier of Europe in a very real sense. Moving westward, the frontier became more and more American. As successive terminal moraines result from successive glaciations, so each frontier leaves its traces behind it, and when it becomes a settled area the region still partakes of the frontier characteristics. Thus the advance of the frontier has meant a steady movement away from the influence of Europe, a steady growth of independence on American lines. And to study this advance, the men who grew up under these conditions, and the political, economic, and social results of it, is to study the really American part of our history. . . .

From decade to decade distinct advances of the frontier occurred. . . . In these successive frontiers we find natural boundary lines which have served to mark and to affect the characteristics of the frontiers, namely: The "fall line"; the Alleghany Mountains; the Mississippi; the Missouri, where its direction approximates north and south; the line of the arid lands, approximately the ninety-ninth meridian; and the Rocky Mountains. The fall line marked the frontier of the seventeenth century; the Alleghanies that of the eighteenth; the Mississippi that of the first quarter of the nineteenth; the Missouri that of the middle of this century (omitting the California movement); and the belt of the Rocky Mountains and the arid tract, the present frontier. Each was won by a series of Indian wars.

At the Atlantic frontier one can study the germs of processes repeated at each successive frontier. We have the complex European life sharply precipitated by the wilderness into the simplicity of primitive conditions. The first frontier had to meet its Indian question, its question of the disposition of the public domain, of the means of intercourse with older settlements, of the extension of political organization, of religious and educational activity. And the settlement of these and similar questions for one frontier served as a guide for the next. . . .

But with all these similarities there are essential differences, due to the place element and the time element. It is evident that the farming frontier of the Mississippi Valley presents different conditions from the mining frontier of the Rocky Mountains. The frontier reached by the Pacific Railroad, surveyed into rectangles, guarded by the United States Army, and recruited by the daily immigrant ship, moves forward at a swifter pace and in a different way than the frontier reached by the birch canoe or the pack horse. . . . Each of these areas has had an influence in our economic and political history; the evolution of each into a higher stage has worked political transformations. But what constitutional historian has made any adequate attempt to interpret political facts by the light of these social areas and changes?

The Atlantic frontier was compounded of fisherman, fur-trader, miner, cattle-raiser, and farmer. Excepting the fisherman, each type of industry was on the march toward the West, impelled.by an irresistible attraction. Each passed in successive waves across the continent. Stand at Cumberland Gap and watch the procession of civilization, marching single file —the buffalo following the trail to the salt springs, the Indian, the fur-trader and hunter, the cattle-raiser, the pioneer farmer—and the frontier has passed by. Stand at South Pass in the Rockies a century later and see the same procession with wider intervals between. The unequal rate of advance compels us to distinguish the frontier into the trader's frontier, the rancher's frontier, or the miner's frontier, and the farmer's frontier. . . .

From the time the mountains rose between the pioneer and the seaboard, a new order of Americanism arose. The West and the East began to get out of touch of each other. The settlements from the sea to the mountains kept connection with the rear and had a certain solidarity. But the over-mountain men grew more and more independent. The East took a narrow view of American advance, and nearly lost these men. Kentucky and Tennessee history bears abundant witness to the truth of this statement. The East began to try to hedge and limit westward expansion. Though Webster could declare that there were no Alleghanies in his politics, yet in politics in general they were a very solid factor.

❖   ❖   ❖

The exploitation of the beasts took hunter and trader to the west, the exploitation of the grasses took the rancher west, and the exploitation of the virgin soil of the river valleys and prairies attracted the farmer. Good soils have been the most continuous attraction to the farmer's frontier. . . .

The farmer's advance came in a distinct series of waves. In Peck's *New Guide to the West,* published in Boston in 1837, occurs this suggestive passage:

Generally, in all the western settlements, three classes, like the waves of the ocean, have rolled one after the other. First comes the pioneer, who depends for the subsistence of his family chiefly upon the natural growth of vegetation, called the "range," and the proceeds of hunting. . . .

The next class of emigrants purchase the lands, add field to field, clear out the roads, throw rough bridges over the streams, put up hewn log houses with glass windows and brick or stone chimneys, occasionally plant orchards, build mills, schoolhouses, court-houses, etc., and exhibit the picture and forms of plain, frugal, civilized life.

Another wave rolls on. The men of capital and enterprise come. The settler is ready to sell out and take the advantage of the rise in property, push farther into the interior and become, himself, a man of capital and enterprise in turn. . . .

A portion of the two first classes remain stationary amidst the general movement, improve their habits and conditions, and rise in the scale of society. . . .

Having now roughly outlined the various kinds of frontiers, and their modes of advance, chiefly from the point of view of the frontier itself, we may next inquire what were the influences on the East and on the Old World.

First, we note that the frontier promoted the formation of a composite nationality for the American people. The coast was preponderantly English, but the later tides of continental immigration flowed across to the free lands. . . . In the crucible of the frontier the immigrants were Americanized, liberated, and fused into a mixed race, English in neither nationality or characteristics. The process has gone on from the early days to our own.

In another way the advance of the frontier decreased our dependence on England. . . . Before long the frontier created a demand for merchants. As it retreated from the coast it became less and less possible for England to bring her supplies directly to the consumer's wharfs, and carry away staple crops, and staple crops began to give way to diversified agriculture for a time. . . .

It is safe to say that the legislation with regard to land, tariff, and internal improvements—the American system of the nationalizing Whig party—was conditioned on frontier ideas and needs. But it was not merely in legislative action that the frontier worked against the sectionalism of the coast. The economic and social characteristics of the frontier worked against sectionalism. . . . But the most important effect of the frontier has been in the promotion of democracy here and in Europe. As has been indicated, the frontier is productive of individualism. Complex society is precipitated by the wilderness into a kind of primitive organization based on the family. The tendency is anti-social. It produces antipathy to control, and particularly to any direct control. . . . The frontier individualism has from the beginning promoted democracy.

The frontier States that came into the Union in the first quarter of a century of its existence came in with democratic suffrage provisions, and had reactive effects of the highest importance upon the older States whose peoples were being attracted there. An extension of the franchise became essential. It was *western* New York that forced an extension of suffrage in the constitutional convention of that State in 1821; and it was *western* Virginia that compelled the tide-water region to put a more liberal suffrage provision in the constitution framed in 1830, and to give to the frontier region a more nearly proportionate representation with the tide-water aristocracy. The rise of democracy as an effective force in the nation came in with western preponderance under Jackson and William Henry Harrison, and it meant the triumph of the frontier —with all of its good and with all of its evil elements. . . .

So long as free land exists, the opportunity for a competency exists, and economic power secures political power. But the democracy born of free land, strong in selfishness and individualism, intolerant of administrative experience and education, and pressing individual liberty beyond its proper bounds, has its dangers as well as its benefits. Individualism in America has allowed a laxity in regard to governmental affairs which has rendered possible the spoils system and all the manifest evils that follow from the lack of a highly developed civic spirit. . . .

From the conditions of frontier life came intellectual traits of profound importance. The works of travelers along each frontier from colonial days onward describe certain common traits, and these traits have, while softening down, still persisted as survivals in the place of their origin, even when a higher social organization succeeded. The result is that to the frontier the American intellect owes its striking characteristics. That coarseness and strength combined with acuteness and inquisitiveness; that practical, inventive turn of mind, quick to find expedients; that masterful grasp of material things, lacking in the artistic but powerful to effect great ends; that restless, nervous energy; that dominant individualism, working for good and for evil, and withal that buoyancy and exuberance which comes with freedom—these are traits of the frontier, or traits called out elsewhere because of the existence of the frontier. . . . What the Mediterranean Sea was to the Greeks, breaking the bond of custom, offering new experiences, calling out new institutions and activities, that, and more, the ever retreating frontier has been to the United States directly, and to the nations of Europe more remotely. And now, four centuries from the discovery of America, at the end of a hundred years of life under the Constitution, the frontier has gone, and with its going has closed the first period of American history.

·2·

WALTER PRESCOTT WEBB

The Great Plains and the
Industrial Revolution

Although he maintained that his ideas were not rooted in
Turner's work, Walter Prescott Webb also emphasized the
great importance of the environment in shaping life and institutions, more unreservedly at times indeed than the older
scholar. But in contrast to many historians of the American
West, who presented a picture of progressive adaptation,
frontier by frontier, Webb argued that a particular region,
the Great Plains, had been uniquely powerful in forcing
Americans to adapt to its unusual features.

The Great Plains environment of the United States may be best defined
in terms of its three major characteristics, of topography, vegetation, and
rainfall:

1. It exhibits a comparatively level surface of great extent.
2. It is a treeless land, an unforested area.
3. It is a region where rainfall is insufficient for the ordinary intensive
agriculture common to lands of a humid climate.

The presence of all three characteristics forms a true plain, of two, a
modified plain. The Great Plains environment comprises one true plains
area plus two modified plains regions. The true plains or *the plains*
occupy a central position, forming a broad belt extending from the Panhandle of Texas northward to Kansas and Nebraska. This region, properly
called the High Plains, is flanked on either side by a modified plain. To
the east lies an irregular V-shaped area, narrow in Texas and broadening
toward the north, which is devoid of timber and level, but it is not arid.
This is the prairie country, named by Van Hise the Prairie Plains. To
the west lies another modified plain which extends from the eastern
foothills of the Rocky Mountains to the Pacific slope, commonly called
the mountain, or inter-mountain region. It may be called the Inter-Mountain Plain. . . .

Source: Abridged from Walter Prescott Webb, "The Great Plains and the Industrial
Revolution," in James F. Willard and Colin B. Goodykoontz, eds. *The Trans Mississippi West* (Boulder: University of Colorado Press, 1930), 309-339.

11

The Great Plains environment is composed of three parallel belts running north and south. The High Plains constitute the middle belt and exhibit all three characteristics: they are level, barren of timber, and semi-arid. East of the central belt or High Plains, lies the V-shaped Prairie Plains which exhibit two characteristics; they are level and treeless. West of the High Plains is the third belt—the Inter-Mountain region—broken as to topography but for the most part without timber and extremely deficient in moisture.

In order to understand the rôle of the Great Plains environment in the development of American civilization, it is necessary to contrast it with the eastern environment, which will be designated as the Eastern Woodland region. The two regions are separated by a broad transition belt extending from Texas northward to Canada and dividing the United States into two almost equal parts. The belt may be spoken of, somewhat inaccurately, as the "timber line," but since the timber line is irregular, it is more convenient, though less accurate, to use a meridian. Some writers use the ninety-sixth, which actually approximates the timber line; some use the one hundredth, beyond which the country is arid; many use the ninety-eighth, the one here adopted as the most convenient. This line separates two environments that are more remarkable for their contrasts than for their similarities. What is present in the one is absent in the other: the outstanding positive features of topography, vegetation, and rainfall in the Eastern Woodland become negative in the Great Plains. The cultural consequences of these contrasts have escaped general attention and study; yet out of such study must come ultimately the key to an understanding of what has happened west of the ninety-eighth meridian. . . .

With the settlement at Jamestown the continuous Anglo-American pioneering experience may be considered as having begun. Though these early colonists found themselves in a new land, the environment was not fundamentally different from what they had known in Europe. The differences they encountered were primarily cultural and social and not geographic. Had England or Scotland been set down on the Atlantic slope, either would have blended as a harmonious detail in the larger American scene. But imagine their incongruity in the middle of the Great Plains!

Once established in the new country, the Anglo-Americans began their journey westward. For more than two centuries, however, they remained in the woods, and in this time they perfected a technique for the utilization of the humid region, and learned to do the things that were necessary for life in the primeval forest. Students of the Westward Movement have often pointed out that the emigrants moved along parallels of latitude. In so doing they kept in the climatic zone where the old lessons could be conned and the old formulas repeated. . . . There appeared to be no unusual physical barrier to westward expansion, and as long as one moved along the parallels one merely changed scenes but not conditions; same houses, same weapons, tools, fences; eventually the same classes of people stratified as to occupation and attitude towards negroes into a North and a South. Everything worked just as it should in each section, just as experience had taught it would in the parent neighborhood. Thus we see, in this exaggerated statement of the process, that in the Eastern Woodland area pioneering tended to become standardized as its technique was perfected.

The American experience in the Woodland constitutes the first epoch in pioneering. In the decade preceeding the Civil War this epoch, which had lasted two and one-half centuries, was approaching its close for the reason that by that time the whole Woodland region, whether east or west of the Great Plains, had been occupied and appropriated. Only the Great Plains remained to be taken; the American experience there constitutes the second and last epoch of pioneering. The transition from one to the other was made between 1840 and 1875 in the neighbor-hood of the ninety-eighth meridian.

Taking the ninety-eighth meridian as the boundary between the two environments, it will not be difficult to indicate what happened when the frontier of occupation—which was essentially that of agriculture—attempted to cross the line from the old region into the new one, attempted to apply the technique worked out in the woods to the conditions on the plains. That the experience was not a pleasant or altogether romantic one is indicated by a writer who said:

From the 98th meridian west to the Rocky Mountains there is a stretch of country whose history is filled with more tragedy, and whose future is pregnant with greater promise than perhaps any other equal expanse of territory within the confines of the Western Hemisphere.

To state an exceedingly complex situation in simple terms, it may be said that *the whole technique of pioneering and the ways of living which had become habitual with the people and had proved so effective as to become standardized broke down completely when carried from the Eastern Woodland region into the Great Plains.* The pioneer could no longer follow the lines of latitude west and remain in familiar, though more primitive, surroundings, either north or south. He had come to a land without logs for houses, or rails for fences, or water for stock; with few living streams, no certainty of rain, no shade from the sun, and no shield from the wind. He had come at last to a physical barrier which he named the Great American Desert.

The attempt of a migrating people to cross this line resulted in social chaos and economic ruin which continued until, through invention and much experiment, new weapons were adopted, new implements invented, new methods devised for getting water, making fences, and farming; until new institutions were evolved or old ones modified to meet the needs of a country that was level, devoid of timber, and deficient in rainfall; until plainscraft took the place of woodcraft. In short, the ninety-eighth meridian became a *fault* line of human affairs comparable to a geological *fault,* at which the ways of life were altered to such an extent that there tended to develop in the West a unique civilization. In speaking of this tendency, Major J[ohn] W[esley] Powell wrote:

The physical conditions which exist in that land, and which inexorably control the operations of men, are such that the industries of the West are necessarily unlike those of the East and their institutions must be adapted to their industrial wants. *It is thus that a new phase of Aryan civilization is being developed in the western half of America.*

When the advancing frontier reached the Great Plains and found its tools, technique, and institutions inadequate there was a pause, a delay, a long interval of waiting until new ways could be devised, and new tools invented or adopted. . . .

There was, of course, a long interval of waiting while the overhauling went on. In the first part of this interval (1825–1860), the trails were thrown across the plains over which trickled the overflow of immigrants who were damming up along the timber line where the machine broke down. In the latter part of the interval (1866–1876), the cattle kingdom, with its origin in Texas, moved northward and westward and appropriated the whole Great Plains area. The cattle kingdom was something distinctly new in American life. . . . It was a plains institution . . . it was made for the plains. Moreover, it was the promise of that new phase of Aryan civilization mentioned by Major Powell, a happy episode in plains life.

By the time the cattle kingdom became well established (1875), the industrial revolution had come to the aid of the agricultural frontier . . . whereupon the farmers resumed their westward course. . . .

Four examples will be given to illustrate the contributions of the industrial revolution to the conquest of the Great Plains in response to urgent and imperative needs. The industrial revolution gave the plainsman a new weapon, the six-shooter; a new fence, barbed wire; a new water machine, the windmill; and new farming implements, and a new method of farming. . . .

•3•

PAUL F. SHARP

Three Frontiers: Some Comparative Studies of Canadian, American and Australian Settlement

Too often in studying the American frontier, we have paid little attention to "other Wests than ours." The comparison of the American West with the frontiers of other nations may well enlarge our understanding of settlement processes significantly. Here Paul F. Sharp urges that historians adopt a comparative approach in studying the frontiers of three of the "new-land" nations.

"If, with our own methods of the occupation of the frontier," announced Frederick Jackson Turner in 1904, "we should compare those of other countries which have dealt with similar problems—such as Russia, Germany, and the English colonies in Canada, Australia, and Africa—we should undoubtedly find most fruitful results."

Fifty years later, Turner's challenge remains unanswered and his stimulating proposal is only partly and unsystematically explored. My purpose here is to suggest some of the "fruitful results" awaiting comparative studies of settlement of regions outside the United States and to examine several such comparisons in Australian and Canadian history. . . .

Systematic, unbiased, and critical examination of "other Wests than ours," . . . provides an opportunity to explore in detail the differences that mark the expansion of western civilization into unoccupied or

SOURCE: Abridged from Paul F. Sharp, "Three Frontiers: Some Comparative Studies of Canadian, American and Australian Settlement." © 1955, by the Pacific Coast Branch, American Historical Association. Reprinted from *Pacific Historical Review*, Vol. XXIV, 369-377, by permission of the Branch and Paul F. Sharp.

sparsely settled areas as well as to investigate the similarities. Historical analysis that fails to measure these differences lacks the perspective essential for sound judgment. No other method, in fact, provides tools to determine similarities or differences in human behavior.

At the outset, it is imperative to define rather sharply the limits of the comparative methodology in studying frontier communities. . . . At least three conditions seem essential for close and profitable comparative analysis. Settlement must occur during the same historical period. The cultural heritage of the pioneers must possess basic similarities and a corresponding technology. Finally, the physical environments must possess a general likeness. Generalizations based upon conditions lacking these three qualifications would probably be too broad to shed significant understanding upon specific problems of frontier settlement, though they might well enrich our understanding of human behavior under dissimilar circumstances and in different historical epochs.

Comparative analysis will not provide new or sweeping interpretations of the role of the frontier in western civilization to replace those already current among us. However, it will broaden our understanding of these interpretations and test their validity. Such studies will enrich our knowledge of the role of institutions inherited from parent societies; they will clarify our understanding of the influence of environment in shaping the new communities; they may well emphasize each settlement as a continuing competition for advantageous sites for production, exchange, or transfer of goods and services; and they will most certainly define the characteristic features of the expanding metropolis as it provides the capital and culture, population and markets, communications and transport for its wilderness offspring.

Unfortunately, initial efforts to compare these frontiers have proceeded from a determination to force Canadian and Australian experiences into a Turnerian mold. Since Turner's views represented theories to be tested rather than laws of history to be applied to frontier phenomena, these efforts have not met with singular success. Nor will they. To explain Canadian and Australian democracy, nationalism, or culture in terms of frontier influences alone can meet with no more success than to interpret American life solely in such terms.

On top of this, neither Canada nor Australia had a steadily or progressively expanding frontier in the American sense. The expansion of British North America was blocked by the Pre-Cambrian Shield, a barren and rocky wilderness. Thus the continuity of the frontier experience was broken, save in the fur trade. This Shield comprised a barrier that forced westward-moving Canadian pioneers southward into the American states of the Old Northwest. When roads and railways finally pierced the Shield, the settlers of the Canadian plains came as easterners, innocent of the influences of a continuous frontier environment. Thus they established institutions possessing a sophistication unfamiliar to plainsmen south of the boundary.

In Australia, on the other hand, a barren, desert heartland confined effective settlement to coastal belts and forced an industrial, urban pattern upon the community relatively earlier than in North America. Sharp conflicts between capital and labor, the predominance of the urban community, and the emergence of a successful labor party in Australia were in part a product of the failure of the continent to provide the geographical base for a nation of small farmers, so familiar in the New World of the northern hemisphere. . . .

Other contrasts, equally basic, make comparative generalizations difficult. Differences in national origins of the pioneers, in their political viewpoints and institutions, and in their cultural inheritance reinforce environmental contrasts to demonstrate the hazards of comparing the total national experiences of the three countries. Canada and Australia developed within an imperial structure, a powerful factor missing from the American development after 1776. Canada's frontier, moreover, emerged under strong influences exerted by the neighboring American republic—influences missing from the antipodes except indirectly and in diluted forms.

These contrasts, along with the similarities, invite analysis. Numerous familiar themes seem appropriate for study: exploration and penetration of the continents, development of agriculture, mining, lumbering, and other exploitative industries, creation of transportation systems adequate to the great distances and unfavorable terrains, as well as the solution of problems of supplying capital and labor, credit and marketing facilities for the new economies.

Certain topics appear peculiarly suited to comparative analysis. Historical study of white and aboriginal contacts and of the painfully slow emergence of government policies would illuminate problems often treated as uniquely American by our historians. In this, anthropologists and sociologists have pioneered with preliminary studies.

In general, the story is much the same on all these frontiers. Smallpox, tuberculosis, and venereal diseases introduced by Europeans decimated and demoralized aboriginal populations. Removals, starvation, wars, and disruption of native religions, cultures, and tribal life hastened their disappearance. . . .

The story is not so simple, of course. Canadian policy on the western plains proved far more successful than either American or Australian treatment of their hapless native populations. Against a background of violence and hatred south of the forty-ninth parallel, the Canadian government conceived and executed an orderly, well-planned, and honorable policy. These successes deserve careful study in contrast to American and Australian failures. In part they were due to the decision to treat the Indians with honesty and respect, to maintain a system of incorruptible agents, and to recognize that the aboriginals could not be expected to forget centuries of neolithic customs over night. Even more important, the Canadian West was virtually uninhabited by white men, save for a scattering of traders. Unlike the American or Australian experiences, the law arrived before the rush of settlement, thus giving the Indians time to adjust to the sedentary life before white settlements engulfed them. . . .

Equally challenging themes emerge from the political and social development of the three frontiers. A comparative study of the "White Australia" policy with "Anglo-Saxonism" in North America would analyze basic social attitudes. Certainly in all three there existed assumptions of superior genetic properties in the foundation stock that found expression in similar agitations and restrictive legislation. Could the Australian frontier, with its homogeneous British population, serve as a control group to measure the influences of North America's diversity? To what degree did the presence of the bloc of French Catholics make the Canadian story different from the others? Again, what were the influences of the numerous half-breeds, especially the métis, along the edge of settlement?

The three communities also developed aggressive nationalisms that looked to the absorption of adjacent lands. In Australia, this expansionism showed itself from the beginnings of settlement in the fear that Dutch, American, or French adventurers might establish footholds on the continent. British naval forces occupied New Holland along the west coast of the continent in the fear that "some foreign power may see the Advantage of taking possession, should his Majesty's Government leave it unappropriated."

A desire to unify the entire continent quickly dominated much of Australian thought. . . . In phrases familiar to the student of American expansion on this continent, nationalist orators and editors proclaimed the gospel of expansionism. "When in the course of Ages," predicted one editor, "the British Lion has waxed old, and the Sun of England's glory and power is dimmed with age, her Australian and New Zealand colonies . . . will carry down her language, her religion, and her might to distant times." . . .

In the United States, the fusion of the national spirit and westward expansion expressed itself in that sense of inevitability known as Manifest Destiny. In Canada, the achievement of political unity in 1867 and a growing sense of nationhood prompted a similar conviction of western destiny that looked to the annexation of the Hudson's Bay Company lands on the western plains. . . .

Dynamic forces similar to those at work south of the boundary led the dominion to expand its boundaries. "The dream of the patriot and the speculation of the political philosopher had been of the destiny that should unite these British people in one nationality from one ocean to the other," William McDougall challenged his colleagues in the House of Commons. Westward expansion seemed as much a divine mandate to Canadians as to Americans, though northern politicians couched their ambitions in less provocative language. "Who cannot see that Providence has entrusted us the building up of a great northern people, fit to cope with our neighbors in the United States, and to advance step by step with them in the march of civilization?" asked George Brown in his influential Toronto *Globe*.

Whether prompted by a spirit of British imperialism or by Canadian nationalism, Canadians were increasingly aware of their "duty" to establish British institutions in the West. A deep conviction of the superiority of British constitutional practices to the republican institutions of their neighbors spurred them to action. Slogans such as "British justice," "British orderliness," and "the Empire" carried the same emotional impact as their counterparts in the American experience. To "save British America for the British Americans" became as potent a drive among Canadians as any Manifest Destiny ambition south of the international boundary.

Frontier extractive industries, such as lumbering and mining, are yet another theme inviting comparative analysis. Gold rushes in the three countries suggest many obvious parallels. The considerable migrations of gold seekers from California to Australia and from both of these to Canada offer particularly valuable data. The reminiscences of Charles D. Ferguson, for example, who spent his life following gold strikes through California to the remote diggings of Australia and New Zealand, emphasize the community of experience shared by gold seekers under different flags. An important theme of the mining industries, and one that appears in other phases of frontier history as well, is the transfer of technological knowledge from one region to another.

Striking differences are as significant as the parallels. Why did the diggers of Australia, unlike those of Canada or the United States, become the heroes of a militant democracy and their Eureka Stockade the symbol of labor's defiance of a tyrannical government? Why were Canada's camps relatively free of crime and disorder so characteristic of the others? These and many other questions need careful study.

Finally, comparative studies of regional developments seem appropriate. Within areas of similar geographic environment, analysis of the problems of adjustment in creating successful economic, political, and cultural institutions yields further insight into the nature of settlement on the world's frontiers. . . . In particular, the Great Plains regions of the Canadian and American Wests and the Australian Outback seem a legitimate theme for historical research. Aridity gives them an inescapable similarity strikingly emphasized by the analogous roles of the hundredth meridian in North America and Goyder's Line in Australia. Beyond each of these the plow "outstripped the rain," forcing material culture adjustments of a similar character. Slowly and painfully, pastoralists and farmers devised systems of land use, experimented with drought resistant crops, and invented new machinery to cope with their problems. In Australia, the invention of the Ridley stripper and the stump-jump plow and the development of new wheat strains by William Farrer parallel familiar developments in North America.

These and many other themes challenge our thoughtful attention. A greater familiarity with these and other frontiers and an enlarged perspective of their relationship to our own will more accurately reveal the meaning of the frontier experience "in the days when the world was wide."

•4•

EVERETT S. LEE

The Turner Thesis Re-examined

In this reading a demographer considers the frontier hypothesis in the light of modern population research. Everett S. Lee believes that the westward movement is best considered as a special case of American migration. But in his comments the historian does find support for the position that frontier society was indeed different from that of some older regions in the United States.

. . . In part, the Turner thesis still commands credence because of the admittedly crucial importance of vast areas of free land during the formative period of American democracy, but another reason for its appeal is that Turner, in emphasizing the frontier, was developing a special case of a more general theory of migration. Most of the effects, desirable and undesirable, that were attributed by Turner to the frontier can, with equal or better logic, be attributed to migration, and in addition, the migration theory does not collapse or depend upon tradition for its maintenance after the frontier is gone. It is not meant by this to substitute one monistic explanation of American development for another. The point is that migration has been a force of greatest moment in American civilization, and that from the magnitude and character of migration within this country certain consequences logically follow. And yet these in turn reinforce the tendency to migrate, so that when we try to arrive at cause and effect we are caught in a never ending circle in which the apparent effects viewed in a different way seem to have produced the very phenomena we first accounted as causes. It is therefore not maintained, paraphrasing Turner, that migration explains American civilization. It certainly does not, but that it was and is a major force in the development of American civilization and in the shaping of American character hardly anyone will deny. The magnitude and uniqueness of internal migration in the United States are, however, not gen-

Source: Abridged from Everett S. Lee, "The Turner Thesis Re-examined," *American Quarterly*, XIII (Spring, 1961), 77-83. © 1961. Trustees of the University of Pennsylvania. Reprinted by permission of the *American Quarterly* and Everett S. Lee.

erally realized, and research on migration differentials is only beginning to reveal the concomitants of continual movement from place to place. . . .

Had our ancestors not been willing migrants and were we as a people not willing to pull up stakes to strike out for greener pastures, American economic development would have been seriously retarded and could not operate with its present efficiency. Modern capitalism demands the quick exploitation of new resources and the abandonment of those which no longer pay well. Here new resources, wherever located, can draw upon a large and almost instantaneous labor supply, and workers do not wait for local resources to be exhausted before moving elsewhere in desperation. The mushrooming mining towns of the West in the 1850's and 1860's have their modern counterparts in the newly established cities that center around defense industries. The exodus of farmers from the rocky slopes of New England into western New York and Ohio has been exceeded in magnitude by the desertion of the dust bowl for California and the Northwest. Contrast this situation with that which is found in some other countries where a labor surplus may exist in a community ten miles from one in which there is a labor shortage, and yet the government finds it hard to persuade unemployed workers to make the short move toward ready employment.

In this connection, it should be pointed out that the true safety valve was not the frontier, even before its alleged disappearance about 1890: it was migration, sometimes to the frontier it is true, sometimes to better farming lands far behind the frontier, but more often it was from the farm to the city. Migration to the city has almost always exceeded the movement to the frontier, and in recent years the migration to Turner's West, however defined, has been to the city rather than to open country. The city has more often been an outlet for the underemployed of rural areas than the farm a haven for the unemployed workers in Eastern industries.

We now know that migrants are not a cross section of the general population. Internal migration as well as external migration is selective, especially for young adults in the ages of greatest productivity and also of greatest reproductivity. The characteristics of migrants between states are somewhat similar to those of migrants from abroad in the days of peak immigration. Males predominate and they are concentrated at ages 20 to 30. Migrants are better educated than nonmigrants, and the highest migration rates are for those at the top of the occupational ladder. The fragmentary studies that exist even suggest that migrants are more intelligent than nonmigrants.

In addition to being young, migrants are likely to be single or in the early stages of family formation. As size of family increases, even when age of head is held constant, there is a decrease in migration. With migration recognized as a part of the way of life, an extra premium is placed upon family limitation. . . . More important, perhaps, than the stimulus to family limitation is the breakdown of the *grossfamilie* system with its encompassed generations and its extension of the privileges and obligations of kinship to cousins of remote degree. By migrating from his clan the individual removes himself from its control and from its protection. Were it not that a highly developed sense of individualism prompted his move in the first place, it would be necessary to acquire it. He and his family become a self-supporting and, to some degree, a self-sufficient little unit. Since he must fight his own battles and provide his own subsistence without the support of his clan he becomes impatient with the demands of distant relatives upon him.

In some persons individualism may manifest itself, as in Turner's frontiersman, in truculence and uncouthness, but most migrants find that a premium is placed upon the ability to adjust to new situations and new people. They learn the value of outward conformity and may come to place great value upon it. They make acquaintances easily—in short, they exhibit many of the characteristics of today's "organization man," and I wonder if the attributes of this gentleman are not largely those in which generations of Americans have been schooled. . . .

A highly mobile population is not one in which an hereditary elite is likely to develop. Migration diminishes the value of blood ties and the possession of a distinguished name may come to mean little. In Massachusetts and South Carolina Adams and Pinckney may be names to conjure with, but what do they mean in Brooklyn and Whisky Gulch? A different set of values distinguishes the mobile from the static society. Land ownership, for example, as a mark of status gives way to more transportable items, among which ability and money are prominent.

It is hardly necessary to note that in the long run nationalism is promoted by interstate migration. Turner, himself, remarked that "Nothing works for nationalism like intercourse within the nation" and that "mobility of population is death to localism." The migrant from Alabama to Detroit is likely to waver in his devotion to state's rights, and the northern metropolis which acquires the product of a South Carolina public school for Negroes is led to wonder whether that state can be entrusted with so important a function as education. Not only does migration promote nationalism and lessen the attachment to a state or locality but it also serves to encourage the extension of the functions of national government into areas once reserved for the states.

With our set of values most of the things we have associated with migration seem desirable. Individualism and equalitarianism are usually associated with democracy, and the creation of a strong central government seems necessary for survival. But tendencies toward conformity and the extension of federal functions may be disturbing. Let us now consider some of the less desirable aspects of migration.

In studying one of our most migratory groups, young executives, researchers noted that though superficial friendships are made readily, there was reluctance to form deep attachments with emotional ties and mutual obligations, partly because they would be interrupted by migration. It would seem that an almost inevitable result of migration with its severing of friendships is the focusing of emotional relationships inward to the immediate family with perhaps too much expected of each member.

Such tensions, if they exist, are minor in comparison with those which result from unsuccessful efforts to adjust or conform, or from rebellion. It is now evident that rates of admission to mental hospitals are much higher for migrants than for nonmigrants and, while this may be true in part because of selection of disease-prone individuals as migrants, the struggle with the changing environment must also play a part. Often the migrant does not understand the reasons for doing things in a particular way in a new community. For example, the detailed sanitary regulations of the northern city may be looked upon as restrictions of freedom by a migrant from the rural South. With rapidly shifting populations, custom cannot be depended upon for controls which are automatically effective in static societies and, since education is too slow and too costly, laws are proliferated.

Migration often breeds carelessness as to immediate surroundings. Few people hope to remain in the slums and not many young people expect to. If surroundings become too bad the quickest and easiest remedy is migration. Local reform movements are hampered and cities remain "corrupt and contented" partly because the natural leaders move to the suburbs. Newcomers are not always aware of the true nature of civic problems and may be tempted by the immediate favors of the political boss to vote against long-range improvements. And, when the newcomer realizes what the situation is, it is much easier to migrate than to attempt reform.

Migrants are likely to meet their numerous new situations with temporary expedients at the expense of long-run solutions. The most characteristic of American philosophies, pragmatism, which stresses continuous short-term adjustments in the conviction that whatever works is best, is a typically migrant philosophy. If, in the long run, we are not dead, we may at least be somewhere else. This carries over into a general emphasis on immediate practicality at the cost of interest in philosophical questions. Perhaps our national bias against basic science or "nonpaying" research is partly due to the spatial restlessness of the American people.

Also, the American penchant for change for change's sake may be associated with our geographic mobility. Migration has been phenomenally successful for Americans. The immigrants from abroad did find superior economic opportunities, and if they were fleeing oppression they found freedom. Within our country the major flows of migration have been from areas of lower to higher economic returns, or from areas in which the amenities were less well developed to those in which they were better developed. The natural interpretation by the migrant is that migration has been a good thing; having done it once he is willing to do it again if another area looks more attractive. This attitude he imparts to his children and to nonmigrants with whom he comes in contact. In itself, migration is one of the most drastic social changes; if this is so generally successful, why not other types of change? . . .

[F]rom a psychological and sociological, as well as from an economic point of view, migration is one of the most important factors in American civilization. There are few characteristics which are shared by so many Americans as migrant status and spatial movement has correlates which are both good and bad. They have not, however, been thoroughly studied. Sixty years ago Turner's thesis set off a round of the most productive studies in American history. A case can be made that his frontier theory is a special case of an as yet undeveloped migration theory. . . .

STANLEY ELKINS
ERIC McKITRICK

A Meaning for Turner's Frontier . . .

In 1954 two young scholars at Columbia University injected
a positive note into the discussion of Turner's theories. Unlike some of the critics of the frontier hypothesis, Stanley
Elkins and Eric McKitrick were willing to admit that there
was a relationship between the West and the development
of democratic institutions in the United States. They suggested
that the major deficiency of Professor Turner's work lay in
the fact that he had failed to present a model of the frontier
experience which could be tested rigorously. Drawing upon
the work of Robert K. Merton and his associates, they tried
to develop such a model. Their derivation of this device
follows.

. . . Suppose that political democracy be regarded as a manipulative
attitude toward government, shared by large numbers of people. Let
it be thought of as a wide participation in public affairs, a diffusion of
leadership, a widespread sense of personal competence to make a difference. Under what conditions have such things typically occurred?
When have the energies of the people been most engaged? What pushes
a man into public activity? It appears that nothing accomplishes this
more quickly than the formation of a settlement.

Our national experience, indeed, furnishes us much material for a
hypothesis. Political democracy evolves most quickly during the initial
stages of setting up a new community; it is seen most dramatically while
the process of organization and the solving of basic problems are still
crucial; it is observed to best advantage when this flow of basic problems is met by a homogeneous population. Now "homogeneity" should
here involve two parallel sorts of facts: not only a similar level of social
and economic status and aspirations among the people, but most partic-

SOURCE: Abridged from Stanley Elkins and Eric McKitrick, "A Meaning for
Turner's Frontier: Part I: Democracy in the Old Northwest," *Political Science Quar-
terly*, LXIX (September, 1954), 321-353. Reprinted by permission of Stanley
Elkins and Eric McKitrick.

ularly a lack of, or failure of, a traditional, ready-made structure of leadership in the community. A simple test of the effectiveness of structured leadership is its ability to command acceptance and respect.

With a heavy flow of community problems, in short, and without such a structure of natural leadership, democracy presents itself much less as a bright possibility than as a brutal necessity. The very incomprehensibility of alternatives has always made it most unlikely that an American should see this. But Tocqueville saw it instantly. "In aristocratic societies," he wrote, "men do not need to combine in order to act, because they are strongly held together."

. . . Among democratic nations, on the contrary, all the citizens are independent and feeble; they can hardly do anything by themselves and none of them can oblige his fellow men to lend him their assistance. They all, therefore, fall into a state of incapacity, if they do not learn voluntarily to help each other.

Before turning to history for a trial of this so simple yet interesting idea, let us set it in yet another dimension by examining a series of extremely important findings in contemporary sociology. Robert K. Merton has conducted a study, whose results are soon to be made public, of social behavior in public housing communities. A theory of political democracy which would meet all our criteria may be derived from Mr. Merton's work; there is little that we shall say from a historical viewpoint which has not already, in a present-day setting, been thoroughly documented by him.

He and his associates have observed two public housing projects, one being designated as "Craftown" and the other as "Hilltown." Craftown, located in southern New Jersey, administered by the Federal Public Housing Authority, and set up originally to house warworkers, was much the more active and interesting of the two. The key to the activity there was a "time of troubles" in the initial stages of the community's existence. The people who settled in Craftown ("homogeneous" in the sense that a majority were employed in nearby shipyards and defense plants) were immediately faced by a staggering series of problems of a fundamental sort, affecting the entire community. These bore on law and order, government, public health, housing, education, religion, municipal services, transportation, and markets. Slovenly construction had resulted in leaky roofs, flooded cellars, and warped floors. There were no schools, no churches, no electricity, no community hall, no grocery stores. Bus service was irregular and the nearest depot was a mile away. There were no hard-surfaced roads or sidewalks and much of the area was flooded during the rainy season. There was a wave of vandalism and no organization for its suppression. There was an epidemic of poliomyelitis. There were no municipal services of any kind; the environing township did not want to assume the cost of such services and by legislative action Craftown was gerrymandered into an independent township—which meant that it had to set up its own institutions for government and for the maintenance of law and order.

Craftown did have a ready-made structure, as it were, of leadership; its affairs were under the administration of a federal bureau, the Federal Public Housing Authority, and handled by a resident manager and staff. Under stable conditions such a structure would have been adequate for most of the community's basic concerns. Yet the problems in Craftown were so overwhelming, so immediate, so pressing, that the residents could not afford to wait upon the government for action. They were therefore forced to behave in that same pattern which so fascinated Tocqueville: they were driven to "the forming of associations." Mass meetings, committees and subcommittees were organized, a township board was set up, officials of great variety were elected; a volunteer police force, fire department and local court were established, with residents serving as constables, firemen and judges. A coöperative store soon came into existence. An ambulance squad, a nursery and child care center, and a great variety of organizations devoted to community needs made their appearance during this critical period. Pressures brought upon the bus company and the government agencies resulted in the improvement of transportation, the paving of streets, repair of houses, drainage of swamps, and the erection of buildings for education, worship and other functions of the community.

This experience resulted in an extraordinary level of public participation by people who for the most part had never had previous political experience; and it produced a political life charged with the utmost energy. Many jobs were created by the crisis—by the flow of problems— and they had to be handled by someone; many roles were created, someone had to fill them. The key was necessity. Persons who had previously never needed to be concerned with politics now found themselves developing a familiarity with institutions, acquiring a sense of personal competence to manipulate them, to make things happen, to make a difference. Thus the coin of necessity had its other side: there were compensations for the individual. With many offices to be filled, large numbers of people found themselves contending for them; the prestige connected with officeholding, the sense of energy and power involved in decision-making, became for the first time a possibility, a reality, an exploitable form of self-expression.

Now Hilltown, in contrast to Craftown, may be regarded as something of a control case. Many factors present in Craftown were present here—but a crucial one was missing. Hilltown, like Craftown, was a public housing project in an industrial area; it too was managed by the Federal Public Housing Authority; its population was likewise characterized by "homogeneity"—insofar as that involved a similar level of social and economic status among the residents. What Hilltown did not experience was a "time of troubles." Unlike Craftown, it was well planned and operated, it was not faced with a failure of municipal services, it was not confronted by lack of transportation, stores, electricity, or facilities for education and religion. The residents, to be sure, had their individual problems—occasional badly fitting doors and the like—but they were not of a community nature, not of a sort that made community organization seem indispensable. Widespread public participation in community affairs was never needed there, and it never took place. Sporadic efforts toward the establishment of a council, the election of officers, and the setting up of community activities aroused little interest and met with failure. The original structure of leadership—the federal agency and its local office—proved quite adequate for the handling of Hilltown's concerns, it was never seriously challenged, and it required no supplementation by resident activity. "Democracy," in short, was unnecessary there.

One more reference to the Craftown episode should be made, in order to note two interesting subsidiary consequences of this problem-solving experience, this wide participation, this sense of individual competence spread among such great numbers. One was a close supervision of the officialdom which the Craftowners themselves had created—and a lesser degree of respect for it than had apparently been the case in their previous communities. The other was a body of shared "traditions," with a common vocabulary, rich with meaning, whereby the experience might be relived and reshared. Although the level of activity was never as high in later times as it was in the beginning—the problems by then had been solved—the intensity of the "time of troubles" served to link the "pioneers" and the later-comers together by a kind of verbal bond. Talking about it was important: once this experience had been undergone, it was not lost. In such a usable fund of tradition, resources for meeting a new crisis, should one appear, would remain always available.

How might such a contemporary model square with the pioneer frontier? No sorcery of forest or prairie could materialize the democrat, yet it should be safe to guess that the periods of wholesale migration to the West forced a setting in which such an experience as that just outlined had to be enacted a thousand times over: an experience crucial in the careers of millions of Americans. Frederick Jackson Turner has stated the undeniable fact—that an organic connection exists between American democracy and the American frontier. The insight is his. But Turner never offered a conceptual framework by which it might be tested. We are proposing such a model; it involves the establishment of new communities. Its variables are a period of problem-solving and a homogeneous population whose key factor is the lack of a structure of leadership. . . .

·6·

ROBERT F. BERKHOFER, JR.

Space, Time, Culture and the New Frontier

Cultural anthropology provides still another perspective from which to study the frontier processes. Here, Robert F. Berkhofer, Jr., well trained in both that discipline and history, uses the concept of culture as a normative system to assess the role of the frontier in the United States. To him the value systems of the American colonists and settlers appear to have been the most important element in the settlement process rather than the physical environment.

. . . In the past two decades the concept of culture has increasingly come to mean a normative system rather than the total social heritage so often used in older textbooks. As such, it is the blueprint or design for behavior rather than the artifacts themselves. Thus a person's culture prescribes what ought to be done, delimits what may be done, and

SOURCE: Abridged from Robert F. Berkhofer, Jr., "Space, Time, Culture and the New Frontier," *Agricultural History*, XXXVIII (January, 1964), 21-30. Reprinted by permission of *Agricultural History* and Robert F. Berkhofer, Jr.

defines what exists, or concerns what are frequently called values, norms, and beliefs. Culture, then, shapes the nature of the institutions in a society and the roles a person plays in them. Culture also filters the perception of reality. What a person accepts as "fact" is highly conditioned by his value-orientation. It is assumed that the various cultural by-patterns, such as subsystems and institutions, fit into an overall configuration that provides that culture's unique integration.

It is important for the frontier historian to distinguish between culture as a normative system as used here and culture as behavior and artifact as was the older interpretation, for the distinction is vital in properly assessing the influence of environment. Climate, terrain, and other physical factors of space affect behavior far more than they do culture. Man adapts his inherited institutions and ways to a new environment only begrudgingly. While his behavior may change, he may not approve of it. A frontiersman may build a log cabin, but that does not mean he will not build a substantial frame house the first chance he gets. For the frontier to have influence, it must change the conception of what is desirable as well as behavior. The impact of environment, furthermore, is proportionate to the technological level of the society. The more technology a society possesses, the less it has to bend its institutions to the dictates of natural environment. Technology as a function of culture can create a secondary environment more powerful than the natural in affecting men's lives, as any modern city proves. At the same time, the distinction between normative system and behavior also means that certain institutions and customs are more subject to environmental modification than others. The less an institution or custom results in behavior or artifacts dependent upon environmental products, the less the environment can influence it. Diet and clothing are far more subject to environment than prayerbooks and church admission. Thus, it would seem that political, social, and religious institutions would be far less influenced by frontier experience than economic ones. . . .

The economic potential of an area is a cultural as well as a physical phenomenon. Natural resources, as David Potter points out in his *People of Plenty: Economic Abundance and the American Character*, are not merely "a storehouse of fixed and universally recognizable assets reposing on shelves until humanity by a process of removal strips them bare. Rather abundance resides in a series of physical potentialities, which have never been inventoried at the same value for any two cultures in the past and are not likely to seem of identical worth to different cultures in the future." The economic value of resources, then, is a matter of what people *want* to exploit and what they *can* exploit. On one hand, the economic organization and technology of a culture at a given time determine the possibility of utilization. On the other hand, the relation of the economic institutions to the overall configuration of cultural values and institutions also determines what may be used in what manner. This is seen on the Atlantic seaboard of the seventeenth century as well as on the plains of the nineteenth.

From the very first landing, American settlers sought economic opportunity as they perceived it. The perception of America as economic opportunity was embodied in the myths of the time. The dreams of gold paved New World cities with the precious metal, and mercantile vision pictured America as a plantation affording the products needed to relieve England at once of specie drain and of dependence on foreign supply. While geography forced the abandonment of Virginia as a producer of gold and figs it did not persuade the colonists to abandon their dreams of pecuniary gain. The colonists soon found tobacco the answer to their hopes; and many historians have attributed tobacco, the plantation system, and even slavery to geographical factors. While the mild climate and rich soil were essential to tobacco cultivation, other crops would have grown as well. In an article that deserves wider readership, Richard Shryock examines the cultural components of the decision to raise tobacco. He finds them in the lack of agricultural tradition and knowledge among the early Virginians, as well as in the demands of the Virginia Company for large profits. Thus, both the Company and the settlers sought the rapid development of a quick money crop in order to survive. Tobacco-raising with its allied institution of the plantation was, in Shryock's opinion, the result of culture and not of geography. If the Germans, who had settled inland, had landed upon the James, far different would have been the history of the Old Dominion. With their traditions of small farms, soil preservation, crop rotation, and livestock improvement, they sought a far different way of life although they, too, were interested in the profits of commercial farming. Thus the comparison between English and German colonists in Virginia shows that we must look beyond the profit motive and economic institutions in order to explain the evolution of society in the colonies.

The English colonists brought a conception of society inherited from the Middle Ages, embodying a hierarchal social structure. Although mobility existed, the stratification was believed rightfully rigid, even God-ordained. A man's status determined his obligations and rights. State and society seemed one, for social respect and political authority reinforced one another. Naturally, political privileges were determined by social status which was in turn connected with economic foundations. Wealth, rank, and power all went together in the same person, and to everyone this unity seemed right. Mobility consisted in obtaining one and getting all three.

On the colonial frontier, the settlers did not abandon this conception of society, but rather filled the structure with new people. The whole English population did not duplicate itself in North America. Rather certain classes came over in numbers disproportionate to others. "Dukes don't emigrate" runs an old proverb, and even most gentlemen would rather risk their purses than their persons. The bulk of English settlers were from the "middling classes" of farmers and skilled laborers. For colonial society to stratify according to the English pattern, this middling class had to fill all levels. Small wonder, then, that the colonial aristocracy was a working one and at best a pale imitation of the mother country's, nor is it strange that Americans possessed those virtues of aggressive individualism that Turner ascribes to the frontier, for they brought these traits from overseas.

The attitude towards land further abetted this process of societal expansion. The social theory that Englishmen held on the eve of settlement was based originally on medieval land tenure. Although other factors had supplemented land as the sole determinant of status in Elizabethan England, still its possession was *the* symbol of rank. Under the medieval agrarian system, emphasis was placed upon land rendering subsistence for the servile population and a living for their lords, but in the new age of agricultural capitalism, stress was more and more laid upon land producing a profit. Land possessed market value, besides determining status, and so speculation in land and leases was prevalent. Not only did large landowners deal in the land market, but so did the yeoman—all the while trying to wring the greatest crop yield, hence profit, from their acres.

This dual attitude of land as commodity and as status determinant sailed with the acquisitive middling class across the Atlantic, where it was reflected in the relationship of economic, political, and social institutions in the Colonial period and goes far to show the importance of land in American history. On the one hand, commercial farming and profit were coincident with settlement, and land-jobbing and speculation were not far behind. On the other hand the abundance of American acres offered the colonists a greater chance than in England to move up the social ladder and gain political rights in line with contemporary social theory. Land made possible a middle class disproportionately large compared to Europe's. The unity of rank, wealth, and power was retained, but the frontier gave the colonist the opportunity to reduplicate it with many new people at a higher level. It was this colonial base of newly-risen people and the larger middle class that appears to have laid the foundations for the unique society that Turner attributed to the Western frontier of the later period.

During the same period in which settlement flowed into the Trans-Appalachian West, a major shift occurred in American ideology. Thus Turner's perception of a new western society was really the recognition of a new social and political outlook which justified self-sufficient farms, social and economic equality, and democracy—not the actual creation of a simplified economic system and elementary democracy as he thought. Historians reconstructing the past of the Old Southwest and the Old Northwest find the extension of the complex institutions and societal network of the East into the new areas of settlement. Cotton grower and grain farmer marched westward with the speculator in the vanguard. Slavery and tenancy likewise travelled over the mountains. So did most of the occupations of the time. All these men were aggressive, and all were looking for the main chance. Forests were cleared and fields culti-vated according to the technology and economic organization of the time. If a farmer was self-sufficient, it was only because he had no access to market. In reality, a much more stratified social system and more complex economic system existed from the earliest settlement west of the mountains than Turner's hypothesis allowed. . . .

It is true that Western political institutions were different from those of the colonial period, but so, too, were those of the East. America's conception of what society *should be* was changing. In the period from Daniel Boone's crossing of the mountains to Andrew Jackson's recrossing of the same mountains to assume the duties of president—the period in which Turner found his new society—Americans as a whole were devel-oping a new value system which conceived the ideal society as one of simple institutions. The individual was the basic unit and all men were deemed equal socially, politically, and with equal economic opportunities. Less emphasis was placed on the unity of the social, economic, and political spheres of life. As a result, status seemed less hard to achieve and opportunity for mobility appeared easier. In no way, however, was there a simplification of the complex structure that was American so-ciety. While the new social philosophy of political and economic indi-vidualism travelled west with the wagons and boats of the settlers, they nonetheless created a complex commercial society, which they judged by the new ideals. In other words, the Westerners, like all Americans, possessed one conception of society but erected quite another. Perhaps this is the true paradox of the Jacksonianism that Turner lauded.

In summary . . . let me present a hypothesis as a guide to further research. The American frontier meant opportunity in the broadest sense, for not only did it mean the possibility for the extension of institutions and trends in the society at the time, but the proliferation and constant founding of institutions enabled a greater number of people to participate at a higher level in them than would have been possible in a society without a frontier. The institutions that sprang up depended more upon the cultural baggage of the migrants than upon the influence of the frontier whether as geography or unpopulated space. Yet, this did not mean the exact duplication of European or Eastern society, for such selective factors as nationality, class background, and the period of time of settlement provided differential cultural bases for institutional growth. Thus German or English heritage, aristocrat or yeoman, 1760 or 1860, accounts more for institutions in a newly settled area as to both similarities and differences from older areas than does forest or climate or terrain. This does not imply that geographical environment played no part; it operated as a limiting factor rather than as a determinant. The limitations were most felt in the speed and direction of settlement and economic activity, but even here, technology modified space.

In this attempt at redefinition, the frontier is viewed not as an area demanding innovation, but as an opportunity for the proliferation of old institutions. The uniqueness of the frontier is basically not one of place, but of time, making possible the rapid extension of certain trends prevailing in Anglo-American society during a given period. To the extent that the frontier afforded this opportunity, it possesses validity as an explanatory factor in American history.

CHAPTER II

Establishing and Expanding
a Western Empire

D URING THE LATE SUMMER and fall of 1782, the Peace Commissioners of the United States of America negotiated with the representatives of Great Britain, France, and Spain in Paris. Suspicious of their French allies and separated from their masters in Congress by the Atlantic waters, they served their country well. Under the terms of the Treaty of Paris which was formally ratified in 1783, the territory of the United States stretched westward to the Mississippi and included the "back lands" across the Appalachians that John Jay had feared the French might treacherously restore to Great Britain. Administering that domain of virgin land beyond the Appalachians, enlarging its area and exploiting its resources were major concerns of Americans for years to come.

The Treaty of Paris did not solve all of the territorial problems of the new nation. The northern boundary of the United States would require further adjudication in both the East and the West. Although the treaty guaranteed that the Mississippi River should remain free and open to both American and British citizens, the Spanish, occupying the Floridas and Louisiana, controlled the lower reaches of that river, as was true of all the other rivers which drained American territory and emptied into the Gulf of Mexico. In an age when trade of any consequence must move by water, this situation could impose frustrating limitations on western development. Almost immediately too, the Spanish contested the claims of Americans to a southern boundary which followed the thirty-first parallel of latitude between the Mississippi and the Chatahoochee rivers.

The future of the western lands was obscure in 1783. It was still uncertain indeed whether the central government or the states were to supervise the development of the West. Under their charters, residents of Massachusetts, Connecticut, the Carolinas and Georgia could argue that the boundaries of their states ran westward from the Atlantic indefinitely into the interior or until the Southern Sea was reached. The Virginia Charter of 1609 described a northern boundary which ran to the northwest, allowing the Virginians to claim a vast empire, embracing not only modern West Virginia and Kentucky but most of the region above the Ohio River as well. Although apparently restricted by charter to lands lying east of the Delaware River, New Yorkers had western ambitions also because the Five Nations had placed their lands under the protection of the province and these confederated Indian tribes claimed suzerainty by conquest over vast stretches of the West.

During the years of the Revolution, the residents of the "landless" states viewed the western claims of more fortunate provinces with suspicion and jealousy. Their less affluent citizens hoped that they or their sons might eventually settle in the West on equal terms with settlers from other states. The spokesmen of the unendowed states suggested that the revenues from western land sales might allow states like Virginia to set taxes so low as to drain the population from less fortunate commonwealths. They professed fear that the landed states would dominate any permanent union of the old British colonies after the western lands were settled. Prior to the Revolution capitalists and land companies, particularly from the unendowed states, had been trying to acquire title to western lands from the British government or directly from the Indians. Those involved in such schemes learned during the 1770's that Virginia's state legislators opposed their pretensions. Such land speculators came to prefer a new nation in which the central government would administer the back country. Marylanders refused to accept the Articles of Confederation until provisions for control of the West were arranged which were more satisfactory to the landless states.

After the New Yorkers surrendered their rather dubious pretensions in the West, the Virginians broke the impasse early in 1781 by surrendering to Congress their claims to the land north and west of the Ohio River. Some Virginia leaders believed that their state would be of ungovernable size if they retained all of their western lands, and they realized also that the government of the United States must have some assets directly under its control if it was to be respected. The Virginians did specify among other conditions, however, that the federal government should not recognize titles in the region, unsanctioned by the state of Virginia. Now the Maryland legislators could no longer in good conscience withhold approval of the Articles of Confederation. Land speculators, however, tried to persuade the members of Congress that they should refuse the cession. Virginia then modified the conditions in a second tender of the lands above the Ohio which Congress accepted in 1784. Now the United States government had a public domain, the Old Northwest. The other states with western claims followed the lead of New York and Virginia, although Connecticut withheld the Western Reserve for its own uses, and other states were laggard or alienated large acreages before surrendering their titles.

The national government's hold on its western domain was most insecure during the first 20 years of national development. Rumors of British plots to reassert control over the Northwest circulated in the West during the 1780's and British garrisons remained in posts along the border that now stood on American soil under the terms of the peace settlement. The Indians of the Old Northwest were restive and cherished hopes that they might retain permanent possession of that region. Not without some provocation, they harried the struggling settlements in Kentucky and on the upper Ohio and remained intransigent until defeated by Anthony Wayne and his troops at Fallen Timbers in August 1794. By then the British were involved in European wars and ready to agree in Jay's Treaty to withdraw their troops from American soil immediately.

In the Southwest the Spanish claimed all of the region beyond the Appalachians and below the Tennessee River. In 1784 they closed the Mississippi to American trade. If the Kentuckians and settlers on the Cumberland River were to prosper, their agricultural produce must travel to market over the Mississippi waterway or other southwestern rivers which drained into the Gulf of Mexico through Spanish territory. The southwestern pioneers also found the Indians hostile and for this they blamed the Spanish. When Congress appeared willing in 1786 to approve a commercial treaty with Spain which surrendered the American claim to free navigation of the Mississippi, westerners were incensed. The Spanish ambassador to the United States then intimated to the Kentuckians that his country might ally itself with an independent western state and open the Mississippi to its citizens. At this point independence became attractive to some Kentuckians, the more so because Congress seemed reluctant to accept Kentucky as a state of the union and apparently could not control the western Indians.

Eventually a number of prominent westerners entered into negotiations with the Spanish. But Spanish intrigues among the men of the western waters failed as the members of Congress came to understand the importance of free navigation on the Mississippi and the federal Constitution of 1787 provided a central government with the power to settle the Indian problems and to establish satisfactory governments in the West. These developments, however, took time and western disaffection persisted into the 1790's. Not until 1795 did Pinckney's Treaty provide that the Spanish would open the Mississippi to western trade, give westerners the right of deposit at New Orleans, accept the thirty-first parallel as the boundary of West Florida, and urge peace upon the southwestern Indians.

If some Americans flirted with Spain during the 1780's and 1790's, others believed that the simplest solution to western problems was to seize the Spanish Floridas and Louisiana. Real and rumored intelligence of Spanish intrigue, separatist schemes and filibusters against the Spanish provinces swirled through the American West. That chapter of our frontier history ended only when James Wilkinson, one-time Spanish agent and now senior officer in the United States Army, accused Aaron Burr of trying to detach the lower Mississippi valley from the United States in 1805. But already Jefferson and his envoys to France had laid the foundation of a new era in western expansion by purchasing Louisiana in 1803.

Now the mouth of the Mississippi lay open to the trade of the American West once and for all, and a magnificent domain between the Mississippi and the Rockies beckoned American enterprise. The vague boundaries of the Louisiana Purchase also encouraged Americans to improve their territorial limits. Almost immediately the federal administration claimed that Louisiana had included West Florida and Madison annexed part of that province in 1810 and the remainder in 1812 after American settlers had arranged a series of uprisings there. Rambunctious General Andrew Jackson later violated Spanish territory by carrying his campaign against the Creek Indians into East Florida and hanging two British traders whom he seized there. Spain then sold the Floridas to the United States under the terms of the Adams-Onìs Treaty in 1819.

In defining the western boundary of Louisiana during the negotiations with Spain, John Quincy Adams, the American secretary of state, surrendered any claim to Texas but persuaded the Spanish to give up their pretensions above the forty-second parallel of latitude to the west of the Rockies. During the 1820's, Mexico encouraged Americans to settle in Texas but restrictions placed upon them at the end of that decade caused Americans there to revolt in 1835 and proclaim a republic in the next year. Despite Texan victories the Mexicans refused to acknowledge their independence. Finally Congress admitted Texas to the Union in 1845. Out of this action and disagreement concerning the settlement of the claims of American citizens against Mexico, the Mexican War developed in 1846. Two years later the Treaty of Guadeloupe Hidalgo ended the war and confirmed the status of Texas as an American state. At this time Mexico also sold to the United States that region below the forty-second parallel and west of Louisiana which comprises the southwestern United States of today, enlarged slightly by the Gadsden Purchase of 1853. Meanwhile British and American negotiators had set the northern boundary of the United States at the forty-ninth parallel between the Mississippi and the Rockies in the Convention of 1818, which also provided that the nationals of the two countries might occupy the Oregon country jointly for the time being. The Webster Ashburton Treaty of 1846 extended the boundary westward to the sea along the forty-ninth parallel. When Alaska was acquired from Russia in 1867, the United States had reached its present continental limits.

In less than one hundred years, Americans had extended the boundaries of the United States west from the Mississippi River to the Pacific and north to the Arctic. This development need not surprise us. For centuries the great European powers had expanded their dominions in North America and their ambitions had clashed repeatedly during the century before American independence. Americans assumed that the United States was to play for continental stakes, and what was more, be the winner. "It is well known that empire has been travelling from east to west . . . ," wrote Jedediah Morse, the leading geographer of the new nation, "probably her last and broadest seat will be America. . . the largest empire that ever existed." Imperial aspirations permeated the words of Hamilton, writing in *The Federalist* No. 11, "Let the thirteen States . . . concur in erecting one great American system, superior to the control of all transatlantic force or influence, and able to dictate the connection between the old and the new world!" The old mercantilist ideal of national self-sufficiency attained, in part, through the development of colonies was well known to Americans and accepted by many.

Americans of the early national period derived a sense of mission from their colonial heritage. The Puritans were convinced that they were God's elect, destined to found a new Canaan in the wilderness. Other colonists too believed that they had been chosen to participate in a great enterprise as well as to make a better life for themselves and their families. In the War for Independence the colonists were called upon to decide whether they had in America something which was worth defending. Victory reinforced their belief that American society and government was far superior to European models. Little wonder that the colonial sense of mission should fuse in many minds with the belief that American institutions were superior. American democracy was destined, Americans believed, to spread throughout North America and even the world. In the rhetorical justification of expansion the sense of mission underwent strange transmutations during the nineteenth century. One author has found in the statements of the expansionists: "metaphysical dogmas of a providential mission and quasi-scientific 'laws' of national development, conceptions of national right and ideals of social duty, legal rationalizations and appeals to 'the higher law,' aims of extending freedom and designs of extending benevolent absolutism." And some historians see the expansive drive of Americans as an expression of the romantic movement in western culture.

At times Americans were expansionists because they feared for the nation's security. European wars might spread to the North American territories of the belligerents and Americans become involved. On occasion they believed that European countries were planning to expand their holdings on this continent. Sometimes they convinced themselves that possession of foreign territory was vital for national defense. Americans knew that many Europeans believed or hoped that their little bark would founder; their feelings of insecurity were well developed. After the Louisiana Purchase and the War of 1812, however, foreign threats to American security did not so much endanger American territorial integrity as threaten to prevent the United States from obtaining and developing territory in the future.

There were, of course, many self-interested advocates among American expansionists. Fur traders longed for the protection of the American flag. Men of commerce dreamed of an all-American passage to the Pacific by land and possession of the great harbors on the Pacific coast. The settlers beyond the Appalachians chafed so long as other nations controlled the outlets of rivers which would carry their produce to the Gulf of Mexico. Frontiersmen protested the raids of Indians who, they alleged, took sanctuary on Spanish or British soil. Land speculators hungered for the opportunities available in new territory and the ordinary run of farmer seemed ever ready to sell his farm at a profit and try his luck in the new settlements. The American missionary was convinced that the red souls of the Pacific Northwest would find God more easily under the sovereignty of the United States. The filibusters of the early Southwest, the American trespasser on the improvements of the Hudson's Bay Company in Oregon and the Fenians along the northern border after the Civil War were all happy to embroil the nation in their own concerns. Indeed we can argue that an unofficial fifth column of subversives played an important part in every acquisition of territory between 1804 and 1850.

Both domestic and external considerations of a general nature conditioned the march of empire. In the early national period, New Englanders feared that territorial expansion would diminish their influence in the nation. Many southerners came to support expansion to the southwest because it would increase the number of slave states, but opposed the acquisition of territory which might provide free states. Some northerners opposed schemes to annex territory which might yield slave states, although they were willing to see the American flag carried to the Northwest or North. But European conflicts and domestic squabbles in the countries of the Old World and in their colonial possessions or former colonies prevented America's rivals from energetically defending their territorial claims. And sometimes the European titles were in effect parchment claims rather than the kind defended by resident settlers. Even so the history of American expansion during the nineteenth century has led some historians to question the moral foundations of this aspect of our foreign policy as well as the precedents it has provided for our relations with other nations in the present century.

JULIUS W. PRATT

Western Aims in the War of 1812

The causes of the War of 1812 have perplexed generations of American scholars. Here Julius W. Pratt summarizes Louis M. Hacker's thesis that land-hungry westerners led the United States into this war and develops an alternative explanation of his own, also stressing the importance of expansionist sentiment in the West. Some historians have emphasized the problems of American traders in trying to maintain their connections with Europe while England and Napoleonic France and their allies were locked in war. Others have stressed the indignation of southern Republican congressmen at successive insults to the national honor of the United States by Great Britain. Any balanced discussion of the question, however, must still give some consideration to the role of the West, its people and their spokesmen.

In an interesting article entitled "Western Land Hunger and the War of 1812: a Conjecture," Mr. Louis Morton Hacker submitted—if I understand him aright—three major propositions.

First, "the West desired Canada and therefore sought war with England."

Second, fear of the Indians, coupled with the belief that the British stood behind the Indian menace, was of little importance as an actual cause of the war spirit in the West.

Third, the true cause of the western enthusiasm for a war of conquest was cupidity for the agricultural land of Canada, induced by a belief that the valuable agricultural land of the United States was nearly all utilized: "Canada stood for great reserves of agricultural land."

Each of these propositions needs, it seems to me, analysis and criticism from an angle somewhat different from that employed by Mr. Hacker.

SOURCE: Abridged from Julius W. Pratt, "Western Aims in the War of 1812," *Mississippi Valley Historical Review*, XII (June, 1925), 36-50. Reprinted by permission of the *Journal of American History* and Julius W. Pratt.

I

With the first—that "the West desired Canada and therefore sought war with England"—I should disagree only in thinking it too narrow a statement of the case. Mr. Hacker's West is too limited an area. He defines it comprehensively enough as "that area of settlement lying back of the frontier line," which in 1812 "ran in a straggling line from southern Maine across the northern edge of the country to the Mississippi and thence east again by way of the Tennessee over the rim of the Appalachians to the sea." But his analysis of the motives that prompted the West to war deals only with those which affected a segment of this great area—the Ohio Valley. The Ohio Valley no doubt desired Canada, and its spokesmen played a great part in bringing on the war; but with the spokesmen of the Ohio Valley, Mr. Hacker himself names not only Grundy of Tennessee, who belonged more to the Southwest than to the Ohio Valley, but Calhoun and Lowndes of South Carolina and Troup of Georgia, who were distinctly southern men. A full account of the reasons why the West desired war in 1812 must explain the motives of the Southwest as well as those of the Northwest. Elsewhere I have attempted to show that the people of the Southwest were quite as anxious for Florida as their northern brethren were for Canada, and that they looked upon the conquest of this territory from Spain (an ally of Great Britain) as a certain fruit of war with England.

The first of Mr. Hacker's three propositions, therefore, I should merely wish to modify to read, let us say, as follows: the Northwest and the Southwest saw as their gains in a war with England the probable acquisition, respectively, of Canada and Florida. My objections to Mr. Hacker's minimizing the British-Indian menace as a cause of the war spirit in the West, and his emphasis of land-hunger as the real cause of the war, I shall attempt to make clear at greater length.

II

Let me . . . emphasize the fact that for the purpose of the subject under discussion we are not primarily concerned with the actual magnitude of the danger from the Indians or the actual nature and extent of the alleged alliance between Indians and British. The object of our inquiry is the Westerner's state of mind, and his state of mind arose not from what we today may know, but from what he then believed. Nor does it seem to me relevant to bring into the discussion the question of right and wrong between Indian and white pioneer. That the Indians were treated inconsiderately, cynically, too often brutally—that they were, in Mr. Hacker's words, "more sinned against than sinning"—may readily be granted. But the question for us to consider is whether, because of this treatment or for other reasons, the Westerner of 1812 regarded the Indians as a menace and held the British partly responsible for their threatening attitude.

At the very beginning of his discussion of this point, Mr. Hacker falls into what I cannot help regarding as a fundamental error in psychology. "Should not the question be," he asks, "not, were the Indians a menace to some isolated areas of settlement where both sides erred in their conduct, but, rather, did the Indians as a host threaten the existence of the white civilization in the Ohio Valley? Conceived in such terms the Indian problem is shorn of its importance." Conceived in such terms most of the vexing problems of history would be shorn of their importance. Now and then comes a danger which actually threatens the existence of a nation or a people, but most international friction and most wars arise from marginal irritations akin to that which existed in 1812 in the Ohio Valley. . . .

No reasonable person would argue with Mr. Hacker when he shows that there was little danger of some 5000 Indian warriors wiping out settlements aggregating nearly 1,000,000 whites. But if the Ohio Valley had little cause for "wholesale fear" of the Indians, it does not follow that it did not feel wholesale detestation of them, and entertain a wholesale determination to render them harmless and punish any who aided them. Mr. Hacker himself pictures the Ohio Valley as possessing a cultural and psychological unity. Would not the center then feel the dangers existent upon the periphery? There can hardly have been a family in the larger and older settlements which had not kinsmen on the border of the wilderness, where men thought of the Indian menace as a very personal matter. . . .

That there were occasional scalping parties and murders by the Indians, that frontier settlements were actually exposed to cruel dangers, Mr. Hacker does not deny. These had always been incidents attendant upon frontier life. The points of his argument are, first, as already stated, that these dangers, real and potential all combined, constituted no real menace to the "existence of the white civilization in the Ohio Valley"; and second, that such outrages and dangers were no real cause for hostility to England and supplied no real motive for wishing to expel the British from Canada.

The reasoning by which Mr. Hacker establishes the second point is not to me entirely clear. After describing the manifold reports of Indian pillage and murder that circulated in 1811, Mr. Hacker states: "The cause for all this was very plain in the mind of the West," and he proceeds to quote widely from newspapers and other sources passages charging that the unrest among the Indians resulted from the operation of British agents. He further states that "of course popular sentiment accepted these accusations." But if the newspapers, Governor Harrison, Governor Scott of Kentucky, popular sentiment, and (as he adds) congressmen from Kentucky and Tennessee, either made or accepted the accusations, if the agency of the British was "very plain in the mind of the West," how are we to escape the conclusion that this belief in a collusion between the Indians and British was a powerful stimulus to war psychology in the West? Why, chiefly because John Randolph stated in Congress that the real motive of the West was "agrarian cupidity." "His utterances," says Mr. Hacker, "are the only contemporary accounts that reveal the affair in its true light." . . .

Again I quote from the article:

Possibly Westerners did not talk of those hopes nearest their hearts as more sophisticated war-makers today do not. The war sentiment was wrapped in the heavy veil of a lofty pretension: horrendous Indians armed to the teeth, led by rascally British, must be faced lest they sweep down upon western settlements and destroy the treasured work of years. . . . Had it not been for the illuminating speeches of John Randolph in the Twelfth Congress it is doubtful whether the true road along which the western men were marching would ever have been completely bared. . . . The western clamor for war and for the conquest of Canada, viewed in the light of his opposition, takes on a new meaning. He questioned the hand of the British in the Tecumseh affair; pointed out the true cause of Indian disaffection [of course the American advance into the Indian country; it needed no very acute mind to see that the Indians objected to giving up their lands]; and, probing deeper, saw western indignation masking a secret policy of agrarian expansion. Here is an understandable motive for the strange desire for Canada.

Leaving for the present the question of the West's "agrarian cupidity," let us see whether it is really necessary to suppose that the great concern over the Indians and their alleged British abettors must have been a "lofty pretension" to cloak some less avowable motive, such as "a secret policy of agrarian expansion," and whether the desire for Canada was otherwise so strange as Mr. Hacker's last sentence makes it appear.

We have seen, by Mr. Hacker's own admission, that the Ohio Valley was almost a unit in ascribing to the British its trouble with the Indians. Now if this is true, and if it is also true that the proclaiming of this grievance as a cause of war was a "lofty pretension," then either the whole Ohio Valley was in a conspiracy, and John Randolph was the only outsider who detected it, or else the Ohio Valley as a unit was bamboozled by its leaders. Neither of these alternatives seems to me probable on the face of it. Furthermore, a little consideration of the historic relations between the United States and the British in Canada will show that it was inevitable that Westerners should lay their Indian troubles largely to the British. From the days of the Revolution, by a virtual continuity of feeling, the British had been regarded as always the potential and frequently the actual allies of the northwestern Indians against the United States; and there was nothing new in the idea that the only perfect cure for Indian troubles would be the expulsion of the British from Canada. . . .

[T]his demand for the expulsion of the British from Canada [then], far from being a new and sudden development of western sentiment, was the perfectly logical culmination of a long contest with the Indians for the secure possession of the Northwest and of a conviction as old as the Revolution that the Indian resistance was supported by the British. If in 1812 it was a "lofty pretension" "masking a secret policy of agrarian expansion," this "lofty pretension" had been sedulously nurtured for thirty-five years.

III

Let us now examine Mr. Hacker's theory that the real motive of the West was the desire for possession of Canadian lands. "Pressing upon men's minds," he says, "was undoubtedly the picture of the good fat fields across the St. Lawrence River that ached for cultivation." What is the evidence? Mr. Hacker admits that "men never said so specifically." After a painstaking examination of western newspapers and the speeches of western congressmen, he is not able to adduce a single statement that these lands were needed or desired. This trifling weakness in the evidence is met by the suggestion that "possibly Westerners did not talk of those hopes nearest their hearts." Too astute to avow their "agrarian cupidity," they invented the British-Indian menace as a mask. On the face of it this suggestion seems to me untrue to frontier psychology; but fortunately we are not left in the dark about the Westerner's habit of concealing his material motives. If he studiously avoided all mention of farming lands as an object of war, why did he not also keep quiet about the fur trade? Was it more wicked, and hence more to be concealed, to covet Canadian lands than to covet the profits from Canadian furs? Yet the fur trade again and again creeps into war speeches and war articles. . . .

In the Southwest, furthermore, where certain material gains were distinctly sought, there was no pretense of excluding them from discussion. Tennesseeans were perfectly frank about stating their cupidity for the waterways of West Florida, and did not hesitate to picture the opportunities for wealth which American conquerors might enjoy in

Mexico, "where the merchant shall see commercial resources unrivalled in other countries; the farmer, a luxuriant soil and delicious climate; where the financier shall be dazzled with gold and silver mines."

It seems highly probable, then, that if the Ohio Valley had been chiefly preoccupied with "vistas of boundless Canadian lands," some newspaper or public speaker would have disclosed this motive. In the absence of any direct evidence from Westerners themselves, Mr. Hacker bases his theory upon two foundations: the charges of John Randolph in Congress, and the argument, painstakingly built up, that the people of the Northwest supposed the good lands of the United States to be nearly all utilized. . . .

Even were Randolph's assertions all consistent, we might be pardoned for giving them slight consideration. His unscrupulous abuse of men and measures he disliked is well known to students of American history. . . .

But Randolph's charges were not even consistent. At one time it was "agrarian cupidity" that urged the war; at another, it was the prospective war profits of the hemp-growers or of those who expected to furnish supplies for the troops; at yet another it was the desire on the part of the northern states "to acquire a prepondering northern influence." It is reasonably evident that Randolph was intent on using any taunt that might sting his opponents or divide their following. To seize upon one of these taunts, ignoring the others, and designate that one as "the key to the desire for Canada," is about as weak a form of historical argument as can be imagined—unless, of course, the charge selected has strong corroboration elsewhere.

The only corroboration offered by Mr. Hacker is drawn from the nature of pioneer agricultural economy and the low value at that time ascribed to prairie lands. Wasteful and inefficient methods of agriculture resulted in rapid exhaustion of the soil, and forced the advance guard of settlement to be constantly on the move, leaving their deteriorated soil to be reclaimed by methods more expensive and laborious. The question might be raised whether the resulting forward pressure was, in 1811–12, quite as urgent as Mr. Hacker assumes, but we may grant that western society was determined to continue its expansion. But why should the Ohio Valley have "turned to Canada for the replenishing of its supply" of land? Because, says Mr. Hacker, "the prairies did not tempt the Ohio Valley," and he then details the numerous difficulties which were supposed to impede prairie agriculture, citing passages from travelers of the period to show that because of lack of water power, and especially of timber for fences, buildings, and fuel, the prairie lands were held to be unfit for settlement. He admits that "no direct references to the prairies are to be found in any of the valley newspapers of the period," but probably there is no reason to find fault with his assumption that the existence of these disadvantages "must have been familiar to the inhabitants of the Ohio Valley."

The weakness of this portion of the argument lies in the assumption that only treeless plains remained unoccupied. A comparison of the census map for 1810 with a map exhibiting the native vegetation of the country shows a vast area of timbered land as yet unpeopled—a third of the state of Ohio, nearly all of Indiana, and fringes of Illinois timbered with hardwood; all of Michigan, Wisconsin, and much of Minnesota bearing hardwood or pine; a great hardwood belt averaging one hundred miles in breadth stretching across Missouri into Arkansas and Oklahoma, with a narrow belt following the Missouri River across the state. . . .

It would appear, then, that the Ohio Valley was not in such desperate straits for land that it must deliberately inaugurate a war of agrarian expansion. The absence from the literature of the war of all mention of those "good fat fields across the St. Lawrence" as one of the objects of the conflict, is best explained by the simplest of all reasons—namely, that there were plenty of "good fat fields" at home. At the same time, if the inferences of this article have been correctly drawn, the Northwest was in reality intensely preoccupied with the Indian danger on its borders and the British hostility thought to be lurking behind it. In other words, we must believe that when newspapers and political leaders almost universally talked about Indians and British they meant what they said, and were not adroitly concealing their real interests. . . .

·2·

FREDERICK MERK

The Oregon Pioneers
and the Boundary

In a reader of this scope we cannot examine all of the steps
by which Americans pushed their territorial boundaries to
the Pacific. Rather we have chosen to present three facets of
the expansion process in the Pacific Northwest. In this
selection from one of his best known articles Frederick Merk
discusses the contribution of the Oregon pioneers to the
settlement of the boundary along the forty-ninth parallel.

It is a truism in American history that the success of the United States
in the Oregon boundary negotiations was due in considerable measure
to the Oregon pioneers. They brought pressure to bear on the British
government during the final stages of the Oregon negotiations, and this
was a factor in winning for their country the empire of the Pacific Northwest. But what the nature of this pressure was, how direct it was, or
how great its effectiveness, are questions that have never been carefully
investigated. . . .

Proper analysis of this subject necessitates at the outset a survey of
the stakes of Oregon diplomacy. They were not as extensive as at first
sight they seem. Nominally the whole of the Oregon country was at
issue, the vast domain extending from the Rocky Mountains to the sea
and from California to Alaska. But the region about which dispute really
centered was the comparatively limited area lying between the Columbia
River and the forty-ninth parallel, the rectangle now constituting the
central and western thirds of the state of Washington. As early as 1818
the British government had intimated a willingness to divide the Oregon
country at the line of the Columbia River and the forty-ninth parallel,
and this it definitely offered to do in 1824, 1826, and 1844. It further
offered in 1826 and 1844 to yield to the United States a large segment
of territory north of the Columbia, intended to satisfy the determined

SOURCE: Reprinted by permission of the publishers from Frederick Merk, *The
Oregon Question: Essays in Anglo-American Diplomacy and Politics*, Cambridge,
Mass.: The Belknap Press of Harvard University Press, 234-254. © 1967, President
and Fellows of Harvard College.

American demand for a share in the harbors of Puget Sound. These proposals the American government had declined. . . .

Similarly, though with somewhat less certainty, the American government stood committed to the line of the forty-ninth parallel. This it had offered as a compromise from the very beginning, and, when in 1844 Calhoun attempted to extend again the field of dispute, Pakenham, the British ambassador, cut him short, informing him that he "was not authorized to treat about any territory lying to the north of the 49th parallel of latitude, which was considered by Her Majesty's Government to form the basis for the Negotiation, on the side of the United States, as the line of the Columbia formed that on the side of Great Britain." So clear had this mutual delimitation of the field of dispute become by the time of the later Oregon negotiations that in 1844 Pakenham recommended to his government that it offer full cession to the United States of the territory south of the Columbia in return for the yielding by the United States of the territory north of the forty-ninth parallel, a proposal which interested Lord Aberdeen but which he did not press because he foresaw that it would be rejected by the American government.

With these facts as a guide we may now turn to assessing the influence of the Oregon pioneers on the boundary negotiations. It has been supposed that they determined the character of the final settlement by simply taking possession as farmers of the territory in dispute. Five thousand American settlers wielded the pen, it is thought, that wrote the Oregon Treaty, demonstrating that in diplomacy possession is nine points of the law. It is a plausible theory. But it collapses at the prick of the fact that in 1846 all or practically all the American pioneers in Oregon were located in the Willamette Valley, on the south side of the Columbia River—just that part of the Oregon country which ever since 1818 the British government had been willing to concede to the United States. American occupation in other words was of an area that did not need to be won.

North of the Columbia River, on the other hand, in the region really at issue, the total number of American settlers was eight. Seven of these with their families under the leadership of M. T. Simmons, famous in the history of the state of Washington as its first permanent white settler, had established themselves in October, 1845, at the head of Puget Sound. At Jackson Prairie near the Cowlitz Landing was an Americanized Englishman. That was the extent of American occupation north of the Columbia; and of American commercial activity here, there was in 1846 none.

British interests, on the other hand, agricultural as well as commercial,

were strong. Fort Vancouver was in this region, on the north bank of
the Columbia River, so located in 1824 in place of old Fort George south
of the river at the special request of George Canning, the British minister of foreign affairs, and so named by Governor Simpson in order to
link the claims to the soil which Great Britain advanced to the discoveries and survey of Vancouver. That this post under the chief factorship
of Doctor McLoughlin controlled the commerce, particularly the fur
trade, of the region north of the Columbia no one can doubt; indeed, it
dominated the commercial life of the whole Oregon country, including
even the American settlements in the Willamette. But this establishment
represented also a powerful agricultural interest. At the fort ten or more
entire sections of land were held for the Hudson's Bay Company. Twelve
hundred acres of this were under cultivation, the remainder pastured
700 brood mares, 1600 hogs, and cattle and sheep to the number of
3400. There were employed here more or less regularly in the fields,
dairies, mills, shops, and stores of the great establishment from 150 to
200 men, who, with their Indian wives and half-breed children, comprised a settlement that already in 1837 was estimated by Lieutenant
Slacum to contain from 750 to 800 souls.

Four other establishments of the Hudson's Bay Company, or of its
subsidiary, the Puget Sound Agricultural Company, lay between the
Columbia River and the forty-ninth parallel. Fort Okanagan, near the
river of the same name, was of minor importance. Fort Victoria at the
tip of Vancouver Island was new but rapidly developing. Fort Nisqually
was the centre of the herding and farming activities of the Puget Sound
Agricultural Company, where on a tract of 167,000 acres there were
pastured 5800 sheep, 200 horses, and 1850 cattle. Cowlitz Farm was another extensive property, embracing 3500 acres, of which 1400 acres
under cultivation produced yearly more than 10,000 bushels of grain
and the remainder pastured 100 horses and sheep and cattle to the number of 1500. Eighty-five men were attached to these four establishments,
who with their families added their quota to the weight of British occupation. Nineteen Canadian families, retired servants of the Hudson's Bay
Company, and a Roman Catholic mission were established near the
Cowlitz River. Clearly British influence outweighed American in this
contested area; and if occupation had determined its fate in 1846, it must
inevitably have become British territory. . . .

But it would be a mistake now to conclude that the Oregon pioneers
did not influence the boundary treaty at all. They did influence it both
indirectly and directly. How much they did it by way of modifying
British public opinion is a difficult matter to determine. No doubt their

presence on the Willamette in growing numbers was a factor enabling the British Cabinet in 1846 to make concessions toward a settlement which would not have been possible before. But on the other hand the London *Times* was well aware that Americans were settled only on the south side of the Columbia, that the disputed region north of the river was in Hudson's Bay Company control, and that to concede the forty-ninth parallel was to surrender important British vested interests. As a potential military force in case of war the Oregon pioneers aroused British apprehension, and perhaps that helped to produce concessions which made a peaceful settlement possible. . . . More effective as a factor in the negotiations was the danger, recognized by both governments, that local conflicts between the pioneers and the Hudson's Bay Company might develop into a general conflagration. No doubt this had considerable influence in hastening a settlement on the basis of mutual concessions.

But there is a positive contribution of real significance which the Oregon pioneers made to the boundary settlement. It is that they led the Hudson's Bay Company to shift its main depot from the old and famous site on the Columbia River to a new location at the tip of Vancouver Island. This they did by arousing in the mind of George Simpson, governor of the Hudson's Bay Company, fears for the safety of the valuable stores concentrated at Fort Vancouver. Simpson profoundly distrusted the Willamette settlers. In his private correspondence he persistently classed all of them together as "desperate characters ". . . . Emigrants en route to Oregon being of the same stamp as those already there, he was concerned for the safety of Fort Hall and warned its chief officer in the spring of 1846 to be on guard against pillaging. Fort Vancouver's vast stores he proposed to put as far as possible out of reach of harm. . . .

Simpson's judgment on the Willamette settlers and on their government was of course warped by prejudice, but his fears for the safety of the stores at Vancouver were warranted. Emigrants to Oregon in this period were no longer God-fearing New England missionaries. Predominantly they were from Missouri and states neighbor to her—communities notorious for turbulence and readiness to self-help. Missouri contributed more than a majority—the state that had just expelled from their homes fifteen thousand Mormon settlers in the dead of winter with a loss of property estimated by Joseph Smith at a million dollars—the state that was soon to win notice again by the exploits of its border ruffians. Southern uplanders, contentious, ignorant, and suspicious, they went to Oregon inflamed against the Hudson's Bay Company by the charges of such men as Kelley, Slacum, and Spaulding, printed in government documents, that it oppressed American settlers in the Willamette, or the atrocious accusation of Benton that it incited Indians to murder American trappers, five hundred of whom had already been slain. Powerful emigrant trains arriving in Oregon destitute and starving, and believing such tales, were capable of attempting any mischief, and it was partly to avert disaster that McLoughlin gave such generous aid to the companies of 1843 and 1844. Residence for a year or two in the Willamette dispelled much hostility, but there were always abundant opportunities for friction in the economic relations of monopoly-hating pioneers with a foreign corporation that dominated, even if benevolently, the life of the community. Particular soreness was felt that a corporation whose charter was believed to grant the right to hold land only for trading purposes had engrossed many of the choicest farming, mill, and town site locations in the country, and this jealousy extended even to the Company's retired servants in the Willamette. A curious echo of Missouri Mormon troubles sounds out of a report brought to McLoughlin early in 1845 of an alleged attempt by some thirty or forty Americans to organize a party whose object was to drive out of the Willamette all the Canadians and others having Indian or half-breed families who held lands there. Similar feeling animated the attempts of bold spirits like Williamson, Alderman, McNamee, and others to stake out claims on lands occupied by the Hudson's Bay Company near Fort Vancouver, and it eventually found successful expression after the Oregon Treaty in the gradual seizure by American settlers, treaty terms notwithstanding, of much the greater part of all the lands and much of the cattle held by the Company and its subsidiary in the region between the Columbia River and the forty-ninth parallel. Beside the danger of spoliation was that of incendiarism, ruffians like Alderman and Chapman, who nursed grievances, having openly threatened to set fire at opportunity to the premises at Fort Vancouver. McLoughlin, as well as Simpson, saw these dangers and took such measures as he could to forestall them, strengthening the defenses of Fort Vancouver in 1844, appealing for naval protection to British authorities in 1845, and, when that brought no response, yielding to the wish of the orderly element among the Americans that he give in his adhesion to the provisional government. . . .

There were, to be sure, other considerations, ordinary requirements of business, that demanded the creation of a new main depot away from the Columbia River. The decline of the fur trade in the valley of the Columbia, the perils of the bar at the entrance of the river, and uncertainties as to the boundary settlement were powerful factors dictating the change. Eventually they would have brought it about even without the intervention of the Americans in the Willamette. Indeed, the Hudson's Bay Company had been contemplating the transfer for at least ten years. But it required the menace of the Willamette settlers to crystallize these factors into action, and action just when the boundary negotiations were at a stage to be influenced by it.

So quietly was this shift of base made that hardly any American understood at the time what was happening; but it did not escape the notice of Lord Aberdeen. He knew of it in 1845 and welcomed it for the promise it offered of a peaceful solution of the Oregon controversy. Sincerely desirous of composing this critical issue he had reconciled himself by March, 1844, to substantially the terms of settlement later laid down in the treaty of 1846. But he had found it impossible to win over Peel, the prime minister, or the remainder of the Cabinet. They no doubt feared the clamor which an active opposition would raise over what was virtually a surrender to the demands of the United States. The Cabinet was still unpersuaded when the news came in 1845 of the shift of base of the Hudson's Bay Company. That event put a new political face on the situation. The Hudson's Bay Company had unwittingly revealed by its move that it no longer regarded the Columbia River as a vital trade route or an indispensable outlet for its western provinces to the sea; that a watercourse which looked imposing on the maps was of so little real promise for anything but a fur-trade commerce that it was being relegated by the British interest which best knew its potentialities to secondary uses. To yield this river to the United States could not involve serious national loss, nor under the circumstances lay the government open to partizan attack or national outcry. And surrender of the Columbia was the key to the peaceful settlement of the Oregon boundary. . . .

American westward expansion was in large measure the work of rough frontiersmen, men who at the cutting edge of civilization had developed habits of direct action and self-help. Such men were hard to control anywhere, and in the Spanish border-lands, weakly held and badly governed, they quickly brought on revolution and annexation to the United States. But West Florida, Texas, and California are not Oregon. In the Pacific Northwest American pioneers were confronted by sterner stuff than Spaniards or Mexicans—the British government and the Hudson's Bay Company. Direct action and turbulence were there held remarkably in leash by the power and wisdom, in considerable part, of a single great corporation. But the Hudson's Bay Company, much feared, was itself afraid. It is a phenomenon by no means new, two hostile elements facing and fearing each other. In Oregon this led, for once, not to war but to peace.

•3•

NORMAN A. GRAEBNER

Maritime Factors in the Oregon Compromise

In contrast to the emphasis which many historians have placed upon the expansionist tendencies of western farmers, Norman A. Graebner has developed another major theme in the history of the Oregon settlement, the demand of commercial interests to obtain permanent control of the great harbors on the Pacific coast. Not only did such interest stimulate expansionist sentiment generally, he argued, but it also shaped the specific terms of the Oregon boundary settlement to an important degree.

Of those factors in American expansionism which sought solution in the Oregon negotiations of 1846, none appeared of greater concern to the people of the United States than the disposition of Asiatic trade. Historians have detected a persistent commercial motivation in this nation's expansion to the Pacific. Foster Rhea Dulles, for example, developed the theme that Oregon and California were not ends in themselves, but rather a "point of departure" for an Asiatic commercial empire. Richard Van Alstyne held that American expansion can be only partly explained in terms of a continental domain. Frederick Jackson Turner also took the broader view of American acquisitions on the Pacific Ocean, the mastery of which, he said, "was to determine the future relations of Asiatic and European civilization."

Mercantile interests in the Pacific, however, explain more than one powerful motive in American expansionism. Maritime calculations augmented the strong inclination of American commercial interests to seek a peaceful solution of the Oregon controversy and actually defeated the

SOURCE: Abridged from Norman A. Graebner, "Maritime Factors in the Oregon Compromise." © 1951, by the Pacific Coast Branch, American Historical Association. Reprinted from *Pacific Historical Review*, Vol. XX, 331-346, by permission of the Branch and Norman A. Graebner.

movement for 54° 40' quite as effectively as the threat of war with Great Britain or Mexico. This ardent quest for ports on the Pacific, moreover, fused Oregon and California into one irreducible issue in the minds of the commercial enthusiasts and thereby played an intensely persuasive role in the eventual delineation of this nation's western boundaries.

When the 29th Congress met in December, 1845, there was still little indication that within six months the settlement of the disturbing Oregon question would be assured. Enthusiasm for the whole of Oregon, engendered by the President's message, rapidly translated United States claims to the Far Northwest into what Albert K. Weinberg has termed a "defiant anti-legalism." It no longer mattered that the American title to territory north of the Columbia was far from conclusive, and above the 49th parallel practically nonexistent. It had become, wrote John L. O'Sullivan of the New York *Morning News,* "our manifest destiny to occupy and to possess the whole of the Continent which Providence has given us. . . ." To 54° 40' proponents that seemed to settle the issue.

It quickly becomes evident from a study of the great debate that this expanding outlook was doomed from the beginning by the patent interests of American commercialism. Too many Congressional eyes were narrowly trained on ports to permit the triumph of agrarian nationalism. For almost a half century the trading empire of Boston and New York had given to Oregon's waterways a peculiar significance in America's future economic growth. Countless early spokesmen for Oregon from John Jacob Astor to Hall J. Kelley had viewed the region primarily as an American window on the Pacific. A decade of attention to trappers, missionaries, and pioneers, furthermore, had not obscured to Congressmen the strategic importance of Oregon to the trade of Asia. Samuel Gordon of New York phrased for the House in January, 1846, his district's cogent evaluation of Oregon: "It is the key to the Pacific. It will command the trade of the isles of the Pacific, of the East, and of China." . . .

Salt spray had also conditioned New England's outlook toward Oregon. Even before the introduction in January, 1846, of the resolution to terminate the convention of 1827, Robert Winthrop of Massachusetts had defined clearly the objectives of commercial America. "We need ports on the Pacific," he shouted. "As to land, we have millions of acres of better land still unoccupied on this side of the mountains." . . .

Agrarian spokesmen of the Middle West also debated the Oregon question in maritime terms, for Oregon held a special commercial significance for their constituents. The Straits of Fuca, saw these ardent expansionists, were the future link between the Mississippi Valley, with its surplus of grain, and the teeming millions of the Orient who in exchange could enrich the great valley with cargoes of tea, porcelain, silks and satins, velvets, sugar, and spices. Through possession of the Straits, moreover, the United States would challenge the commercial supremacy of England in the Pacific. . . .

What alarmed these nationalists, however, was the fact that the constant reiteration of the commercial value of Oregon bespoke compromise at the 49th parallel, for that boundary would give the United States access to the Straits. Representatives of commerce who wished to settle the issue and secure permanent title to the magnificent inlet pointed out that the United States could acquire all the excellent harbors in Oregon and still proffer an olive branch to England. . . .

Uncompromising Democrats were driven by the logic of the commercial argument to assume the task not only of proving the value of Oregon north of 49°, but actually of doing so in realistic commercial terms. The acquisition of the Straits alone, they sought to illustrate, hardly touched the commercial possibilities of the Northwest coast. They reminded Congress that a compromise would lose the islands of Vancouver and Washington with their sturdy forests for American shipbuilding, their excellent harbors, their unparalleled fisheries, and their commanding position on the sea lanes. With such a settlement would go also other valuable islands and the bays and harbors which indented the coast. They demanded to know why the United States would voluntarily grant such enormous commercial advantages to Great Britain. . . .

Actually the South, like the Northeast, revealed its inclination to compromise in commercial terms. No American publication called the attention of its readers to the importance of Asiatic commerce in more ebullient terms than did *DeBow's Commercial Review* of New Orleans. . . .

Even those who believed that the trade of Oregon would accrue to the benefit of other sections insisted on the preservation of the Straits. But they would court no conflict by demanding more than 49°. To Jefferson Davis this guaranteed American interests in Oregon: "Possessed, as by this line we should be, of the agricultural portion of the country, of the Straits of Fuca, and Admiralty Inlet, to American enterprise and American institutions we can, without a fear, intrust the future."

Widening emphasis on the Fuca Straits developed public opinion for compromise in 1845 and 1846. Perhaps more significant was the role of Pacific commerce in diverting attention from Oregon to the harbors of California. Whereas the excellence of the Straits as an ocean port was widely recognized, their northern position blinded many to their potential value. All agreed that harbors were of real consequence in the development of commerce in the Pacific, but the known quality of San Francisco and San Diego harbors to the south convinced many travelers, politicians, and members of the press that the commercial growth of the United States in the Pacific was contingent upon the acquision of the California ports. When by 1845 this ardent quest for ports encompassed the question of both Oregon and California, it increasingly motivated compromise at 49° and actually determined the fate of the Pacific coast from Lower California to Alaska. . . .

Several noted writers and travelers, when they ignored the Straits of Fuca and recounted in detail the inadequacies of the Columbia, stimulated the intensive desire of Americans to acquire ports in California. Albert Gilliam warned that Oregon was so devoid of harbors that if the United States did not secure ports in California it would ultimately lack sea room. Similarly, Waddy Thompson, seeing no hope for commercial greatness in Oregon's waterways, praised San Francisco Bay. . . .

It is not strange that many Americans were willing to trade off varying portions of Oregon for an opportunity to acquire California. That Daniel Webster had little interest in land empires but enormous enthusiasm for spacious ports for his Yankee constituents is well known. In 1843 he attempted to cede all of Oregon north of the Columbia in exchange for the acquisition of San Francisco from Mexico through British intercession. By 1845 the tremendous burst of enthusiasm for California which followed the passage of the Texas resolution had convinced many commercial expansionists that America's real interests lay to the south of Oregon. In March, Webster revealed his true interests in the American West: "You know my opinion to have been, and it now is, that the port of San Francisco would be twenty times as valuable to us as all Texas." In July, Thomas O. Larkin of Monterey in a letter to the New York *Journal of Commerce* found the solution of the Oregon question in the expanding commercial interest in California. He wrote: "If the Oregon dispute continues, let England take eight degrees north of the Columbia, and purchase eight degrees south of forty-two from Mexico, and exchange." The *Journal* concurred in the view that California was this nation's real objective and therefore the United States could well settle at the Columbia and still retain ten degrees of coast. John Tyler never lost the vision of Webster's tripartite proposal. . . .

Other California enthusiasts desired to compromise the Oregon controversy but were far more sanguine in their objectives. Increasingly the American dream of empire on the Pacific included the ports of both Oregon and California. Writing to President James K. Polk in July,

1845, Charles Fletcher, the Pennsylvania railroad booster, pictured an American union expanding from the Atlantic to the Pacific and from the 30th to the 49th degree of north latitude. The St. Louis *Missourian* demanded both the Straits of Fuca and San Francisco harbor to fulfill the maritime destiny of the United States. . . . By 1846 this unitary view of the Pacific coast had penetrated the halls of Congress where Meredith P. Gentry of Tennessee observed: "Oregon up to the 49th parallel of latitude, and the province of Upper California, when it can be fairly acquired, is the utmost limit to which this nation ought to go in the acquision of territory."

Even the British press saw the impact of American interest in California on the Oregon question. Before the news of the Mexican War had reached Europe, the London *Times* insisted that "if any incident should lead to the declaration of war against Mexico, the seizure of Port St. Francis and of Upper California, would be considered all over the Union as a sufficient pretext for adjourning the discussion of the Oregon Convention."

It was more than the desire for San Francisco Bay that caused the California issue to prompt compromise on Oregon. The pervading fear that England was negotiating for California had not only designated that province as an immediate objective of Manifest Destiny in 1845, but also it now convinced certain American observers that the United States might well compromise on Oregon to diminish British pressure in California. . . .

By early 1846 the metropolitan expansionist press was fostering compromise vigorously. Because of its addiction to California, the New York *Journal of Commerce* succumbed early to the desire for compromise at 49°. By January, 1846, both the New York *Herald* and the New York *Sun* had joined the trend, as had also the Washington *Union* and the St. Louis and New Orleans press. The leading compromise editors stressed the maritime significance of the Pacific coast, denounced members of Congress who still favored the whole of Oregon even at the cost of war, and minimized the worth of Oregon's soil, especially as compared to that of California. . . .

Even after the outbreak of the Mexican War, expansionist editors continued uninterrupted in their commercial outlook toward the Pacific. To them the settlement with England had been made particularly acceptable by the anticipation of adding certain Mexican ports to the American union. As war broke out in May, 1846, the New York *Herald* urged the United States to seize San Francisco so that men would forget the whole of Oregon. One California correspondent predicted the result of the speedy occupation of the Pacific ports by the American naval commander:

We shall have then a country, bounded at the North latitude by 49 degrees, to the Pacific—and the South on the same ocean by 32 degrees—and the western and eastern boundaries, being what Nature intended them, the Pacific, with China in the outline, and the Atlantic with Europe in the background.

Such prospects pleased the editor of the New York *Herald*. He noted that the proposed boundaries gave the United States 1,300 miles of coast on the Pacific, several magnificent harbors, and "squared off our South-Western possessions." One writer for the New York *Journal of Commerce* in December, 1846, rejoiced that with the acquision of New Mexico and California the territory of the United States would "spread out in one broad square belt from one ocean to the other, giving us nearly as much coast on the Pacific as we possess on the Atlantic." Obviously the imaginary line of 42° meant little to the American commercial expansionists of a century ago. . . .

Although it is true that there was tremendous pressure placed upon the President to avoid war with England, it must be remembered that long before Polk forced the Oregon issue upon Congress and the British ministry in his message of December, 1845, his vision of America's future position in the West had been fashioned by the Pacific. It was largely his interest in ports that turned his attention to California in 1845. He admitted to Senator Thomas Hart Benton in October that in his desire to limit British encroachment in North America he had California and the bay of San Francisco as much in mind as Oregon. He demonstrated this interest when he attempted to purchase that port from Mexico in the Slidell mission of November, 1845. Yet at no time did the President lose sight of the Straits of Fuca. In his first message to Congress he declared that the United States could never accept a settlement in Oregon that "would leave on the British side two-thirds of the whole Oregon territory, including the free navigation of the Columbia and all valuable harbors on the Pacific." Finally, in late December, 1845, Polk noted in his diary that he would submit to the Senate for its previous advice any British offer that would grant to the United States the Straits of Fuca and some free ports to the north.

This brief analysis of the maritime objectives of the national leaders would indicate that the Oregon settlement was no compromise at all, for Polk and Aberdeen were essentially in agreement over an equitable distribution of Oregon waterways even before the great debate of 1846.

For large portions of both the British and American people, however, the final settlement was viewed as a sacrifice. The task of leadership in the crisis consisted of bringing public opinion in both nations to an acceptance of the 49th parallel. Since the unequivocal language of Polk's message tied his hands, the movement for compromise in the United States had to come from Congress and the metropolitan press. For Aberdeen the task of securing support was more difficult, since Britain, unlike the United States, was forced to retreat from its traditional offer.

Both nations as a whole were content with the distribution of land and ports. During the closing argument on the Oregon treaty Benton passed final judgment on the 49th parallel: "With that boundary comes all that we want in that quarter, namely, all the waters of Puget's Sound, and the fertile Olympian district which borders upon them." The Oregon treaty brought to the business community on both sides of the Atlantic relief from the evils of suspense and uncertainty. . . .

• 4 •

EDWARD GAYLORD BOURNE

The Legend of Marcus Whitman

The traveller who drives over the roads that follow the general route of the Oregon Trail can hardly escape noticing the historical markers which commemorate the role of Marcus and Narcissa Whitman in the early migration to the Oregon country and in the history of that region. Even more than the Lee brothers, the first American missionaries of the Pacific Northwest, Whitman came to symbolize the role of the missionary impulse in that story. Edward Gaylord Bourne's devastating analysis of the Whitman "legend" deeply shocked the local historians of the Northwest and sharply revised the estimates of the missionary contribution to the winning of Oregon.

[In 1834] . . . Marcus Whitman, a physician in Wheeler, Steuben Co., N. Y., received an appointment from the American Board of Com-

SOURCE: Abridged from Edward Gaylord Bourne, *Essays in Historical Criticism*, (New York: Charles Scribner's Sons, 1901), 3-100.

missioners for Foreign Missions to assist the Rev. Samuel Parker in establishing a mission among the Indians of the Oregon Territory. Upon their arrival at Green River (in Wyoming) Dr. Whitman decided to return to enlist more help. Early the next year he started out again with his bride, accompanied by the Rev. and Mrs. Henry H. Spalding and Mr. W. H. Gray, whom he had induced to join him in his arduous enterprise. Eleven years later, in November 1847, the energetic and faithful missionary with his wife and twelve other persons were massacred at their Station Waiilatpu, now Walla Walla, by the Cayuse Indians. . . .

Fifty-two years later, in the most careful appraisal of human achievement in America that has ever been made, the voting for the Hall of Fame at New York University, Marcus Whitman received nineteen out of a possible ninety-eight votes to be ranked as one of the fifty greatest Americans. In the class of missionaries and explorers he stood fourth, being surpassed by Adoniram Judson with thirty-five, Daniel Boone with thirty-four, and Elisha Kent Kane with twenty-one votes, and followed by Frémont and George Rogers Clark with seventeen, Houston with fourteen, and Meriwether Lewis with thirteen votes. . . .

. . . [T]he frontier missionary in less than half a century is transformed into a great historic figure who shaped the destiny of the far northwest and saved the Oregon territory to the United States. Such a transformation can be accounted for only in two ways: either the historians and public men of fifty years ago were unaccountably ignorant of an epoch-making achievement of their own day, which has since become known through the discovery of authentic sources of the history of that time at once explaining previous ignorance and establishing the real facts; or, an extraordinary legend has sprung up and spread until it has entirely overgrown and concealed the true history of a great transaction in our national life. If the last is the case it throws new light on the possibility of the development of unhistorical narratives and renders nugatory so much of apologetic criticism as is based on the belief that legendary narratives cannot grow up and displace the truth in a few years in an age abounding with documents. . . .

In this case of the story of Marcus Whitman a critical investigation will show that it is the second alternative which is forced upon us. No new sources of value relative to the history of the Oregon question have been discovered and the extraordinary posthumous fame of Marcus Whitman is found to rest upon the unsubstantial foundation of a fictitious narrative first published many years after his alleged achievement.

When a traditional narrative is subjected to criticism two questions present themselves: "Is it true?"—and if not: "How did it come to be believed to be true?" In other words, "What is its origin and history?" . . .

I shall investigate the second question first. To enable the reader to follow such a study a brief outline of the accepted story must be given.

About the first of October, 1842, and during the period when the Oregon country was under the joint occupation of the United States and Great Britain, while Dr. Whitman was dining at a trading post of the Hudson's Bay Company at Fort Walla Walla the news comes of the arrival of a colony of Canadians from the Red River country. The assembled company is jubilant and a young priest cries out "Hurrah for Oregon! America is too late, and we have got the country." Whitman realizes that if Canadian immigration has really begun the authorities at Washington ought to know it, and a counter American immigration ought to be promoted, so that when the joint occupation of Oregon is terminated, the presence of a majority of American settlers may turn the balance in favor of the United States by right of possession. The government must be informed as to the value of Oregon and its accessibility by overland emigration. In spite of the protests of his fellow missionaries, he immediately starts for Washington where he arrives March 2, 1843, most opportunely to secure the postponement of negotiations looking to the surrender of Oregon by pledging himself to demonstrate the accessibility of the country by conducting thither a thousand immigrants, which he does during the ensuing summer.

The essential points in this statement are the cause and purpose of Dr. Whitman's journey to the East in 1842, his influence on the Oregon policy of the government and his organization of the great immigration of 1843. Incidental or collateral assumptions usually accompany this statement to the effect that great ignorance and indifference in regard to Oregon prevailed in Washington and generally throughout the United States, and that Dr. Whitman was able to dispel the ignorance and to transform the indifference into a deep and widespread interest. In both the essentials and the explanatory details the story of how Marcus Whitman saved Oregon is fictitious. It is not only without trustworthy contemporary evidence, but is irreconcilable with well established facts. No traces of knowledge of it have ever been found in the contemporary discussion of the Oregon question. The story first emerges over twenty years after the events and seventeen years after Whitman's death and its conception of the Oregon policy of the government is that handed down by tradition in an isolated and remote community.

The evidence advanced in support of this story is exclusively the oral testimony of a small group of people who have alleged that their accounts rested on Whitman's words or upon their own recollections. None of this testimony is of earlier date than 1864, and nearly all of it is subsequent to the publication of the story in its most complete form. As much of it repeats the gross historical errors of the story as originally published, it is difficult to escape the conclusion that if these witnesses derived these errors from the printed narrative they probably derived other features of their testimony from the same source. If this is made probable, it does not necessarily convict these witnesses of conscious dishonesty. No one who appreciates the fallibility of human memory as an instrument of precision and understands the subtle influence upon the mind of suggestion need be confronted by the painful dilemma that either they must reject the evidence of their reasoning powers or believe that venerated friends have been dishonest. Again most of the controversy in regard to this matter has involved religious and sectarian interests and has been conducted in large measure by people at once untrained in weighing evidence and profoundly interested in the final judgment. . . .

The original account of Whitman's journey, its causes, purpose, and results was first published in a series of articles in *The Pacific,* a religious paper in San Francisco, in the fall of 1865, contributed by the Rev. H. H. Spalding, a colleague of Dr. Whitman in the Oregon mission. . . .

By articles III and IV of the Oregon Treaty of 1846 the possessory rights of the Hudson's Bay Company and of all British subjects in lands or other property were to be respected and the lands and property belonging to the Puget's Sound Agricultural Company were to be confirmed to it or purchased by the United States at a proper valuation. Settlers encroached upon the lands claimed by these companies and the Oregon land grants were also in conflict with the claims. Much annoyance and litigation resulted and the only settlement possible was for the United States to buy out the rights of these two corporations. A treaty providing for such a purchase at a valuation to be determined by a joint commission was concluded between England and the United States in July 1863 and proclaimed March 5, 1864. The commission began its labors in January 1865. . . . The claims of the Hudson's Bay Company aggregated over $4,000,000 and those of the Puget's Sound Agricultural Company over $1,100,000. September 10th, 1869, the commission awarded the two companies $450,000 and $200,000 respectively.

Many of the old settlers in Oregon cherished a resentment against the Hudson's Bay Company for real or fancied wrongs and the thought of such immense claims being preferred by foreign corporations was exasperating. The feeling was intensified by the belief that the Hudson's Bay Company had intrigued against the interests of the United States during the joint occupation. On the other hand, for one reason or another, the most of the land claims of the Protestant missions were forfeited because they were not actually occupied at the time of the passage of the land law. The title to all the stations of the American Board lapsed in this way except that to Waiilatpu, where the occupants had been massacred. In 1862 the Board put in a claim to Lapwai, Mr. Spalding's station in the Nez Percés country, but it was disallowed, and he devoted years to the effort to secure a reversal of the decision. That the mission claims should be rejected while those of the Hudson's Bay Company were recognized by the National Government seemed an outrage to Spalding. To cap the climax, just about this time it came to his attention that an attack on the work of the missionaries of the American Board had been given an extensive publicity by being included in a public document.

At the time of the Whitman massacre Spalding had undergone a terrible nervous and physical strain from which apparently he never recovered.

He believed the massacre had been instigated by the Catholic missionaries, and this belief made him almost if not quite a monomaniac on the subject of Catholicism. He charged the Catholic missionaries repeatedly with having instigated the massacre. These charges were echoed by others, and in their morbid imaginations, behind the scenes, as the concealed prime movers of the tragedy, stood the Hudson's Bay Company, vindictive at the loss of Oregon through the activity of the missionaries. A fierce controversy arose whose embers are still smoldering. The Vicar-General of Walla Walla, the Reverend J. B. A. Brouillet, prepared a reply to these charges which was published in New York in 1853, and later in 1858 was included by J. Ross Browne, a special agent of the Treasury Department, in a report which he prepared for the Commissioner of Indian Affairs on the *Indian War in Oregon and Washington Territories.*

Brouillet's reply was temperate in tone and in marked contrast to the tremulous passion of Spalding's articles, but he made assertions about the attitude of the Indians toward the Protestant missionaries, about the inefficacy of their work, and the worldly interests which influenced them which Spalding and his missionary colleagues regarded as slanders. But to have this Catholic disparagement of their labors distributed as a public document, of which he became aware as has been said at about the same time when the claim to the Lapwai Mission station fell through, and the Hudson's Bay Company's claims were recognized, incensed Spalding beyond endurance and roused him to ceaseless efforts to overwhelm the Catholics with obloquy and to demonstrate the injustice of the forfeiture of the title to the Lapwai Mission Station. He began writing and lecturing on what the missionaries had done for Oregon, upon the work of Whitman, and the massacre. . . . [I]n 1870 he came east, where through the influence of William E. Dodge, the Vice-President of the American Board, he was enabled to get the material which he had compiled and collected in defence of Whitman and of himself published under the title: *Early Labors of the Missionaries of the American Board, etc., in Oregon, etc.,* as *Executive Document 37* (Senate), 41st Congress, 3d session.

It was as an element in this extraordinary campaign of vindication that the legendary story of Whitman was developed. Nothing could more effectively catch the public ear and prepare the public mind for resentment against the Catholics than to show that Whitman saved Oregon to the United States and then lost his life a sacrifice to the malignant disappointment of the "Jesuits" and the Hudson's Bay Company. . . .

It may be questioned if the emigration of 1843 would have met with disaster if Whitman had not been with them, or, if it had, whether that would have really made any difference in the history of the Oregon question. . . . The value of Whitman's services in 1843 was great and need not be questioned. That they were indispensable there is no reason to suppose.

Two questions may now be considered which have frequently been urged in support of the legend. First, if the fate of Oregon was not at stake, but only the continuance of the mission, why did Whitman make the perilous winter journey; why did he not wait till summer? The answer is twofold. First, by starting immediately he hoped to reach the settlements before winter set in. If successful he would have time to get up his party of Christian lay helpers and return the following summer. If he waited till summer he would be absent from his mission and his wife two years. The second question is, why did he go to Washington first if his main business was in Boston? The answer to that is that as his business in Washington was to urge government measures to make emigration to Oregon easier and safer, he could not delay because the people he wished to see might scatter to their homes. His main purpose in going to Boston would not be affected one way or the other by a delay of a week or two, but his opportunities in Washington to urge his plan for protecting and aiding emigration might be seriously diminished by a few days' delay after the adjournment of Congress.

That the generally accepted story of Marcus Whitman is entirely unhistorical has been demonstrated. There was no political crisis in Oregon affairs in 1842–43 either in Oregon to give occasion to Whitman's ride, or in Washington to render his arrival and information important. There is no reason to suppose that the course of events in Oregon or in Washington would not have gone on just as they did if Whitman had stayed in Waiilatpu.

The real history of Marcus Whitman is briefly as follows: Sent out as a missionary to the Oregon Indians in 1836, he established a prosperous station which proved a haven of rest for the weary emigrant and traveller. In 1842 he is ordered to give up the station, but at the very time when the orders come a large emigration party arrives much reduced by the hardships of the journey from Fort Hall. Their leader, Dr. White, announces that the United States are going to occupy the country and that many are preparing to come the following year.

If the mission station is abandoned it would be giving up Protestant mission work just at the time when the Catholics had begun to come in and when the country was going to be settled, and when the mission station would be of especial service to the emigrants. If it were still kept up, more help must be secured: clergymen for religious work and Christian laymen to attend to the increasing business of the mission station, the farms, the mill, the sheltering of the sick and orphans, etc. If emigration on a grand scale was to begin, the government ought to protect it and establish supply stations. If anything was to be done to reverse the action of the Board it must be done at once, or a year would be lost.

Dr. Whitman was an energetic, impulsive man, of sanguine temperament, and he revolted at giving up the station at the time when its best opportunity to render material and tangible services to Oregon was at hand.

The missionaries gather and discuss the situation. Before they separate he is resolved. He will listen to no dissuasion. After presenting the needs of the emigrants at Washington and securing the reversal of the decision of the Board at Boston he returns. The mission increases in its usefulness to the emigrants. It is a hospital and orphan asylum and a refuge for the sick and helpless. The Indians, however, for whom it was established, foresee the inevitable. Disease and death invade their ranks; superstition and jealousy, distrust and resentment, take possession of their minds, and the dreadful tragedy of Waiilatpu follows.

That Marcus Whitman was a devoted and heroic missionary who braved every hardship and imperilled his life for the cause of Christian missions and Christian civilization in the far Northwest and finally died at his post, a sacrifice to the cause, will not be gainsaid. . . . But that he is a national figure in American history, or that he "saved" Oregon, must be rejected as a fiction.

·5·

WILLIAM H. GOETZMANN

The West and the American Age of Exploration

Too frequently we see historical events in rather narrow nationalistic terms. Critics have argued that this has been particularly true of the historians of the westward movement in the United States. William H. Goetzmann maintains that American expansionist sentiment can be usefully viewed in very broad perspective indeed; the high tide of American expansionism was "an age devoted to exploration and the romantic desire to see ever outward from the immediate circle of one's own existence to the remote frontier of the universe."

It has always been permissible, of course, for the Western historian to say with Turner, that "to the frontier the American intellect owes its striking characteristics." But perhaps in celebrating and studying the great story of the westward movement the Western historian has taken too narrow a view. Perhaps he has really been guilty of underestimating the extent of this impulse to move into the unknown and uncharted wildernesses of the world. Might it not be possible that this experience in the American West was an experience that was characteristic of the whole of America rather than just a part of it? Indeed, there is reason to suspect that the impulse for expansion over the globe might even be as characteristic of European civilization as a whole as it was for those hardy pioneers way out West. It might even be that one of the

Source: Abridged from William H. Goetzmann, "The West and the American Age of Exploration," *Arizona and the West*, II (Autumn, 1960), 265-278. Reprinted by permission of *Arizona and the West* and William H. Goetzmann.

reasons for the enthusiastic acceptance of the myth of the American West was its very centrality to the whole of American experience at that particular time and place in the nineteenth century and perhaps even today. . . .

Let us abandon for the moment the traditional narrow view of the expansion impulse and take up another point of view. Let us focus upon the history of exploration in the American West as part of the general history of American and European culture between the years 1800 and 1860, a quite arbitrary time span but one that is central to the course of American westward expansion. In this period public enthusiasm for the discovery and exploration of exotic places reached a culmination due to the impetus of the romantic imagination and the rapid development of scientific techniques. So widespread was such enthusiasm that one might almost be justified in calling this sixty-year period "The American Age of Exploration." . . .

Stimulated by the eighteenth-century voyages of Captain Cook, the daring adventures of Alexander McKenzie, and the exotic excursions of Alexander von Humboldt into the green world of the Amazon Basin, Europeans and Americans alike increasingly began to undertake important expeditions—with the result that by about 1900 virtually all the interiors of the great continents had been explored, the sea lanes charted, and the Arctic and Antarctic discovered and to some extent explored.

Humboldt was a key figure of the period not only because of his work in South and Central America, but because somehow he combined the cosmopolitan rationalism of the eighteenth century with the newer romantic feeling for the grandeur and exoticism of nature into a scientific approach that could be understood and imitated by those who came after him. His purpose was as clear as any in that time of romantic strivings. From his field headquarters in the heart of the Andes he wrote:

The ultimate aim of physical geography is . . . to recognize unity in the vast diversity of phenomena. . . . I have conceived the mad notion of representing, in a graphic and attractive manner, the whole of the physical aspect of the universe in one work, which is to include all that is at present known of celestial and terrestrial phenomena, from the nature of the nebula down to the geography of the mosses clinging to a granite rock. . . .

Throughout the period he remained a kind of spiritual godfather and grand adviser to great numbers of American and European scientists and explorers. . . .

At the outset certain geographical areas and problems were of special interest to various nations. Since Napoleon's campaigns in Egypt,

French, British, and German explorers roamed over the continent of Africa in increasing numbers, searching for everything from gorillas to the source of the Nile. Men like Speke, Burton, du Chaillu, Krapf, and Livingstone were heroes of the hour as they searched out the secrets of the dark continent. In North America the central focus was for a long time upon the discovery of a Northwest Passage, or at least a satisfactory trade route to India. McKenzie's great Canadian explorations had not entirely solved this problem, and it was not until Lewis and Clark marched down the Columbia to the Pacific, that any satisfactory answer was forthcoming. National rivalries over the priority of discoveries developed a particular intensity, not only in North America and Africa, but even in such remote areas as the Antarctic. . . .

Although these various expeditions throughout the world were based to a large extent upon the exigencies of national economic and political considerations, they were motivated also by an insatiable scientific curiosity. Most of the explorers seemed bent on collecting, examining, and classifying all of the various phenomena of nature which, in and of itself, seemed a vast and infinitely mysterious thing. Darwin's voyage on the *Beagle* (1832–36), inspired by the work of Humboldt, is an outstanding example of such intellectual activity.

In all of this furious activity the young republic of the United States played an important part. Under the guidance of Thomas Jefferson, Americans turned after 1800 to the task of exploring the Great West. Official expeditions were sent out under Lewis and Clark, Dunbar and Hunter, Dunbar and Freeman, Pike, and Stephen H. Long. Private John Colter of the United States Army, on detached duty from the Lewis and Clark Expedition, became the first American to see the marvels of Yellowstone Park. It was Jefferson who played the key role not only in the planning of the expeditions but in devising a proper way to present the projects to an economy-minded Congress little interested at the time in the possible contributions of "pure science." Invariably these expeditions were presented to Congress as economic and political necessities, with their scientific objectives appearing to be an afterthought.

In considering the total picture of American achievement in exploration it would, of course, be a serious mistake to overlook the private interests that accomplished so much between 1806 and 1842. The mountain men, in particular, formed one of the most spectacular groups of explorers in all history as they roamed free and unrestrained (except by the Indians) all over the western half of North America. Jim Bridger, Jedediah Smith, and James Pattie were among the first Americans to see such geographical landmarks as the South Pass, the Great Basin, the Great Salt Lake, and the Grand Canyon. Fur magnates like John Jacob Astor, Pierre Chouteau, William H. Ashley, and Charles Bent, sponsored expeditions of their own which searched out the hitherto secret places of the West. On numerous occasions they afforded opportunities for savants, like the botanist Thomas Nuttall, or the geographer Joseph Nicollet, to extend their researches into the West.

By 1842, however, the day of the mountain man was about at an end, and in that year Jim Bridger settled down to the life of a trader in his fort at the South Pass in the Rockies. Then a new era began, one that was dominated by the United States Army's Topographical Engineers, of which the most representative figure was the boyish hero John C. Frémont. . . . Unlike the mountain men, these new explorers were interested in mapping the West and making its resources known to the generations of pioneers that would follow them. For the most part the Topographical Engineers considered themselves men of science, and they rarely failed to utilize the opportunities afforded them by their Western expeditions to record and publish their scientific data to the world. . . .

When these Army officers returned to make their findings known, they were assisted by the leading scientific men in the country—men like John Torrey, Asa Gray, James Hall, John Strong Newberry, and Louis Agassiz. F. V. Hayden's work with Lieutenant G. K. Warren in the Dakotas helped to launch the serious study of vertebrate paleontology in the United States. Some of the scientists who accompanied the expeditions were so enthusiastic in the pursuit of knowledge that they even attempted to pickle some of the Indians and bring them back to the Smithsonian in a jar! . . .

The maps, the reports, the illustrations, the scientific data, and most of all the accounts of the expeditions themselves all added up to a picture of the American West as a vast and exotic place—a land of gigantic sunless canyons, towering mountains, burning lakes and fountains, mud-daubed Indians who lived in sky-high palaces, locust-eaters scarcely out of the Stone Age, immense herds of buffalo stretching for miles over the limitless horizon—all virtually untouched by the hand of civilization. And though these reports were intended as scientific documents, they helped to set the tone of an age devoted to exploration and the romantic desire to see ever outward from the immediate circle of one's own existence to the remote frontiers of the universe, just as Humboldt had dreamed of being the single genius who would capture all knowledge of the cosmos in one massive compendium. This compulsion, as much as the often-stressed desire for free land, drove the spearhead of American civilization into the West during the so-called period of Manifest Destiny.

This aspect of Manifest Destiny, however, was not confined solely to the desire to explore the Western land frontier. While most of the agrarian states were urging Federal sponsorship of Western surveys, maritime interests on the Eastern seaboard and professional scientists in Washington saw to the launching of naval expeditions to all parts of the world, some of them with the admitted purpose of maintaining the national prestige in competition with the other nations bent on exploring and subduing the globe. . . .

One further form of exploration during this period was the semi-private expedition in which a man received a governmental post which sent him to the place where he could do the exploring that he desired. The most notable examples of this were John Lloyd Stephens and Ephriam George Squier, who were sent to Central America on diplomatic missions so that they might explore the jungle regions. Stephens produced the monumental *Incidents of Travel in Central America, Chiapas, and Yucatan* which, with its magnificent illustrations executed by Frederick Catherwood, gave the first clear picture of the lost civilization of the Mayas. Squier also produced some highly important archaeological works on Central America.

Most of these men belonged to a curious literary group, interested in travel books, which met at Bartlett and Welford's bookstore in New York's Astor Hotel. The patriarch of the group was the aged Albert Gallatin; it also included such figures as Dr. F. S. Hawks, William Kennedy, George Folsom, and Brantz Mayer, author of *Mexico As It Is and As It Was*. On occasion, Edgar Allan Poe dropped in for meetings and gathered material for his own fictionalized versions of the travel book. The guiding spirit of the group was John Russell Bartlett, who got himself made United States-Mexican Boundary Commissioner in 1852 so that he could go to the Southwest and write a sequel to Stephens' enormously successful work on the Mayas. Bartlett proved to be a colossal failure as Boundary Commissioner; but he produced still another interesting travel book, his *Personal Narrative of Exploration in Texas, New Mexico, California, Sonora, and Chihuahua,* which is one of the most delightful books in the entire literature of the American West.

In general these men produced works on the borderline between serious science and romantic travel literature in which the strange and the exotic were the most important objectives. As it was for Humboldt himself, it was quite difficult for them to separate the two because the main impetus for scientific investigation seems to have been generated

by the romantic interest in the unique and the marvelous—in the minutiae of nature as well as in the extremities of the cosmos—that hung
over and dominated the entire period.

Much of the literature of the day contributed to and drew inspiration
from this spirit, suggesting that it was all part of an imaginative whole.
Books like Francis Parkman's *Oregon Trail* or Washington Irving's
Astoria & the Adventures of Captain Bonneville were romanticized
chronicles that nevertheless also contributed factual information about
the West at a time when such information was sorely needed. . . .
They conveyed much useful data about the West; but their chief significance was that they presented a picture of the West as an exotic
unknown, a place of adventure for the man of spirit and daring to go
and make his mark. In the 1840's and '50's the West was our Africa,
or Polynesia, or the Road to Xanadu. Yet the majority of serious economic and political historians tend to take this for granted—if they do
not scorn it entirely as a motive for moving West. The color and spirit
of the West have been left to Hollywood, as if it never really did matter
as an operative force which spurred people westward. But surely such
a spirit played its part in the settlement of Western America and should
not be overlooked. It was an integral part of the age. . . .

If we put all of these aspects of American culture together—the
scientific, the literary, the impact of the frontier, the rational techniques
and the romantic enthusiasms—we get a somewhat different perspective
on this period of American history. What was happening on the trans-
Mississippi frontier was akin to the activities on the Eastern seaboard.
The drive for maritime expansion, as Professor Norman Graebner has
recently pointed out, had as much to do with the course of Manifest
Destiny as the desire for free land. All aspects of American expansionism
were to some extent part of a larger impulse which was world-wide and
extremely competitive. Intellectually, this might be explained by the
fact that at this moment the scientific and rational mind of the eighteenth
century was exposed to a true world horizon—and, as that mind went
to work in the effort of comprehension, it became romantic. Whatever
was but dimly known became irresistibly attractive, and it was this attraction itself that had much to do with stimulating the impulse of Manifest
Destiny on a global basis.

Viewed in this way, the experience in the American West seems
somewhat less than unique. Rather it appears as a part of a much larger
whole—a great synthesis which extends all the way from the picturesque
trappers' rendezvous in Cache Valley to the dimly lit study of Humboldt
in Potsdam.

CHAPTER III

The Challenge of
Indian Relations

T HE WESTWARD MOVEMENT in the United States is a chronicle of
success and progress; but it is also a story of tragedy, particularly in the
history of relations between the Anglo-Americans and the North American Indians. The first Americans played a number of roles in our early
history. They might appear as friends or benefactors of the colonists,
advising them about the crops of the New World or explaining the
relations between different tribes. Most spectacularly some friendly
Indian might save unwary colonials from capture or death at the hands
of hostile natives. As a collector of furs, the Indian became a part of the
colonial economic system, even serving as middle man between the
traders and far distant tribes. So strategic was the position and so large
the size of some tribes that they played the role of allies in the game of
colonial diplomacy, their friendship eagerly sought by the officers of
England, France or Spain.

Most important of all the Indian owned land that the American settlers
desired for their own use. From the beginning the English were prepared to recognize a possessory right in the Indians which they must
purchase, but eventually, as individuals cheated the Indians and complicated colonial Indian policy, such negotiations became the exclusive
right of the colonial or imperial governments. Although most Indian
tribes depended to some extent at least upon agriculture, their use of
the land was much less intensive than that of the colonial farmers.
Nor did they understand land ownership in terms of individual holdings
as did the Anglo-Americans; rather the tribesmen held their lands in
common. The goals of the two cultures were different and to even well-
disposed settlers the Indian was an inconvenience, occupying lands
which they coveted for themselves or others like them. And to many
pioneers the Indian was merely the scourge of the frontier.

A grim pattern of relations between the two cultures developed during the colonial period. Traders of European origin used the Indians to collect furs and entrapped them in the colonial economy. But as the wild animals decreased in number in a region and the tide of settlers moved closer, a second stage of cultural contact began. Now government officers cajoled, intimidated or tricked the tribesmen into selling part of their lands. During this process the pressures upon the Indians might produce warfare in which government troops or the frontiersmen eventually subdued the Indians. When white colonists crushed Indian uprisings, the Indians must often do additional penance by ceding more lands. Sometimes the shattered tribal remnants coalesced with other tribes. At other times the Anglo-Americans allowed them to stay on a reservation, some undesirable remnant of their once extensive hunting grounds. Typically during these developments the diseases of the white man and his alcohol created more distress among the tribesmen than did warfare. During the wars with France of the late seventeenth and the eighteenth centuries, good relations with the major Indian tribes became so important that the British government finally developed a centralized system of administration, designating northern and southern superintendents of Indian affairs.

Under the Constitution of 1787, the federal government assumed responsibility for Indian relations and Congress provided that the Secretary of War should supervise Indian affairs. Henry Knox and his successors developed a system of administration similar to the old British establishment. Superintendents administered Indian relations in particular regions and agents were allocated to tribes or to groups of tribes as the course of events dictated. After an initial period when the Americans maintained that some western tribes had forfeited their lands by siding with the British during the Revolution, the new government accepted the imperial interpretation of the Indian right of prior occupancy. Henry Knox wrote that the lands of the Indians could not be "taken from them unless by their free consent, or by the right of conquest in case of a just war. To dispossess them on any other principle, . . . would be a gross violation of the fundamental laws of nature, and of that distributive justice which is the glory of a nation."

Until 1871 relations between the American government, its citizens and any particular tribe of Indians was governed to a considerable extent by the treaties between the United States and that tribe; thereafter by agreements between the two. Although the treaty policy may appear disingenuous in retrospect, the numbers, military strength and strategic location of some of the tribes or tribal confederations made the policy appear reasonable in the colonial and early national period and perhaps facilitated negotiations. In the treaties with the tribes the historian finds the description of the various land cessions which the Indian groups yielded and the terms on which they surrendered them. Usually they received annuities in return for their lands, running sometimes in perpetuity and at others involving only a specific period of years. Sometimes the treaties provided that agents would live on the reservations left to them, as well as blacksmiths or other craftsmen and farmers responsible for teaching the Indians the agricultural methods of the Anglo-American civilization. Also, the United States Congress approved general legislation concerning the tribesmen, notably the Indian intercourse laws, specifying the conditions under which white men might enter Indian lands and trade with tribesmen, as well as laws related to the affairs of specific tribes. The treaties, agreements and legislation together now constitute a massive monument to our relations with the original Americans.

If Americans were willing to negotiate with the Indians they were also on occasion prepared to use force. When Indian agents failed to keep their charges contentedly on reservations or when negotiations between government officers and the Indians failed to prevent war, the Army restored peace on the frontier. The Secretary of War was directly responsible for the administration of Indian policy until the Department of the Interior was created in 1849. This fact, some believe, was tacit admission that Americans considered the Indian to be primarily a military problem during the first 60 years of the Republic. Yet there were humanitarian elements in American Indian policy also. Some Anglo-Americans did try to alleviate the distress of the Indians as their culture decayed and to help them adjust to new conditions. The treaty provisions which provided that agricultural training be given to the tribesmen reflected such sentiment. Some churchmen labored among the Indian tribes and the government encouraged the missionaries by allowing them to use the educational funds provided in some treaties and by making other small contributions to their efforts to "civilize" the tribesmen (see Chapter XV).

Educated Americans pondered both the Indian's place in Anglo-American culture and their obligations to him, usually maintaining during the first half of the nineteenth century that the Indian was living in a stage of civilization that their own forefathers had passed through many generations earlier. Intensive farming forced the land to yield more than did the mixed agriculture and hunting of the Indian; it was therefore superior to the Indian way. Bible-reading settlers found it easier to draw parallels between the utopias of scripture and their own culture than with the way of the Indian. When the objectives of the two cultures clashed, there was little doubt in the minds of Anglo-Americans, therefore, that their wishes should prevail. They could agree that the fate of the Indian was tragic but they could see no alternative but to make the Indians over in their own image. A clause of the Northwest Ordinance read, "The utmost good faith shall always be observed towards the Indians. . . ." But good faith in the Indian view would have allowed them to retain their lands and way of life. In the long run this was exactly what the central government and its Indian service could not allow if the settlers moving relentlessly westward were to have land.

During the early national period, the government realized that Indian policy might have important effects upon the relations of the United States with foreign powers. At that time the Indians above the Ohio River still looked to the British provinces for guidance; the tribes of the Southwest maintained close contacts with the Spanish authorities in the Floridas. American leaders must ask themselves whether their policies would make the Indians more or less amenable to these foreign influences. By the end of the War of 1812 the tribes of the Old Northwest were no longer a military threat of great significance. Although their numbers still made the southern tribes formidable at this time, the Spanish decision to cede the Floridas to the United States in 1819 removed the danger of foreign influence in that region. Despite occasional incidents thereafter, the Indians had ceased to be a major consideration in American diplomacy by 1820.

Given the importance of Indian affairs during the early years of the Republic, it is not surprising that the federal government developed one of its most enlightened Indian programs during this period and terminated it in the early 1820's. This was the government factory system. President Washington recommended the development of a system of government trading posts which might on the one hand counter British or Spanish influence and traders among the Indians, and also provide a place where the Indian could be sure of honest treatment. (See Chapter X.) But after the foreign danger was removed, Congress capitulated to the pressure of the fur traders and ended the system. Congressmen and members of the executive branch had found the administrator of the factory system to be a useful source of information about the Indians. In this development historians see the origins of the Bureau of Indian Affairs, established in the War Department during the mid-1820's to supervise the operation of the government's Indian policy.

More significant than the factory system during the years before 1840 was the development of the removal program. Remnants of some shattered or demoralized tribes had drifted before the settler's frontier throughout the colonial period. Now a majority of Americans came to favor a formal policy of removal. Westerners favored it because the transfer of an Indian tribe or band elsewhere typically freed lands for white settlement. But humanitarians also favored removal. Some missionaries who were ministering to Indian tribes wished to remove them from the corrupting influences of the border settlements and educate them so that the tribesmen could compete in the white man's world on equal terms. President Jefferson recommended that part of the Louisiana Purchase be used as a home for the Indian tribes then living east of the Mississippi. The idea became increasingly popular and Congress passed a general Indian Removal Act in 1830, authorizing the President to provide lands west of the Mississippi for eastern tribesmen. This law did not provide for coercive removal but in some cases that was the final result. By 1850 most of the surviving eastern tribes were in locations beyond the great river.

There was a depressing similarity in many of the tribal removals. Government commissioners often urged the reluctant tribesmen to accept treaty terms by every means short of outright force, while neighboring Anglo-Americans invaded their lands and stole their livestock. Civilian contractors supplied the equipment and rations for the journeys and provided a bare minimum or less for the subsistence of the Indians. Frequently many Indians died on the way west and during the period of adjustment in their new location. The shallowness of the American rationalization for removal was best revealed perhaps in the case of the Cherokees. The Indians, advocates of removal maintained, must make way for a superior civilization. But many of the Cherokees had already adopted the ways and values of the dominant culture. That fact did not prevent American soldiers from removing them from their lands at bayonet point, nor "The Trail of Tears." Many of the northern tribes endured removal after removal until finally they were settled more permanently, usually in the Indian Territory.

By the 1850's the American government was applying the familiar processes of its earlier policy to the tribes of the Trans-Missouri West. The specification of tribal territories, their constriction, the allocation of reservations and removal of tribes to concentration areas all became familiar elements in Indian policy in the western half of the country. In the Plains region the federal government moved the tribesmen particularly to Indian Territory and to Dakota Territory. For a time the policy promised to concentrate all of the Plains Indians in the former area, but the residents of neighboring states protested and the federal government did not carry the program to its logical conclusion.

Although there had been widespread unrest among the western Indians during the 1860's, old soldier Ulysses S. Grant refused to place sole reliance upon military measures after he became president in 1868. Army leaders urged that the Bureau of Indian Affairs be returned to the War Department, but he rejected their advice. He began a policy of selecting Indian agents from the nominees of the various church groups in the United States. During his administration the Board of Indian Commissioners was established. This group of unpaid philanthropists became a source of ideas for the Indian administrators, the conscience of the Bureau of Indian Affairs and an organ of public education. But the new policies did little to ease the adjustments of the western tribes as Anglo-Americans continued the development of the plains and mountain regions. The military campaign of the 1870's against western tribes climaxed the coercive phase of American Indian policy.

Despite the Indian Wars of the 1870's, popular concern with the plight of the first Americans began to increase. Although struck down and left for dead at peace negotiations during the Modoc War, Alfred B. Meacham began to agitate vigorously for reform; Helen Hunt Jackson became the literary star of the movement and her book, A Century of Dishonor, its creed. During the early 1880's the reformers formed a number of organizations to carry on the struggle. Spectacular or tragic events of the 1870's and early 1880's stimulated the critics and made the public more receptive to their pleas. Corruption in the Bureau of Indian Affairs shocked Americans, and they were sickened by the ruthless way in which frontiersmen tried to force the government to open Indian lands to settlement. The miners who invaded the Black Hills illegally during the mid-1870's helped to produce the Sioux Wars of that period. During the early 1880's "boomers" tried to force the opening of Indian Territory by squatting on the lands below the Kansas border. The gallant running battle of the Nez Percés in 1877 and the pitiful efforts of Cheyenne and Ponca Indians to flee Indian Territory and return to northern hunting grounds also increased the sympathy of the American people for the Indian. Evidence was accumulating also in this period that the tribesmen could respond to the challenge of acculturation. The efforts of various tribes or bands to do their own freighting and to police the reservations were impressive. The success of General Samuel C. Armstrong and Captain R. H. Pratt in training Indians at the Hampton and Carlisle Institutes seemed to promise that education would bridge the gap between the cultures.

In 1887 Congress approved the Dawes Severalty Act. A number of the treaties of the early and mid-nineteenth century had provided individual allotments of land for tribal members. Although the earlier allottees had usually sold or lost their land in short order, the Dawes Act provided that the reservations might be divided into individual holdings and distributed to the tribesmen in severalty, 160 acres to each adult head of a family and lesser amounts to other adults and children. The government would recompense the tribes or bands concerned for the excess reservation acreage left after allotment. The law stipulated that the allottees could not sell their land for 25 years. The Dawes Act also clarified the citizenship status of the Indians. During the mid-1880's the Supreme Court held that natives who had renounced tribal life were not citizens of the United States. Ironically the first Americans could apparently only become citizens by naturalization or by act of Congress. The Dawes Act provided that Indians who received allotments were to become citizens at that time. The reformers hoped that the Severalty Act would encourage the tribesmen to adopt the values and the way of life of the Anglo-Americans. Some western supporters of the law were more interested in the Indian lands which they expected it would release than in improving the lot of the Indians themselves.

Should the United States government have developed a different Indian policy? If so, what should its major features have been? Or could any other policy, short of leaving them in possession of most of their hunting grounds, have averted the Indian Wars and the cultural demoralization of the Indians? What do Anglo-American relations with the tribesmen tell us of relations between stronger and weaker peoples and between folk of different cultures? In the answers to these questions and others like them lie the lessons of American Indian policy.

ROY HARVEY PEARCE

The Indian in American Life and the Idea of Savagism

In retrospect Americans frequently conclude that the Indian policy of the United States during the eighteenth and nineteenth centuries was both cruel and disgusting. How they ask, could Americans have salved their consciences? Roy Harvey Pearce provides one answer to such questioning. Drawing upon the social theorizing of Europeans as well as upon their own observations and analysis, educated Americans, at least, accepted the concept of savagism. This idea did not blind them perhaps to the tragic impact of Anglo-American culture upon the Indians but it did convince them that it was inevitable.

Americans who were setting out to make a new society could find a place in it for the Indian only if he would become what they were—settled, steady, civilized. Yet somehow he would not be anything but what he was—roaming, unreliable, savage. So they concluded that they were destined to try to civilize him and, in trying, to destroy him, because he could not and would not be civilized. He was to be pitied for this, and also to be censured. Pity and censure were the price Americans would have to pay for destroying the Indian. Pity and censure would be, in the long run, the price of the progress of civilization over savagism. . . .

The basis of their understanding had long been part of the grand rationale of westward-moving colonialism. This was the tradition of the natural and divine superiority of a farming to a hunting culture. Universally Americans could see the Indian only as hunter. That his culture, at least the culture of the eastern Indians whom they knew best until the second quarter of the nineteenth century, was as much agrarian as hunting, they simply could not see. They forgot too, if they had ever known, that many of their own farming methods had been

---

Source: Abridged from Roy Harvey Pearce, *Savagism and Civilization: A Study of the Indian and the American Mind* (Rev. ed. Baltimore, 1965), 53, 66-68, 73-76, 87, 103-104. Reprinted by permission of the Johns Hopkins University Press.

taken over directly from the Indians whom they were pushing westward. One can say only that their intellectual and cultural traditions, their idea of order, so informed their thoughts and their actions that they could see and conceive of nothing but the Indian who hunted.

Biblical injunction framed their belief; and on the frontier practical conditions supported it. The Indian with his known hunting ways needed many square miles on which to live, whereas the white farmer needed only a few acres. The latter way was obviously more economical and intelligent; it was essentially the civilized way. Therefore the Indian would have to move on to make way for a better and higher life. If the Indian's fate was a sad one and civilized men should be properly moved by it, still, in the long run, the prospects were exciting and ennobling. Thus an historian towards the end of the eighteenth century:

... His agonies, at first, seem to demand a tear from the eye of humanity; but when we reflect, that the extinction of his race, and the progress of the arts which give rise to his distressing apprehensions, are for the increase of mankind, and for the promotion of the world's glory and happiness; that five hundred rational animals may enjoy life in plenty, and comfort, where only one Savage drags out a hungry existence, we shall be pleased with the perspective into futurity.

Yet belief in the glorious possibilities of a culture built out of cities and cultivated fields was based on something more than Biblical injunction and economic necessity. "Those who labor in the earth," Jefferson had written in 1784, "are the chosen people of God, if ever He had a chosen people. Whose breasts He has made His peculiar deposit for substantial and genuine virtue." This is agrarian idealism, the belief that men, having a natural right to their land by occupation and labor, achieve status and dignity by exercising that right and becoming free-holding farmers. It is a deep-rooted belief, whose theoretical ground derives from the Lockean theory of the free individual and the metaphysics and sociology of his freedom. For Locke—and virtually all Americans were, in the most general sense, Lockeans—man achieved his highest humanity by taking something out of nature and converting it with his labor into part of himself. His private property, conceived of in terms of the close, personal relationships of an agrarian society, was his means to social maturity. It gave him stability, self-respect, privacy, and the basis for civilized society itself. For Americans the Lockean theory must have made savage society seem loose, immature, virtually anarchic, full of the false freedom of doing as one pleased; likewise, for Americans the theory now must have made it all the more possible to see how Indians could become truly rational animals. All, indeed, that an Indian would need to be on his way to civilization was, in the words of the Secretary of War in 1789, "a love for exclusive property. . . ."

Pity, censure, and their justification are the qualities we must distinguish in American thinking about the Indian between the Revolution and the period of Removal. We need not try to get directly at the psychological roots of such qualities. At best, knowing now what we know about our fundamental psychological nature as humans, we can only guess at such roots. We can say that the American, as the self-consciously civilized and civilizing man, could envision the possibilities of a life free from what he somehow felt to be the complexities of civilization. Envisioning that life, he might very well yearn for it. But seeing it, as he thought, in disturbing actuality to the west, he hated himself for his yearning. He was tempted, we might say; and he felt driven to destroy the temptation and likewise the tempters. He pitied the tempters, because in his yearning for a simpler life, he could identify with them. He censured them, because he was ashamed to be tempted, and he refused to deny his higher nature.

All this, perhaps, is too much to psychologize the situation and to ask too much of the evidence we have. I mean it only to suggest the possible roots of the pattern of pity and censure and to suggest that it derives from polarities deep in the American character, deep in all human character. It reflects the simple fact that the tensions of any way of life suggest to men that there is a simpler way, with fewer tensions, perhaps none, and that how men face up to the fact—and how they rationalize and symbolize their facing up to the fact—is an expression of the meaning that they at once find in and give to their situation in history. Our concern, however, is not with what their separate and collective unconscious made Americans be, but with what their conscious life and imagination told them they were.

What these nineteenth-century Americans were aware of was degradation and destruction of the Indian, removal, desperate drives to civilize and to Christianize before it would be too late, abhorrence of the perverse cruelties of white man on the frontier, frightening glimpses of the Indian as the vanishing American. If they were to be borne, if men were to live with them, all these attitudes and impulses had to be shown to be products of a civilizing process whose good finally negated the evil in them, even if it did not make that evil immediately less painful. When this came to pass, when the destiny of the savage was fully comprehended in its relationship to the destiny of the civilized man, the Indian had been mastered not only as individual but as symbol. . . .

American double-mindedness about the Indian issued rapidly into a theory of his life—an idea of savagism, as it was called. As all ideas should be, this one was for its time true. That is to say, it consisted of a set of interrelated propositions which held together and made logical sense of all that was known and felt about the Indian, and it made for understanding, belief, and action. As data about the Indian accumulated, the idea was first filled out, then modified, and finally broken through. By the time the idea could no longer contain the data—it was then the 1850's—psychological as well as physical Removal had been effected, and the Indian had become a creature of philanthropic agencies, scientific ethnology, and dime novels. Savagism no longer seemed to exist. At least, it no longer seemed seriously to threaten civilized existence. . . .

In spite of the nationalism which forced its growth, the American understanding of the Indian depended on an idea of savagism whose main structure derived from European sources. American theorizing about the Indian owed its greatest debt to a group of eighteenth-century Scottish writers on man and society, to their historical method, and to the one of the group who wrote on the North American Indian. The group was the historians belonging to the Scottish school of common sense and moral sentiment; their method was that of the historical analysis of social process; and the one who wrote on the North American Indian was William Robertson, in his *History of America* (1777).

The grand intention of the eighteenth-century Scottish historians and writers on society—among them, Francis Hutcheson, Thomas Reid, Adam Ferguson, Lord Kames, and Robertson—was to construct a sociology of progress, a theory which would make comprehensible at once social stability and social growth, which would explain to Christians how they could originally have fallen and yet have come to such a high and noble state in their enlightened century. The Scots' thinking had evolved ultimately out of a Protestant theology in which the millennium had been rationalized from a certainty of the second coming of Christ into a certainty of the God-ordained, intelligent self-sufficiency of modern man to work out his own way with his common sense, his analytic reason, and his special moral sense. The Scots held that it might be conjectured back from empirical evidence how God was revealing His Word to modern man slowly but surely, how modern man was thus slowly but surely progressing to high civilization, how he had left behind him forever his savage, primitive state. This was the grand Christian, civilized Idea of Progress. . . .

Part of the empirical data which this idea of progress comprehended was that concerning primitive peoples, past and present. To this end, the

Scots constructed what they called conjectural histories—their translation of *histoire raisonée*—and gave the primitive his due, placing him in their past and present, as they felt, for good and for bad. A typical analysis, that of Adam Ferguson's *Essay on the History of Civil Society*, begins with an attack on the notion that the state of nature was one of simple animality. Man, Ferguson insists, is by nature social. Civilization itself is natural to him; at every stage in his evolution he lives for a group; his is, in its fullest sense, the life of the family. Thus, Ferguson can conclude, every state is a state of nature, social nature, and man is limited only by the society in which he lives. . . .

What generally emerges from Ferguson's *Essay*, and from others like it, is a simple and clear demonstration from conjectural history of a proposition which Americans, in their feelings of pity and censure over the fate of the Indians, needed desperately to believe: that men in becoming civilized had gained much more than they had lost; and that civilization, the act of civilizing, for all of its destruction of primitive virtues, put something higher and greater in their place. Americans could see this proposition demonstrated again and again. It was clear that primitive life carried with it concomitant virtues and defects, the products of the social form in which they were produced. Thus it was not a matter of mourning the destruction of primitive virtues. Rather, it was a matter of analyzing the virtues and defects, necessary in the very scheme of things, of a given stage of social evolution. As it happened, savage courage, fortitude, and freedom could all be developed only in a primitive society. But there were also more unfortunate products of that society—hardship, cruelty, warfare, lack of "social affections" and of refined religion, philosophy, and learning in general. Good qualities and bad were both part of a social whole which could not be broken down suddenly, but which should slowly evolve toward something better. Civilizers were agents of that evolution and that progress, and they should come to know that they were, even as they should be deeply and charitably moved by the fate of the savages over whom they were progressing. Scottish theory seemed to bear out American practice.

A special problem still existed, however. Why had American Indians not progressed to high civilization as had Europeans? What had happened to the historical line? The terms of the answer were simple: isolation and the overpowering effect of environment. . . .

Operating from a moral absolute—that involved in the theory of man's social destiny—Americans were able to achieve a satisfactory kind of cultural relativity. Before one judges the Indian, so their argument went, one must understand him. And when one understands, one will see that judgment of the savage as being noble or ignoble is precluded. Savage life and civilized life are realms apart, separated by centuries of cultural history, or by entirely different environmental situations, most likely by both. Hence what is good for a savage is not necessarily good for a civilized man. The ideals of a savage society are built around the hunt and warfare; and its members can develop no further, no higher, than their life will let them. To follow up a favorite example, in an Indian society women must do all the manual labor, because in order for that society to survive, the men must be occupied with nothing but the basic problem of feeding and defending it. The Indian is not a beast because he treats his women as he does; our saying that he is, is tantamount to our judging behavior in a savage society in terms of behavior in a civilized society. Even as what seem to us to be the Indian's inferior traits are the products of his immature and inhibited society, so are his superior traits. American writers noted again and again that the Indian's ability to bear tremendous physical pain stoically makes him neither better nor worse than the civilized man, but rather is simply a characteristic result of the natural ideals and aims of a warrior-dominated society in which all men must expect to do just that, grow used to doing just that. Savage virtues, then, like savage vices, are uniquely savage.

The simplest way to describe the Indian would be to say that he was uncivilized. The simplest way to evaluate him would be to say that his virtues and vices, his bravery and cruelty, were products of his being uncivilized. One would thus be evaluating not so much the qualities of an individual as those of a society; and one would be placing that society in relation to one's own in such a way that history, and the idea of progress which gave meaning to history, would solve the problem of evaluation. The idea of history as progress made it possible fully to comprehend the culturally earlier as the morally inferior, even as an environmentalist analysis of societies made it possible to account for the contemporaneity of that which should have been part of the past. Savagism could be known only in terms of the civilization to which, by the law of nature, it had to give way. . . .

MARY E. YOUNG

Indian Removal and Land Allotment:
The Civilized Tribes and Jacksonian Justice

Historians believe that the presidency of Andrew Jackson was
extremely important in the development of American democratic institutions. In his administration Congress also confirmed the policy of removing the eastern tribes beyond
the Mississippi, which had been developing under earlier
presidents. Here Mary E. Young analyzes the policy of
granting individual allotments to members of the great
southern tribes during the government's efforts to purchase
the title of their remaining lands. It is both a complex and
a disturbing story.

By the year 1830, the vanguard of the southern frontier had crossed
the Mississippi and was pressing through Louisiana, Arkansas, and
Missouri. But the line of settlement was by no means as solid as frontier
lines were classically supposed to be. East of the Mississippi, white
occupancy was limited by Indian tenure of northeastern Georgia, en-
claves in western North Carolina and southern Tennessee, eastern Alabama, and the northern two-thirds of Mississippi. In this twenty-five-
million-acre domain lived nearly 60,000 Cherokees, Creeks, Choctaws,
and Chickasaws.

The Jackson administration sought to correct this anomaly by removing
the tribes beyond the reach of white settlements, west of the Mississippi.
As the President demanded of Congress in December, 1830:

What good man would prefer a country covered with forests and ranged
by a few thousand savages to our extensive Republic, studded with cities,
towns, and prosperous farms, embellished with all the improvements which
art can devise or industry execute, occupied by more than 12,000,000 happy
people, and filled with all the blessings of liberty, civilization, and religion?

The President's justification of Indian removal was the one usually

---

SOURCE: Abridged from Mary E. Young, "Indian Removal and Allotment: The
Civilized Tribes and Jacksonian Justice," *American Historical Review*, LXIV (October,
1958), 31-45. Reprinted by permission of Mary E. Young.

applied to the displacement of the Indians by newer Americans—the superiority of a farming to a hunting culture, and of Anglo-American "liberty, civilization, and religion" to the strange and barbarous way of the red man. The superior capacity of the farmer to exploit the gifts of nature and of nature's God was one of the principal warranties of the triumph of westward-moving "civilization."

Such a rationalization had one serious weakness as an instrument of policy. The farmer's right of eminent domain over the lands of the savage could be asserted consistently only so long as the tribes involved were "savage." The southeastern tribes, however, were agriculturists as well as hunters. For two or three generations prior to 1830, farmers among them fenced their plantations and "mixed their labor with the soil," making it their private property according to accepted definitions of natural law. . . .

The "civilization" of a portion of these tribes embarrassed United States policy in more ways than one. Long-term contact between the southeastern tribes and white traders, missionaries, and government officials created and trained numerous half-breeds. The half-breed men acted as intermediaries between the less sophisticated Indians and the white Americans. Acquiring direct or indirect control of tribal politics, they often determined the outcome of treaty negotiations. Since they proved to be skillful bargainers, it became common practice to win their assistance by thinly veiled bribery. The rise of the half-breeds to power, the rewards they received, and their efforts on behalf of tribal reform gave rise to bitter opposition. . . . Furthermore, many of the new leaders had valuable plantations, mills, and trading establishments on these lands. Particularly among the Cherokees and Choctaws, they took pride in their achievements and those of their people in assimilating the trappings of civilization. As "founding Fathers," they prized the political and territorial integrity of the newly organized Indian "nations." These interests and convictions gave birth to a fixed determination, embodied in tribal laws and intertribal agreements, that no more cessions of land should be made. The tribes must be permitted to develop their new way of life in what was left of their ancient domain. . . .

To Jacksonian officials, however, the tactics of the half-breeds and the struggles among tribal factions seemed to reflect a diabolical plot. Treaty negotiators saw the poverty and "depravity" of the common Indian, who suffered from the scarcity of game, the missionary attacks on his accustomed habits and ceremonies, and the ravages of "demon rum" and who failed to find solace in the values of Christian and commercial civilization. Not unreasonably, they concluded that it was to the interest of the tribesman to remove west of the Mississippi. There, sheltered from the intruder and the whisky merchant, he could lose his savagery while improving his nobility. Since this seemed so obviously to the Indian's interest, the negotiators conveniently concluded that it was also his desire. What, then, deterred emigration? Only the rapacity of the half-breeds, who were unwilling to give up their extensive properties and their exalted position.

These observers recognized that the government's difficulties were in part of its own making. The United States had pursued an essentially contradictory policy toward the Indians, encouraging both segregation and assimilation. Since Jefferson's administration, the government had tried periodically to secure the emigration of the eastern tribes across the Mississippi. At the same time, it had paid agents and subsidized missionaries who encouraged the Indian to follow the white man's way. Thus it had helped create the class of tribesmen skilled in agriculture, pecuniary accumulation, and political leadership. Furthermore, by encouraging the southeastern Indians to become cultivators and Christians, the government had undermined its own moral claim to eminent domain over tribal lands. The people it now hoped to displace could by no stretch of dialectic be classed as mere wandering savages.

By the time Jackson became President, then, the situation of the United States vis-à-vis the southeastern tribes was superficially that of irresistible force and immovable object. But the President, together with such close advisers as Secretary of War John H. Eaton and General John Coffee, viewed the problem in a more encouraging perspective. They believed that the government faced not the intent of whole tribes to remain near the bones of their ancestors but the selfish determination of a few quasi-Indian leaders to retain their riches and their ill-used power. Besides, the moral right of the civilized tribes to their lands was a claim not on their whole doman but rather on the part cultivated by individuals. Both the Indian's natural right to his land and his political capacity for keeping it were products of his imitation of white "civilization." Both might be eliminated by a rigorous application of the principle that to treat an Indian fairly was to treat him like a white man. . . .

The technique used to effect this object was simple: the entire population of the tribes was forced to deal with white men on terms familiar only to the most acculturated portion of them. If the Indian is civilized, he can behave like a white man. Then let him take for his own as much land as he can cultivate, become a citizen of the state where he lives, and accept the burdens which citizenship entails. If he is not capable of living like this, he should be liberated from the tyranny of his chiefs and allowed to follow his own best interest by emigrating beyond the farthest frontiers of white settlement. By the restriction of the civilized to the lands they cultivate and by the emigration of the savages millions of acres will be opened to white settlement.

The first step dictated by this line of reasoning was the extension of state laws over the Indian tribes. Beginning soon after Jackson's election, Georgia, Alabama, Mississippi, and Tennessee gradually brought the Indians inside their borders under their jurisdiction. Thus an Indian could be sued for trespass or debt, though only in Mississippi and Tennessee was his testimony invariably acceptable in a court of law. In Mississippi, the tribesmen were further harassed by subjection—or the threat of subjection—to such duties as mustering with the militia, working on roads, and paying taxes. State laws establishing county governments within the tribal domains and, in some cases, giving legal protection to purchasers of Indian improvements encouraged the intrusion of white settlers on Indian lands. The laws nullified the legal force of Indian customs, except those relating to marriage. They provided heavy penalties for anyone who might enact or enforce tribal law. Finally, they threatened punishment to any person who might attempt to deter another from signing a removal treaty or enrolling for emigration. The object of these laws was to destroy the tribal governments and to thrust upon individual Indians the uncongenial alternative of adjusting to the burdens of citizenship or removing beyond state jurisdiction. . . .

Congress in May, 1830, complemented the efforts of the states by appropriating $500,000 and authorizing the President to negotiate removal treaties with all the tribes east of the Mississippi. The vote on this bill was close in both houses. By skillful use of pamphlets, petitions, and lobbyists, missionary organizations had enlisted leading congressmen in their campaign against the administration's attempt to force the tribes to emigrate. In the congressional debates, opponents of the bill agreed that savage tribes were duty-bound to relinquish their hunting grounds to the agriculturist, but they argued that the southeastern tribes were no longer savage. In any case, such relinquishment must be made in a freely contracted treaty. The extension of state laws over the Indian country was coercion; this made the negotiation of a free contract impossible. Both supporters and opponents of the bill agreed on one cardinal point—the Indian's moral right to keep his land depended on his actual cultivation of it.

A logical corollary of vesting rights in land in proportion to cultivation was the reservation to individuals of as much land as they had improved at the time a treaty was signed. In 1816, Secretary of War William H.

Crawford had proposed such reservations, or allotments, as a means of accommodating the removal policy to the program of assimilation. According to Crawford's plan, individual Indians who had demonstrated their capacity for civilization by establishing farms and who were willing to become citizens should be given the option of keeping their cultivated lands, by fee simple title, rather than emigrating. This offer was expected to reconcile the property-loving half-breeds to the policy of emigration. . . .

The Crawford policy was applied in the Cherokee treaties of 1817 and 1819 and the Choctaw treaty of 1820. These agreements offered fee simple allotments to heads of Indian families having improved lands within the areas ceded to the government. Only 311 Cherokees and eight Choctaws took advantage of the offer. This seemed to bear out the assumption that only a minority of the tribesmen would care to take allotments. Actually, these experiments were not reliable. In both cases, the tribes ceded only a fraction of their holdings. Comparatively few took allotments; but on the other hand, few emigrated. The majority simply remained within the diminished tribal territories east of the Mississippi.

The offer of fee simple allotments was an important feature of the negotiations with the tribes in the 1820's. When the extension of state laws made removal of the tribes imperative, it was to be expected that allotments would comprise part of the consideration offered for the ceded lands. Both the ideology which rationalized the removal policy and the conclusions erroneously drawn from experience with the earlier allotment treaties led government negotiators to assume that a few hundred allotments at most would be required. . . .

Widespread intrusion on Indian lands began with the extension of state laws over the tribal domains. In the treaties of cession, the government promised to remove intruders, but its policy in this respect was vacillating and ineffective. Indians whose allotments covered valuable plantations proved anxious to promote the sale of their property by allowing buyers to enter the ceded territory as soon as possible. Once this group of whites was admitted, it became difficult to discriminate against others. Thus a large number of intruders settled among the Indians with the passive connivance of the War Department and the tribal leaders. The task of removing them was so formidable that after making a few gestures the government generally evaded its obligation. The misery of the common Indians, surrounded by intruders and confused by the disruption of tribal authority, was so acute that any method for securing their removal seemed worth trying. Furthermore, their emigration would serve the interest of white settlers, land speculators, and their representatives in Washington. The government therefore chose to facilitate the sale of allotments even before the Indians received fee simple title to them.

The right to sell his allotment was useful to the sophisticated tribesman with a large plantation. Such men were accustomed to selling their crops and hiring labor. Through their experience in treaty negotiations, they had learned to bargain over the price of lands. Many of them received handsome payment for their allotments. Some kept part of their holdings and remained in Alabama and Mississippi as planters—like others planters, practicing as land speculators on the side. Nearly all the Indians had some experience in trade, but to most of them the conception of land as a salable commodity was foreign. . . .

It is not surprising that the common Indian's legal freedom of contract in selling his allotment did not necessarily lead him to make the best bargain possible in terms of his pecuniary interests. Nor did the proceeds of the sales transform each seller into an emigrant of large independent means. A right of property and freedom to contract for its sale did not automatically invest the Indian owner with the habits, values, and skills of a sober land speculator. His acquisition of property and freedom actually increased his dependence on those who traditionally mediated for him in contractual relations with white Americans.

Prominent among these mediators were white men with Indian wives who made their living as planters and traders in the Indian nations, men from nearby settlements who traded with the leading Indians or performed legal services for them, and interpreters. In the past, such individuals had been appropriately compensated for using their influence in favor of land cessions. It is likely that their speculative foresight was in part responsible for the allotment features in the treaties of the 1830's. When the process of allotting lands to individuals began, these speculative gentlemen made loans of whisky, muslin, horses, slaves, and other useful commodities to the new property-owner. They received in return the Indian's written promise to sell his allotment to them as soon as its boundaries were defined. Generally they were on hand to help him locate it on "desirable" lands. They, in turn, sold their "interest" in the lands to men of capital. Government agents encouraged the enterprising investor, since it was in the Indian's interest and the government's policy that the lands be sold and the tribes emigrate. Unfortunately, the community of interest among the government, the speculator, and the Indian proved largely fictitious. The speculator's interest in Indian lands led to frauds which impoverished the Indians, soiled the reputation of the government, and retarded the emigration of the tribes. . . .

Besides embarrassing the government, the speculators contributed to the demoralization of the Indians. Universal complaint held that after paying the tribesman for his land they often borrowed back the money without serious intent of repaying it, or recovered it in return for over-priced goods of which a popular article was whisky. Apprised of this situation, Secretary of War Lewis Cass replied that once the Indian had been paid for his land the War Department had no authority to circumscribe his freedom to do what he wished with the proceeds.

Nevertheless, within their conception of the proper role of government officials who dealt with the tribes tried to be helpful. Although the Indian must be left free to contract for the sale of his lands, the United States sent agents to determine the validity of the contracts. These agents some-times refused to approve a contract that did not specify a fair price for the land in question. They also refused official sanction when it could not be shown that the Indian owner had at some time been in possession of the sum stipulated. This protective action on the part of the govern-ment, together with its several investigations into frauds in the sale of Indian lands, apparently did secure the payment of more money than the tribesmen might otherwise have had. But the effort was seriously hampered by the near impossibility of obtaining disinterested testi-mony. . . .

A superficially ironic consequence of the allotment policy as a method of acquiring land for white settlers was the fact that it facilitated the engrossment of land by speculators. With their superior command of capital and the influence it would buy, speculators acquired 80 to 90 per cent of the lands allotted to the southeastern tribesmen.

For most of the Indian beneficiaries of the policy, its most important consequence was to leave them landless. After selling their allotment, or a claim to it, they might take to the swamp, live for a while on the bounty of a still hopeful speculator, or scavenge on their settler neigh-bors. But ultimately most of them faced the alternative of emigration or destitution, and chose to emigrate. The machinations of the speculators and the hopes they nurtured that the Indians might somehow be able to keep a part of their allotted lands made the timing of removals less predictable than it might otherwise have been. This unpredictability compounded the evils inherent in a mass migration managed by a gov-ernment committed to economy and unversed in the arts of economic planning. The result was the "Trail of Tears."

The allotment treaties of the 1830's represent an attempt to apply Anglo-American notions of justice, which enshrined private property in land and freedom of contract as virtually absolute values, to Indian tribes whose tastes and traditions were otherwise. Their history illustrates the limitations of intercultural application of the Golden Rule. In a more practical sense, the treaties typified an effort to force on the Indians the alternative of complete assimiliation or complete segregation by placing individuals of varying levels of sophistication in situations where they must use the skills of businessmen or lose their means of livelihood. This policy secured tribal lands while preserving the forms of respect for property rights and freedom of contract, but it proved costly to both the government and the Indians.

•3•

ROBERT F. BERKHOFER, JR.

Protestants, Pagans, and Sequences among the North American Indians, 1760-1860

Anglo-American culture penetrated Indian society in many ways, weakening its social and political structure and demoralizing the individual tribesman. No agent of white society was more revolutionary in his demands upon the Indians than was the Protestant missionary. In this selection Robert F. Berkhofer, Jr. describes the sequences of social interaction which developed when Protestant churchmen began to minister to the members of Indian tribes or bands.

. . . Examination of the actual work in the field reveals few differences in aim among the missionaries of various denominations during the hundred years under study. Though many controversies raged in the religious periodicals over the best methods of saving savages, and the century witnessed the transformation from the lonely missionary sponsored by a small society to the erection of giant manual labor boarding schools financed by prosperous national societies, all missionaries consciously and unconsciously spread much the same mixture of religion

Source: Abridged from Robert F. Berkhofer, Jr., "Protestants, Pagans, and Sequences among the North American Indians, 1760-1860," *Ethnohistory*, X (Summer, 1963), 201-231. Reprinted by permission of *Ethnohistory* and Robert F. Berkhofer, Jr.

and secular pursuits. While most missionaries did not enter the Lord's vineyard to preach houses and hoes as well as Heaven, they did so, for as the American Board of Commissioners for Foreign Missions admitted in the most sophisticated statement of the period:

Missions are instituted for the spread of scriptural self-propagating Christianity. This is their only aim. Civilization as an end, they never attempt; still they are the most successful of all civilizing agencies, because (1) a certain degree of general improvement is involved in a self-propagating Christianity, and must be furthered as a *means* thereto; and (2) a rapid change in the intellectual and social life is a sure growth therefrom.

For this reason the sacred and profane were combined in the minds of missionaries, and the version of their culture which they propagated may be called, as some of them termed it, "Christian Civilization." Therefore the only good Indian from their point of view was a copy of a *good* White man, or as a Methodist missionary wrote, "In school and in field, as well as in kitchen, our aim was to teach the Indians to live like white people." . . .

Like other Whites, missionaries viewed the Indian as the lowest rung on the ladder of social evolution and believed that progress and civilization must triumph over savagery. In fact, they felt they were in the vanguard of the movement to force the aborigine up the ladder to the American apex.

Yet the missionary was only one among many Whites in contact with the Indian. Soldiers, traders, and government agents usually preceded the Protestant missionary to the tribe. Although he was only one among many acculturative agents, he *demanded* more change on the part of the Indians than any other. The traders only wanted a simple bartering system implemented and perhaps a squaw. The soldiers wanted peace except when bored. The government agents desired fulfillment of treaty obligations. The blackcoat, on the other hand, sought not only religious converts but the complete transformation of Indian life. Of all the forces for acculturation between 1760 and 1860, the missionary pushed more aggressively for change than any other White. . . .

By the time the missionary arrived at . . . a village or band in the century under consideration, much acculturation had occurred, but the changes had not affected the basic social structure or cultural patterning inherited from aboriginal times. As the missionary gained converts to his program of Christian Civilization, more and more Indians accepted new values and aspired to a new way of life, for just as the missionary could not really separate religion and secularism, so the Indians could not unravel the two when the blackcoat preached. For this reason, the Indians normally reacted to missionaries as to the whole of American civilization. Each culture opposed the other as a totality in this stage. Psychologically speaking there seemed to be no half-way point. Once an Indian fully surrendered to Christ, he not only observed the Sabbath and attended church, but he dressed in White man's clothing, sent his children to school, took hold of the plow, cleared his fields, began a garden, erected a house, and married his wife in a Christian ceremony— or, at least he knew he should even if he did not reach these goals. . . . Both missionaries and Indians recognized that the two cultural systems clashed, and the missionaries called the adherents of the two systems the Pagan Party and the Christian Party. . . .

The success of the missionary in causing such a cultural division forced the Indians who retained the old customs to realize that they must meet the challenge to their way of life. First, the Pagan Party employed the methods of social control normally used to correct any deviation within the tribe upon those converts within the community. Social pressure ranged from mild derision to threats of personal violence against the converts. . . . Secondly, the Pagan Party persecuted the missionary in hopes of driving him away, and in extreme cases, massacred him. At this stage of contact, the Indians frequently failed to differentiate between missionary and other American contact, so pique, whether at government agent or God, led to slaughter of mission cattle, stolen clothes, burned mission fences, and sabotaged grist and saw mills. . . .

Somewhat more complicated is the second possible sequence which involves a social as well as cultural division. Societal disruption naturally followed from missionization, for the acceptance of new values as well as Pagan persecution demanded new social relationships. Sometimes conversion merely meant the end of polygamy. At other times couples separated because one spouse had been converted. In still other instances, people left their villages to settle in places more favorable to Indian Christianity. In extreme cases new villages or bands were formed entirely of White-oriented Indians. Thus in this sequence, after the initial cultural divisions, the cleavage worsens, and instead of reuniting as in the first sequence, the community breaks into two physically separate groups which enables each one to live in its own community in which culture and social structure coincide. . . .

[The way was now prepared for the third possible sequence.] As more and more missionaries arrived and more Whites settled around the reservation, the coincidence between culture, social structure, and community broke down not only in one village as in the preceding sequence but in many towns in the tribe. To heal the divisions, attempts were made at political organization on the tribal level. Such attempts were reinforced by the activities of government agents and missionaries. Since the Indians bordered on rapidly expanding White settlements, the governmental authorities constantly bargained for tribal lands. The peculiar ethical views of the dominant society necessitated the signing of a contract by the tribe as a whole through some legal representatives and thus fostered the notion of a more elaborate tribal government. At the same time the ever-diminishing reservation impressed the concept of territoriality, which is so essential to the modern idea of the state, upon Christian and Pagan alike. At the same time, the idea of more formal government was assisted by the missionaries who not only trained Indians in governance through church and voluntary associations organized by this time along tribal lines, but who had always strongly advocated better Indian government, that is, White law and organization. With missionary encouragement and the experience gathered in church societies, the members of the Christian Party naturally attempted to form a tribal-wide government in order to force their new culture and social relations upon their fellow tribesmen. In order to counter this move, the Pagans were compelled to expand the traditional political system in functions and authority, if not in offices, to meet the challenge. . . .

In the ideal development of this sequence, the form of government presented by the Christians for tribal use was modeled after that of the dominant society: a written constitution provided for elective officers to fill positions in a government of divided powers. Though the Pagans opposed the aims and even the mechanism of the Christians' political system, they would be forced at this stage to gain power through elections and capture the new government established by the Christians. If all had gone well, genuine political parties would have arisen. Yet a smoothly-functioning political party system was never realized, for neither Christians nor Pagans consented to the other faction controlling the government in this period. The Pagans, when they won an election, dedicated themselves to destroying the government—or they paid no attention to the new government at all! . . .

. . . [There was another] possible sequence of missionization. Given conditions of advanced acculturation and tribal division, missionaries entering a tribe then were thrown into an already existing faction rather than aiding in the creation of one. Such a possibility is seen in Cherokee and Choctaw history, where missionaries were automatically involved in factional politics revolving about removal and later slavery, in spite of their efforts at dissociation. Under these circumstances, Indian church members switched religious affiliation according to politics. For instance, a leading Choctaw left the church of a Presbyterian missionary from the North and organized a Cumberland Presbyterian Church which was more in line with his sentiments toward the Negro. In other words, the Indians had acculturated to the point where they could not only differentiate the various elements of American civilization, but were themselves divided according to their perceptions of the various elements.

Although this last sequence points to the eventual and complete assimilation of the Indian, such was not to happen after the Civil War. Instead, greater fragmentation followed acculturation, and Americans always have refused final acceptance of the Indian because of racial prejudice. Furthermore, as the government took over work in the field, the missionary became less significant as the major acculturative force. . . . Yet, when the missionary was the chief force, he and the response to him provide many clues to the nature of cultural change.

RAY H. MATTISON

The Indian Reservation System on the
Upper Missouri, 1865–1890

The Anglo-Americans encountered a considerable population of Indians in the upper Missouri region. After 1850 the United States government established several dozen reservation agencies supervising these Indians, most notably perhaps the Dakotas, who have come to typify the mounted warrior culture of the Northern Plains country. Ray H. Mattison gives an account of the policies which the agents of that region were expected to follow and some of the characteristics and shortcomings of the agency system in this region.

. . . With the ending of the Indian wars and the placing of the various tribes on reservations, the role of the military in controlling the red man decreased. For many years the Army had pointed out the numerous frauds and instances of mismanagement of the Indians by the Interior Department to which they had been transferred in 1849. Through its friends in Congress, the military continued its pressure through the late 1860's and throughout the 1870's to have the Indian Bureau again placed under the War Department. Proponents of this change introduced bill after bill in Congress to achieve this end. The friends of civilian control were able to build up an equally strong case for their cause, so all the measures proposing transfer met defeat. After 1879 this pressure subsided, and the friends of the Indians sought more fundamental reforms.

Public opinion, on the other hand, was to play an increasing part in shaping the Nation's policies toward its charges. Prior to 1865 the West was openly hostile to the red man, while the East was indifferent to him. From 1865 to 1880, a number of public-spirited individuals, such as William Welsh, Bishop H. B. Whipple, and George Manypenny, who were sincerely sympathetic toward the Indians, were particularly active

SOURCE: Abridged from Ray H. Mattison, "The Indian Reservation System on the Upper Missouri, 1865–1890," *Nebraska History*, XXXVI (September, 1955), 141–172. Reprinted by permission of *Nebraska History* and Ray H. Mattison.

in promoting the interests of the Upper Missouri River tribes. Numerous frauds, the invasion of the Black Hills by the whites, and the Ponca Removal from Nebraska in 1877 and its aftermath all stimulated public opinion in favor of the red man. The period from 1879 to 1885 was to see the formation of several groups, such as the Women's National Indian Association, the Indian Rights Association, the Lake Mohonk conferences, the National Indian Defense Association, all of which were dedicated to the protection of the Indians' interests. These organizations were very active in propagandizing for Indian reforms.

By the late 1870's the Indian Bureau was in a position to compel all of its reluctant wards to conform to its policy or starve. With the aid of the Army, it had accomplished its first objective of placing them on reservations and making the Indians entirely dependent on the Government for subsistence. Its next main objective was to make them self-supporting like their white brothers so they could take a place among the latter as citizens. . . .

The Bureau found many established habits and customs in the Indian's mode of living which were obstacles in its program for reforming him. His communistic concepts of property were alien to the whites. His marriage, divorce, and burial customs, his so-called "loose" morals, the practice of polygamy and plural marriages were particularly offensive. The red man's tribal village life, characterized by the dominance of chiefs and medicine men, was regarded as an obstacle to progress. His unsanitary habitations were breeding grounds for diseases. His native dances were regarded as relics of barbarism. The Indian's roving habits prevented him from settling down to agricultural pursuits. His native garb and language prevented him from being assimilated by white communities. The practice of women doing the more arduous and routine tasks, a holdover from the hunting stage economy, was repugnant to the whites. While some advancement had been made in remedying these alleged evils, the Indian still had to make a great deal of "progress" before he could take his place by the side of the white man. . . .

The success of the program depended in a large measure on the quality of the personnel who administered it, particularly the Indian agent. Earlier he was assisted by interpreters, farmers, blacksmiths, and mechanics who were directly under his control. The missionaries, although not under agency control, usually gave moral support to the agent, particularly if he were interested in the Indians' welfare. In case the agent wished to expel some obnoxious white from the reservation, he was authorized to call upon the military to assist him. However, as long as the Indian was not dependent upon the Government for his livelihood, the agent could not normally exercise more than nominal control over him.

The power of the agent grew as the Indians' dependence upon the Government increased. By the late 1870's it was practically absolute, particularly among the Plains tribes. He could and frequently did bend the Indians to his wishes by cutting off their rations. About the only recourse the Indian had was to complain to the commanding officer of the nearest military post who might write a letter of complaint in his behalf or submit a petition for him to the Great White Father in Washington.

Too frequently the quality of the man selected for agent left much to be desired. The Indian Bureau repeatedly complained that it was difficult, if not impossible, to obtain qualified agents for a salary of $1,500 a year and urged that the stipend be increased. The agents also complained of their inadequate salaries. . . .

The combined factors of inadequate salary and unfavorable living conditions resulted in frequent change in agents. This, of course, was reflected in turn in poor administration of Indian affairs. The agent at Fort Berthold in 1879 attributed the lack of progress on the part of his wards to the fact that there had been five agents at that place in the preceding eight years. The special agent at Fort Peck wrote, "Four agents in four years is sufficient in itself to account for the disreputable conditions found to exist here."

The period from 1876 to 1890 was to see a number of administrative changes which included the establishment of new machinery and new laws and regulations—most of which were designed to strengthen the position of the Indian agent. To assist him in enforcing regulations and with routine tasks, Congress in 1878 authorized the establishment of the Indian police. In 1883, the Secretary of the Interior authorized the creation of the Court of Indian Offenses to try Indians for infractions of rules promulgated by the Bureau. An act approved March 3, 1885, made the Indians on reservations answerable to the United States courts for certain crimes. . . .

It was the objective of the Bureau to compel the Indians to settle down to farming. This could not be accomplished as long as they were permitted to travel at will from one reservation to another. To curtail their roving propensities the Bureau issued an order requiring that its wards be required to have passes, signed by their respective agents, authorizing them to visit other agencies. Although the issuance of such permits was discouraged, the Indians somehow obtained passes and continued their traveling. The Standing Rock agent in 1879 reported that 207 Fort Berthold Indians had recently visited his agency. They had spent five days with his Indians "dancing, feasting and exchanging presents," during which time the "corn-fields and hay, at the most critical time, were entirely neglected." . . .

Following 1876 the Government intensified its educational efforts. The Treaty of 1868 provided compulsory education for children from six to sixteen years of age for all the Sioux bands which signed it. Prior to the Sioux War the Government had done little toward providing schools for the Indians in the Dakotas and Montana. Since the Bureau's program for the civilizing of the Indians, put in operation toward the close of the war, provided for universal education of their children, the Government pushed forward its program of supplying them with schools. At first the agents encountered some opposition from the parents. Some of the officials found it necessary to cut off the rations from entire families before the parents would co-operate in sending their children to school. By the end of the 1880's most of this opposition had ceased. The Cheyenne River agent reported in 1889 that most of the parents sent their children to school without any compulsion and that it was rarely necessary to use the police to compel attendance. They were, however, reluctant to send their children to schools away from the reservation.

The period from 1876 to 1890 was also one of great missionary activity in most of the Upper Missouri reservations. Owing to the greater interest evinced in Indian affairs by eastern philanthropic groups and individuals, various missionary and church groups supplemented the educational work of the Government. Prior to that time, the Presbyterians and Congregationalists had established mission schools among the Omahas, the Santee and Yankton Sioux and the Cheyenne River Indians. After 1876 these denominations continued to be active, and the Episcopalians, Catholics and Methodists built a number of mission schools. Some of these missions, known as contract schools, received subsidies from the Government. . . .

By the end of the 1880's most of the reservations on the Upper Missouri had provided educational facilities for the Indian youth. In 1889 the Commissioner reported that the Bureau was conducting eighteen day and eleven boarding schools there. In addition to these, religious denominations were operating six boarding schools under contract. Two boarding schools were maintained jointly by the Government and religious societies. . . . These schools provided both general and vocational training. The day schools offered only elementary courses to the Indian children. At the boarding schools the boys were given vocational training in addition to their regular courses, while the girls were instructed in household arts. The Government also operated nonreservation schools, such as Hampton Institute, Genoa School, Carlisle Institute, and Haskell Institute, where young Indian men and women were given advanced training. Many of the more promising Upper Missouri Indian youths attended these nonreservation schools.

The Government also took an increased interest in the physical well-being of its wards. In addition to encouraging them to improve their housing, which was frequently a breeding ground for vermin and disease, it provided each of the agencies with one or several physicians. At first these men met considerable competition with the native medicine man in whom most of the older generation had confidence. As time passed his influence decreased, and the Indians more and more utilized the services of the agency physicians. . . .

Perhaps with the view of impressing the Commissioner with their alleged efficiency, most of the agents in the late 1870's and during the 1880's painted glowing pictures of their charges' progress. The Indians, they wrote, were emerging from a condition of barbarism and dependence upon the government. With the assistance of the schools and churches, the Indians would soon become, when the older generation passed away, self-supporting and able to fit into society as citizens. . . .

In spite of the optimistic reports of most of the agents, the Indians by 1890 were far from being self-supporting. It was becoming increasingly evident that the Dakota and Montana reservations were not suited for farming. Although the Indians' efforts to raise crops occasionally met with success, they were, for the most part, partial or complete failures. . . . The failure of these Indians to become successful farmers forced them to continue to rely on rations. A study of the contracts made by the Bureau during the period from 1876 to 1885 inclusive indicates that an average of 14,000,000 pounds of beef was driven annually to the Upper Missouri agencies. In 1885 they received approximately 10,000,000 pounds. In justification of the feeding policy the Commissioner argued that it was much cheaper to support the Indians than to fight them. At Crow Creek and at the Yankton Agency the agents attempted to make their wards more self-reliant by reducing rations. Their subsequent reports do not indicate whether their efforts met with success. However, by 1890 most of the Upper Missouri Indians were apparently relying largely on the Government for their livelihood.

During the 1880's white pressure for reducing the Indian lands on the Upper Missouri reservations steadily increased. In the Nebraska agencies where the Indians were already living on their allotments and had made considerable progress in farming, this pressure soon resulted in giving the Indians individual titles to lands and opening the remainder of their reservations to white settlement. . . . Meanwhile the process of restoring large portions of the huge reservations in the Dakotas and Montana to the public domain continued. . . .

Only among the Plains Sioux did the Government encounter open resistance to its program. While the majority appeared to accept the dictates of the Indian Bureau without complaint, there was a strong and influential minority group of unprogressives or "irreconcilables" who resented the Government's efforts to force them to conform to white man's civilization. The causes of the Sioux outbreak of 1890–1891 were described as "complex," "obscure and remote." Among the more remote causes was the general feeling of insecurity among the Indians which resulted from the disappearance of game, the sudden attempts of the Bureau to compel them to settle down to farming on lands unsuited for agriculture, the long series of treaties, cessions, and removals and a widespread lack of confidence in the motives of the Government. Among the immediate causes were the unfulfilled promises made by the Sioux Commission in 1888, the large reduction of the reservation, and the cutting down of the rations. The leaders of the Messiah Craze such as Sitting Bull readily exploited the unrest to restore their lost prestige. The outbreak culminated in the killing of Sitting Bull and the Battle of Wounded Knee in December 1890. . . .

The next two decades which followed were to witness additional changes in the status of the Indians on the Upper Missouri, particularly in the Dakotas and Montana. The Bureau undertook the complex task of surveying and allotting the lands to individual Indians. With the completion of these allotments, some of the reservations were opened to white settlement. Many of the officials in the Indian Service were placed under classified civil service and removed from political influence. The government schools largely replaced the earlier mission schools. However, many of the policies evolved and much of the administrative machinery developed from 1865 to 1890 for the governing of the Indians became permanent features of the reservation system.

CHAPTER IV

The Multi-Purpose Army

I N THE TAPESTRY of Western history runs a thin thread of blue—the United States Army. Indelibly etched in popular imagination along with the bark of the six-gun and the war cry of the Indian is the blare of the bugle and the flash of the sabre. "U.S. Cavalry to the rescue" is a common theme in the drama of the West, and if soldiers failed to attain the heroic proportions of John Wayne, we are led to believe that the fault lies primarily with history.

The origins of the United States Army were deeply rooted in the need to protect the frontier against Indian attacks. With the exception of the War of 1812 (1812–15), the Mexican War (1846–48) and the Civil War (1861–65), most members of the Regular Army spent their lives before 1890 in isolated posts dotting the frontier where dull routine was occasionally interrupted by brief periods of relatively small-scale fighting. The story of the "Indian Wars" is a sorry chapter in our nation's history, often marred by broken treaties, brutality, corruption, and injustice. The Army wrote much of that chapter. The confrontation between soldier and brave spanned more than a century, and from the reorganization of the Army shortly after the Revolutionary War until the "closing" of the frontier during the 1890's, regulars engaged in more than 60 campaigns and expeditions in 19 fairly well-defined wars against the Indians.

From the earliest days of the Republic, citizens, statesmen, and politicians recognized the need for frontier defense, but not all agreed that a professional army should perform the task. Americans emerged from the Revolutionary War believing strongly that a standing army of professional soldiers might threaten both republican principles and personal liberty. The citizens of the young nation had grounds for concern, for all too often the standing armies of European powers had been employed as instruments of coercion and oppression. The success of the colonial army during the struggle for independence supported the belief that citizen soldiers could defend the nation without threatening individual rights. If, however, the national interest demanded the creation of a Regular Army, Americans insisted that it should be kept as small as possible.

Except during the three major wars the military establishment of the United States consisted, between 1790 and 1890, of numerous state militia units and a small regular force which rarely exceeded 30,000 men. The Militia Act of 1792 authorized the establishment of the militia and it was a rare community that did not boast of at least one company. Most of these units never gained any degree of military ability or discipline, but their enthusiasm compensated for their lack of professional polish. Many community leaders, and especially frontier politicians, who openly denounced standing armies, actively sought the command of the local volunteers in order to obtain the title of captain or colonel. Americans believed that militia manned and commanded by local residents was no threat to their freedom.

Scholars have often viewed the westward advance of the American people as a procession of frontier types. The Army cannot be assigned a single position in this movement for it influenced every stage of the westward migration. As Francis Paul Prucha has written, "Few frontiers would have developed as they did without the presence near at hand of a military force."

Active service against the Indians was only a small part of the antebellum Army's duties on the frontier. The Army's role as a police force was far more important to the development of the West. Once the Indian's spirit of resistance was broken in battle the military assumed the responsibility of seeing that the tribes no longer harassed the settlements. The presence of even a small detachment of soldiers to show the flag was often enough to intimidate neighboring Indians. Resplendent in blue and brass, the military presided at most treaty negotiations, supervised the process of putting the covenants into operation and were a constant reminder to the Indians of the power available to enforce the terms of the treaties.

The sword of the frontier army was two-edged and dismayed frontiersmen learned that the military also protected the Indians from incursions by the settlers. When Anglo-Americans ignored treaty provisions and surged onto Indian lands, they were forced back by patrols from military garrisons. The troops seized the whiskey of peddlers who attempted to sell such goods to the Indians. The Army's efforts to protect the Indians from ruthless frontiersmen were sharply criticized as impeding the march of civilization. Despite these accusations many frontier settlements owed their safety to the protection provided by the regulars. Thriving communities sprang up in the shadow of frontier posts and those venture-some individuals who lived on the edge of Indian country took comfort from the knowledge that the troops would come to their aid if needed.

Because of the spectacular nature of Indian campaigns most writers have concentrated on the military and police actions of the frontier army, often ignoring the nonmilitary duties of the soldiers. It has been estimated that the average soldier was under fire only once during a three-year enlistment in the peacetime army prior to the Civil War. If the military on the frontier did not always assume an active role, neither did the soldiers stagnate safely behind the walls of the forts and garrisons. Even more important perhaps than the Army's peace-keeping duties were its activities as a trained, disciplined, and mobile labor force. The military pacification of the frontier preceded the physical assault on the wilderness, but as Professor Prucha has noted of the years between 1815 and 1860, regulars spent more of their time with broadaxes than with bayonets.

If fur traders and settlers cut paths through the forest, soldiers transformed those primitive trails into well-engineered roads. The need to move men and supplies to the frontier and between garrisons necessitated the construction of additional roads. To insure the rapid delivery of supplies to forts located on waterways, soldiers improved rivers and streams by removing obstacles and building dikes and levees. While the labor of troops on internal improvements could be justified in terms of military necessity, much of the effort was clearly designed to facilitate the settlement of the frontier.

The employment of soldiers as laborers was not a matter of chance, but rather the official policy of the men who commanded the Army. Congress and the military hierarchy approved of soldier-labor and believed that it helped to preserve discipline and health among the troops as well as being in the public interest. Soldiers, however, argued that they had enlisted to fight Indians rather than to dig ditches and strongly objected to being used constantly as laborers. Few enlisted men saw any justice in receiving Army pay for doing a civilian laborer's work at half the wage. Officers noted that resentment of extra duty labor was a major cause of desertion.

While enlisted men contributed their sweat and muscle to the physical conquest of the wilderness, another element of the Army worked to expand the knowledge of the nation's vast public domain. The Lewis and Clark expedition was only the most famous of the explorations conducted by the Army during the early national period. After the establishment of the United States Military Academy in 1802, Army officers were often well trained in the natural sciences, and during the next 75 years they led many exploring parties into the West. Organized in 1838, the small Corps of Topographical Engineers led the scientific assault on the wilderness between that date and the outbreak of the Civil War. These Engineers were not solely interested in exploration but tried to describe all of the western phenomena as accurately as possible. In addition to exploring the unknown, mapping the terrain, and examining the local flora and fauna, members of the Topographical Corps often assisted in the construction of roads, bridges, and other internal improvements. So broad were their duties that William H. Goetzmann described the Topographical Corps as a "department of public works" for the West.

Between 1820 and 1850 many Americans considered the country west of the Missouri's northern course to be a "Great American Desert" and unfit for agricultural settlement. As a result the government uprooted many eastern woodland tribes and forceably moved them into the region. Army posts like Fort Crawford, Fort Des Moines, Fort Leavenworth and Fort Smith marked a line which some government officers expected would remain a "Permanent Indian Frontier." But the migration to Oregon, the acquisition of the Mexican Cession and the Gadsden Purchase destroyed the concept of a clearly defined Indian frontier. During the 1830's and 1840's most of the Army's troops were serving in posts to the east of the Mississippi but by the 1850's the majority of regulars manned stations scattered from the Dakota region, south across the plains to Texas and New Mexico, and along the Pacific coast. The sudden expansion of the national domain had greatly increased the Army's responsibilities. But vast expanses of territory, climatic extremes, the shortage of such essentials as fuel, food, and water in some regions and its small size impaired the Army's effectiveness.

To aggravate these conditions the Indian tribes of the plains, mountains, and deserts had adapted well to the environment. They had learned to live in a forbidding land and, of more importance to the Army, how to turn the hostile features of the terrain to military advantage. Well mounted and often well armed, the western Indians presented a formidable challenge to the regulars. Napoleonic and Clausewitzian concepts of warfare were of limited use in subduing enemies that had mastered the principles of guerilla warfare. Young West Pointers schooled in traditional European concepts of war soon realized that the military pacification of the West demanded the development of new tactics and strategies.

Guided by the dictates of economy and the traditional opposition to a large standing army, Congress severely limited the capabilities of the ante-bellum Army by restricting the size and composition of the regular force. The Army, however, never recruited the authorized numbers, and deaths, discharges, and desertions further reduced its strength. In 1853 slightly fewer than 7000 men garrisoned the 54 posts west of the Mississippi, an average of less than 130 soldiers at each station. Under such circumstances it is not surprising that Indians raided with impunity while settlers rebuked the troops for failing to protect frontier communities adequately.

Congress also fixed the composition of the Army. Military leaders insisted that mounted troops were best suited to the frontier, but statistics demonstrating that the cost of maintaining a mounted regiment in the field for a year was nearly four times that required to support a foot unit hardly encouraged Congressmen to loosen their grip on the federal purse strings. Cavalry rarely constituted more than a third of the force on the frontier during the 1840's and 1850's, but the futility of trying to subdue mounted Indians with infantry was apparently lost on the legislators.

In 1855, the Army included four regiments of artillery, ten of infantry, and five of cavalry. Low pay, long enlistments, and the general unattractiveness of military service discouraged many from joining the Army. Few Americans of ability were willing to exchange the opportunities in an expanding society for the hardships of frontier service and the paltry monthly wage offered by the military. Although some men of good character were found in the ranks, the majority of the regulars were an unimpressive lot recruited from the lower levels of society and the newly arrived immigrants from Great Britain, Ireland, and Europe.

Two types of men composed the officer corps, those who had entered the Army from civilian life, usually after militia service, and those who had graduated from the Military Academy. Most of the senior officers during the 1840's and 1850's were not West Pointers and a high proportion were veterans of the War of 1812. By the middle of the 1850's, nearly three-fourths of all Army officers were West Pointers and young, ambitious graduates of the Academy like Lee, McClellan and Longstreet, who had demonstrated their ability during the Mexican War, were anxious to assume higher commands. But promotions were slow in coming and the absence of a retirement system effectively blocked the upward mobility of the younger men and burdened the higher ranks with ancient officers unable to perform their duties. It was not until after the Civil War that West Pointers provided most of the leadership in the United States Army.

During the Civil War volunteer regiments replaced the regular units on the frontier. Boastful frontiersmen and critics of the Army had long claimed that civilian soldiers familiar with frontier conditions were better equipped to deal with Indians than the regulars. The success of the Texas Rangers supported their claims, and few dared to dispute the fighting ability of the individual frontiersman. Although the size of the volunteer force in the West during these years was double that of the regular contingent before the war, a series of major Indian wars erupted on the frontier. In 1862 state troops, some having served in Grant's campaign down the Mississippi, were assembled in Minnesota to put down the uprising of the Santee Sioux which claimed the lives of several hundred whites. In the Southwest volunteer troops commanded by General James H. Carleton and Kit Carson, who had accepted a colonelcy in a New Mexico regiment, spent much of the war fighting Apaches and Navajos. In 1864 war exploded on the Central Plains as the tribes allied to revenge the attack on a band of Cheyennes by Colorado militiamen commanded by Colonel John Chivington. The Sand Creek Massacre showed once again that not all savages in the Indian wars had red skin.

Other than a substantial increase in size, the Army underwent few organizational changes during the Civil War. The Reorganization Act of 1869, which provided the basic framework for the regular force until the Spanish-American War, authorized 25 regiments of infantry, 10 of cavalry, and 5 of artillery. A significant addition to the Army occurred when Congress specified that two of the infantry and two of the cavalry regiments were to be composed of black soldiers. The calibre of the average soldier in the post-Civil War Army differed only slightly from the frontier veterans of the 1840's and 1850's. Large numbers of foreigners continued to enlist and with few exceptions the native American recruits continued to be drawn from the lower social and economic strata of the population. The officer corps experienced a significant transition as the older commanders retired or resigned and younger, more dynamic men replaced them. Many of the men who accepted regular commissions in the reorganized Army had brilliant records in the Civil War, and Sherman, Sheridan, Crook, Miles and Mackenzie quickly demonstrated their abilities as Indian fighters. The annual increment of West Pointers injected fresh blood into the corps, and nearly 80 percent of the officers serving during the 1880's had graduated from the national military academy.

After four years of bloody civil war most Americans busied themselves with the problems of political reconstruction, urbanization, and industrialization and willingly delegated the task of subduing the Indians and protecting the trans-Mississippi West to the Army. While the details may be hazy, few readers are unfamiliar with the basic theme of the Indian campaigns. Geronimo, Sitting Bull and Custer's Last Stand are prominent in the nation's popular history. Despite the "bugles in the afternoon" myth of the movies and television, not all Indians were noble savages fighting a civilization which threatened to destroy their way of life and, often as not, the military failed to arrive in the nick of time to save an imperiled wagon train or frontier settlement. With the exception of a few major campaigns most military action consisted of brief skirmishes or long patrols in which there was no contact with the enemy.

Congressional legislation specified an Army of 25,000 men, but, as in the prewar years, there were again too few troops, too many Indians, and too much territory. Army officers and government officials quarrelled over the most appropriate means of implementing Indian policy. Some military leaders advocated that the Army be given full authority over the Indians. Officers charged that politicians, safe behind their desks, were bemused by idealistic and humanitarian impulses and misunderstood the real nature of our relations with the tribesmen. Civilians in turn indicted the military for advocating simplistic and brutal solutions to the Indian problem. Such controversy undoubtedly contributed to the contradictions and confusion which sometimes marked American Indian policy.

Postwar regulars spent much of their time in the field. In their capacity as policemen, soldiers served as guards for road, railroad and telegraph construction crews. Immigrant trains, overland freighters and mail and stage coaches crossed the frontier protected by military escorts. In the cattle country regulars often guarded drovers when herds passed through Indian territory. Road building continued to be a common military operation and regulars were perhaps more proficient with shovel and pick than with their rifles. Scattered in small contingents of two and three companies at posts along the frontier, regulars usually looked forward to little more than hard work, and routine military duty.

Although the conquest of the frontier depended in large part upon the Army's ability to defeat Indians in battle, it is misleading to examine the role of the frontier Army in military terms alone. Expeditions commanded by Lewis and Clark, Stephen Long, John C. Frémont and other army explorers helped open the West as much as any military victory over infuriated tribesmen. In the absence of civil officers, Army officers were sometimes policeman, judge and government administrator all in one in the first days of new settlements. The pacification of the Indians eliminated one of the principle obstacles to the westward advance of the Anglo-Americans, but the improvements which the soldiers made to road and stream greatly facilitated the settlement process.

Although other emissaries of American society sometimes preceded them in the new regions of the West, blue-clad soldiers were seldom far behind. The flag, the sword, the bugle and their other symbols uniquely represented the stability and authority of government. Often unheralded or even unnoticed, the peacetime army was a living shield, protecting the settlers of the American West. But as we have seen, the soldiers were more than protectors, they were members of a truly multi-purpose Army.

By and large Democracy's Army did what needed to be done in the era of the westward movement. Could it have done it better? Did the nineteenth-century officer too often regard the Indian campaign as an exercise in big game hunting rather than a police action in force to be performed as humanely as possible? Was there not also in the Army's intolerance of civilian control of Indian policy, after the organization of the Department of the Interior in 1849, a disturbing prophecy of the statements of those Army officers in the twentieth century who have believed that political considerations have no place in warfare and that civilian administrators should not question their recommendations? Or on the other hand have we honored our military men too little, paid them miserable wages, asked the impossible of them in time of war and forgotten them in times of peace? What is indeed the place of the Army in a democratic nation and are the precedents, established in a nineteenth-century nation with a free land frontier, valueless to Americans of the twentieth century?

•1•

BERNARD DEVOTO

The Significance of the Lewis and
Clark Expedition

From the beginning of the early national period military men explored the frontier regions and the maps and reports prepared by Army explorers helped to draw settlers into the West. The journey of Captains Lewis and Clark is the most familiar example of the exploratory role of the military. Although the principal result of the expedition was the accumulation of geographical knowledge about the Louisiana Purchase and the Pacific Northwest, Bernard DeVoto shows that the findings of the two captains significantly affected later developments in Indian policy, the fur trade and American expansion into the Pacific Northwest.

. . . The expedition did not win any other tribes so permanently as . . . [the Flatheads and Nez Percés] . . . but it established so great a good will as to make the early years of the fur trade era a good deal less violent than they could possibly have been without it.

This climate of approval extended far beyond the tribes which the expedition actually met and it made a kind of culture hero of William Clark. All the Plains and Northwest tribes knew of the Red Headed Chief and came to depend on him for friendship and, if not justice, at least advocacy. He was the white man whose tongue was straight, our elder brother. Miracles were expected of him, indeed he was able to perform miracles on their behalf, but if he had been able to obtain for them any substantial measure of justice it would have been a transcendent miracle. He did what he could; he was able to procure occasional decencies and often able to prevent or moderate indecencies and he accomplished more for the Indians than anyone else in Western history. If a delegation of Indians went to St. Louis, it sought out Clark first of all; if a fur company sent a brigade up the Missouri or into the mountains, it provided itself with a passport in the form of messages and

SOURCE: Abridged from Bernard DeVoto, (ed.), *The Journals of Lewis and Clark* (Cambridge, 1953), xlviii-lii. Reprinted by permission of Houghton Mifflin Company.

greetings from Clark. If the U.S. government had to send an embassy to the Indian country it began by trying to get Clark to accompany it, and if Clark consented he was invariably able to get fairer treatment for the Indians and more amenable behavior from them. This subsequent function is a bright strand in a dark history. It has had less attention than it deserves from those who write history; sometime it should be described in detail.

Creating such a predisposition, however insecure, in the Far West must be accounted one of the important results of the Lewis and Clark expedition. Those results were so numerous that little can be said about them in an introduction but they must be characterized. They were of various orders of immediacy and significance.

The first major achievement was the demonstration that the last area of North America in which a commercially practicable water route to the Pacific might exist did not contain one. In the long arc of history this ended the search for the Northwest Passage. And ending that chapter, it closed the volume which opened with the first voyage of Columbus.

Lewis's reluctance to accept the fact which his journey had demonstrated, attested in two of his reports to Jefferson, strikingly signalizes the intensity of the hope. Nevertheless the demonstration was immediately accepted by commercial interests to which an inland water route would have been supremely important. When John Jacob Astor organized a fur company to fulfill the commercial (and incidentally the political) vision of Jefferson, he based the organization solidly on salt-water transport, though he also sent an overland expedition to reconnoiter other areas and to check the results of Lewis and Clark. But unquestioning acceptance of those results was among the reasons why his partisan, Wilson Price Hunt, abandoned the Upper Missouri route and crossed to the south of it.

With the transcontinental water route, Jefferson's hope of engrossing the Canadian fur trade, or at least, its carriage, disappeared too. It was not a realistic hope anyway, even if such a route had existed, but on the other hand in the outcome this potential wealth was not missed. Lewis and Clark established that the American West was a treasury of beaver and its exploitation began at once. The amazing solitary pair of trappers whom they met near the mouth of the Yellowstone in 1806, Dixon and Hancock, were the portents that heralded developments to come. St. Louis capital was behind the venture of Manuel Lisa the next year, 1807. Lisa hired three of the expedition's veterans, Drewyer, Potts, and Wiser, and, meeting Colter on his way downriver from his winter with the forerunners, persuaded him too to return to the fur country. Lisa's first Missouri voyage is the beginning of the Western fur trade, and he was bound for the fields that Lewis and Clark had most highly recommended, the Three Forks and the valley of the Yellowstone. The Western trade, roughly divided between two regions, the Upper Missouri and the Rocky Mountains, was continuous thenceforward and steadily increased in importance till the break in beaver prices toward the the end of the 1830's. The "mountain men" whom the trade developed completed the exploration of the West that Lewis and Clark had begun.

It may be that to secure the Columbia country—Oregon—was the earliest as it was certainly the most urgent of Jefferson's purposes. The expedition served it vitally; in fact, one is justified in saying, decisively. The land traverse bolstered the claim established by Robert Gray's discovery and was of equal or greater legal importance; in international polity the two combined to give the United States not only a prior but a paramount claim. More, it was the journey of Lewis and Clark that gave the American people a conviction that Oregon was theirs and this conviction was more important than the claim. And pragmatically, the establishment of Fort Astoria by Astor's party won the British-American race to the Pacific. Astor's American Fur Company and Pacific Fur Company were established not only as a result of the expedition's reports but in exact accordance with Lewis's analysis of the practices required.

Here we may glance at a map. The route of the Western emigration was to be that of the Platte Valley, pioneered in 1824 and 1825 by William Ashley and his subordinates when the Arikaras tried their hand at closing the Missouri. The emigration had to be by land travel; distances and geographical conditions necessitated it. They also made the Platte Valley the route of the Pacific Railroad. Nevertheless, despite the circuitousness of the Missouri and the hazards and difficulties of traveling it by boat it remained an important route to the West, the Rockies, and the Northwest till the end of the steamboat age. And the railroads which ended that age on the Missouri followed its valley, and beyond it, in great part followed the route of Lewis and Clark to the Northwest. How minutely the expedition pioneered one main course of American economic development a list of names reveals at once: Kansas City, Leavenworth, St. Joseph, Atchison, Omaha, Council Bluffs, Sioux City, Yankton, Pierre, Bismarck, Williston, Miles City, Billings, Bozeman, Fort Benton, Great Falls, Helena, Dillon, Salmon, Missoula, Lewiston, Walla Walla, Portland, Astoria.

A century and a half later, it is still impossible to make a satisfactory statement about the scientific results of the expedition: qualified scientists and historians have not been interested in making the requisite studies. Lewis's untimely death in 1809 prolonged the already serious delay in the issuance of a detailed official account of the expedition. Unquestionably he would have written one if he had lived and he was in a better position to formulate findings than Biddle, who wrote the invaluable *History*. As it is, the only "literary" results that were not indirect are anthropological. The voluminous notes on Indian tribes, mainly by Lewis, which were sent to the War Department from the Mandan villages in 1805, were codified and tabulated and published as "A Statistical View of the Indian Nations Inhabiting the Territory of Louisiana . . ." This report was at once immensely important and, as the first survey of the trans-Mississippi tribes, is permanently important.

The "Statistical View" defines the nature of Biddle's *History*, through which mainly the "literary" purposes of the expedition were fulfilled. Lewis's carefully assembled Indian vocabularies were lost but Biddle worked into narrative an enormous amount of the information about Indians that the journals contained. He also wrote several extended passages of generalization, based not only on the journals but on communications from Clark and discussions with George Shannon, and these too are amazingly sound and useful. The *History* is the first detailed account, and one may add the first reliable account of whatever length, of the Western tribes. It put a valuable bulk of knowledge at the disposal of anyone who had interest in or use for knowledge relating to the Indians of the West. So it has always been a prime source for anthropologists and historians.

But that, of course, is true of much more than anthropology. History is not so divisible as to permit us to say exactly how important the Lewis and Clark expedition was in securing Oregon, as a physical possession, to the United States, though its paramount importance is self-evident. But it gave not only Oregon but the entire West to the American people as something with which the mind could deal. The westering people had crossed the Mississippi with the Louisiana Purchase and by that act had acquired the manifest destiny of going on to the Pacific. But the entire wilderness expanse, more than twice the size of the United States at the beginning of Jefferson's administration, was a blank, not only on the map but in human thought. It was an area of rumor, guess, and fantasy. Now it had been crossed by a large party who came back and told in assimilable and trustworthy detail what a large part of it was. Henceforth the mind could focus on reality. Here were not only the Indians but the land itself and its conditions: river systems, valleys, mountain ranges, climates, flora, fauna, and a rich and varied membrane of detail relating them to one another and to familiar experience. It was the first report on the West, on the United States over the hill and beyond the sunset, on the province of the American future. There has never been another so excellent or so influential. So it was rather as a treasury of knowledge than as a great adventure story that the *History* became a national and international favorite, reprinted, translated, pirated, and counterfeited. It satisfied desire and it created desire: the desire of the westering nation.

That, the increase of our cultural heritage, the beginning of knowledge of the American West, must be accounted the most important result of the Lewis and Clark expedition.

·2·

FRANCIS PAUL PRUCHA

The Physical Attack Upon the Wilderness

> The conquest of the frontier did not depend entirely on the pacification of the Indians. Francis Paul Prucha, who has studied the role of the Army on the Indian frontier, considers the nonmilitary duties of soldiers as important to the development of the West as the Army's peace keeping activities. In Professor Prucha's view the frontier Army was an organized labor force, and in this reading he describes the variety of tasks performed by soldier-laborers.

The regular army on the Northwest frontier was only intermittently engaged in hostilities with the Indians. Detachments of troops made frequent forays into the Indian country to apprehend Indians who had committed crimes, to overawe war parties who threatened the peace, or to remove trespassers from the Indian domains, but even these quasi-military activities occupied only a small portion of the soldier's time. Garrison duties, including a strict schedule of drill and parades, were

SOURCE: Abridged from Francis Paul Prucha, *Broadax and Bayonet: The Role of the United States Army in the Development of the Northwest, 1815–1860* (Madison, 1953), 104–135. Reprinted by permission of the State Historical Society of Wisconsin. We have allowed the title of Chapter VI to stand over materials from Chapter VII and VIII as well.

an integral part of the soldier's life, but a recital of this calendar of events would result in a formalized and distorted picture of garrison life. Respectable inactivity, so often associated with a peacetime army, had little place in a frontier post, and recruits who joined the army for a life of leisure or adventure were soon disillusioned. In truth, the lot of the private soldier on the frontier was steady hard work. Common labor consumed the greater part of his working hours. . . .

The energy expended by the soldiers, however unwillingly, had tangible and impressive results. Entering a country little changed from a state of nature, the army, like a giant pioneer, worked a transformation in it. Land was cleared and fields sown. Roads were carved through forests and etched across the prairie openings, and staunch garrisons, like the citadels of medieval days, reared their heads along the waterways. The works of the white man were becoming manifest. . . .

The weakness of a lone pioneering family, symbol of the advance of the agricultural frontier, is a pathetic contrast to the power and resources of an army garrison. The one, struggling to clear a patch of land that would yield a meager subsistence, depending upon wild game to augment its simple diet, and relying on the kindness of its neighbors for help in raising a house or barn, could take only a nibble at the wilderness. The other, a compact, well-organized, and well-directed labor force, acting on the authority of the United States government and deriving subsistence and equipment from Eastern sources, bit out sizable chunks at a time. The army, despite the weaknesses of its personnel, possessed a pool of manpower and skill which is seldom associated with the remote frontier. Most of the men who enlisted in the regular army in the peacetime years before the Civil War were not the most highly skilled artisans, but they represented a multitude of trades. A listing of the civilian jobs of the soldiers reads like an occupational directory. Unskilled laborers head any tabulation, but they constitute only a small percentage of the total. Carpenters, cabinet-makers, bricklayers, coopers, farmers, weavers, tailors, masons, clerks, musicians, blacksmiths, and painters appear frequently on the rolls. . . .

The use of army troops as a labor force on the frontier was not a matter of chance, but the considered policy of those who directed the army's destinies. Not only did army commanders sanction the practice provided it did not interfere seriously with military duties, but Congress gave it the legal stamp of approval. The employment of soldiers in the building of military roads and erection of fortifications was regarded as necessary to the preservation of health and discipline among the troops as well as advantageous to the public interest.

What the War Department advocated was "moderate" use of the troops as laborers, for too great an emphasis on non-military duties could be prejudicial to the morale and military performance of the men. But on the remote frontier it was not easy to employ the soldiers up to a certain point and then stop. There was no one at hand to continue the work; and forts had to be built, hay procured, and fuel gathered for the winter. The absence of civilians to furnish these necessities—to say nothing of the War Department's repeated economy drives which precluded the purchase of services—created the situations which the privates and the inspectors deplored. Year after year Inspector General Croghan found on his tours of the Western posts that the men were too much occupied with non-military duties. Not only did they show deficiencies in drill because of a lack of practice, but—what was worse—they seemed to have lost the military spirit. . . .

But the labor of the troops for these purposes could not be dispensed with. Granted that the forts did not need to be elaborate affairs of stone, certain minimum quarters and minimum supplies of forage and fuel were required. The problem was never squarely faced. It was necessary to use the troops to reduce expenses even if other labor could be procured, and army commanders still clung to the idea that moderate labor was beneficial to the troops and made a man a better soldier. Whenever work needed to be done at the frontier posts, therefore, the troops were usually called upon to do it. . . .

The building of a frontier fort was a difficult undertaking. An imposing fortification that would symbolize American power to the Indians called for extensive lumbering and quarrying operations to provide material for the bastions or pickets guarding and enclosing the garrison. Even the less imposing structures required to meet the everyday needs of garrison life—barracks and storehouses, a hospital and stables, a sutler's store and laundresses' quarters—were erected only with the commanders' dogged goading of their ungainly crews of workmen. Then there was the problem of upkeep. Wood construction was less tedious and time-consuming than stone construction, but it resulted in buildings that required constant repair and frequent replacement. Indeed the maintenance of a fort taxed the capabilities of the men little less than did the initial building. . . .

As the frontier advanced and the Indian migrations created new needs, other forts were built. Time and again the soldiers of the United States army shouldered the task of the pioneer, gathering building materials and fashioning them into living quarters and palisades. Not until new fortifications were erected west of the Mississippi was a substantial portion of the construction work consigned to civilians. The time had come when it was no longer possible to rely wholly on soldier labor; the limited number of troops on the Northwest frontier were sufficiently occupied with the heavier military duties that were being imposed on them. Larger appropriations were made for the new posts, which permitted the employment of civilian mechanics and laborers, now fairly numerous in the West. Whereas Fort Snelling had been built almost entirely by the troops—at an almost negligible cost to the government—the new forts in Iowa were largely the product of civilian labor, and their cost ran into high figures. . . .

Although sometimes diverted during the thirties and forties from its original policy of relying exclusively on soldier labor, the War Department returned to it in the early fifties when an economy drive swept the department. New directives from Washington forbade the hiring of civilians in any capacity without express authority from division headquarters, and any who were then in the employ of the posts were to be discharged immediately. Again it was upon the troops that the army was forced to rely for labor on the frontier. . . .

The government trading factors and the Indian agents also depended upon the soldiers in their vicinity for whatever construction work they needed to have done. There was no one else to turn to and, as the agent at Sault Ste. Marie wrote in 1822, "the soldiery, who embrace mechanicks of every description, possess the resources of building almost wholly within themselves." The United States factors at Green Bay and Prairie du Chien, for instance, applied to the army commanders for help in erecting their buildings, and they paid the soldiers an allowance of money and whiskey for their work. The army officers also delegated soldiers to help the factors pack and beat furs and peltries preparatory to shipment East. . . .

The fortifications and other structures built by the troops on the Northwest frontier were tangible evidence of American power. More than that, they were the first attempt to set up in the wilderness some symbols of American culture. In areas that were completely devoid of settlement or touched only by the primitive communities of traders a fort was an entirely new element. Each became the visible center of impending change, a nucleus of rapid and amazing growth.

The frontier army was regularly engaged, likewise, in time-consuming agricultural activity, for the remoteness of the Western posts made some measure of self-sufficiency imperative. Difficult enough was the task of delivering on time the subsistence stores and military equipment which could not be produced in the West. To offset the danger that supply contracts would not be fulfilled, it was highly desirable, if not absolutely necessary, that the Western garrisons have an independent supply of the goods that could be produced locally. From the standpoint of health it was important that the staples of army diet—salt pork and beans and bread—be supplemented by fresh vegetables. Because there was no way to preserve them during transportation, such foods had to be grown in the vicinity of the posts. Moreover, there was the War Department's constant preoccupation with economy. Production by the troops would materially reduce the drain on its coffers and would eliminate the ruinous charges for transportation to the frontier.

Vegetable gardens were therefore established at every permanent Western post. Land on the military reservations close to the forts was assiduously cultivated by the soldiers, who became expert at drawing from the soil a remarkable variety of vegetables. Such gardening had been part of established army policy almost from the beginning, and in 1818, when the advance of the military frontier was dotting the Northwest with remote and isolated garrisons, it became a specific responsibility of the frontier commanders. They had no help from higher headquarters; expenses for seeds, utensils, and fences were met not by army disbursing agents but by the officers and men who were to consume the produce. . . .

These gardening activities, however, were merely routine, almost insignificant, as compared with the field cultivation that was undertaken in pursuance of the order of 1818. Garden truck alone represented little saving of War Department funds, for it merely supplemented the basic rations and in only small measure lessened dependence on Eastern sources of supply. Wherever feasible, more extensive farming operations were initiated. The posts on the upper Mississippi, at Green Bay, and at Chicago were directed to begin large-scale farming that would provide wheat for the soldier's bread, peas and beans, turnips, potatoes, and cabbages for the staples of his diet, and oats and corn for the forage of the livestock. . . .

This auspicious beginning little suggested what disappointments were in store for the military farmers. The insufficiency of teams and farming implements restricted production, as did the men's want of experience and skill. . . .

The field cultivation program never really fulfilled its purpose. Estimates of needed supplies had to be submitted and contracts signed long before the goods were to be consumed at the frontier garrisons. The uncertainties of farming made it impossible to estimate what proportion of the stores could be supplied by the troops. In the long run crop failures at the posts were no less serious than the non-fulfillment of contracts, and subsistence and quartermaster officers spent many a day frantically trying to arrange for the last-minute purchase and transportion of grain which they had expected the garrisons to produce. . . .

Rounding out the private's career as a farmer was his care of the livestock which every post required in its building activities, for plowing, and for hauling wood. To feed and care for the "public cattle" was a never-ending duty. The permanent herds were seldom very large, but they were augmented greatly at the more remote forts by beef cattle driven in for the subsistence of the troops. Unless some settler close at hand could provide the garrison with fresh beef two or three times a week—and this was rare in the early days of a Northwest fort—it devolved upon the local commissary officer to purchase beef on the hoof, maintain the cattle, and butcher them at frequent intervals. The care of the animals was not always an easy task. Wintering them was a special difficulty, and by spring they were often too emaciated either to serve for food or to work. Strays, which as often as not fell prey to Indians, were a constant drain upon the beef supplies. At Fort Snelling an earnest effort was made to maintain a herd of swine to provide pork as well as beef for the soldiers' rations, but this enterprise failed as a result of the lack of corn for feed, a shortage of hands to care for them, and depredations by the Indians.

The onerous duties of haying and wood cutting took a great deal of time and manpower, but they worked important transformations in the areas about the forts.

The forage needed for the livestock consisted partly of corn and oats raised by the soldiers or bought on contract, partly of the prairie hay which grew wild in many areas. Military sites were chosen with an eye to abundant and easily accessible prairie land, and gathering hay was a primary garrison duty until such time as it became expedient to buy forage from local settlers. Haying was one of the harder and more unpleasant tasks of the soldier—and certainly an "un-military" one—but the War Department insisted that it be performed by the men of the garrison. . . .

To the soldiers also fell the task of gathering the tremendous quantities of fuel that were consumed during the course of the rigorous Northern winter. Barrack fireplaces had no regard for human limitations, and their cavernous mouths greedily consumed cord after cord of fuel. Fortunately the Northwest abounded in hardwood forests which yielded excellent firewood, but its acquisition grew progressively more difficult as the supply close at hand became exhausted and more distant spots had to be exploited. At certain times of the year wood gathering was the chief activity of the garrison, for until the supply on the military reservation and neighboring public lands had been exhausted, no wood was purchased from civilians. . . .

A frontier military post was no stronger than its lines of supply and reinforcement. To maintain a frontier fort demanded careful logistical planning, for unless contact with the interior communities was well established the garrison could entertain little hope for survival. So it was that military sites were selected with careful regard for lines of communication and transportation, and that the posts were built where they would be served by the natural features of the region. . . .

But it was not always possible, nor even advantageous, to rely entirely upon lakes and rivers for transportation from one settlement or military post to another. A river, after all, had an immutable course which might not carry the soldier or the pioneer to his destination. And at best it did only part-time service, for the winter's freeze-over and the summer's dry spells halted traffic for many months of the year. . . .

To supplement the water routes, roads were built through the frontier wilderness, and again the army furnished the manpower. Garrison troops, their muscles hardened and their hands calloused from the building of forts, cut trails through the forests, bridged rivers and streams, built up or drained the swamps, and marked out routes across the prairies. It was hard labor with a vengeance, but labor that made a lasting contribution to the development of the frontier communities.

The utility of public roads for purposes of defense and the prudence of employing soldiers to build them were commonly agreed upon once government officials had overcome their early doubts as to the constitutionality of using military troops for such a purpose. In a country having almost interminable seacoasts and frontiers to defend, the small numbers of troops authorized by Congress could be used effectively only by maintaining maximum mobility. If they could be rapidly dispatched to points of danger, army commanders agreed American security could be preserved. Hence the military value of good roads—whether they were strictly "military" roads or not—was never disputed. . . .

For some of the roads the military was only indirectly responsible, in that the forts merely furnished the reason—or in many instances the rationalization—for their construction. Wisconsin, Minnesota, and Iowa all acquired a network of roads built by civilians under contracts let by the War Department. Construction was superintended by army engineers, but beyond that the military personnel was not actively involved. Of the roads built by the troops themselves, some were definite projects sponsored by the War Department, others were little more than rough trails cut by the army supply wagons as they crossed the prairies. Much construction that was considered desirable was impossible because of the shortage of troops, but the fact remains that the army built roads that proved to be of more than immediate military importance. . . .

·3·

LONNIE J. WHITE

From Bloodless to Bloody:
The Third Colorado Cavalry and the
Sand Creek Massacre

Although the task of defending the frontier was primarily the responsibility of the Regular Army, volunteer or militia units manned by Westerners participated in many of the Indian campaigns. On occasion, however, the frontier citizen soldiers used their temporary military status to vent their hatred of Indians. In this selection, Lonnie J. White describes the notorious Sand Creek Massacre.

. . . The Third Colorado Cavalry began organizing in about mid-August [of 1864]. Recruiting, however, proceeded slowly, and in Arapahoe County which included Denver, the major center of population, [Colonel John M.] Chivington declared martial law in an effort to speed up enlistments evidently in both the "Hundred Day Service" and the militia. . . .

The volunteers at Camp Evans, while they waited for equipment and supplies, drilled, paraded, listened to speeches, and played. Editor Hollister, who observed them on parade, stated in the *Journal* that they were "a magnificent set and as well drilled and soldierly as could be expected under the circumstances." He also noticed that the "gambling halls" of Denver were "very lively, and they and the streets are full of

SOURCE: Abridged from Lonnie J. White, "From Bloodless to Bloody: The Third Colorado Cavalry and the Sand Creek Massacre," *Journal of the West*, VI (October, 1967), 535-581. Reprinted by permission of *Journal of the West* and Lonnie J. White.

men and boys covered with lemon stripes 'sashaying' gaily round on their dignity just as if it twasn't their business to get killed immediately." . . .

But all was not well with the volunteers, for the populace of Colorado was anxious for them to go after the Indians. When the volunteers were not immediately supplied and equipped, Coloradans began "grumbling that nothing was likely to be done, hounding the authorities, and taunting the officers and soldiers in camp . . ." As the days turned into weeks and the weeks into months and the regiment still did not embark on a campaign, the taunting presumably became sharper and harder to endure. The "Bloodless Third" was still in camp and its one hundred days of life was rapidly expiring. . . .

One of those persons severely criticized for the Third's inaction was the district commander, Colonel Chivington. Chivington was forty-three years old, a big man physically, and a Methodist minister. . . . In 1862 Major Chivington turned in an outstanding performance against a Confederate invasion force at Apache Canyon, New Mexico Territory. The same year "the fighting preacher" was made a colonel and placed in command of the District of Colorado. . . . In 1864 the anti-state opposition apparently succeeded in making it appear that Chivington had not acted vigorously enough in protecting the territory against the Indians. . . . Chivington probably now looked for some means to restore his waning popularity. An expedition against the Indians was certain to elevate him in the eyes of his fellow-citizens! It seems possible, too, that Chivington was simply spurred to action by the pressure of the citizenry and the discontent of the volunteers. . . .

At about eight o'clock p.m. in the evening, November 28, the expedition broke camp and headed toward the Cheyenne village on Sand Creek. Precisely how many troops it numbered is unknown since the estimates of contemporaries vary. [Colonel] Shoup stated that there were about "one hundred and seventy-five men of the First Colorado, a small detachment of the First New Mexican [Infantry], and about six hundred and fifty of my regiment." Chivington gave the number of Thirdsters as about four hundred fifty and that of the First Colorado as about two hundred fifty. The expedition picked up one hundred twenty-five troops and two howitzers at Fort Lyon. . . .

Throughout the cool, clear night the volunteers marched rapidly in columns of fours until at daylight they came upon the nearly dry Sand Creek. The Indian camp stood to their front on the north side of the creek where the stream made an east-west bend. It numbered one hundred thirty Cheyenne and eight Arapaho lodges.

Chivington began the attack immediately by sending [Lieutenant]

Wilson's battalion across the creek to cut the Indians off from one of their two pony-herds. The other herd, which was southwest of the village below the creek, was subsequently secured by two companies of the Third. As the result of this stratagem, the surprised Indians were forced either to stand and fight or to run on foot. Wilson's troopers, after accomplishing their objective, dismounted and began pouring in a galling fire upon the village from the northeast. The two companies of the Third, after capturing the other herd, also turned and began firing on the village from the south.

Meanwhile, [Major] Anthony's battalion crossed the stream, dismounted, and opened fire from the southeast. The Third, which was to make the main attack between Anthony and Wilson, was the last to enter the fray. Halting the men briefly in the bed of the stream, Chivington ordered them to "throw off all superfluous luggage." "I don't tell you to kill all ages and sex," he is reported as saying, but "remember our slaughtered women and children." The command then advanced on foot to a position behind Anthony's. For a short time the Thirdsters shot through and over their comrades of the First, but Anthony presently corrected the situation by moving to the left. Pressing forward under a cover of artillery fire, the volunteers were soon moving westward through the village and along the stream.

The Indians thought when they first heard the soldiers coming that the noise was that of a buffalo herd. Pro-Indian sources would have us believe that Black Kettle tried unsuccessfully to stop the attack by displaying both an American flag and a white flag over his tipi. The Thirdsters generally denied that he did so, which may not mean that there were no flags but that in the confusion and from where they were they may not have seen them. We are told that White Antelope also attempted to halt the assault by running toward the troopers with his hands up and shouting to them not to fire. When they did not stop, he stood steady with his arms folded over his chest as a gesture of friendship. But he was shot down for his trouble. . . .

Fleeing from the village, a large number of Indians, many of them women and children, formed a battle line of sorts a short distance above where the creek made its eastward bend. Digging holes in the loose sand, they fought for their lives. Chivington and others later claimed that these holes were rifle pits which the warriors prepared before the fight, though it was not the custom of the Plains Indians to fortify a village. Although the Indians suffered heavy losses in this combat, a number of them survived, and they and others gathered after dark in a ravine about ten miles above the village.

One surmises from the conflicting accounts of the battle, that the soldiers, after the initial advance, fought in considerable disorder and without much direction from their officers. The fighting spread to include a wide area and much of it was at close range, in some instances hand-to-hand with knives and rifles. Apparently, vicious atrocities were committed. First Lieutenant James D. Cannon of the First New Mexico Volunteers, who allegedly came along only because he was ordered to by Anthony, subsequently stated:

. . . I did not see a body of man, woman, or child but was scalped, and in many instances their bodies were mutilated in the most horrible manner—men, women, and children's privates cut out . . .

There seems little doubt that the soldiers scalped and mutilated bodies Indian fashion, though it may be that the extent of it was, in the aftermath of the affair . . . exaggerated somewhat. Even had Chivington tried to stop the carnage, and the evidence seems to indicate that he did not, it is doubtful that he would have been successful, for the record indicates that western volunteers were not inclined to show mercy to Indians in any instance.

The battle ended about mid-afternoon and in the evening the expedition went into camp on the battleground, the men sleeping on their arms. There Colonel Chivington evidently wrote two reports, one to General Curtis and the other to the acting assistant adjutant general of the District of Colorado in Denver, each giving essentially the same account of the fight. He had struck a Cheyenne village containing some "900 to 1,000 warriors," killing "between 400 and 500" Indians and capturing about "500 ponies and mules." Several of the Indian dead were chiefs, one of whom he mistakenly identified as Black Kettle. That he had struck a hostile band Chivington did not doubt for he was shown "by my Chief Surgeon, the scalp of a white man taken from the lodge of one of the Chiefs, which could not have been more than two or three days taken; and I could mention many more things to show how these Indians, who have been drawing Government rations at Fort Lyon, are and have been acting." His own losses were nine men killed and thirty-eight wounded.

Other sources indicate that Chivington grossly exaggerated the number of Indians in the village and that of those killed. There were only about five hundred Indians in the village, of which probably some one hundred fifty were killed. Precisely how many of the killed were women and children is unknown since the sources are in disagreement. . . .

News of the fight at Sand Creek reached Denver on December 7.

The next day the *News* printed two private letters giving its details. One was from Colonel Shoup to a Denverite. Shoup estimated the Indian losses at "about 300" killed. "Our men," he said, "fought with great enthusiasm and *bravery*, but with some disorder." There was no truth in the "story" that "Indians are our equals in warfare." The other letter was from Major Anthony to his brother, also of Denver. "I never saw more bravery displayed by any set of people on the face of the earth than by those Indians," he declared. "They would charge on a whole company singly, determined to kill some one before being killed themselves. We, of course, took no prisoners. . . ."

The *Journal*, which learned of the battle from a letter of Captain H. M. Orahood to his wife at Black Hawk, expressed similar sentiments. "It is impossible to estimate the value of this occurrence to Colorado." The *Journal* did not care who got the "credit" for the victory—Connor, Chivington, Shoup, "even Gov. Evans—some one deserves credit and they shall have it . . ." The territory had been saved "from ruin." In subsequent issues both the *Journal* and the *News* printed the official reports of a number of the ranking officers who had participated in the battle. One notices that in none of them was there more than a hint of the atrocities committed by the soldiers upon the Indians.

On December 22 the Third Colorado arrived in Denver from Fort Lyon amidst the plaudits of the multitude. Its "return" was, declared the *News*, "the grand feature of to-day." . . .

Soon after the Third's arrival, Denver's "streets, hotels, saloons and stores" were "thronged with strangers, chiefly 'Indian killers'." And a "high old time there was" during the ensuing night. According to the *News*, the volunteers, happy to be home, talked freely and with considerable exaggeration about their experiences. And "no two men give the same version of the big battle, and, of the stories of a score of them, there ain't three alike, respecting the minutiae of the great glorious victory."

The soldiers also exhibited and sold trophies of the fight. A number of Sand Creek "trappings, beaded garments, scalps, and so forth" were hung "as curiosities" in "some of the bars." A "Navajoe blanket" taken from a "defunct Indian" was "rafled off" for $150.00. And on several occasions during the ensuing weeks "striking trophies" were displayed at the Denver theater.

The troopers remained in Denver until December 28, when they were finally mustered out. . . .

ROBERT G. ATHEARN

War Paint Against Brass: The Army
and the Plains Indians

After the Civil War the Army confronted a very different
situation than that faced by earlier generations of American
military men. Instead of occupying posts along a fairly well
defined Indian frontier, regulars were scattered in small
garrisons across a vast wilderness. Now great distances combined with the usual shortage of troops to reduce the effectiveness of the frontier army. In this selection Robert G. Athearn
discusses this problem and its solution.

The surrender at Appomattox was more than a death knell to the Confederate forces; it also marked the beginning of a period later called
the Federal Army's "Dark Ages." While the gray-clad soldiers disconso-
lately stacked their arms, knowing that militarily their cause had ended,
the day of triumph for the boys in blue was only momentary. Within
weeks demobilization seriously decimated their ranks and a year later
the force that once numbered nearly a million men was a mere shadow
of an army. Subsequent reductions cut it to a corporal's guard.

Yet, during the post-war years events in the American West demanded
a larger frontier force than ever; a fact never quite fixed in the public
mind. . . .

Army men were placed in the dilemma of having the responsibility of
peace in the new West and yet treading carefully to avoid offending the
sponsors of the *beau savage*. General W. T. Sherman, who commanded
the Western Army, expressed the military view when he said, "My own
opinion is that unless we have absolute control of Indian affairs, we cannot
be responsible for harmony of action, and the safety of the Frontiers. . . ."
His belief was unnoticed in the crescendo of maudlin sympathy voiced
for the oppressed race. Both he and his subordinates were placed in the
false position of being called "exterminationists." Except for a few young

SOURCE: Abridged from Robert G. Athearn, "War Paint Against Brass: The Army
and the Plains Indians," *Montana: the Magazine of Western History*, VI (Summer,
1956), 11–22. Reprinted by permission of *Montana: the Magazine of Western History* and Robert G. Athearn.

and ambitious warriors like George Custer and Nelson Miles, Army men wanted neither Indian war nor extermination. To thinking military men the question was one of law and order. They believed that if the races were to be separated the operation should be done with strictness and equity. Those Indians assigned to reservations ought to be fed and cared for, just as the Interior Department advocated, but should they transgress the law and stray they must be returned, by force if necessary. In short, reservation Indians were to be regarded as good Indians and so treated; those who wandered and committed depredations were to be regarded as hostile and punished accordingly. . . .

Army men, driven to near desperation by the hard-fighting, shifty Plains Indians, showed a surprising understanding of the enemy's dilemma. Those who knew the western country saw what was happening. From the East came settlers, cattlemen, and miners, while from the Pacific Coast the mineral frontier edged through Oregon and Nevada into Idaho and Montana, closing the vise, cutting off further retreat. Treaty by treaty the Indians gave up land, moved to reservations, and tried to understand their shrinking boundaries. . . .

It was the high plains that witnessed the most violent struggle between the Indians and settlers, for over this region ranged the nation's fiercest red warriors. Mobile, well-armed, and able to live off the buffalo herds, they posed a threat that puzzled the best military minds. Sherman, studying the empire of grass lying between the Mississippi and Rocky Mountains, admitted that "It is plain to me that we cannot undertake to keep any part of our army massed according to the systems of Europe, but will be forced for years to come to adapt our conduct to the prevailing sentiment and necessities of the Frontier." The adaptation proved to be difficult for with each succeeding army appropriation fewer troops were available. To divide up and pursue the small Indian bands to the death was theoretically sound, but it required a superior force and the army did not have it. . . .

Concerned by increasingly complicated problems of command, General Sherman endeavored to lay out some comprehensive plan that would at once protect the settlers and then do justice to the tribes in the land-rush years that followed. As he wrote to his old friend, Admiral David Dixon Porter, the Plains resembled the high seas in their limitless extent and uncharted paths. It was a comparison that was widely employed, so striking was the parallel. Far out in the grassy waters were little islands of settlement, and occasional military outposts. Sherman's primary task was to maintain communications with these widely scattered strongholds and prevent them from being engulfed by a red population that still controlled much of the land. Once the permanency of major routes was guaranteed, additional roads could be developed and protected. Ultimately the West would be interlaced by travel routes and whites easily could go to any part of it, a situation that in itself would help to contain the tribes. Meanwhile, troops must stay close to the few main roads, even at the expense of the more isolated settlements, and work at the problem from the standpoint of military defense. . . .

As the post-war population movement increased an alarming number of off-shoots from these main lines were developed by travelers. Already the Bozeman Trail, branching north from the Overland Road at Fort Laramie and hooking around the Big Horns into Montana, was disturbing the Sioux. Other branches, like the Niobrara Road across Nebraska and present South Dakota put pressure on the tribes. Sherman saw that a showdown was shaping up as a result of the white pressure and he warned Grant's office that clashes between the two races lay directly ahead. . . .

Even Westerners were alarmed at the recklessness with which newcomers crossed Indian country, ignoring all signs of danger, taking any short-cuts available, bent only upon reaching the yellow metal. The *Montana Post* agreed with Sherman's desire to control the traffic and warned that those who had "cut-off on the brain" risked not only their own scalps but invited a general Indian war. Such warnings were lost in the din of preparation for the great treasure hunt beyond the Missouri and those who saw gain for themselves discounted warnings by gloomy army officers. . . .

The great emigrant road along the Platte River was a continuous cloud of dust during the travel season as settlers and freighters churned along it in their heavy wagons. In a period of only six weeks during the summer of 1865 no less than six thousand wagons, each carrying from one to four tons of freight, passed Fort Kearny in Nebraska. Sherman himself, fascinated by the westward rush, could not suppress the enthusiasm he shared with those who were bound for new lands. . . .

At the same time he realized the effect of the movement upon his own problems and warned headquarters that with the growth in importance of the mountain regions military protection of the routes connecting them was an absolute necessity. The nomadic tribes, however friendly, were increasingly obliged to live, in part, by raids upon wagon trains and small settlements. The very presence of white men offered a temptation that meant trouble.

The Indians were not the only ones tempted by the presence of another race; the whites themselves found it difficult to refrain from attacking the natives. In the new states and territories governors frequently re-garded the solution of local Indian problems as falling within their province. They knew that such duty normally belonged to the Federal Army but in cases of emergency, local volunteers had in the past been called upon. The governors were too often guilty of yielding to local clamor and declaring a state of emergency before the facts warranted such action. They were torn between a desire to wait for the Army, or take to the field at the head of locally raised troops with an oppor-tunity for personal glory in the offing. . . .

Another of the Army's great enemies in the West was distance. Tiny settlements, hundreds of miles apart, demand protection that could not be given. No sooner did soldiers go to the aid of one of them, than another cried out for help. The hit and run tactics of the Indians kept the soldiers constantly moving. . . . "With almost everything to do you can understand they have not much chance to hunt down horse-thieving Indians whose lodges are in the Black Hills of the Cheyenne 400 miles off," wrote Sherman from Fort Laramie in 1866. "It is these awful distances that make our problem out here so difficult."

Fortunately a great shrinker of distances was poised at the Missouri River, ready to move across the forbidding stretches to the West. For decades the Army had faced the problem of supplying its remote frontier outposts. Now with its area of operations swelled to new proportions, the coming of the railroad offered the only hope of combatting appar-ently insoluble problems of logistics. . . .

Army men were delighted at the expansion of the railroad in the Trans-Mississippi West during the years immediately following the war. From the time Sherman took command of the Military Division of the Missouri, in the summer of 1865, to his retirement in 1883 he regarded it as the final solution to the Indian problem, and said so repeatedly. . . . Within a few years the parallel lines marked off a wide corridor of country from which the Indians were driven. Now a wedge of white population projected westward to the mountains, shoving aside the tribes like a great snowplow. It was the beginning of the Indians' final stand. . . .

Upon the completion of the Pacific Railroad, Sherman, now command-ing the Army of the United States, turned his attention to other sections of the West. He advised Phil Sheridan, who had succeeded him in the western command, to watch the construction of the new Northern Pacific with particular care for "it will help to bring the Indian problem for a final solution." Even the Indian Bureau had to agree. In 1872 its commissioner admitted that the new line would "solve the great Sioux problem" and serve as part of a great corral for that warlike tribe. In places like Colorado, Utah, Arizona and New Mexico the coming of the railroad would accomplish a like result and "multiply fourfold the striking force of the Army in that section."

Sherman had said these things for some time and as the rail network spread, he continued to preach its worth. . . . After touring the West with President Hayes in 1880 the General was willing to say that the railroad had completely revolutionized the country during the past few years. In his final report, written in 1883, he attributed the general condition of peace in the West to three principal factors: The presence of the Army, the heavy influx of settlers, and the railroads. Of these factors he called the railroads the most significant.

Gradually the West was fenced off, and as the rails criss-crossed its great stretches of mountain and plains the tribes were surrounded. Meanwhile, along the sprouting branches of steel, settlements clung like fungi, gradually spreading over the land. When danger from the Indians threatened, troops were quickly dispatched, traveling in a single day distances that formerly took them a month. At last the great enemy—distance—was controlled. . . .

The defense of the last frontier had presented the American Army with problems that were both unique and perplexing. If the great plains altered methods of farmers who had learned their trade in the tree area east of the Mississippi, the change was no less true for the soldiers. . . .

Gone now was the earlier notion of a fixed frontier, a chain of protective posts to fend off Indians from the West. The frontier's advance guard now plunged headlong into Indian country in a frontal attack and was momentarily swallowed up in a land of illimitable distances. So rapid was the ensuing change, so fluid the situation, that the military frontier was never quite fixed until the final battle had been fought. Like a traveling road show the troopers periodically struck their tents and moved on. They were, in Sherman's words, the picket line of civilization. . . .

THOMAS D. PHILLIPS

The Black Regulars

Prompted by the need for a large military force in the West
after the Civil War, Congress authorized the enlistment of
Negroes in the Regular Army. Although black soldiers encountered racial discrimination within the military establishment and suffered abuse from white frontiersmen, many
Negroes found military service preferable to civilian life.
Few historians have examined the contributions of minority
groups to the development of the West, and here Thomas
D. Phillips summarizes some of his research on black soldiers
in the "Indian Fighting Army."

Despite the commendable performance of the nearly 200,000 blacks
who served as volunteers during the Civil War, the U. S. Army maintained a strict color line throughout the conflict and refused to enlist
Negroes as regulars. The situation which existed at the close of the war,
however, forced military and political leaders to modify this exclusionist
policy. If the Rebel yell was a thing of the past, the war cry of the
Indian sounded with ever increasing frequency along the frontiers of
the trans-Mississippi West. To meet the need for additional troops in the
West, Congress debated the possibility of enrolling Negroes. The Reorganization Act of 1869 specified that two regiments of infantry, the
Twenty-fourth and Twenty-fifth, and two cavalry regiments, the Ninth
and Tenth, be composed of blacks. It was assumed that the officers of
these regiments would be white men.

From 1869 until President Harry S. Truman ordered the desegregation
of the armed forces in 1948, these four regiments constituted the only
Negro units in the Regular Army. During the period of the Indian
Wars Negro regiments represented ten per cent of the Army's effective
strength and in many western commands black soldiers made up more
than half of the available military force. For nearly 15 years black soldiers
served in Texas and helped protect ex-Confederates and former slave
owners from Commanche and Kiowa war parties. In New Mexico and
Arizona black cavalrymen, commanded by Crook and Miles, participated
in the long campaigns against the Apaches. Black soldiers removed

the "Boomers" from the Indian Territory and were called in to restrain small ranchers and cattle barons during the Johnson County War in Wyoming. The Army's desperate need for troops in the West forced military commanders to employ Negro soldiers in the same manner as white troops, and in nearly three decades of frontier service against the Indians black regulars amassed an impressive military record.

It would be absurd to suggest that white frontiersmen, civilian and military, harbored no prejudices against Negroes during the decades following the Civil War. Although some scholars have emphasized the democratizing influence of the frontier experience, the West, nevertheless, witnessed the transfer and fertilization of racial biases. Several military historians have asserted that commanders harbored such prejudices and attempted to minimize racial friction by segregating Negro troops from white soldiers and civilians. Military necessities on the frontier, however, prevented Army commanders from adopting a strict policy of segregation.

Between 1869 and the end of the Indian Wars in the 1890's, black soldiers served in most of the western states and territories, and with few exceptions commanders assigned troops on the basis of military need rather than racial considerations. The absence of large urban centers in the West somewhat mitigated the problem of garrisoning Negro troops near large concentrations of white civilians, but throughout the period blacks served in the vicinity of frontier settlements and on several occasions garrisoned posts adjacent to populous frontier communities.

Civilian reaction towards the Negro garrisons depended in large part on the geographic origins of the residents of frontier communities. Persons of southern extraction living in Texas and New Mexico vehemently objected to the presence of black soldiers. To the north in Montana, Wyoming, and the Dakotas, settlers from the Midwest and the sizeable foreign-born element were less hostile to the blacks. Negroes, of course did not always constitute the bottom rung of the social ladder in the West, and Chinese, Mexicans and especially the Indians were often the principal targets of racial violence, prejudice and discrimination on the frontier.

Frontiersmen rarely applauded the arrival of a Negro detachment, and local editors frequently printed the usual stereotyped reports of black social behavior. The newspaper comments, however, suggest that the editors were less concerned about the presence of an unwelcome racial group than with the arrival of armed blacks. Although ante-bellum southerners had feared the possibility of a slave revolt, apparently some of the anti-Negro sentiment in frontier communities was generated by the apprehension that black soldiers would turn their guns on the whites.

White racists had traditionally employed violence to preserve the subordinate status of Negroes, but frontiersmen quickly realized that armed
Negro troops were equipped to meet that force in kind.

Although racism flourished in most frontier communities, certain
factors minimized the extent of racial conflict. Townsmen near posts
garrisoned by Negroes found themselves in a serious dilemma; although
they resented the presence of such troops, the soldiers were an important
source of income for local merchants. Supplying the garrisons with food,
forage and fuel, and the soldiers with goods supplementary to those
of the post quartermaster, might be a lucrative business and many merchants catered to the soldiers regardless of their color. In addition to
economic considerations, military necessity often mitigated racial hostility.
Frontiersmen demanded military protection, but the Army simply did
not have enough white troops to garrison every post. Critics always
derided the effectiveness of the Negroes, but they helped provide the
military protection which frontier residents demanded. Racial conflict
frequently marred relations between Negro soldiers and white civilians,
but the need for military security and the purchasing power of the blacks
convinced many westerners of the folly of antagonizing the Negro
soldiers and contributed to an uneasy racial truce in garrison communities.

Throughout the Indian campaigns white and Negro soldiers often
served at the same posts. Separate company barracks and messing facilities at each garrison reduced racial contact somewhat, but in military
duties the color line was obliterated. On occasion white and Negro
soldiers did fight each other, but a white officer best summarized the
conditions at the "mixed" garrisons when he wrote, "There appears to
be no trouble or bad feelings between the white and colored troops . . .
they do not mix, neither do they quarrel."

Although the Army insisted on racial equality in all military functions,
officers did not believe in dictating the social relations of their troops.
White soldiers usually shunned their black comrades and members of
both races participated in their own social and recreational activities.
Segregated company athletic teams were found at many posts, but garrisons did sponsor integrated teams when competing with groups from
other posts or civilian organizations. Blacks occasionally attended dances
given by white soldiers but always under the tacit understanding that
they would bring their own companions and would not attempt to
dance with white women. War Department records suggest that the
attention of Negro soldiers to white women precipitated most of the
quarrels between white and Negro regulars. Despite such conflict, the
daily military contact and social relations between the races and the

fact that Negro soldiers shared equally in the dangers and boredom of frontier service probably dissipated some of the prejudices held by members of both groups.

In the campaigns against the Indians the record of the Negro regiments fully demonstrated the effectiveness of black soldiers. Although some other regiments saw more action, the Adjutant General's report of 1891 showed that of the 2704 Indian engagements fought by the frontier army between 1866 and 1891, black troops participated in the following number: Ninth Cavalry—68, Tenth Cavalry—49, Twenty-fourth Infantry —9, Twenty-fifth Infantry—15.

During the Indian Wars the War Department awarded those soldiers who distinguished themselves in action either the Congressional Medal of Honor, a Certificate of Merit, or an Order of Honorable Mention. Between 1869 and 1890, officers nominated 52 Negro soldiers for various decorations. The War Department and Congress honored each of the applications and black regulars received 14 Medals, 9 Certificates, and 29 Orders. One scholar has suggested that officers and legislators preferred to ignore black heroism, fearing to tacitly admit that the Negro soldier was the equal of the white in combat. Such acknowledgement would have destroyed the myth perpetuated by whites that blacks were innate cowards and did not possess the manly virtues. But apparently officers did not hesitate to nominate Negroes for decorations, nor did the War Department and Congress refuse to approve them. The text of the citations accompanying the awards to black soldiers, usually repeating the words "bravery," "courage" and "gallantry," showed that practice did not follow preference and that the Army acknowledged acts of extraordinary heroism performed by blacks in the presence of the enemy.

Little distinguished the activities of Negro and white soldiers on the military frontier, but in some respects the behavorial patterns of Negroes were markedly different from that of white soldiers. Desertion was extremely common in the frontier army; the annual attrition in some regiments reached between fifteen and twenty per cent of total strength. The Negro regiments, however, never lost more than 10 per cent of their strength and only rarely did desertions exceed 5 per cent per year. General James Parker, who served on the frontier between 1872 and 1897, noted, "Negro troops were proud of the [military] profession and enlisted practically for life." A high proportion of Negro regulars re-enlisted and by the 1880's a substantial number of soldiers in each of the four Negro regiments were hardened veterans of the Indian campaigns.

Black soldiers probably did not join the Army from a sense of duty or other patriotic motivation. The Army offered Negroes a better existence than they could often find in civilian life. Recruiting officers offered steady pay, food, shelter and clothing to Negroes who wished to enroll, and these same material advantages probably convinced black veterans to remain in service. Because Army records furnish only fragmentary information about the personal lives of the black soldiers, it is extremely difficult to determine why Negroes enlisted in the Regular Army. One historian of the enlisted man in the "Indian Fighting Army" stated the obvious when he wrote that each soldier "saw fit to take on of his own free will and for varying reasons," and it seems probable that blacks enlisted for many reasons also.

In 1866 Congress specified that a school be established at each permanent army post, but the legislators neglected to provide for the enlistment of qualified teachers and the War Department rarely allocated funds to construct school buildings and classrooms. In the Negro regiments especially, few of the soldiers had ever obtained any formal education and the officers had to perform most of the duties which noncommissioned officers normally attended to. A lieutenant in the Ninth Cavalry accurately described the educational deficiencies of many Negro soldiers when he wrote of the men in his company, "Few indeed could read and scarcely any were able to write even their own names."

The regimental chaplains, two of whom were Negroes, were responsible for educating the black soldiers. Until the Army instituted a system of compulsory schooling for all enlisted men in 1889, the chaplains labored under extremely difficult conditions to give the men a satisfactory education. Officers encouraged their men to attend classes and in the two Negro infantry units the regimental commanders refused to promote any soldier to the rank of noncommissioned officer unless he could read and write. Many black soldiers enthusiastically seized the opportunity to educate themselves, and Chaplain George Mullins of the Twenty-fifth Infantry maintained that the men who learned to read and write soon developed "a sense of self-respect and a pride of soldiership." The desire of Negro soldiers to learn and the efforts of Chaplains and officers together enabled the black regiments to claim a literacy rate by the late 1880's which nearly equaled the average of the entire Army.

Despite the excellent service record of Negro soldiers, the Army staunchly maintained a color line and only assigned blacks to the four segregated regiments. Army regulations, however, did not prohibit the commissioning of Negro officers and between 1870 and 1889, twenty-three young Negroes received appointments to the United States Military Academy. Twelve passed the difficult entrance examinations, but only three managed to graduate: Henry O. Flipper in 1877, John H. Alexander in 1887 and Charles Young in 1889. The next Negro to complete the Academy course, Benjamin O. Davis, Jr., graduated in 1936. Of the three nineteenth-century graduates, only Flipper served on the frontier, but he was court-martialed and dismissed in 1882.

In the winter of 1890–91, black troopers of the Ninth Cavalry participated in the last engagement of the Indian Wars, the Battle of Wounded Knee. For over 20 years Negro regulars had been an integral part of the frontier army which finally brought peace to the trans-Mississippi West. During the course of the Indian campaigns military leaders evaluated the capabilities and performance of Negro soldiers on military rather than racial considerations. Many Americans held a stereotyped and highly uncomplimentary opinion of Negroes, but the Army simply could not afford to look at the Negro soldiers through such prejudiced eyes. To be sure, a blue uniform could not hide a black skin, but the very nature of the military establishment, its small size, its concepts of professionalism and its authoritarian principles, helped to insulate military leaders from the mainstream of American society and permitted them to judge the Negroes primarily on their ability as soldiers.

The Army during these years did not, unfortunately, try to guarantee the complete equality of Negro regulars, and blacks found themselves segregated in four regiments commanded by white officers. It is conceivable that military leaders could have tried to eliminate all manifestations of segregation and discrimination in the Army, but the prevailing attitude among officers was that the military could not serve as a field for social experimentation. In this they undoubtedly reflected the biases of the white society which produced them.

CHAPTER V

Developing a Territorial System

DAVID HOWELL, a member of Congress, wrote to a friend in February, 1784:

There are at present many great objects before Congress; but none of more importance, or which engaged my attention more than that of the Western Country. . . . The western world opens an amazing prospect as a national fund, in my opinion; it is equal to our debt. As a source of future population and strength, it is a guarantee to our independence. As its inhabitants will be mostly cultivators of the soil, republicanism looks to them as its guardian.

But how was the great region to be governed? The failure of the British Government to meet a similar challenge successfully helped to produce the American Revolution. Could the government of the United States succeed where the leaders of the British Empire had failed? No question concerning the western domain was more important than this.

A committee of Congress, led by Thomas Jefferson, provided the first answer to the problem of developing western governments in 1784. Its members recommended that numerous small states be created in the West, none to be larger than 150 miles square. They also recommended that the westerners should have self-government from the beginning. Settlers free and of "full age" on territory which the federal government had purchased from the Indians might adopt the constitution and laws of any one of the original states for their governance. After the number of people in such a region had risen to 20,000 they might convene a constitutional convention and draft their own constitution. When they equalled the population of the least populous state of the original 13, their government was to be admitted to the Union as a state equal in every respect to all of the other states.

Although Congress adopted the report of Jefferson's committee as an ordinance, it was never applied to any region of the western country. To some conservatives the Ordinance of 1784 seemed excessively democratic and it also promised such a large number of new states that their delegations might eventually come to dominate the Congress. And some members of Congress regretted that the Ordinance of 1784 did not prohibit slavery in any part of the West. These were considerations which in varying degrees influenced the thinking of members of Congress concerning the Ordinance of 1784. Some three years later they approved the Ordinance of 1787, providing for "the government of the Territory of the United States northwest of the River Ohio."

The Northwest Ordinance provided that the region beyond the Ohio was to be organized as a territorial district, under a governor and three judges; a territorial secretary assisting the chief executive. The governor and judges were to draft criminal and civil codes, drawing upon the laws of the original states for specific provisions of the various laws. The governor was commander-in-chief of the militia and authorized to appoint magistrates and other local officers of government as this seemed necessary. Not until 5000 free male inhabitants lived in the territory was there to be an elected legislature. This body consisted of a legislative council and a house of representatives, but Congress was to choose the members of the council from a list proposed by the members of the territorial house of representatives. After its organization the territorial legislature was to assume the legislative duties that the governor and judges had discharged until that time. The governor enjoyed a veto of the acts of the legislature and could prorogue and dissolve it as he saw fit. To the house of representatives and the territorial council jointly fell the task of electing a representative to Congress, who could speak on behalf of the territory but was not given a vote in that body. Contrary to the earlier act, the Ordinance of 1787 provided that there were to be no less than three and no more than five states created from the territory above the Ohio. When one of the territorial jurisdictions should have 60,000 residents, it was eligible to enter the Union as a state, but such admission was not automatic as in the Ordinance of 1784.

In drafting the Northwest Ordinance, the members of Congress retained a number of restrictions upon the territorial residents which had appeared in the earlier act. The westerners were not to supervise the primary disposal of the land; the federal government retained that function. The settlers must not tax the property of the United States nor levy higher taxes upon the lands of nonresidents than upon those of residents. The people of the territory were held responsible in both ordinances for their share of the national debt. Time would prove these to be judicious provisions.

The Ordinance of 1784 had provided independent, representative government from the beginning but under the Northwest Ordinance the western settlers must endure a period of administrative rule. The earlier law had authorized manhood suffrage initially at least; the later statute required that the territorial voter must own a 50-acre freehold and members of the territorial legislature a somewhat more substantial holding. On the other hand the Ordinance of 1787 forbade the institution of slavery above the Ohio River, a most important proviso as history would show. And the Northwest Ordinance included a bill of rights which guaranteed western residents the enjoyment of freedom of religion, habeas corpus, trial by jury, judicial procedures in accordance with common law and representation in proportion to population—significant guarantees invoked specifically in judicial proceedings before the Supreme Court as recently as the pleading of the apportionment cases of the early 1960's. Howard R. Lamar has written that the Northwest Ordinance was "an internal colonial system, a device for eventual self-government, a guarantor of property, and a bill of rights rolled into one act." Despite personal reservations about the phrasing of some clauses and the results of other provisions, as well as about the motivations of some of those involved in drafting it, Theodore C. Pease maintained:

. . . a precious part of the world's heritage in distant ages to come . . . will be the ideas that men may not permanently by their brothers be held in political subordination and clientage; and that the highest and most sacred guarantee, the most practical and stable cement of states and governments is the free and unforced covenant and agreement of man and man.

But some scholars have contrasted the Ordinance of 1787 with that of 1784 and interpreted its provisions as evidence of conservative reaction in the new nation.

In July of 1788 the Governor of the Northwest Territory, General Arthur St. Clair, arrived at Marietta in the western wilderness and began to put the Ordinance of 1787 into effect. Soon Congress organized the region below Kentucky into the Southwest Territory, drafting an organic act which was virtually identical with the earlier law, except that slavery was allowed. Although its drafters could hardly have expected so much, the Ordinance of 1787 served as the foundation for the system of government given to every new territory within the contiguous United States and in Alaska and Hawaii as well. Of course Congress changed the early patterns somewhat as it established new territories and passed legislation, supplementing the organic acts, when local problems demanded it. Since the economic foundations, and the politics which reflected them, also varied somewhat from territory to territory, the distribution of political power in one dependency might differ considerably from that in another.

Despite this fact the political systems of the new territories were similar in many important respects during the nineteenth century. Initially territorial politics were fluid, reflecting the inward movement of people which could change the political complexion of the population in short order. In a sense the federal appointees formed a ready-made political apparatus, but long-established cliques or machines were of course lacking. Instead one found aggressive young men scrabbling for a start, as well as political has-beens who were hoping to start new careers by capitalizing on past experience and avoiding the errors which had ruined them back in the states. There were in most dependencies also men with large financial stakes in the new country who hoped to shape policy to their best interests. And there was, in addition, the great mass of settlers, composed of men who hoped to improve their economic and social positions in the new territory, who were keenly interested in politics and who, as a result, provided some of the leaders of the territory from their numbers as well.

As in the first territories, the territorial officers of the nineteenth century were underpaid in proportion to the labor and responsibility involved in their positions. Sometimes they were interested in land speculation or other frontier business opportunities and the position of governor or judge both produced additional income and placed the incumbent in a strategic position to protect or to enhance his financial interests. Others hoped to use their territorial offices as the foundation of a political career which might carry them to the governor's office of a new state or to Washington as a member of the House of Representatives or of the Senate. William Henry Harrison is an excellent example of such a man; successively a territorial secretary, a territorial delegate and governor, he finally became president of the United States. Usually the territorial officers came from the ranks of the political party in control of the national government at the time of their appointment. A class of professional administrators never developed as in the British Empire despite the example of Harrison and of a few other men.

The initial problems of government were much the same in most territories. Drafting the first codes of laws, establishing local administrative units, locating territorial boundaries, maintaining satisfactory relations with the Indians, guiding or tempering sentiment for statehood—these were to be the concerns of government officers in all of the territories. And in a surprising number of instances the territorial officials found the energy to bicker among themselves about proper policies and procedures.

National politics had much to do with the time when the people of particular territories won admission to the Union. If a majority of the voters were supporters of the political party in control of the national government, they might expect admission much more promptly than if those in control at Washington believed that the new state would send unfriendly representatives and senators to the capitol. But westerners were often in disagreement among themselves on the question of statehood. Its advocates typically argued that a state government would be more responsive to local needs and allow the natural resources of the region to be developed more effectively than did the territorial officials appointed in Washington. But in the territorial stages the federal government paid the salaries of the governor and other dignitaries and some additional costs of government as well. Almost invariably some westerners contended that statehood would bring higher taxes. Let statehood be deferred, they demanded, until the territorial population was clearly adequate to support the additional costs of state government.

During the first 30 years of our national history it was extremely important that the territorial system should operate successfully. Powerful Indian tribes or alliances existed in both the northern and southern territories, looking to the British for aid and comfort in the North and to the Spanish in the South. Although the British had recognized the independence of the United States, they were our most powerful rival in settling the remainder of the continent. If the Spanish were less formidable, their territory still provided a haven whither Indian raiders might retire after ravaging the settlements of the southern frontier. Briefly too in this era the French re-acquired Louisiana, causing Americans considerable concern. The territories were buffers between the older settlements of the United States and the possessions of jealous foreign powers; it was essential that they be governed vigorously and efficiently and their residents remain satisfied with the United States government.

The outstanding ability of many territorial governors prior to 1820 reflected this situation. Undoubtedly too these circumstances help to explain some of the concessions to democracy which the federal government made to territorial residents in the early national period. The stage of administrative government was soon abandoned, territorial residents were allowed to elect their territorial delegate, as well as both houses of their assemblies and most of their county officers. Manhood suffrage became the rule in the territories. At the same time Congress provided a somewhat more conservative system of government in those dependencies where French or Spanish populations had become accustomed to forms of government, law and land tenure that differed from the Anglo-American style, as in Louisiana, Florida and Michigan.

The democratic trend which so greatly changed American institutions prior to 1850 also modified territorial government, but many westerners were dissatisfied with the territorial system at mid-century. Apparently the Oregonians in particular resented the way in which their territorial government worked. In 1851 one of the founding fathers of the Oregon Territory, Jesse Applegate, challenged the United States government to restore their political rights to the Oregonians by allowing them to adopt their own form of government, choose their own government officers and share in the councils of the nation by allowing them to vote in presidential elections. Applegate also argued that federal officers who performed duties mainly for the people of Oregon should be selected from the territorial residents. He asked also that the military forces stationed in Oregon be subject to the control of the civil government there. Congress should support the territory financially, he maintained, until the territory contained residents equal in number to the total required to give a state an additional member in the House of Representatives. At that point a territory should automatically enter the union of states under the action of a general law, rather than by the demeaning method of petition to Congress.

Critics like Applegate attracted little notice while the slavery crisis deepened during the 1850's. The problem of conciliating sectional views on the institution of slavery almost destroyed the territorial system at this time. We cannot develop that story here in detail. Some national politicians sought a solution in the concept of popular sovereignty—that is, the practice of allowing territorial legislators to legislate or not to legislate on slavery as they saw fit. Developed in the compromise legislation of 1850 and the Kansas–Nebraska Act of 1854, this formula, they argued, merely continued the process of extending self-government and democracy in the territories which had been under way since the birth of the Republic. The argument was both ingenious and to some extent true, but it failed to convince northerners of antislavery conviction. Theoretical disputation yielded to violence on the rolling prairies and along the wooded streams of eastern Kansas and the larger question of whether slavery was to survive was settled only after the southern states had left the Union.

After Appomattox territorial administration entered a new phase in the United States. No longer could the caliber of territorial executives or judges significantly affect international relations as had been the case in earlier years. No longer was it necessary for the members of Congress to consider seriously whether conditions in a territory might cause the westerners to leave the Union. Gripped by the nationalism of the postwar years, the members of Congress administered the territories in casual disregard of the feelings of their residents. Yet at the same time they frequently demanded that the territorial government be meticulous in meeting the niggling administrative regulations which Washington prescribed. But, during this period, a very large amount of the continental land mass still remained under territorial governments. Between the outbreak of the Civil War and 1888 there were 13 western territories in all, of which Congress admitted only 4 to statehood. The new states of 1889 and 1890 comprised approximately one-sixth of the area of the contiguous United States. After Utah, finally purged of polygamy, entered the Union in 1896, there were still Oklahoma, Arizona and New Mexico to come, among the contiguous states, and Alaska and Hawaii were not welcomed into the union of states until 1958 and 1959.

Territorial residents writhed at the "ignorance, lack of inerest, selfishness or sheer inertia" of "salt-water despots" that kept them in colonial dependence for long years. Yet it is a fact that the early pleas for statehood in some territories were extremely unrealistic and it is also true that the long struggles for statehood in some territories generated a sense of community and identity which territorial residents carried into the statehood experience with beneficial results.

Indeed the territorial process frequently imparted more than a sense of self-awareness to territorial residents. After studying Dakota Territory, Howard R. Lamar concluded that "many basic and distinct political patterns and economic attitudes," characteristic of the States of North and South Dakota, originated during the territorial years. In that era, he believed, the economic and physical environment caused Dakotans to develop attitudes which were essentially colonial in nature. This heritage in turn helps to explain the nature of Dakota Populism and the history of the Non Partisan League. Similar generalizations can be made concerning other territories.

In comparison to the history of the national, state and local governments, the territories have inspired surprisingly little study. Perhaps there has been a widespread feeling that territorial organization was a transient phase in any region and that its greatest success led only to its demise. Yet the story of the American territorial system may hold the answers to much that is important about the American experience. Can we really say that Americans solved the colonial problem that Great Britain failed to master? Would a different system have perhaps prevented the territories from serving as the focal point of sectional animosities? Does the administration of the system after the Civil War give the lie to many of our cherished assumptions about the political freedom and rights which Americans have supposedly enjoyed? To what extent did the territorial experience and institutions shape subsequent developments in the emergent states? Did the law making and the drafting of constitutions of the territorial process serve as a school for democratic institutions or were they merely exercises in imitating the laws, institutions and practices of older states? Are there lessons for the administrators of dependencies today and the people of emerging nations in our territorial experience? Are we a significantly different kind of nation today because of the territorial system of government? These are questions inherent in our territorial experience.

•1•

ROBERT F. BERKHOFER, JR.

The Republican Origins of the American Territorial System

> In this reading Robert F. Berkhofer, Jr. reviews the back-ground of both the Ordinance of 1784 and the Northwest Ordinance. He suggests that the differences between the two acts have been overstressed. Nor does he believe that Jefferson and the drafters of the 1784 ordinance viewed the frontiersmen very sympathetically. His position has interesting implications both for our understanding of Thomas Jefferson and other assessments of the two ordinances.

To American historians, the year 1787 calls immediately to mind two great documents: the Constitution, which federalized the government of the new nation, and the Northwest Ordinance, which provided for the expansion of that nation upon new principles. While recent interpretation of the first document has moved to placing it within the broader cultural context of its times, the still standard interpretation of the second document is the generation-old economic one of conservative counter-revolution. In this view, the evolution of territorial government from

---

SOURCE: © 1969, Robert F. Berkhofer, Jr. Printed by permission of the author.

Jefferson's Ordinance of 1784 to Nathan Dane's Ordinance of 1787 was a shift from liberalism to conservatism. Jefferson's plan is portrayed as an embodiment of revolutionary idealism and faith in frontier democracy, while Dane's draft is depicted as a reactionary law designed to exploit western inhabitants for the economic benefit of eastern conservatives.

Categorization of the two ordinances in terms of twentieth-century political ideology emphasizes the differences between the two documents at the expense of their similarities. Regional suspicions did prevail in a nation more politically than socially united, but all members of Congress agreed fundamentally that the lands west of the Appalachians should be formed into new states equal in status with the original thirteen, and that such statehood should be achieved only after a previous territorial stage under Congressional authority. This evolutionary scheme was deemed essential by all republicans as a result of their assumptions about the nature of the frontier and its inhabitants.

From the very beginning of the Revolution, Americans believed that their "Western Territory" should be laid off as new states. During the Congressional debates on the cession of lands claimed west of the Appalachians, all sides to the controversy favored the creation of new states there. As the Virginia delegates proposed in an amendment (October 10, 1780):

... all the appropriated lands that may be ceded or relinquished to the United States, by any particular states, . . . shall be disposed of for the common benefit of the United States and be settled and formed into distinct republican states, which shall become members of the federal union, and have the same rights of sovereignty, freedom, and independence, as the other states.

Furthermore, this amendment, which established the basis for Virginia's eventual cession and hence the foundation of the territorial system, specified that these states be no less than one hundred nor more than one hundred fifty miles square.

That all participants in the prickly cession controversy should have accepted the creation of equal new states is not surprising in light of their own history. On the eve of the Revolution, many leading Americans subscribed to an idea of an empire of colonies coordinate with England and united by loyalty to one king. The Declaration of Independence repudiated this loyalty, thus the colonies, now states, became equal in sovereignty, although confederated as the United States in Congress Assembled. As a result of this transformation, what were once proposed as western colonies before the war must now also become independent states, if Americans would be consistent with their ideals. Thus was laid the foundation for a new kind of colonial system consonant with other American innovations. As a young foreign friend of Thomas Jefferson wrote in admiration, Congress in the Ordinance of 1784 intended "establishing a colossal empire, a Union which new nations, not yet in existence, will consent to join as time goes on."

Equally well agreed upon by the end of the Revolution was the principle that such statehood must evolve from a previous condition of "infancy," as one Congressman phrased it. Accordingly, Congress resolved on October 15, 1783, that a committee was

to report a plan, consistent with the principles of the Confederation, for connecting with the Union by a temporary government, the purchasers and inhabitants of said district, until their number and circumstances shall entitle them to form a permanent constitution for themselves, and as citizens of a free, sovereign and independent state, to be admitted to a representation in the Union; provided always that such constitution not be incompatible with republican principles, which are the basis of the constitutions of the respective states of the Union.

This resolve required the committee to produce a plan reconciling republican government with the necessity of governmental evolution. Since the earlier cession resolution restricted the size and shape of the new states, and other men had suggested the minimum population required for statehood, the originality of the committee was severely restricted. Thus Jefferson's work on this Ordinance, like so much of his writing, was a summation of the ideas of his time.

The scheme as reported out of Jefferson's committee embodied four aspects: the delineation and naming of new states, the provision for temporary governments, the general rules for temporary and permanent governments, and the so-called articles of compact. Committee member David Howell summarized succinctly the first part of the report:

It is proposed to divide the country into fourteen new states, in the following manner. There are three tiers of states:—One in the Atlantic [original], one on the Mississippi, and a middle tier. The middle tier is to be the smallest and form a balance betwixt the two more powerful ones.

The originality of this part lies in its division of both ceded and yet-to-be-ceded lands as well as in the immediate division of the territory into the full number of states required by the Virginia amendment of October 10, 1780. Thus it rejected a preliminary government in one or several territories before final state boundaries were to be drawn, as had been previously advocated. Some have wondered why Jefferson named some of these proposed states. Howell's explanation of the naming shows that its purpose was to make the exact stage of governmental evolution very evident to the inhabitants of the new states:

As settlers will always readily know in which states they are, for the states are to be named as well as numbered, when a number of settlers shall have planted themselves in any particular state, either on their petition, or the order of Congress, they are to hold a general meeting of all the free males, and to choose, out of all the constitutions of the present thirteen states, one constitution, and to adopt the laws of such state, also, which are to be subject to alterations by their ordinary legislature. They are also, in this first and general meeting, to divide the state into counties or towns, for the choice of their legislature; and this government is to be originated among them. From this period they are to be subject to pay a quota of taxes by the same rule as the other states, and they are to have a setting member of Congress with a right of debating but not of voting. This is the first stage. After the settlers in any such state shall consist of ___ souls, the free males shall have a right to call a convention, and to form a constitution for themselves, which is to be permanent, of the republican form, and agreeable to the spirit of the Confederation. This is the second stage.

After the settlers in any such state shall consist of a number of souls equal to the least numerous of the thirteen original states, such state shall be admitted as a member in full of the Federal Union, and vote as well as debate, on subscribing to the Articles of Confederation.

Essentially, the report of 1 March 1784 contained these thoughts but in more formal language. The figure of twenty thousand souls was inserted as the requirement for entrance into the second stage of permanent government but not for the third stage of admission to Congress with vote as well as voice. In addition, the report required that the states under temporary and permanent governments be established upon certain principles: they were to remain forever a part of the United States of America; they were to be subject in persons, property, and territory to the government of the United States in all cases in which the other states were subject; they were to pay their share of Confederation debts; their governments were to be republican; they were not to admit to citizenship any holder of hereditary title; and finally they were to exclude slavery after 1800. All of these provisions were to be formed into a "Charter of Compact" as "fundamental constitutions between the thirteen original states and those now newly described, unalterable but by the joint consent of the United States in Congress assembled, and of the particular state within which such alteration is proposed to be made." Here, then, was a document which embodied the recapitulation of the governmental history of the original states complete with colonial agent, taxation with representation, and admission to statehood upon attaining a population equal to the smallest state. At the same time, the success of the republican experiment was to be assured even to requiring the selection of a constitution from one of the original states during the period of temporary government.

The discussion of the Report as recorded in the scanty notes of the *Journals of the Continental Congress* indicates little dissatisfaction with the document except for twelve votes on amendments. The slavery prohibition clause came under attack immediately. Jefferson and Howell voted for retention as did the delegates from all the states north of Pennsylvania, but the delegates from Maryland and South Carolina as well as Jefferson's colleagues from Virginia voted for its deletion. The provision against hereditary titles was also questioned and struck out; as Jefferson explained to James Madison, the delegates voted against the provision not because they approved of such honors, but because they thought it an "improper place to encounter them." Interestingly enough, it was Jefferson who seconded Elbridge Gerry's motion that lands and improvements of non-resident proprietors should not be taxed higher than those of residents within the states before admission into Congress. Howell opposed this attempt to benefit absentee speculators but succeeded only in deleting improvements from the amendment. Yet both Howell and Jefferson agreed to the imposition of stronger government upon the settlers prior to the formation of temporary government. Both men voted for a proposed amendment placing these initial settlers under Congressional regulations and Congressionally-chosen magistrates. Such denial of local autonomy needed only one more state's vote for passage; so two days later a milder proposition, perhaps drafted by Jefferson, permitted Congress to take measures "necessary for the preservation of peace and good order" among the new states' settlers before the organization of a temporary government. Thus Congress adopted a policy for the expansion of a republican empire, which embodied an entirely new colonial principle of providing, as the New Hampshire delegates phrased it, for the admission of "those states into the Union when they shall be of sufficient maturity to be entitled to that privilege."

Jefferson's Ordinance never took effect because the Northwest territory was not cleared of Indians, and so settlers could not enter the area legally. Yet frontiersmen located beyond the Ohio River in violation of Congresssional authority. Such affrontery caused many Congressmen to wonder whether stronger control ought not be asserted. Among these men was James Monroe, who after a tour of the West, moved to amend

Jefferson's Ordinance as to the number of states to be formed from the territory. He proposed no fewer than three nor more than five states be formed, in order to allow these new states to enter sooner with the prescribed minimal population.

Monroe's action reopened the whole issue of territorial government at a time when the activities of frontiersmen only reinforced the idea of greater control during the initial stages of dependency. Jefferson's young friend became head of a committee instructed to study whether further government should be provided before the institution of temporary government under the Ordinance of 1784. How Monroe saw the question before his committee provides insight into this new turn of events:

Shall it be upon Colonial principles, under a governor, council and judges of the U.S. removable at a certain period of time and then admitted to a vote in Congress with the common rights of other States, or shall they be left to themselves until that event?

From this committee in 1786 came the outline of what was to become the Northwest Ordinance of the next year. At first the inhabitants would be subject to a congressionally-appointed government composed of a governor, a council of five, a secretary, and a court of five judges. During this period, the government would operate under the laws of one of the original states, and the governor would command the militia and lay off townships and counties. When the territory contained a certain but unspecified number of free males, Congress would authorize the election of delegates to a lower house. Both the voters and their representatives had to possess a certain but unspecified amount of property. The governor held an absolute veto and power to convene, prorogue, or dissolve the assembly at will. After the formation of the general assembly, the inhabitants were entitled to send a delegate to Congress with voice but no vote. Full statehood would be achieved when the number of free males equalled that in the smallest of the thirteen original states "for the time being."

To Monroe, as he wrote Jefferson, this act retained all "the most important principles" of his friend's Ordinance, whose repeal the report recommended:

It is in effect to be a colonial government similar to that which prevail'd in these States previous to the revolution, with this remarkable and important difference that when such districts shall contain the number of the least numerous of the '13. original States for the time being' they shall be admitted to the Confederacy.

In the sense that this plan continued the idea of evolution, Monroe was correct, but the addition of a quasi-military organization in the first phase harkened back to earlier plans for enforcing law and order from the start of settlement. Now the evolution idea had been extended and specified more concretely than before in order to, in the words of the report, "protect the persons and rights of those who may settle within such districts in the infancy of their settlement."

Later versions more or less liberal than this, depending upon how the blanks were filled, appeared from various committees, but this plan provided the basic structure and sequence of territorial government. It was the appearance of the Ohio Land Company representatives, who sought to purchase a large area of land, that sparked the final version of what is now called the Northwest Ordinance. In record time, still another version of the Monroe report appeared, and it was adopted almost unanimously.

Under the guidance of Nathan Dane, this report, in line with previous Congressional debate, placed the entire territory under one temporary government. The first part provided for the conveyance of property by transfer and inheritance. The second part retained the structure and sequence of the evolution of territorial government in the first and second stage, but the governor, secretary, and judges had to meet newly-imposed property qualifications as did the legislative members, who were selected through a more elaborate procedure. The report also restored the oaths required of all officers in the government and reinstated a Congressional representative in the second stage. Thirdly, it revived Jefferson's idea of compact articles between the United States and the future states in order to extend "the fundamental principles of Civil and religious liberty which form the basis whereon these republics, their laws and Constitutions are erected; to fix and establish those principles as the basis of all laws [,] Constitutions and Governments, which forever hereafter shall be formed in the said Territory." Articles one and two covered religious freedom, habeas corpus, trial by jury, and other rights common to state bills of rights at the time. Some of these had been urged by Dane earlier; there also appeared for the first time the non-impairment of contracts clause. The third article vaguely urged the encouragement of religion and morality, as well as good faith in dealing with the Indians. The next article specified that the territory and new states were to remain forever part of the United States, that they were to pay a proportional part of federal debts in the manner requested by the Ohio Company representative, that they were never to interfere with nor tax the federal lands, that they were never to tax non-resident higher than resident proprietors, nor to create perpetuities. Lastly, this article guaranteed free navigation of waters leading into the Mississippi and the St. Lawrence. Most of these clauses were taken from Jefferson's Ordinance or from subsequent debates in Congress over Monroe's plan for reducing the number of states. The latter was the source of the fifth article which divided the territory into three to five possible states which would gain admission to Congress upon reaching a now-specified population of sixty thousand. In record time, Congress read the bill for a third time and passed it with few changes and one dissenting vote. Among the minor changes were a deletion in the descent clause, the elimination of the perpetuity clause, and changed wording in article three to encourage schools rather than religion as such. Most significant was the addition of an anti-slavery sixth article of compact.

Just as Monroe had written to Jefferson that his revision of the latter's plan was not too different from the Ordinance of 1784, so Congressman William Grayson assured Monroe that while the new Ordinance was somewhat different from his correspondent's ideas, the departure was not "so essential but that it will meet your approbation." And given the perspective of the period, the Ordinance of 1787 was not very different from the Ordinance of 1784. Both documents provided for the evolution from temporary government to permanent government and admission, with equal status, to the Union. Although Jefferson had provided no formal requirements for the stage before organization of a legislature, he and many other Congressmen had voted for Congressional control over settlers during this initial period. While it is true that temporary government was organized by the state's inhabitants under his plan, they still had to operate under a constitution selected from those of the original states. This requirement restricted voting rights and the nature of government anyway. Lastly, his Ordinance gave statehood upon obtaining the population of the least populated state, which given the census of 1790 meant 59,096 inhabitants, or about the same as the Northwest Ordinance. Surely Jefferson would have no objections to the bill of rights, and both the anti-slavery clause and the compact notion were his ideas in the first place. Apparently the new Ordinance did not bother Jefferson enough to complain about it at the time, or at least there is no surviving evidence that he did.

The similarities between the two ordinances must be ascribed to the fundamental agreement among republican legislators upon the character of frontiersmen, and therefore the necessity for social and governmental evolution before property and nation would be safe. Jefferson, like Crèvecoeur, Benjamin Rush, and other Americans of the period believed that the initial settlers upon the frontier were halfway between "tractable people" and "Indians," to use his own words. Under this impression, all republicans felt some Congressional authority must be prescribed during the period of early settlement, although they might differ over the specific amount. On the other hand, Jefferson, Dane, and their colleagues were equally certain that these early inhabitants would be pushed westward and replaced by respectable landowners who obeyed the law. Their faith in eventual settlement by such ideal citizens meant that full-fledged statehood could be extended without qualms, but that statehood ought only come when the higher stage of social progress had been reached. Therefore an evolutionary governmental sequence was incorporated into the framework of both Jefferson's and Dane's Ordinances. With the coming of democratic ideals in the next century the territorial stage would become simplified in line with a new image of frontiersmen, but the republican ideology that lay at the foundation of the territorial system was too deeply imbedded in the very framework of the system to erase some period of colonial dependency entirely.

ROBERT R. RUSSEL

Constitutional Doctrines with Regard to Slavery in Territories

During a fruitful career of teaching and writing, Robert R. Russel has carefully studied various aspects of sectionalism in the United States prior to the Civil War, particularly as it involved the territories. We draw upon one of his articles for a summary of the various interpretations which Americans advanced in those years, concerning the constitutional status, of slavery there. Explaining both the number and the variations in these interpretations is a very considerable challenge to the student of American history.

It is very uncertain what powers the framers of the Constitution intended the federal government to have in territories. The provisions of the Constitution that may have been intended to relate to the matter are capable of differing interpretations, and the available records of proceedings in the Constitutional Convention shed surprisingly little light on the subject. However, all students of our history have agreed that within a few years after the Constitution had gone into effect it had come to be the prevailing view in all the states, although not in the territories themselves, that Congress had complete or almost complete legislative power in the territories and could not only apply to them the laws applicable to the country generally, such as revenue laws, currency laws, and navigation laws, but could also legislate for them in all matters on which state legislatures might legislate for their respective states.

In accord with this view of its power, Congress continued the practice begun in the Confederation period of organizing portions of the "territory" of the United States into political units, which shortly came to be called "territories," and providing for the organization of "territorial"

SOURCE: Abridged from Robert R. Russel, "Constitutional Doctrines with Regard to Slavery in Territories," *Journal of Southern History,* XXXII (November, 1966), 466–486. © 1966, Southern Historical Association. Reprinted by permission of the Managing Editor and Robert R. Russel.

governments therein. And it also early came to be the practice of Congress when organizing a territory to provide for an elective legislature and to authorize that body to legislate on "all rightful subjects" except for a short list of reserved matters. However, bills passed by a territorial legislature might be vetoed absolutely by the territorial governor, an official appointive by the President of the United States with the advice and consent of the Senate, and those bills approved by the governor must nevertheless be sent to Congress for review and possible disallowance.

Chief Justice John Marshall accepted this prevailing view of the powers of Congress in the territories and lent it the support of his great prestige; he seemed to assume that the matter was so clear as not to require argument or demonstration. . . .

As to the particular subject of Negro slavery in territories, it was the *early prevailing view,* in accord with the prevailing view of the general powers of Congress in the territories, that Congress could exclude slavery from a territory, or legalize it there, or continue in effect the laws on the subject that had been in effect there prior to the annexation to the United States of the district involved, or delegate to the territorial legislature the power to legislate in regard to slavery. It was entirely in accord with the then prevailing view of its power that Congress by the famous eighth section of the Missouri Enabling Act, 1820, prohibited slavery "forever" in that portion of the Louisiana Purchase which lay north of 36° 30' north latitude and was not within the bounds set for the contemplated state of Missouri. Of all those whom President James Monroe consulted before he signed the Missouri Compromise and for whom we have records, only former President Madison said that he did not think the imposition of such a restriction was "within the true scope of the Constitution," and even he said no blame could attach to "those acquiescing in a conciliatory course. . . ."

In the 1840's three virtually new views of the powers of Congress as to slavery in territories were presented to the public; and each of these in the troublous years that followed gained a considerable number of adherents among concerned citizens generally as well as among constitutional lawyers.

The first of these new views to appear may, perhaps, best be denoted the *free-soil doctrine.* In its more specific form the doctrine was briefly this: That portion of the Fifth Amendment of the Constitution which says, "No person shall be . . . deprived of . . . *liberty* . . . without due process of law," prohibited and was intended to prohibit slavery in territories, the District of Columbia, and all other places under the exclusive jurisdiction of the federal government. Congress, the executive department, and the courts were under a constitutional obligation to give effect to this provision. A variant of the doctrine was that the prevailing view at the time of the making of the Constitution was that freedom, not slavery, was the natural and proper status of people of African descent, as well as of white people, therefore the framers of the Constitution must have intended to embody this idea of liberty in the Constitution and therefore Congress was under a constitutional obligation to exclude slavery from the territories and other places under the exclusive jurisdiction of the federal government. . . .

The second virtually new view of the powers of Congress as to slavery in territories presented in the 1840's was that which has most commonly been called the *Calhoun doctrine* but whose subscribers chose to call "nonintervention." It could perhaps better be called the "common-property-of-the-states" doctrine. It was first stated publicly in something like its final form by Robert Barnwell Rhett of South Carolina in the House of Representatives January 15, 1847, and then, more logically, by John C. Calhoun in a set of Senate resolutions on February 19. The doctrine was briefly this: Sovereignty is indivisible. The states were sovereign; the United States was not. The federal government was only the agent or trustee of the states in matter expressly delegated to it by the Constitution. The territories were the common property of the states, as co-owners, not of the United States as an entity. The government of the territories was necessarily left to the federal government, as agent or trustee for the states. But in governing territories the federal government was under obligation not to discriminate in any way among the various states or among their citizens. It must admit into the territories and protect there as property anything, slaves, for example, which a citizen of any state might choose to bring with him and of which he had been legally possessed in the state whence he had come; for to do otherwise would be discrimination between states and between citizens of different states and, therefore, unconstitutional. And if Congress could not prohibit slaveowners from bringing their slaves into the territories but must protect them there in their property rights, a territorial legislature could not exclude slaves or deny protection to slave property, for a territorial legislature was but a creature of Congress and could not be authorized to do what its creator could not do. . . .

A third new view of the constitutional powers of Congress as to slavery in territories—or perhaps one should say a view that was revived in the 1840's after a long period of dormancy—was the "squatter-sovereignty" or, better, the *Cass doctrine*. It was first prominently advanced by Senator Lewis Cass of Michigan in a well-publicized letter to A. O. P. Nicholson of Tennessee dated December 24, 1847, and was refined and elaborated by Cass and others in the next several years. Very briefly, the doctrine was this: While from the very necessities of the case, Congress must have power to mark off new territories and provide and ensure them, as incipient states, republican forms of government, it had no constitutional authority to regulate their internal policies in matters not put under federal jurisdiction by the Constitution. The regulation of these latter matters must be left to the people of the territories themselves acting through their elected representatives; and whether or not to permit slavery was one of these matters of local, internal concern. . . .

The Utah and New Mexico territorial acts, 1850, and the Kansas-Nebraska Act, 1854, provided for practical squatter sovereignty in the territories to which they applied. The congressional debates during the proceedings leading to the passage of these acts contributed nothing toward agreement on the constitutional issues involved. But incidents during the debates and proceedings and some of the actual provisions of the acts, especially the Kansas-Nebraska Act, were almost tantamount to an invitation by majorities in Congress to the Supreme Court to step in and settle the constitutional controversy if opportunity should afford.

No slave case reached the Supreme Court under either of the statutes mentioned; but a Missouri case, the Dred Scott case, which could be made to involve at least some of the constitutional issues did reach the Court and was there heard and decided, the decision being announced in March 1857. . . .

Of the eight justices who passed upon the constitutionality of the Missouri Compromise, two said it had been constitutional, that is, that Congress had power to exclude slavery from the territory concerned; six said it had been unconstitutional, that is, in effect, that Congress did not have power to exclude slavery from the territory. . . .

Justices McLean and Curtis in their opinions presented the older, prevailing view as to the powers of Congress in territories, and Curtis gave perhaps the most thorough argument in support of it that has ever been made. It is the view which, with minor qualifications, has prevailed in court and out since the Civil War and requires no further description here.

The four majority justices who wrote their opinions reached the conclusion that the Missouri Compromise had been unconstitutional by *four distinctly different* lines of reasoning, only one of which—that of Justice Catron—resembled at all closely any one of the four constitutional doctrines described thus far in this article. . . .

Chief Justice Taney (Justice Wayne concurring) said Congress possessed extensive power to legislate for territories acquired since 1789. Its power to do so was limited only by the specific prohibitions imposed upon the federal government by the Constitution. The specific prohibition pertinent to the case before the court was, he said, that portion of the Fifth Amendment which reads, "No person shall be . . . deprived of . . . *property,* without due process of law . . . ." Without saying that he was making such an assumption, he assumed that the Fathers had somehow embodied in the Constitution the rule that things of every class of things commonly regarded as property at the time the Constitution was made should be so regarded by the federal government. He cited at length evidence designed to show that at the time of the making of the Constitution our people generally in all parts of the country regarded slavery as the proper and normal status of persons of African descent and that both the common law and the law of nations at the time sanctioned slavery. From these alleged facts, and from the fact that the Constitution in two—he said two—separate clauses recognized the existence of slavery in the country, and without offering one scintilla of direct historical evidence to show that a single member of the Constitutional Convention had ever thought of doing any such thing, and with complete disregard of a great deal of historical evidence that the convention intended the Constitution to be neutral in the matter, he concluded that the Fathers had incorporated into the Constitution the recognition that persons of African descent were among the objects normally and rightly held as property. Slave property, he said, was as much entitled to protection as any other class of property. And to deprive a citizen of property (Dred Scott and his wife Harriet), as the Missouri Compromise had undertaken to do, just because he had taken it across the line into a territory into which he had a legal right to go certainly was not due process of law. Therefore, the Missouri Compromise had been unconstitutional and void.

It will have been observed that the Chief Justice was employing substantive due process of law, just as the free soilers would do; but whereas they invoked it to protect a *liberty*—freedom from slavery—which they claimed was recognized by the Constitution as the rightful condition of all human beings, the Justice resorted to it to protect a right of *property* in persons of African descent held in slavery, which right, he said, was recognized by the Constitution. Taney, as was also true of the free soilers, offered no explanation as to how or why the phrase, "due process of law," could or should be construed to govern the substance of laws affecting life, liberty, and property as well as the procedures by which the laws were enforced. He did not cite a single precedent.

Justice Daniel said Congress had only a limited amount of power to legislate for territories. Just how much it was unnecessary to determine. But it did not have the power to exclude slave property. By a line of reasoning almost impossible to follow he concluded "that the only private property which the Constitution has *specifically recognised,* and has imposed it as a direct obligation both on the States and the Federal Government to protect and *enforce,* is the property of the master in his slave. . . ." "Congress was made simply the agent or *trustee* for the United States, and could not, without a breach of trust and a fraud," exclude from the territories any portion of the citizens of the United States because they were owners of slaves. The Missouri Compromise, therefore, had been unconstitutional and void. . . .

Justice Campbell, as had Daniel, found that the Constitution gave Congress only a limited amount of power to legislate for territories. The history of the times, which he reviewed, indicated, he said, that the Fathers did not intend Congress to have power to determine the internal "polity" of the territories or to adjust the domestic relations of the people there or to determine who might lawfully enter them. At this point logic would seem to require him to have said that such matters must be left to the territories themselves as bodies politic—as the Cass doctrine had it. Instead, he took a different tack. Both the state and federal governments, he said, were "agents and trustees of the *people* of the several States, appointed with different powers and with distinct purposes, but whose acts, within the scope of their respective jurisdictions, are *mutually obligatory.*" It was left to the *states* to determine what might and what might not be held as property. Whatever they or any of them recognized as property [slaves in this case], it was the duty of the federal government to recognize as property in the territories; for to do otherwise would *endanger* the *"social system"* of one or more states and would, therefore, be repugnant to the federal compact and accordingly unconstitutional. . . .

Justice Catron agreed with Taney that Congress had extensive legislative powers in the territories. However, he said, the Missouri Compromise had been void from the start because Article III of the Louisiana Purchase treaty had stipulated that the property laws in effect in the region at the time of the purchase by the United States should remain in effect, and those laws recognized and protected slavery. But the Justice did not stop there; *the treaty aside,* he said, the Missouri Compromise had been unconstitutional: The territories were "the common property of all the States united." The citizens of any state derived the right to go into the territories and "enjoy the common property" not from the United States but from their state. The federal government governed the territories as trustee for the *states*. The Constitution made the states equal in political rights and the right to participate in the common property. For Congress to exclude slavery from the territories would in effect exclude slaveowners, and to do that would violate the "great fundamental condition of the Union—the equality of the States." Catron's view, it will be noted, was quite similar to the Calhoun doctrine except that he did not assert the sovereignty of the states.

Both Justices Curtis and McLean in their written opinions acknowledged the weight of Campbell's and Catron's contention as to the equality of the states and their citizens under the Constitution. Curtis said it may have been unfair to slave states and to slaveholders to prohibit slavery in the territory concerned, but whether it was or not was a political question to be decided by Congress. The Court could only decide as to the constitutional power of Congress, and Congress had acted within its powers. McLean went a little farther. He said, ". . . with one-fourth of the Federal population of the Union, they [our Southern brethren] have in the slave States a larger extent of fertile territory than is included in the free States . . . ." As for the territories, "The repugnancy to slavery would probably prevent fifty or a hundred freemen from settling in a slave Territory, where one slaveholder would be prevented from settling in a free Territory." . . .

. . . [T]his writer has no disposition to try to magnify the constitutional controversies herein described into a major explanation of the causes of secession and civil war. However, not only did great constitutional lawyers grapple with the constitutional issues described, but also hundreds of thousands of their fellow citizens took these issues seriously and debated or pondered them earnestly and intelligently. Historians should strive to understand these constitutional matters and the positions individuals and parties took upon them and treat them neither lightly nor carelessly in their general accounts of the causes of secession.

EARL POMEROY

Carpet-Baggers in the Territories 1861 to 1890

Earl Pomeroy received the Beveridge Prize, one of the major awards granted to American historians, for the research of which this selection was a part. Here he describes one of the more important reasons why territorial residents were critical of the territorial system during the late nineteenth century and implicitly raises questions about the effectiveness and fairness of the American system of government during that period.

Not All Carpet-Baggers were in the southern states during reconstruction. When the epithet became current, it fitted to a turn the easterners who had been filling offices in those other federal dependencies, the territories, since Arthur St. Clair headed down the Ohio in 1788. St. Clair himself was a political successor of the royal governors who had carried their commissions from London to New York rather than from New York to Cincinnati, or than from Washington to Prescott.

The new boundaries set up after secession began, between the Colorado act of 1861 and the Wyoming act of 1868, substantially gave the west its political framework until the admissions of 1889–90. Stabilized boundaries, however, did not mean stability in administration. There was never a territorial service in the sense that European powers evolved colonial services. Of four hundred and twenty-four governors, secretaries, and judges of this period, two hundred and eighty-eight did not fill out their four-year terms, and only sixty were recommissioned. Many renounced frontier discomforts and inadequate federal salaries when better prospects opened; many others were removed to make room for new political bankrupts. Too often the men sent out were merely "young men or men out of employment, who would not be assigned to like positions in the States . . ."

Source: Abridged from Earl Pomeroy, "Carpet-Baggers in the Territories, 1861 to 1890," *The Historian*, II (Winter, 1939), 53-64. Reprinted by permission of *The Historian* and Earl Pomeroy.

The number of nominees with claims to territorial residence fluctuated without rising much above one-third of the total in any administration. The number who exceeded formal satisfaction of legal residence requirements probably was much less. . . . An appointee might renounce his eastern "allegiance" upon arriving in the territory, or he might be commissioned a third time as resident of a state. Governor Ferry of Washington (1872–80) was considered a resident, although twice commissioned as from Illinois. The informal designation of "bona fide resident" was reserved by territorial citizens for men whom they accepted as one of them, regardless of legal qualifications.

Aside from patronage considerations, there were always persuasive arguments for limiting offices to easterners. During the Civil War, it was urged that disloyalty and the "Pacific Republic" project increased the "importance of having *good reliable Republicans* in office . . ." Only rarely were territorial residents absolved of all competence for office, though former Delegate Todd of Dakota affirmed that "outside the officials, there is not a man . . . that has the legal knowledge or qualification" for a judgeship. Appointment of residents often satisfied territorial citizens more in principle than it produced a better service in practice. Some were actually dishonest, such as Holmes of New Mexico, Gilson of Idaho, Webb of Montana. It was difficult to choose a resident, for endorsements might be obtained by fraud or threat. A common objection emphasized the bitterness of intraterritorial politics. Attacks against residents were often as savage as against non-residents; to appoint a member of any faction was to embarrass the party as a whole. In general the executive impulse to appoint from the territories was sporadic and needed no better answer.

Before the election of 1884, the Democratic House passed a bill requiring that all those appointed governor be two-year residents, while the Republican Senate gave comprehensive expression to the conservative point of view:

[I]n many instances, owing to party complications and unhealthy alliances . . . , it was almost impossible to select impartial and unprejudiced persons . . . from residents . . . It often happens that schemes exist in the Territories, or a certain policy prevails that Congress is anxious to suppress . . . , with which every resident otherwise fit to be governor is not only identified, but is exerting himself to maintain . . . , and to limit the selection to residents . . . would in such cases amount to encouraging strife and discord. . .

The Territories being the common property of the United States . . . , the Committee can see no good reason why these Territorial officers may not be selected from the States having an interest in these Territories.

A month later the Republican convention at Chicago adopted a plank affirming the principle maintained by the House, without limiting it to governors and without advocating a statutory requirement:

Resolved, That appointments by the President to offices in the Territories should be made from the bona-fide citizens and residents of the Territories wherein they are to serve.

The Democrats followed suit in July.

During Arthur's last month in office he made two notable resident appointments: Edward J. Curtis as secretary of Idaho, and Francis E. Warren as governor of Wyoming. The delegate from Wyoming had urged the importance of holding a future state:

They [the people] do not want a sick man or a politician sent from elsewhere. The prominent republicans say very freely that they had rather have a decent resident democrat fill the place than the best non-resident republican. . . You know, that if the republican party would again come into power . . . that it must be done through the progressive western States and Territories.

Warren, supported by the Union Pacific and aided by a split among Wyoming Democrats, remained in office until November, 1886. His suspension followed charges of collusion in a territorial "salary grab" and of enclosing government land. George W. Baxter of Wyoming, his successor, was asked to resign after a month in office when it appeared that he, too, was implicated in illegal enclosures.

By 1886–87 Cleveland was besieged by the spoilsmen, and doubtless the Wyoming experience was not encouraging. Baxter's successor was Moonlight, recently defeated for the governorship of Kansas. Governor Samuel T. Hauser of Montana, like Warren, incurred the displeasure of Land Office Commissioner Sparks, and gave place to a Kentuckian. After 1886, fewer residents were appointed. The House Committee on Territories reversed the stand it had taken under a Republican president in 1884, reporting that

while . . . , wherever practicable the Territorial offices should be filled by appointment of . . . qualified electors . . . , . . . it would be unwise to require by statute that this should be done in all cases.

In their 1888 platform, the Democrats attacked the Republican stoppage of admissions and said nothing of appointments. The Republican convention resolved that

Pending the preparation for statehood, all officers thereof should be selected from *bona-fide* residents and citizens of the Territories wherein they are to serve.

It was easy for the Republicans to be virtuous in renouncing territorial patronage in 1889: the reward of a few months of virtue was to be a sizeable block of Republican votes in Congress. Cleveland's good intentions may have been more disinterested, but they met with unpropitious circumstances. Harrison from the first made strictly partisan appointments, from among partisans within the territories. Far from limiting his resident appointments to the territories that were immediate candidates for statehood, however, he extended them also to Utah, New Mexico, and Arizona. The practice thus founded, encouraged perhaps by the imminence of further admissions, continued through the admission of the last state in 1912. In 1933 proposed elimination of the statutory requirement for governors of Hawaii was denounced as "resurrection of the old-fashioned carpetbagging . . ."

In the territories non-residence of officers was a stigma and a source of suspicion. Men from the states, without local sources of income, were under disadvantage in living on consistently low federal salaries:

Think of a judge receiving a salary of $2,500 . . . , sent out for . . . four years and liable to be removed by the President at any time, with questions involving millions to decide, in a new country where the expense of living is very great, far exceeding his salary! . . . It is hard to make people believe . . . that it is possible for him to be willing to sacrifice himself in a country like that. . . . There is universal distrust of him.

When such officers attempted to maintain former business connections by trips to the east, their absences often were real grievances. These became acute at such times as during the Dakota Indian wars of 1862.

Distrust of officers without supplementary incomes was paralleled by distrust of officers whose incomes came from without the territories. There was a feeling that men with their material interests in the states could not share the territorial point of view; . . . .

Territorial wants and interests were held to be unique and impenetrable to eastern understanding. . . . Governors from the states were no doubt satisfactory in other territories, but

not so . . . with respect for New Mexico. Nearly a whole term is here required to fit an intelligent appointee for Governor from the East for his duties. . . .

Distaste for "imported" territorial officers naturally gave rise to comparisons of an unpopular governor with George III, to descriptions of the territories themselves as

mere colonies, occupying much the same relation to the General Government as the colonies did to the British government prior to the Revolution.

Territorial politicians found attacks against federal officers a popular and profitable line of campaigning even when there was no immediate prospect of winning state office. The Idaho legislature refused to allow bounties for Civil War volunteers because, after nine months of no government at all, the United States had sent "tax gatherers and officials to rule over them and eat out their substance." The position of stressing colonial aspects was so customary that the *Rocky Mountain News* could greet news of admission legislation with the comment that "The Colorado bill has passed both branches of Congress, and Colorado is now in America." According to the *Vermillion Republican,* Dakotans were

not even wards of the government, but a party subject to the whims of political leaders, the intrigues of schemers and the mining of party rats. . . . When shall we slough off this chrysalis or bondage and be free, independent and self governing?

By the time of the Omnibus Bill, the evils of non-resident appointments had been recognized in both territories and states. Doubtless they were aired, and probably they were exaggerated, for partisan interests outside the territories. Minority Democrats orated in Congress against "carpet-bag officials who have been intriguing, blundering, and domineering in the Territories as they used to do in the South . . ." Likewise, much of the territorial protest against "carpet-baggers" may have come from recent arrivals expecting offices under statehood. Yet there was a genuine antipathy for officers appointed from the states, as there were practical reasons for appointing men acquainted with territorial as distinct from state problems. Montana Democrats viewed with complacency the tenure of a Republican governor because "it will keep the [Republican] party divided and we stand a much better show to defeat them in the elections." Territorial candidates for positions, alienated by appointments from the states, might join the opposition party.

When Harrison handed over to the Senate his lists of nominees for territorial offices in 1889, practical politicians could not well quarrel with the new policy of selecting resident rather than non-resident Republicans. There was little unsupported idealism in the new course, as there had been little idealism in the course of nominations in the first hundred years of territorial government just concluded. Good men and bad men came out from the east, men who could not wait expiration of their terms to entrain for the states and men who remained for service and honor in new homes. The ordinary territorial carpet-bagger, however, was an unhappy figure, thwarted by the legislature, unsupported by the national government, with few thanks and little pay for his discomforts and labors. When statehood became possible, he was not the least of the considerations that turned western electorates to a more complete self-government.

•4•

BAYRD STILL

An Interpretation of the Statehood Process, 1800 to 1850

Very few historians have tried to analyze the impact which the territorial experience had upon the institutions and government of the states. Bayrd Still developed an interesting hypothesis about this subject which has attracted far too little attention in the historical profession. Not only does he seek to explain constitutional development in the new states during the first half of the nineteenth century but, if he is correct, his findings have important implications for our understanding of the growth of state political parties and national politics in the same era.

State making is one of the constants of the American experience. The ever recurring practice of creating and revising state constitutions has produced, in delegates' debates and popular reaction, a record of changing political attitudes in the United States and some suggestion of the motivation of the change. Thus, for example, state constitutional activity between 1800 and 1850 reveals a consistent cycle of first, expansive trust in, then rigid curtailment of, government activity. The consistency of this pattern, as well as the reflection of significant political ideas, either accepted or in the making, is well exhibited in the popular attitude toward the legislative branch of government.

In "first-constitution" movements of the period, the words of the framers manifested a wide trust in the representatives of the people. Of

SOURCE: Abridged from Bayrd Still, "An Interpretation of the Statehood Process, 1800 to 1850," *Mississippi Valley Historical Review*, XXIII (September, 1936), 189-204. Reprinted by permission of the *Journal of American History* and Bayrd Still. Professor Still kindly provided us with a revised draft of the original article.

this, Ohio (1802), Indiana (1816), Mississippi (1817), Illinois (1818), Alabama (1819), Missouri (1820), Michigan (1835), and Arkansas (1836) provide excellent examples; while Florida (1838-39), Iowa (1844 and 1846), Wisconsin (1846 and 1847-48), and California (1849), though somewhat critical of the legislative branch because of the economic experience of the sister states, conform in the essential tendencies. Citing the Jeffersonian maxim: "Where annual meetings end, tyranny begins," the framers of these first constitutions insisted upon the annual election of representatives to insure a quick responsiveness to the popular will. They expressed their confidence in legislative discretion by leaving most of the details of government to later legislative enactment. Jealous of encroachment upon the legislator's function, they opposed any move to restrict the activity of the people's agents. Wide powers of appointment, of administrative officers and judges, were left in the hands of the legislature. In short, the conduct of state government, in these as in the first Atlantic-coast constitutions of the Revolutionary period, was to depend largely upon the legislative will. As a corollary, the executive function was minimized by checking the governor's appointing power, by limiting his term of office, and by weakening his veto.

An aggrandizement of the legislature at this stage of governmental experience is understandable. It was a response quite natural to framers of first constitutions. The attainment of statehood was accompanied by a self-pride and self-confidence which gave promise of accomplishment by the people, an accomplishment most readily to be achieved by the agents whom that people chose. Territorial experience had brought dissatisfaction with executive dominance and sympathy for legislative discretion. Among the delegates were many of the same political leaders of the frontier community who had sat in the territorial assembly; consequently, they were inclined to favor that branch of government and to exalt its function. Since statehood was usually achieved at a moment of expansive growth rather than at one of restriction and reaction, a spirit of expansion rather than of limitation was likely to govern the grant of power to the legislative department. Even the delegates who met to make first constitutions in a period of economic restriction, as in Iowa and Wisconsin in the 1840's, were convinced that the people as the true source of power never erred, that if a legislator made a mistake he would not be reelected, and that the Jeffersonian principle of governments quickly responsive to the popular will had the greatest likelihood of success.

By contrast it was the experience with popularly-managed government colored by discontent due to economic causes—the late "revulsion" they called it in Louisiana—that engendered the "second constitution" attitude characteristic of the revision movements of the three decades after 1820. Criticism centered now upon the excess of government activity resulting from the powers originally granted, that allegedly had brought debt and disaster, and especially upon the legislators who had been responsible for this expansion. The criticism became especially bitter and widespread after the crisis of 1819 and 1837. Delegates to New York's convention of 1821 expressed criticism of legislative excess, and throughout the twenties similar arguments were heard in Indiana and some of the states of the South. In the revision movements of the thirties (in Delaware, Mississippi, Georgia, Tennessee, North Carolina, and Pennsylvania), when economic conditions had improved, advocates of curtailment met difficulty in winning their point; but delegates to conventions from 1844 to 1851 (in New Jersey, Louisiana, Texas, Missouri, New York, Illinois, Kentucky, Michigan, New Hampshire, Ohio, Indiana, Maryland, and Virginia), held during and in the wake of dark years of economic distress, were universally and consistently outspoken in their condemnation of the havoc legislatures and government had brought about.

Now it was claimed that the people's delegates were foolish, rash, extravagant of time and money. Legislation was excessive, unstable, personal. As a remedy, special legislation for individuals, such as for divorce, was abolished. The "curse" of legislation was to be checked by biennial or triennial sessions, by limiting the number of days legislatures might meet, by reducing the lawmakers' salaries. Now critical of legislative discretion, some states required a majority of all members elected to pass laws; it was suggested that the aye and no on all measures be recorded; a two-thirds vote in the legislature or popular approval by the electorate were often made prerequisite to the creation of banks or internal improvement schemes. The pent-up opposition to the evils of over-expansion of banks and corporations was leveled against the creators of these institutions. A definite limit was set upon the amount of debt which the legislature could contract. The desire to remove all matters from legislative discretion led to adding much actual "legislation" to the frames of government. As the legislature was curtailed, the governor was aggrandized, both directly, through desire to have him check legislative excess, and indirectly, since to weaken the legislature would lead, as one delegate said, to an increase in executive power. Almost everywhere the governor's veto power was strengthened and his appointive power increased.

A marked confidence in the people's agents was apparent among delegates to the first constitutional conventions in the Old Northwest. Ohio denied a veto to the governor in 1802 and exhibited a hostility to judicial encroachment upon the legislature which resulted in a denial of judicial review of state legislation from 1805 to 1811 in the state. Strong objection was raised to incorporating in Indiana's constitution of 1816 provisions fixing the seat of government and limiting the salaries of certain public officials. These, it was claimed, were purely legislative functions. Mississippi's annually-elected legislators were empowered to appoint the secretary of state, the attorney-general, treasurer, and auditor of public accounts, as well as the judiciary. In 1816 the inhabitants of territorial Illinois urged the abolition of the executive veto and the grant of wider appointive power to the legislature. According to the *Western Intelligencer* for August 21, 1816, the colonial situation which they had experienced in the territorial stage had withheld from "the people, the only true source of all power, a participation in those rights guaranteed by the constitutions of every state in the Union." Yet despite this implication that the activity of the legislature could be synonymous with the popular will, the framers of Illinois' first constitution expressed some criticism of the "over-legislation" of the territorial assembly when one said: "Our laws on some subjects have become so confused, that, to use a common adage, a 'Philadelphia lawyer' could not tell what these acts mean, nor even how much of them is in force." Nevertheless, the legislature, as set up in 1818, was still to have predominant power in the new state government. . . .

Experience with expansive legislatures in the period prior to the crisis of 1819, both in New York and in other eastern states, had been disillusioning to conservatives. "Not many years ago," one said, "a law had passed the legislature enabling all who were dishonestly inclined to defraud their creditors of their honest dues. . . . Very many honest men lost their property, and roguery and corruption were encouraged." Banks had literally overrun the country. Ezekiel Bacon could not "shut his eyes to the occurrences which had taken place in the various legislative assemblies in this country." He cited Pennsylvania's plight when her legislature had projected a program of banks which looked like "madness to every man whose wisdom had not grown up within . . . legislative halls." Though the "Jeffersonians" continued their opposition to this implication that the "representatives of the people are not the people," the fears engendered by the legislative expansiveness of the years previous to the crisis of 1819 gave the conservatives backing for their contention that the executive and judiciary were the best safeguards against legislative irregularity.

Even some of the western states which had bestowed broad grants of power upon their legislators were beginning now to exhibit criticism of and exasperation with their "trusted representatives." No longer was there so great an anxiety to keep the legislature close to the people. Already in the early twenties, Indiana was complaining of her legislators. About ten thousand dollars was being spent annually on "fruitless legislation," it was held. "Much of the time of the session was taken up repealing acts of the previous session. . . . If the General Assembly met biennially [and some even said triennially] the laws would be as wholesome, more permanent, and the expense would be materially reduced." In many southern states the same criticism was heard throughout the period from 1822 to 1834. . . .

The "vicious habits" of the legislatures were condemned more bitterly in the years following the crisis of 1837. In New Jersey, criticism of legislative divorce, annual sessions, and executive weakness led to reform in 1844. A delegate to Louisiana's convention of 1844–45 contended that "from the language of gentlemen one would suppose that the legislature was a body at war with the people and entirely independent of them." Moving to curtail the legislature's power to create debt, one delegate said, "If you open the floodgates, we shall be again submerged by extravagant and profligate appropriations of money after the revulsion through which we have passed." The New Orleans *Weekly Picayune* praised the article which prevented the state from becoming a subscriber to joint stock companies. Biennial sessions limited to sixty days would remove the "curse" of "excess of legislation" at great saving to the public treasury. The legislature was not to interfere in the choice of the executive or with his appointive powers. A strengthened veto was praised as "the first check on the wild spirit of internal improvements . . . the greatest check that can constitutionally be put on partial or hasty systems of legislation." . . .

Despite the criticism of legislative excess that characterized constitutional revision in the established states from 1830 to 1850, conventions creating new governments continued to exhibit a predominant trust in the legislative arm. This became increasingly difficult to maintain in the forties; and yet the majority attitude among delegates to first conventions in Iowa and Wisconsin, though framed in the wake of economic difficulties, conformed in spirit more closely to the "first-constitution" pattern than did other constitutional movements of the period. The impetuous frontiersmen who met to frame Michigan's first constitution in May and June, 1835, constituted a legislature directly and immediately responsible to the people. Proposals to lengthen terms, restrict sessions, and limit numbers were rejected. The framers were anxious that internal improvements should be "encouraged by the government of this state." The executive power was to be organized "for the most limited term comporting with the exigencies of the country." The Arkansas convention, held in 1836, was less expansive, but nevertheless so favored the legislature at the expense of the executive that Governor James S. Conway remarked that most of the sister-states gave the governor greater power than he had. Many champions of legislative discretion were among the delegates to Iowa's first convention held in October and November, 1844. J. C. Hall considered that to question the legislature was "a step that struck at the representative form of our government. It was taking from the legislature what had been its right and its province. If the legislature passed a law that made taxes oppressive, we, the people, would not select them or any others to do the same thing again." This constitution was rejected, among other reasons, because it was not "sufficiently Jeffersonian." Although the second attempt at constitution-making incorporated some of the currently popular restrictions on the legislative arm, the *Iowa Standard* reported: "The people were anxious to go into the Union; and a small majority of voters was found who voted for it from motives of temporary expediency, believing that amendments could be made before any serious inconvenience could result from some of the foolish restrictions imposed upon the legislature."

Delegates to Wisconsin's first constitutional convention—October to December, 1846—had reason, through experience and the eagerly watched example of their neighbor states, to distrust legislative excess and especially the institutions, such as banks, which legislators were likely to create; yet they did not wholly forego their "first-framer" confidence in the peoples' representatives. An annually elected assembly was provided. Considerable and outspoken objection was raised against the attempt to strengthen the governorship with what the majority deemed a necessary salary. . . .

Thus a pattern of confidence in the legislature, as agents of and synonymous with the people, appears to have prevailed in new states at the same time that the residents of the older states, through experience with the operation of state government had developed a different philosophy concerning the ability of the representative to serve the interests at least of those groups now most dominant in the revision conventions. The first phase of the statehood process took place under conditions that invariably, in this half-century of rapid frontier expansion, enhanced the prestige of the agents of the people. The second phase, one of curtailment, indicates that popular attitudes were now affected by a generation of experience with expansive self-government, by the periodic recurrence of economic depression, or by the appearance of newly dominant groups in the community. This succession of forces ultimately found a reflection in the constitutional structure of the states. . . .

CHAPTER VI

Disposing of the Public Domain

After prolonged controversy, the leaders of the revolutionary generation agreed that states claiming territory beyond the Appalachians under their charters or by other authority, should cede these titles to the national government. These cessions bestowed assets upon the central government which enhanced its prestige and promised a flow of income from land sales that would allow it to support itself and to reduce the debts remaining from the Revolutionary War. Initially of course this public domain stretched only to the Mississippi and did not include the Floridas. But acquisition followed acquisition and Americans extended their territorial boundaries until the purchase of Alaska rounded out the continental limits of the nation in 1867. The Texans, however, retained management of their public lands when they entered the Union in 1845.

Some members of the revolutionary generation believed that the public domain of the nation was to be the foundation of a new American empire, perhaps the greatest empire that the world had ever seen. They visualized spreading farms, growing cities and enhanced prosperity for all. Others reacted with ominous forebodings. Some delegates to the Constitutional Convention feared, for instance, that legislators from new western states might soon wrest control of the Union from the original incorporators.

When the first state cessions gave the Confederation a public domain, the Old Northwest, the federal treasury was bare and fiddle-footed settlers were already drifting into the region, intensifying the irritation of the Indians. The members of Congress promptly decided that they should devise a system of land sale and title for that region. The Land Ordinance of 1785 provided for the survey of seven ranges of townships along the western border of Pennsylvania above the Ohio River. The provisions of this act applied only to the seven ranges and government officers put them into effect slowly. The clause in the law which provided that the lands were to be put to sale in the original states was surely no convenience to the frontiersmen. The members of Congress felt so little bound by the basic principles of the Ordinance that they shortly sold several large tracts in the Ohio country to land companies on much more generous terms. But much of the procedure which the Ordinance provided was to become a basic part of American land policy in which federal officers removed the Indian title from tracts of land and others surveyed them into townships, six miles square, set in a grid oriented to true north. Interior surveys of these townships divided them into 36 lots each a mile square, the familiar section of today. Then officers of the federal government offered the lands at auction, accepting no bids below a specified minimum price and ultimately the federal government gave patents or deeds to the purchasers. Congress reserved some lands in each township, notably for the support of education.

In future years the members of Congress established local land offices in the West and modified the price and certain other sale provisions of the Ordinance of 1785, but the basic system of survey which it provided was to prevail throughout the public domain of the United States, excepting only a few special congressional grants, legitimate Spanish and French grants and some extremely mountainous regions. Periodically critics have ridiculed the rigidity of the straight boundaries and the rectangular tracts which this system has produced, arguing that it separated lands more appropriately left together for administrative purposes and impeded the development of soil-conserving practices and the organization of economic farm units. But relatively unskilled surveyors found it easy to apply the American system of land survey in the field and it was both simple and cheap to administer. During the last half of the nineteenth century a small number of government surveyors, land officers and clerks surveyed and issued patents to huge acreages of land each year.

Alexander Hamilton wrote in 1790:

. . . on the formation of a plan for the disposition of the vacant lands of the United States, there appear to be two leading objects of consideration; one, the facility of advantageous sales . . . the other, the accommodation of individuals now inhabiting the Western Country, or who may hereafter emigrate thither.

The former, as an operation of finance, claims primary attention; the latter is important, as it relates to the satisfaction of individuals now inhabiting the Western Country, or who may hereafter emigrate thither.

Hamilton believed that it was both desirable and practical to conciliate the two objectives but he was primarily interested in revenue. Land sales provided a major source of income for the federal government prior to the Civil War and the forthright nationalist, John Quincy Adams, maintained that this flow of income should be used to support the construction of a great system of internal improvements as well as other beneficial projects of national importance. Subscribing to such a revenue and development policy, Henry Clay and other Whigs of the 1830's preferred to distribute excess national revenue to the state governments rather than to lower the price of federal land or to modify the tariffs which they believed were necessary to insure the development of manufacturing industries.

At a very early date some Americans were ready to reverse Hamilton's emphasis. Frontiersmen, particularly, maintained that the country could best be developed if land policy fostered the needs of the small farmer. If such individuals could easily acquire land, they would add to the wealth of the country by creating new units of production. Critics of the revenue policy buttressed this argument by invoking the Jeffersonian idea that the independent yeoman possessed unique political virtues, an argument still used to justify special treatment of the nation's farmers.

During the nineteenth century the land policy of the United States revealed concessions to both the revenue and the agrarian theories. The Ordinance of 1785 provided that alternate townships in the Seven Ranges were to be sold as units and the remaining in sections of 640 acres at a minimum price of $1 per acre plus surveying fees. Such terms of sale attracted mainly the well-to-do and in 1796 the members of Congress actually raised the minimum price of public land to $2 per acre. But thereafter the federal lawmakers acknowledged the complaints of the frontier farmers, the men of small capital and their champions, and made the terms of sale more attractive to such individuals. They decreased the minimum size of the unit which the government would sell from 640 acres to 320 acres in 1800 and, after further reductions, reduced it finally in the 1830's to 40 acres. Although specifying a minimum price of $2 per acre the Land Law of 1800 allowed the purchaser four years of credit and Congress soon reduced the price somewhat. But the credit provisions of the Act of 1800 encouraged both small and large purchasers to buy beyond their needs and means in the hope of making speculative profits. The depression of 1819 struck the purchasers of government land with such force that the land accounts of the United States Treasury fell greatly in arrears. The members of Congress, therefore, eliminated the credit provision from the land code in the Act of 1820 which retained the land auction and set the minimum price of federal land at $1.25 per acre.

After 1820 westerners began to demand a right of preemption which would allow the settler to buy the claim, which he had developed on the public lands, before the local land sale took place. Congress gave a special right of preemption to deserving groups of settlers during the 1820's and 1830's and passed a permanent Preemption Law in 1841, allowing the settler on surveyed public lands to buy up to 160 acres of land at $1.25 per acre prior to the local land auction. Now settlers who qualified under the law need not bid for their homes against large buyers or local rivals at the land sale. In 1854 the members of Congress passed the Graduation Act lowering the price of government land below the $1.25 minimum in proportion to the length of time that it had remained unsold after being offered for sale at the land auction. Speculators bought such lands in large amounts and Congress repealed the law in 1862. Meanwhile the advocates of liberalization had continued their fight and apparently won their greatest triumph when Congress passed the Homestead Law of 1862, giving the settler title to 160 acres of land after five years of residence and the payment of nominal fees.

Although it became progressively easier for the man of limited resources to obtain land from the government during the first 60 years of the nineteenth century, men of greater capital continued to purchase large holdings which the farmers of developing regions must ultimately buy from them. And the members of Congress used the public domain for purposes only indirectly related to the demand of western settlers for farms. They granted land bounty warrants to the veterans of all the wars prior to the Civil War. Many of the old soldiers or their heirs sold these warrants at a discount to brokers or speculators and individuals often used large numbers of them to buy great acreages of land for speculation. Buyers using military warrants, for instance, purchased about one-third of the state of Iowa. Congress also donated land grants to support the building of wagon roads, canals, and eventually railroads, most frequently using the states as intermediaries. One of the later railroad grants, that of the Northern Pacific, totalled some 40 million acres. Settlers would eventually purchase most of the land in such grants. Upon entering the Union new states received land to assist in the construction of government buildings, to support their common schools and to help them establish institutions of higher learning. The educational grants culminated in the Morrill Act of 1862, granting claims on the public domain to each state in the amount of 30,000 acres for each member of its congressional delegation for the support of a college of agriculture and mechanic arts. The Swamp Lands Act of 1850 had bestowed title to swampy and overflowed land upon the states on the condition, generally ignored, that their legislators provide for draining these lands. As a result of all these laws, great acreages of land passed into the hands of large holders who sold tracts to settlers at prices considerably above the minimum price that the government charged at the land sales.

The Homestead Law of 1862 did not effect an immediate revolution in the land disposal program of the United States. Those lands which the government had offered at auction unsuccessfully before that date were still available to purchasers at private entry by paying the minimum price of $1.25 per acre. The federal lawmakers did not terminate the railroad land grant policy until 1871. Speculators bought land grant college scrip and military bounty warrants and used such land paper to purchase land in the public domain that homesteaders might otherwise have acquired. The Preemption Act remained in force. And the Homestead Law itself contained a provision that an entryman might convert his application to a cash purchase at $1.25 per acre after six months.

By 1862 the settler's frontier was pushing into the Great Plains, where diminishing and erratic rainfall frustrated hopeful farm makers and where they found inadequate amounts of timber for fences and buildings, in sharp contrast to earlier frontiers. In response to the timber shortage, Congress approved the Timber Culture Acts during the 1870's, allowing settlers to enter tracts at the district land offices on condition that they plant trees on a part. If a sufficient number of trees were surviving after seven years, the farmer or his descendants obtained full title to the land. Although we may deride legislators who believed that rainfall sufficient to support grass must also be adequate to maintain trees, or even thought that planting trees would increase the rainfall, not all timber claims were failures. Even so, the legislation was a bizarre indication that American legislators still had much to learn about the vagaries of the great western grassland. More sensible was the Desert Land Act of 1877, which allowed westerners to purchase a section of land for irrigation purposes. But Congress passed no law to meet the special problems of the stockmen, who were building a grazing empire in the West during the 1870's. The grazers needed acreages far greater than the Homestead Law provided and they maintained that its provisions actually encouraged settlers to try and make farms in "cow country," where small holdings were doomed to failure.

The settlers moving into the Plains country generated a tremendous demand for lumber. This contributed in part to the rapidity with which lumbermen exhausted the great pine stands of the Lake States. Through most of a century, Congress had failed to recognize, except in a most perfunctory way, that special policies were required for the lands that were valuable chiefly because timber was growing upon them. The law-makers were perhaps even more delinquent in failing to provide and en-force legislation which regulated the exploitation of mineral lands. A leas-ing policy, applied in the lead lands of Missouri and the states of the upper Mississippi valley, was unsuccessful and thereafter Congress allowed miners to extract massive riches from the placers and lodes of the public lands without any regulation except that provided by the miners them-selves and their local governments. During the 1860's, Congress began to develop a mineral lands code, providing for their sale as such and in the Timber and Stone Act of 1878 allowed the sale of timber land in limited amounts on the western public domain. But in neither case were the laws adequate to the complexity of the problems involved.

From the earliest days of the Republic, there were critics of the land disposal system and every major change in the land laws followed the criticism of the existing statutes from some quarter. The defenders of the frontier settlers agitated for liberalization of the land laws and excoriated the speculators who were spawned, so they believed, by the land system. During the early nineteenth century, some New Englanders feared that liberalization of the land laws would drain needed labor from the growing manufacturing industries of their region. This attitude had dissipated to a considerable extent by the late 1850's as the significance of the western market became clear to eastern manufacturers. But in the meantime representatives of the eastern working class had come to support a free homestead law, believing that it would draw workers to the frontier thereby raising eastern wages. Some southerners opposed more liberal land laws lest new free states develop so rapidly that slavedom's emis-saries be overwhelmed in Congress. Northern freesoilers on the other hand worked to accomplish this very thing. Only vestiges of these northern and southern attitudes remained after the Civil War, but westerners remained critical of a system which restricted their freedom to exploit the public domain.

In the years following the Civil War many Americans became con-vinced that the land laws inadequately protected the ordinary citizen's interest in the public domain. By this time great capitalists and cor-porations, some of them alien, had amassed principalities from what Henry George called the "unfenced land," the precious resource which had produced "all that we are proud of in the American character; all that makes our conditions and institutions better than those of older countries. . . ." Instead of insuring just distribution, critics believed that the land laws had cloaked the fraud of unconscionable malefactors. They suspected that railroad companies, lumbermen, mining corporations and cattle barons were intimidating legislators, bribing government officers, using dummy entrymen and employing other subterfuges to obtain large holdings from the public domain. Investigations showed, however, that even the humble settler was often willing to falsify the facts in preparing the affidavits required under the Homestead, Timber Culture and Pre-emption laws. Tabulating farm tenants in the United States for the first time, the federal census takers of 1880 discovered that one-quarter of the nation's farmers were tenants and far more than that number in some areas—shocking evidence to many that a land system designed to foster the independent yeoman had failed. Horrified by the rapid depletion of the nation's forests and eager to apply the knowledge accumulated by the great scientific surveys of the West during the postwar years, scientists began to demand more rational use of the nation's natural resources. In his report on the arid lands of the West in 1879, John Wesley Powell urged that the remaining public lands be classified into land use categories and policies developed which were appropriate to each classification.

Against this background, the members of Congress approved a notable reform of the land code in 1891. The legislators repealed the Timber Culture Acts and the system of land sale by auction and private entry. In future homesteaders could convert their entries to cash purchase only after 14 months of residence, rather than the 6 which had encouraged fraudulent entries. Suspecting the Desert Land Act of assisting the speculator and the cattleman more than the irrigator, the lawmakers modified it, allowing acquisition of only 320 acres instead of 640. In effect these changes made the Homestead Law the major instrument of public land disposal. Attracting relatively little attention, the twenty-fourth section of the act allowed the president to set aside forest reserves, thereafter to be closed to entry under disposal acts. Using this clause, conservation-minded presidents developed our great system of national forests.

Interested Americans have always realized that much was at stake when federal legislators designed and amended the land laws. Economic power, gained by the recipients of special favors under the land disposal system, might become political power and this in turn might be used to enhance the position of such favored individuals still more. The demand of Jeffersonians for a land policy which fostered the independent yeoman reflected their understanding of these economic and political realities. In general the critics have argued that some Americans were indeed favored unduly. Paul Wallace Gates has maintained that many individuals who speculated heavily in the public lands of the Middle West used their profits to establish themselves as leaders in the new western communities—roles which some of their descendants still play. To him this result was unfortunate. But we can also argue that the large buyers and landholders contributed importantly to the building of the communities of the West. They advertised their lands for sale and attracted settlers; their sale contracts gave impecunious farmers the credit which the national land system denied them after 1820; and they often provided more than their share of the taxes which the new communities needed to support schools and road building. When speculators set prices on their lands which settlers could not pay, the large landholders may have retarded the development of the farms and trade centers in the locality where their lands lay. But it is doubtful that the speculators were the useless parasites that some contemporaries and later historians have suggested.

Historians have written a good deal about the fraud that characterized the transfer of land from the national government to private parties, and the gap between "high intentions and low performance" was on occasion shocking. But in general the government did its job honestly and chicanery was sometimes a local response to unrealistic legislation. In broadest perspective the task of the legislator was to develop land laws which would most effectively attract labor and capital to the West on terms that would provide the optimum amount of economic development in the nation. Could our land disposal system have been changed so as to stimulate economic growth still more? And if so, what would have been the effect of such alteration on our political system? These are questions which are of particular interest to scholars who are investigating the history of the public lands at this time.

HENRY TATTER

State and Federal Land Policy During the Confederation Period

Settlers of British origin had been taking up new lands and developing farms for almost 200 years when the British government acknowledged the independence of the American states. To the dismay of the colonists, the British had tried to tighten and centralize the administration of the land disposal process in the colonies immediately prior to the Revolution. During that struggle and immediately afterwards, the states developed their own policies. Here, Henry Tatter argues that the members of the national Congress ignored the generous precedents developed by the state governments and created a federal land system which was a reversion to the repressive imperial policies.

The study of comparative legislation concerning land policies during the first years after the formation of the United States requires a few broad introductory statements. The new policy of exclusive governmental agreements with Indian tribes for cessions of land prior to white settlement gained wide acceptance with the Proclamation of 1763 and similar colonial enactments. The colonials were no longer able, either individually or in groups, to negotiate directly with the Indians for land; the exercise of this right became so vested with public interest that governments assumed control without reservation, and the new Federal Government became heir to this practice.

After 1766, the formulation of plans by the British Lords of Trade for the assurance of larger revenue receipts from the disposal of land in America and for a controlled social order evolved into a drastic modification of the land system. . . . The comprehensive plans of the new British policy called for extensive surveys before sale, progressive sale of contiguous parcels of land, and sale at auction to the highest bidder above a defined minimum after due advertisement. . . .

SOURCE: Abridged from Henry Tatter, "State and Federal Land Policy During the Confederation Period," *Agricultural History*, IX (October, 1935), 176-186. Reprinted by permission of *Agricultural History*.

Having claims to western lands which the Crown rather completely ignored after 1763, the landed colonies, particularly Virginia and New York, reasserted their claims vehemently. The popular protest against the British Acts and Orders in Council in 1774 and 1775 relating to land policy was widespread. These measures seemed as tyrannical to the frontiersmen as the Intolerable Acts did to the people of the coast. A stake in the land was their stake in life. To circumscribe it with burdensome conditions was a threat to the fundamental basis of happiness on the frontier.

In the years immediately preceding the American Revolution an ever-increasing stream of pioneers filtered into the valleys of western Pennsylvania, western Virginia, Tennessee, and Kentucky—into and through the neutral strip created by the Proclamation of 1763 and subsequent Indian treaties. These squatters ignored even the liberal requirements of the colonial land laws. The land offices were too far from the scenes of pioneering activity to enable the settler to make his entry before or immediately after his location of the land. As a result, a series of settlement rights sprang up which became recognized as a customary method of acquiring a land claim. The usual requirement of building a cabin, clearing a few acres, planting a crop of corn, and blazing or otherwise marking the exterior bounds of the claim and residing on it, which constituted the foundations of a cabin, corn, or settlement right, now often gave way to the practice of deadening a few trees to mark the rough bounds of a tomahawk claim. When the tomahawk claimant actually settled on the land but without a warrant of survey or a patent, frontier opinion sustained him until his rights were recognized in law, and protected him from all who sought to eject him with the weight of a superior legal title. . . .

Not having made adequate provision for the squatting situation in the west, North Carolina and Virginia were besieged with petitions and threats from the far-off settlers in Tennessee and Kentucky, demanding legal right to their lands since they had undergone the perils and hardships of pioneering. The Virginia Convention of Delegates meeting in the spring and summer of 1776 considered this problem seriously, and the summation of its land legislation typifies the radical agrarian measures of Revolutionary legislatures. It was ordained "that all persons who are now actually settled on any unlocated or unappropriated lands in Virginia shall have the preemption, or preference in the grant of such lands." . . .

The Virginia legislature enacted an amendatory law in 1777 and elaborated it two years later, granting those who had settled on the "Western Waters" before 1778 a preemption right to 400 acres, and an additional preemption to land adjoining their improvements gave them the right to a total of 1,000 acres. Those settling after January 1, 1778, were given preemption to 400 acres including improvements, no warrant of location being necessary. The price to preemptors was two and one-half cents an acre in addition to a small certificate fee.

In Tennessee as in Kentucky the settlers depended on their numerical strength, their persistence, and their years of actual occupancy to win the preferential right to acquire title from the Government. It was not long in coming, for in November 1777, the Assembly of North Carolina granted each settler and each prospective settler during the next two years 640 acres for himself and an additional 100 acres for his wife and each child at the reasonable charge of 40 s. for each 100 acres. . . .

Maryland, leader in the movement to require the states with western claims to cede them to the Federal Government, provided preferential rights to settlers on its remaining public domain to purchase land on very reasonable terms, based entirely on the value of the land in its native condition.

Squatting in Maine during the Revolution was encouraged by the belief that the lands of the proprietors, many of whom were Tories, would be confiscated for the benefit of actual settlers. The General Court of Massachusetts ordered a committee of five to investigate intrusions on lands of the Commonwealth and to arrange "fair adjustments with all such as were disposed to do right, upon principles of equity, good faith, and duty." After three years the committee suggested that townships be laid out to prevent emigration to other States and to accelerate settlement. Special inducements were offered to actual settlers. Large blocks of land in the new townships were to be granted in 100-acre tracts to those who settled on the land; and title was to be confirmed to such settlers after four years of residence and cultivation. . . .

After the close of the Revolution, Pennsylvania attacked its land-disposal problem with vigor. In doing so, it was influenced by strained State finances, military bounty promises, the pressure of surplus population, a wild agrarian spirit, and a natural competitive zeal to attract new immigrants. The General Assembly ordered the opening of new areas to sale in 1784, and the sale at auction of the Depreciation Tracts followed. The average yield of all auction sales was thirty-four cents an acre, and this method of sale was abandoned in 1787. The compact with Virginia recognized the property rights of the settlers in the disputed area. An act of December 1784 gave those who settled prior to 1780 a preemption right to 300 acres. . . .

Vermont went furthest during this agrarian period in the development of the law, assuring the settler the value of his improvements on the land of another. The Betterment Act of 1781 entitled the occupying claimant who lost in a title dispute to bring action immediately for the value of his improvements; it declared that a judgment in his favor was a lien on the land. The amendatory laws of 1785 also gave the dispossessed claimant one-half of the improved value, or the rise in the value of the land since his possession.

Turning from these examples of individualism and liberality toward the actual settler let us glance at the Federal situation. The first concern of the Continental Congress with the public domain then being formed by the cessions of western lands was to prohibit intrusions on the Indian lands and thus thwart causes of friction. With reference to the settlers on the Ohio, Timothy Pickering wrote to George Washington in 1778 that "The inhabitants appear, many of them, to be a wild ungovernable race, little less savage than their tawn neighbors," and asked for sufficient regulars to quiet and protect the frontier. As an immediate consequence, Captain John Clark was ordered to the Wheeling region to dispossess settlers on Indian lands. In the same year, Virginia prohibited settlement northwest of the Ohio River. In September 1783, Congress issued a proclamation forbidding "all persons from making settlements on land inhabited or claimed by Indians" beyond the limits of the States, as a step essential to the maintenance of harmony and friendship with the Indians. However, the Treaty of Fort McIntosh, completed in January 1785, was a signal for settlers and land speculators to invade the territory. They anticipated the soldiers sent down the Ohio River to patrol the ceded region, and were their principal concern. . . .

The unsatisfactory relations with the Indians of the Northwest before 1795 forced further emphasis upon the policy of keeping the pioneer squatters from encroaching on Indian lands. The Federal policy toward intruders also included those on Federal lands destined for sale. The prospect of profitable disposal of the public lands won by the "common blood" and for the "common benefit" of the entire Nation placed the Federal Government in opposition to squatters from the beginning.

The fact that the cessions of western land claims to the Federal Government and the financial crisis were concurrent was ominous. The young Nation parted at once with the colonial precedents of recognizing individual rights in the heritage of unsettled land. The leaders in the struggle for Independence cast aside their liberal concepts of the natural right of man to a fair allotment of whatever unused land he might find, and embraced the idea that the vacant lands in the west should be used as the basis for a fund to extinguish the Nation's debts. . . .

The statesmen of the time had to change their opinions radically before they could espouse the principle of using the public domain as a source of public revenue. Jefferson is the classic example. Having opposed the recent efforts of the Lords of Trade to reorganize the system of colonial land disposition on a profit basis he asked his compatriots of 1776: "is it consistent with good policy or free government to establish a perpetual revenue?" . . . A few years later Jefferson spoke of the western lands as a "precious resource" for the extinguishment of the public debt, and he looked eagerly to the immediate perfection of the land-disposal system. . . .

Pelatiah Webster's plan of 1781 came close to the final ordinance that inaugurated the Federal land-disposal system. He proposed survey before sale, sale before settlement, strict forbiddance of intrusions, the auction system of sale with an upset price of one Spanish milled dollar per acre, a curt preferential right to settlers already on the land to purchase their holdings at the average auction price "excluding every idea of favor to which they may think themselves entitled for their *first migration and cultivation*. For I esteem all this very wrong and injurious to the public, which rather deserves punishment than reward." . . .

The Ordinance of 1785 was a compromise between the internal and external interests of the States as well as between the New England and Southern land systems. . . . The auction system of sale of wilderness land was in direct opposition to the pioneering process. The conflict between the internal and external interests of the States is suggested in the auction system, in the high upset price of one dollar, and in controlled settlement where the suggestion was implicit that policy should limit the number of townships to be put on sale not merely to maintain the value of land for the benefit of those who had already purchased, but to control thereby the exodus from the old States. This was rank imperialism.

Land sales under the Ordinance of 1785 were a dismal failure. No sales of full townships and forfeiture upon default of smaller parcels characterized the first efforts. But the system under the Confederation is distinguished for large sales to land companies and later equitable adjustments to their financial distress. The confirmations of foreign land grants launched under the Confederation were liberal to real and supposed grantees in marked contrast with the Federal attitude toward its own settlers.

For fifty years the actual settler found himself out of grace with the Federal Government. When thereafter he came into political power the pendulum swung to the opposite extreme, and the full effect of the belated and exhaustive application of the Homestead Law of 1862 are with us now. As the Federal public domain was being formed, the new

Nation in its Federal capacity fell heir or victim to the recent plans of the British Board of Trade that were a break with colonial practice. It saw strength and wealth in a similar centralization of land disposition. With the perspective of a century and a half we see that the dedication of the new Federal domain to the extinguishment of the public debt created by the Revolution was an error, even as the Crown was in error in seeking revenue from similar sources for the extinguishment of the debts due to its imperial wars. While the representatives of the sovereign States legislated in the Federal Congress for high revenues, controlled settlement intended to limit settlement, and opposed squatting in woeful disregard of the pioneering process, the respective State legislatures developed most liberal land disposal innovations for their remaining vacant lands in a concerted, competitive effort to attract new settlers. While the right to a free homestead was granted by some of the States and liberal preemption rights by all others, mere preemption was rejected by the Confederation. . . .

·2·

ALLAN G. BOGUE

The Iowa Claim Clubs: Symbol and Substance

In many frontier communities between 1820 and 1862, the settlers organized themselves in squatters' associations or claim clubs, which regulated their members in "staking out" claims and protected them against claim jumpers and the capitalists who might bid up the price of claims at the government land auctions. Many historians have interpreted the clubs as a manifestation of the frontiersman's capacity for democratic action. Some years ago, one of the editors discovered evidence which countered that view and concluded after further study that some claim clubs at least were instruments of coercion and speculation.

. . . . Although claim clubs existed elsewhere in the Middle West, the Iowa variety has occasioned particular comment. When historians have believed citation to be in order, Jesse Macy's early study of institutional beginnings in Iowa, the records of the claim club in Johnson County, Iowa, edited by Benjamin F. Shambaugh, and Shambaugh's article on "Frontier Land Clubs or Claim Associations" have been standard exhibits. To Shambaugh, who built upon Macy's work, the claim club was an organization which the settlers used to protect their claims on the public domain until they could obtain title from the federal government. Squatters organized such clubs, he suggested, so that they might forestall the land speculator and the claim jumper. Although pointing out that the claim club did allow settlers to transfer claims to which they had not received legal title, and that technically the squatters were trespassing, Shambaugh emphasized that these squatters were "honest farmers," establishing homes and improving their claims. Representing "the beginnings of Western local political institutions," the clubs fostered "natural justice, equality, and democracy." . . .

Of the twenty-six counties in which claim clubs of the usual type existed, nineteen lay contiguous one to the other—outliers running north, south, and east from a solid block of nine counties located in the third

SOURCE: Abridged from Allan G. Bogue, "The Iowa Claim Clubs: Symbol and Substance," *Mississippi Valley Historical Review*, XLV (September, 1958), 231–253. Reprinted by permission of the *Journal of American History*.

and fourth tiers of counties north from the Missouri border and lying in the east central portion of the state. Most of these counties were settled during the 1830's and 1840's, but they were not the only counties settled in that period. In general, also, considerable numbers of settlers of southern stock settled in these counties, although not to the same degree as in the counties in the two southern tiers. Those counties in which the southern stock mingled with Yankee or alien settlers made up the central block of claim club counties. Whether the tensions generated by the mixing of cultural stocks stimulated the formation of organizations designed to deal with the basic problem of control of the land in these frontier settlements can only be conjectured. Very definitely, however, club activity was not linked solely to the absence of a preemption law. In the first place limited preemption laws applied to many of the settlers who moved to Iowa prior to 1841, and secondly the claim clubs in sixteen of the twenty-six counties were active considerably after the passage of the general preemption act of 1841.

The county histories contain all or a portion of the club laws in nineteen cases, and in a few instances the original manuscript records are still available. . . . The club laws ranged all the way from the general to the specific, depending in part, perhaps, on the degree of pressure to which the organizers believed themselves subject and in part on the predilections of those who drew up the regulations. Granted such local variations the regulations covered the size of the claims allowed; directions for marking, registering, and transferring claims; and the procedure to be followed when club members contested each other's rights, when members were threatened by claim jumpers, and when the date of the land sale arrived.

In any re-evaluation of the role of the squatters' associations the responsibilities and the privileges of the members must be carefully considered in order to discover whether they were consistent with the avowed purpose of the clubs. The pioneers justified the organization of claim clubs on a variety of grounds. In some cases formal justification was given as a preamble to the club regulations. Most common was the wording,

Whereas it has become a custom in the western states, as soon as the Indian title to the public lands has been extinguished by the General Government for the citizens of the United States to settle upon and improve said lands, and heretofore the improvement and claim of the settler to the extent of 320 acres, has been respected by both the citizens and laws of Iowa . . .

Other clubs emphasized the need of protection against "reckless claim jumpers and invidious wolves in human form," or the need "for better security against foreign as well as domestic aggression." In a number of cases the acquisition and peaceable possession of land were given in the preamble as objectives of the settlers. . . . In no case did a preamble specifically mention preservation of the home.

The squatter could expect that his comrades in the club would come to his assistance if claim jumpers threatened his holding and that similarly his friends would intimidate speculators who might seek to outbid him at the land auction. The settlers who organized the Jackson and Mahaska county clubs agreed to protect each other in the enjoyment of their claims for a period of two years, if necessary, after the land sales. The squatters usually placed an upper limit upon the size of the claim to be protected. In ten out of fourteen cases the maximum was set at 320 acres, but in two instances 480 acres was specified, and on one occasion 200 acres. Club members in another county limited themselves to 160 acres, but allowed each other to reserve an additional 160 acres for a non-resident friend. In Poweshiek, Johnson, and Webster counties, where the manuscript claim records were preserved in rather complete form, one did not have to be a resident to enjoy the protection of the club. Nor was it necessary in some clubs for a settler to have attained his majority. In two cases the minimum age of members was set at sixteen years, in one instance at seventeen, and in two others at eighteen. None of the clubs forbade members to sell their claims; indeed the right to make such transfers was specifically guaranteed at times and the purchaser assured of the protection of the club.

If the squatters of a claim club expected to benefit from membership they also assumed responsibilities. They pledged that they would assist their officers in maintaining club law in their districts should it be challenged. They promised to co-operate with the other members in intimidatory action at the land auction if necessary. In some clubs members paid small sums to the recorder or other club officers for their services. Regulations prescribing the degree to which the member must improve his claim appear in the manuscript records of the Poweshiek, Johnson, and Webster county associations, but not in the selections of the club laws printed in the histories of other counties. The members of the Webster County or Fort Dodge club agreed to expend labor worth $10 on their claims each month after the first month. The members of the Poweshiek Protection Society pledged in their revised by-laws to put in $30 worth of labor on their claims within six months of registration and $30 additional labor for each succeeding six months the claim was held. In the Johnson County club, however, only non-residents were compelled to improve their claims to the extent of $50 worth of labor for each six months held. If the squatters actually envisioned developing their holdings into productive farms and homes it would seem reasonable to expect more frequent and more stringent improvement requirements in the club laws.

Questions might also be raised concerning the motives of the members in protecting the claims of minors, who were ineligible to purchase land under the pre-emption law. Allowing membership to minors was no doubt justified in the eyes of members on the grounds that the minor might well be of age by the time of the government land sales, but it might also have been used by squatters to acquire additional land through their children. The club laws also reveal that although all clubs regarded the public auction as the main reason for their existence, a number of them pledged themselves to maintain control of the claims beyond the date of the land sales. In addition, most club regulations provided that the squatters could claim an acreage which was much larger than needed for a farm unit in the mid-nineteenth-century Middle West.

Local historians often viewed club activities in the same light as did Shambaugh. Extralegal though its activities might be, the claim club was justified, they said, because it protected the honest squatter against the claim jumper and the land speculator and allowed him to improve his claim and protect his home. As one local historian put it, "the thought was intolerable that speculators, or eleventh-hour newcomers who knew nothing of the burden and heat of the day should enter upon land which actual settlers had staked out and tilled, and upon which they had builded homes." Some writers admitted that inequities perhaps resulted from club action, but they obviously believed that these were trifling in comparison to the beneficial achievements of the clubs. In nine of the twenty-six accounts, however, the authors introduced material which ran counter to the usual interpretation, some apparently not realizing the conflict. For example, a local historian of Cedar County wrote:

Early in the country's history, a ring of mercenary characters, anticipating immigration, claimed all the untaken groves and wooded tracts in the county, and when an actual settler—one who wanted land for a home and immediate occupancy . . . settled on a portion of the land rings' domain, he was immediately set upon by the bloodhounds, and it was demanded of him that he either abandon the claim or pay them for what they maintained was their right. If the settler expressed doubts of their having previously claimed their site, the ring always had one or more witnesses at hand to testify to the validity of the interest they asserted. The result was nearly always the same. These settlers, more to avoid difficulties than for any other reason, would purchase their pretended right for forty, fifty or one hundred dollars, more or less, according to value after which the ring was ready for operation in some other locality.

Such activity, continued the writer, led the "settlers who came to find homes" to form mutual protection leagues to resist such bogus land claimants. . . .

An incident in Clinton County reveals the possible inequities of claim club activity. David Hess and his family, late-comers to the county, wished to settle near the town of Lyons, where they had discovered former neighbors from the East, but they "found that the 'claim-makers' had ploughed their furrows and set their corner stakes around all the land near the river, leaving their agents to 'sell-out' while they had sought new fields for similar enterprise." The Hesses decided to go elsewhere, but their old neighbors interceded with the other residents of the settlement and they were "informed that they were at liberty to settle upon any lands not occupied by an actual settler, and that the settlers would protect them against all claimants." . . .

Daniel H. Pierce, one of the early settlers in Clinton, later wrote:

Some of the chivalry, or gentlemen of elegant leisure, followed the business of making claims and selling them to emigrants as they came through. As soon as a new settler arrived, the above named gentry would ascertain his "pile," by some means best known to themselves. They would then have a claim to suit the newcomer's purpose and purse, and, if he demurred paying anything to them, contending that his right to the public land was as good as theirs, they would very soon convince him of his error. He would be summoned to appear before a justice of the peace as a trespasser, or, as they called it, a "claim jumper." The magistrate issuing the summons belonged to the fraternity, and the poor settler would have to sell out or leave, and, even if he went, would have to go a poorer if not sadder man. . . .

In his history of Marion County, William M. Donnel pointed out that the spirit of monopoly was not confined to speculators. He wrote:

Many settlers were not content with the amount of land the law entitled them to, but made pretended claims to so large a portion of the territory, that in some instances, it was difficult for a buyer to find an unclaimed lot. Of course such claims were without improvements, but the pretended claimants, by representing themselves as the real owners thereof, would frequently impose upon some unwary buyer, or, by threats extort from him sums, varying in proportion to the supposed value of the claim, or whatever sum could be obtained. . . .

Analysis of the variant accounts in the county histories would seem to cast doubt on the traditional assumption that claim clubs were always a wholesome manifestation of democracy at work on the frontier. Instead, another pattern of club activity seems to emerge, in which the clubs were organized by claim speculators rather than by settlers, and in many instances were actually used against the best interests of the very same settlers who have usually received the credit for creating and operating them. The soundness of this alternative interpretation can perhaps best be tested by a more detailed analysis of the information contained in the manuscript records of the Johnson County club.

Professor Shambaugh argued that the Johnson County claim club was "in its organization and administration, one of the most perfect . . . in the West." . . . In all, 325 individuals either signed the compact of the claim club, filed claims, or participated in transactions noted by the recorder between March, 1838, and January, 1843. The members of the group fell into at least nine discernable categories. Ninety-six settlers filed from one to three claims under the auspices of the association. Another seventy-three signed the compact but did not appear in the claim and deed record of the club. In contrast to the members of this group, forty-three individuals appeared in the record four or more times; Samuel Bumgardner, indeed, was a party in twenty-two entries. Although filing no original claims of their own, forty-two settlers purchased from one to three claims. Seventeen pioneers filed claims and also sold claims, not always the same ones. Three groups, each consisting of sixteen individuals, either filed original claims and also purchased claims, or purchased a claim and sold one, or merely sold claims not originally registered in the club records. Finally, a small group of six filed one claim, purchased one claim, and sold one claim.

Further analysis of the Johnson County club membership sheds light on the motivation of these pioneers. The settlers who merely filed claim entries made up only about 30 per cent of the group, although the simple filing of a claim supposedly characterized the Macy-Shambaugh stereotype of a claim club member. . . . Close examination of the transactions in which members with multiple entries were involved shows that many of them were dealing in claims—they were, in other words, claim speculators. Six of the first seven men who signed the club compact in Johnson County appeared in four or more entries on the club record and of the eighteen officers who served the club, thirteen fell into the same category. Although the members might describe their activities as "garding our rights against the speculator," the land dealer and the engrosser were actually in their midst.

Of course the claim dealer's operations were petty in comparison to those of land speculators who purchased large holdings at the land sale or entered considerable acreages at private entry after the auction. But in Johnson County even flagrant land speculators were not excluded from membership in the claim club, despite the worthy resolutions of the squatters. Morgan Reno, who entered one claim on the club record, proved to be anything but an impecunious settler when the land was offered by the federal government. In the townships subject to club law in Johnson County, Reno purchased 2,834 acres, enough land, probably, for thirty farm units. He also purchased land in at least one nearby county. . . .

Further light is shed upon the role of the Johnson County claim club by a close examination of one of the incidents in which the club exercised its punitive power. Shambaugh gave a detailed account of the incident, drawing upon an unfinished history of Johnson County, which was written by two former members of the association, Cyrus Sanders and Henry Felkner. These writters described the efforts of the club members in 1839 to drive a "man named Crawford" from a claim owned by William Sturgis. When Crawford refused to abandon the claim, even though Sturgis offered to pay for the improvements, some sixty members of the club under the leadership of its marshal tore down Crawford's substantial log and clapboard cabin. Crawford then rebuilt the cabin and moved his family into it. The club members returned to the claim, however, and this time Crawford "adjusted" the matter to the "full satisfaction" of Sturgis.

To both Shambaugh and Roscoe Lokken, the historian of public land disposal in Iowa, the Sturgis-Crawford incident was illustrative of claim club action. Lokken cited it as an illustration of "pioneer justice." The action of the aggrieved squatter Sturgis, however, did not conform to the pattern of squatter democracy sketched by Macy, Shambaugh, and those who have relied upon them. Sturgis apparently had not made any improvements on the claim. . . . Between April 1, 1839, and March 9, 1843, the name of William Sturgis appeared repeatedly on the club record. He filed three claims, purchased five additional claims for an outlay of $270, and sold five claims for sums totaling $400. The amount of the "adjustment" with Crawford does not appear in the claim record. At the land sales, Sturgis purchased 463 acres—much more than any pioneer farmer needed for farming operations. Patently he was no hard-pressed pioneer defending his home; and in the Crawford incident he was playing the role of a claim speculator who used the club for support in extorting tribute from late-comers to the community. That the club membership would twice mobilize to support Sturgis illuminates the sympathies and aspirations of his colleagues in the association. . . .

·3·

THOMAS LE DUC

History and Appraisal of U.S. Land Policy to 1862

> During the last twenty years, Thomas Le Duc has published a number of thoughtful articles on the operation of the federal land laws during the nineteenth century. Here, he reviews various special programs of land disposal which were begun before 1862 and concludes that "by and large, the land program before 1862 tended to retard economic development."

. . . Now if Turner had bothered to tally the records of land disposal, he would have discovered that the supply of free, arable, humid land was pretty well exhausted by 1870, twenty years earlier than the date he assigned. In the two decades before 1870 the pace of disposal had accelerated markedly. Much of this land was still idle in 1870, but it was not free.

To this increased rate of desocialization a sustantial contribution was made by sales under the Graduation Act of 1854. In an effort to head off the demand for free homesteads, Congress finally adopted the principle of differential pricing of the land. Had this measure been enacted thirty years earlier and administered in conjunction with a program of limiting the amount of land offered on the market, the country would certainly have been better off. Apart from the gains to the Treasury, the policy would have insured compact settlement, with correspondingly lower social costs for roads and schools. Rejecting such a program, Congress had so saturated the market that a backlog of unsold land, amounting perhaps to 100 million acres, had accumulated. Some of it had been on the market for thirty years or more; almost 80 million acres had been on the market for at least ten years. By pricing it on a sliding scale, Congress managed to put into private hands almost 40 million

SOURCE: Abridged from Thomas Le Duc, "History and Appraisal of U.S. Land Policy to 1862," in Howard W. Ottoson, *Land Use Policy and Problems in the United States* (Lincoln, 1963), 3-27. Reprinted by permission of the University of Nebraska Press and Thomas Le Duc.

acres before the act was repealed in 1862. The original provision of the Act of 1854 (that the buyer must occupy and develop his purchase) was soon modified and, while we are not certain, it is believed that much of the land went into the hands of those who wanted the timber or the minerals, or who planned to hold it speculatively.

Even more significant than graduation as a factor in speeding up disposal was the stepping up of the rate of donations after 1847. Despite the enormous volume of cash sales in the 1850's, accumulated donations continued to exceed accumulated sales. . . . One may be permitted to view many of the land grants, as well as the spending of land-sales proceeds, as kinds of deficit spending in which the government spent off its capital to support current policies, instead of levying taxes and appropriating the revenue.

By and large, donating land seems to have proven a poor way to support the public policies for which the grants were assertedly made. In many categories, small cash grants would have done a better job. . . .

Take, for example, the donations to military veterans. During the War of 1812, Congress provided for grants to the soldiers and officers. After the war, three large tracts were reserved for the satisfaction of the veterans' claims. As a matter of historical fact, most of the veterans never even visited the lands granted to them, but sold out to itinerant solicitors who offered them modest cash settlements. The net effect was that the soldiers realized little. The government had conveyed a lot of choice land through the hands of the veterans to a second group of intermediaries who hoped to unload it profitably on genuine settlers. It is interesting to note that Congress, notwithstanding the history of this transaction, embarked in the years from 1847 to 1855 upon an even bigger program of land bonuses to veterans. . . . All told, [military] warrants for 61 million acres were issued. After 1852, the warrants were fully negotiable and they came to be traded in the open market like other government obligations. Most of the veterans sold their warrants for less than $1.25 an acre, and most of the land paid for with warrants fell into the hands of intermediaries rather than farm makers. The issue of the warrants undermined the cash marketing of land; it undermined any intent to restrict to genuine farm makers the initial entry on the public lands; and it speeded up exhaustion of the supply of public, humid, tillable land. . . . The whole experience . . . so completely fulfilled the expectations of those contemporaries who asserted that later bounty acts were designed to promote speculation, one is forced to conclude that in issuing the warrants Congress was far less interested in either soldiers or settlers than in speculators.

Somewhat akin to soldiers' bounties were a series of grants to settlers in specified areas. As early as 1842, Congress tried to promote settlement in northern Florida by offering free homesteads to those who would settle, cultivate five acres, and remain five years. The act was an almost complete failure and even the lifting of the cultivation requirement did not attract settlers. . . .

For years Missouri politicians had talked of rewarding migrants to Oregon with free land. The act, as finally passed, provided that a man could take 320 acres and his wife could take an additional half-section, while latecomers arriving between 1850 and 1853 could qualify for half these quantities. The sole condition of the grant was occupancy for four years. What happened under this act is highly revealing. Most of the beneficiaries had no use for as much as 320 acres, much less 640. They lacked the capital to develop that amount and the man power to farm it. What they wanted was a negotiable title that could be sold. Congress came to their rescue with a law permitting them to buy their land at $1.25 an acre after two years' residence. Bona fide settlers could sit out their four-year term and get the land free, but 72 per cent of the claimants elected to buy their land. . . . [T]he main effect of the Oregon Donation Act was to create another large group of petty intermediaries whose interest in the land was purely speculative.

These several programs of donations to individuals were dwarfed by the donations made to the public-land states. . . . Eventually the magnitude of the surrender would approach 200 million acres, far more than the aggregate sales from the beginning.

The performance of the states in conscientiously applying earlier grants to the public purpose for which they had been made was so lax that one is puzzled by the action of Congress in giving them ever greater quantities to mishandle. The best explanation, perhaps, is that Congress interpreted the Constitution as authorizing land subsidies to the states to encourage the performance of functions not within the powers of the federal government.

At an early date, the federal government had entrusted to the states small grants in support of elementary education. A restriction against sale of these lands was met by more or less perpetual leases to political favorites. Eventually, the early states were released from the trust and they, like the newer states, were allowed to sell the lands. . . . By a variety of devices, the interests of buyers were put ahead of fiduciary responsibility. Congress made no effort to introduce controls that would assure fulfillment of the terms of the trust and indeed proceeded, in the 1840's, to double the rate of grant.

Even more grotesque is the story of the donation of the wet or swampy lands to the states in which they were situated, on condition that they reclaim them by drainage. . . . The entire idea of reclaiming swampland was so preposterous that the sober mind is astonished it should have been suggested at that stage in American development. . . .

It is not surprising, therefore, to find that while few of the 64 million acres donated to the states under this act were ever reclaimed by them, much land valuable for timber or hay or minerals passed through their hands with little regard for the public interest.

In the 1820's, several unrelated developments converged to support the idea that investment in transportation facilities should be undertaken by the states and supported by a program of federal land grants. The completion and instant success of the Erie Canal demonstrated that cheap transportation would permit a cash-crop specialization that could liberate the interior from the penury of subsistence farming. New York's achievement seemed also to justify confidence that other states could build and operate facilities of comparable character and magnitude. It was recognized, of course, that the western states and territories possessed neither the tax base nor the credit standing that would enable them to finance any sizable program of public works. This difficulty would be overcome by a federal land grant sufficient to serve as collateral security for borrowing the construction outlays. . . .

To justify the federal land grants it was argued that they would speed the sale and enhance the market price of the federally owned lands. Altogether, almost 56 million acres passed to the states under the guise of aids to transportation.

We can see now that the western states were not the optimum agencies to carry out federal policy. The record is not all bad, but it is filled with mismanagement and corruption. One must recognize, however, that the ability of the states to raise money on the security of the land grants was steadily impaired by the cheap-land policy of the federal government. Financing in many instances was so retarded that by the time the roads or canals were built they had already been rendered partly obsolete by the technical superiority of the steam railroad.

Although it was clearly understood that the railroad could not serve as a public highway but must function as a common carrier, there was little opposition to a policy of allowing private interests to develop it and much support for land grants that would entice private capital into tapping undeveloped areas. . . . I should . . . like to say a little about what might be called "nonpolicy." The heart of this nonpolicy is the failure of Congress to formulate and support a program for the protection of the public interest in timber, coal, and metals found on the public property. These resources were neither managed affirmatively nor opened to private development on a basis that would guard the people's equity. Congress chose, instead, to tolerate depredation and depletion of such resources as did not pass by sale or donation under laws contemplating the transfer of lands suited primarily for agriculture.

If one is inclined to think the whole idea of conservation and public ownership is a recent concept, it may be worth noting that the Land Ordinance of 1785 reserved to the public an interest in minerals and that early in national history one finds a number of measures surprisingly modern in their recognition of the public interest. The year 1807, which saw Congress authorize the President to use the army to expel intruders from the public lands, saw also passage of a law authorizing the leasing of the Missouri lead lands in consideration of payment of royalties on the ore extracted. The system was later extended to the lead lands in Illinois and Wisconsin, but it must everywhere be written off as a failure. Although a challenge to the constitutionality of leasing was successfully met, the system was systematically and successfully sabotaged by private interests. . . .

Despite occasional indications of Congressional interest in differentiating mineral lands from other types, intelligence could not be sufficiently mobilized to protect the public interest and, as a result, such substantial resources as the iron and copper lands of the upper Great Lakes were either given away or sold at token prices.

Coal lands, not considered mineral lands until 1864, were not differentiated from agricultural lands even where the deposits appeared at the surface. Except for a few tracts of Indian tribal trust land that never came into the public domain, the whole mid-continent coal field, extending from Indiana to Kansas passed into private ownership under laws intended for the conveyance of farm land. Only then did Congress lock the stable door.

The most spectacular display of the incompetence of democratic government is seen in the way the precious metals were mishandled. Until 1866, Congress not only did nothing to regulate the removal of 1 billion dollar's worth of gold and silver from public property, but actually bought and paid for ores taken from federal lands. When one state attempted to lay a tax on the ores, the taxpayer asserted the ores could not be taxed because they were federal property. The Supreme Court did not acquiesce in this reasoning; on the contrary, it became an accessory to the crime by holding that the metal, although unlawfully removed from federal land, had become private property. In the light of such a relaxed attitude on the part of federal authorities, and in view of the negligible amount of capital needed in the enterprise of carrying gold from the public lands to the public mint, it is not surprising that California and Colorado magnetized labor that might better have been left in productive work.

Finally, Congress achieved an almost perfect record of ignoring the public interest in timber resources. Except for the designation of minor tracts with stands of timber especially needed for construction of naval vessels, valuable timberlands were not reserved or segregated from the mass of public land subject to disposal under the regular laws. Even where the timber was extremely valuable and the land surface was unsuited to tillage, the government made no effort to introduce a system of administered stumpage. As a result, most of the pine land of the three northern Lake states and the timberlands of Arkansas and the Gulf states passed either by donations or by sales at token prices. Before this happened, however, a great deal of the best timber had been removed by depredators. Although timber trespass had been made a criminal offense in 1831, Congress failed to provide adequately for enforcement and the law was generally ignored.

The matter of federal nonenforcement must be put in its proper context. While it is my assignment here to deal with public resources, I do not want to leave the impression that Congress was singularly blind in this one field. We should recognize that, by and large, federal criminal laws were not effectively enforced in the period here dealt with. It is true that for many crimes grand juries would not indict and trial juries would not convict. . . .

Americans seem to have felt a greater need for ritualistic declaration of a moral code than for achieving even minimal adherence to it. Why this was so I must leave to the cultural anthropologists. . . .

It is my contention that, by and large, the land program before 1862 tended to retard economic development. Low prices, together with free grants, tended to put land in the hands of intermediaries between the federal government and the ultimate farm makers. One need not argue the question of the profitability of this ownership. Certainly, the endless flooding of the market with public land and grant land disappointed the expectations of many a speculator, big and little. But the dream of easy profits never died and it tended to channel into mere ownership capital that might have flowed into development. Because they thought land was cheap, settlers beggared themselves trying to control more land than they could develop or operate. To buy land they borrowed heavily and so raised interest rates on development capital. And, so far as they engaged in agriculture, their enterprise was skewed towards the crops that required minimum capital and minimum labor. . . .

·4·

PAUL WALLACE GATES

The Homestead Act: Free Land Policy in Operation, 1862–1935

In 1936 Paul Wallace Gates published an article entitled "The Homestead Law in an Incongruous Land System" in the *American Historical Review* and pointed out that the famous act of 1862 did not immediately revolutionize the system of land disposal in the United States. Going further some historians concluded that the law was a failure. After the publication of several books and numerous articles on the American land system, Professor Gates returned to the subject and in this selection he describes the specific results of the Homestead Law.

. . . A common error in appraising the Homestead Law has been the assumption that homesteading was only important in the Great Plains and Interior Basin where the unit of farming characteristic of the more humid regions was not suitable. The fact is that 23 per cent (689,000) of all original homestead entries were filed in the states east of the Mississippi and in the first tier west of that river. Twenty-four per cent of the homestead entries that went to final patent were located in this region. During the first ten years of the operation of the Homestead Law, Minnesota outranked all states in number of final entries of homesteads and was exceeded only by Kansas in the number of original entries. Altogether, 82,845 free homesteads were patented in Minnesota. This constitutes 66 per cent of the farms of Minnesota of 100 acres or more as listed in the census of 1920. It probably would not be far from the truth to say that the abstracts of two-thirds of Minnesota farms trace

SOURCE: Abridged from Paul W. Gates, "The Homestead Act: Free Land Policy in Operation, 1862–1935," in Howard W. Ottoson, *Land Use Policy and Problems in the United States* (Lincoln, 1963), 28–46. Reprinted by permission of the University of Nebraska Press and Paul W. Gates.

back to the patent of the homesteader. East of the Mississippi, 143,360 homestead entries for 15,990,533 acres were carried to patent, mostly in Alabama, Florida, Wisconsin, Mississippi, and Michigan.

In all the states around the Great Lakes, in the South, and in the first tier west of the Mississippi, a considerably higher proportion of the original filings were carried to final entry than elsewhere and there were fewer commutations.

In substantial portions of the second tier of states beyond the Mississippi (extending from Dakota to Oklahoma), the 160-acre unit of farming was not altogether unsuited for farm practices in the late Nineteenth Century. The line of 20-inch rainfall begins roughly just west of the Red River of the North and extends in a gentle southwestward direction. East of that line is perhaps a fifth of North Dakota, a third of South Dakota, more than half of Nebraska, and two-thirds of Kansas. The line of 24-inch rainfall leaves, to the east, a small corner of South Dakota, a fifth of Nebraska, and half of Kansas. To and somewhat beyond the 24-inch rainfall line, corn flourished and the 160-acre unit of agriculture seemed reasonably well adapted to farming. I have conservatively estimated that 150,000 homestead applications were filed in the more humid portions of the Great Plains. This means that, together with the 689,000 entries previously mentioned, 839,000 homesteads or 28 per cent of the total number of homesteads were commenced in areas generally suitable in the Nineteenth Century for 160-acre farm units.

Furthermore, it is important to note that of these early homesteads established from Kansas north to Dakota territory before 1881, 58 per cent of those in Kansas were successfully carried to final entry, 61 per cent in Nebraska and 52 per cent in Dakota. Sixty-seven per cent of the entries in Dakota made before 1876 were patented by 1880. This is perhaps the best test of the applicability of homestead to these areas. For the country as a whole, slightly less than 50 per cent of the original homesteads were carried to patent. . . .

A second error frequently observed in appraisals of the Homestead Act is forgetting that it took five years, later reduced to three (veterans' military service could be counted), for the original entries to mature. Actually, even more than five years was required for many homesteaders who were driven out by drought, grasshoppers, or other misfortunes, and who had to be allowed extensions of time in which to prove up.

In the land selection process many choices were made by settlers and speculators who were misled by the descriptions on the surveyors' plats; by the land lookers who for fees guided settlers to what soon proved to be questionable locations; and by settlers themselves who may have had little knowledge of the quality of land in the vicinity of the 100th meridian. Some settlers, like those who participated in the great rushes into Oklahoma or who desperately tried to get a claim on the Rosebud Reservation in South Dakota, had no time to pick and choose but had perforce to take the first vacant land they could find. Inevitably, mistakes were made. . . . In the absence of land classification, settlers made many errors that resulted in a high rate of failure on homesteads.

Nebraska well illustrates this tendency to err in the selection of land. When homestead was adopted, or shortly thereafter, the grants to the state for educational purposes, and to railroads for aid to construction had reduced the public domain to less than 37 million acres. Of this amount speculators quickly grabbed up an additional million acres. Yet the records show that settlers filed on nearly 51 million acres either for homesteads or timber-culture claims. Some of these filings led to contests between homesteaders and the railroads or between different homesteaders; other filings proved to be unattractive and were abandoned or relinquished, and perhaps the rights transferred to others. For Nebraska, 51 per cent of the homestead entries and 46 per cent of the combined homestead and timber-culture entries were carried to patent as free land. If commuted entries are included, the percentages reaching patent becomes 58 and 53. Those that did not reach patent were either relinquished for a fee to others or simply abandoned for better selections elsewhere. What is important is that ownership of 74 per cent of the land available for homesteading in Nebraska was actually achieved either through the Homestead Act or the Timber Culture Act, with their privilege of commutation. Or, we may go one step farther and say that at least 80 per cent of the land area of Nebraska available for settler location became owned by homesteaders through settler-oriented laws, though some of this ownership was quite unstable and was not acquired by the first owner for farming. . . .

Not long after the hungry land seekers crossed the Missouri they came into contact with a region where rainfall was less than they had been accustomed to and the variations greater from year to year; where drought, winter blizzards, and grasshopper plagues were met, and where more extensive farm practices were essential. These conditions made larger farm units necessary. It is interesting to note how the average size of farms in Kansas increased with a certain regularity from east to west as is shown by the census of 1920: 153 acres was the average in Miami County on the eastern Kansas front, 167 in Osage County, 192 in Lyons County, 244 in Morris County, 354 in Ellsworth County, 590 in Ness County, and 900 acres on the western border in Greeley County.

Historians have been troubled that the homestead unit was fixed at 160 acres just when, as they say, settlers were preparing to break into the less humid region of the Great Plains where larger farm units were desirable. Paradoxically, they have also been troubled that the Preemption Law which, with homestead, made possible larger farm units, was kept on the statute books. Following the judgment of the Commissioners of the General Land Office who harped on the amount of fraud involved in preemption, they have given undue emphasis to this aspect and insufficient attention to the fact that preemption was consciously retained by Congress surely because of the greater flexibility it allowed settlers in adapting themselves to farming in the dryer portions of America where land was not offered. . . .

In 1872 and 1873 the two houses of Congress finally came to agreement on a bill to encourage the planting of trees on the Great Plains. An additional quarter section was thereby offered to settlers who would plant and care for forty acres of trees (later reduced to ten acres) for a period of ten years. An effort to limit its benefits to settlers who had not taken up a preemption or homestead failed. Timber culture was designed further to adapt the post-1862 land system to farming in sub-humid America. . . .

With preemption and homestead it provided a flexibility that after its repeal was to be assured by the more direct method of enlarging the homestead unit to 320 and then 640 acres.

How significant was the Homestead Law in enabling settlers to acquire land and to establish themselves on going farms? It is clear that it was most successful in the period from 1863 to 1880 when the greater proportion of homesteads were being established in the states bordering on the Mississippi River. It was successful also in parts of Kansas and Nebraska well east of the 98th meridian where there was abundance of rain, and where commutations, relinquishments, and abandonments were fewer than they were to be in other areas later. In these eighteen years, homesteaders filed on 469,000 tracts and by 1885 had made their final entries and were in process of getting title on 55 per cent. Doubtless some would complete their residence requirements in later years.

The misuse of the Homestead Law was becoming common between 1880 and 1900. As shown, misuse was by persons not primarily interested in farm making but concerned to sell relinquishments to immigrants or to transfer rights to cattle, timber, and mining companies. But the most glaring abuses occurred later. Between 1880 and 1900, approximately half of the homestead entries were filed in the six states and territories extending from Oklahoma to North Dakota and including Minnesota. These all were major farm states and the Homestead Law was contributing largely to the development of farm ownership, notwithstanding its abuses.

In these states and territories, free government land, advertised by the America letters which earlier immigrants had sent back to their families in the Old World, by the government immigration bureaus, by even the colonization departments of the railroads and land companies, provided the lodestone, the directing force, that set in motion continued waves of settlers in search of free land. It was the prospect of disposing of their lands to these settlers and transporting their goods that made possible the financing and construction of the railroads through the Plains, into the Interior Basin and to the Pacific Coast. Homestead, above all other factors, made possible the fast growth of the West and all the problems this rapid growth brought with it.

Altogether, 1,413,513 original homestead entries were filed between 1863 and 1900, but even more were to be filed in the twentieth century for a substantially larger acreage. The great day of farm making with the material aid of Uncle Sam was over, however. True, some twentieth century entries were made with the enlarged units for small stock raising farms or ranches or even wheat farms but the evidence seems strong that the great bulk of the entries filed after 1900 were for large ranching, mining, and lumbering companies. The numbers of original and final homestead entries, when compared with the number of farms in the Rocky Mountain States, provides startling evidence that the homesteads were being assimilated into larger aggregations of land. Using round figures, we find that Idaho had 92,000 original homestead entries, 60,000 final entries and in 1910–1930 its highest number of farms was 42,000. Colorado had 205,000 original, 107,000 final entries, and at its most 59,000 farms. Arizona had 38,000 original, 20,000 final entries, and 9,000 farms. Wyoming had 115,000 original, 67,000 final entries, and 15,000 farms. In six mountain states the original entries came to 848,000, final entries 492,000, and the maximum number of farms 217,000. Thus it seemed to take about four original entries and two final homestead entries to produce a farm, and most of these homesteads were of the enlarged variety.

Major John W. Powell's recommendation of 1879 that the public lands be classified for use and that a 2,560-acre pasturage homestead be established for lands fit only for grazing was somewhat premature, but certainly by 1900, land classification and larger homestead units were essential. Yet the evidence is strong that the enlarged units of 1904, 1909, and 1916 were not altogether wise or successful. The old evils of careless drafting of land legislation, weak and inefficient administrations (inadequately staffed), and the anxiety of interests to take advantage of loopholes in the laws, all brought the Homestead Acts into contempt and censure. But their noble purpose and the great part they played in enabling nearly a million and a half people to acquire farm land, much of which developed into farm homes, far outweigh the misuse to which they were put.

·5·

DOUGLASS C. NORTH

Land Policy and the Westward Movement, 1785-1890

Scholars have been critical of the American system of land disposal, particularly stressing fraudulent transfers and the land speculator whose activities they usually believe to be harmful or at best unnecessary. Douglass C. North, one of the "New Economic Historians," argues that historians have frequently disagreed with each other because they have generalized from particular cases. Also they have failed to use economic theory systematically and test hypotheses derived in this way "by careful empirical research." Historians he suggests have been asking the wrong questions and using the wrong methods. After quoting extensively from a number of historians he continues as reprinted below.

. . . These quotations do more than simply show the contradictory interpretive positions that riddle the literature on the subject. They point up the inability of the historian to come to grips with the problems without the systematic use of theory to examine the issues and the testing of resultant hypotheses by careful empirical research. I do not

SOURCE: Abridged from Douglass C. North, *Growth and Welfare in the American Past: A New Economic History* (Englewood Cliffs, N.J., 1966), 131-135. © 1966. Reprinted by permission of Prentice-Hall, Inc., Englewood Cliffs, N.J. and Douglass C. North.

mean to suggest that each and every quotation is not founded upon some detailed story of the vast panorama of settlement of the public domains. It is. And this very fact reflects the immensely rich and variegated story of this westward movement. But from these particular stories, the historian has generalized the consequences of the entire public land policies. It would be possible to accumulate an endless number of such stories, but they do not add up to an over-all appraisal of the policies. If we are to assert that the policies adversely affected economic growth, then we must assess the policies in terms of the determinants of economic growth; or if we are to assess them in terms of their effects upon welfare or equity, we must do so in terms of a careful examination of the consequences of the policies on the distribution of income. . . .

Examination of public land policies, to determine their effect on growth and welfare in the nineteenth century is complicated by (1) the number and variety of laws related to public land policies; (2) the wide variety of types of land and resources that were exploited in the course of the westward movement; (3) inadequate, poor administration of public land policies; and (4) graft and corruption that was characteristic of all levels and all kinds of people involved in the settlement of the public domain.

Continuous repetition of the word "speculator" and "land monopolization" throughout the literature requires precise examination of these terms before we can go further. Just what does constitute speculation? When anyone buys an asset with a resale value, he is indulging in speculation. Buying that asset, he foregoes buying other assets, all offering prospective income streams that he takes into account. He is guessing about the future value of that asset. In contemplating the purchase of a fixed-yield bond, for example, he speculates not only that he will get the specified return, but whether the general level of prices will rise or fall, so that actually his return will be of lesser or greater value than was indicated. Speculation is endemic to any system of private ownership of assets. It is therefore hard to imagine any way that one could dispose of public lands without speculation. Moreover, the speculator performs the important function of bearing risks in a market economy and of improving knowledge about the available alternative opportunities, thereby making the market work more perfectly.

The term "land monopolist" is simply a misuse of "monopolist." There is no meaningful sense in which a monopoly of land existed at any time in the nineteenth century. In fact, availability is the one clearly evident characteristic of the opening up of the public domain. There were immense amounts of land continuously available from a large number of different sources. People who wanted land of any quality could always get it from a host of sellers in addition to the government. Merely to record that large blocks of land were at times bought by individuals is in no sense an indication of land monopoly, unless the buyers actually acquired such an appreciable percentage of all available land that they could influence its over-all price.

Examining these salient features of public land policy in the context of the determinants of economic growth, we might, on the face of it, expect them to have very little effect upon economic growth. While a system of land distribution by auction or by giving it away (under the Homestead Act) would certainly have consequences for the distribution of income, it is not obvious that such policies would have any striking effects upon the growth of the economy. These methods of distribution generally lead to efficient resource allocation. This statement perhaps begs the issue, because the historian's implicit or explicit criticisms have been that some hypothetical alternative would have yielded a higher rate of growth. However, I know of no hypothetical alternatives, either explicitly advanced by historians or implicit in their criticisms, that would produce such a result.

One explicit hypothetical alternative that has been advanced is based on the contention that the unlimited amounts of land made available had adverse effect upon economic growth. Actually, just the reverse is true. The notion that limiting the amount of land made available would have accelerated growth is incorrect, since such action would have decreased the supply of productive factors from those that were, in fact, available. And since in this case the productive factor that would have been limited was land of superior quality, compared to that in production, any restriction would have had an adverse effect on the growth of the economy.

If speculators deliberately held land out of production (which should have had an adverse effect upon growth for the reasons just described), it would be surprising. The purpose of speculation is to make money, and by following a withholding policy, the speculator would have been doing just the reverse. That is, to the extent that speculators bought up great tracts of land and held them for appreciation, they were tying up large sums of money in the initial cost of acquiring the land and were foregoing income from that money used in another way—such as buying bonds. It would have been to their advantage, while holding the land, to rent it out, but buyers were easier to find than tenants.

With so much land available free or at very low prices, a settler had an opportunity for a windfall in acquiring land of his own, rather than renting or working as a tenant.

Land grants to railroads should have accelerated economic growth. First, railroad construction was consistent with improving the rate of growth. Second, this construction would have been slower, or in some cases perhaps lacking, without the land grants, because the private rate of return from railroad building was too low to encourage investors to put their funds to this use. Third, the land grants gave impetus to construction by permitting investors to share, through the appreciation of land values, in some of the social rate of return from railroad building.

Public land policies had few adverse effects on economic growth, none of them very significant, but four might be mentioned. One, giving away land under the Homestead Act probably encouraged some inefficiency by attracting to agriculture people who would have been more productive in other employments. Two, until the Graduation Act, large parcels of land were left idle because the potential capitalized income stream from them was lower than the minimum price set by the government. Clearly, the Graduation Act should have come in earlier, so that these lands could sooner have been put to productive use. Three, the unit of 160 acres set by the Homestead Act became increasingly inappropriate as available land dwindled to nonarable pasture land for which any efficient use would require much larger tracts. Admittedly, the ultimate result of this would be gradual consolidation into larger parcels of land as settlers recognized the facts; in the short run, however, and with the settlers' imperfect knowledge about agricultural and farming possibilities, it probably led to poor utilization of the land. Four, the alternate sections in railroad land grant areas—that is, those sections retained by the government to be opened up for homestead use—were held off the market for varying periods of time. It would have been a gain to national income to have opened up the settlement as rapidly as possible, since the sections were areas where the potential income was greatly enhanced by availability of lower cost transportation.

The broad, tentative conclusion to be drawn, therefore, is that subject to the exceptions just noted, land policies in general were consistent with a high rate of economic growth, and it would be hard to develop a hypothetical alternative that would be a very great improvement. These conclusions follow, however, only if the tentative hypotheses advanced above withstand empirical tests, and very little systematic work has given us evidence for testing. . . .

The major effect of public land policies was upon the distribution of income. Did they, as so many historians say, favor the rich at the expense of the poor? Without the necessary evidence, the following conclusions are tentative. First of all, giving away the land instead of selling it is a redistribution of income in favor of the homesteader and against the taxpayer (rich and poor): the government must get revenue from sources other than land sales, and the homesteader is getting a windfall in free land that has positive value. Next, it is probable that large speculators did better than small ones. They were better informed, had better knowledge of the complex laws involving land disposal, had better knowledge of the possible alternatives, and—in a somewhat imperfect capital market—had better access to capital than the small speculator. We would expect, therefore, that their rate of return on investment in land would typically have been higher than that of the small speculator or of the individual settler. Third, the results of the railroad land grants are more uncertain. They added to the income received by the railroads, but the alternate sections retained by the government were ultimately put into the hands of settlers and farmers, to whom they brought windfall gains, the land's value having increased as a result of nearby, low-cost transportation. . . .

CHAPTER VII

Transportation Problems

IN MOST HISTORICAL ATLASES of the United States, maps show the major roads, waterways and ultimately the railroads of the United States in various years of the nation's history. Taken in chronological order, these maps show the development of the American transportation system. Thin lines and thick lines, dashed lines and dotted lines, sometimes even red, blue or green lines, show a thickening network in the northeastern region of the United States, a more fragmentary arrangement in the South and a projection westward of the whole system over time. Dull or abstract as such patterns may seem, they are of the utmost importance in this nation's history; in reality they show the circulatory system of a growing giant—Young America. The maps, of course, omit a great deal; historians have never completely recaptured the changing variety of the early regional road systems or the short-run significance of particular canals, river routes and western cutoffs. The differences in gauge between the connecting lines of early railroads seldom appear on the maps. And cartography can only suggest the mobility patterns of people and things, the technological and institutional sequences, and the economic and political processes that explain the development of transportation facilities in the United States.

When the American colonials chose war and independence in preference to peace and the frustrations of dependence, only Daniel Boone and a few thousand other venturesome souls had moved beyond the Appalachians. That people could live on the bounty of the forest and the produce of the frontier clearings none can doubt. But few of the pioneers went west because they wished to live in that way; they went rather to grow up with the country and to share in the development of its wealth. Such goals demanded the production of surplus and the growth of commerce and these in turn required the development of transportation routes and facilities.

Although hunter, trader or soldier first probed the back country of the settlements, the pioneer settler followed soon after. And as the settlers moved westward a primitive road system developed, carrying them to the new lands and serving them after they had established themselves. There was an evolutionary quality in the development of many of the major arteries of land travel during the later colonial and early national period. The strategically located trail of the Indians became the path of far-ranging hunters and the first of the pioneer farmers. As these forelopers improved the trail to allow pack animals to pass, it became a trace. Soon the pioneer farmers were chopping obstructive trees from the trace, rolling off rocks and smoothing the sides of gullies to allow the passage of their wagons and carts. A few years more and the trail had become a post road and stagecoach route. Such was the development of the famed Wilderness Road of Kentucky, which settlers by the thousands followed from Cumberland Gap to new homes on the western waters. The sons of the pioneers later watched the puffing engines and rickety cars of the early railroads, running on rights-of-way that followed routes first known as the Lake Shore Trail or the Mahonning Trail. Across the Mississippi, the wagons of traders, emigrants and freighters etched the Santa Fe Trail, the Overland Trail and other less famous routes deep into the soil of the Plains country and the rock of the western mountains.

As settlement thickened in any region, a system of local trails and roads developed. These were the roads over which the pioneer farmers carried their surplus to market in the frontier villages and trade centers on the banks of navigable streams or lakes, or lying on major overland routes. Wherever found, the early local roads were usually crude and rough. The settlers provided the cash outlays necessary for such roads from tiny tax levies; they themselves did most of the roadwork under the direction of local overseers, pathmasters or roadmasters. We know something of the statutes which authorized such roads in the frontier territories and states. We know much less about the actual maintenance, the stages by which such systems developed and the amounts of traffic which they carried.

During the early national period, large numbers of settlers used a few major land routes which traversed the Appalachians to the new lands of the West. Some travellers and westerners urged that the federal or state governments should improve and maintain such interregional links. The National Road, authorized by Congress in 1806, was the federal government's major concession to such thinking. The enabling act, which authorized the people of the Northwest Territory to establish the state of Ohio, provided that the federal government would spend two per cent of the proceeds of land sales in the new state to build roads leading to it. The national government made its initial contributions to the National Road from this source. The great thoroughfare had linked Cumberland, Maryland and Wheeling, West Virginia by 1818. After 1825 it was extended through Zanesville and Columbus, Ohio, and plans provided that it should extend to the Mississippi. Because strict constructionists had long argued that it was unconstitutional for the federal government to charge tolls and maintain the road, Congress progressively surrendered control of the highway to the states through which it passed. The federal legislators approved their last appropriation for the National Road in 1838 and surfacing was still incomplete in Indiana and Illinois when the governments of those states assumed control of the road within their boundaries.

The National Road was not the federal government's only contribution to western road building. The Ohio Enabling Act also provided that the state government should receive three per cent of the public land revenues for use in the construction of roads within the commonwealth. The enabling acts of Alabama, Mississippi, Missouri, Indiana and Illinois subsequently allocated five per cent of the revenue from federal land sales for this purpose. Congress also used the public lands to support the improvement of western transportation somewhat differently. In both the Mississippi valley and regions farther to the west, the federal lawmakers provided land grants to defray the cost of building wagon roads along important routes. During the early years of the Republic, the postal department supported the construction and maintenance of a number of western roads over which postal officers wished to send mail to major western centers. More important were the contributions of the United States Army. During the War of 1812 and various Indian campaigns, both earlier and later, Army detachments built stretches of road over strategic routes which settlers later used. But the Army Engineers surveyed and supervised the construction of many miles of western roads during years of peace as well, linking posts in the western system of forts or opening up areas of the western country. Army officers admitted that some of these roads were of little military value but agreed that they would be useful in the development of the country.

The contributions of the federal government were not enough to fill the West's need for interregional connections. Many lawmakers of the early national period believed that turnpike corporations could develop the routes which drew heavy traffic. State and territorial legislatures chartered turnpike companies in large numbers during this era, which assumed the maintenance of important thoroughfares and charged tolls in return for the service provided. The western immigrant of the 1820's could choose a number of routes to the West which had been more or less improved in this fashion, including the Genesee and Catskill Pikes in New York and the famed Pennsylvania Pike, traversing Pennsylvania from Philadelphia to Pittsburgh. If the traveller's destination lay below the Ohio River, he could ride the famed Valley Road through western Virginia and enter Kentucky through Cumberland Gap. The so-called Upper Road and the Fall Line road system carried travellers into the lower South.

Great numbers of migrants travelled west over the major land routes during the early national period and many thousands of tons of essential merchandise reached the western country in freighting wagons, rumbling over the National Road and other major thoroughfares. But the West would have developed slowly indeed if its residents had been forced to depend on road transportation alone. During those years transportation costs consumed the value of a wagonload of wheat in some 200 miles and that of a load of corn in less than 150 miles. During the early nineteenth century westerners depended particularly upon the magnificent inland water system of the Mississippi River and its major tributaries which allowed them to ship their agricultural surplus south to the lower river ports, particularly New Orleans, and thence, if necessary, to the eastern seaboard, the West Indies or Europe.

Various types of craft plied the western waters of the nation during its early years, but the keelboat and the flatboat were of particular importance in western commerce. Sharp of prow and stern and capable of carrying from 15 to 50 tons of cargo, the keelboats could be hauled or poled upstream, laborious though this task was. Boasting greater capacity than the keelboats and easily constructed by farmers or semi-skilled labor, the boxlike flatboats floated downstream only and were usually broken up after discharging their cargo. Such were the craft that carried most of the agricultural produce of the Ohio valley to southern markets during the nation's early years. For their return trip from New Orleans the keelboat captains usually loaded cargoes of eastern or European merchandise.

Introduced on the Ohio and the Mississippi in 1811 after its introduction on eastern waters, the steamboat revolutionized transportation on the western river system. Between 1816 and 1828 the rate for carrying goods upstream fell from 6 cents per ton mile to between .6 and .5 cents per ton mile. The keelboats and their roistering crews soon disappeared from the western waters as a result. Fewer than twenty steamboats plied the western rivers in 1817 but more than 700 were churning the waters of the great inland river system by the 1850's.

Not only did the technology of western water transportation change tremendously between 1800 and 1850 but the water routes of the northern United States were extended ingeniously by the construction of canals. Some of these channels merely improved river courses by circumventing shoals or rapids, but the most important of them opened new routes of trade. It was the Erie Canal which most fundamentally changed the economic and political destiny of the West. Built between 1817 and 1825, the "Big Ditch" provided low-cost water transportation through the Appalachian barrier. After the completion of this channel a growing flood of western agricultural products began to move eastward on it. Not to be outreached, Pennsylvania politicians authorized a remarkable system of canal and portage railroad west to Pittsburgh, but this system was never as successful as the Erie Canal.

As the Erie Canal proved itself a success, an epidemic of canal fever swept the western country. Frustrated by the inadequate storage facilities in New Orleans and the unpredictability of that market, residents of the Ohio valley dreamed of canals that would allow them to choose between the New York and southern markets. Eventually Ohioans built two major canal systems: The Ohio Canal, linking Cleveland, Marietta and Portsmouth, and the Miami Canal, connecting Cincinnati and Toledo. The Hoosiers linked the Ohio River and Lake Erie by building the Wabash Canal, and their neighbors in Illinois constructed the Illinois and Michigan Canal, joining the Illinois River and Lake Michigan. But only a fraction of the canal projects which western businessmen or legislators visualized were completed. During the 1830's the scattered residents of the western states lightheartedly planned canal systems that were more elaborate and more difficult to construct than had been the Erie and which could not possibly attract the amount of traffic that flowed along that waterway. And some of these projects were only part of ambitious internal improvement projects which also included railroad linkages. Unfortunately the depression of 1837 and internal improvement debts brought some western states to the verge of bankruptcy. Despite such misfortunes the canal network of the United States had grown to some 3300 miles by 1840, most of it so located as to benefit western producers. Westerners completed some important canal links after 1840 but most of them were beginning to understand that the railroad was the real key to the destiny of their region.

Water transportation played a major role in opening up the Pacific frontier after the Oregon settlement and the acquisition of California. Indeed, the appearance in 1836 of the paddle-wheel steamer, Beaver, owned by the Hudson's Bay Company, antedated the American era. Steamers plied the interior rivers of California, the Columbia system and the Puget Sound region to serve the miners and other settlers. Some of the vessels were good enough to carry men but unsafe for treasure, as the saying went, and irritating monopolies developed in both California and on the Columbia system, but river traffic was as important in the early development of these regions as in parts of the Mississippi valley.

The railroad mileage in the United States in 1840 was almost equal to the mileage of the canals. By 1850 the canal system of the nation had extended an additional 400 miles, but the miles of track in the railroad network had risen from approximately 3300 to 9000 miles. By 1860 this figure had become 31,000 and by 1900 it stood at 194,000. A number of building patterns emerged during the construction of the railroad system which were of great importance to western development. Imaginative men realized that the railroad could conquer the Appalachian barrier and the trunk lines verified their vision. Pioneer among them was the Baltimore and Ohio, but the Pennsylvania, the New York Central and the Erie illustrated the type as well. The promoters of these lines had originally hoped to tap the eastern edge of the trans-Appalachian West, but, once through to the Ohio or to Lake Erie, the ambitions of the railroaders soared and they raced to establish terminals in Chicago or St. Louis. Meanwhile east-west connections were developing in the South as the businessmen of both Charleston and Savannah dreamed of systems that would reach the Mississippi and tap the intervening territory. Fatefully these connections were incomplete when the southerners left the Union in 1861. The leaders of New Orleans and Mobile tried to defend their commercial hegemony by planning lines to run north from the Gulf, including the Mobile and Ohio, designed to meet the Illinois Central, building south from Chicago.

Although interrupted by the Civil War, several important building patterns developed in the valley of the Mississippi and the regions farther west between 1850 and the early 1870's. Highly important to the economic development of the Upper Midwest were the lines which terminated in Chicago, and ran south and west into the Missouri River region, to be know eventually as the Granger roads, The Burlington, the Rock Island and the Northwestern are included in this group. Roads like the St. Louis and Iron Mountain and the Missouri, Kansas and Texas built south from St. Louis and the lower Missouri to impose another important construction pattern on the trans-Mississippi West. Most impressive were the transcontinentals. Since such projects demanded much construction in undeveloped territory, many Americans believed that federal action was essential if rails were to join the Pacific coast and the Mississipi valley.

Interregional jealousies prevented the members of Congress from agreeing on the details of a transcontinental project until the southerners raised the assorted flags of the Confederacy. Then Congress passed the Pacific Railroad Act, which gave land grant and loan assistance to the Central Pacific, the Union Pacific and to various railroads that were intended to link points in the Missouri valley with the main trunk of the Union Pacific in central Nebraska. The Union Pacific and Central Pacific railroad companies joined their lines in Utah in 1869 to provide the first transcontinental connection in the United States. During the next 25 years, the Southern Pacific, the Atchison, Topeka and Santa Fe, the Northern Pacific and the Great Northern all reached terminals on the Pacific Coast; with the exception of the Great Northern, all had received major federal land grants. When the construction crews of the Southern Pacific joined that company's track with those of the railroad system in the Pacific Northwest during 1887, steel rails bounded the entire country.

The development of transportation facilities in the United States, particularly in the western regions, was a story of technological achievement. Although they benefited to some extent from European example, the American canal builders met the challenges of American terrain with impressive ingenuity. The huge freighting wagons that groaned over road and trail and the sturdy stagecoaches reflected the unique needs and intimidating distances of western America. Both the annals of the steamboat and the history of the railroads and their rolling stock are chronicles of innovation. While the pioneers worked to develop the resources of the West and while residents of the older regions of the country endeavored to provide the capital and equipment necessary for such growth, a revolution in the industrial use of power was under way. To the power generated by muscle, wind and water, Americans now added the power of steam. It was the application of this energy to transportation in steamboat and railroad engines that transformed the transportation of the country and solved a major problem of the western country. The revolution was of course progressive in nature. The western steamboat of the 1850's differed immensely from the pioneer vessel of 1811, the puny New Orleans. The Great Northern's proud locomotives of the 1890's little resembled the puffing pygmies of the Baltimore and Ohio in 1835.

Roads, canals, rails, vessels and vehicles did not mobilize themselves of course; this was the task of business organization. During the early national period, Americans increasingly used the corporation to raise funds for transportation projects. What were the obligations of such companies to their stockholders and how best could they organize their energies for efficient operation and profit? One historian argues that the railroads were the first of the really great corporations of the American business world and pioneered the art of large-scale business management. But their innovations ultimately shocked and angered many Americans.

What were to be the proper relationships between government, transportation agencies and producers? Initially Americans raised this question concerning the degree to which government should assist in the improvement of transportation facilities. Few denied that local governments should assume the costs of building local, common roads. Most welcomed the contributions of men of capital, organized in turnpike corporations, ferry or bridge companies, although some deplored the monopoly inherent in some charter grants to such groups. When private capital was believed to be inadequate during the first half of the nineteenth century, state lawmakers willingly endorsed the mixed corporation in which both the state and private investors purchased stock, as in the case of numerous turnpike companies. The canals required even greater commitments from government and the state governments built, owned and operated much of the American canal system, although chartered companies sometimes shared in its development. The federal government meanwhile donated land grants to support the construction of some western wagon roads and canals. The unhappy experience of state lawmakers in canal financing and the magnitude of many railroad projects caused westerners to urge that the federal government increase its aid to transportation projects. In 1850 the members of Congress bestowed land grants upon the Illinois Central and the Mobile and Ohio railroad companies, and continued the policy with mounting generosity until 1871. As we have seen, the railroads of the first transcontinental system received both land grants and loans of federal bonds as well. Eager to expose their regions to the stimulating effect of railroads, western residents often ignored the lessons of the canal era and supported state and local aid to such companies. Their legislators gave state lands and other assistance to railroads and the residents of both counties and lesser municipalities approved bond issues or other aid to attract railroads.

Prior to 1850 Congress and state legislatures exercised control over transportation corporations by specifying their obligations and privileges in the charters granted to them. After 1850 the importance of carrying agencies to the growth of the country became increasingly apparent. It became obvious also that the railroad companies possessed large resources that might be used for ill as well as for good. As the economy became increasingly intricate, large, and commercial, economic interest groups almost inevitably became more and more critical of the transportation agencies that so largely controlled their destinies. To many users the rates which railroad companies charged appeared discriminatory, capricious and excessive. Evidence accumulated that major railroad companies had used government aid to benefit insiders rather than the stockholders in general or the public. Critics, therefore, asserted the public responsibility of transportation agencies and demanded that the state and federal governments regulate them in the public interest.

Was indeed mixed enterprise the most effective way of providing the transportation that a growing nation demanded? Did the entrepreneurs of transportation construct a system that was duplicative and inequitable? Should the federal government have planned, constructed and operated the major links in the nation's transportation network? Many historians have suggested that the railroad land grants were a waste of the nation's resources, but even today, railroad men maintain that the nation obtained a colossal bargain when the federal lawmakers insured that railroad companies would build thousands of miles of vital track by giving them grants of land in the public domain. Who is to be believed—historians or corporate spokesman? Were those who sought to regulate freight rates after the Civil War merely hysterical ignoramuses, nescient of the basic economics of transportation or were they realistic critics of industrial America? Such are a few of the questions that we can ask about the way that Americans solved the fundamental problem of linking West and East within an industrial economy.

•1•

CARTER GOODRICH

American Development Policy:
The Case of Internal Improvements

Several generations of speakers from the American business community have extolled the merits of our system of "free enterprise." Such a characterization is misleading today and is, indeed, inaccurate as a description of the American system at any time in our national history. In this reading Carter Goodrich considers the development of the internal improvement system in the United States and finds a unique pattern of governmental action, "profoundly affected—for better or worse—by the traditional American characteristics of individualism, of localism, and of the habit of voluntary association."

. . . It is not quite true that the United States just "growed" like Topsy or that the American empire of the West was settled and developed in a fit of absence of mind. Throughout our history statesmen have been concerned with devising measures to promote economic growth, and individuals and corporations have often come to governmental agencies with demands for encouragement and assistance. Many of the great debates on political issues have turned on what would today be described as development policy. . . .

In an examination of American development policy, I believe that particular interest attaches to the case of internal improvements. Here the aim was directly and unmistakably developmental and the amount and variety of governmental activity quite extraordinary. Recent studies have increased our knowledge of the number of cases, and they have shown that the volume of government investment was greater than had been believed, both in absolute figures and in relation to total canal and railroad investment, to total national investment, and to the total budgets

SOURCE: Abridged from Carter Goodrich, "American Development Policy: The Case of Internal Improvements," *Journal of Economic History,* XVI (December, 1956), 449-460. Reprinted by permission of the *Journal of Economic History* and Carter Goodrich.

of governmental authorities. Yet, half a century ago, the first modern student of the subject, Guy Stevens Callender, was able to point out that our supposedly individualistic America had had in the early and middle nineteenth century a certain world prominence as an example of the extension of the activity of the state into industry. He asked what conditions had given "rise to this remarkable movement towards State enterprise here in America, where of all places in the world"—he said —"we should least expect to find it."

This movement, however, appears less paradoxical if it is examined in the light of the economics of development. The conspicuous contrast was with England. English canals and railways were built entirely by private enterprise. American canals and railways were for the most part products of governmental or mixed enterprise or the recipients of government aid. But consider the difference in economic circumstance. A railway between London and Liverpool ran through settled country and connected established centers of trade. It could expect substantial traffic as soon as completed. On the other hand, a route across the Appalachians to the largely unsettled West or a railroad running from Chicago west across almost empty plains could hardly be profitable until settlement took place along its route and at its terminus. Jerome Cranmer uses the words "exploitative" and "developmental" for these two types of enterprise. Exploitative canals or railroads were built to take advantage of an existing opportunity. With them early returns could be expected and private enterprise could operate without subsidy. On the other hand the developmental undertaking depended for most of its traffic on the settlement that its own construction was to bring about. But such development could not in the nature of the case be immediate, and substantial early returns on the investment were hardly possible. The ultimate benefits might be very large but they were certain to be deferred and likely to be widely diffused. Such undertakings, therefore, could hardly be carried to success by unaided private means. They required either government enterprise, subsidy to private enterprise, or else extraordinary illusions on the part of the original investors. . . .

There were certain railroad companies, particularly on the Atlantic seaboard, exploiting the opportunities of trade between established centers, which were profitable from the beginning and neither asked nor needed government aid. . . . But these were exceptions. Most of the canals and early railroads depended for their traffic on the growth of the areas into which they were extended. They were developmental in character and, like developmental undertakings almost everywhere, they were in considerable part built with government funds and credit. . . .

Aid was given by local authorities, in varying amounts, in every state that formed part of the Union before 1890; and in some fourteen states it continued to be given after the abandonment of state programs. It may be said that governmental participation at one level or another persisted in most sections of the country as long as "developmental" conditions continued to exist, and perhaps in some cases beyond that point.

In general the relationship between developmental conditions and the various ways of government activity can be readily traced. For the Federal Government the building of the National Road and the formulation of the comprehensive internal improvement plans of Gallatin and Calhoun took place when the geographical obstacle to development was the Appalachian Mountains; and the major extension of actual aid to the transcontinental railroads took place when the obstacle was that of the Rocky Mountains and the Great Plains. Government activity in internal improvements was in large measure a frontier phenomenon, a great instance of frontier collectivism. In any given area it tended to diminish and die out as settlement and traffic became more dense and also as the business corporations themselves grew in strength and in the ability to raise large sums of money and commit them for long periods. . . .

If, then, we think of nineteenth-century America as a country in process of development, the experience of other countries in a similar situation suggests that extensive government investment in the means of transportation was not paradoxical but something entirely to be expected. What would really have been surprising would have been the spectacle of communities eager for rapid development but waiting patiently for their canals and railroads until the way was clear for prudent private investment to go forward without assistance. Yet neither an analysis of the economics of development nor analogy from foreign experience would account for all the peculiar forms and shapes taken by the American movement for internal improvements. Among its characteristics were three general shortcomings that would at once be obvious to anyone attempting to advise the underdeveloped countries of today on the organization of their programs of public improvement.

The first of these deficiencies was the failure to develop a workable economic criterion for the selection of projects for government support. Perhaps the sheer abundance of developmental opportunities made the question seem less crucial than it is for countries with more limited resources. . . .

A second shortcoming was the failure to develop and apply criteria for

the assignment of projects to the different levels of government authority
—federal, state, and local. . . .

The third shortcoming lay in the nature of the government agencies
themselves. They were sometimes subject to corruption, the danger of
which increased as the railroad corporations graduated from the stage
of infant enterprises. Moreover, they were in most cases poorly equipped
to discharge the responsibilities of planning programs of internal improvement and of operating the undertakings effectively or of protecting
the public interest in those that received public support. . . . The deficiency became more glaring as public aid came more and more to rest
on the decisions of local authorities. Little planning could be expected of
village or township boards deciding whether to recommend "whacking
up" the contribution demanded by the railroad agent, or to risk letting
the road go through the neighboring crossroads instead. Their chance
to protect the public interest consisted mainly in making sure that the
company really ran cars through their village in exchange for the contribution. . . .

As long as the common purpose was that of getting the much-desired
improvement made, those who took part in the movement were not very
much concerned if in many cases the method employed came close to
being public enterprise under private management. To the Missourians
on whom James N. Primm reports, as to many other Americans of the
same period, "The details of ownership and control were secondary . . .
to the principal objective, the establishment of a comprehensive system of
public improvement in the interests of the general welfare." . . .

Throughout the developmental period individual citizens donated land
for railroad rights of way, permitted the use of stone and timber from
their lands, and supplied the labor of their slaves or their teams—occasionally even their own labor—to what was considered the common
cause. Often, though not always, these services were paid for in shares
of the stock of the enterprise. Appeals for cash subscriptions to canal or
railroad stock were frequently based on grounds of civic duty as well
as on prospects of financial return. Citizens were urged to bear an
honorable part in what was often described as a great state or national
work. . . . The building of the American network of transportation
gained support from the local patriotism and the booster spirit of the
city, town, and small community. It may be pointed out that the Com-
munist practice of carrying regimentation and the party apparatus
down into the smallest units, and the very different methods of "community development" of India and other countries, represent deliberate
efforts to obtain popular participation at the local level in the processes

of economic development. In the United States, vigorous local participation took instead the spontaneous forms that have been described. . . .

Our record demonstrates a preference, though by no means universal or doctrinaire, for government partnership or subsidy rather than for purely public enterprise, and for leaving management largely in the hands of individuals and corporations. In this American experience differs from that of many foreign countries but not of all. Our record also shows that a large amount of this government action was taken by local governments, often of small communities. In this American experience is unique. In our case, moreover, governmental effort has been accompanied and abetted by the voluntary activity of a host of unofficial civic organizations, for which I am sure no parallel can be found in the history of other developing countries. Our policy with respect to internal improvements has thus been profoundly affected—for better or worse—by the traditional American characteristics of individualism, of localism, and of the habit of voluntary association.

LELAND H. JENKS

Railroads as an Economic Force in American Development

Although historians have not overlooked the importance
of canals and river transportation in American economic
development, they have usually emphasized the tremendous
contribution of the railroads. Leland H. Jenks has written
a classic statement of the importance of these carriers, discussing the impact of the railroad as an idea, as a construction enterprise and as a carrier. His analysis of the "linkage"
effects of the railroad is a major milestone in the historical
study of economic growth in the United States.

Any attempt to discuss the way in which railroads have promoted the
rise of the American economy must assume some theory of economic
evolution. The following analysis is based upon Schumpeter's theory of
innovations. Briefly this theory holds that economic evolution in capitalistic society is started by innovation in some production function, that is,
by new combinations of the factors in the economic process. . . .

Railroad development has had three phases or moments which have
involved innovation in distinctive ways. I shall consider (1) the railroad
as an idea, (2) the railroad as a construction enterprise, and (3) the
railroad as a producer of transportation services.

I

By the railroad as an idea is not meant the original design of steam
locomotion on rails. It pertains to the inception in particular areas of
particular projects, conceived as likely to be appropriate opportunities
for business enterprise. In this sense the idea of any major innovation,
such as the railroad, is a potent economic force. For once railway projects
have been conceived and plans for their execution elaborated, it becomes
easier for other innovating ideas to be entertained. . . .

SOURCE: Abridged from Leland H. Jenks, "Railroads as an Economic Force in
American Development," *Journal of Economic History*, IV (May, 1944), 1-20. Reprinted by permission of the *Journal of Economic History* and Leland H. Jenks.

The first railway projects emerged in the United States in the thirties in a situation in which the psychological risks had already been appreciably lowered by the general passion for internal improvements displayed in a plethora of projects for canals, turnpikes, plank roads, bridges, banks, and other enterprises. The earliest railways paralleled, supplemented, or improved transport systems that were already in being. The real railway revolution dates from the forties, prior to the California gold discoveries, in projects to cross the Appalachians, to link the seaboard with the interior, the Ohio Valley with the Great Lakes, and, breaking away from the contours of water transport, to unite distant points by more direct routes. It was the determination to build railroads in advance of traffic that gave the "railroad idea" prolonged force in American economic life. The conviction that the railroad would run anywhere at a profit put fresh spurs to American ingenuity and opened closed paddocks of potential enterprise. . . .

II

The second moment of the railroad as an economic force came with the actual construction of new lines. The statistics of net mileage added in each year from 1837 to 1937 give a quantitative measure of this contribution of the railroad to development. . . . Two general statements are strikingly supported by these data. In the first place, railway building proceeded in an undulating pattern, paralleling closely the general contours of major business cycles until the First World War. From 1850 to the nineties, omitting the years of the Civil War, the rise and fall in new construction in fact led by a perceptible interval most other indices of business conditions. . . .

But how did railway construction as such act as an economic force? How could it be a pace setter? The answer is broadly that it operated directly to create a demand for various factors of production. In response to this demand there were rises in prices or increases in supply or both. Increase of supply could come only from some sort of further innovations, such as the drawing of fresh increments of land, labor, or capital into economic uses or the transfer of such factors to more effective combinations. This process meant the periodic dislocation of the economic structure as well as the disruption of the activities of individuals and communities. At the same time it enhanced the opportunities for enterprisers having a high degree of flexibility, pioneering individuals and groups, the agents of innumerable innovating firms and procedures.

The land for railroad construction was largely new land, previously not of economic use. It cost virtually nothing to the railway companies, and not very much to anyone else. Socially the land devoted to railroad purposes more than paid for itself by the increment in productivity of adjacent land. . . .

The demand for labor initiated a chapter in the history of immigration and colonization. It also disciplined migratory and local labor power to co-operative industrial effort. But it had wider repercussions. Laborers were paid wages and the wages were spent for goods. They went to market to buy the produce of American farms and mills. Thus the demand for labor stimulated the spread of market economy and the more extensive production of goods and services for distant markets, and thereby contributed to the spread of economic specialization.

The demand for capital functioned in parallel to the demand for labor. I am speaking of real capital, of goods, of the picks and shovels, sleepers and steel rails, engines and rolling stock and bridgework and culverts and ordinary building material, which make up the physical plant of a railroad. The construction moment of railway history brought an initial demand for these durable goods. . . . [T]he initial impetus of investment in railway construction led in widening arcs to increments of economic activity over the entire American domain, far exceeding in their total volume the original inputs of investment capital. To this feature of modern capitalism, John Maynard Keynes and others have applied the term "multiplier." . . .

I have spoken of inputs and investment. In our economy the demand for land and labor and capital has meant another demand, a demand not for an independent factor of production, but for something equally essential, a demand for money capital. In fact, without a supply of money capital there could have been no effective demand for any of the real factors, no railways, and no stimulus from them for economic development. Hence it is convenient to think of the building of railroads as an investment of money capital. To this investment there corresponded in the long run the accumulation of savings. . . .

In final analysis, the funds for railway construction came from the extension of credit by American banks and from foreign exchange supplied by European investors. This was accomplished by many devices which called into play the charitable cupidity of contractors and iron manufacturers on both sides of the Atlantic, and the lively anticipations of property owners in the area which the railroad was to develop. Some of the shares were sold at a heavy discount to local residents, but more were given outright for land, for legal and legislative services, for banking accommodation, or as a bonus to promote the sale of bonds. Frequently there was a construction company, analogous to the Crédit

Mobilier, which took all the securities in payment for the road and operated it pending the completion of construction. . . .

Whatever the source or timing of the application of money capital, the financing of railroad construction encouraged innovations in financial enterprise: the development of stock exchanges and their techniques; the specialization of firms, old and new, in investment banking and in security brokerage; the specialization of banking institutions (especially trust companies) as trustees and registration agents for securities, and as agents for distributing capital and interest payments; the rise of legal firms specializing in corporation law and in adjusting construction activities to the intricacies of the American political system. . . .

With financial innovation came a transformation of the role of the enterpriser in connection with particular railway systems. In the initial moments of construction, the typical enterpriser was still pretty much the omnicompetent pioneer, the individual of imagination, daring, and energy. . . .

Such enterprisers were rarely able, however, to cope with recurrent financial involvements. The elaboration of the superstructure of railroad securities sooner or later compelled a more formal division of tasks and responsibilities in the continuance of construction. In some cases this involved a shift of the center of decision from the engineer-promoter to financial and legal experts either within or outside the railroad organization. . . .

III

The third moment to be surveyed is that of the railroad as a going concern, a complex of tracks and engines and cars and managers and employees engaged in the business of carrying passengers and freight. By rendering this transportation service, the railroad in operation has doubtless added directly to the real income of the United States, and indirectly to economic expansion. There appears to be no satisfactory technique for giving a precise measure to the extent of this contribution. . . .

It is commonly assumed that the great contribution of railroad transportation came from the reduction of shipping costs. As compared with pre-motorized forms of highway transportation, the advantage of the railroad has always been obvious. There is no convincing evidence, however, that railways have ever carried freight at lower costs either to shippers or to society than canals or waterways. The advantages that early railways showed over canals, such as speed, flexibility of service, and special adaptability to short hauls, are analogous to those of modern highway transport over the railroad. It was far more important that the railroad brought transportation to areas that without it could have had scarcely any commercial existence at all. . . .

Holmstrom's study of the cost characteristics of various forms of transportation brings other considerations to the forefront of analysis. He shows that the traffic potential of the railroad per unit of installation is even now far greater than that of any other form of transportation that he considers. . . . Thus an initial and continuing potential contribution of the railroad has come from the volume of traffic it has been able to carry.

The converse of this proposition is the fact that the railroad constitutes a case of increasing return, with special features that give a decisive bent to its impact upon economic structure. Its social costs per unit of traffic decrease rapidly with traffic density. A familiar manifestation of this condition was the well-known shift from passengers and light traffic as principal sources of revenue in the early railroad days to bulk traffic. . . .

That the railroad tends to attract factors of production to its right of way needs no comment; this perception lay at the heart of the American railroad innovation. As Holmstrom points out, however, this supply of potential traffic does not distribute itself at random. It is polarized first about line terminals, and secondarily about traffic intersections. There is a further tendency. Irrespective of rate differentials, the service of the railroad is of greatest advantage to large shippers requiring a fairly regular flow of traffic. Thus railroad transportation provides a considerable addition to the external economies that firms can realize from large-scale operations. . . .

As early as the eighties, railway systems that had been daring ventures only a decade before found themselves embarking on extensions and improvements, not as acts of innovating faith, but to enable them to handle traffic that had been offered them or to keep somebody else from getting the business. In region after region development initiated by the railroad outran the plans of the projectors. . . .

IV

This general interpretation of the role of the railroad as an economic force suggests what might be undertaken in greater detail to apply the innovation theory to the history of particular companies and of the railroad system as a whole. What was the impact of the railroad upon technological, locational, structural, and organizational alterations in particular firms, industries, and regions? Parallel inquiries could be made regarding the part played by other major innovations, such as the more recent rise of the electromotive industries. It is not a question of applying the facts of economic history to verify an economic theory. It is a question of using a theory as a tool to coherent understanding of the facts. Economic historians seem increasingly willing to make use of conceptual aids for this purpose. It is one of the most prominent symptoms of what may be a wider tendency to employ analytical procedures in historical studies. . . .

•3•

ROBERT WILLIAM FOGEL

A Quantitative Approach to the Study of Railroads in American Economic Growth . . .

Depending more heavily upon economic analysis than many earlier economic historians and committed to the use of quantitative methods, the "Cliometricists" are trying to find precise answers to questions about American economic development that we have hitherto answered in general terms only. In this selection Robert William Fogel describes one method of calculating the importance of railroads in the interregional carriage of agricultural products. In his larger study Professor Fogel concluded that railroads were responsible for approximately five per cent of the national income in 1890.

The idea of a crucial nexus between the railroad and the forward surge of the American economy following 1840 appears to be supported by an avalanche of factual evidence. There is, first of all, the impact of the railroad on the growth of cities. Atlanta was transformed from a spot in the wilderness to a thriving metropolis as a result of the construction of the Western and Atlantic. Chicago eclipsed St. Louis as the

SOURCE: Abridged from Robert William Fogel, "A Quantitative Approach to the Study of Railroads in American Economic Growth: A Report of Some Preliminary Findings," *Journal of Economic History*, XXII (June, 1962), 163-197. Reprinted by permission of the *Journal of Economic History* and Robert William Fogel.

commercial emporium of the West by virtue of its superior railroad connections. And Louisville throttled the growth of Cincinnati by its ability
to deny the "Porkopolis" rail connection with the South. Further, the
decisive victory of the railroads over canals and rivers in the contest
for the nation's freight is beyond dispute. . . .

Finally, there is the high correlation between new railroad construction and both population growth and commercial activity. Illinois,
Michigan, and Ohio, for example, experienced a marked increase in
population, construction, and manufacturing following the completion of
rail lines within and across their borders. . . .

The evidence is impressive. But it demonstrates only an association
between the growth of the rail network and the growth of the economy.
It fails to establish a causal relationship between the railroad and the
regional reorganization of trade, the change in the structure of output,
the rise in per capita income, or the various other strategic changes that
characterized the American economy of the last century. . . .

The question to be considered is: did the interregional distribution of
agricultural products—a striking feature of the American economy of
the nineteenth century—depend on the existence of the long-haul railroad? To answer the question, I define a concept of "social saving" in
interregional transportation attributable to the existence of the railroad,
and propose a method of measuring it. . . .

The massive change in the geographical pattern of agricultural output
during the nineteenth century has been a leading theme of American
historiography. The meager data at the start of the century strongly
suggest that the main sections of the nation were agriculturally self-
sufficient. By 1890 the North Atlantic, South Atlantic, and South Central
divisions, containing twenty-five states and 60 per cent of the nation's
population, had become a deficit area in various agricultural commodities,
particularly foodstuffs. . . . The local supply of foodstuffs in the deficit
regions appears even more inadequate when the product needed for the
export market is added to domestic consumption. In the North Atlantic
division, for example, local production of wheat supplied only 24 per
cent of the combined local and export requirement.

In contrast to the decline in regional self-sufficiency in foodstuffs in
the East and South, the North Central division of the country had become
a great agricultural surplus area. Virgin territory at the start of the
century, these twelve states were producing 71 per cent of the country's
cereal grains by 1890 and were also the national center of cattle and
swine production. . . .

The process by which the agricultural surpluses of the Midwest were distributed can be divided into three stages. In the case of grain, the first stage was the concentration of the surplus in the great primary markets of the Midwest: Chicago, Minneapolis, Duluth, Milwaukee, Peoria, Kansas City, St. Louis, Cincinnati, Toledo, and Detroit. Over 80 per cent of the grain that entered into interregional trade was shipped from the farms to these cities. The second stage involved the shipment of the grain from the primary markets to some ninety secondary markets in the East and South. . . . The third stage was the distribution of the grain within the territory immediately surrounding the secondary markets, and exportation abroad. The distributional pattern of meat products roughly paralleled that of grain. Perhaps the most important difference was that the first stage of the distribution process—concentration of livestock in the primary markets—was dominated by only four cities: Chicago, St. Louis, Kansas City, and Omaha. . . .

For the purposes of this paper, "interregional distribution" is defined as the shipments of commodities from the primary markets of the Midwest to the secondary markets of the East and South. . . . The hypothesis to be examined in this paper . . . can now be stated as follows:

Rail connections between the primary and secondary markets of the nation were a necessary condition for the system of agricultural production and distribution that characterized the American economy of the last half of the nineteenth century. Moreover, the absence of such rail connections would have forced a regional pattern of agricultural production that would have significantly restricted the development of the American economy.

In the year 1890, a certain bundle of agricultural commodities was shipped from the primary markets to the secondary markets. The shipment occurred in a certain pattern, that is, with certain tonnages moving from each primary market city to each secondary market city. This pattern of shipments was carried out by some combination of rail, wagon, and water haulage at some definite cost. With enough data, one could determine both this cost and the alternative cost of shipping exactly the same bundle of goods from the primary to the secondary markets in exactly the same pattern without the railroad. The difference between these two amounts I call the social saving attributable to the railroad in the interregional distribution of agricultural products—or simply "the social saving." . . .

If the calculation shows the saving to be zero, then obviously the absence of the interregional railroad would not have altered the existing productive pattern. On the other hand, if the social saving turns out to be very large, say on the order of magnitude of national income, it would be equally obvious that in the absence of the interregional rail-road all production of surpluses in the Midwest would have ceased. . . . The crucial question is not whether the absence of the railroad would have left agricultural production in a different regional pattern, but whether such a pattern would have significantly restricted economic growth.

The social saving is calculated in my estimates for only one year, 1890. . . .

By 1890 the average cost of railroad transportation was less than a cent per ton-mile. On the other hand, the cost of wagon transportation was in the neighborhood of twenty-five cents per ton-mile. According to estimates made here, approximately 7.7 million tons of corn and 5.0 million tons of wheat entered into interregional transportation. Taking the differential between rail and wagon transportation at twenty-five cents per-ton mile, the social saving involved in moving these 12.7 million tons one mile would have been $3,180,000. Assuming that on the average the corn and wheat shipped interregionally traveled nine hundred miles, the total social saving would have been $2,860,000,000. Even this figure is low, since wagon rates did not reflect the cost involved in road construction and maintenance. If account were taken of these and other omitted charges, and if a similar calculation were performed for livestock, the figure for the social saving would probably increase by 50 per cent, to four billion dollars, or more than one third of gross national product in 1890. . . .

Water transportation was a practical alternative to the railroad in interregional transportation. A glance at a map will show that all of the primary market cities were on navigable waterways. . . . The lakes, inland rivers, canals, and coastal waters directly linked the primary market cities to most of the secondary market cities. Of the forty-three most important secondary markets, thirty-two were located on navigable waters still in use in 1890. Seven were on waterways that had been forced into inactivity as a result of railroad competition, but which could have been used in the absence of the railroad. Only four cities were without direct water connection to the Midwest, and each of these was within a rela-tively short wagon haul of a major water artery.

The importance of a water-route alternative lies in the fact that on a per ton-mile basis, water rates were not only less than wagon rates but also less than railroad rates. The all-rail rate on wheat from Chicago to New York, for example, was about 0.52 cents per ton-mile, or nearly four times as much as the ton-mile rate by water. This fact does not, of course, imply that the social cost or even the private cost on a given tonnage was less when shipped by water. Water routes were much more circuitous than rail routes, and the time in transit was considerably greater. Loss of cargo was more frequent. Terminal charges were higher. These and other problems raised the cost of water transportation to a point where shipments between most primary and most secondary markets were cheaper by rail than by boat. . . .

Until now, the discussion has been carried on as if all the agricultural commodities that entered into interregional trade were to be included in the estimate. In fact, the estimate will be based on only four commodities: wheat, corn, beef, and pork. These four accounted for 42 per cent of income originating in agriculture in 1889. Neglect of the other products is not so serious as it first seems. What is important is not the share of wheat, corn, beef, and pork in total output, but their share in that part of output which entered interregional trade. . . . [N]eglected items probably do not account for more than 10 per cent of the goods entering into interregional trade, and would not justify the effort required to include them. The most direct method of determining the social saving is to find the 1890 pattern of the shipments of the four commodities, and then estimate both the actual cost of the pattern and the cost that would have obtained if the pattern had been executed with only boats and wagons. . . .

The starting point of the calculation is the difference between the average ton-mile transportation rate by water and by rail. Various experts on transportation have pointed out that water rates were generally less than railroad rates. Thus, over the route from Chicago to New York, the average all-rail rate on wheat in 1890 was 0.523 cents per ton-mile while the average all-water rate was 0.139 cents per ton-mile. Casual examination of the available data suggests that these figures are approximately the same as those applying to all grains on this and other routes. Hence, for the purposes of calculation it will be arbitrarily assumed that the New York to Chicago all-water rate per ton-mile on wheat equaled the average all-water rate (per ton-mile) on all grains over all the relevant routes. The assumption to be made on the all-rail rate is symmetric.

For the crude calculation of the social saving, the average national rate at which grain was actually transported in 1890 is needed. This actual rate must have been less than the all-rail rate. Not all grains shipped interregionally were carried exclusively by rail. Considerable quantities were shipped by a combination of rail and water or completely by water. In contrast to the 0.523 cents all-rail rate per ton-mile on wheat transported from Chicago to New York, the lake-and-rail charge was 0.229 cents, and the lake-and-canal charge was 0.186 cents.

The average of these three rates, weighted by the quantities of grain shipped under each one, is 0.434 cents. . . . This last figure will be taken as the "actual" national average rate on grains per ton-mile in 1890. . . .

In the case of meat and livestock products, the calculation is based on the St. Louis to New Orleans rates on pork. The all-rail rate was 1.07 cents per ton-mile and the all-water rate was 0.45 cents. Again, these rates are comparable to those that prevailed on other meat products shipped on this and other routes. Furthermore, since the quantity of meat shipped by water was a small part of the total interregional tonnage, no further adjustment need be made; that is, the all-rail rate on pork will be assumed to equal the actual average rate on all meat products.

The quantity of corn, wheat, pork, and beef shipped interregionally in 1890 was approximately equal to the net local deficit of the trading areas plus net exports. Assuming that half of the meat products was shipped as livestock and half as dressed meat, the amount transported interregionally was 15,700,000 tons.

If rates and ton-miles were the only elements entering into the cost of transportation, it would have been cheaper to have shipped interregionally by water than by rail . . . [T]he social saving calculated on the basis of these elements is negative by about $38,000,000. This odd result is not difficult to explain. While the estimated actual cost of transportation includes virtually all relevant items, the estimated cost of water transportation does not. In calculating the cost of shipping without the railroad, one must account for six neglected items of cost not reflected in the first approximation: cargo losses in transit, transshipment costs, wagon haulage from water points to secondary markets not on water routes, the cost resulting from the time lost when using a slow medium of transportation, the cost of being unable to use water routes for five months out of the year, and finally, capital costs not reflected in water rates.

When account is taken of the six neglected costs, the loss attributable to the railroad will be transformed into a saving. How big must the neglected costs be to produce a positive saving of 1 per cent of national income? In 1890 gross national product was about $12,000,000,000, and 1 per cent of this amount is $120,000,000. Without the neglected costs, interregional shipment of the four commodities would have been $38,-000,000 cheaper by water than by rail. Consequently, in order to reach a social saving of 1 per cent of gross national product, the neglected costs will have to be approximately $158,000,000.

The literature on the interregional transportation of agricultural products indicates that cargo losses were greater on water shipments than on rail shipments. Insurance rates can be used to estimate the cost of these water transit losses. . . . The cost of insurance (cost of cargo losses) in the absence of the railroad would have been approximately $6,000,000. Subtracting this figure from $158,000,000, there is left $152,000,000 to cover the remaining costs.

Transshipping costs were incurred whenever it became necessary to switch a cargo from one type of vessel to another. Grain shipped from Chicago to New York, for example, was transferred at Buffalo from lake steamers to canal barges. In the absence of the railroad there would probably have been an average of two transshipments on each ton carried from a primary to a secondary market. At a cost of fifty cents per ton per transshipment, transshipping charges on the grain and meat products in question would have been $16,000,000. Subtracting this amount from $152,000,000, there is left $136,000,000 to cover the remaining costs.

The two indirect costs of water transportation most frequently cited are the cost of time lost in shipping by water and the cost of being unable to use water routes for about five months out of each year. . . .

The key to quantifying the cost of the time that would have been lost in water transportation is the nexus between time and inventories. If entrepreneurs could replace goods the instant they were sold, they would, *ceteris paribus,* carry zero inventories. Inventories are necessary to bridge the gap of time required to deliver a commodity from its supply source to a given point. If, on the average, interregional shipments of agricultural commodities required a month more by water than by rail, it would have been possible to compensate for the time lost through an inventory increase in the secondary markets equal to one twelfth of annual shipments. Hence the cost of the time lost in using water transportation was the 1890 cost of carrying such an additional inventory.

The problems inherent in the limited season of water transportation could also have been met by an increase in inventory. Since water routes were closed for five-twelfths of the year, I will assume that the absence of railroads would have increased the inventories of agricultural commodities held in secondary markets by five-twelfths of the annual interregional shipment. It should be noted that this assumption overstates the additional inventory requirement. Abstracting from risk considerations, the limited season of navigation would—at least with respect to grains—have had no effect on the inventory requirements of the nation. A crop once harvested was placed in inventory and drawn down throughout the year. A shorter transportation season would only have affected the way in which a fixed total inventory was divided between the Midwest and the secondary markets. Exclusive reliance on water routes would have increased the inventory total only if risk factors were operative. Under conditions of risk, the availability of a central depository reduces the size of the stock that must be held by a given set of cities. Nevertheless, the five-twelfths assumption will be adopted to simplify the computation.

The cost of time lost in water transportation and the limited season of navigation would thus not have exceeded the cost incurred in carrying an inventory equal to one half of the annual amount of agricultural products that were transported interregionally. . . . [T]he Chicago wholesale value of the corn, wheat, beef, and pork shipped interregionally was about $550,000,000. Another $43,000,000 should be added to approximate wholesale value at seaboard. Hence, in the absence of the railroad, the limited season of navigation would have required an increase in the value of inventories of about $297,000,000. The cost of carrying such an additional inventory would have included the forgone opportunity of investing the same amount elsewhere. If it is assumed that on the average capital earned 6 per cent in 1890, the alternative cost of the investment in additional inventory would have been about $18,000,000 per year. To this, one must add about $30,000,000 for storage charges. Subtracting $48,000,000 from $136,000,000 leaves $88,000,000 to account for the two remaining costs.

Cities receiving approximately 10 per cent of the interregional shipments were not on water routes. If these cities were an average of fifty miles from the nearest water point, the cost of wagon haulage (at twenty-five cents per ton-mile) would have been $20,000,000. Subtracting this amount from $88,000,000 leaves $68,000,000 to account for the last item —neglected capital charges.

Water rates failed to reflect capital costs to the extent that rivers and canals were improved or built by the government and financed out of taxes rather than tolls. If a complete statement of these uncompensated expenditures were available, one could easily estimate the neglected capital costs. . . . [A]t an interest rate of 6 per cent the neglected capital costs would have been about $18,000,000—$50,000,000 short of the amount required to bring the social saving to 1 per cent of gross national product.

Thus casual examination of the available data suggests that the social savings attributable to the railroad in the interregional transportation of agricultural products was about 1 per cent of national income. The calculation is, of course, subject to considerable error; but there are

grounds for having confidence in the result. Four of the estimates—
those dealing with transshipment, wagon haulage, time lost, and the
limited season of navigation—probably overstate the actual cost of water
transportation. While the estimates of some of the other items may be
too low, it does not seem likely that the errors are large enough to alter
substantially the magnitude of the indicated social saving. . . .

·4·

GEORGE H. MILLER

Origins of the Iowa Granger Law

The enthusiasm of some westerners for improved transportation curdled during the years after the Civil War, when they
learned that water or rail connection, or even both, did not
provide the prosperity which they had expected. During the
1870's midwestern legislatures approved legislation to regulate the rates and other practices of railroads and warehousing
agencies, often called the "Granger Laws," because they
were believed to reflect the agitation of farmers and their
organization, the Grange or Patrons of Husbandry. In this
passage George H. Miller shows that the background of the
Iowa Granger Law was complex and that the activity of
commercial interests was more important in promoting it
than the efforts of the farmers.

The Granger laws are prominent mileposts in the history of American
public-service law. Their enactment in the 1870's precipitated a constitutional crisis from which there emerged a fundamental restatement of
state rights with respect to "private enterprise." As contributions to substantive and procedural law they figured prominently in the evolution
of a system of railroad rate regulation which later was embodied in the
pioneer Interstate Commerce Act of 1887. To their adoption has been
traced the very beginnings of modern industrial control in the interest
of the public welfare.

SOURCE: Abridged from George H. Miller, "Origins of the Iowa Granger Law,"
Mississippi Valley Historical Review, XL (March, 1954), 657-680. Reprinted by
permission of the Journal of American History and George H. Miller.

The body of state legislation referred to as the Granger laws derives its common name from the farmers' organization known as the Patrons of Husbandry or Grange. The standard interpretation as to the origin of these measures holds that during the decade following the Civil War, "militant farmers," oppressed by the exorbitant and discriminatory charges of railroads and warehousemen, "seized control" of Western state legislatures and enacted a series of radical and stringent rate-control statutes. . . .

But the farmers' movement which brought the Grange into national prominence during the early 1870's was by no means coextensive with the movement leading to the adoption of the Granger laws. . . .

It can be shown conclusively that the Granger railroad laws passed by the states of the upper Mississippi Valley between 1871 and 1874 were all concerned primarily with the problem of rate discrimination. . . . The primary target of these measures was discrimination against localities, a form of unequal treatment against which the existing common law of carriers offered no protection. They are part of a chain of historical development which begins with the introduction of prorata bills in New England state legislatures during the 1840's and 1850's and continues through the adoption of the Interstate Commerce Act of 1887. This series of proposals for rate-law reforms, sponsored for the most part by merchants and businessmen, can scarcely be interpreted as agrarian attacks upon the business community. On the contrary, they were designed to protect vested commercial interests in the face of disruptive economic forces engendered by discriminatory railroad rate-making practices; and to this general rule the Granger laws were no exception. The legislative history of the Iowa law of March 19, 1874, provides abundant evidence in support of this thesis.

During the early years of railroad operation in the United States the power to regulate the charges of common carriers by statute was freely exercised by state legislatures. It is quite probable that most of the railway mileage of the United States in the year 1850 was being operated under some form of legislative restriction with regard to rate levels. As far as the courts were concerned rate fixing was a normal operation of the police power and was exercised without benefit of judicial review unless the right to regulate was specifically granted away by charter. The two decades between 1850 and 1870, however, were marked by a general curtailment of the regulatory function. In the interest of railway promotion many state legislatures refrained from using their power of police over rates, and in some cases made outright grants of immunity from statutory control. For a short time the established practice of carrier rate restriction gave way to a liberal policy of freedom and encouragement for railroad development. . . .

The first Iowa railroads—those put into operation during the 1850's—were planned as feeder lines for the towns along the Mississippi River. They were conceived as connecting lines between the River and the interior—as improved highways over which the grain of the prairies could be brought to the mills and landings at McGregor, Dubuque, Clinton, Davenport, Muscatine, Burlington, Fort Madison, Keokuk, and other ports along the banks of the great north-south waterway. . . .

But to the river towns of Iowa the railroads soon proved a mixed blessing. Beginning in 1854, Chicago and Milwaukee rail lines reached the River at points opposite the Iowa terminals. The Milwaukee, the Illinois Central, the Northwestern, the Rock Island, and the Burlington laid their tracks to the River's edge, contemplated the bridging of the great barrier, and established running connections with roads on the other side. The impact of the Chicago and Milwaukee "invasion" upon the commercial life of the state was tremendous. The easy-going collection and distribution system established by merchants serving the older river trade was no match for the aggressive, highly competitive organizations serving the Great Lakes ports. Ignoring the existing terminals, Eastern grain buyers and wholesale merchants moved into the interior, going straight to the rural markets. Lumber for prairie farmhouses began to roll westward from Chicago to interior Iowa communities without using the facilities of the river-town markets. In like manner grain and hogs were billed through directly to the Lakes from local Iowa collecting points. Virtually overnight, the Mississippi ports had become mere way points on trunk lines serving the lake cities. Dubuque, Davenport, and Burlington in their position as primary markets were forced into direct competition with Chicago for the business of their own state.

The market price of grain at each step in the chain of sale was that offered at the next terminal collecting point minus freight charges and the customary dealer's commission. Dubuque merchants in other words, paid either St. Louis or Chicago prices less the cost of transportation to these markets; the grain buyers at Waterloo, Iowa, now paid either Dubuque or Chicago prices less the cost of shipment to one of these two points. If Dubuque were to compete with Chicago for the grain of Waterloo and realize the profits of a primary grain market, it obviously had to pay a price equal to that offered by Chicago; but its ability to do so depended in large measure upon the structure of rates on the Illinois Central and its Iowa connection. . . .

The reaction of the state assembly to the introduction of the railroad rate problem into Iowa politics [in the 1860's] was decidedly hostile. The majority felt strongly that it would be "state suicide" to legislate in an unfriendly manner with respect to railroads at that time. Since Iowa was unable to supply sufficient capital to build her own roads and since no Eastern capitalist would invest money in a railroad over which he and his associates could not exercise control, rate restrictions were considered inimical to the best interests of the state. The need of the day was for more railroads. Accordingly each of the rate-control measures was rejected. . . .

By 1870, Iowa was well integrated into the national railway net and more than ever tributary to the Chicago market. The railroads continued to defeat the commercial ambitions of the river towns by their rate-making policies and by their political strength in the state assembly. By steadily reducing their rates from interior points to Lake Michigan they had virtually neutralized the competitive possibilities of the River; and by playing upon the promotional aims of the have-not areas they had helped to prevent the adoption of active control laws and charter provisions. The rapid development of the railroad system, however, was giving rise to other forms of local inequalities in the rate structures of the different roads. The wave of discontent was moving westward across the state in the wake of railroad construction.

The legislative history of the Iowa Granger law [of 1874] shows clearly that the movement to impose legislative restrictions upon intrastate railroad rates in Iowa grew out of complaints of unjust discrimination against the trade and commerce of the state. It shows further that the hardships inflicted by the carriers upon certain mercantile interests remained a decisive factor in the movement down to the time of legislative enactment. Neither the agrarian revolt of 1873-1874 nor the appearance of the Anti-Monopoly party in 1873 can be credited with any decisive influence upon the course of the movement in the legislature or upon the substance of the law. The issue was decided by the extension of the railway net over the unserved part of the state and by a political compromise of the strong-weak road problem [allowing roads with low earnings to charge higher rates]. This does not mean that agrarian interests were without influence in the movement for rate regulation. It means simply that the organized or "militant" farmers were not in control of the movement and that a rate-control measure would almost certainly have been adopted by the general assembly of 1874 had there been no Granger revolt.

These conclusions with respect to Iowa find added confirmation in the parallel experiences of neighboring states. In Illinois and Minnesota the pattern of protest is found to be very similar, and the origins of the railroad rate legislation enacted by these states between 1869 and 1874 are different only in detail. Here, too, the merchants and shippers complained of uneven rate structures and were the first to ask for Granger-type legislation. The organized farmers and Anti-Monopolists joined the movement only after it was well under way and in no instance came to dominate it. In Iowa the leadership of the river-town interests gave to the movement a special character which led to the adoption of fixed statutory maxima. In Illinois and Minnesota the interior way-point interests came to dominate and brought about the passage of long-and-short-haul measures supplemented by commission control.

In Wisconsin, where the most radical of all the Granger laws was adopted, the movement for regulation had similar beginnings but followed a different course from 1867 on. Strong agitation for controls virtually disappeared from the political scene for a period of six years and then suddenly re-emerged in the election campaign of 1873. The passage of the famous Potter law by the state legislature of the following year was so confused by partisan politics that it is difficult to determine the true objectives of the sincere advocates of controls. The Potter law was little more than a Republican trick designed to embarrass a Reform party administration. It was neither sponsored nor approved by the Grangers.

If the Grangers and Anti-Monopolists contributed in any significant way to the adoption of these laws it was in their promotion of a public attitude which was hostile to certain railroad practices and which was sufficiently strong to overbalance for a time that hunger for more railroads which had led to freedom from regulation in the first place. In an atmosphere charged with anti-railroad sentiment it was difficult for state legislators to find a satisfactory solution to the rate problem. Consequently much of the Granger legislation was premature and ill-advised, and only the Illinois law of 1873 survived the reaction of the late 1870's. Such a contribution is of considerable historical importance. But it does not alter the fact that rate discrimination, a source of discontent in nearly every state, was primarily a problem for merchants and shippers and that the remedies adopted in all of the Granger laws were geared to the needs of commercial interests. The same remedies had been and were being demanded in areas unaffected by the farmers' crusade. . . .

CHAPTER VIII

Building the Urban Nucleus

The first academic historians of the American West were more interested in the fur trader, the miner or the pioneer farmer than in the western town promoter, merchant or banker. Although these scholars were aware of the activities of the town dwellers, they took their contributions for granted. In retrospect we can understand that the early western historians reflected prevailing agrarian prejudices against townsmen. They believed them to be less important than the primary producers, as well as predatory or even corrupt. The western stereotype of the townsman charged excessively for forwarding furs, for smelting ore, or shipping grain to terminal markets, and for filling the grocery basket of the countrywoman. When William Jennings Bryan looked out upon the sweating delegates of the Democratic Convention in 1896 and intoned "burn down your cities and leave our farms, and your cities will spring up again as if by magic; but destroy our farms, and the grass will grow in the streets of every city in the country," he expressed the values and understanding of millions of Americans. And certainly, throughout great stretches of the western regions of the United States prior to the twentieth century, the town dwellers were but a fraction of the total population. But their cities and their towns were the foci of economic activity and townsmen themselves were significant beyond their numbers. Some writers now emphasize the preeminence of urban residents in developing the West—it is probably more accurate to stress the interdependence of the urban and rural populations.

Whether village, town or city, the growth of any urban center depended upon the ability of its residents to provide goods and services and to profit in the process. Even when Americans pushed beyond the Appalachians, they never completely escaped the influence of urban populations in the East. Indeed, much of the economic development of the West reflected the competition among businessmen of major eastern ports to win as much of the trade of the western regions as possible for their cities.

Despite recurrent dreams of commercial empire in the West, Boston's business leaders learned during the first half of the nineteenth century that their greatest opportunities lay in shaping the industrialization of New England, in fostering the settlement of that region's northern fringe and in sending capital to the West. Meanwhile the businessmen of New York, Philadelphia and Baltimore struggled to capture the commerce of the trans-Appalachian West, to serve as the starting point for immigrants to the western country, to supply them with goods and equipment and to become the major destination of their surplus production. During the first 60 years of the nineteenth century, the mercantile rivalry of these hopeful metropolises stimulated the improvement of transportation facilities through the Appalachian barrier. To Philadelphia merchants, the National Road which channeled western produce to Baltimore and carried settlers and manufactured goods from that port westward was a threat indeed, and the Pennsylvania Pike was their response. New York's men of commerce did not command such direct land routes to the Ohio valley as did their rivals in Philadelphia and Baltimore, but they discovered to their joy that the Erie Canal gave them the best commercial connection to the West yet devised.

The Pennsylvania canal system terminating in Pittsburgh and Baltimore's Chesapeake and Ohio Canal were only feeble answers to the Erie Canal. This fact explains the early interest of Baltimore's civic leaders in the Baltimore and Ohio Railroad. When one of the competitors had accepted the logic of railroads, all must per force accept it as the best solution to the problem of communications with the western regions. New York businessmen won the lion's share of the western trade but this victory was not the only reason that New York grew mightier than her seaboard rivals. To the western prize her businessmen added much of the mercantile trade from overseas and the city's dominance in the southern cotton trade also swelled its commerce and rewarded its financiers. The western trade, however, made the members of the mercantile communities in all of these cities usually willing and eager to support improvements in transportation to the West. Nor was such "commercial fever" confined to the northern seaboard. South of Baltimore the business leaders of other cities nurtured western ambitions, notably in Charleston and Savannah, but the prizes of western commerce were smaller there and the efforts to win them less impressive.

As population thickened beyond the Appalachians, western cities aspired to empire also. The great movement of people to the West between 1800 and 1860 was mirrored in the population statistics of the major cities of the United States, although western towns or cities did not rival the eastern giants. New York and Philadelphia in 1810 boasted populations of 96,000 and 92,000 respectively; New Orleans, the southern entrepôt of the Mississippi valley, ranked fifth among the nation's cities in that year, having 17,000 residents. The second most populous city of the West, Cincinnati, was twelfth largest in the country, claiming 12,500 inhabitants. By 1860, the giant of the American cities, New York, had pushed beyond the million mark in population, outstripping eastern competitors as well as dwarfing the fledging metropolises of the West. But five of the western centers were now among the nine largest American cities, ranging from New Orleans, claiming 169,000 residents through Cincinnati, St. Louis and Chicago to Buffalo, a city of 80,000 people. During the next half-century, the interior cities continued to grow, some, particularly Chicago, more rapidly than others, and other regional giants developed on the fringe of the Plains, within the mountain regions and on the west coast. Businessmen of the western cities competed with regional or local rivals in developing transportation routes and facilities much as the great rivals of the northern and central seaboard had struggled to control western traffic and commerce during the early nineteenth century. After the transportation network was established, western producers and middle men became feverishly interested in the rate structure which could spell success or failure for their enterprises and their city.

We distort the picture of western economic growth if we consider only the large urban centers that developed in the new regions. The hopeful residents of hundreds of hamlets aspired to urban greatness and contributed to the settling of the western country, although only a few of their urban centers achieved regional empire. Historians have usually pictured some real, or imagined geographical advantage as the seed of urbanism, the magnet that drew a nucleus of merchants, tradesmen, craftsmen and professional folk. The head of navigation on river or creek, the junction of road and canal, a sheltered lake port, a portage around falls or rapids on a major river, the fall in stream or the configuration of bank that promised abundant supplies of power for grist or saw mills, the meeting place of trail or interregional road with waterway, the presence of a good ford or a convenient ferry site on a stream of consequence, the presence of mineral deposits, salt, coal, lead or other useful or precious metal—these were locational advantages which singly or in combination have been used to explain the development of urban centers at particular places in the West of the nineteenth century.

Considerations of defense and government administration also might affect the process of sifting and selection which determined the success or failure of sites with one or more natural advantages. Little clusters of population sought protection beside the early army posts of the Ohio valley. When the soldiers moved on to new frontiers, a center's usefulness in the economic development of the region determined its future. Most nineteenth-century Americans believed that the seat of government should be located in the center of its constituency, although there were scandalous exceptions to the rule. Thus some locations were considered more appropriate as the sites of territorial or state capitals or county seats than others. In retrospect, indeed, we find that some western capitals and county seats had only their central location to commend them.

Scholars have agreed that the development of the railroad changed the game of city building somewhat. Interior cities, having less than adequate water connections, could now play an important role in the economic development of a considerable region. But the aspirations of business leaders in such cities depended on their success in obtaining adequate railroad linkages with all of the cities that would benefit their trade. To achieve this end urban promoters might have to convince the disdainful officers of several railroad companies that they should provide new connections or reroute projected lines. When such overtures were fruitless, town or city fathers sometimes tried to organize their own railroad companies. Beyond the Mississippi and particularly beyond the Missouri, the railroad companies constructed track in thinly settled country, and shaped urban developments significantly by the location of their lines and stations. Sometimes the railroad corporations actively promoted the towns along their lines or created affiliate companies to do so as in the case of some land grant roads. "Whereas Eastern cities built railroads," wrote one author, "in the West railroads built cities."

The particular locational advantages of some western cities are often emphasized. At Pittsburgh, immigrants and goods, in part land borne from the East, could transfer to the Ohio River system. Louisville grew fat on the portage business generated by the fall of the Ohio there. The rich valleys of the Miami rivers poured out their agricultural surplus at Cincinnati. At Buffalo, the Erie Canal tapped the traffic of the lakes. Rail shipments from huge western hinterlands found their most direct or convenient route eastward through Chicago, a canal terminus and lake port as well. St. Louis stood at the junction of the Missouri and Mississippi rivers and accepted traffic from the Ohio as well. New Orleans guarded the outlet of the magnificent inland water system formed by those great rivers and their tributaries. Natural harbors and river outlets, it is said, explain much of the success of the frontier metropolises on the west coast. Between the Missouri and the coastal ranges of the Pacific slope the story is admittedly more complex. The specific influence of river, trail, railroad builder and resource location have often seemed less than obvious there.

The social scientist who is concerned with locational theory is skeptical of the heavy stress on natural advantages, so frequently found in historical accounts of urban development. Agricultural regions, as was much of the American West, some of them suggest, would generate service centers at appropriate spatial intervals even if there were no sites with unusual locational advantages. The location of such elemental settlements, to quote one economist, would "depend upon the equilibrating interaction of transportation costs and specialization and size. . . ." A second stage of growth might begin if some characteristic of the site promised attractive profits to local entrepreneurs. This is the point at which most of the factors so frequently stressed by historians would come into play. Still further growth would occur if "urbanization economies or a pull upon market oriented industries" was generated. In general historians have not successfully integrated these and related or alternative concepts of location theory into their descriptions of the development of American urban centers. The nineteenth-century town and city promoter seems to have thought in terms very similar to those used by most historians. This is not surprising because historians have been influenced by the rhetoric and reminiscences of the promoters.

Although they were happily ignorant of the fine points of "comparative site advantage, scale economies in transportation or agglomeration . . . the ordering effect of distance on the spatial distribution of activities," or even the concept of the urban center as an ecosystem, many westerners sensed that the road to riches lay in detecting the urban promise of a location and promoting it so that it reached its full potential. Eager town promoters purchased town sites from the federal government or from less perceptive westerners, obtained town charters under the territorial or state laws, platted the property into town lots, and hawked them to immigrants and nonresident investors. Some promoters worked singlehanded, others organized town site companies and still other urban property owners worked in informal concert with their neighbors. An efflorescence of western town promotion inevitably marked the upward swing of the business cycle during the nineteenth century. No matter how beautiful the promotional literature or how magnificent the promoter's conception, economic realities shaped the outcome. Some westerners made fortunes in urban real estate but many a promoter platted subdivisions during the nineteenth century which are still cornfield, hay meadow or sagebrush flat. This is not to discount the entrepreneur's influence. There were after all many locations in the West with fine natural advantages; the logic of geography did not necessarily decide that a city must dominate its particular region. The natural advantages at alternate sites might be almost equally impressive. In such a case the efforts of local promoters to provide excellent wharves and warehouses, to police local business practices, to find a source of eastern capital for mill or stockyards, to mobilize local resources in building a bridge or in providing the inducements to attract an additional line of railroad might be crucial in ensuring the success of one urban center to the detriment of the others. Town promoters besieged western legislators in the hope of bringing the capitol, the state university, a normal school, the penitentiary or the insane asylum to their budding metropolis. The imaginative local government, the aggressive board of trade, or the enthusiastic chamber of commerce all contributed to urban success stories in the West. The mongering of scandalous rumors about the present situation and future prospects of rivals was also common and the "booming" editor who could sing the praises of his city and convincingly consign its rivals to limbo was much in demand.

As Charles N. Glaab has pointed out, a class of western promoter-intellectuals, such as William Gilpin, developed in the American West who argued that internal commerce would inevitably create large cities in the interior of the nation and that centers like St. Louis, Chicago, and Kansas City were destined to become great international trading centers because they stood astride "the natural paths of world commerce." Such publicists were equally at home in drawing upon von Humboldt's theories that world population was moving westward "along an isothermal zodiac," and that great cities developed in those latitudes where temperatures were particularly favorable, or in resort to classical and Biblical imagery. At the other extreme promoters bribed legislators, hired gunmen and stole county records in the county seat "wars" which western towns waged with rivals during the latter half of the nineteenth century.

We portray western urbanism too simply if we accept the town boomer's picture of united urban communities determined to prosper whatever the odds. Even in tiny urban nodes residents sometimes disagreed with their fellows because their economic interests differed. Some merchants served the local farmers; other citizens, during the pre-railroad age, specialized in the forwarding business; and other businessmen might wish to develop industry. Factions among the real estate promoters tried to foster new business or home construction on their lands and divert

it from the holdings of rivals. The location of the post office, a new
bank or office building could be crucial in such maneuvering. Robert R.
Dykstra has described the conflict in Kansas cattle towns between
those businessmen who wished to serve the Texas drovers and those
who were more interested in encouraging farmers to develop farms in
the vicinity. Urban communities developed power or leadership structures
very early and an influx of new entrepreneurs or new supplies of capital
might ignite power struggles of great importance to their later development.

Commerce, local trade and the provision of local services were usually
the central concerns of the residents of new urban centers. But the details
and variety of such functions were almost infinite. In smaller centers,
merchants, and in larger communities, commission merchants and forwarding agents, shipped the agricultural produce of the Western regions
as did the factors of the South. In time such men developed systems
of warehouses, elevators, and even commodity exchanges to facilitate
the work. Other merchants handled the flow of supplies and equipment
into the region, breaking bulk, wholesaling and jobbing. Quite early in
their history many towns and cities of the upper Mississippi valley began
to develop processing industries, concentrating bulky products for shipment out of the region. Distilling, milling, livestock packing and canning
were common activities of this type. The capital accumulated in such
industries was soon moving into more complex industry. Cincinnati was
the first western city to benefit spectacularly in this way; but other urban
centers of the region moved in the same direction, some to succeed in
part and others to fail.

Unique concentrations of effort gave a special character to some
western towns and cities. Between 1820 and 1870 this was true of the
outfitting towns located along the elbow of the Missouri River. At Westport, Independence, Nebraska City and several other such centers,
merchants and traders loaded freighting wagons for passage to Santa
Fe, Salt Lake City, the western military posts and the mineral frontiers
of the mountain regions. From these towns also, settlers and miners
launched themselves into the trans-Missouri country. Briefly after 1866,
the cattle towns of the Plains country developed a colorful commerce.
From Missouri to Minnesota, businessmen of the Mississippi River towns
developed a thriving saw mill industry, processing logs which were
floated out of the magnificent pineries of Wisconsin and Minnesota.
This midwestern milling industry inherited traditions rooted in the New
England lumbering industry and passed them on as the pineries of the
Lake states became exhausted to newer mill towns in the far West and

in the South. The mining towns of the mountain and Pacific coast territories and states had a character of their own as well. The business of government imparted a unique tone to at least one town in every western county. This was the county seat; local residents and visiting lawyers came to its courthouse, to use the local machinery of criminal and civil justice, of probate, of land and property transfer and, less happily, of taxation, or to consult the county officers who were usually also local political leaders. Federal land offices attracted a motley crowd of speculators, moneylenders, settlers and lawyers to the towns in which they were located. And to the territorial and western state capitals, the flow of customers was even more varied.

Nearby fields and the presence of family milk cows and driving horses gave a rural tone to much town life in the West, but urban dwellers had common problems which set them apart. Not only must they find some measure of agreement in the cause of economic development, they must unite in providing healthful water supplies, adequate sanitation systems, police protection and, in large centers, local transportation facilities. Within the urban clusters stood the masonic lodges and the halls of the Oddfellows or Knights of Temperance. To the village, town or city came the travelling lecturers and entertainers. Here many of the ladies had the leisure to busy themselves in good works or in organized social life. In such activities social distinctions might appear very early in the history of western communities and indeed social and economic stratification was generally present in western as well as eastern towns and cities. Leadership in the economic, social and cultural life of their localities and regions did not win the universal gratitude that urban dwellers believed their due. The line between city or town folks and country folks was drawn early in the new settlements; the countryman suspected that the urban resident gouged him and was certain that town women were "stuck up" or "put on airs." Prairie and plains country farmers demanded a herd law which would require the owners of livestock to keep them enclosed; townsmen wished to allow their animals to graze at large in the countryside. In this and many other petty sources of conflict we find the roots of the rural–urban distrust which reached fever heat in the days of the Granger and the Populist.

Despite the growing research in urban history the western townsman is still a rather elusive figure. Did he migrate from eastern urban centers, or was he an eastern or western farm boy? Was he more or less mobile than the members of the farming, mining, and lumbering labor forces that passed through his store, shop, office or place of work? Was he in general of the same ethnocultural background as the people whom he served? Was he more or less successful in amassing wealth than were they? To what extent was he better educated than residents in the rural hinterland? We have some partial answers to such questions but they by no means are fully answered yet.

In retrospect the energy and achievements of the western town builders are as impressive in every way as the tenacity and fields of the agricultural pioneer. Yet the waste in human energy and capital entailed in competitive town promotion has also impressed scholars. In an earlier age, European princes developed their frontier domains by establishing towns to serve as nuclei of settlements. The United States government went no further in this direction than an abortive attempt to have its surveyors select locations which were to be sold as town sites. Would closer government supervision of the urban process in the West have produced urban services and leadership more effectively and cheaply than was the case? To this question, the historian cannot give a firm answer.

RICHARD C. WADE

Urban Life in Western America, 1790–1830

Other scholars had described the early history of some
western towns and cities before Richard C. Wade published
the article from which this reading is taken. But none
had so directly considered the relation of urbanization to the
westward movement and frontier institutions as did he. Based
upon study of the leading towns of the Ohio valley during
the pioneer period, his generalizations provide the historians
of other urban frontiers with useful insights and the basis
for both comparison and contrast.

The towns were the spearheads of the American frontier. Planted as
forts or trading posts far in advance of the line of settlement, they held
the West for the approaching population. Indeed, in 1763, when the
British drew the Proclamation Line across the Appalachians to stop the
flow of migrants, a French merchant company prepared to survey the
streets of St. Louis, a thousand miles through the wilderness. Whether
as part of French and Spanish activity from New Orleans or part of
Anglo-American operations from the Atlantic seaboard, the establishment of towns preceded the breaking of soil in the transmontane
West. . . .

Furthermore, these urban outposts grew rapidly even in their infant
decades. By 1815 Pittsburgh, already a thriving industrial center, had
8,000 inhabitants, giving it a slight margin over Lexington. Cincinnati
estimated its population at 4,000 at the end of the war with Great Britain,
while farther west Louisville and St. Louis neared half that figure. . . .

Not all the towns founded in the trans-Allegheny region in this period
fared as well, however. Many never developed much beyond a survey
and a newspaper advertisement. Others, after promising beginnings,
slackened and settled down to slow and unspectacular development. Still
others flourished briefly then faded, leaving behind a grim story of de-

SOURCE: Abridged from Richard C. Wade, "Urban Life in Western America,
1790–1830," *American Historical Review*, LXIV (October, 1958), 14-30. Reprinted
by permission of the author.

serted mills, broken buildings, and aging people—the West's first harvest of ghost towns. . . .

Despite many failures, these abortive attempts to plant towns were significant, for they reveal much about the motives of the people who came West in the early period. Many settlers moved across the mountains in search of promising towns rather than good land, their inducements being urban opportunities rather than fertile soil. . . .

The West's young cities owed their initial success to commerce. All sprang from it, and their growth in the early years of the century stemmed from its expansion. Since the Ohio River was the chief artery of trade and travel, the towns along its banks prospered most. Pittsburgh, where the Allegheny meets the Monongahela, commanded the entire valley; Cincinnati served the rich farm lands of Kentucky and Ohio; Louisville fattened on the transshipment of goods around the Falls; and St. Louis, astride the Mississippi, was the focus of far-flung enterprises, some of which reached to the Pacific Ocean. Even Lexington, landlocked in a country of water highways, grew up as the central mart of Kentucky and Tennessee. . . .

As these commercial centers grew, some inhabitants turned to manu-, facturing. Indeed, this new interest spread so rapidly in Pittsburgh that in 1810 a resident likened the place to "a large workshop," and already travelers complained of the smoke and soot. . . .

As the cities grew they staked out extensive commercial claims over the entire West. Timothy Flint calculated that Cincinnati was the central market for over a million people, while a resident asserted that its trade was "co-extensive with steamboat navigation on the western waters." Louisville's economic penetration was scarcely less impressive. As early as 1821, a local editor declared that "the people of the greater part of Indiana, all Kentucky, and portions of Tennessee, Alabama, Illinois, Missouri, now report to this place for dry goods, groceries, hardware and queensware." St. Louis' empire touched Santa Fe on the south, Canada on the north, and the Pacific on the west. "It is doubtful if history affords the example of another city," wrote Hiram M. Chittenden, "which has been the exclusive mart for so vast an area as that which was tributary to St. Louis."

In carving out these extensive dependencies, the young metropolises overwhelmed their smaller neighbors. The rise of St. Louis destroyed the ambitions of Edwardsville across the Mississippi, which once harbored modest hopes of importance. Pittsburgh's recovery in the late twenties condemned Wheeling and Steubenville to minor roles in the upper Ohio region. And Louisville's development swallowed two Kentucky neighbors while reducing Jeffersonville and New Albany on the Indiana side of the river to mere appendages.

Not satisfied with such considerable conquests, the cities reached out for more. Seeking wider opportunities, they built canals and turnpikes and, even before 1830, planned railroads to strengthen their position. Cincinnati, Pittsburgh, and St. Louis tried to tap the increasing trade on the Great Lakes by water links to the North. Pennsylvania's Iron City also hoped to become a major station on the National Road, and for a decade its Washington representatives lobbied to win that commercial bond with the East. Lexington, suffocating in its inland position, frantically strove for better connections with the Ohio River. A turnpike to Maysville was dashed by Jackson's veto, technical difficulties made a canal to the Kentucky River impractical, but some belated hope rose with the possibility of a railroad to Louisville or Cincinnati.

The intensive search for new advantages brought rivalry and conflict. Though the commerce of the whole West lay untouched before them, the cities quarreled over its division. Thus Louisville and Cincinnati fought over a canal around the Falls of the Ohio. The Kentucky town, feeling that its strength depended upon maintaining the break in transportation, obstructed every attempt to circumvent the rapids. Only when Ohio interests threatened to dig on the Indiana side did Louisville move ahead with its own project. Likewise, harsh words flew between Wheeling and Pittsburgh as they contended for the Ohio River terminus of the National Road. Smaller towns, too, joined the struggle. Cleveland and Sandusky, for instance, clashed over the location of the Ohio Canal, the stake being nothing less than control of the mounting trade between the Valley and the lakes. And their instinct to fight was sound, for the outcome shaped the future of both places. . . .

Despite inadequate charters and modest incomes, urban governments played a decisive role in the growth of Western cities. Since these were commercial towns, local authorities paid special attention to mercantile requirements. They not only constructed market houses but also extended municipal regulation over a wide variety of trading activity. Ordinances protected the public against adulterated foods, false measurements, and rigged prices. Some municipalities went even farther and assumed responsibility for seeing that "justice is done between buyer and seller." In search of this objective, officials fixed prices on some goods, excluded monopolies from the market, and tried to equalize opportunities for smaller purchasers. To facilitate access to the exchange center, they lavished time and money on the development of wharves and docks and the improvement of streets.

Municipalities also tackled a wide variety of other problems growing out of urban life. Fire protection, at first casually organized, was placed on a more formal basis. Volunteer companies still provided the manpower, but government participation increased markedly. Local councils legislated against many kinds of fire hazards, and public money furnished most of the equipment. Moreover some places, haunted by the image of Detroit's disaster in 1805, forbade the construction of wooden buildings in the heart of the city, a measure which not only reduced fire risks but also changed the face of downtown areas. The development of adequate police was much slower. By 1830 only Lexington and Louisville had regular patrols, and these were established with the intent more of control of slaves than the general protection of life and property. In other towns law enforcement was lax by day and absent at night, though the introduction of gas lighting in Pittsburgh and Cincinnati in the late twenties made the after-dark hours there less dangerous than before.

Congested living created new health hazards and especially increased the likelihood of epidemics. Every place suffered, but none like Louisville, which earned a grim reputation as the "Graveyard of the West" because of the constant visitations of yellow fever and malaria. Cities took preventive measures, such as draining stagnant ponds and clearing streets and lots, and also appointed boards of health to preside over the problem. Municipal water systems, introduced in Pittsburgh and Cincinnati before 1830, made life healthier and certainly more comfortable, while the discussion of installing underground sewers pointed to still more extensive reform in sanitation.

In meeting urban problems, Western officials drew heavily on Eastern experience. Lacking precedents of their own, and familiar with the techniques of older cities, they frankly patterned their practice on Eastern models. There was little innovation. When confronted by a new question, local authorities responded by adopting tested solutions. This emulation characterized nearly every aspect of development—from the width of streets to housing regulations. No major improvement was launched without a close study of established seaboard practices. . . .

As transmontane cities developed they created societies whose ways and habits contrasted sharply with those of the countryside. Not only was their physical environment distinct, but their interests, activities, and pace of life also differed greatly. . . .

One of the most conspicuous differences was in social structure. The stratification of urban societies was in marked contrast with the boisterous equality of the countryside. Social lines developed very quickly in the city. Though not as tightly drawn as in the East, they represented the meaningful distinctions in Western communities. The groupings were basically economic, though professional people were set apart by their interest and training, and Negroes by their color. No rigid boundaries divided the classes, and movement between them was constant. Yet differences did exist; people felt them and contemporaries thought them significant. . . .

These divisions deepened in the postwar years. As the cities grew the sense of neighborliness and intimacy diminished, giving way to the impersonality characteristic of urban living. To old-timers the changing social configuration bred a deep nostalgia and raised the image of happier, simpler days. . . . Having come from places where differences mattered, early city dwellers tried to re-create them in a new setting. The urge for status was stronger than the appeal of equality, and as the towns expanded cleavages deepened.

Urban ways were further distinguished from rural habits by the collective approach to many problems. City living created issues which could not always be solved by the highly individualistic methods of agrarian society. Local governments assumed an ever wider responsibility for the conduct of community affairs, and voluntary associations handled a large variety of other questions. . . .

Rural and metropolitan West were also separated by distinctive social and cultural developments. The towns very quickly produced a surprisingly rich and diversified life, offering opportunities in many fields similar to those of Eastern cities but lacking on the farm or frontier. They enjoyed a virtual monopoly of printing presses, newspapers, bookstores, and circulating libraries. Theaters sprang up to encourage local players and traveling troupes, while in larger places museums brought the curious and the scientific to the townfolks. In addition, every week brought numerous lectures and debates on all kinds of topics, keeping urban residents abreast of the latest discoveries and developments in every field. . . .

This leadership extended into almost every field. For example, the educational opportunities of town children greatly exceeded those of their rural neighbors. Every municipality developed a complex of private tuition schools topped by an academy and, in every place except Louisville, a college. Moreover, the cities organized the movement for public schooling. . . .

Nor was this urban leadership surprising. The cities, as the great population centers, felt the educational pressure first and most acutely. In addition, they alone had the wealth needed to launch ambitious projects for large numbers of children. Hence the towns were ready for comprehensive public programs long before the countryside. . . .

No less striking than cultural cleavages were the differences in rural and urban religious development. Progress in the cities was steadier and more substantial—though less spectacular—than in the back country. Traveling ministers might refer to Pittsburgh as "a young hell, a second Sodom," and Francis Asbury might complain in 1803 that he felt "the power of Satan in those little, wicked western trading towns," but both churches and membership multiplied rapidly in urban centers. Furthermore, the growth owed nothing to the sporadic revivals which burned across the countryside at the beginning of the century. These movements were essentially rural, having their roots in the isolation of agricultural living and the spiritual starvation of people unattended by regular services. The city situation, with its constant contacts and settled church organizations, involved neither of these elements. Instead, religious societies proliferated, sects took on such additional functions as charity and missionary work, and congregations sent money back East to aid their seminaries. Far from being sinks of corruption, Western cities quickly became religious centers, supplying Bibles to the frontier, assisting foreign missions, and, in the twenties, building theological schools to provide priests and ministers for the whole region.

Political life also reflected the growing rural-urban division. Though the rhetoric of the period often obscured them, differences existed from the very beginning. Suspicion of the towns led states to avoid economic and cultural centers when locating their capitals. Nearly all of these cities sought the prize, but none was successful. . . .

Of course, farm dwellers easily outnumbered urbanites, but the latter wielded disproportionate power. The case of Jefferson and Oldham counties in Kentucky was illustrative. In the mid-twenties the combined vote reached 3,200, Louisville residents casting roughly a quarter of them. Yet the state senator and both representatives came from the city. . . . The situation was the same elsewhere. At one time all of Missouri's representatives in Washington—two senators and one congressman—as well as its governor came from St. Louis.

The cities' political influence rested on their ability to produce leadership. As the economic and intellectual centers of transmontane life they attracted the talented and ambitious in all fields. Politics was no exception. Nearly all the great spokesmen of the West had important urban connections and their activity often reflected the demands of their town constituents. Henry Clay was one of Lexington's most prominent lawyers when he went to the United States Senate in 1806. Thomas Hart Benton held local offices in St. Louis before moving on to the national scene, and William Henry Harrison, though he lived in nearby North Bend, had deep roots in Cincinnati affairs through most of his long public life. . . .

By 1830, then, the West had produced two types of society—one rural and one urban. Each developed its own institutions, habits, and living patterns. The countryside claimed much the larger population and often gave to transmontane affairs an agrarian flavor. But broadcloth was catching up with buckskin. The census of 1830 revealed the disproportionate rate of city growth. While the state of Ohio had four times as many inhabitants as it counted in 1810, Cincinnati's increase was twelvefold. The story was the same elsewhere. Lousville's figure showed a growth of 650 per cent compared with Kentucky's 50 per cent, and Pittsburgh tripled in size while Pennsylvania did not quite double its population. By 1830 the rise of these cities had driven a broad wedge of urbanism into Western life.

Though town and country developed along different paths, clashes were still infrequent. The West was large enough to contain both movements comfortably. Indeed, each supported the other. The rural regions supplied the cities with raw materials for their mills and packinghouses and offered an expanding market to their shops and factories. In turn, urban centers served the surrounding areas by providing both the necessities and comforts of life as well as new opportunity for ambitious farm youths. Yet the cities represented the more aggressive and dynamic force. By spreading their economic power over the entire section, by bringing the fruits of civilization across the mountains, and by insinuating their ways into the countryside, they speeded up the transformation of the West from a gloomy wilderness to a richly diversified region. Any historical view which omits this aspect of Western life tells but part of the story.

·2·

CHARLES N. GLAAB

Business Patterns in the Growth of a Midwestern City: The Kansas City Business Community Before the Civil War

Here Charles N. Glaab summarizes the various patterns of business enterprise which contributed to the early growth of Kansas City. Of particular interest to him is the way in which businessmen adapted their activities to the economic realities of urban development and from his study he derives a hypothesis to explain the success of the leaders who accumulated fortunes.

. . . During the 1830's and 1840's, a complex of small trading towns —Independence, Parkville, Weston, Westport, and Kansas City—had sprung up along the Missouri-Kansas border to serve commerce. For the first fifteen years of its existence, Kansas City was little more than a collection of warehouses and general stores at the junction of the Kaw and Missouri rivers. The settlement functioned as an entrepôt of the river-caravan trade, a convenient location where goods could be easily transferred from steamboat to wagon for shipment to a distant hinterland. There is no evidence that the group of traders and merchants who platted the town site in 1839 foresaw that it would ever be much more than this.

By 1858, however, Kansas City had begun to eclipse these local rivals and until the Civil War was steadily to increase in population, wealth, and trade. The rapid settlement of Kansas Territory after 1854 had posed a new possibility—the development of a more general commercial center. The new territory provided a rich trade area that could furnish the base for the rise of a regional city, and, in the light of this possibility, local businessmen accepted the challenge to modify their lines of activity.

SOURCE: Abridged from Charles N. Glaab, "Business Patterns in the Growth of a Midwestern City: The Kansas City Business Community Before the Civil War," *Business History Review*, XXXIII (Summer, 1959), 156-174. © 1959, Graduate School of Business Administration, Harvard University. Reprinted by permission of the *Business History Review* and Charles N. Glaab.

In spite of the large immediate profits that were made in the overland trade down to the Civil War, participation in it was not the real basis for permanent fortune in the city. The careers of early local business leaders and their families show that long-range business success was the result of willingness at an early date to respond to the challenge of accommodating individual business ambitions to the broader design of building a city: to shift from Western merchandising to other fields such as banking and real estate, which were directly related to urban economic functions, and to organize joint business efforts and community projects necessary to foster city growth.

Because of the unspecialized character of frontier enterprise, these adjustments in patterns of business activity in the transition from trading depot to city cannot be described with exactness. From the beginning, all business arrangements in the town were fluid and informal; no trader or merchant operated without a number of partners who came and went, moving from one firm to another. Nearly all mercantile houses combined to some degree the functions of the general store and the commission agent; not until shortly before the Civil War did any significant specialization take place. All local merchants invested in land; such investment in a frontier environment was almost a reflex action.

Nevertheless, it is possible to divide into two main groups the early local business leaders who were closely involved in the process of town building. First, there were traders and merchants who selected the town as a site for their operations in the western trade, sometimes moving well-established businesses from neighboring communities. Later many of them were drawn to other interests related to town growth and especially to the promotion of city additions. By the time of the Civil War many of the early commission men and merchants had sold their warehouses and stores to outside interests, notably St. Louis investors, in order to devote full effort to real estate development. Secondly, there was a diverse group of casual land buyers who had purchased tracts of land in the locale long before it became a townsite and accordingly had a direct stake in its growth. . . .

There was, however, another group among the landed in the Kansas City business community who were more deliberately speculative. They came West with money after the Kansas-Nebraska Act, looking for ripe investment opportunities which they found in the young town. These late arrivals were vigorous and systematic town boomers who brought to the development of their holdings astute promotional techniques. They accompanied a new stage in the city's development, for they reinforced the conviction developing among the early leaders that success lay in tying individual business ambitions to the broader ambition of building a city and provided much of the means for achieving this goal. . . .

The most important organization established to back the necessary programs was the Kansas City Chamber of Commerce. For all practical purposes, the Chamber was the effective government of the city in the years before the war, and its actions indicate the range of the business community's interests. Efforts were made to persuade the federal government that Kansas City should be the starting point for mail service to California; to improve navigation facilities on the Kansas River; to obtain state charters for local insurance and banking companies; to extend the city limits; to import goods directly from Europe by way of the Gulf of Mexico; and to remove the Indians from Kansas Territory. Most important, the Chamber was the organization through which the city leaders expressed their railroad program. This was the central concern of local businessmen, for they recognized that if their design for a great city was to be realized, and city additions and other properties were to be profitable speculations, railroads built into the region would have to pass through Kansas City.

By 1860 Kansas City's business leaders were beginning to regard the city's future as secure. Population growth had been rapid and steady—reaching over 4,000 according to the census reports, although local estimates were much higher. The Santa Fe trade, the government freighting business, the proposed terminus of the Pacific Railroad of Missouri all were located there. "Complete the Pacific and our future is safe," asserted Van Horn in the *Journal.* "We have but to finish what we have so well begun and all is well. The beginning has already more than gratified our expectations and the end will perfect our hopes."

The outbreak of war shattered this optimism and brought about drastic changes in the organization of the economic life of the city. By and large, the city founders were of Southern descent. A majority held slaves and were pro-Southern in attitude. In the pre-Civil War controversies, however, and particularly during the Border Troubles, local business leaders adopted an attitude of careful political neutrality. This position was in sharp contrast to the attitudes of neighboring communities where politics was emphasized at the expense of business. Reid and McGee modified their pro-Southern positions and [Kersey L.] Coates softened his equally intense pro-Northern view to conform to a more practical consensus. But with the outbreak of fighting, this studied neutrality broke down. Unsettled conditions along the border, depredations on the Santa Fe trail, the expulsion of pro-Southern businessmen caused an enormous upheaval. The current of immigration came to a standstill, and the town's population declined by over a half. All government freighting and much of the private traffic was transferred to better protected Leavenworth in 1861. Kansas City lost its position as the freighting capital of the plains, and the coming of the railroads during the war was to destroy the overland caravan trade for all time.

The ranks of the city's business community thinned out. Some were expelled; others left of their own accord to weather out the storm elsewhere. Many of the early prominent merchants such as Franklin Conant and Jesse Riddlesbarger were ruined by the war. But a majority of the business leaders held on or returned to build fortunes. And it is significant that they did so almost exclusively through real estate. Livestock, grain, and meat packing, the industries which constituted the basis for the city's revival and its rapid and spectacular growth, were controlled in large part by outside investors, such as the Armours in meat packing, or by those who transferred well-established businesses from other locations. Not one instance of a prewar merchandising, wholesale, or commission business surviving into the postwar era under the same ownership has been found. But those who owned city additions and other property and who kept their holdings, as most of them did, and who took up the task of redevelopment at war's end were frequently rewarded with large fortunes. Business success in Kansas City thus bore a fundamental relation to participation in an identifiable "urban enterprise." Early town founders and business leaders made large-scale profits largely through shaping their aspirations at an early date to the most optimistic forecasts concerning the town's future, investing in enterprises in accordance with this possibility, and concentrating their collective efforts on intensive community promotion. In this fashion, individual business interest in early Kansas City came to bear a striking relationship to what can be called the general interest of the city. The example of Kansas City suggests that a major source for business profits in the development of the West lay in a nearly complete identification with the fortunes of a town site from the first stages of its growth.

·3·

ROBERT R. DYKSTRA

Wild Bill Hickok in Abilene

How was law and order to be maintained in the frontier town? The question was unimportant in some of the hamlets of the agricultural frontier. But when frontier resources, and the business based upon them, attracted large numbers of transients, town builders often faced the difficult problem of preventing violence and punishing crime while maintaining the good will of those who brought custom to local business-men. West of the Mississippi the frontier lawman sometimes played a role in resolving the dilemma. Robert R. Dykstra probes the myth of one of the most famous, "Wild Bill" Hickok.

"I was raised," remarked Dwight Eisenhower in a 1953 speech, "in a little town. . . . called Abilene, Kansas. We had as our marshal for a long time a man named Wild Bill Hickok." The town had a code, said the President. "It was: Meet anyone face to face with whom you disagree. . . . If you met him face to face and took the same risks he did, you could get away with almost anything, as long as the bullet was in front." This invoking of a curious "fair play" symbol in the depths of the McCarthy era illustrates perhaps more pungently than could anything else the continuing status of James Butler Hickok (1837–1876) as a hero for Americans. . . .

The traditional view of Hickok in Abilene—the grim, vigilant peace officer who single-handedly imposed a cast-iron rule on the worst of tempestuous frontier towns, but who had to kill frequently in doing it— lives on in formal American social history as well as in media wherein one more readily expects to find it: television, motion pictures, and children's literature.

What are the facts? In what ways does the traditional image, as well as the image modifications, reflect them? Municipal records have sur-

SOURCE: Abridged from Robert R. Dykstra, "Wild Bill Hickok in Abilene," *Journal of the Central Mississippi Valley American Studies Association* (Fall, 1961), 20-48. Reprinted by permission of *Midcontinent American Studies Journal* and Robert R. Dykstra.

vived. Consisting of the *City of Abilene Minute Book* and the *City of Abilene Ordinance Book,* they contain, respectively, the minutes of the Abilene city council which met in regular session one or two evenings a week, and the texts of city ordinances passed and revised by the council. Together they record an official view of Hickok's marshalship.

Wild Bill's name appears first in the minutes of the meeting of April 15, 1871: "J. B. Hicocks appointed by the Mayor as Marshall. Unanimously confirmed[.]" Four days later a section of an ordinance was unanimously approved in an otherwise stormy session which set Hickok's salary at $150 per month, plus 25 per cent of fines against violators arrested by himself. At the meeting of April 21 his bond was set at $1,000 and section five of a new ordinance laid out his duties:

> The marshal shall be industrious & vigilant, not only in preventing any infraction of the ordinances of said city, and bring[ing] offenders against them to justice, but also in causing the prosecution or punishment of offences against the penal laws of the State of Kansas committed within said City, and in suppressing disturbances, affrays, riots, and other breaches of the peace therein. He shall keep an account of all moneys received by him for the use of said City, and pay the same to the treasurer thereof on the first Saturday of every month and take his receipt therefor, and do & perform all such other duties as are now or hereafter may be required of him by said Council.

By April 24 the new marshal was at work. . . .

June 24 witnessed a new "Miscellaneous Ordinance" which made the carrying and discharge of firearms within city limits, as well as the carrying of dirks and bowie knives, a crime. The same document reaffirmed the compensation schedule for the marshal, but in addition made him street commissioner at no additional pay. In this capacity Hickok was delegated to investigate complaints about street obstructions and nuisances, to have the same removed by employing prisoners from the jail or hired laborers, and in general to "see that all laws, ordinances[,] Resolutions, and contracts passed or entered into by said Council and regulating or in any way referring to the streets, alleys, sidewalks[,] gutters[,] conduits or bridges of said city be strictly enforced." Later in the summer the commissioner also was made responsible for hiring surveyors for proposed thoroughfares, initiating the submission of labor cost estimates for street improvements, and for hiring and supervising labor for certain small jobs authorized by the council.

At the regular meeting of June 28 the marshal was authorized payment of 50 cents "for killing each and every dog not properly registered as required by ordinance." . . .

On July 8 Councilman Smith was appointed "to confer with the City

Marshall, defining him certain duties to be performed." The council then ordered that "A" Street be cleared of obstructions. A week later Hickok was ordered "to stop dance houses and the [presumably unlicensed] vending of Whiskeys[,] Brandies &c in McCoys Addition," the brothel district southeast of town. On July 22 he was directed "to close up all dead & Brace Gambling Games and to arrest all Cappers for the aforesaid Games"—that is, to suppress crooked gambling. . . .

The files of the weekly Abilene *Chronicle* for 1871, marred by only occasional missing issues, provide . . . an insight into the local attitude toward Wild Bill—that is, the public view of his marshalship. No issues of the paper survive covering the date Hickok was sworn in; the first mention of the new marshal is in the edition of May 18, wherein the mayor was criticized for his handling of the absconding councilman affair. "The councilman was arrested and carried into the room by the Marshal," noted the editor. "There was not the least shadow of law for such a proceeding, there being no ordinance to compel the attendance of councilmen. Of course the Marshal simply obeyed orders—whether legal or not—and is not to blame." The editor was especially angry that Mayor McCoy as a joke had an engraving made in Topeka of Wild Bill carrying the councilman on his shoulder over the title "Who's Mayor Now?" The same edition, which printed several anti-McCoy items, carried a signed statement by two councilmen that the mayor had tried to influence their voting on a controversial saloon tax issue. The two councilmen stood for a high tax, the mayor for a low one. The difference, McCoy was alleged to have said, would be made up by having Hickok, "(who Mr. McCoy said would do anything he wanted,) when the gamblers and bad women came into the city, collect fines from them . . . and no one wo'd be the wiser for it." The editor endorsed this laying-bare of the scheme, but did not comment on the marshal's proposed role in it.

On June 8 the paper noted with pleasure that Hickok "has posted up printed notices, informing all persons that the ordinance against carrying fire arms or other weapons in Abilene, will be enforced." Throughout the summer the paper documented the city council's campaign against organized sin in Abilene, but made no mention of Hickok's part in it. The July 13 *Chronicle* criticized policeman McDonald who "under orders" arrested a stranger for gambling after he had lost $1,025, but who ignored the professional gambler taking the money. Apparently the marshal did not figure in the incident. The issue of August 3 noted that Lake's Circus had exhibited in Abilene, but no specific mention was made of the future Mrs. Hickok.

The first mention of the marshal since early June, and the first extensive notice of his activities, occurred with the October 12 writeup of the Coe–Hickok gunfight.

SHOOTING AFFRAY
Two Men Killed

On last Thursday evening a number of men got on a "spree," and compelled several citizens and others to "stand treat," catching them on the street and carrying them upon their shoulders into the saloons. The crowd served the Marshal, commonly called "Wild Bill," in this manner. He treated, but told them that they must keep within the bounds of order or he would stop them. They kept on, until finally one of the crowd, named Phil. Coe, fired a revolver. The Marshal heard the report and knew at once that the leading spirits in the crowd, numbering probably fifty men, intended to get up a "fight." He immediately started to quell the affair and when he reached the Alamo saloon, in front of which the crowd had gathered, he was confronted by Coe, who said that he had fired the shot at a dog. Coe had his revolver in his hand, as had also other parties in the crowd. As quick as thought the Marshal drew two revolvers and both men fired almost simultaneously. Several shots were fired, during which Mike Williams, a policemen [sic], came around the corner for the purpose of assisting the Marshal, and rushing between him and Coe received two of the shots intended for Coe. The whole affair was the work of an instant. The Marshal, surrounded by the crowd, and standing in the light, did not recognize Williams whose death he deeply regrets. Coe was shot through the stomach, the ball coming out through his back; he lived in great agony until Sunday evening; he was a gambler, but a man of natural good impulses in his better moments. It is said that he had a spite at Wild Bill and had threatened to kill him—which Bill believed he would do if he gave him the opportunity. One of Coe's shots went through Bill's coat and another passed between his legs striking the floor behind him. The fact is Wild Bill's escape was truly marvelous. The two men were not over eight feet apart, and both of them large, stout men. One or two others in the crowd were hit, but none seriously. . . .

A third source of information offers an insight into the private life of Abilene's marshal. While gathering materials on local history, J. B. Edwards, an Abilene businessman and antiquarian, gained contact in the 1920's with one Charles F. Gross of Chicago. Gross, a native Illinoisian, had been brought to Abilene as a young man by Joseph McCoy. In a series of letters, which on Edwards' death were obtained by the Kansas Historical Society, Gross proved an amazingly uninhibited informant, with a memory for detail balanced by a fondness for piquant generalization. . . . [Here follows an excerpt from one of the Gross letters.]

[In] The many talks I had with Bill I do not now recall any remark, or refference to any Woman other than those he made to the One he lived with in the Small house & he did not Ever show bifore me any Especial affection for her—What he called her I do not recall but *I do Know he was on Guard Even against her*[.] I was there alone with the two Many times but I was Very carefull never to go unless I knew Bill was Home & always there was good reason for my going. Having to go Early one morning Bill was still in Bed & when I went to the door and the woman came to let me in she saw through the window who I was.—she was only just up & was still in night dress[.] Bill said "let him in; you dont give a Dam for Gross seeing you"; but she did and showed it in looks. she went into the next room & Bill got up leasurely and as he sat side ways on the Bed I saw he had his 6 shooter in his right hand and on the Bed spread lay a sawed off shot Gun (Double Barreled) with a strap on it so he could swing it over his shoulder and Carry it under his Coat out of sight[.] I dont think the Barrell was More than a 1-1/2 feet long—to my surprise as soon as Bill was dressed, all but Coat & Hat—he went carefully to the door [,] looked all arround for several mts & then Emptied one 6 shooter. He had the one in Each hand, returned to the room[,] cleaned & reloaded it, then went to the door & Empt[i]ed the Other one & reload[e]d it the same way. . . . so I said, did you get your Guns damp yesterday Bill? he said "*no*, but I aint ready to go yet & I am not taking any chances, when I draw & pull I *must be sure*. You are the Only person in Abilene I will go to sleep with in the same room that I do not make things as sure as I Know how when I awake." I went fishing with Bill once at Hoffmans Dam & when we got in the Buggie Bill threw on 2 extra pistols and on our way home we stopped at a clear spot by some Cotto[n] woods & he & [I] put up a piece of paper on a tree as near the size of a mans body as we could guess & about the h[e]ight of Navel—(a 6 foot man) [.] the paper was about 6 in long with a spot in the Center half way. We stepped off 20 feet & he asked me to "wait a few moments," he Kind of slouched and did not appe[a]r to be looking at anything[.] he said "Keep talking & then suddenly without any hesitation in your talk, say *Draw* (Kinder qu[i]ck)"[.]

He shot six times so quick it startled me, for his 6 was in his Holster when I said "Draw"[.] I was looking directly at him and only saw a Motion & he was firing. No use to ask how he drew[.] I dont Know[.] I only saw his arm was not straight and stiff[.] there was a preciptible Curve to his arm, but very slight—Every shot was in the paper and two in the spot. . . . He said "I never shot a man with my left hand Except the time when some drunken Soldiers had me down on the floor & were trampling me & then I used both hands. I do not recall that I ever heard Bill say "Killed"[.] He always said "shot"[.] I have wandered away from Your question & I will now return to it only pausing to say, Bill said "Charlie I hope you never have to shoot any man, but if you do[,] shoot him in the Guts near the Navel. *you* may not make a fatal shot, but *he* will get a shock that will paralize his brain and arm so much that the fight is all over—

Now Edwards I dont think Bill Ever was married[.] if he did it was before the War & back in Ills. . . .

When Mrs Lake the Widow of "Old Lake["] of Circus fame Came to Abilene she set up her tent Just West of the D[rovers] Cottage on the Vacant ground[.] Bill was on hand to Keep order. Bill was a Handsome man as you Know & she fell for him hard, fell all the way *Clear to the Basement,* tried her best to get him to marry her & run the Circus[.] Bill told me all about it. I said why dont you do it—He said "I Know she has a good show, but when she is done in the West, she will go East & I dont want any paper collar on, & its me for the West. I would be lost back in the States, and she has a [obscenity deleted] like a Horse Collar anyway—No it wont do." . . .

How does the folk-image of Hickok in Abilene contrast with available documentation? The official records of Abilene in 1871 show Hickok, as city marshal and street commissioner, to have been an essential cog in the routine of municipal management, with an especially important role to play as marshal in the city council's campaign against prostitution, crooked gambling, and illegal liquor-retailing. As street commissioner his duties were also important, yet whether these duties actually occupied his time to any extent is problematical; they of course are not part of the traditional image. There was one recorded case of friction between Hickok and one of his deputies. . . . Some of the modifications of the Hickok image imply similar friction between Wild Bill and the city government. . . . Perhaps more important, the traditional Wild Bill seems to be in a sort of free-agent status as marshal, motivated only by a kind of personal commitment against lawlessness, completely divorced from the prosaic duties of the modern police officer or the discipline and direction of a municipal employer. Modification of the traditional image seems in order on this perhaps subtle but important point.

The public view in Abilene of Wild Bill was evidently unqualified approval—if the *Chronicle* does accurately reflect, as it seems to do, the view of Abilene at large. . . . The editor seems to have known little about routine activity in the disreputable part of town, "Texan" Abilene below the railroad tracks, and this seems to portray the same lack of knowledge by "respectable" Abilene. In short, the majority of the public, like the newspaper, never was well acquainted with Marshal Hickok, but it had the impression that he was a conscientious, nearly single-handed mainstay of law and order in that unstable, dangerous section of town seemingly inhabited by a criminally-oriented population. In this way . . . Abilene citizens apparently took a view of Hickok that conforms rather closely to the Hickok image that is with us today.

The C. F. Gross letter, finally, reveals a Wild Bill far from the controlled, inflexibly fearless traditional type. On the contrary, Hickok appears greatly, perhaps morbidly, fearful of assassination. What occurred, especially after his gunfight with Coe, may have been a kind of occupational paranoia. . . .

Of course, the picture of Wild Bill's pervasive and somewhat unorthodox sex life is most destructive of tradition, with the cruelly offhand remark concerning the woman he was later to court and marry especially damaging. In general, Hickok emerges from the Gross letter as a human being (if of an irritatingly male variety), displaying all the stresses and strains many men would have, given the ordeal of his official position.

One important modification of the tradition, however, remains unverified. This is the assertion that Hickok was willing to stretch the law he was hired to uphold. According to the [Ben] Thompson biography, Hickok was involved with Abilene's authorities in robbing the town's transients. This smacks of the scheme exposed in the *Chronicle* as having been proposed by Mayor McCoy; as a matter of fact, raising civic revenue by regular "fines" levied on semi-legal or illegal elements was commonly done in the Kansas cowtowns, sometimes quite overtly. Hickok may indeed have been party to such a program in Abilene. [John Wesley] Hardin maintained that Hickok also modified the letter of the law in several specific incidents. It is also not improbable that this was the fact, but documentation is lacking.

In conclusion, it can be seen that the traditional image of the Great Lawman diverges in certain fundamental ways from what was probably the real Wild Bill Hickok in Abilene. Perhaps it is fair therefore to speak of a "Hickok Legend," even though . . . accounts of Abilene's marshal have been entwined more or less with the essential facts. In any event it seems most useful to view the 90 years of Hickok literature as a study in the materials of hero-making. What the heroic, larger-than-life image exactly signifies in American civilization is beyond the scope of this study; that it exists should no longer be subject to question.

LEWIS E. ATHERTON

The Midwestern Country Town—
Myth and Reality

In this reading Lewis E. Atherton has attempted to place the midwestern country town in historical perspective; ranging in his discussion from the pioneer period to the 1920's. We have, therefore, in this essay, both some description of the unique problems of the frontier era and some suggestion of the ways in which these related to the urban style of the later urban community. Thorstein Veblen's critique of the country town was a damning one; Professor Atherton is not prepared to accept it without major qualifications.

The appearance of Edgar Lee Masters' *Spoon River Anthology* in 1914 provided midwestern intellectuals with a damning indictment of the spiritual and cultural aridity of the small town from which so many of them had fled. In epitaph after epitaph Masters depicted barren, mean, and vicious lives of villagers, and created for his readers a picture of moral and intellectual depravity softened only occasionally by reference to heroic individuals or humanitarian impulses. . . . Six years later, in 1920, Sinclair Lewis published his famous novel, *Main Street*, in which he succeeded in reaching a large audience. Almost overnight Gopher Prairie and Carol Kennicott came to symbolize sterile towns and despondent heroines who found it impossible to change village cultural patterns for the better. Didactic and simply written, *Main Street* penetrated the consciousness of even the more intellectually obtuse, and in doing so it joined with *Spoon River* in completing an indictment which now attracted the attention of all classes of Americans. . . .

Spoon River and *Main Street* were timely books in the sense that they marked a peak of disillusionment with small towns. Americans were ready for them and more than willing to examine their claims, even if only to scoff and jeer at their conclusions. For several generations Amer-

SOURCE: Abridged from Lewis E. Atherton, "The Midwestern Country Town— Myth and Reality," *Agricultural History*, XXVI (July, 1952), 73-79. Reprinted by permission of *Agricultural History* and Lewis E. Atherton.

icans had at least pretended to believe that log cabins surpassed mansions in producing statesmen, that agriculture and country towns constituted the proper environment for creating leaders in the arts and professions, and that pastoral pursuits contributed to virtue, the good life, and happiness. Masters and Lewis challenged all this, and in doing so they served a new age of industry, urbanization and revolution by weakening the credo which had justified agricultural America. . . .

Writing in 1923, the distinguished American economist, Thorstein Veblen, provided an economic analysis of the country town which was as devastating as the literary efforts of Masters and Lewis. In Veblen's words, "The country town is one of the great American institutions; perhaps the greatest, in the sense that it has had and continues to have a greater part than any other in shaping public sentiment and giving character to American culture." This was true, in Veblen's estimation, because the country town was and is the perfect flower of self-help (rugged individualism) and cupidity. In elaborating this theme, Veblen's incisive language and his gift for irony enabled him to lay bare in a most effective manner the shortcomings of the country town as they appeared to him. . . .

One example involves derogatory generalizations concerning small-town business psychology. As an unfriendly critic, Veblen stated a number of propositions critical of business men in country towns. He accused them of trying to monopolize the farm trade and of exploiting the farmer to the extent that monopoly could be achieved. Needless duplication of overhead and personnel and a virtual monopoly in their own areas led merchants to levy charges at the very peak of what farmers would pay without being driven away. In groceries and banking, where Veblen thought the monopoly was most complete, top price levels often were reached, but seldom in the conduct of ordinary trade. In the latter, the dominant note was "circumspection" or "salesmanlike pusillanimity." This meant that storekeepers attempted to avoid all offense, to cultivate good will without suffering financial loss in so doing, and to exploit a rival merchant's disabilities in every possible way. Veblen also accused storekeepers of being aggressively and truculently conservative. Much prestige value came from contributions to causes which fitted accepted community beliefs, and business men made much of this in their quest for trade. When the chains arrived and began to sell goods on *price* competition, the storekeeper was snared by the competitive philosophy which he had preached over the years. Lastly, in Veblen's opinion, farmers and townsmen cooperated only to boom real estate values; otherwise relations were marked by hostility.

In stating such clear-cut propositions Veblen failed to distinguish between motivations and the extent to which these were realized. He was also guilty of ignoring the full range of motivations which governed the actions of small-town business men. For these reasons, his analysis, like that of many other unfriendly critics, resulted in an unbalanced picture both of purposes and results as these worked out in country towns.

Newspapers and other records sustain Veblen's charge that small-town business men desired trade monopolies, a not unusual purpose in all occupations, but the same records indicate how far he missed actuality when he postulated a theory of competition under monopolistic conditions. Normally, even in the age of horse-drawn transportation, the farmer had a choice of trading centers. Even the railroads, agencies of long-distance transportation, contributed to this end. . . .

Granger complaints, and those of Veblen himself, that merchants priced their goods on the basis of obtaining all that the traffic would bear have to be considered in the light of this competitive condition. Veblen should have stressed elementary and even outmoded merchandising techniques as more important than monopolistic conditions in maintaining high prices. . . .

In spite of the mutual interdependence of town and countryside, some evidence supports Veblen's charge that hostility prevailed between the two. The Granger movement of the late 1860's and early 1870's was a case in point. Perhaps, however, passive indifference or acceptance of the farmer's patronage as a natural advantage constituted the more usual relationship. Storekeepers in country towns were satisfied to let farmers work out their social life around schools and churches in their own townships. Concentrated organized efforts by business men were likely to go in the direction of seeking new industries so that their villages could ape the tremendous growth in numbers, wealth, and real estate values already taking place in larger American industrial centers. . . .

Aspirations to become city people made the inhabitants of country towns sensitive to the realization that they were almost as rural as the farmers who thronged their streets on Saturday afternoons, and they were inclined to look askance at country ways. The very similarity of culture in countryside and town and the ease with which individuals moved back and forth from one to the other only added to the need for villagers to search for evidence of their superiority. The revolutions in transportation, manufacturing and management which developed in the post-Civil War years created new competitive threats to the domination of farm trade by business men in country towns. Preceding this, they perhaps should have attempted to build a cultural, social, and economic affinity with the countryside to serve as a powerful ally in the trying days ahead. The urge to become industrial centers and indifference to their rural heritage rather than Machiavellian efforts to exploit the farmer constituted the error of small-town business men.

The great volume of literature on the problem of the rural town in the twentieth century has served to create a second debatable assumption in regard to the history of such communities. In reading such studies one is likely to assume that country towns underwent little change and experienced little difficulty before the automobile destroyed their isolation and threatened their very existence. In actuality, the country town received the same constant hammering as the rest of the United States, first from the westward movement and then from the revolutions in transportation, manufacturing and management. The advertising of new agricultural frontiers and of new towns located within these antagonized and frightened owners of property in areas which had passed beyond the frontier stage of development. . . .

Competition from a plethora of frontier towns was only the beginning for these supposedly sleepy midwestern communities. Attention has been called to the industrial craze which swept over American urban communities and which has not yet subsided. Midwestern country towns staged feverish campaigns to raise money to subsidize the establishment of local shoe factories or to obtain some new form of transportation. Some succeeded, many had to settle for axe-handle factories, and others were denied even that solace. Whatever the outcome, such campaigns stimulated dissatisfaction with existing conditions and a determination to bring about a change. . . .

Decade by decade the revolutions in transportation, manufacturing and management modified the economic life of midwestern country towns. The electric trolley car, rural free delivery, mail-order houses, the telephone, chain stores, the automobile and truck all contributed to shifting patterns of operation and helped to determine the degree of prosperity which prevailed in any particular town. Some profited by the changes being wrought in economic life and others suffered, but all felt the impact of constant change.

Lack of recognition of this long-continuing pattern of change in midwestern country towns has contributed to a third common opinion which partakes of myth more than reality, namely, that the country town is a dying institution. The growth of metropolitan centers and the ease of reaching these by automobile, truck and bus has seriously injured and even destroyed many country towns. Vacant buildings along Main Street offer compelling evidence of the changes under way and apparently provide irrefutable proof that the country town is rapidly disappearing from the American scene.

Viewed historically, however, the picture takes on new meaning. Vacant buildings and declining population in a considerable percentage of towns seems to have been characteristic of midwestern history for almost every decade from the beginning of settlement. County histories testify to the number of ghost towns which fell prey to destructive forces or were still-born long before the automobile. In 1930, for instance, Iowa, which became a state only in 1846, had 2,205 completely abandoned towns, villages, hamlets and country post offices. Reasons for this high mortality in less than a hundred years were legion. Loss of the county seat to a larger or more aggressive town; abandonment of a military road; exhaustion of coal veins; declining importance of grist and saw-mills; declining importance of river traffic; shifts in locational advantages with the coming of railroads—all these and other factors contributed to a heavy mortality before the automobile age. In this earlier period, however, few people expressed any fear concerning the future of the midwestern country town. . . .

In view of the declining farm population in the Mid-West, it is evident that the country town has displayed an astonishing capacity to survive. Moreover, the figures definitely indicate the mythical nature of the assertion that the midwestern country town is a dying institution.

Lastly, the charge that such communities have been and are barren and sterile culturally and intellectually needs reappraisal in terms of surviving historical records. Space permits attention to only one class of these, the autobiographies of people born in midwestern country towns who went on to achieve prominence in the arts or professions. On the basis of such records it is thoroughly evident that country towns were not creative centers. They were addicted to the cult of the immediately useful and the practical. Financial success in an artistic career brought recognition from the masculine inhabitants of Main Street but artistic matters were left primarily to the womenfolk, who insisted that art must first of all be moral. Professional men like the fathers of William Allen White, Edgar Lee Masters, and Thomas Hart Benton, the Missouri artist, strongly opposed the inclinations of their sons to turn to artistic careers. . . .

On the other hand, lawyers, doctors, newspaper editors, preachers and teachers found employment and encouragement in the country town. Moreover, citizens of such communities were eager to aid promising youngsters. . . .

Too many creative intellects were awakened in small-town Mid-

America for one to conclude that Main Street destroyed creative impulses. Nor should one necessarily condemn the small town because its distinguished sons often sought training and companionship in cultural islands in larger cities. Preparation in the arts and professions has generally demanded more even in the way of material resources than the country town has been able to provide.

For generalizations to have validity they need to be based on a multiplicity of records and data that encompasses, and at the same time transcends, purely personal experiences. Only through such an approach can one hope to separate myth and reality as they relate to the midwestern country town.

CHAPTER IX

Shaping Western Economic Development

Ⅰ N HIS ESSAY on the significance of the frontier Frederick Jackson Turner presented a model of the economic development of the western regions of the United States. The West, he explained, was developed successively by fur traders, miners, cattlemen and farmers who succeeded each other in any region. Different types followed each other among the farmers also: the hunter-farmer, the small intensive farmer and a third class of men who possessed greater capital and enterprise. Finally, he wrote, city and factory organization developed in the regions of intense agriculture. From the members of each pioneer group there remained a few who stayed to participate in the subsequent stages of economic exploitation in a particular region.

Turner's model still has its usefulness, if we are prepared to qualify and supplement it. We know for instance that some steps in the Turnerian sequence involved many more people and much more capital than did others. We know also that these contrasts varied from region to region. We are aware that the lumberman was an important figure also in some territories or states. Lumbermen who were based in villages or towns harvested great stretches of timber in regions where the cattlemen and farmer had not yet penetrated and sometimes never would, in a significant way. Several of the economic types were sometimes active at the same time in relatively small areas. Nor was the economic succession necessarily from east to west in any particular district; resources were used less intensively as the distance to shipping points increased. Settlers first penetrated major river valleys and moved from there into the intervening country, whether that lay to the west, east, north or south. Nodes of settlement grew on western rivers or western lakes simultaneously with the spread of pioneer farmers throughout the adjacent regions. We have often ignored the invisible threads of credit and capital which linked frontier industry and the older settlements. Critics

have pointed out that Turner's model described the economic development of the Middle West rather well but is much less satisfactory as a
description of the settlement and economic growth of other regions.
But the Turnerian formula did identify major agents of western
economic development and it emphasized the increasingly intensive
nature of economic activity in the newer regions. The fur traders and
the hunters who supplied them could support themselves only by ranging
over great stretches of territory. The typical farmer settler in the great
central valley of the United States needed only 80 acres to support himself
and his family.

Between 1787 and the end of the next century millions of people
settled in the trans-Appalachian West and developed a complex industrial
economy in the process. In part the natural increase of the older settlements fed the western population, mostly rural in background but urban
to some degree as well; these settlers were united with the children of
the new western communities, and the immigrants from abroad and their
children. Some historians of American immigration have stressed that
many immigrants preferred to settle in the older regions, freeing the
residents there to participate in the western movement. Undoubtedly this
was true to some extent, but many immigrants moved to the newer regions
of the country soon after their arrival. Sometimes they clustered in urban
centers there but often they went to the land. German and Scandinavian
names dot the early census rolls of midwestern states and the Mormons
trekking westward after 1850 were often British or Scandinavian in
origin. The Irish were western farm makers as well as town dwellers
and the western miners were strikingly cosmopolitan in origin. Another
important population group shared in the migration to the frontiers of
the Southwest prior to the Civil War. Here planters and prosperous
farmers brought slaves and a complex internal commerce transferred
still more of these workers to the Southwest from their birthplaces in
the older South. Partly in response to such competition perhaps, immigrants were less common in the new South than in northern frontier
states and territories. But Irish, Germans, and immigrants of other
national origins contributed to the development of southern frontiers
also.

Some who moved to the West were men of capital, able to buy large
tracts of virgin land from the government or to become merchants,
millers, mine owners, bankers or moneylenders. But many such businessmen required additional capital beyond their own resources; eastern
merchants allowed western merchants to purchase inventories on credit;
local and nonresident land speculators sold land to pioneers on time;

eastern banks, insurance companies, and investors loaned money to western farmers or bought the stocks and bonds of western corporations. During the course of the nineteenth century some of these processes became increasingly obvious and institutionalized. During the 1830's and 1840's, for instance, settlers borrowed funds from nonresident capitalists or their agents who attended the federal land sales in the West. But the homesteader or preemptor of the 1880's in the Plains states was besieged by the agents of mortgage companies offering funds which they had obtained from eastern investors.

The fur trade did not attract large numbers of people to the West. Mining drew many more settlers westward, and the agricultural frontier was still more important in the settlement process. Generations of pioneer farmers and planters devoted themselves to the production of livestock in the West or to cultivation of the great agricultural staples, notably cotton, wheat and corn. In explaining economic growth during the period between 1815 and 1840, some economic historians emphasize the unique significance of the development of the Cotton Belt. Foreign and domestic demand for cotton, they point out, induced Americans to open up lands for cotton production very rapidly throughout the lower South during those years. The southern plantation economy in turn generated a demand for grain and livestock in excess of the region's production. Settlers poured into the Old Northwest to supply the deficiency. Flatboats and western steamboats carried the surplus livestock and grain of the states above the Ohio to southern destinations. Impressed by the surging American economy, British investors purchased large quantities of the bonds that American state legislators authorized to finance internal improvements which they believed would encourage still greater economic growth in turn. Agriculture became increasingly commercial in both the Northwest and the Southwest, but the results were very different. The slave and staple crop economy of the Southerners did not beget industry to any great extent. In the Old Northwest, however, agricultural processing industries developed and ultimately heavy industry as well. Such is the picture of the West's role in American economic development after 1815 that a number of historians present. Some, however, disagree about the relative importance of the southern market to the northwestern farmers of this era.

After the 1840's the economic foundations of western development are much less easy to describe. The livestock and grain of western states moved to markets on the west coast, to the industrial East and abroad, as well as to the South. The output of western mines was governed by the demand of both domestic and foreign users of their production. The occupation of the grassland frontiers as well as the demands of industrial America stimulated the lumbermen to strenuous exertions in the Great Lakes states, the South, and subsequently the Pacific Northwest. We cannot, therefore, explain the exploitation of frontier resources in this era largely in terms of the demand for one major staple. After 1850 also the spread of the railroad network, the use of telegraphic communication, the development of futures trading and highly organized commodity markets, all helped to revolutionize the trade in agricultural commodities. Soon westerners suspected that evil and rapacious men were controlling the new marketing agencies, stealing the just earnings of primary producers and enmeshing them in a web of economic colonialism.

In modern terms the frontier process illustrated sequential economic growth. Individual Americans and the American government decided when and in what quantities new bodies of western resources were to be added to the resource base of the Anglo-American economy. Apparently the economic, social and political rewards of development were highly attractive to the decision makers of the nineteenth century in the United States because they exploited the frontier's natural wealth very rapidly. Of course, the newly opened resources provided new jobs and the workers in these jobs added to the national product. But more was involved in the process of development than this. As each new area was integrated into the American economy there was a very considerable investment in social overhead capital; that is, in the roads and transportation improvements necessary to link the region to the older settlements, as well as in the public buildings, the schools and the churches which the residents of the new country needed to govern themselves properly, to educate their children and to lead socially rewarding lives. In addition the frontier resources demanded initial outlays of capital that need not be repeated in such massive amounts in the future. So the very process of opening new western resources generated a demand for labor and capital, in addition to that required in the normal operation of farm, shop or manufactory.

Most Americans of the nineteenth century believed that the development of resources and the peopling of the continent from sea to sea were highly desirable objectives. They did not always agree on the way in which these objectives were to be achieved. Southerners or northerners might oppose developmental legislation because they feared that it threatened their own regional interests or institutions, or would assist the residents of other regions more than themselves. In general southerners feared to expand federal powers lest they eventually be turned against slavery. More specifically, many southerners opposed

liberal land policies that they believed would encourage the development of new free states more rapidly than the creation of new slave
states. Selling their cotton to a considerable extent in England, southerners
opposed tariffs to protect northern industry, which, they feared, would
increase the cost of the manufactured goods that they must buy. Some
western farmers on the other hand desired protection against foreign
wool or hoped that tariff-supported industry would enlarge the domestic
market for their grain or livestock. The federal policies which affected
western growth were necessarily, therefore, the product of interregional
compromise. Most specifically such political compromise dictated that
the developers could freely use slave labor in the West only below
the Ohio River, in Missouri, in regions of the Louisiana Purchase below
Missouri's southern boundary and in Texas.

The territorial system guaranteed that western settlers would enjoy
political institutions similar to those in the older states. The provision
in the Northwest Ordinance and later territorial organic acts that forbade
residents of the territories from taxing the lands of nonresidents at
higher rates than their own removed a potential impediment to the
flow of capital westward. Some westerners demanded that the federal
government surrender the remaining public lands to the new states as
they entered the Union. The members of Congress refused but they did
use the public domain to foster western development. We have described
these policies of the national government in some detail in Chapter VI.
Undoubtedly, the federal lawmakers could have used federal resources
more generously in building major roads, canals, and railroads to the
western regions and within them. But the assistance was enough to allow
the westerners to exploit large areas of the West very rapidly. In the
eyes of some historians, indeed, the federal government's contribution,
particularly the railroad land grants, was needlessly prodigal.

In meeting the economic needs of the West, the national lawmakers
were, perhaps, least helpful in providing credit and banking services.
They contributed capital to the First and Second Banks of the United
States but these were primarily commercial banks. Insofar as they aided
the movement of western staples to market, and insofar as their loan and
discount operations and currency issues insured a stable monetary
system, they did assist western development. But these banks did not
satisfy the needs of an agricultural economy for land credit and westerners believed that the officers of the Second Bank of the United States
were unnecessarily harsh in their efforts to force banks operating under
state charter to maintain adequate specie reserves behind their note
issue. After Andrew Jackson vetoed the bill to recharter that institution,

the states could develop their banking systems unhindered by outside agencies. Then began the golden age of western wildcat banking. Jackson's war against the B.U.S. [Second Bank of the United States] and the excesses of some state-chartered institutions contributed to a severe reaction against banks and a number of western states forbade them for a time. When federal lawmakers created the system of National Banks in 1863, they again ignored the need of farmers for credit on the security of land and agricultural products, although they soon ended the worst excesses of state banking by placing a prohibitive tax on the currency issued by state banks. Such regulation, however, diminished the credit available to westerners and further concentrated control of the American monetary system in eastern banking institutions.

In discussing the activities of the western state governments in encouraging economic growth, historians have stressed their role in the construction of internal improvements and this was indeed a most important aspect of state developmental policy down to the 1850's. Between 1820 and 1840, frontier legislators not only transferred federal land grants to transportation corporations but they invested state funds in the stock of turnpike companies and in the construction of canals and railroads. The Depression of 1837 and its aftermath, as well as the mismanagement of some state projects, convinced many westerners that they should restrict the participation of their state governments in such activities. The western state governments still continued, however, to allocate federal land grants to transportation companies and this was an important function. On various occasions western legislatures reclaimed land grants and assigned them to other corporations, more eager or more able to construct railroads. And, although the state governments became more conservative after 1840 in assisting economic development, county and other municipal governments invested large sums in developing transportation connections, particularly by issuing bonds in order to make gifts or loans to railroad corporations or to buy their stocks. Western legislators also pressed the federal government for military roads and urged it to remove obstructions from their rivers. They developed road codes, outlining the ways in which the taxpayers were to provide road funds and local government officers disburse them. Prior to the Civil War the obligation of western lawmakers to approve the charters of turnpike, plank road, bridge and ferry companies was sometimes of crucial importance in fostering regional growth. After that conflict western legislators somewhat reluctantly attempted to regulate transportation agencies in the interests of producers and users.

Transportation policy was not the only concern of western lawmakers.

A number of western states set up state banks between 1815 and 1840. Throughout the nineteenth century western legislators became increasingly interested in providing education for the youth of the West. Realizing the crucial importance of immigration to economic development some western lawmakers established state immigration bureaus. They bestowed financial aid upon state agricultural societies to assure prospective settlers that agriculture was being encouraged in the new commonwealths. The state and county fairs sponsored by the societies and their published reports advertised the new state as well as educating their farmers. Adverse possession laws protected western farmers from sharpers who might challenge the titles to their land, and homestead legislation protected the debtor's home in the West.

Mingled with the desire of western lawmakers to entice people to the West was their desire to attract and hold capital. Maximum legal interest rates were usually high in the West in comparison to the East; during the mid-years of the nineteenth century some western states set no limit on rates whatsoever. The deed of trust, allowing foreclosure of real estate security without court proceedings, was common in many western states. Western legislators sometimes ignored the need for laws which gave the debtors a period in which to pay court judgements before their security was put to sale, or effective redemption laws, providing delinquent borrowers with the opportunity to redeem foreclosed property after the sheriff's sale.

Eastern capitalists found it profitable to buy land at the tax sales in the counties of western territories and states, since they were reimbursed with a return of 25 per cent or more per annum on their investments after the delinquent owners had settled up with the county treasurer. If such property holders did not redeem their lands, the eastern investors were entitled, after a waiting period, to exchange their certificates of payment for tax deeds. Many western legislatures tried to provide that such deeds would completely supersede the chain of title originating in the federal government. Impecunious western pioneers, trying to develop farms, crafts or industries, detested such credit and tax laws, particularly in times of depression. To some extent western legislation on such matters reflected the economic climate prevailing when it was passed. During times of prosperity western lawmakers deferred to the "developers" and altered the credit and tax laws in ways that were attractive to investors. In times of depression they modified the laws in the interests of debtors. When western commercial interests and producers first demanded the regulation of railroad rates and practices many legislators feared that such legislation would cause the railroad companies to stop extending their lines and retard the development of their states. Such feeling explains the reluctance of some of the lawmakers to act.

The growing markets of the West stimulated eastern industry and business in many ways. On occasion also western producers, particularly the farmers, provided such vigorous competition that major changes resulted in eastern production patterns. Despite such domestic dislocations western resources helped to fuel a dynamic and productive economy. The economists George S. Murphy and Arnold Zellner believe that sequential economic growth based on western resources raised per capita income and employment, encouraged economic and social mobility, and made legislators sympathetic to the needs of labor in the United States. Technological innovation, a "growing stock of capital," and the "successive geographic frontiers" helped Americans to produce the "nineteenth century's highest level of per capita income and rate of increase in per capita income." Should Americans be satisfied with this historical performance? Or have the economic achievements, which were based in part on free land, diverted attention from the failures of conscience and the economic and social inequities that were present in nineteenth-century America? Or is it the task of the historian to raise such queries?

DOUGLASS C. NORTH

Agriculture in Regional Economic Growth

Why did a significant industrial sector fail to evolve in the ante-bellum South while major industrial activity developed in the midwestern regions of the North? In this passage Douglass C. North develops a theory to explain regional differences in economic development, involving the natural resources available, the characteristics of the export industry, the technological limitations of that industry and the possibility of transferring resources from it to other local industrial uses. In these terms the West of the free states had potential for economic diversification and industrialization that were lacking in the South.

. . . The first step in the analysis of regional economic growth consists of an exploration of the determinants of the export sector of the region. However, a necessary additional step is to examine the disposition of the income received from without the region. Certainly one of the perplexing problems in the study of economic growth has been the differential progress as amongst different regions resulting from an increment to income from the export sector. Why does one area remain tied to a single export staple while another diversifies its production and becomes an urbanized, industrialized region? Regions that remained tied to a single export commodity almost inevitably do not achieve sustained expansion. Not only will there be a slowing down in the rate of growth in the industry which will adversely affect the region, but the very fact that it remains tied to a single export industry will mean that specialization and diversion of labor are limited outside that industry. Historically it has meant that a larger share of the populace has remained outside the market economy. The answer lies (a) in the natural endowments of the region (at any given level of technology), (b) in the character of the export industry, and (c) in changes in technology and transfer costs. It is worthwhile to examine each of these in turn.

Source: Abridged from Douglass C. North, "Agriculture in Regional Economic Growth," *Journal of Farm Economics*, XLI (December, 1959), 943–951. Reprinted by permission of the *Journal of Farm Economics* and Douglass C. North.

The natural endowments of the region dictate the initial export commodities of the area. If these endowments are such as to result in a tremendous comparative advantage in one commodity over any other, then the immediate consequence will be for resources to concentrate upon its production. If, on the other hand, the region has broad production possibilities such that the rate of return upon the production of a number of goods and services is not too much less than upon the initial export commodity, then with the growth of the region and accompanying change in factor proportions the production of other goods and services is likely to be a simple process.

The character of the export commodity in influencing regional growth is more complicated since there are several facets to it. A number of important consequences stem from the technological nature of the production function. If the export commodity is a "plantation" type commodity which is relatively labor intensive and in which there are significant increasing returns to scale, then the development will be in marked contrast to one in which the export commodity may be produced most efficiently on a family-size farm with relatively less absolute amounts of labor required. In the first case there will tend to result an extremely unequal distribution of income with the bulk of the population devoting most of their income to foodstuff and simple necessities (much of which may be self-sufficient production). At the other end of the income scale, the plantation owners will tend to spend most of their income upon luxury consumption goods which will be imported. In short, there will be little encouragement of residentiary types of economic activity. With the more equitable distribution of incomes, there is a demand for a broad range of goods and services, part of which will be residentiary, thus inducing investment in other types of economic activities. There will tend to develop trading centers to provide a wide variety of such goods and services, in contrast to the plantation economy which will merely develop a few urban areas devoted to the export of the staple commodity and the distribution of imports.

A natural consequence of the divergent patterns described in the previous paragraph will be the attitude towards investment in knowledge. Under the plantation type with very unequal income distribution, the planter will be extremely reluctant to devote his tax monies to expenditures for education or research other than that related to the staple commodity. As a consequence skills and knowledge not directly related to the export commodity will be at a low level. In contrast, the region with more equitable income distribution will be well aware of the stake in improving its comparative position through education and research and will accordingly be willing to devote public expenditures in these directions. The result will be to relatively improve its comparative position in a variety of types of economic activity and therefore broaden the resultant economic base.

Equally important is the investment induced by the export commodity or service. If the export is such as to require substantial investment in transport, warehousing, port facilities and other types of social overhead investment, then the external economies are created which facilitate the development of other exports. Furthermore, if the export industry induces growth of subsidiary industries and if technology, transport costs and resource endowments permit these to be locally produced rather than imported, then this will induce further development. Both in the case of social overhead investment and investment in subsidiary industry the consequence is to promote urbanization and increased specialization and development of additional residentiary activity geared to the increasing local demand for consumption goods and services. At the other extreme is the export industry which requires only the immediate development of a few centers for the collection and export of the commodity and entails the development of little subsidiary industry or perhaps entails the development of such subsidiary industry and marketing facilities, but they are of a nature to be most efficiently imported.

Changes in technology and transport may completely alter the region's comparative advantage either favorably or unfavorably. Technological change may increase the potential rate of return in the production of other goods and services and lead to the exploitation of new resources and a shift of resources away from the old export industry. The initial development of transportation facilities to implement the export industry tends to reinforce dependence upon it and inhibit more diversified economic activity in several ways. The early development of transport typically (under competitive conditions) leads to a rapid fall in the transport rate and therefore increases the comparative advantage of the export commodity. Moreover, with newly settled regions the transportation is typically one way. The outward shipment of a bulky product having no counterpart in the inward shipment which must be made mostly empty or in ballast. In consequence, inward freights are very low and compete with locally produced goods. As a result a good deal of local industry which had been protected by high transport costs or might develop if high transport costs continued, faces effective competition from imports. In summary the disposition of income earned from export industry plays a decisive role in the growth of the region. Related to this argument is the region's propensity to import. To the extent that a region's income directly flows out in the purchase of goods and services rather than having a regional multiplier-accelerator effect, then it is inducing growth elsewhere, but reaping few of the benefits of increased income from the export sector itself.

Let me briefly illustrate the argument of the preceding pages by contrasting the economic structure of the South and the West in the years prior to the Civil War.

Both regions enjoyed a thriving export trade in the years between the end of the second war with England and the Civil War. The cotton trade of the South accounted for more than half of total U. S. exports during the period, with rice, sugar and tobacco as subsidiary commodity exports. The value of cotton exports alone increased from $17.5 million in 1815 to $191.8 million in 1860. The West enjoyed an expanding trade in wheat and corn and derivatives thereof (pork bacon, lard, flour, whisky) first with the South and then increasingly after the mid 1840's with the Northeast and Europe. However, at this point their similarity ends. Let me point up the contrasts.

1. The South was characterized by its concentrated production for the market of a single export staple with a comparative advantage so great that even in periods of low cotton prices, resources could not receive an equal return from alternative types of economic activity. The West had no overwhelming comparative advantage in a single commodity but rather branched out into mining (lead in Missouri, copper in Michigan and iron at Pittsburgh) and various kinds of processing.

2. Large scale organization typified the southern plantation and a resultant extremely unequal pattern of income distribution reinforced, of course, by the institution of slavery. Wheat and corn in the West could be produced most efficiently on the "family size farm" given early 19th century technology. In consequence the pattern of consumer demand was markedly different. The South was almost totally lacking in urban development during the period (with the exception of New Orleans which served as an entrepôt for western foodstuff for the southern planter and as a port for cotton exports), and its states were conspicuously at the bottom of the list of retail stores per thousand population in the 1840 census. A large percentage of the South's population remained outside the market economy. In contrast small community centers dotted the West to serve the local populace and served as nuclei for residentiary industry and trade and services. While these early developed to serve local consumer needs, with the gradual expansion of the market and the development of external economies many came to serve an increasingly large area and become export industries. With each surge of expansion

in the West (1816–18, 1832–39, 1849–57), an increasing percentage of western farmers shifted out of self-sufficiency and became a part of the market economy.

A further consequence of these contrasting structures was the differential investment in education. The South had the highest illiteracy rate (as a percentage of the white population), the lowest ratio of pupils to (white) population, and the smallest number of libraries. Even western states that were just emerging from the pioneer stage were conspicuously higher than the South in educational investment.

3. Little additional investment was necessary for the efficient export of southern cotton. Neither transportation development nor extensive subsidiary industry were required. The Factor with his ties with northern credit and shipping served as both the exporter of the planter's cotton, and importer of his foodstuff (from the West) and manufactures (from the Northeast and Europe). Large scale investment in the South was devoted solely to the opening up of new cotton lands and the acquisition of slaves. Extensive investment in transportation (as well as other facilities to implement the export of goods) was essential to opening up the West. Moreover, there were important locational advantages to processing wheat and corn products into flour, corn meal, ham, bacon, salt pork, lard, and whisky within the region rather than without. In consequence a variety of such manufacturing grew up and promoted urban development in the West.

4. The unique characteristics of the ocean freight trade which resulted in one-way cargoes from the cotton ports resulted in back hauls of manufactured goods being imported into the cotton region at very low rates. As a result there was no protection for local consumer oriented industries from the cheap imports of the Northeast and Europe. In contrast manufactures had to come to the West either over land or via the long route back up the Mississippi, and the protection thereby assisted the early development of consumer oriented industries in the West. . . .

A positive restatement of the thesis elaborated above is that the development of a successful agricultural export industry [as in the West] will result in an increase in income to the region, and under the favorable conditions outlined above will lead to:

(1) Specialization and division of labor with a widening of the regional market;

(2) The growth of facilities and subsidiary industry to efficiently produce and market the export commodity;

(3) The development of residentiary industry to serve local consumers, some of which may, in consequence of expanding markets and external

economies developed in association with the export industry, lead to a broadening in the export base;

(4) As a natural consequence of the above conditions, the growth of urban areas and facilities;

(5) An expanded investment in education and research to broaden the region's potential.

Under these circumstances, a good deal of industrial development will occur naturally as a consequence of the conditions described above. Indeed as the regional market increases in size, more and more manufacturing firms will find it feasible to establish branch plants there. . . .

·2·

DOUGLAS F. DOWD

. . . Economic Development in the American West . . .

Some historians have suggested that the literature describing economically underdeveloped areas may increase our understanding of the growth of the American West. Douglas F. Dowd maintains that current definitions of underdevelopment do not fit the western experience in the United States. If his line of argument is convincing, should we develop another terminology to describe the economic relations between the eastern and western sections of the American economy during the nineteenth century?

. . . Out of the hubbub over underdeveloped areas that has sounded for the last decade or two, we should be in a position to state simply the major defining characteristics of such areas, in terms of quantity, quality, and process. Quantitatively, underdevelopment is expressible in terms of per capita income, the degree of surplus (savings and investment), levels and patterns of consumption and investment, and productivity; in measures of health, education, etc., where the bias is heavily

SOURCE: Abridged from Douglas F. Dowd, "A Comparative Analysis of Economic Development in the American West and South," *Journal of Economic History*, XVI (December, 1956), 558-574. Reprinted by permission of the *Journal of Economic History* and Douglas F. Dowd.

toward lowness and inadequacy. Qualitatively, the underdeveloped society exhibits a structure of production, ownership, and control which, taken together with thin and shallow markets, and an absence of adequate financial institutions and the factors making for external economies, combines to keep the quantitative achievements of the society at a low level. Often there is an associated population problem that holds back growth and wipes out gains. In terms of process, the underdeveloped society is one that is spinning its wheels in the mud; which, to use the more common metaphor, is revolving slowly and helplessly within a series of intertwined vicious circles.

Did the American West fit this definition? Of course not. We may note that the productive structure of the West has been dominated by primary production; that much of the ownership (particularly in railroads, mining, cattle, and timber) was nonwestern; that Westerners were faced with unfavorable terms of trade in their dealings with the more powerful East; that the per capita income of Westerners throughout our period and to this date is lower than that of those to the east of them above the Mason and Dixon line, and lower than those in the Far West. These and other particular characteristics often associated with underdevelopment may be found in the West. What *cannot* be found is the over-all quality of underdevelopment: the matrix of inhibiting institutional relationships is almost totally absent. The West, from its inception as a settled area, was possessed of vitality; it continually changed and expanded.

The West was settled and exploited in a series of *booms*: railroad booms, cattle booms, farming booms, mining and timber booms. These booms were in time followed by the rise of commercial and financial nuclei, and by the growth of secondary industries. That much of the profitability of the booms may have drained out to eastern (and some foreign) owners is true, but because the West was an integral part of the society to which the largest part of it went, the drain did not have a long-run negative impact on development possibilities, although it did affect the distribution of income as between West and East.

In its critical period of development, the thirty years or so following the Civil War, the West was of course subjected to falling prices for its goods—as was the rest of the nation, and the rest of the world. As is well known, price drops were a consequence of newly opened food lands, and a connected rapid improvement in technology, transportation, and communications. Western resources were exploited ruthlessly and often stupidly, as were western miners, farm workers, and loggers; and many western farmers sank into tenancy or were pushed out of farming. But through it all western production and productivity grew, so much so as to provide simultaneously a rising level and improving quality of life for Westerners, cheap food and raw materials for the rest of the country, and a surplus of foodstuffs that played a crucial role in our balance of payments.

In brief, the West was never a region faced with a development *problem*. It developed as an outcome of the needs of the rest of the nation, and out of its inherent possibilities as an area empty of people (except the easily brushed-aside Indians), and relatively well equipped with natural resources. Extravagant and some not so extravagant hopes pulled people and capital out of the regions of the East and from Europe—both on the make, the people ambitious and relatively flexible, the capital speculative and always forthcoming; albeit at high rates.

The story of the impact of technology on western farming has been told frequently and well. The point of it, for present purposes, is that the West was quick to adopt relevant new techniques on a general scale. If settlement was to take place in the West, it had to take place with a more capital-intensive agriculture than had existed in the regions to the east and south. Fencing and barbed wire, deep wells and windmills, seeds and agricultural science; all had to be experimented with if the Plains were to be cultivated. Given the climate and soils, a labor-extensive agriculture had to be practiced, and cultivation had to be mechanized. The needs were faced, the technical problems were solved, and settlement rapidly followed the solutions. What is true of agriculture—the necessity of adopting new techniques—is true of cattle raising, of mining, and of timber exploitation, though fewer people and therefore less drama were involved. This was an area that innovated quickly and extensively, held back only briefly by preconceived notions, driven on by a "boomer" optimism and a materialistic social philosophy.

Puritanism in Kansas and Mormonism in Utah, to mention the most striking cases, combined religion and economics to promote rapid development. For the region as a whole, it is clear that the social outlook of the people was completely in harmony with sustained economic growth, particularly with the prodding of an East and a world hungry for raw materials and food. Though we may deplore wheat cultivation in lands better suited to grazing, though many "busted" in Kansas and points west and north, though we may muse on the ultimate meaning of wasted mineral and timber resources, we cannot argue, at this point in our history, that economic growth was sickly, or its results unfortunate in the West.

Perhaps it was the relatively lower levels of income in the West that led to the notion that it was underdeveloped. Perhaps it is the still wide-open spaces. But if underdevelopment is to have any serious meaning, that meaning must lie in the realm of comparing actual with potential. Looking back at the West, it is hard to imagine how, given the technology and markets of the period 1865–1930, much more could have been made of the area.

The West remained empty until its resources could fit the needs of the vigorous East. As such, vested interests and inhibiting forms of economic and social organization were absent. There were no significant institutional obstacles to the maximum development of western resources. And when settled, the West was thinly settled, by people whose eyes were fixed on the main chance. . . .

ELLEN VON NARDROFF

The American Frontier as a Safety Valve...

The possibility that the western lands served as a kind of
economic safety valve has been the subject of much scholarly
discussion. Ellen Von Nardroff has published a critique of
the literature on the subject along with a restatement of the
impact of western resources on eastern labor. She identified
a number of variants of the theory, including the "potential
safety-valve," suggesting that some eastern farmers were
able to migrate to new farms in the West rather than joining
the industrial labor force; the "natural-resources-safety-valve
theory," in which the broad impact of western resources on
the economy was stressed; and the "socio-psychological"
variant, emphasizing the importance of the impact which
easterners believed that the free lands had upon American
life rather than the actual effect of the free lands on Americans. In the passage presented here, the author develops her
own assessment of the importance of the doctrine.

. . . Our proposition now reads: Did the process of developing this
area contribute to the high wage level and the social outlook of the
United States? And the answer becomes absurdly obvious. To respond
other than in the affirmative is to reason that both would have been the
same if United States development had been confined to the thirteen
original colonies. The various safety valve "theories," however, were
more nearly designed to answer the question of *how* the great continental
frontier contributed.

Explaining how continental development mitigated class consciousness
in North America consists largely in restating the socio-psychological
safety valve theory and reiterating that it has never really been challenged in any systematic fashion. Two additional comments, however,
should be made. Even if the multilingual, multi-ethnic nature of the
American labor force is considered the prime deterrent to early unioniza-

SOURCE: Abridged from Ellen Von Nardroff, "The American Frontier as a Safety
Valve—The Life, Death, Reincarnation, and Justification of a Theory," *Agricultural
History*, XXXVI (July, 1962), 123-142. Reprinted by permission of *Agricultural
History*.

tion, this factor may be indirectly attributed to the frontier. It is generally maintained that mass immigration was the result of the pull of free land (actual or mythical) or of high wages. The former is obviously a frontier phenomenon. So is the latter, to the extent to which high wages are traceable to the existence of the frontier.

Of utmost importance to the socio-psychological safety valve notion is the effect of the frontier on the distribution of conventional symbols of wealth and status. In the western world no such symbol has been so important as the ownership of private property, especially land. In the early colonial period it was the ease with which land could be acquired that did much to lessen the awe with which the lower classes viewed their traditional betters. It is also suggested that even in later periods in the East, ownership of some bit of real estate was not only possible for large segments of the society (including wage earners) but quite prevalent in comparison to elsewhere. Land vacated in urban environs as commercial agriculture moved westward was at least available for homes. Even possession of a fifty-foot lot with a house of sorts and a couple of rows of radishes makes one a landowner.

We are now left with the effect of the frontier on the wage level, and propose to surmount this final hurdle by consolidating fragmentary expositions of the resources safety valve and asserting that it, also, has yet to be seriously challenged. The discussion can be most logically divided into the major components of wage determination: demand, supply, and productivity.

The effect of the frontier on the supply of labor to industry was due to the factor that has been most obvious all along; namely, that the agricultural sector was expanding physically. What some of the more violent anti-safety valvists would like to forget is that this is something of an anomaly in economic development. Both in Europe and in the typical underdeveloped country today, initial industrial development was and is based on exploitation of an agricultural labor surplus, meaning that the marginal productivity of labor in agriculture is or is approaching zero, that labor already engaged in agriculture may be withdrawn without reducing the total product of the sector significantly, and that the supply of labor to industry, for a time, at least, is infinitely elastic at subsistence wages. No such state of affairs ever existed in this country despite the fact that historians dearly love to use the term "surplus labor" without ever saying what they mean. As a result, American industry was relatively capital intensive from the start and continues to be so.

The absence of an agricultural labor surplus does not mean that agricultural labor could not be drawn into industry. Obviously it was. It seems safe to assume that the marginal productivity of labor in agriculture was rising so long as prime virgin land was available to exploit, fell as the soil was gradually mined, and rose again with the application of improved technology. If at any time the productivity of labor in industry was rising faster or falling less fast than in agriculture, it could attract labor from the agricultural sector—but at a price higher than would have been obtained had not agricultural expansion rendered the supply of labor to industry less elastic. Like all such analysis, the above possibly assumes a greater mobility of labor than actually existed. However, immobility works both ways (as all kinds of safety-valvists have pointed out) and there is no reason to assume that one sector benefited more than the other.

It is true, on the other hand, that mass immigration was a partial substitute for the absence of an agricultural labor surplus and that as a result of immigration money wages fell in the nineteenth century. In other words, demand, in the form of high returns to labor in both agriculture and industry, seems to have created its own supply. However, the immobility principle may be invoked here with even more validity than in the domestic case. Whereas employment opportunities determined the *fact* of immigration, its *extent* was exogenously determined. Given this, the competition for labor between two expanding sectors created a floor below which wages could not fall and two important characteristics of that floor should be delineated. First, the floor was low enough to permit industrialization. As Kemmerer points out, had wages remained as high as in the colonial period, industrialization might well have been impossible. It seems unlikely that anyone would argue that the absence of an industrial sector would in the long run have benefited anyone— and least of all labor. Secondly, the floor was high enough to insure, as has been pointed out earlier, that real wages did not fall in the nineteenth century. It would seem, then, that endogenous and exogenous factors combined to balance demand with supply of precisely the right magnitude and elasticity to sustain expansion without lowering the standard of living of labor.

In a sense, the above analysis is an elaboration of the potential safety valve thesis. Unlike potential safety-valvists, however, we do not maintain that labor supply is the whole story.

In the preceding treatment of labor supply it is clearly indicated that the westward expansion of agriculture increased the productivity of labor in that sector. The same relationship exists between development of western resources in general and productivity in the industrial sector.

As C. W. Wright pointed out long ago, obviously the productivity of all labor is higher when applied to abundant and prime resources. This effect, it should be added, does not necessarily depend on the number of people who migrate to the resources. So long as there is sufficient migration to maintain the extractive industries and the transportation system, the effect of the resulting abundance is the same on processing industries wherever they may be located.

One of Clarence Danhof's conclusions is that "fundamentally the productivity and profitability of eastern industry made high wages possible. Rapid growth guaranteed that such wages would actually be paid." Essentially, he is referring to the increasing effective demand of industry for labor. The growth on which this expanding demand was based was, of course, dependent on the rate of investment and the productivity of capital. In any underdeveloped country initial capital shortage is somewhat offset by the fact that marginal returns to capital are high. There is no reason to question that when the resource base is expanding the returns to capital will either increase or fail to diminish as soon as when the base is limited. It may well have been this extra yield which permitted the extensive expansion via "plowing-back" that was so characteristic of American industrial growth.

Industrial growth may also depend on agricultural growth. In the first place, an inadequate agricultural sector may be a bottleneck to industrialization purely and simply because it cannot support an urban working class. This was the case in Russia and is still one of their most bothersome problems. In many presently developing countries limited agricultural productivity is also a matter of prime concern. This was conspicuously not the case in the United States. As Louis Hacker points out:

The free lands of the West were not important, however, because they made possible the creation of a unique "American spirit"—that indefinable something that was to set the U.S. apart from European experience for all time—but because their quick settlement and utilization for the extensive cultivation of foodstuffs furnished exactly those commodities with which the U.S., a debtor nation, could balance its international payments and borrow European capital in order to develop a native industrial enterprise.

In other words, agricultural expansion westward not only supported industrialization and urbanization directly, it also indirectly contributed to a high rate of investment in the inital stages of industrialization.

In the above discussion we are by no means trying to imply that the mere fact of expansion into a frontier area will insure a high wage level or that it was expansion alone that sustained wages in the United States. Other people have expanded over vast areas with no such result. Such expansions arose from different social structures and different levels of technological development; and they expanded at different rates into different terrains. While varying degrees of emphasis may be placed on the institutional structure and technology from which migration proceeded in this country, we are suggesting that the net effect on the rate of economic growth and on wages of American expansion into the American West was positive.

•4•

CHARLES M. GATES

Boom Stages in American Expansion

Hopeful western promoters dreamed of the time when the economic development of their region would accelerate rapidly or boom and make them and other early settlers rich. Charles M. Gates defines the characteristics of "booms" and describes such a crucial period of frontier development in the Pacific Northwest. Important in his analysis are the businessmen who played the role of "facilitating agents," in the service of eastern capitalists, but underlying the boom were basic economic "accelerator forces."

. . . The purpose of the present essay is to explore the ramifications of what we may call the boom stage in the development of a regional economy in the American West. The observations to be offered are based upon a case study of the Pacific Northwest, and the illustrations and examples are taken from that study. But it is to be hoped that a consideration of this locality will be helpful and suggestive for the study of other sections as well. The general thesis to be advanced is that new areas, as they were settled in various parts of the American West, typical-

SOURCE: Abridged from Charles M. Gates, "Boom Stages in American Expansion," *Business History Review*, XXXIII (Spring, 1959), 32-42. © 1959, Graduate School of Business Administration, Harvard University. Reprinted by permission of the *Business History Review*.

ly passed through a transitional period in their progress from frontier beginnings to more advanced post-frontier stages of growth. During this transition, changes of great importance occurred very quickly, growth was extremely rapid, and opportunities for unusual economic gain presented themselves; opportunities which were unlike those existing either earlier or later. Such a "boom stage" of development deserves to be differentiated from the stage of first occupancy which preceded it, and from the more stable regional economy which followed.

The economic analysis of boom stages confronts us, first of all, with problems of quantitative measurement. We must have barometers or indexes of some kind that will enable us to compare the levels of economic activity during significant intervals of time. It will pay us to pore over the reports of the Bureau of the Census and to go as far as we can with calculations that suggest significant comparisons between different states and different decades. Comparative rates of increase will be useful when considering statistical series under such headings as Population, Estimates of Wealth, Value of Farms and of Agricultural Products, Manufacturing Employment, and Values Created by Manufacturing. . . .

Statistics of commercial and banking activity and production figures for significant resource industries may likewise be used as partial indexes, and will be helpful in quantitative studies of the boom stages of development. . . .

The Pacific Northwest study indicates a rather clear pattern in which the statistical levels and indexes rise comparatively slowly during the years of early growth, then sharply during the boom stage, then level off again suggesting a kind of equilibrium with other sections of the country thereafter. Growth continued, to be sure, and gains were registered, at times more rapid gains than in other places. But there has been no recurrence of the spectacular changes and gains of the boom stage, and we may doubt that there will be.

Basically the rapid growth of the region during the years 1880–1910 was a matter of economic integration with the rest of the country. The completion of the transcontinental railroads marked the beginning of the boom stage, and railroad transport was a crucial factor in lifting the level of the regional economy very abruptly during the next quarter-century. Population mobility was completely changed as tens of thousands of travelers went West "by the cars" who never would have gone by wagon train or schooner.

Hardly less important was the role of the rail carriers in bringing Northwest commodities to market. In 1907 nearly 8 million tons of freight moved over the Northern Pacific for a total of 1.4 billion ton-miles of traffic within the State of Washington alone. More than two-thirds of this represented interstate service, and perhaps one-third of it lumber shipments that traveled some 1,500 miles to midwestern points. Great Northern shipments were of lesser volume, but the general character of freight service was essentially similar to that of the Northern Pacific. Lime, cement and metal ores, livestock, grain, fresh fruit and canned salmon, all found their way in considerable quantities over long distances, and resource industries were enormously stimulated as these new outlets were reached.

At the same time, the railroads were themselves enterprises which spent large sums of money in the Far West and gave employment to a considerable work force. By 1896 the main sections of the Northern Pacific in Washington State represented an outlay of more than $25 million. Ten years later the railroad paid out in 12 months' time $5.7 million in compensation in Washington State and estimated the replacement cost of its system in that state at $61.6 million. The transportation revolution thus brought about heavy capital investments and spurred spectacular gains in population and in the growth of resource industries. . . . Once the system was built and the rate structure was stabilized, the transport factor became more constant, subject only to comparatively minor revision. During the boom stage, however, the rails brought about dynamic changes, the importance of which can hardly be exaggerated.

The process of knitting together the Northwest with the rest of the nation involved a whole complex of economic operations which, once achieved, never needed to be done again in the same formative way. Services of supply and distribution were revolutionized along with the system of transport. Wholesale houses established direct and continuous commercial contact with manufacturers and eastern suppliers and materially changed the feel of things for the drummers who invaded the region from vantage points outside. Waterfront facilities were greatly enlarged to meet the needs of an expanded trans-Pacific commerce. This was the critical era when the practical requirements of international trade were gauged and met. The banking system was transformed so that local institutions which had been starved for resources, came to command assets of perhaps $10 million to $12 million each. These large banks served as a channel for the movement of investment capital, provided the means of financing both commerce and construction, and became intermediaries through which reserve funds, as they accumulated in the smaller rural depositories, were transferred to the major financial centers of the country. Management and entrepreneurial patterns were fundamentally altered as out-of-state companies launched or expanded their operations in Washington or Oregon, and local men found themselves associated in various ways with nonresidents who ventured into the Far West in a business way, but who never really became identified with the western community.

The boom stage was a time when "ground floor" opportunities were particularly promising and aggressiveness won many special advantages that had to be established early if they were to be established at all. This was the period when the basic pattern of utilities and improvements took shape. During these years James J. Hill argued persistently and successfully with municipal authorities in Seattle over the concessions he thought necessary for the Great Northern Railway. Private landowners shrewdly bought up tidelands at low prices, and Stone and Webster, the Boston utility company, established itself in the Far West with favorable franchises in Washington cities and excellent water power sites in the mountains. The "inner business circle" of stores and banks and office buildings, constructed at that time in Seattle, has continued to be the heart of the city from that day to this.

The speculative transactions, maneuvering, and litigation that were characteristic of "ground floor" enterprises will form an important part of the chapters of regional histories that deal with the boom stages. Now and again emerged an individual figure who represented and exemplified the new entrepreneurial patterns. Such a man was Thomas Burke of Seattle.

It has been said in Burke's behalf that "he built Seattle." This, of course, is a great exaggeration, yet we cannot dispute the fact that he and men of similar principles and ambitions had much to do with the way the city was built. His ideology was very simple. Economic development required capital and it was therefore axiomatic to him that capitalists and entrepreneurs should be allowed such inducements as might be necessary to attract them. Burke seems to have had no second thoughts as to whether the ground floor operator might enjoy his advantage later at the expense of the rest of the community. He considered it his business to get what he could for himself or his clients within the provisions of the law, and to modify the law to the advantage of the entrepreneur whenever opportunities arose.

Burke thus became a prime facilitating agent, rendering assistance in many ingenious ways to those who would derive gain from the developments of the boom stage. Did some out-of-state corporation seek escape from the restraints of Washington's residence requirements?

Burke helped them set up a suitable, and obedient, local administration. Did railroads wish to bring in their tracks in front of the city along the full length of the waterfront? Burke helped them secure Railroad Avenue which did just about that. Did the establishment of inner and outer harbor lines threaten to curtail the activities of those who held the tidelands? Burke had a hand in obtaining a ruling which dissolved the difficulty by administrative interpretation. . . . He was a remarkably articulate spokesman for the select but important company of men who came to some western frontier on the eve of its boom stage, rode the tide of progress, and made themselves intermediaries between the locality and the larger world of capitalism and investment.

Burke concerned himself primarily with three facets of regional development: railroad construction, the rise of metropolitan centers, and the exploitation of regional resources under conditions of expansion. We have spoken of the first. The other two merit a few words of further comment.

The building up of the resource industries was one of the major developments of the boom stage. In sensing this, Burke was shrewd enough, but unfortunately he was wedded to the wrong resources and the wrong industries. We should not be too critical, however, for nobody knew very much about the iron deposits in the Cascade Mountains, and even experienced steel manufacturers failed to recognize the factors that were to make the Pacific Coast dependent upon Chicago and Pittsburgh for many years to come. . . .

The lumber industry, agriculture, and the fisheries were more richly endowed, and they all expanded rapidly under conditions of economic integration. Great tracts of magnificent forests, which formerly had very little commercial value, now changed hands quickly, sometimes bringing tenfold profits in a single transaction. . . .

During the boom stage, agriculture developed the general pattern of specialization and diversification which has continued with some modifications to the present. . . .

Meanwhile the salmon streams and halibut banks beckoned to fishermen from Norway and New England, California and the Dalmatian coast. The ownership of pounds and traps was bitterly contested, ships from Puget Sound challenged ships from Gloucester, and catch records increased so rapidly that the industry faced problems of depletion and overproduction before the boom stage generally was well advanced.

In all these resource lines there were fortunes to be made not so much from speculation as from skill and good management. The middle years were years of opportunity, but the conditions of success were exacting, for the far westerner must match his wits and his ingenuity against competitors who were experienced and well established. The boom stage gave him his chance, but he must prove his worth. Little in life was free.

So far as urbanization goes, the pattern of urban and metropolitan development in the Pacific Northwest was largely set during the boom stage and deserves therefore to be studied particularly for that period. . . . The boom stage was the formative era, and if we want to know how and why a certain balance of metropolitan centers, secondary cities, and rural areas was established in the region, the period to study is the interval from 1880 to 1910. . . .

In our interpretation of the significance of the boom stages in American expansion, the conclusion of the era of transition will be as important as the beginning of it. Every boom has had its climax and its fade-out. Sometimes the ending has been violent. As often, perhaps, it has been a matter of gradual adjustment devoid of crash or catastrophe. If we eliminate the psychological elements of mania and panic for which the over-zealous boosters and speculators were largely responsible, we can see more clearly the essential character of the movement. The principal accelerator forces of the boom stage were (1) basic changes of transport and accessibility which made possible a rapid economic integration; and (2) a lag in the upward movement of land and resource values which for a time put them out of line with the new conditions. Such a lag made possible, briefly at least, exceptionally high profit margins for those who bought in early enough to realize them. This generalized situation included a great number of variations produced by the specific economics of land use, resource exploitation or urbanization in individual instances, or by considerations of time and lag. As values edged higher, the margin of advantage in the boom section as compared with other sections narrowed and perhaps disappeared. As resources were exploited, they were weakened and depleted. Shrinking profits and declining yields progressively diminished the attractiveness of the area either for investment or population migration. When newness and favorable value no longer produced development at rates higher than the national average, we may say the boom stage was ended.

From such an analysis it will be evident that in this interpretation the boom stage of development in a particular locality was a nonrecurring transition. It was not, however, simply a youthful malady. On the contrary, it was a period of formative change that is deserving of special study for the Pacific Northwest and, I suspect, for other regions as well. . . .

·5·

LEWIS E. ATHERTON

The Services of the Frontier Merchant

For a time in the development of most areas of the West, the general merchant played a most important role, concentrating diverse functions in his hands which would pass to specialists as the regional economy became more complex. Here Lewis E. Atherton examines the varied services that the frontier merchants performed in the Middle West and concluded that "they were the services which had to be performed if the West was to pass from a self-sufficient economy to the stage of economic specialization."

. . . If the story of the frontier is to be told solely in terms of classes like the cowboy and the farmer the process of transforming such an area into a modern specialized community will remain a closed book. At one period or another all America was in the pioneer stage. How the transition to a specialized economy occurred has not been studied, and the story of this transition should prove as valuable as the descriptions of other western developments in explaining American life. When told it will be in terms of the merchant class and professional groups— lawyer, doctor, and teacher. . . .

Hunters, farmers and land speculators naturally preceded the business classes, a market for their services being necessary to attract the latter. Thus, peddlers were the only source of merchandise until settlement became sufficiently large to justify merchants in permanently locating at one place, unless the settler was willing to travel to distant markets for his goods. A traveler down the Mississippi River in 1833 commented on the presence of from ten to twenty flatboats at every village along the stream. Foodstuffs, brooms, cabinet-furniture, cider, plows, cordage, and similar articles from towns farther upstream, like Cincinnati, were offered for sale by these floating stores. If the market at one village proved too limited for the disposal of supplies it was an

SOURCE: Abridged from Lewis E. Atherton, "The Services of the Frontier Merchant," *Mississippi Valley Historical Review*, XXIV (September, 1937), 153–170. Reprinted by permission of the *Journal of American History* and Lewis E. Atherton.

easy matter to move to other villages down the river. Such peddlers disposed of their boats when the goods had been sold and returned home by steamboat. . . .

Inducements were frequently offered to merchants to settle in new towns. An elementary form of town life attracted professional men, and a store was the most important attribute of western towns. Real estate promoters, anxious to start a new town, realized the imperative necessity of attracting merchants and frequently offered town lots free to those agreeing to erect store buildings. . . .

In analysing the western merchant it should be borne in mind that frontier conditions demanded a type of business more varied than that found in the East. Merchandising was only one of the merchant's activities. Ninian Edwards of Illinois owned and supervised five stores in Illinois and three in Missouri, practised law, engaged in farming and real estate speculations, operated saw and grist mills, served as governor of Illinois while it was in the territorial stage, and as governor and United States Senator after Illinois entered the Union as a state. In the four volumes of his correspondence only a few letters were devoted to storekeeping. . . .

The firm of James and Robert Aull at Lexington, Missouri, operated stores there and at Liberty, Richmond, and Independence, Missouri, in the thirties. In addition they owned and operated a grist mill, flour mill, and hemp factory, invested in river steamboats, and exported farm crops. Jared Warner at Millville, Wisconsin, engaged in trade, lumbering, and farming. As exporters of farm produce such merchants departed from a limited conception of their function as retailers of manufactured goods, but in so doing they enabled farmers to devote more time to the now primary object of producing a surplus of agricultural products for sale. Varied interests were the rule rather than the exception, and in this respect merchants were conforming to the pattern of western life; but their activities were of such a nature that other residents of their communities were able to specialize to a greater degree than had formerly been the case. As a result, the western merchants speeded up the process of developing a modern economy by remaining entrepreneurs of varied interests when they first entered a pioneer community.

As a citizen of the small western villages, which he helped to create, the merchant's first, and most obvious, service was as a retailer of manufactured goods and groceries. In this capacity he offered escape from the self-sufficient stage in which the community lived when he first appeared. In his varied stock of drygoods, hardware, groceries, and drugs was the power to liberate the resident of the West from the necessity of being a jack of all trades and a master of none. For example, C. B. Fletcher at Vandalia, Illinois, in 1826 advertised drygoods, hardware, crockery, and groceries. When such a store appeared in a new community farmers no longer found it imperative to spin their own clothing, to rely on handmade, crude tools, or even to produce all the foodstuffs essential to existence. They were now able to concentrate on the production of those crops which offered the greatest return on the investment.

If the merchant had been satisfied to stop with this service the West would have taken a much longer time to reach economic maturity than proved to be the case. Money was scarce, and the most bountiful supply of goods was worthless without some medium of exchange. Banks and a market for western crops would solve the problem, but neither existed in the early communities. In this situation the merchant had no choice but to assume the double function of banker and dealer in agricultural crops.

The simplest and most pleasant banking operation consisted of caring for the funds of farmers who feared to keep their money at home. . . . Customers withdrew the money as needed or took it out in goods, the merchant profiting both from the additional sales and the use of the money as capital on which to operate. Here the usual process was reversed, however. As a rule the merchant supplied the capital for business operations and rare indeed was the customer who had a balance in his favor at a store.

Storekeepers obtained credit from eastern wholesale houses without great difficulty, the usual terms being six months' credit, payable in twelve, with interest ranging from six to ten per cent after the first six months. Papers of western merchants indicate the great extent to which credit was asked in the East. . . .

Such a credit system allowed twelve months in which to make remittances for eastern goods, and in turn influenced the credit policy of western shopkeepers. Customers were allowed credit for six months, but were expected to settle their accounts twice a year, January first and June first being the usual time for such settlements. . . . As money was scarce in the West the mercantile credit system did much to facilitate trade.

Furthermore, the merchant soon realized the need for banks. Many bought their goods directly in the eastern cities, a practise which called for annual remittances of large sums of money to those centers. An estimate of the percentage of merchants who bought goods in the East is difficult to make. That the number was large, however, is attested by the frequency of advertisements announcing the return of a merchant with goods bought in Philadelphia, Baltimore, or New York markets. Storekeepers located in the Mississippi Valley generally visited the East sometime near the first of the year in order to get their goods home in time for the spring trade. The trip was expensive, kept a merchant away from his store for a month or six weeks, and involved many difficulties. . . .

But eastern markets had certain well defined advantages over western wholesale centers, and for the larger merchants these seemed to outweigh the difficulties involved in purchasing goods at such a distance from home. Close contacts with European firms permitted seaboard wholesalers to undersell western competitors. Liberal credit terms, close attention to the needs of customers, and larger stocks of goods from which to make selections added to the supremacy of the eastern firms. With such advantages in their favor it is easy to understand why they drew storekeepers from the farthest reaches of the frontier.

But whether he purchased in eastern or western markets, a storekeeper living in a village without banking facilities had to send paper money through the mails to the larger western cities in order to purchase bills of exchange with which to make his remittances. The uncertainty of the mails made the transfer of money by that means extremely hazardous. To lessen the risk bills were frequently cut in two and the separate parts sent in different mails. If one mail was lost the money could still be redeemed by presenting the remaining half to the bank which had issued it. Even more of a problem was the transfer of specie. This often was moved to the larger cities in the wagons of freighters or concealed in shipments of produce. . . . An investigation of the lives of one hundred and forty merchants, chosen at random from biographical encyclopedias for the states of Missouri, Ohio, Illinois, Wisconsin, Iowa, and Kentucky, showed that fourteen per cent of them ultimately transferred from merchandising to banking. This was due in part to the fact that men originally engaged in more general enterprises could specialize as the West became more settled, but the difficulties faced by such men in the early days of storekeeping contributed to the realization of the need for financial institutions.

The barter system employed by the merchants to dispose of their goods also helped to ease the money situation. Farmers exchanged their crops for groceries and drygoods, thereby escaping the necessity of purchasing with currency. Furs, meats, wheat, beeswax, flax, hemp, honey, whiskey, ginseng—anything of value, could be exchanged at the neighborhood store for goods. Only through this means was the storekeeper able to dispose of his wares to a population that lacked ready cash with which to buy. . . .

All over the West this pattern of bartering goods for produce was practised, the merchant serving as a middleman to a much greater extent than is the case today. The farm crops taken in exchange for goods were consigned to commission merchants in the larger western cities and in New Orleans, the proceeds from the sale easing the merchant's burden of obtaining the credits necessary to meet his bills to the eastward. . . .

The services of the merchants did not end with the marketing of the farmer's crop. Many of them were interested in farming and operated farms of their own. Better read and more widely traveled than the average western farmer, they exhibited an interest in scientific farming and took the lead in fostering it. . . .

Furthermore, the mercantile class played a prominent part in developing manufacturing. James Wier at Lexington, Kentucky, owned and operated a rope walk and yearly sent large quantities of bagging and rope to Charleston and New Orleans in the South and to New York City. Through this means he was able to establish funds in eastern cities with which to meet his wholesale bills. Thus in 1811 Wier drew on a New York City firm for $3,000, payment to be made within one hundred and twenty days. Before that time had expired he had sent his eastern creditors a shipment of hemp, tobacco, and yarn. . . .

The Aull mercantile firm owned a rope walk at Liberty, Missouri. Operations were started in the autumn of 1829, with Aull shipping between 60,000 and 70,000 pounds of bale rope to New Orleans in the first year. The shipments increased in size in succeeding years, with New Orleans as the chief market. In enterprises of this type the merchant achieved his most advanced position in the pre-Civil War period. Goods from the Atlantic seaboard were bartered to the western farmer for his leading crop. The farm crop was then processed by the merchant, which enabled him both to reduce the bulk and increase the value before paying freighting charges. The commodity was often sold in the South, fulfilling the West's place as the source of supply for the South in the three cornered trade so typical of that period. Through the process credit was built up in New Orleans, and this was transferred to the eastern cities to meet the wholesale bills which the merchants contracted in the winter months. . . .

When all these services by the mercantile class are totalled—the building of towns, wholesaling and retailing, banking, the development of a market for farm crops, the promotion of agriculture, and the start of manufacturing—they are seen to be of the same general significance.

They were the services which had to be performed if the West was to pass from a self-sufficient economy to the stage of economic specialization. Without them an advanced economic order was impossible; with them the West rapidly worked itself out of the pioneer stage. It is because of their leadership in this transition period that the merchant class deserves a place in the story of the frontier.

PART TWO

Consequences and Continuities

SECTION 1

Patterns of
Local Exploitation

CHAPTER X

The Fur Men

MAULED AND FEARFULLY TORN by a grizzly, and left for dead some days later by his remaining companions, Hugh Glass survived to stagger hundreds of miles back to Fort Kiowa. During fantastic journeys through the mountains, deserts and forests of the far West, Jedediah Strong Smith twice escaped massacres that claimed some of his companions, only to die on Comanche lances while travelling the Santa Fe Trail. Dramatic chapters abound in the history of the North American fur trade. The incredible hardships and the courage and the fortitude of some of the fur men and the fact that they were violent and colorful men, imparts a kind of epic quality to the history of the fur trade which has stirred the interest of many serious scholars and fiction writers.

But the color and the drama of the fur trade has sometimes obscured its basic realities. In most of the interior of North America from the Gulf of Mexico northward, the fur trade was the first important pattern of resource use which the Europeans developed. The fur trade drew the French into the interior from their post at Quebec and the British colonists were soon bartering for furs among the Indians adjacent to their settlements. The aspirations of European dynasties and the frictions generated by imperial ambitions on four continents underlay the series of wars between France and England in the years between 1689 and 1763. But in North America the fur trade of the continental interior was clearly the first prize of empire. As elsewhere there was a very important economic dimension in the international politics of North America.

Historians of the fur trade in the United States have particularly emphasized the traffic in beaver fur and the exploitation of the fur fields in the Northern Plains and western mountains which reached its climax during the early 1830's. Recently Professor James L. Clayton has challenged both the significance of the fur trade in American economic development and the emphasis which scholars have placed upon the years between 1800 and 1835. During the early nineteenth century most furs gathered in the United States were exported, representing about one per cent of all the exports from the United States each year. The percentage actually remained at about that level throughout the remainder of the century. Since American exports increased substantially between 1835 and 1900 and a considerable domestic market for furs developed also, fur production obviously increased.

Many historians have suggested that the fur trade declined after the western fur companies and the mountain men had reaped the richest harvests from the western beaver lands, but Professor Clayton points out that the increased importance of raccoon skins, obtained in the Middle West, buffalo robes, skunk, mink and seal skins more than compensated for the declining yield of beaver fur. Nor did the fur trade always remain on the western margin of settlement. Since the Great Lakes states were the source of most raccoon skins, that region produced more fur during the mid-nineteenth century than did the Far West. An insignificant proportion of the full-time workers in the United States was engaged in collecting fur at any given time. Trappers and traders of European origin probably never numbered more than 1500 during the classic days of the beaver trade during the 1820's and 1830's. Monopolizing both the Canadian and the Oregon trade, the Hudson's Bay Company employed about 1300 men during the mid-1830's. In the late 1820's the value of the furs exported each year from the United States, was perhaps no more than an eighth of the value of the lead which the miners were producing annually in the Galena lead district of the upper Mississippi valley.

We can push this line of argument too far, however. The fur trader did bring the Indian into the American business system. Several substantial fortunes were made in the fur trade, in an era of American history when such fortunes were uncommon. In a capital-scarce economy the value of mobilized wealth goes far beyond its amount. A major center of western enterprise and development, St. Louis, derived significant economic impetus from the fur trade for many years. Many lads on the farming frontier of the nineteenth century, as well as part-time trappers, supplemented their incomes by trapping raccoon, mink and skunk.

Although dozens of historical novels picture the wild, free and sometimes gay life of the mountain men, ironically enough, their era was one in which the American fur trade illustrated imperfect competition, if not outright monopoly. In 1784 young John Jacob Astor arrived in the United States and within two years had become the proprietor of a small fur store in New York. He rapidly developed a flourishing whole-sale business in furs which he sold both in the domestic market and abroad. By the beginning of the new century he was shipping furs to China and taking the proceeds in oriental goods. In 1808 he incorporated his business as the American Fur Company and began to move energetically into the business of supplying the traders who bought furs from the Indians. He purchased an interest in the Mackinaw Company, an organization of British traders who were active in American territory to the west and south of Michilimacinac, and negotiated an agreement with them which allowed the American Fur Company to share the field. Next he tried to establish the American trade in Oregon by planting Fort Astoria there but members of the North West Fur Company, based in Montreal, used the War of 1812 as an excuse to oust the traders of his Pacific Fur Company. Such setbacks were rare in Astor's career and when Congress barred British traders from American soil in 1816 he acquired the assets of those who had been trading in the region between the Great Lakes and the Rocky Mountains and below the forty-ninth parallel.

Assisted by the young Auguste Chouteau, the fur trader, Pierre Laclede established the tiny settlement, which he called St. Louis, in 1764. From that date forward, residents of this strategically located village endeavored to develop the fur trade of the region. There were pelts to be purchased to the north, along the Mississippi River and its upper tributaries, but the Missouri particularly seemed the gateway to a veritable empire of fur. By 1800 a community of capable traders had developed at St. Louis, most notable among them, Manuel Lisa. Associated through much of the period with the Missouri Fur Company, this wily trader directed most of the efforts to tap the upper Missouri country during the next 20 years. Although Astor purchased furs from the St. Louis men and sold trade goods to them, they strongly resisted his efforts to place traders in the Missouri and trans-Missouri fields. During the early 1820's, Astor acquired control of one of the St. Louis trading firms and developed the Western Department of the American Fur Company on the foundation which it provided. Thereafter the American Fur Company steadily expanded its trade up the Missouri and in the adjacent mountain regions, absorbing a number of major competitors in the process, most notably the Columbia Fur Company which became the upper Missouri outfit of the Astor enterprises.

Astor never completely throttled his rivals in the region and the Missouri businessman, politician and militia officer, William H. Ashley, made the greatest contribution to opening up the fur lands of the northern Rockies. During the mid- and late 1820's, Ashley and a series of partners and successors, mobilized a cadre of Anglo-American trappers who worked the mountain beaver lands and met their suppliers at a spring rendezvous in convenient locations in the mountains. Many of the most celebrated of the mountain men emerged from this organization. Ashley himself won a modest fortune from the business and several of his lieutenants or field partners accumulated competencies. But the members of the last of the partnerships which emerged from the old Ashley organization, the Rocky Mountain Fur Company, enjoyed meager returns, so vicious was the competition generated by the American Fur Company and minor rivals. West of the Great Divide the trapping brigades of the Hudson's Bay Company held most of the field. The partners of the Rocky Mountain Fur Company sold its assets to the American Fur Company in 1834 and in that same year, John Jacob Astor disposed of his interest in that organization to his major associates. There was little prime fur left in the Rockies by this time and the market for beaver pelts was shrinking rapidly because the hat of beaver felt was giving way to other types of headware. Perhaps the most colorful chapter in the history of the fur trade in the United States was coming to an end.

By 1834 the American Fur Company was handling about three-quarters of the fur exports of the country, although some of these furs had been collected in the field by rivals. In some regions the company was completely dominant. John Jacob Astor's shrewdness in selecting associates and his other business skills, as well as his vision and ruthlessness, explain the success of the American Fur Company in large measure. But characteristics of the fur trade in these years help to explain the development of imperfect competition as well. The traders operated at great distances from the outfitting bases and considerable organization was required to carry equipment and trade goods into the fur country and to bring the furs out most efficiently. The danger of Indian attack and of the unpredictable catastrophes of life in the wilderness made the fur man much safer as the member of an organization. The large firm with established contacts abroad could both purchase trade goods on better terms and sell its furs more profitably than could the individual trader or small firm.

Although the western Indian superintendents and the Army exercised some supervision over the fur trade, most traders and trappers gathered fur outside the institutions of government and beyond the scrutiny of the agencies of law and order in the border settlements. When undercutting prices or giving excessive credit failed to eliminate pestiferous small rivals, foul play was feasible and apparently occurred sometimes. The officers of the American Fur Company saw to it that the prices paid for fur in the field, the wages paid to employees and the returns to its trading partners were as low as hard and ruthless bargaining could make them, and woe betide the trapper or trader of any company who deserted to a rival. While tenderfoot writers gaped at the rowdy horseplay of the rendezvous, the representatives of the fur companies totalled the accounts of a business which was as predatory in its way as the carnivores that lurked in the surrounding wilderness.

Writers portray the mountain man or white trapper in various ways as William H. Goetzmann explains in the fifth selection of this chapter. His reinterpretation is a most interesting one. It is also of some interest to consider that the trappers who gave themselves to the mountain life for considerable periods of time created a halfway culture—drawing both upon the mores of the white settlements and the life ways of the Indians. If left to their own devices in the older communities, it was said, most of the trappers frequented the barrooms and other centers of lower class entertainment. With some notable exceptions they were of extremely low status in Anglo-American society. In the mountains they created a new society, where they enjoyed a higher social position than ever before. Their skills, their weapons and their relative affluence allowed them to pick wives as they willed among the Indians. In this environment they were men of consequence; they had actually risen in social stature by choosing the life of the mountains.

Although it is possible to qualify older descriptions of the fur trade, the business certainly did have important economic, political and social implications for the development of the American West. Until almost 1850 the fur business was also of unique international significance. Although Americans expected to inherit the fur trade in the region below the Great Lakes after Great Britain recognized the independence of the United States in 1783, British traders based in Montreal proved difficult to dislodge from the region. When British troops withdrew from posts on American soil, such as Detroit and Mackinac, following Jay's Treaty in 1794, American traders became more successful to the east of Lake Michigan but beyond that body of water British traders continued to penetrate deeply into American territory.

The activity of American traders along the coast of the Pacific Northwest, including Captain Robert Gray's discovery of the Columbia demonstrated American interest in the region, as did the Lewis and Clark expedition some years later. Although unsuccessful as a business enterprise, the Astoria venture demonstrated the continuing interest of Americans in that region. In the discussions which produced the Convention of 1818, providing for joint occupation of the Oregon country, British negotiators conceded that the men of the Pacific Fur Company had indeed been within their rights in establishing and trying to maintain Fort Astoria. Meanwhile domestic traders had convinced Congress that British rivals should be barred from American territory to the east of the Rockies.

After the North West Fur Company and the Hudson's Bay Company merged in 1821, the latter held the trade of the northern Pacific coast firmly in its grasp for many years and its employees in Oregon worked strenuously during the 1820's and 1830's to prevent American traders from sharing in the fur harvest of that region. The determination of the Hudson's Bay Company to monopolize the trade there undoubtedly stimulated the ambitions of Americans to possess that region. Thus national policy and the economic interests of the fur traders were linked together. Although the American and British traders were rivals for the fur of much of the continent, the American trade drew both personnel and expertise from the British industry. Many American traders had first worked in one or other of the British companies, French-Canadian engagés served as boatmen on the Missouri River, and business practices and procedures in the trade were colored by the Canadian heritage. Indeed John Jacob Astor chose his wife from one of the Scottish fur trading families of Montreal.

The fur men made a very considerable contribution to the exploration of the West. Jedediah Smith linked the geography of Lewis and Clark and the geography of the Spanish explorers in the Southwest. A land party of Astorians discovered South Pass, the great avenue through the Rockies which was later used by so many parties of transcontinental travellers. The fur traders accepted the logic of the Platte route to the mountains and drove wagons over the future Overland Trail as far as Fort Hall on the Snake River. Only the Indians had seen the natural wonders of the Yellowstone country before them and the fur men knew the lay of the land in hundreds of western localities before official explorers ventured there. From the ranks of the traders and trappers emerged many of the guides who accompanied official exploring expeditions and many of the wagon companies that crossed the continent during the 1840's and 1850's. The knowledge which the trapping fraternity accumulated about the plains and the approaches to the mountains undoubtedly did much to dispel the myth of the Great American Desert which was based on the reports of early army expeditions to the mountain barrier. The fur traders first recognized the locational advantages of the sites now occupied by Omaha, Bismarck, Laramie and other western cities.

Nor can we ignore the impact of the fur traders upon the Indians, although some have deplored it with good reason. The fur trader was the representative of American business among the Indian tribes, and incidentally an important agent of acculturation. Using the tribesmen as fur collectors, he rewarded them in return with the trinkets, utensils and hunting equipment of the Anglo-American culture. He brought both alcohol and new diseases among the Indians, debauching them on the one hand and killing them on the other. The debts which the Indians owed to the traders were sometimes used as leverage in extracting cessions of land from them. The traders came, therefore, and Indian culture crumbled in their wake. Yet it is possible that the impact of the white man upon Indian society would have been even more tragic had there been no fur trade. Despite the gouging and the demoralization, in a very real sense the trade allowed the two cultures to come to terms with each other. In the fur trade Indian and Anglo-American found a community of interest. The fur trader offered the Indian a useful role of a sort that he understood. How much more devastating in effect might the conflict between Indian and Anglo-American have been if the latter had offered only the white man's agriculture to the tribesmen.

What should the relation of our government have been to the fur men? Some have suggested that our government was less accommodating than the British government, which provided the Hudson's Bay Company with a trading monopoly over a huge northern empire. The government of the United States established a factory system which competed with the traders. The embargo which Thomas Jefferson fashioned against foreign exports struck the domestic fur men with paralyzing effect. Had the United States government supported the Astoria venture, it has been argued, Oregon would have become American territory many years before the fact. American traders resented the supervision of the Indian service and the official prohibition against the use of alcohol in the trade. It is hard to accept such reasoning as anything but the self-interest of the members of an American economic interest group making a typically American argument for special treatment. The government did bar English traders from American soil in 1816 and it abolished the factory system. Discharged Indian agents sometimes charged that they had lost their jobs because they had incurred the wrath of the fur men. Such eminent western politicians as Thomas Hart Benton and Lewis Cass guarded the interests of their fur trading constituents with particular solicitude.

Although the fur men were few in number and the capital invested and the returns from the trade were suprisingly small in retrospect, they did make a unique contribution to the making of Western America.

·1·

WAYNE E. STEVENS

The Organization of the British Fur Trade, 1760-1800

The great British fur companies, the North West Company and the Hudson's Bay Company, influenced the fur trade of the United States in many ways. The Hudson's Bay Company obtained exclusive privileges to trade in the vast watershed of Hudson's Bay from the British Crown in the year 1670. In the following narrative, Wayne E. Stevens describes the background of the British fur trade in the Great Lakes region and the formation of the North West Company.

. . . The reduction of Canada . . . meant the overthrow of the entire business organization which had been built up by French merchants in the days of the old regime. Henceforth, goods destined for use in the Indian trade would be imported from England, while the peltries for which they were exchanged would find their way to London instead of to Paris; all this was in accord with the mercantile theory of the time, which regarded colonies as producers of raw materials and as consumers of goods manufactured in the mother country. . . . There were left in the Indian country, however, a great many *engagés* and small French traders, who must either accommodate themselves to the new order of things or seek new fields of endeavor. The easy-going disposition of the French-Canadian led him to choose the former alternative, and the result was that when the British merchant entered the country, he found ready to hand a large class of persons, skilled in the more or less

Source: Abridged from Wayne E. Stevens, "The Organization of the British Fur Trade, 1760–1800," *Mississippi Valley Historical Review*, III (September, 1916), 172-202. Reprinted by permission of the *Journal of American History*.

technical processes of the trade, who formed a substructure upon which might be reared a stable business organization. The system of posts erected in the interior by the French was also at the disposal of the British when they arrived, and formed convenient centers of trade. . . .

Very little is known concerning the early history of the merchants who came to Canada after 1760, and their rise to wealth and power can be traced only through such glimpses of their business activities as it is possible to obtain. Their vigor and industry, however, are amply attested by the rapid growth of the fur industry during the period of British rule in the northwest. Establishing their headquarters at the city of Montreal, they extended their operations southwestward into the Illinois country, and westward into the wilderness beyond the Mississippi river; while their representatives penetrated far into the country beyond lake Superior, establishing posts in regions unknown to the French. From out of this vast range of territory were annually carried hundreds of thousands of furs of many varieties, including those of the beaver, marten, otter, mink, muskrat, raccoon, and cat, along with the skins of the deer and the bear. Estimates as to the value of the furs annually exported from Canada to the London market during the period of the revolution and the following decade vary somewhat, but it is probable that the annual returns did not fall far short of £200,000 sterling. . . .

In the early days of the British period, traders frequently obtained their outfits in person at Montreal, or in New York; carried them to some post in the interior; bartered them with the Indians, assisted by a few clerks and interpreters; and carried the furs obtained back to market. . . . But for one man to obtain his goods in person and carry them to the interior involved the loss of a great deal of time and rendered it impossible for the trader to spend each winter in the Indian country. Describing his operations during these early years, [Alexander] Henry makes a significant statement. He says that in 1765 he began to prosecute the Indian trade anew, and that he purchased an outfit consisting of four canoe loads of goods, at twelve months' credit, at the post of Michillimackinac. This little incident reveals how there was being developed a complex mechanism of distribution, based upon a division of labor, the function of which was to effect the interchange of peltry and merchandise which has been described.

As a matter of fact, the group of men represented by the trader in the buckskin shirt and raccoon cap formed only one of a number of classes of persons who were interested in the peltry trade. Regarded collectively, the various groups constituted a business organization which extended from the city of London to the most remote depths of the North American wilderness. At the top of this vast industrial system were the great London firms. . . . An enumeration of the London houses interested in the northwest fur trade would include the names of many of the great merchants of the United Kingdom, men who did not hesitate to apply to his majesty's ministers in their own interests or those of their correspondents on the other side of the water.

Next in order came the great mercantile houses of Montreal, firms often referred to collectively as the "merchants of Montreal," whose business formed the backbone of Canadian commerce. . . . Many of the great fur barons of Montreal were Scotchmen, who had come to Canada soon after the conquest and supplanted the French merchants who had hitherto reaped the benefits of the peltry trade of the great lakes and upper Mississippi. . . .

A step further down in this commercial hierarchy were the merchants who were located at Michillimackinac and Detroit and supplied outfits to those who traded at the various dependencies of these posts scattered throughout the interior. These merchants were men of lesser means, usually, than the members of the Montreal firms. . . . It is very probable that certain of the Montreal concerns supplied outfits directly to the small traders, who went among the Indians, through representatives at the upper posts; still there were numerous merchants who made their headquarters at Michillimackinac and Detroit and acted as middlemen between the Montreal firms and the petty traders dwelling in the interior. A great many of the traders established at these two posts were French who had simply remained in their places after the conquest and accommodated themselves to the new commercial system which was inaugurated by the British.

Still a fourth group may be distinguished, made up of traders who spent the greater part of each year in the Indian country, dealing with the savages at the dependencies of Detroit and Michillimackinac. Probably the greater number of these small traders scattered throughout the interior were French-Canadians who had gone out into the wilderness as traders and *engagés* during the French régime and remained after the coming of the British. There were in addition, however, numerous petty traders of English, Scotch, and Irish descent. . . .

Taking up for consideration the manner in which these different groups of merchants and traders coöperated, it will be convenient to begin by describing the business relationship which subsisted between the small trader living in the remote interior and the merchant who made his headquarters at Michillimackinac or Detroit. . . . A trader coming in from the Illinois country to Michillimackinac . . . went to the merchant at that post with whom he was in the habit of dealing, and presented a memorandum of certain articles which he desired for his trade the following winter. If the merchant considered his credit good, he made up an outfit of the goods desired and turned it over to his customer at a certain price, with the understanding that the latter should settle ·for it when he brought in his returns the following season. When the trader came in from his wintering ground in the following spring with the peltry he had succeeded in obtaining from the Indians, he might either sell his returns in the open market at Michillimackinac and then settle with his outfitter, or he might turn them over to the latter at the market price, the proceeds to be applied on his account. Still another alternative was open to him, for, instead of disposing of his furs at Michillimackinac, he might consign them to Montreal or even to London, at his own risk, in order to obtain the advantage of the higher prices which they might be expected to bring in those markets. . . .

The connection between the Montreal firm and the merchant at Detroit or Michillimackinac was rather similar to that which existed between the latter and the trader in the Indian country, which has just been described. The goods which were imported into the upper country were obtained through the medium of the great Montreal houses, who imported them from England on commission, and supplied them to the merchant at the upper post at a certain "advance" on the sterling cost. There were certain articles of merchandise, however, known as "cash goods," such as rum, for example, for which the Montreal outfitter was obliged to pay ready money; and he charged the merchant interest on all goods of this sort which were furnished on credit. . . . The agent at Montreal superintended the business of making up the outfits . . . a task which involved the supervision of a good many details of one sort and another. . . .

All these details were attended to by the Montreal concern and the expense involved was charged to the account of the customer at Detroit or Michillimackinac. In addition to the services which have been enumerated, the firm at Montreal acted in the capacity of banker for its customers. Thus, if a merchant at Michillimackinac desired to pay the wages of his *engagés,* or meet any other obligation in fact, he might draw upon his agent at Montreal in favor of the person to whom he was making the remittance and thus the conduct of his business was greatly facilitated.

Besides supplying goods to the merchants in the upper country, the Montreal firm also acted as agent for the returns in peltry which

were sent down from time to time, either in sailing vessels by way
of the lakes or by canoe down the Ottawa or Grand river. The merchant
usually consigned the peltry he had on hand to his agent, who was
instructed either to sell it as advantageously as possible in the market at
Montreal, or to ship it to England to be sold in the London market. . . .

Just as the Montreal concern acted as agent for the merchants and
traders in the upper country, so the London merchant performed a
similar service for his correspondents in Montreal. Besides supplying
his customers with goods, he superintended the marketing of the furs
which were exported from Canada, seeing that they were properly
unloaded and stored away in warehouses and later preparing them for
the annual fur sales. . . . In brief, the London firm transacted all the
business incidental to the marketing of the furs, for which service a
commission was charged on the proceeds of the sale as well as interest
on sums of money which it was necessary to advance from time to time.

From the foregoing description, it is apparent that practically every
step in the entire process known as the fur trade was based upon credit.
The merchants of Montreal almost invariably obtained their supplies
from the London firms on credit, making the goods up into outfits which
they advanced to their customers at the upper posts. In the spring the
small trader came in to Michillimackinac or Detroit from the Indian
country with his peltry and set out again in the late summer or fall,
with an outfit obtained from the merchant with whom he dealt, still on
credit. The proceeds derived from the sale of the furs he carried in with
him were almost invariably used to pay for the outfit which had been
secured the preceding season and which had been consumed during
the past winter in trading for the same peltry which he carried in with
him. Considering the basis upon which the trade was conducted throughout its various stages, it is not difficult to understand how poor returns in
furs, owing to war, unsuccessful hunting, or any other cause, would
affect the whole industry. . . .

The character of the fur trade rendered it desirable—indeed, almost
necessary, that there should be a considerable degree of coöperation
among those who were engaged therein. The small trader was handicapped by the fact that his limited capital and resources compelled him
to lead a sort of hand-to-mouth existence in the conduct of his affairs,
while he was obliged to depend upon another merchant, his agent,
to transact a large share of his business. During the last quarter of the
eighteenth century there was a very marked tendency toward centralization in the fur trade, and it was during this period that the great companies which dominated the northwest trade in the early part of the

nineteenth century had their origin. The types of business organization which were developed varied from the simple agreement between individual traders or firms, to the rich and powerful North-west company. . . .

The fur trade which was carried on from Montreal reached its highest development at the hands of the North-west company, which included some of the ablest men of all Canada. The origin of the concern may be traced back to the early days of the English occupation, though the company was not definitely organized until the winter of 1783 and 1784, when a number of traders operating in the region beyond lake Superior consolidated their interests by the formation of a sixteen-share company at Montreal, which was to last for a period of five years. No capital in the form of money was put into the enterprise but each share holder furnished a certain proportion of goods to be used in the trade. . . .

Certain of the share holders were entrusted with the management of the affairs of the company in the upper country, making their general headquarters and place of rendezvous at Grand Portage, near the western end of lake Superior. They were called "wintering partners," to distinguish them from the members of the concern who had their headquarters at Montreal. The numerous posts of the company which were scattered throughout the vast region beyond lake Superior were in charge of hired clerks, or "bourgeois," as they were called, some of whom by reason of their industry in time rose to the rank of wintering partners. The important fact to be noted is that the company conducted its own business through all the various stages, importing such goods as were required from London, and dividing the net profits among the various partners in proportion to the shares which they held. The goods were the property of the company, however, from the time they left Montreal until they were bartered for furs at the various posts of the interior. Thus the conduct of the trade in the far northwest was systematized, and so successful was the enterprise that the competition of small individual traders in the region was completely destroyed; in time, the concern was even able to challenge the supremacy of the Hudson's bay company in its own territory. . . .

The northwest fur trade enjoyed a much more vigorous growth under the British régime than it had while the French were still masters of Canada, due in part to the inauguration of a system of free competition instead of legal monopolies, and in no small measure also to the character and ability of the English, Scotch, and Irish merchants who flocked to Canada after the conquest; under their direction the industry was extended westward to the head waters of the Missouri river, and far into the vast Canadian wilderness lying beyond lake Superior. For vigor and enterprise, the world has probably seen very few groups of men superior to those who have been referred to so often in the preceding pages as the "merchants of Montreal." Not only did they direct their respective business enterprises in masterly fashion, but they worked together to secure the favor and coöperation of the government of Canada, and even of the British ministry itself. As a class, they were possessed of great power and influence; they addressed memorial after memorial to the administrative heads of the government of Quebec, and it is no exaggeration to say that their influence made itself felt in the course of Anglo-American diplomacy during the years which followed the revolution. . . .

EDGAR B. WESLEY

The Government Factory System Among the Indians, 1795–1822

Typically the fur traders were the first white men to have business dealings with any particular tribe or band of Indians. If the traders were particularly irresponsible or grasping in bartering for furs, they might render the Indians hostile to Americans in general, encourage them to patronize foreign traders, or even provoke the natives into raiding the settler's frontier. During President Washington's administration, the members of Congress established a system of government trading posts which might have insured fair dealing in the fur trade if it had been properly managed and maintained.

. . . The law of 1796 definitely established a system which had been merely tried out under the law of the preceding year. The president was directed to appoint factors to reside at the posts and sell goods to the Indians. They were to report twice a year to the secretary of the Treasury and account for all money, furs, and supplies. They were to take oath for the faithful performance of their duties and to furnish bond as the president directed. No factor was to be engaged in the trade on his own account, and he was prohibited from receiving presents from the Indians or any furs except in exchange for government goods. The appropriation of $150,000 brought the total capital to $200,000, and goods were to be sold at such prices as would merely maintain the principal. The sum of $8,000 annually was provided for maintenance. The Act was limited to two years, plus the duration of the Congress then in session. The purpose of the bill establishing the government factory system may be summed up as (1) diplomatic, since its purpose was to destroy British influence and secure the friendship of the Indians, (2) economic, in that it sought incidentally to eliminate British traders, and (3) military, as a system of controlling the Indians. . . .

Source: Abridged from Edgar B. Wesley, "The Government Factory System Among the Indians, 1795–1822," *Journal of Economic and Business History*, IV (May, 1932), 487–511. © 1932, Graduate School of Business Administration, Harvard University. Reprinted by permission of the *Business History Review*.

The general plan of operation was well established. The superintendent of Indian Trade sent out order blanks, and the factors sent in their requisitions, basing their estimates upon past business, the condition of the market, the competition of traders, and future prospects. The superintendent endeavored to supply all goods which the factors ordered. . . . He was limited to the domestic markets and thus sometimes failed to secure goods of high quality. During the early years of the system the office of the superintendent was located at Philadelphia and most of the goods were purchased at that place. After the removal of the office to Georgetown, about 1808, that city became the principal supply market.

The transportation of goods to the factories was an expensive, time-consuming, and often wasteful process. Since most of the factories were located in remote places, goods had to be reshipped several times. The principal distributing centers were New Orleans, St. Louis, and Detroit. A forwarding agent received the goods and sent them on to the factories by boats, wagons, or pack-horses, depending upon the local conditions. Under the circumstances freight charges were high. It cost from $4.00 to $9.00 to ship a hundred pounds of goods from Washington to St. Louis. In 1821 the cost was $4.24. . . . It is thus apparent that the factory prices on heavy articles of little value would have to be greatly increased over their original cost, if each article was to be sold at such a price as would maintain the capital fund undiminished. . . .

The factor sold his goods to various groups and by various methods. Indians were the principal customers, and for them the factory system was maintained, but the number of stores was hopelessly inadequate for supplying all tribes and villages. In order to reach those who lived at great distances from the factories and to offset the competition of private traders, the factors sent goods to these traders, even into remote villages. This practice was bitterly denounced by private traders, but it had the approval of the superintendent of Indian Trade and was in entire accord with the purposes which had led to the establishment of the system. The Indians usually gave furs, skins, beeswax, tallow, bear oil, feathers, and other products in exchange for factory goods, whereas soldiers, private traders, travelers, and other white customers usually paid cash. The factor shipped the furs, skins, and so forth that he had received to the forwarding agent at the nearest distributing center, who sometimes sold them locally but more frequently forwarded them to the superintendent, who sold them at auction.

Instructions were sent to factors to guide them in the details of their work. Those sent out in 1808 by John Mason, superintendent of Indian

Trade, are condensed and summarized as follows:

1. Bear in mind that the object of the factory system is to win and retain the friendship of the Indians.
2. The cost of goods should be figured as approximately 68 per cent advance over the marked cost. Watch carefully that the Indians do not sell you inferior furs, for they are likely to be made the instruments of unprincipled traders. On the other hand, do not sell any inferior goods without calling attention to the defect and making allowance for it.
3. Sell to Indians only. If it is necessary to sell to whites, do so by charging 10 per cent more than when selling to Indians. Give credit cautiously and mostly to chiefs.
4. You will be furnished with sufficient guards and with an interpreter if necessary.
5. You are forbidden to carry on any trade on your own account.
6. In no case will you sell or dispense liquors.
7. Send in your requisitions early and mark them explicitly.
8. Send your furs to Joseph Saul at New Orleans or General William Clark at St. Louis.
9. Invoices should be sent to the superintendent of Indian Trade.
10. Keep careful and correct records of all transactions. . . .

From 1809 to the close of the system in 1822 the trading fund amounted to $290,000. In addition to the trade fund, annual appropriations were made for the salaries of all employees. . . . The War of 1812, however, was a serious blow to the factories. Those at Chicago, Mackinac, Sandusky, Fort Wayne, and Fort Madison were captured or destroyed by the British, entailing a loss of $43,369, and the others suffered a diminution of business. . . .

Following the War of 1812 there was a steady rise in the volume of business until the panic year of 1819. . . .

The factors needed commercial sense and diplomatic skill. They were tested by wary Indians eager to sell their furs at high prices and secure goods at bargain rates. Dissatisfied groups required considerate treatment, and the laws of hospitality were subject to great strains. Rival traders often misrepresented the purposes of the factors and incited worthless Indians to buy goods on credit at the factories. Some of the factors took their families with them and lived the life typical of the frontier. Lost goods, spoiled skins, bad debts, commercial rivalries, and Indian alarms occasioned much worry and prevented the factors from leading an idyllic life.

The connection between the factory system and the army was close. Factories were usually located at fortified posts, occasionally occupying one of the rooms within the fort. The soldiers were ordered to assist the factors in transporting goods, beating and packing furs, and erecting buildings, for which extra-military services they were rewarded with a gill of whiskey and fifteen cents a day. . . . Protection, however, was the chief service of the army to the factories, and in most cases the mere presence of the troops was all that was needed.

The opponents of the factory system were the fur companies, individual traders, and many disinterested persons who really believed that it was a failure. The system had its defects and its enemies took delight in pointing them out; in many instances they added misrepresentation to honest criticism. In one instance the Indians were told that the factory system was for the purpose of inducing them to run into debt so that the United States could seize their lands. Traders told Indians that the factors *sold* goods which were intended by the government as *presents,* and that the agents stole half of the presents. . . .

The opponents of the factory system were divided as to what system should supplant it. The most frequently mentioned plans were those for the establishment of a large factory at St. Louis which would sell to traders only, and the formation of a company guaranteed and regulated by the government. . . .

The supporters of the factory system included many people well disposed toward the Indians, most public officials, and the factors themselves. They upheld it because of its supposed benefits to the Indians. It was repeatedly sustained by committees of Congress and by Congress itself in the face of opposition. . . . One Indian agent said that the factories were rallying centers where the Indians felt at home and that they considered them "as their father's houses." . . . The supporters blamed the enemies of the system for many of its faults. Factor George C. Sibley was one of the most vehement critics of the fur traders and fur companies. He said that the practices of the fur companies rendered the factories useless. He aroused the ire of more than one by hinting that the American Fur Company smuggled its goods into the country.

Early in 1822 a Senate committee, with Thomas H. Benton as chairman, began to gather evidence against the factory system. Benton claimed that he, being from a frontier State, understood the operations of the factories. In his account he observed, "it cost me a strenuous exertion" to accomplish their downfall. It is, however, difficult to escape the suspicion that Benton was serving . . . influential fur dealers who were his constituents. . . .

Thomas L. McKenney, superintendent of Indian Trade, presented an able defense. He said that the unscrupulous conduct of traders and the open competition had prevented the factories from proving their worth. He submitted many letters and tables to prove that he secured the best quality of goods to be had in the United States, and that they were similar to those which the traders sold. . . .

Conditions favored the opponents of the factory system. The steady rise of the American Fur Company was a menace to the success of the factories. In its early years the Company chose to concentrate its efforts in the region of the Great Lakes. The declining volume of business of the factories at Mackinac, Green Bay, and Chicago is evidence of the success of the Company. About 1815 the fur traders of St. Louis became conscious of the part which the factories were playing in the fur trade. Consequently they became hostile and began agitation for the abolition of the system. They were fortunate in securing the services of Senator Benton when he entered the Senate in 1821. In addition to the combined efforts of the great fur traders the opposition also found convincing proof in the financial affairs of the system. . . .

From the inception of the system the opposition had been sufficiently strong to limit the duration of the continuation of the laws to one, two, or three years. The new nationalism, so pronounced in the period following the war, favored the laissez-faire policy. Thus the specific opposition secured the aid of a widespread feeling that private business should not be injured by official undertakings. The fiery and astute Benton was able to unify the opposing forces and secured the passage of an act on May 6, 1822, repealing the entire system. . . .

The factory system lasted twenty-seven years. It failed to justify the sanguine expectations of its friends and afforded many just grounds for the criticism of its enemies. The factories were inaugurated during a period when private capital was unable to meet the situation and when traders were powerless before the stronger organization and greater experience of the British. During the period of their existence, the War of 1812 enabled the United States to shake off British influence and thus open a more unhindered field to native traders. The system was probably unnecessary after that event, but its abolition led to unrestrained competition, and the *engagés* of great companies fought each other in more than commercial ways. Following the abolition of the factory system, the government made little effort to protect the Indians against the outrages of the trader, and the rapid development of the fur-gathering industry almost dispensed with the need of the Indian at all. Within a decade after the abolition of the factories the fur region east of the Rockies was rapidly being depleted. . . .

RAY H. MATTISON

The Upper Missouri Fur Trade:
Its Methods of Operation

During the first half of the nineteenth century, the fur traders were the only representatives of the American business system who were active in the upper Missouri country. Here, as elsewhere, they fashioned a unique society, part North American Indian and part Euro-American in character. Professor Mattison describes the characteristics of the fur business and the life of the fur traders in that region.

Before the United States had acquired Louisiana, President Thomas Jefferson, probably with the view of wresting the control of the region from the British, took initial steps toward exploring the Missouri River to the mountains and finding a route to the Pacific. The purchase of Louisiana was consummated in 1803, and the following year in accordance with their instructions, Captains Meriwether Lewis and William Clark and 48 young frontiersmen, set out on their epic journey to the Pacific. . . .

Stimulated by glowing reports of the newly-discovered fur-bearing regions on the Upper Missouri, Manuel Lisa, prominent St. Louis trader, in 1807, embarked on his first ambitious trapping expedition on the Upper Missouri. Inaugurating a new system of operating the business, he built strong permanent forts at strategic places where white hunters and trappers rendezvoused. These posts also served as trading houses and depositories for furs and peltries. . . .

In the decade and a half following the War of 1812 there was a sharp decline in the fur trade, following which there was a great revival in the business. The 1820's saw four strong outfits competing on the Upper Missouri—the Missouri Fur Company . . . the Rocky Mountain Fur Company supported by General William [H.] Ashley and Major Andrew Henry; the Columbia Fur Company backed by strong St. Louis interests

---

SOURCE: Abridged from Ray H. Mattison, "The Upper Missouri Fur Trade: Its Methods of Operation," *Nebraska History*, XLII (March, 1961), 1–28. Reprinted by permission of *Nebraska History* and Ray H. Mattison.

and under the operation of former Northwest Company employees; and
the Western Department, American Fur Company, organized in 1808
under the powerful leadership of John Jacob Astor and supported by
the Chouteaus and other prominent French families in St. Louis. Within
less than a decade after the merger of the two last companies in 1828,
the new subsidiary firm, operating under the name of Upper Missouri
Outfit, had driven its two other principal rivals and a number of lesser
ones from the field.

Although frequently challenged, the Upper Missouri Outfit, generally
called the American Fur Company, for the next three decades, monopo-
lized the fur trade on the river. It was always known as "the company."
Those competing against it, whether an individual trader or a powerful
rival, were known as "the opposition."

By the early 1830's the company had a number of permanent trading
posts on the Upper Missouri. In 1833 there were Cabanne's Post,
located near Council Bluffs, Forts Pierre, Clark, Union and McKenzie.
All, with the exception of the first, were stockaded posts with bastions
and were constructed to withstand attacks by strong war parties of
Indians. . . . All of these principal posts were under the charge of an
agent usually called a "bourgeois," who was responsible to the company
for its operation.

In addition to principal and subsidiary posts there were a number
of wintering houses, which were usually block houses or log houses,
at which three to six men were normally employed. These were usually
erected for a winter among the Indian villages within the range of their
trade and abandoned the following spring if the tribe moved to a new
location. The furs from these places were sent to such depots as Forts
Union or Pierre.

The main permanent trading establishments were quite self-sufficient
institutions. In 1833 the company had listed on its payroll, at Fort Union,
12 clerks and 129 men. At this post the trades of tailor, gunsmith, blacksmith, tinner, cooper, carter, hunter and trapper were represented. . . .

In the early period much of the taking of the furs, particularly of
the beaver, was done by the white trappers. There were two classes of
these, the hired trappers and the free trappers. Hired trappers were employed by the company, normally for a term of three years, for a stipulated sum. They were usually engaged for from one to two hundred
dollars a year paid off in goods at company prices which were very
high. . . .

The free trappers, on the other hand, were more of an independent
class. They supplied their own horses and equipment, could hunt and

trap where they pleased, and could dispose of their furs to the highest bidder. Occasionally, when in dangerous country, it was necessary for the trapper to attach himself to some other trader for protection. In such circumstances he was compelled to conform to the ordinary rules for trapping and to the rules of the camp. He was also required to dispose of his beaver to the trader who commanded the camp. . . .

In the Rocky Mountain region, much of the beaver trapping had been done by bands of white trappers traveling through the country. On the Upper Missouri, on the other hand, a large part of the trapping, particularly of the small fur-bearing animals such as muskrat, racoon, otter, and ermine was done by the Indians. The buffalo robe and a substantial tongue business, important items in the Upper Missouri trade, continued to be largely in Indian hands. . . .

Each year the company sent out its Indian trade goods to its various posts on the Upper Missouri. Prior to the use of the steamboats in the 1830's the keelboat was largely used. Goods were shipped to the principal posts where stock valued at from fifteen to twenty thousand dollars was kept. Those shipped by the larger posts to the temporary posts varied in value from five hundred to two or three thousand dollars. . . .

The Indian trade at the posts was frequently conducted with considerable ceremony. During his visit to Fort McKenzie in 1833, Maximilian, Prince of Wied, was very much impressed with the elaborate ritual which preceded the trade. When a trading party approached, the post hoisted the flag and discharged cannon signalling that trade was about to commence. Then the principal chief and the head men, dressed in the colored great coats and round hats with tufts of feathers, given them by the company, and bringing horse or beaver skins for gifts, arrived at the trading post, they were welcomed with a salute of guns and met by the bourgeois who shook hands with them. The chiefs, after delivering their colors on a long ensign staff in military style, were followed by the warriors, all of whom were admitted to the fort, seated, fed, and given drinks and tobacco by the company. This was followed by an exchange of oratory in which the bourgeois sometimes rewarded those loyal to the company and to the whites with special presents. After dispensing with the ceremonies, trade began. This ritual, with some variations, apparently continued to be observed for several decades at the Upper Missouri posts. . . .

Although the ostensible profits from the fur trade appear to have been excessive, the real ones were not as great as they appeared. The goods traded in the 1830's for buffalo robes and beaver skins, at the place of exchange, would indicate that the trader received a profit of from 200 to 2,000 percent. Denig wrote about 1854 that "all goods are sold at an average profit of 200 percent." However, the expenses involved above original cost, in carrying out this business, were immense. . . .

The American Fur Company officials always contended that competition was undesirable in the business. "The Indian trade does not admit of competition," wrote Denig. "The effects of strong rival companies have been more injurious and demoralizing to the Indians than any other circumstances that have come to our knowledge, not even excepting the sale of ardent spirits among them." Its methods in crushing the opposition were not unlike those of many of the large companies, such as the Standard Oil Company and others, which established monopolies and fortunes in the 19th century.

Coute que coute and *ecrasez toute opposition* (cost what it may and crush all opposition) seems to have been the standing order in the instructions of [the] American Fur Company to its traders. The first step was to crush the opposition by competition. Kenneth McKenzie, bourgeois at Fort Union, explained "it is not a good policy to buy out opposition, rather work them out by extra industry and assuidity" and if "the opponents must get some robes, let it be on such terms as to leave them with no profits."

If competition failed, the company then tried force. If the latter did not succeed, it would then endeavor to buy out the opposition. Many are the stories of its methods of liquidating small traders. . . .

Much of the routine work of the early trade was conducted by the *engagees* or *voyageurs*. They represented many different nationalities, half breeds, mulattoes, and negroes and came for the most part from St. Louis. The Canadians were in majority. The engagees were called *"mangeurs de lard"* or "pork eaters" because most of them were imported from Canada and in the course of their trip from that country lived largely on a diet of pork, hard bread and pea soup. Prior to the use of the steamboat, many of these "pork eaters" used to man the keelboats on their trips up the river. . . .

Above the engagees were the clerks and the bourgeois. The work of the clerks appears to have varied but seems to have been principally the supervision of the normal operations of the post. . . .

The clerk's salary seems to have varied according to his length of service and the responsibility of the position. In 1834 the American Fur Company engaged inexperienced clerks for a three year period for $500 and a complete suit of clothes of fine broadcloth. . . . [C]lerks and traders who had a knowledge of the Indians at the particular post at which they were stationed, commanded a salary from $800 to $1000 a year. . . .

There was a caste system at the larger posts such as Fort Union and social amenities were observed. Clerks and the bourgeois were served at the first table which was furnished with such luxuries as flour, bread, bacon, cheese, butter and milk. The bourgeois sat at the head of the table, on which was spread a white tablecloth and was attended by waiters. The employees were seated in accordance to rank. . . .

Many of the agents, clerks and other personnel of the trading posts, married Indian women. These "Indian marriages," as they were called, were normally of a temporary character and when the white trader moved to another station or returned to the States, often to his white wife and children, he abandoned his Indian wife and his half-breed offspring. Men in charge of the fur trading posts endeavored to marry into prominent and influential Indian families because by such connections their adherents were increased and they made greater profits. The Indian relatives remained loyal and traded nowhere else. . . .

The life of the fur trader was attended with numerous dangers. Some lost their lives in boat wrecks transporting furs and merchandise on the Missouri. While the Indians were normally friendly toward the fur traders, they sometimes attacked and pillaged small parties. . . .

The trader was frequently in danger at the posts themselves. The Indians, being a primitive people, were very suspicious. They blamed the white man for such plagues as the small pox and cholera which carried away many on the Upper Missouri. During these epidemics, the traders' lives were often in danger. The Indians' code was "an eye for an eye and a tooth for a tooth." Every injury real or imaginary called for revenge. They were always unpredictable. . . .

The habitations of the traders, except perhaps those of the bourgeois in the larger posts, were generally primitive. Kurz described his quarters at Fort Clark as "A dark room, lighted only by a tiny window, the panes of which seem never to have been washed." It was equipped with "A large fireplace and two wooden bedsteads, which I found upon closer inspection to be inhabited by bedbugs." . . .

The larger posts were not without their social life. Balls were occasionally held at Fort Benton and Union. . . .

The fur trading posts were frequently the scenes of carousals, drunken brawls, and violence in which the red men as well as the trading fraternity took part. Practically all of the river boats smuggled liquor into the country, so for a day or so following the arrival of a steamboat, a grand spree would take place among the drinking employees of the fort.

"Great drunken frolic took place last night liquor being obtained from the Steamer agnes which arrived from [Fort] Benton, " wrote Larpenteur in 1867. However, drinking bouts were not confined to the male members of the fort personnel. Larpenteur recorded:

Sept. 15 [1865] . . . Great Row among the Squaws at night having Smuggled down a five gallon Keg of whiskey upon which they immediately Commenced. . . .

With the approach of white civilization on the Missouri in the middle of the 19th century, the once flourishing fur trade declined. Fort Pierre was sold to the Government in 1855. Although several other fur trading establishments sprang up in the vicinity, these had a short life. . . .

The fur trading fraternity's contributions to the development of the Upper Missouri region, have been both positive and negative. Stories of the rich fur-bearing resources of the region no doubt resulted in encouraging many adventurous individuals to come into the region and explore every stream and ravine. In this way they made it easier for the permanent settlers.

The fur trader did very little toward furthering the civilization of the red man. Instead, he greatly exploited the Indian largely in the interests of a few absentee owners in St. Louis and New York. Although some instances may be cited where he materially helped the red man, these are far outweighed by those in which he plied the Indians with liquor, cheated him, and prostituted his women. He also introduced white man's diseases among the various tribes which killed thousands. As a result, the Indians became suspicious of all whites, a feeling which a century of consistent effort by the Government has been unable to eradicate.

The fur trader contributed little toward the permanent development of the region. He discouraged farming and permanent development since these would interfere with his business. Unlike his counterparts in Canada, as represented by the Hudson's Bay Company, the American trader destroyed the wild life very quickly and left the country in search of more fertile fields.

HIRAM MARTIN CHITTENDEN

The American Fur Company:
Methods and Men

In 1902 a scholarly captain of the Corps of Engineers of the
United States Army, Hiram Martin Chittenden, published a
general history of the fur trade in the United States that has
been indispensable to all later students of that subject.
In the following passage, he described some of the "special
features" that distinguished the American Fur Company
from other firms in the trade.

The chief elements of strength which made the American Fur Company such a power in the Indian country were the great wealth and
business sagacity of its founder. Its formidable financial backing gave
to its operations a degree of force and stability which none of the other
American fur companies possessed. Reverses which would have ruined
an ordinary concern scarcely caused a ripple on the current of its affairs.
If competing traders stood in the way, and could not be crushed by
opposition, the exhaustless reservoir of Mr. Astor's pocket-book could
buy them out. The onward march of the company was therefore that
of resistless power and even the great opposition of the St. Louis traders
was finally forced to give way.

The operations of the company, moreover, were always conducted
with caution and sound judgment. Its career was marked by few brilliant strokes of policy, but rather by a conservative and continuous
advance so fortified and supported that each step was permanent progress. It permitted other and more adventurous concerns to break the
ground in new and dangerous territory rather than run the risk of
invading those untried fields. Thus every point of its territory on the
upper river had previously been occupied by the Missouri or Columbia
Fur Companies or by General Ashley. . . .

The goods for the trade were generally imported or purchased in

SOURCE: Abridged from Hiram Martin Chittenden, *The American Fur Trade of
the Far West* (New York: Francis P. Harper, 1902), I, Chap. XXIII, 375–380.

New York under the immediate direction of the home office. Those going to the Northern Department were sent to Lake Erie and shipped from Black Rock to posts on the lakes and the Upper Mississippi. Those bound for the Western Department were generally sent by way of New Orleans, particularly after the advent of steamboats. Shipments were also often made by way of Pittsburgh, and occasionally by way of the lakes. . . .

The goods in their long journey from Europe to the interior of this continent, passed through three distinct agencies before their final destination was reached. They were generally furnished by Mr. Astor at a fixed advance upon cost and charges. They went through the house at St. Louis, where the various outfits for each year were made up. Here there was a second regular advance. To this point the profits were fixed and certain, and the chances of loss very small. It was not until the traders at the company houses in the interior were reached that the struggle of the business began. The trader's profits were largely dependent upon his own efforts. He ran the risks of loss from hostile Indians, competing traders, and the many other difficulties that beset his business. On the whole the trade arrangements of the American Fur Company were grossly one-sided and unfair. They threw the risks of loss upon those who had the burden of the work to perform. . . .

It is not a pleasing reflection that the profits of this extensive business found their way into a few hands while those who bore its hardships and dangers beyond the frontiers of civilization and the comforts and luxuries thereof, generally ended their careers in comparative poverty if not in actual want.

In the multitudinous details of a business like that of the American Fur Company, covering half the area of the United States, it is not surprising that it should appear in different lights from different points of view. One may search in vain the correspondence of Astor or Crooks for any evidence of irregular methods. The conduct of affairs at the home office, however vigorous and aggressive it might be, was always strictly within the law. Very different was it at the other end of the line, where the business came in contact with the lawless element of the wilderness. Thus, while McKenzie was making preparations to establish a distillery at Fort Union whereby he would be able to evade the Federal statutes, Crooks was writing to Chouteau strongly deprecating his course, and urging the agents of the company to stand upon higher ground. . . . The St. Louis house had a more difficult rôle to fill, for it was midway between New York and the wilderness—between the law-abiding management of the company's affairs and the law-defying agents at the distant posts. One does not need to scan very closely the correspondence of the Western Department at St. Louis to see that it had one code of business when looking toward the east and quite a different one when looking in the other direction.

Owing to the great power of the American Fur Company it was opposed by all other traders. It had no allies. An "opposition company" was one opposed to the American Fur Company. However much the smaller traders might fight among themselves, there was one enemy against whom they made common cause—one flag under which all could rally. The opposition to the company was, it is true, more numerous than formidable, and considering their uniform experience of failure, the number of competitors is at first thought surprising. A great part of the opposition to the company was a species of blackmail. It was a common thing for employes who had been trained in its service until they had acquired some knowledge of the fur trade, to quit their employment and set up for themselves. Sometimes they did this from personal spite, because they had a grievance against the company, and at others because they actually felt that they might meet with some success. Occasionally the more experienced would enlist eastern capital in their enterprises and would themselves ascend the river as agent or principal in the business. As a general thing, however, these smaller concerns, like minor political parties, had no real expectation of accomplishing anything by themselves, but hoped, by embarrassing their powerful competitor, to force it to buy them out or to make profitable concessions to them. To this end they would ascend the river and settle down near some important outpost of the company and ply their skill to the utmost to debauch the Indians and secure their trade. Not having any character to defend they were reckless of measures. They could easily smuggle through the small quantities of liquor they wanted, and were often better equipped at particular points with this decisive weapon of trade than were their opponents. These irresponsible traders were in fact an unmitigated nuisance in the Indian trade. They were not powerful enough to stand the least chance of crippling their adversary, any more than summer flies can cripple a horse which they annoy, but they could and did succeed in causing it infinite embarrassment, and its whole career was one prolonged effort to exterminate the myriad pests that were always swarming about it.

Notwithstanding the discreditable motives which lay behind most of these adventures the sympathy of the public was always with them. The great company was looked upon as an oppressive monopoly, resolved to crush whatever lay in its way, and its acts were judged by a stricter standard than were those of its less powerful rivals. The government inspectors were as a rule more severe with it, perhaps from sympathy with the smaller traders, but probably because they could more easily detect its shortcomings.

The attitude of the company toward these competitors was always severe and merciless, for, knowing their character and motives, it held them in the utmost contempt. As a general thing it fought them with their own methods until it had won all the trade away from them, when they would find themselves stranded and helpless and would sue for mercy. Others of the more respectable class it would buy out, receiving them again in their service. With still others who were really powerful rivals, like the Columbia Fur Company, it formed coalitions on advantageous terms to the company absorbed. In one way or another it held the field against all competitors and only retired at last when its work was done and a new order of things had come over the field of its extensive operation.

For the rest, the company's affairs were conducted on the same principles which control the business world today. It knew perfectly well the power of political influence. . . . More than once it escaped exclusion from the Indian country where a more obscure party would have had no show whatever. The company also understood to perfection the value of favors to those who were in a position to help or injure it. Free passes were provided on its steamboats; scientific enterprises were generously promoted, and everything was done that would redound to its praise or credit. It may indeed be said that the history of the company upon the Upper Missouri was uniformly on the side of the advancement of knowledge and its assistance to enterprises of this character was of permanent value. But to the average individual the American Fur Company was the personification of monopoly, determined to rule or ruin, and hence it was thoroughly hated even by those who respected its power.

WILLIAM H. GOETZMANN

The Mountain Man as Jacksonian Man

Although the fur trade stretches back to the earliest colonial
ventures of the French and English in North America and
still goes on, the trapper or mountain man, who roamed
the beaver meadows of the Rocky Mountains for a brief
period, is frequently pictured as the symbol of the American
trade as well as the epitome of free, primitive life. Here
William H. Goetzmann presents a "collective biography" of
the trappers and argues that the mountain man was really
that same type of "expectant capitalist" whom Richard Hofstadter has identified as the typical Jacksonian man.

One of the most often studied and least understood figures in American
history has been the Mountain Man. Remote, so it would seem, as
Neanderthal, and according to some almost as inarticulate, the Mountain
Man exists as a figure of American mythology rather than history. As
such he has presented at least two vivid stereotypes to the public imagination. From the first he has been the very symbol for the romantic banditti
of the forest, freed of the artificial restrictions of civilization—a picturesque wanderer in the wilderness whose very life is a constant and
direct association with Nature. . . .

On the other hand, to perhaps more discerning eyes in his own day
and down through the years, the Mountain Man presented another image
—one that was far less exalted. Set off from the ordinary man by his
costume of greasy buckskins, coonskin cap and Indian finery, not to
mention the distinctive odor that went with bear grease and the habitual
failure to bathe between one yearly rendezvous and the next, the
Mountain Man seemed a forlorn and pathetic primitive out of the
past. . . .

Both of these stereotypes embody, as do most effective stereotypes,
more than a measure of reality. The Mountain Man traveled far out ahead

SOURCE: Abridged from William H. Goetzmann, "The Mountain Man as Jacksonian
Man," *American Quarterly*, XV (Fall, 1963), 402–415. © 1963, Trustees of the
University of Pennsylvania. Reprinted by permission of *American Quarterly* and
William H. Goetzmann.

of the march of conventional civilization, and the job he did required him to be as tough, primitive and close to nature as an Indian. Moreover, it was an out-of-doors life of the hunt and the chase that he often grew to like. By the same token because he spent much of his time in primitive isolation in the mountains, he very often proved to be a poor business-man ignorant of current prices and sharp company practices. Even if aware of his disadvantageous position he could do nothing to free himself until he had made his stake.

The fact is, however, that many Mountain Men lived for the chance to exchange their dangerous mountain careers for an advantageous start in civilized life. If one examines their lives and their stated aspirations one discovers that the Mountain Men, for all their apparent eccentricities, were astonishingly similar to the common men of their time—plain repub-lican citizens of the Jacksonian era.

Jacksonian Man, according to Richard Hofstadter, "was an expectant capitalist, a hardworking ambitious person for whom enterprise was a kind of religion." He was

the master mechanic who aspired to open his own shop, the planter, or farmer who speculated in land, the lawyer who hoped to be a judge, the local politician who wanted to go to Congress, the grocer who would be a merchant. . . .

To this list one might well add, the trapper who hoped some day, if he hit it lucky and avoided the scalping knife, to be one or all of these, or perhaps better still, a landed gentleman of wealth and prestige. . . .

Marvin Meyers has added a further characterization of Jacksonian Man. He was, according to Meyers, the "venturous conservative," the man who desired relative freedom from restraint so that he might risk his life and his fortune, if not his sacred honor, on what appeared to be a long-term, continent-wide boom. Yet at the same time he wished to pyramid his fortune within the limits of the familiar American social and economic system, and likewise to derive his status therefrom. Wherever he went, and especially on the frontier, Jacksonian Man did not wish to change the system. He merely wished to throw it open as much as possible to opportunity, with the hope that by so doing he could place himself at the top instead of at the bottom of the conventional social and economic ladder. . . .

The structure of the Rocky Mountain fur trade itself, the life stories of the trappers and on rare occasions their stated or implied aspirations all make it clear that if he was not precisely the Meyers-Hofstadter Jacksonian Man, the Mountain Man was most certainly his cousin once removed, and a clearly recognizable member of the family. . . .

Ambiguous though the Mountain Man's approach to it may have been, it is abundantly clear that the Rocky Mountain fur trade was indeed a *business*, and not an invariably individualistic enterprise at that. The unit of operation was the company, usually a partnership for the sake of capital, risk and year-round efficiency. Examples of the company are The Missouri Fur Company, Gant and Blackwell, Stone and Bostwick, Bean and Sinclair, and most famous of all, the Rocky Mountain Fur Company. . . . These were the average company units in the Rocky Mountain trade and much of the story of their existence is analogous to Jackson's war on the "Monster Bank" for they were all forced to contend against John Jacob Astor's "Monster Monopoly," the American Fur Co., which was controlled and financed by eastern capitalists.

Perhaps the most interesting aspect of the independent fur companies was their fluid structure of leadership. There was indeed, "a baton in every knapsack" or more accurately, perhaps, in every "possibles" bag. William [H.] Ashley, owner of a gun powder factory and Andrew Henry, a former Lisa lieutenant, and lead miner, founded the Rocky Mountain Fur Company. After a few years of overwhelming success, first Henry, and then Ashley, retired, and they were succeeded by their lieutenants, Jedediah Smith, David Jackson and William Sublette, three of the "enterprising young men" who had answered Ashley's advertisement in the St. Louis *Gazette and Public Advertiser* in 1823. When Smith and Jackson moved on to more attractive endeavors first William Sublette and Robert Campbell, then Tom "Broken Hand" Fitzpatrick, James "Old Gabe" Bridger, Henry Fraeb, Milton "Thunderbolt" Sublette and Jean Baptiste Gervais moved up to fill their entrepreneurial role. . . .

In addition to the fact of rapid entrepreneurial succession within the structure of the independent fur companies, a study of 446 Mountain Men (perhaps 45 per cent of the total engaged in this pursuit between 1805 and 1845) indicates that their life-patterns could be extremely varied. One hundred seventeen Mountain Men definitely turned to occupations other than trapping subsequent to their entering the mountain trade. Of this number 39 followed more than one pursuit. As such they often worked at as many as four or five different callings.

Moreover beyond the 117 definite cases of alternative callings, 32 others were found to have indeterminate occupations that were almost certainly not connected with the fur trade, making a total of 149 out of 154 men for whom some occupational data exists who had turned away from the trapping fraternity before 1845. Of the remaining men in the study, 110 men yielded nothing to investigation beyond the fact that they had once been trappers, 182 can be listed as killed in the line of duty and only five men out of the total stayed with the great out-of-doors life of the free trapper that according to the myth they were all supposed to love.

From this it seems clear that statistically at least the Mountain Man was hardly the simple-minded primitive that mythology has made him out to be. Indeed it appears that whenever he had the chance, he exchanged the joys of the rendezvous and the wilderness life for the more civilized excitement of "getting ahead." . . .

Two further facts emerge in part from this data. First, it is clear that though the Jeffersonian agrarian dream of "Arcadia" bulked large in the Mountain Man's choice of occupations, it by no means obscured the whole range of "mechanical" or mercantile pursuits that offered the chance for success on the frontier. Indeed, if it suggests anything a statistical view of the Mountain Man's "other life" suggests that almost from the beginning the Far Western frontier took on the decided aspect of an urban or semi-urban "industrial" civilization. Secondly, though it is not immediately apparent from the above statistics, a closer look indicates that a surprising number of the Mountain Men succeeded at their "other" tasks to the extent that they became regionally and even nationally prominent. . . .

If the Mountain Man was indeed Jacksonian Man, then there are at least three senses in which this concept has importance. First, more clearly than anything else a statistical and occupational view of the various callings of the Mountain Man tentatively indicates the incredible rate and the surprising *nature* of social and economic change in the West. In little more than two decades most of the surviving enterprising men had left the fur trade for more lucrative and presumably more useful occupations. And by their choice of occupations it is clear that in the Far West a whole step in the settlement process had been virtually skipped. They may have dreamed of "Arcadia," but when they turned to the task of settling the West as fast as possible, the former Mountain Men and perhaps others like them brought with them all the aspects of an "industrial," mercantile and quasi-urban society. The opera house went up almost simultaneously with the ranch, and the Bank of Missouri was secured before the land was properly put into hay.

Secondly, as explorers—men who searched out the hidden places in the western wilderness—the Mountain Men as Jacksonian Men looked with a flexible eye upon the new land. Unlike the Hudson's Bay explorer who looked only for beaver and immediate profit, the Mountain Man looked to the future and the development of the West, not as a vast game preserve, but as a land like the one he had known back home. . . .

Tied in with this and of the greatest significance is a third and final point. Not only did they *see* a settler's future in the West, but at least some of the Mountain Men were most eager to see to it that such a future was *guaranteed* by the institutions of the United States Government which must be brought West and extended over all the wild new land to protect the settler in the enjoyment of his own "vine and fig tree." The Mexican Government, unstable, and blown by whim or caprice, could not secure the future, and the British Government, at least in North America, was under the heel of monopoly. France was frivolous and decadent. Russia was a sinister and backward despotism. Only the free institutions of Jacksonian America would make the West safe for enterprise. . . . It may well have been this spirit that settled the Oregon question and brought on the Mexican War.

Settlement, security, stability, enterprise, free enterprise, a government of laws which, in the words of Jackson himself, confines "itself to equal *protection*, and as Heaven does its rains, showers its favors alike on the high and low, the rich and the poor," all of these shaped the Mountain Man's vision of the West and his role in its development. It was called Manifest Destiny. But long before John L. O'Sullivan nicely turned the phrase in the *Democratic Review*, the Mountain Man as Jacksonian Man —a "venturous conservative"—was out in the West doing his utmost to lend the Almighty a helping hand. . . .

CHAPTER XI

The Miners

THE LURE of easily accumulated wealth in the form of previous metals provided the impetus for the exploration and settlement of much of the Americas. Early charters granted by European sovereigns bore witness to the lure of gold and silver in sixteenth-century exploration and seventeenth-century settlement. Spanish explorers criss-crossed great regions of the American continents in their persistent search for the elusive metals, finding only enough gold and silver to whet their appetites. Although the Seven Cities of Gold proved a myth, the *conquistadores* found traces of gold in Georgia, the Rocky Mountain region, and on the Pacific slope, all to be important mining regions in the future.

After the deterioration of the Spanish-American empire in the seventeenth century and the establishment of French settlement in Canada and English colonies in Virginia and Massachusetts, settlers in the New World devoted less energy to the vain quest for precious metals. Revealing the pragmatic process of settlement building, the English colonists exploited furs, timber, and some lead and iron deposits. The latter two metals were indispensable in growing settlements; silver and gold were only desirable.

Perhaps the first American mining "boom" took place in the upper Mississippi valley lead region in the area around Galena, Illinois. Colonial charters had established the precedent of retaining the right to a percentage of all metals for the crown. Consistent with this practice, the Land Ordinance of 1785 reserved one-third of all gold, silver, lead and copper found on the public domain. In 1807 Congress passed legislation to implement this policy in Missouri and the Old Northwest, lowering the government's share to one-tenth. This mercantilist policy failed in Missouri because it conflicted with established mining practices and the private ownership of mineral lands. Reservation and federal taxation was highly popular among the miners of the Galena district, however, because there this policy encountered no conflicting traditions. With the clearing of Indian titles to the region, old Missouri miners led the rush to the upper Mississippi mines in the mid-1820's, and the miners reacted favorably to the paternalistic federal policy which ordered most aspects of their lives. Landholding and usage, mining practices, and marketing procedures conformed to governmental directives.

The public mining system fell into disuse in the 1830's because of administrative apathy, policy conflicts between the mining officials and the General Land Office, and hostility on the part of some western politicians and entrepreneurs. Pressure from the miners led to the reinstatement of the leasing system for a brief period in the 1840's, and also caused the extension of this practice to the Lake Superior copper mines and the lead mines of Arkansas, but in 1846 Congress terminated this experiment in mineral land policy.

The discovery of gold in the late 1820's on the Cherokee lands of northeast Georgia temporarily diverted national attention to the Southeast. Working the accessible placers and some veins in Georgia and North Carolina, miners learned techniques which would serve them well in the far West.

When James Marshall discovered gold near Sutter's mill on the American River in California in January 1848 he set the stage for the greatest and most dramatic of the American mining rushes. And while the western mining booms, from California to Cripple Creek and the Klondike, captured the imagination of Americans—and the world—for the next half-century, certain precedents relating to mining technology and claim regulation had been established long before the discovery of the American fields. In California miners applied the knowledge accumulated in the Georgia placer fields, in the deep shafts of the upper Mississippi and Missouri, in the stopes of Cornwall, in the mining schools of France and Germany, and in the small-scale Mexican mining industry of the Southwest.

The California mines were not in all respects the most important of the West. But as the first of the major precious metal frontiers, California was a testing ground for mining technology and the California legal processes became the foundation of western mining law. The experiences on later mining frontiers in other western territories and states often followed the pattern of California, thus the latter serves as an adequate —if by no means perfect—model for the mining frontier.

Fortunately for the many naive amateurs who followed any of a number of long and difficult routes to California, a great deal of placer gold lined the streams and banks near the foothills of the western Sierras. Placer gold had eroded from its natural vein and been deposited on stream beds or on the slopes of hills by downward-rushing streams.

There were few obstacles to mining the metal in this state. To "wash" the gold in pans or sluice boxes did not require a mining engineer. Most of the precious mineral produced in California during the first few years came from simple placer operations. This enabled some Californians to accumulate capital and others to gain mining experience, both of which were essential for the later assault on the more deeply held and tightly gripped mineral treasures of the mining West.

In a somewhat transitional phase between placer mining and intensive deep mining, the Californians often resorted to hydraulic mining and river mining. In the former the miners forced water against a hillside under enough pressure to clear away the soil and rocks that covered the auriferous dirt. In river mining a group of miners—using dams and canals—literally turned the course of rivers and streams so that they might work the gravel on the river bed. These ventures required capital and labor to an extent unknown in placer mining, but cooperative ventures were probably more common than corporations or companies.

As the miners exhausted the major placer deposits, they increasingly turned their attention to the lodes or veins from which the placer gold had eroded. These ventures called for technical skill and capital investment far beyond that which the miners had earlier required. Miners encountered problems in blasting and in removing waste rock, in controlling water seepage and timbering unsafe ground as well as in the persistent problem of removing the precious ores with a minimum of waste. Once the ore reached the surface, serious problems remained. Some California miners used the centuries old stamp mill—an apparatus similar to a huge mortar and pestle—or modified the Spanish *arrastra* for crushing the ore-bearing rock. The use of quicksilver then usually sufficed to separate the gold from the waste rock. In areas where gold was chemically locked with other elements, generally sulfides, metallurgical treatment was necessary to extract the gold. The latter process was, fortunately, not usually required in California because the gold there was generally in a free state. Some miners used sluice boxes, riffles, and even coarse blankets, to separate the gold from the crushed rock after a washing process.

As might be expected, waste was quite high in such crude processing operations. Estimates placed the amount of gold recovered under these conditions at one-fifth to one-third of the metal actually in the ore. Marginal mines could not function profitably at this rate, and many were closed, to be reopened later in the century when improved techniques made their operation profitable. Nevertheless, by 1858 an estimated 279 stamp mills in California were processing the output of deep mines, while in 1855 there had been only 32 mills in operation. These figures revealed the rapid transition of California mining, and similar patterns appeared in other western states as the mining frontier moved eastward.

As profitable placer mining declined and large-scale deep mining commenced, the California miners—at least those who wished to continue mining—had only two choices open to them: to become wage employees in the mines or to drift to the Pacific Northwest or across the Sierras in search of new placer deposits. It was to the benefit of western mining generally that a good number of Californians made the latter choice. In the years following the 1849 gold rush California miners joined the rushes to the Fraser River in British Columbia, to Idaho, to Montana, to Nevada, to Arizona, and some even made the long trek back across the Continental Divide to Colorado. And these ubiquitous prospectors usually searched every gully and stream between these distant points, in spite of extremes of temperature, rough terrain and the danger of Indian attack.

The presence of veteran Californians in later camps permitted the application of skills gained through experience in the California mines. But in many cases California techniques ill suited the particular geological or metallurgical problems of other areas and at times the California experience slowed recognition of unique characteristics in areas to the east. On the rich Comstock lode in the Washoe district of Nevada, for example, the early miners—mainly old Californians—cursed and discarded the "blue stuff" which marred their placer operations. Silver generally had not been found contiguous to gold in California; consequently, the early miners on the Comstock threw away the dark dirt which was incredibly rich silver ore. In Colorado, early reliance on the stamp mill and quicksilver processes to separate gold from pyrites resulted in the loss of from 50 to 90 per cent of the mineral.

In spite of such examples the California miners had learned to be flexible and innovative. Although the early miners failed to recognize the silver of the Comstock lode immediately, they soon made the mines there one of the finest examples of advanced mining technology. If the first Colorado miners were baffled by the chemical combinations in which they discovered gold, they soon modified American techniques by introducing European smelting processes so that the Centennial State became one of the richest producers of gold and silver in the world.

Problems of governmental organization plagued the early settlers in all mining camps. The mining frontier differed from the agricultural frontier in that the miners had often literally rushed hundreds of miles beyond the established settlements. This placed the mining camps an equal number of miles from the nearest government. With the exception of the rushes to the Galena district and to British Columbia, most mining camps found no governmental officers waiting to regulate procedures and adjudicate disputes. Vigilance committees, claim clubs, and mining codes were the pragmatic responses to this condition. These institutions minimized—but by no means eliminated—conflicts in what essentially was an anarchic situation. Contrary to popular stereotypes, however, these groups often abused their powers. The first arrivals might use claim clubs to maintain special privileges and vigilance committees too frequently subordinated due process in their desire for order. Generally the members of both of these groups systematically discriminated against minority-group members.

Because of the attraction which the American mining frontier held for the people of all nations, the mining camps were often ethnic polyglots. Behind the democratic institutions which have impressed historians such as Charles Howard Shinn, an ethnic pecking order quickly developed which placed black Americans, Spanish-Americans, Indians, Kanakas and Chinese at the bottom of the social scale. The fact that members of these groups, unaccustomed to the living standards of eastern America, often agreed to work at lower wages than the other miners, intensified the racial prejudice of the white settlers. Often the latter excluded nonwhites from the camps until the remunerative, early placers were worked out. Frenzied mobs assaulted the Chinese particularly, destroyed their property, and sometimes even murdered them. The anti-Chinese riots of 1871 and 1880, in Los Angeles and Denver respectively, were natural outgrowths of a society in which racial prejudice was more the rule than the exception.

The mining codes of the camps and diggings were a most important contribution to the development of local western government. Varying from simple regulations to elaborate legalistic compilations, these codes provided methods of acquiring and holding claims and arbitrating conflicts between miners. These were important needs prior to 1866 because Congress had refused to sell mineral lands and at the same time failed to provide any administrative apparatus for the western mining districts. In most cases the mining codes of the West were retained when formal governmental institutions extended their control over the camps. Constituent assemblies, state legislatures, and the courts came to recognize the codes as permanent, even though the regulations at times conflicted with common law practices recognized in the East and England. These conflicts caused no small amount of consternation and litigation among the nonresident owners of western mines.

In 1866 the United States Congress gave statutory recognition to the codes of the individual mining districts. At the same time Congress provided for the sale of lode claims to miners, an action extended to placer claims in 1870. By these actions the federal government abandoned direct control over the exploitation of the nation's minerals, a policy which was not reversed until the twentieth century.

As placer mining declined in each of the states and territories of the mining West, capital and organization became essential for the assault on the deep lodes. San Franciscans who had accumulated wealth in California mining invested in the development of the mineral resources of some of the areas, notably the Comstock, but generally there was little indigenous western capital that could be invested in the mining companies. Capital from the Midwest, the East and Europe, especially England, became essential for the development of the western mining industry. This process involved the incorporation of American mining, with all of its attendant problems. By 1902, 39 per cent of the metal mines in the United States were corporate-owned; these mines accounted for nearly 90 per cent of the production in that year. Absentee ownership often resulted in mismanaged properties and bad relations with the mine laborers.

The term "miner" usually brings to mind a doughty old prospector with beard, pick, knapsack and burro, and popular vignettes of drama, romance and humor. In point of fact, however, this individual was common for only a short time in the history of any mining district. When the placers played out and corporate deep mining began, the western mining camps became, in the words of Rodman Wilson Paul, "industrial islands in the midst of forest, desert, or mountain. . . ." And the miners became industrial laborers. There was little drama, romance or humor in the life of such western mine workers. Long hours, low real wages, danger to life and limb and extremely difficult working conditions were their lot. It was perhaps then only natural that western miners became active in some of the most radical of American labor unions, particularly the Western Federation of Miners, founded at Butte, Montana, in 1893 and the Industrial Workers of the World, organized in 1905. The armed warfare which broke out in bitter strikes at Butte and Cripple Creek, Colorado, and numerous other mining camps, made them among the most violent in American labor history.

American mines produced an estimated $25 million in gold and silver from 1792 through 1847. The 1849 production alone, mainly from California, totalled $40.5 million, and this yearly figure steadily increased until the domestic mines were producing well above $100 million of gold and silver a year in the 1890's. In the 50 years after the California discoveries, United States gold and silver production exceeded $3.5 billion. As coin for international payments and as bullion for sale on the international market, this tremendous production favorably affected the United States position in world trade.

Domestically, mineral production influenced United States monetary policy which in turn had wide political repercussions. Prior to 1873 the United States mint purchased all silver presented to it at a fixed price ratio with gold of approximately 16 to 1. Little silver found its way into circulation, however, because the market price of silver exceeded the mint price; the bullion value of a silver dollar was greater than a dollar.

In 1873 Congress demonetized silver, giving statutory recognition to monetary reality. Shortly thereafter silver production increased greatly as miners struck the bonanzas of the Comstock and discovered rich ore veins at Leadville. World demand for silver diminished, as other nations demonetized silver, at the very time that supply was increasing. The price of silver dropped from $1.30 a fine ounce in July of 1873 to $1.15 in July 1878. From the middle 1880's onward silver generally remained at less than a dollar an ounce, and the bullion value of a standard silver dollar was less than 50 cents by 1894.

The Populist protest of the 1890's politicized the silver issue, and inflationists and some silver miners joined in common cause. The United States never again adopted complete bi-metallism, however, and marginal silver mines either closed down or became dependent upon the production of subsidiary metals. By 1909 the value of precious metal production ranked behind that of coal, petroleum and natural gas, copper and iron in the United States mining industry.

After the initial assault on California in 1849, the mining frontier moved eastward during the next 30 years. Finally miners met the westward moving farmers in Colorado and the Black Hills. With this achieved, most of the frontier of the contiguous states and territories had been touched by civilization. The agricultural settlement of the Great Basin, California, and the Pacific Northwest, as well as the western Plains, and the extension of the grazing empire through the high Plains continued. But in the vicinity of many mining camps or towns, the desire of the miners for agricultural produce stimulated commercial agriculture long before the cattlemen or farmers would otherwise have appeared. Similarly the miners stimulated railroad building. But the frontier miners were seldom permanent settlers. Usually they hurriedly exploited an area's resources and then left like the earlier fur traders, having exploited nature even more ruthlessly. For they had mutilated the earth, diverted and polluted the streams, and stripped the timber. Their abandoned towns stood as monuments to the impermanence of their labors. But if this was their legacy to the agrarian frontier, so also were San Francisco and Denver and a host of subordinate cities between. So also were the early government institutions of some western territories and states. In the transition from the simple placer claims of the 1850's to the capitalized, industrial mining of the late nineteenth century, the miners accelerated the settlement process from the Rocky Mountains to the Pacific Ocean.

· 1 ·

RODMAN WILSON PAUL

Mining Frontiers as a Measure of Western Historical Writing

Rodman Wilson Paul has written extensively about the mining frontiers of western America. In this essay he discusses the place of the mining frontier in the broader analysis of western history. Professor Paul calls attention to post-frontier developments on the mining frontier as a fruitful—if often undramatic—field for historical study.

. . . The relationship between the frontier phase and the subsequent industrialization of mining is a curious one, not easily comprehended. During the frontier days, gold or silver was found at many different places. Disorderly crowds stampeded into the wilderness, mountains, and desert in response to each rumor of discovery. Mining of a simple type was started at once, on limited capital, while camps, towns, roads,

SOURCE: Abridged from Rodman Wilson Paul, "Mining Frontiers as a Measure of Western Historical Writing." © 1964 by the Pacific Coast Branch, American Historical Association. Reprinted from *Pacific Historical Review*, Vol. XXXIII, 25–34. Reprinted by permission of the Branch and Rodman Wilson Paul.

stores, saloons, gambling houses, and other essential facilities were hastily built.

Subsequently, this initial pattern in each area was bound to change greatly. If the deposits began to dwindle, the area declined in population and commercial activity, and usually at a much faster rate than the actual reduction in mineral yield. Even if the deposits continued to pay well, still they were bound to require a very different kind of mining as greater depth was reached and the ores took on a more complex character. At such a point in the history of most mining areas, an extensive change in population could be observed. The original crowd was a motley one in which Americans of modest means predominated. Their successors were very apt to be foreigners. In districts devoted to superficial placers, Chinese usually replaced the original miners, because they were content with the small income that the worked-over placers still afforded. In areas of vein mines, the work underground was taken over most commonly by Irish or Cornish immigrants, with some Germans, Canadians, and later south Europeans also joining the labor force. Handling of machinery was often preempted by mechanically inclined Americans, while direction of operation was divided between Cornish mine captains and American, Irish, or German superintendents and owners. Later, graduates of the great European mining academies began to play an important role. Meantime such mines became centers for heavy investment and heavy machinery.

In short, an extensive change in personnel characterized the transition from the frontier phase to the more mature era. The historian who attempts to tell the story finds that he is dealing with two different groups of people, and that there is real reason for distinguishing between the frontier and what followed. And yet the patterns established during the earlier period continued to influence the later one. The ownership of claims was established, on a highly unsystematic basis, by the original crowd. Towns were started on locations that proved increasingly inconvenient for the later citizens. Habits, attitudes, and practices proved surprisingly resistant to   change. And in each town or camp a few determined individuals stayed at their posts throughout all vicissitudes. This was especially true of merchants, who often emerged as a continuing force of great influence. . . .

In any synthesis the historian finds himself dealing with the question of natural environment, which looms so large in the work of Frederick Jackson Turner's disciples. It would be difficult to think of any western industry save arid-land agriculture that has been more subject than mining to the influence of physiographic conditions. The basic controlling factors in any region were the presence or absence of profitable deposits, the availability of water and wood, the height and abruptness of the mountains, the distance from established supply centers, the winter and summer extremes of temperature. Perhaps one should add the effectiveness of the Indian opposition, which was essentially a part of the natural setting. Inferior deposits located in remote, difficult, and dangerous country could mean that a region would draw only limited attention after being prospected and partially opened. This was the fate of much of Arizona, New Mexico, and Utah, and of many northwestern areas, until railroad transportation greatly reduced the obstacles during the last two decades of the nineteenth century. Until then economic and social development was severely restricted.

The negative effect of the natural environment is thus quite obvious. The positive effect is the speculative opportunity that was there if promising mineral deposits existed. It is difficult for a modern reader to appreciate the financial and personal risks ambitious men would take in order to tap hidden treasure. The 190 miles of underground shafts and galleries on the Comstock Lode is perhaps the supreme example, but the whole mountain West is dotted with shafts, waste dumps, rusting mills, pock-marked river courses, and zigzag mountain roads that were once capable of handling ore wagons hauled by sixteen-mule teams.

What is particularly interesting about this massive assault on the western landscape is to see how heavily the mining West drew upon the accumulated knowledge of both the older East and Europe. Turner's emphasis on the West as a land of innovation needs qualification. In mining techniques, the West was not so much originator as adapter and accelerator. There were some true inventions, such as hydraulic mining, but most of the technical progress came through borrowing practices, processes, and machines long known to Europe or Spanish America, altering them to suit the special conditions of the American West, such as high-cost labor and capital and the demand for quick profits, and then speeding up the improvement of any given process or device by spending money to the point of extravagance. Starting in the middle and late 1860's, technological and scientific guidance was often provided by engineers and geologists who came directly from famous European academies, such as Freiberg, the École des Mines, or the Royal School of Mines. I suspect this may be an instance unique in western history of an influential university-trained professional group moving directly from Europe to the Far West. In national origins, many of these products of European training were Americans.

If the Far West's debt to Europe was large in mining technology, so was it in mining law, where again the process was one of selecting portions of long-established precedents, adapting them, and experimenting in unsystematic fashion. What makes western mining law and western mining technology so different from their European ancestors is not so much the degree of innovation as the prevailing psychological atmosphere. Western mine owners wanted quick results, they did not expect their properties to last for generations, as in Europe, and they showed little concern over wasted natural resources, operating inefficiencies, or the high cost of paying legal blackmail to rival claimants who found loopholes in the carelessly kept records of legal titles to mining claims.

Earl Pomeroy has asserted that "the Westerner has been fundamentally imitator rather than innovator." As Pomeroy points out, the basic patterns for local, territorial, and state government, like the architecture of western buildings and the format of western newspapers, was a conscious attempt to reproduce in the new setting the familiar arrangements of "home." This seems only natural. The social scientists would call it a case of cultural determinism.

Yet there may be an important difference between forms and substance. The key here is the question of individualism, long a major concern of Turnerians. America has been built by the operation of the desire for personal profit and power, as partially and uneasily counterbalanced by the insistance of a minority that the public welfare must also be considered. In the mining West, considerations of community well-being often were decidedly inferior to the propelling force of the desire for fortune and the restless love of excitement and movement.

When the original gold rush crowd of 1849 arrived in California, their elaborate joint stock companies, so carefully devised before leaving home and intended to give mutual support and collective profit in the new land, immediately disintegrated. The business partnerships that replaced the joint stock ventures were more often changeable associations than enduring ones. A few months or a season was the life span of most. Political institutions showed a similar instability. Up in the mountain towns and in San Francisco, Sacramento, and the other new cities, the forms of American local government were established, with a little borrowing from Mexican practice. But most people were too busy with their own concerns and with the high cost of living to stand for office themselves or to help elect good men. Nor did they regard themselves as permanent citizens of their towns or even of California. They were transients who had come to make money, share in an exciting adventure, and return home. Therein is the explanation for the weakness of local government and the too frequent resort to vigilantism and lynching. Not enough people could be induced to show a real interest in civic affairs until the criminal minority had gotten so out of hand that the majority of the atomistic society of the camps and cities found itself forced momentarily to drop individual concerns in order to think and function as a group. This same cycle of neglect followed by extralegal action was to be repeated on all subsequent mining frontiers.

When the moment for action came, the presence of a few leaders, of a few men with a developed sense of responsibility for the community, became of critical importance. Whether "popular justice" succeeded in a given camp or city, and whether it kept its vengeance within bounds, depended largely on the quality of leadership. What is more, the men who came to the fore in these moments of crisis sometimes won so much prestige that thereafter they served for considerable periods as a stabilizing and cohesive influence. As local leaders, they often found their readiest allies among the merchants, who had an understandable concern for the permanence and well being of the community.

In business life, similarly, there emerged first in California and then elsewhere in the West, a group of outstanding men who became the leaders in mining investments throughout the region and often had also great influence in politics—partly because of their ability to pay the party's bills. Examples were Marcus Daly, George Hearst, William M. Stewart, Nathaniel P. Hill, William Andrews Clark, Samuel T. Hauser, and John P. Jones. By the 1870's and early 1880's the names of these men were appearing repeatedly as investors in a succession of mining ventures from the Pacific Coast to the Black Hills, while many of them sought election to the United States Senate or tried to control the selection of candidates for the Senate and other high offices. In other words, as the mining West matured, something like an elite emerged. Society was still fluid, in that the individual in so volatile an occupation as mining might move with remarkable rapidity from povery to riches, or vice versa, but nevertheless a privileged group had developed, strong in wealth and personality.

Mining life was different from other frontier societies in that it led so quickly to cities rather than just the hamlets created by other western industries. The primitive mining camp was not greatly elevated above a Great Plains cow town or a temporary construction settlement at the end of the railroad tracks, because all existed solely to provide recreation and supplies for an exclusively male population of a not very refined kind. But as the more prosperous camps grew into towns and cities, amenities multiplied far more rapidly than in an agricultural or pastoral region. Theaters, book stores, locally printed newspapers, daily contact with the outer world by stagecoach and telegraph, luxuries of food and drink, fraternal organizations, and even discussion groups could be found in the more substantial towns and supply centers. Religion and feminine influence were less important than in farm communities, but self-education was more so.

Yet there was always an air of impermanence about mining centers, and development was lopsided, because the town had no reason for existence save for its one industry. The big supply centers and points of transshipment, notably San Francisco and Denver, were far more normal communities, since they had additional sources of support as well as mining, and since within the field of mining they drew business from many different localities rather than just one. Capital for investment accumulated in these major supply centers, from both local and absentee holders, and thereby made substantial funds far more available than would have been true in a farm economy. Thanks to the need for heavy machinery in the mines, iron foundries and machine shops prospered despite the high cost of labor and materials. It is clear, then, that the rôle of towns and cities was an important one, not to be overlooked in writing of the mining West. . . .

CHARLES HOWARD SHINN

California's Golden Prime of Forty-Nine

Charles Howard Shinn was perhaps the earliest of the professional historians to study the mining camps. Influenced by
the "germ theory" of history which Frederick Jackson Turner
found incompatible with the American experience, Shinn
argued that the great technical and social developments in
the camps were attributable to the Teutonic origins of the
American settlers.

. . . The mining camps, whose white tents and rude cabins rose so
rapidly beside the rivers of "New Colchis" in early "Forty-Nine," have
found a place in literature; the Argonaut himself has become one of the
heroic figures of the past, and is likely to become as strong a type in
the romance of American history as Viking or Crusader are in that of
Europe. But it is the place held by the Argonaut as an organizer of
society that is of greatest historical importance. Literature has too often
depicted him as a dialect-speaking rowdy, savagely picturesque, rudely
turbulent; in reality he was a plain American citizen, cut loose from the
authority, freed from the restraints and protections of law, and forced
to make the defense and organization of society a part of his daily business. In its best estate the mining camp of California was a manifestation
of the inherent capacities of the race for self-government. Here, in a
new land, under new conditions, were associated bodies of freemen,
bound together for a time by common interests, ruled by equal laws,
and owing allegiance to no higher authority than their own sense of
right and wrong. They held meetings, chose officers, decided disputes,
meted out a stern and swift punishment to offenders, and managed their
local affairs with entire success. . . .

To many cheerful, impetuous, and intelligent men the ups and downs
of mining life seemed full of wild fascination; to be there was to be a part
of a scene that each thoughtful miner knew in his heart was as evanescent
as it was brilliant—an episode whose intensity corresponded accurately to

SOURCE: Abridged from Charles Howard Shinn, "California's Golden Prime of
Forty-Nine," *Magazine of American History*, XII (November, 1884), 433–443.

its briefness. Reports filled each camp, almost every week, telling of "new diggings, where from $100 to $1,000 might easily be collected in a day." Down came the tent-ropes, the claims were abandoned; the epidemic gold-rush fever had seized each Argonaut in the camp. They went to Gold Lake, Gold Bluffs, and a hundred other as loudly trumpeted regions, till the habit of following with swift feet each new excitement became as much a part of the Argonaut's nature as the habit of running after a fire is a part of the nature of a healthy boy. . . .

Fortunately, there were some, even from the first, who had "come to California to remain and make homes," who recognized vast resources other than mineral, and by whose unswerving fidelity to justice the best elements of camp life were evolved. A fine example of this was afforded in what were called the Southern Mines, the camps of Tuolumne. The several hundred dwellers in and about the Mexican, or "Sonoranian" Camp, were reinforced as early as July, 1849, by about 15,000 foreigners, chiefly from Sonora, Chili, and the Isthmus. Some of them were outlaws and desperadoes, and they speedily made the country unsafe. The camp in which they most congregated became notorious for its bull-fights and fandangoes. Opposed to them was a little camp of Americans, who had elected their own "alcalde," or chief officer of the camp, the previous autumn. By the united action of the Americans the foreign invasion, for it can hardly be called less, as many of the Mexicans came in armed bands, was held in check, controlled, and finally conquered and partially dispersed before the close of the eventful year of "Forty-nine." In some of the American camps, "good and true men" were at once chosen alcaldes; in some the direct intervention of "Miners' Courts" was preferred; in camps of a third class, committee government was restored to. But government of an efficient and judicious sort, the Americans in the invaded region secured for and of themselves.

The mountain land over which mining became for years the chief industry of men was a region fitted by nature to attract and firmly hold the affections of a hardy and energetic race. Its physical features are most inspiring even now, when the valleys and foothills are subdued to agricultural purposes. But when the miners of Forty-nine began to pitch their tents in the wilderness it was unfenced, unclaimed, and almost unexplored. Everywhere the land had a charm for men that no language can describe. . . .

Even today the smallest of these decaying camps is worth patient study. . . . Go down and talk with those ghost-like inhabitants of the ancient camps, and they will set your blood tingling with tales of the past. Twenty years! Thirty years ago! Why, it is centuries!

The saddest of all possible sights in the old mining region is when there are not even half a dozen miners to keep each other company, but where, solitary and in desolation, the last miner clings to his former haunts. He cooks his lonesome meals in the wrecked and rotting hotel, where, a quarter of a century before, then young, gay, prosperous, and, like the camp, in his prime, he had tossed the reins of his livery team to the obsequious servant, and played billiards with "the boys," and passed the hat for a collection to help build the first church; he sharpens his battered pick at a little forge under the tree on which he had helped to hang "the Mexican who had stabbed Sailor Bill;" he looks down in the cañon where vines and trees hide all but the crumbling chimney of the house where the "Rose of the Camp" lived, sweetening their lives with her girlish grace and purity as she tripped over the long bridge to the little school-house, and waved her hand to her friends toiling waist-deep in their claims on the hillside or by the river. But that was long ago, and the bridge has fallen into the torrent, and the snow-storms have shattered the school-house, and he has not seen her for years and years.

Not one of all the thousands of men who hurried into the "Camps of Forty-nine" ever paused to consider how these camps would look if deserted, nor imagined themselves old and lonely pioneers sitting over the ashes of departed fires. The work they did is sufficiently shown by the facts of the gold yield. In 1849, by official record, the miners took out $23,000,000; in 1850 this yield was more than doubled. It is certain that a large percentage, perhaps one-fourth part or even one-half, of the gold taken from these early placers was never reported to express company or custom-house. The typical camp of the "Golden Prime of Forty-Nine" was flush, lively, reckless, flourishing, and vigorous of speech and action. Saloons and gambling-houses abounded. Every man went around, and felt fully able to protect himself. Gold dust was currency at a dollar a pinch. In the camp, gathered as of one household, under no law but that of their own making, were men from North, South, East and West, and from nearly every country in Europe, Asia, North America. They mined, traded, gambled, bought, discussed camp affairs; they paid fifty cents a drink for their whisky, and fifty dollars a barrel for their flour, and thirty dollars apiece, at times, for butcher-knives with which to pick out the gold from the rock crevices. They talked, as one who knew them well has written, "a language half English and half Mexican," and he might have added, wholly their own. Even Bret Harte has failed to reproduce it; the dialect of his miners leans too far toward the Missourian. These lawless, brave pioneers, risked their lives for each other, made and lost fortunes, went on lonely prospect tours, died lonely deaths or perished by violence; some, wiser or more fortunate, than these, became farmers when the mining era closed, sowed wheat-fields, planted fruitful orchards.

There were times in almost every camp when the rowdy element came near ruling, and only the powerful and hereditary organizing instincts of the Americans ever brought order out of chaos. In every such crisis there were men of the right stamp at hand to say the brave word and do the brave act; to appeal to Saxon love of fair play; to seize the murderer, or to defy the mob. Side by side in the same gulch, working on claims of eight paces square, were, perhaps, fishermen from Cape Ann, loggers from Penobscot, farmers from the Genesee Valley, physicians from the prairies of Iowa, lawyers from Maryland and Louisiana, college graduates from Yale, Harvard and the University of Virginia. From so variously mingled elements came that terribly exacting mining-camp society which tested with pitiless tests each man's individual manhood, discovering his intrinsic worth or worthlessness with almost superhuman precision, until, in the end, the ablest and best men became leaders in the free and self-governed camps of the Sierra.

HARWOOD HINTON

Frontier Speculation: A Study of the Walker Mining Districts

Charles Howard Shinn and others have been impressed by the
early establishment of codes and administrative structures
in the western mining districts. They have used these developments as examples of the flowering of American democracy. Harwood Hinton has discovered a different genesis
for these codes in his research on the Walker mining districts
in Arizona. In this case the mining codes resulted from the
attempts of the early prospectors to profit from their holdings
rather than from democratic propensities.

On November 4, 1863, a commentator in the San Francisco *Evening
Bulletin* blasted the practice of prospectors converting mining districts and their codes into vehicles for speculation. . . . Neither prospector nor capitalist, he concluded, could expect protection or encouragement when "on a few days' notice, a corporal's guard assembles, and,
on simple motion, radically changes the whole system." From 1863 to
1865, the Walker mining districts in central Arizona illustrated the
extent and significance of these practices on one part of the mining
frontier.

Late in May, 1863, twenty-five dusty prospectors, led by the experienced guide, Joseph Reddeford Walker, reached the Pima villages on
the Gila, with news of a gold discovery in the mountains of northern
Arizona. . . . Before returning to the villages, the Walker party re-enacted
a scene common to the mining camps of the West. On May 10, by a voice
vote, they constituted themselves a sovereign body, elected a temporary
chairman, and proceeded to erect a placer mining district and to draft
a proper code. They included in their "Pioneer District" all the gulches
and ravines entering the Ookilsipava, from its head to a "tree below the

Source: Abridged from Harwood Hinton, "Frontier Speculation: A Study of
the Walker Mining Districts." © 1960, by the Pacific Coast Branch, American
Historical Association. Reprinted from *Pacific Historical Review*, Vol. XXIX, 245–
255, by permission of the Branch and Harwood Hinton.

falls, at the foot of the mountains," and decreed that "no claims be taken for persons outside of original prospectors until they have definitely settled."

Many of those present had helped organize mining districts in California and Colorado; all knew the rudiments of a placer code. In their domain, the sovereigns continued, a mining claim would be one hundred yards square—one hundred yards along and fifty yards back on each side of the stream. An individual could stake two claims—one by right of discovery and one by pre-emption—and could secure title to each merely by registering it and paying a filing fee of two dollars and fifty cents. All altercations, laws, elections, and other affairs of the district would be settled by a majority vote at duly announced meetings. Two annually elected officers—a president and a recorder—would administer the business of the district.

In several of the bylaws, the Walker party expanded, encouraged, and guaranteed their position in the new district. First, they required that their names be entered on the minutes as the "original prospectors." Next, they banned Mexicans from the diggings for six months, assumed the privileges of relocating claims on unclaimed ground anywhere in the district, and declared themselves exempt from any filing fee. Finally, they resolved that each member of the party would draw two claims by lottery immediately upon his return from the Gila.

The next day, the prospectors, anxious to report their gold strike, cached the remaining supplies and headed south. They knew that their return to the settlements would signal a wild rush to the diggings, and by forming a placer district and a code they hoped to regulate the ensuing boom. Being prospectors, not miners, and speculators, not laborers, they hoped to protect, enhance, and sell their claims before the placer interest ended. If they could uncover gold-bearing quartz, they would locate claims and hope for a buyer, or would merge their interests with others, wait for the appreciation that actual mining would bring, then sell. To protect their claim values over an extended period, they had to limit further prospecting. Only by controlling the voting at subsequent meetings could they do this. Their control, they knew, could be easily destroyed. Members of the party, because of claim sales, scarcity of supplies, or Indian menace, could scatter to other districts; new groups could enter the diggings, buy up and locate claims, and vitally affect the voting balance. . . .

Soon after reaching their camp in the mountains, the Walker party assembled with others to alter both district and code. Anticipating other placer deposits nearby, they expanded the boundaries of their domain, east, west, and north, practically doubling its area. Next, they amended the mining regulations, thereby initiating a practice which persisted throughout the history of the diggings. An individual could hold a claim one year without working it only if he had marked it with stakes or rocks and properly recorded it within ten days of location. He could hire Mexicans to occupy his holding if he registered each laborer at "four bits" per head and informed the recorder of all dismissals.

The assembly adopted several amendments to regulate situations which could arise in the enlarged district. In no instance, they asserted, could an individual register claims for nonresidents of the district. This amendment struck at the basis of absentee ownership. Though relaxing the barrier against Mexicans, the lawmakers manifested no tolerance toward the Chinese. They banned the race completely from the diggings. Then, in anticipation of gold-bearing quartz discoveries, they set the length of a quartz claim at 200 feet along the outcropping. In conclusion, the group closed the district to all but members of the Walker party for two days. . . .

On July 12, the men remaining in the placer district held their last summer meeting at the recorder's office, which had been moved to Lynx Creek. As at previous assemblies, they amended their code to favor the interests of the Walker party. They declared that only "original prospectors" could hold more than one pre-emption, granted them ten days in which to relocate their initial claims anywhere in the district, and placed the group in control of committees to measure and stake new claims and to certify who were Mexicans. These acts indicated that the Walker influence over local mining legislation remained strong. The prospecting privilege, the control over committees to validate claims and to select the labor force, and the restrictions on claim holding all served to protect and enhance their interests. The fame of the Arizona placers, however, had traveled far. At that moment, numerous groups who would substantially affect activities in the Walker domain were hurrying to the mines.

On August 19, the surveyor general of New Mexico, John A. Clark, with a cavalry escort, rode into the diggings. . . . Clark's visit signaled an abrupt shift in prospecting in the Walker district. Since the Ookilsipava strike four months before, the local residents had expended their energies in the placers. One day after his arrival, however, Clark, with eight others—five were prominent nonresidents of the district—filed the first quartz claim. . . . A rapid increase in absentee ownership had accompanied the sudden interest in quartz, but Lynx Creek residents made no move to arrest the development. Their inaction was due to the nature of the mining organizations which had appeared in the diggings.

On Lynx Creek, as elsewhere on the mining frontier, companies formed to open quartz mines experienced little restraint. But, as a mining investigator explained, the men who organized these early ventures generally had other ends in mind. In each new diggings, he said, one or several prospectors, whether authorized or not, would include the names of personal friends, notable businessmen, or territorial officials when constituting a new company. These individuals, upon being informed of their good fortune, either bought out their known, or unknown partners, sold them their interests for a small sum, or simply forgot the matter. Whatever the result, prospectors knew that influential names on the district records enhanced the over-all speculative values of their diggings. In the quartz companies organized on Lynx Creek during the early fall of 1863, there were many who had engaged in an agent-client capacity in other districts. Here, as elsewhere, prospectors scrambled for mining claims, not for themselves but for sale to others.

The rising interest in quartz quickly dampened all enthusiasm in the placers. The owners of placer claims, believing the sudden appearance of quartz companies would unsettle claim values, began selling or transferring their holdings. Through October and early November their transactions continued, as falling temperatures and chilling winds drove many south to warmer climes. The placer boom in the Pioneer District was over.

On November 24, Walker prospectors and others on Lynx Creek braved the mountain cold to meet in the recorder's office and discuss their changing circumstances. The discussion shifted from the interest in quartz to the possibility of an army post—and perhaps the territorial capital—being located nearby. To protect their claims and to regulate more closely any subsequent quartz boom, they decided to erect a quartz district. . . .

In framing the quartz code the law makers drew heavily on their placer experience. From their placer code they extracted directly the provisions dealing with the duties of district officers; the principles of settling disputes, laws, and elections; the restrictions on Mexicans and Chinese; and the specifications for a quartz claim. They veered away from the placers, however, in their instructions for claim validation. To secure title to a quartz site, an individual or a group, within sixty days of locating on a mineral vein, must present to the recorder an ore specimen, a copy of the posted claim notice, and pay a filing fee, assessed at fifty cents per name. To hold a claim, the interested party must occupy and work it three days per quarter for one year, or twelve days continually within three months of location. The legislators, however, postponed for four months the effective date of the work stipulation. In conclusion, they elected one set of officers to function over both the placer and quartz districts, restricted their tenure to six months, and adjourned.

The Walker influence became blurred in this meeting. Several members of the party served on the committee to draft quartz bylaws; the final code contained many of their placer regulations. In no way were their holdings and their opportunities limited. But, for the first time, the Walker party received no special privileges. Everyone in the diggings, however, stood to benefit by the formation of the new district. Few in number, with the weather conditions precluding any immediate accretion, they were in a favorable position to locate the richer claims. This opportunity, however, proved short-lived. . . .

During the late spring, the Walker quartz district sparkled with activity. Prospectors recorded four times as many claims in May as they had in the preceding month. Sales and transfers were few. The quieting of the Indian menace, the ease in securing claims—merely by registration—and a flood of new gold-seekers combined to produce the briskness. The mounting enthusiasm, however, caused growing unrest in some quarters. For weeks the Walker group had seen soldiers from Fort Whipple swarm into the diggings to prospect and to record claims of unauthorized size. On May 22, at a routine meeting to elect new officers, the disgruntled element spoke out. Without forewarning, George Coulter, who had been with Walker since 1861, suddenly suggested that all persons "in the service of the United States" be prohibited from filing claims in the district. This would alleviate the increasing disregard for local regulations and stifle the growing atmosphere of competition—conditions which could unsettle property values. After a short discussion, the assembly adopted the proposal.

The Walker edict was untimely. It vitally affected a group that had acquired extensive holdings in the diggings—the territorial party, composed of civil and military officials and their friends. As property owners with grounds for complaint, they reacted immediately. At their request, the district president called a meeting of the Lynx Creek community on May 29. The meeting was short and decisive. By a quick voice vote, those attending quashed the onerous edict and threw the diggings open to "all citizens of the Territory." By this action they swept from the district the Walker influence. . . .

On Friday, September 29, the first territorial legislature of Arizona convened at Prescott. The next day, Governor Goodwin, in his message

to the members, outlined a program which stressed the need for territorial regulations of quartz mining. For this industry to develop, he
explained, the great confusion among district laws must be rectified.
Placer codes could continue, for they were ephemeral, but local quartz
laws must be superseded by a territorial code. Capitalists, he concluded,
would not invest in the mines unless they could obtain clear and uniform
titles. The following week, the legislators began discussing a detailed
code which William T. Howell, a territorial judge, had prepared the
preceding spring. On November 10, when the session ended, they had
enacted, and the governor had approved, the major portion of Howell's
proposals. By this act, the territorial party imposed its control over
Arizona's richest natural asset. . . .

From the beginning, activity in the Walker districts had centered upon
the location and sale of mining claims. The Walker party, in particular,
had made every effort to control the district voting so as to protect and
enhance the value of their holdings. In this endeavor they were eminently
successful for nearly a year. Then, new prospectors and a new governmental organization swept their influence from the diggings. During
their brief span of activity, however, the Walker party had re-enacted
a drama which gave credence to the charge that prospectors erected
mining districts and enacted codes primarily for speculative ends.

CLARK C. SPENCE

British Investment and the American Mining Frontier, 1860–1914

When placer operations subsided in any mining district, capital became essential in order to open deep mines and process the ore. The western miners had to secure this money in the East or from foreign sources. In this selection Clark C. Spence analyzes the role of English investors in western mining development. In spite of the political rhetoric of some westerners to the contrary, the investors were as often the exploited as the exploiters.

"England is a lake of money, bank full and running over." So wrote the San Francisco editor of the *Mining and Scientific Press* in 1895. Many fellow Americans were inclined to agree and undoubtedly the relatively heavy investments of British capital that had already splashed over into the West had much to do with creating this attitude. Although the pound sterling was attracted to many types of enterprises—vineyards, railroads, and ranching among others—between 1860 and 1914 at least 584 joint-stock companies, with a total nominal capitalization of not less than £81,185,000, were registered with the Board of Trade in Great Britain to engage in mining or milling activities in the intermountain West and Southwest, exclusive of the Pacific Coast proper. . . .

Such figures must be approached gingerly. Often the gap between nominal and actual capital was a wide one. The British public might fail to respond, with the result that part of the nominal capital remained unsubscribed; large blocks of shares might be granted fully paid to vendors in full or partial payment for property; sometimes non-British shareholders—American or Continental—accounted for a proportion of the subscribed capital. . . .

On the other hand, these general figures—and, indeed, this paper—are

---

SOURCE: Abridged from Clark C. Spence, "British Investment and the American Mining Frontier, 1860–1914," *New Mexico Historical Review*, XXXVI (April, 1961), 121–137. By permission of the *New Mexico Historical Review* and Clark C. Spence.

concerned with only part of the story of British investment in western mines. Undoubtedly much capital cannot be pinpointed. . . .

But whatever its extent and through whatever its media, the flow of investment into western mines was but part of a much broader movement of British capital into all corners of the mineral world, ranging from Aruba to the Yukon, from Coolgardie to Zanzibar. The American West was not peculiarly favored; competing with other regions it received only a fraction of British overseas capital. In 1890 only 17.1 per cent of all new capital offered by mining concerns registered in England was destined for any part of the United States; probably about 3.5 per cent of similar capital offered in 1900 was earmarked specifically for the American West. And British investments made up only a small portion of the total capital that developed western mineral industries. . . .

After a brief and unhappy experience in California during the 1850's, English investments were not especially noticeable in western mines until after 1870. The confusion and uncertainty fostered by the Civil War acted as a deterrent, as did the condition of the mineral industry itself. Depression struck in the mid-sixties, as Eastern companies succumbed to "process mania" and installed fantastic new contraptions for "frying, roasting or stewing precious ores" which had been devised by so-called "experts" who knew "as little about practical milling as the lunatic in Swift did about extracting sunbeams from cucumbers." The resulting costly and spectacular failures by many American firms could not help but leave the British public cool to western investment schemes.

Moreover, British capital had a tendency to lag until some semblance of "civilization" became apparent in the West. It tended to move more readily, for example, into regions where the Indians provided the least trouble and where railroads were early available. Thus Nevada, Colorado, and Utah were favored with overseas capital at an earlier date than Idaho, Montana, New Mexico, and Arizona. . . .

In general the decade of the sixties brought only limited British investment (actually sixteen companies, with a total capitalization of £1,525,000), but the stage was being set for a more substantial flow. . . . In the early 1870's came a speculative flurry which focused attention sharply on Colorado, Nevada, and Utah. In spite of momentary scares emanating from the confusion of the Franco-Prussian War and the *Alabama* claims question, the year 1871 produced a bumper crop of Anglo-American mining companies—a total of thirty-four, capitalized nominally at £4,550,000, of which twenty, with a capital of £3,211,000, actually operated. The boom leveled out in 1872 and 1873, then fell off sharply as the cold wind of depression swept across the West, chilling the ardor of the investor and leaving in its wake a mass of corporate wreckage. . . .

Stiff competition from the booming new Indian fields and a mild financial crisis in 1878 did nothing to relieve the situation, but except for a sharp downward trend in 1880 and again in 1885, the eighties brought a general increase, the year 1886 being the best since 1871; 1887 and 1888 were the two peak years of the entire period. . . .

Despite a near panic in 1890 when the Barings crashed, the level of investment remained high until 1892; then a fall in metal prices and another international financial dislocation were to cause the flow to ebb momentarily. British concerns throughout the West were hard hit and often never recovered. A few prospered, most muddled along, many . . . liquidated their American interests and reinvested in gold mines abroad. But new capital was attracted again after 1894, although the pre-depression level was never again reached. . . .

If profits are any indication, the degree of success of the average Anglo-American mining concern fell far short of expectations. At least fifty-seven of the companies registered in the 1860-1914 era paid dividends aggregating about £ 11,700,000 prior to 1915. Numerically this would mean that one company in every ten ultimately paid some kind of dividend. But many of these were but token payments to appease stockholders or to sustain share prices artificially. . . .

If dividends were not ordinarily forthcoming and if mountainous debts of half a million pounds sometimes piled up, wherein lay the blame? It was not merely that "salted" properties were passed off on the naive British investor. . . . The over-all story is much more complex, with a number of contributing factors combining to spell disillusionment and disappointment.

The whole process of promoting mining enterprises in England left the way open for gross misrepresentation and the transfer of shoddy goods across the trans-Atlantic counter. Worthless claims, labeled "prospect holes" in Colorado or Arizona, became "permanent mining investments" in London. Disputed titles and an occasional hidden mortgage passed into British hands. Prospectuses spoke in glowing terms of "mountains of silver" in New Mexico and of "probable dividends of 200 to 300 percent" in Nevada, and in their optimism rivaled accounts from Sinbad the Sailor, or as unhappy investors more often insisted, from the tales of Baron Munchausen. Extreme statements came to be expected as a regular part of western mine promotion. . . . Unfortunately, too many of the projects presented in this fashion could not hope to live up to promotional claims and left the average investor with a slim purse and an attitude which, in the words of a contemporary, "generally assays about two tons of regret to the square inch."

Many joint stock enterprises collapsed from weaknesses in capital structure. . . . As a result, having plunged most of their capital into the purchase of property, most companies sorely lacked working capital. Next to the cry of "fraud" (usually unsubstantiated) the most common plea heard in company meetings in London was for additional operating funds.

Another factor contributing to a lack of success was the inability to find satisfactory solutions to problems of management across an ocean and three-quarters of a continent. Boards of direction selected for their appeal to the "lord-loving public," rather than for administrative or mining experience, too often proved inept or disinterested. Most concerns refused to entrust their property to unpredictable Yankees and insisted instead on British engineers or mine captains. Probably the majority of such men sent from the home islands were well-trained and competent; indeed, many of them would have been regarded as top-flight mining experts in any setting. Many of them brought with them ideas and processes stemming from years of experience in mines and smelters the world over and were to be of more than passing importance for their contributions to the development of the trans-Mississippi West.

But a sizable minority were neither able nor qualified for the positions of responsibility they were sent to fill. To the end of the era, British companies never completely discarded the idea "that a man having been a Sunday school teacher, or a most exemplary tradesman, or a needy relative of the president, or one of the directors is sufficient qualification to enable him to manage a mine successfully." Nepotism was common; so were misfits. . . .

If by chance an Anglo-American concern were fortunate enough to have acquired paying property, had sufficient capital to work it, and a trustworthy manager of ability, it might well be sure of being dragged through legal proceedings of some sort. . . .

To be sure, litigation was the bane of the mining world and was by no means confined to British firms in the West. But English companies, because of their general lack of familiarity with the labyrinths of American mining law, were particularly susceptible to legal ensnarlments. The adverse effects of this were to act as a brake to discourage investments from abroad, as well as literally to force a number of concerns from the western field.

Probably federal restrictions did not deter investments or bring corporate failure to any great extent, except indirectly, protests of interested bystanders to the contrary notwithstanding. By law no alien or alien corporation could locate a mining claim or obtain a patent directly from the government, although a foreign concern could always acquire patented property from an American citizen. In actual practice because decisions of the Land Office and of federal courts were not ordinarily enforced, British firms often left title in American hands while patents were being obtained. But rather than resort to this subterfuge and run even the slightest risk of confiscation, many English companies were careful to purchase patented claims at the beginning. Thus, since patented property was more expensive than unpatented, federal mining laws indirectly contributed to boosting prices against foreign firms. Attempts of the Foreign Office to intercede in favor of modification that would permit aliens to obtain patents directly met with no success.

The controversial Alien Land Law, which in 1887 technically barred any foreign citizen or corporation from acquiring or holding real estate in the territories, presented no real threat to British mining interests. It was not retroactive and might easily be evaded by leasing rather than buying property or by the established device of leaving title in the name of subsidiary concerns or American managers. . . .

Failure, then, might be attributed to any one or a combination of several causes, of which federal policy was unimportant: a certain amount of chicanery—or at least misrepresentation; overcapitalization, yet a lack of working capital; exorbitant prices paid for property; the perils of management across vast distances; and the perplexities of American mining law. More basic was the fact that mining in general is fundamentally the story of risk. There was much truth in the old miners' proverb that only a fool predicted beyond the end of his pick. An innate gambling spirit and the hope of striking the mineralogical jackpot prompted many an investor to plunge on the market, often with little distinction between undeveloped mines and those actually producing. British investment was but part of the larger whole; part of the unchecked plundering of America's natural resources at an unprecedented rate; part of what Vernon L. Parrington calls the "Great Barbecue." Human nature being what it is, if investors—British or otherwise—stood too close to the pit and were singed, that was not unexpected.

RODMAN WILSON PAUL

Colorado as a Pioneer of Science in the Mining West

Geological features and metallurgical problems varied greatly on the mining frontier. Nearly each new district called for modification of old techniques or for innovation. The mineral resources of Colorado posed particular problems for the miners, and Rodman Wilson Paul argues that the government and scientific researchers collaborated in Colorado to develop new methods for the location, extraction and processing of mineral resources.

Different states and regions have made quite different contributions to the history of the mining West, and more particularly to the history of that part of the mining West which owed its being to the search for gold and silver. . . .

What was Colorado's contribution? Was there some respect in which Colorado stood forth as the pioneer of trends that were of importance to the whole Far West? . . .

Such an inquiry is easier for us today than it would have been for an earlier generation, because the distracting emphasis on the dramatic and colorful side of mining now seems thoroughly dated, whereas the circumstances of our own modern lives help to make us instinctively receptive to considerations of quite a different sort, such as the role of science in the mining West. In Colorado, science became important at a surprisingly early date, and a heavy reliance on scientific advice has been a distinguishing characteristic of Colorado mining ever since. To understand why Colorado, more quickly than other western boom areas of that day, came to accept the guidance of metallurgists, geologists, and chemists, one must compare the successive stages in Colorado's development with similar epochs in the history of other mining commonwealths. . . .

SOURCE: Abridged from Rodman Wilson Paul, "Colorado as a Pioneer of Science in the Mining West," *Mississippi Valley Historical Review*, XLVII (June, 1960), 34-50. Reprinted by permission of the *Journal of American History* and Rodman Wilson Paul.

The cycle started, in most cases, with a real or alleged discovery—it might be either—in an area little known to white men. Quite commonly the area was one of difficult topography or climate. After a very brief period of concealment by the original discoverers, rumors would leak out and quickly become exaggerated. A crowd would then come rushing in to the new El Dorado. Usually the crowd was led by a few veterans of previous similar excitements, but the bulk of the population, being quite inexperienced, was bound to suffer disappointment and hardship.

As the crowd came pouring into the new diggings, the early discoverers were apt to sell out to tenderfeet or to men with capital, and push off on prospecting trips into the surrounding, more rugged terrain, thereby greatly increasing the known area. If there was anything worth the effort, flush production would develop rapidly, based on placer deposits and perhaps on the easily worked upper parts of veins. . . .

The period of flush production was bound to be brief, usually no more than half a dozen years, sometimes only half that time, sometimes only a season. As the flush period passed, the former boom area faced either of two fates. It might survive a period of depression and start up once more because of new discoveries, usually accompanied by and made possible by greater capital investment and technological improvements. Or the area might for a period of years support a constantly shrinking population of small-time operators, who struggled to eke out a living from the dwindling annual output. . . .

How does Colorado's history of mining precious metals compare with this typical life cycle? Its first phase was, of course, the gold rush. . . . Like most gold and silver rushes, the affair of 1859 and 1860 was based upon disorderly individual enthusiasms rather than upon plan or logic. The important gold discoveries were made *after* the vanguard of the gold rush crowd had arrived, which means that the hysteria started before there were any discoveries sufficiently rich to justify such a movement. . . .

Colorado was never as isolated from the settled part of the nation as was California prior to the completion of the Pacific railroad. Because of its geographical position, Colorado's ties were with the Middle West. The censuses of 1860, 1870, and 1880 all show a preponderance of middle westerners among Colorado's population, and a lesser degree of cosmopolitanism than had characterized California in its similar period. For precisely these several reasons, Denver seems not to have developed the economic independence or cultural vitality that made San Francisco so notable a community in the 1860's and 1870's.

Nor was Colorado as closely linked to California as were the other new mining regions that were springing up contemporaneously in the vast region from the western Rockies to the sea and from British Columbia to the northern provinces of Mexico. . . . The facts of geography seem to have set the eastern Rockies apart, and thereby to have given Denver a chance, at a much later date, to become the headquarters for mining engineers who operated up and down the line of the Rockies from Montana to New Mexico.

It is true that in 1859 and 1860 prospecting and mining in Colorado tended to be dominated by "Old Californians," who were sometimes also veterans of the Georgia mines, but thereafter the "old Californians" seem to have straggled off to the new diggings in Idaho and Montana. Similarly, some of the earliest mining equipment seems to have been built at Burlington, Iowa, from plans obtained from the experienced San Francisco manufacturers. Soon, however, local experience was suggesting modifications in the original California designs, and in any case California's technological influence was bound to diminish because Colorado's mining machinery was "mostly supplied from Chicago" and other middle-western cities. . . .

In Colorado, to the usual problems that are always encountered with depth was added the special question of how to treat the ores. The ores at or near the surface presented no new problems, because they had been oxidized by weathering. Simple stamp mills, copied from California or even Georgia models, and a few Spanish arrastras sufficed to break up the ore and render it ready for the action of mercury, through the familiar process known as amalgamation. But at depths of one hundred feet or more, the Colorado gold ores were found to be in chemical combination with sulphides, thus constituting what miners called "sulphurets," or pyritic or "refractory ores," by which they meant ores that resisted amalgamation. . . .

This was essentially a problem in metallurgy and chemistry. The fact that it was encountered so early in Colorado's history suggests one of the fundamental distinctions between Colorado's experience and that of either California, which had preceded Colorado by a decade, or the Comstock Lode, which was essentially simultaneous with Colorado. The California ores were virtually free milling, and the silver ores of the Comstock were only a little more complex. . . .

At the risk of oversimplifying, it can be said that the greatest contributions of California and the Comstock Lode, other than their enormous output of treasure, were twofold. First, by a process of trial and error, intelligent practical millmen worked out relatively simple ways of treating ores, techniques that were well suited to the particular ores at hand.

. . . Second, California and Nevada developed some extraordinarily competent engineers who built the great water systems used by both placer and lode mines, made brilliant progress in mechanical design, and excavated the greatest underground workings seen in America up to that time. . . .

These great accomplishments were what modern scientists would call engineering solutions to mining problems. The Coloradans also needed engineering solutions, although their most striking achievements of that sort were probably in the field of railroad and tramway construction; but even more than engineering the Coloradans needed *scientific* solutions. That is to say, they needed an understanding and a set of processes that could come only from chemistry, metallurgy, and geology. . . .

In the later 1860's . . . one could reasonably have argued that Colorado had run through its flush period and was gradually dwindling into extinction. The population figures would have supported such pessimism. If one makes adjustments for changes in boundaries, and if, for the present purpose, one excludes the immigration of Spanish-speaking farmers and ranchers into the southern counties, then there were fewer people in 1870 than in 1860. . . .

From this low point in its fortunes Colorado was rescued by several simultaneous developments. The first was a slow improvement in the way the existing gold lode mines were being handled. Working miners replaced absentee corporations, by buying or leasing idle properties. Adjacent claims were consolidated into more efficient units. Out of the tons of abandoned equipment and scrap iron that cluttered the Territory after the failures of the middle 1860's, the new operators reconstructed stamp mills on a more sensible basis, free from the fancy eastern and European notions. . . . In an attempt to lessen the inhibiting effect of the sulphides, the Coloradans now built mills that would give the refractory ores a longer and finer crushing and a longer period during which the crushed rock would be exposed to the action of mercury. This meant reducing the daily tonnage of the mill by more than one half, and accepting a loss of gold that one government mining expert estimated at 40 to 50 per cent, and another at 30 to 70 per cent. . . .

Appropriately, it was in Gilpin County that the second of these several simultaneous improvements was inaugurated. Nathaniel P. Hill, while teaching applied chemistry at Brown University, won the confidence of a group of New England industrialists. With their backing he made trips to Colorado to examine the losses under existing milling practices, and trips to Britain and continental Europe to study well-established techniques for smelting ores. The great advantage of smelting was that it saved virtually all of the valuable metals in the ore. . . .

Despite innumerable obstacles, Hill succeeded in building at Black Hawk, Gilpin County, a smelter that was largely copied from those used in Wales. His smelter was technologically successful from the time it went into operation in 1868, but its operating costs were so high that only the richest ores could be worked. Most of the ores continued to be treated in stamp mills, despite the waste. . . .

Precisely as Hill was putting his smelting plant into operation for the treatment of gold ores, a whole new field opened up with the beginning of silver production in Clear Creek County, adjacent to Gilpin County. Silver had been discovered there at the end of 1864, but until 1869 little silver ore was produced and smelting facilities were minimal. This delay did not check the development of a vigorous little boom and the discovery of silver lodes at points widely scattered over Colorado. The state's silver production, after a modest beginning at $600,000 a year in 1869 and 1870, rose to more than $1,000,000 in 1871, to over $2,000,000 in 1872, and to over $3,000,000 in 1874. In the last of these years the value of the silver output exceeded that of gold for the first time.

Fundamental to all this success was the advent of the railroads. Two different railroads linked Denver with the nation's transportation system in 1870, and at almost the same time the first of many local railroad lines wound its way up from Denver to tap the mining regions. Prices for all commodities, including labor, began to decline, and a marked reduction took place in the cost of transporting ores and fuel to the smelters and mills. . . .

As one examines the simultaneous reorganization of stamp milling, beginning of smelting, discovery of silver in Clear Creek County and elsewhere, and the coming of the railroads, it becomes apparent that the decade from 1867 to 1876 can be regarded as a period of gradual recovery from the collapse of the middle 1860's. In the typical mining cycle this is the period of depression that so often follows flush times, depression that lifts as the region responds to new discoveries, greater capital investment, and technological improvements. . . .

By the year 1877 Colorado had experienced all of these stages of recovery except the final one, the discovery of a true bonanza. One of the richest of the old placer gold camps of the early 1860's had been California Gulch, located in Lake County, at an altitude of 10,000 feet. Just as the early placer miners on what became the Comstock Lode were irritated by heavy "blue stuff" in their gold claims, so the placer miners of California Gulch, Colorado, cursed the heavy sands and rocks that interfered with their gold washing. A decade later, in 1874–1875, two miners with a good analytical sense correctly guessed that the decaying gold camp was probably rich in silver. By great good fortune, in 1876 the St. Louis Smelting and Refining Company sent into that area a well-trained metallurgist, August R. Meyer, a graduate of European mining schools. After demonstrating that the ores were lead carbonates, in 1877 Meyer built a smelter for his employers at the little hamlet that became known as Leadville. . . . Its annual output of silver soon surpassed that of any foreign nation except Mexico, and its auxiliary production of lead was nearly equal to England's. There were apprehensions that Leadville would overstock the world's markets in both metals. Among American silver districts, only the Comstock Lode had surpassed it in importance up to that time, and the Comstock was then in its decline. According to the uncertain local statistics, from 1877 to 1884, inclusive, Leadville produced nearly $96,000,000 in bullion. . . .

Perhaps the best way to summarize Leadville's importance to Colorado is to state that it was as if Colorado mining had been born again, but with the advantage of being born this time into a family of experienced and educated people who had money in the bank and transportation in the garage. What is more, the Leadville mining men soon had available scientific advice of a new kind. In 1879 the United States Geological Survey was formed by consolidating several existing government surveys. A Rocky Mountain division, with headquarters at Denver, was set up under the leadership of Samuel F. Emmons. . . . In August and September, 1879, Emmons put topographers to work in the Leadville region, and in December, 1879, he began studying the Leadville deposits himself. Throughout 1880, despite fifteen to twenty feet of snow in winter, he kept the project going, with a crew of chemists, metallurgists, and petrographers supplementing his own understanding. By the autumn of 1881 his collaborative project was far enough along that a substantial abstract could be published for the immediate guidance of the miners. Publication of the full monograph had to wait five years for congressional appropriations.

Emmons' monograph on the *Geology and Mining Industry of Leadville* genuinely deserves that over-used phrase "epoch-making." Even today it is still referred to as "the miners' bible." More than any other event, the publication of this scientific study convinced skeptical mining operators that they could learn something of cash value from university men. . . .

At Cripple Creek, near Pike's Peak, gold was discovered in 1890–1891. Skepticism as to the genuineness of alleged discoveries in so well-known a district retarded the usual rush during the first two years, but thereafter Cripple Creek became the new El Dorado of the West. A cow ranch in 1891, it had become a town of 10,000 in 1894. . . .

It's ores occurred in an unusual setting, in the throat of an old volcano, and in an unfamiliar form, as tellurides. Richard Pearce, now a veteran of more than twenty years in Colorado, took the lead in bringing science to the aid of the puzzled mining industry. Pearce presented two papers on Cripple Creek ores to the Colorado Scientific Society at its meetings in the winter and spring of 1894. . . . His associates were Richard A. F. Penrose, Jr., of the University of Chicago, and Edward B. Mathews, of Johns Hopkins University. With the permission of the director of the United States Geological Survey, Cross and Penrose presented preliminary reports to the Society on June 4, and these reports were printed at once in pamphlet form for quick distribution. . . .

[I]n Colorado, after a generation of struggle, science had triumphed over the hostile doubts of self-trained mining men, with their instinctive jeers at the unintelligible researches of an intellectual minority. Now the industry was eagerly seeking guidance, and it was able to find it because a vigorous local scientific society was prepared to join with the federal government in insuring that key analyses and explanations were made available at a time when the Cripple Creek district was still young enough for the guidance to be useful.

If this seems a heavy stress on the role of science, it is because a brief essay leaves room only for the central theme. There were some notable engineering achievements in Colorado mining—for example, the introduction of electricity as a source of power. This seems to have come more quickly and on a wider scale in Colorado than anywhere else in the mining West because of the peculiar difficulties involved in hauling fuel to precipitous locations. Or again, power drills for driving mine adits were used for the first time in Colorado.

There were other achievements that could be cited, just as one could lay much more stress on the favorable economic changes produced by better transportation, the use of Colorado-produced coal and coke, and the development of local food supplies. Yet all of these are auxiliary to the central problem, which was how to work profitably ores of unusual complexity and unusual variety. For this problem the Fifty-Niners and the later gold rushers, however romantic they may seem, could supply no answer. Nor could even the best minds in the region, until a painful decade of readjustment and the arrival of well-trained scientists had prepared Colorado for the new era that opened with Leadville in 1877 and carried on through a series of remarkable discoveries that extended down to the end of the century.

CHAPTER XII

The Grazers and Drovers

O F ALL THE WESTERNERS the cowboy has become the best known symbol of America's frontier heritage. Beginning with the dime novelists of the late nineteenth century, several generations of American writers have elevated the cowboy to a place in the national imagination reserved for true folk heroes. It matters little to readers apparently that neither the dime novelists nor their more sophisticated descendants have described the cattle business and the cowboy accurately. Although western cattlemen dominated the Great Plains for little more than a generation, the cattle kingdom contributed greatly to the development of the West and the legacy of that empire has exerted a considerable influence on the pattern of American popular culture.

While large-scale ranching developed mainly in the trans-Mississippi West during the years after the Civil War, stockmen had grazed their herds on the frontier since the early colonial era. From the Carolinas to the New England frontier, farmers drove their cattle to the markets of more densely populated regions or sold their surplus animals to drovers who did so. The pattern was continued in the trans-Appalachian territories and states. As settlers moved in increasing numbers to Indiana and Illinois after the War of 1812, the rich prairies there attracted the cattlemen. Paul Wallace Gates has shown how "Cattle Kings of the Prairies" developed a profitable and highly organized type of ranching on the midwestern grasslands. Before the coming of the railroad, cattlemen drove midwestern herds to eastern markets, often fattening them on corn for some months in Ohio before delivering them to markets in the seaboard states. While these stockmen did not encounter the same problems as the cattlemen of a later era on the Great Plains, the distance from midwestern prairie to eastern market often equaled that between Texas and some of the Kansas cattle towns.

The far western cattle industry had its origins on the Texas plains before the Civil War. During the 1840's and 1850's, Texan cattlemen marketed the longhorn descendants of Spanish cattle in New Orleans, in the mining camps of the Southwest and California, and occasionally in the Middle West. The Texas cattle also supported a considerable trade in hides.

At least since Walter Prescott Webb published *The Great Plains* in 1931, most students of the cattle industry have accepted his contention that Anglo-Americans with little or no herding tradition began the Texan cattle industry in the coastal region between the Rio Grande and the Guadeloupe rivers after Mexican ranchers were driven from the area between 1836 and 1846. The Americans, he claimed, adopted the methods of the Mexican ranchers, as well as taking their land and some of their cattle. Recently Terry G. Jordan has suggested that Webb and his followers were incorrect, and argues that Americans from the herding fringe of the southern frontier brought cattle ranching with them to Texas between 1820 and 1840, establishing themselves on the coastal prairie between the Sabine and the Guadeloupe rivers. Expansion of the industry then continued from this region into the section of lower Texas which Webb considered the cradle of the cattle industry in his state. The methods of the early cattle ranchers in Texas, Professor Jordan maintained, were a blend of Anglo-American and Spanish precedents and the cowboys who assisted the first Anglo-American ranchers and the members of their families were usually black slaves rather than Mexican *vaqueros.*

The Texan herds increased in size rapidly during the Civil War and by 1865 several million cattle were grazing in the southern portions of the state. War time demands had depleted midwestern herds and the industrial and urban population of the northern states was growing rapidly. Now northern buyers offered up to $40 a head for Texas cattle while an animal could be purchased in Texas for a few dollars. Now drovers tried to deliver "the four-dollar critter to the forty-dollar market" and exchange southern steers for northern dollars. The thousand-mile journey north to market did not deter the Texans, and when they pointed the first herd north in 1866 the era of the "long drive" had begun.

Many of the drovers of 1866 planned to sell or ship their herds at Sedalia, Missouri, but historians disagree on the number of cattle that actually reached this point on the Missouri Pacific Railroad. Indians and outlaws harassed some trail drivers; cattle accustomed to the open range stampeded in the woods of Missouri; and irate farmers in Missouri and eastern Kansas halted herds that they feared might infect their own stock with the dreaded Spanish or Texas fever or trample their crops. The more successful drovers apparently disposed of their stock at various towns on the midwestern frontier such as St. Joseph and Baxter Springs, but the difficulties of the herdsmen on the Sedalia Trail doomed the future of the Missouri railhead as a cattle town. If the long drive was to continue, the drovers must find a more satisfactory route northward, and a shipping point with satisfactory facilities for handling the herds and supplying the needs of both buyers and sellers.

In 1867 Joseph G. McCoy, an Illinois livestock dealer, offered a solution to the marketing problem, when he began to develop Abilene, Kansas as a livestock terminal, safely beyond the thickly settled farm lands of eastern Kansas. By early summer of that year he had constructed cattle yards and pens, and in July he sent riders south to inform trail drivers of the new shipping point. Between 1868 and 1871, northern buyers perhaps purchased more than a million cattle in Abilene.

Throughout the 1870's the long drive was an important element of the western cattle business. As farmers thickened in the vicinity of that village, Abilene surrendered the trade; for varying lengths of time Baxter Springs, Wichita, Ellsworth, Newton and Dodge City were flourishing cattle towns as was Ogallala, Nebraska. During most of the year these communities slumbered, but districts in them blossomed into gaudy and tinseled pleasure marts when the herds arrived during the late spring and summer months. Saloons, gambling dens and prostitutes served the drovers and the cattle buyers. Respectable citizens of the cattle towns faced a serious dilemma; although they heartily condemned the lawlessness of the cowboys and other unsavory individuals attracted by the profits of the cattle trade, they were afraid to antagonize the men who brought so much business to their communities. Robert R. Dykstra has correctly stressed that writers have exaggerated the amount of violence in the cattle towns, but frontier lawmen did not eliminate it completely.

Trail driving was an important part of the Texas cattle industry for only a short time and various factors severely reduced the profits. Stock lost weight on the trail; disease, stampedes and Indian raids reduced the value of the trail herds. Some Indians collected toll when herds crossed their reservations in Indian Territory. But the farmers most seriously impeded the northward-bound herds. Steadily pushing the farm frontier westward through Kansas, they feared the tick-borne fever which the cattle sometimes spread, and stormed when Texan stock destroyed their crops. Sometimes they repelled invaders with shotguns, but more effective was the pressure which they exerted upon the state legislators. Kansas lawmakers, and those in other midwestern states as well, approved herd laws which allowed county residents to vote to enclose all livestock and some legislatures also approved quarantine legislation. The Kansas legislators, for instance, barred Texan cattle from the settled areas of the state during those months when splenic fever was most to be feared. During the mid-1880's, stockmen, particularly the Texans, requested Congress to establish a national cattle trail over the public lands, but the northern cattlemen were now much less dependent upon Texas as a source of foundation and stocker cattle. The measure died in Congress.

While some cattlemen devoted their energies to the trailing business, others were expanding the cattleman's domain in the Southwest; some moved into northern and western Texas and others pushed into New Mexico and Arizona or negotiated grazing leases with tribes in the Indian Territory. In the beginning the cattlemen usually did not hold title to their ranges and they subscribed to an unwritten code which gave the first comer control of the lands on which his cattle grazed. But farmers began to settle in central and northern Texas and nearby states, threatening this system. At first cattlemen reacted violently to the invasion of their domain, but accepting the inevitable, they gradually abandoned the open range and began to obtain title to land and fence it. By purchasing only a few thousand acres along streams some cattlemen insured that they would be able to use great stretches of unwatered lands adjacent to their holdings. But particularly in the 1880's some ranchers or cattle companies acquired legal title to large holdings. Established during the mid 1880's, the XIT owned more than three million acres of land in ten counties of the Texas Panhandle. The XIT was unique but ranch holdings of many thousands of acres became common. Land acquisition stabilized the cattle industry and permitted southwestern ranchers to improve the quality of their livestock by introducing blooded sires.

While such changes were occurring in the southwestern cattle industry, the northern range cattle business was also expanding. During the 1850's overland freighters and Army contractors had discovered that livestock could survive the harsh winters on the Northern Plains. By the 1870's ranchers were grazing herds on the high plains of Colorado, Montana, Wyoming and Dakota Territory, attracted in part by the markets provided by mines, Army posts and Indian reservations. These cattlemen also adopted the open range system.

The pacification of the northern tribes during the 1870's, the construction of branch lines by the Union Pacific and other railroad companies and the advance of the Northern Pacific Railroad into the Northern Plains all contributed to a ranching boom in that region. Accounts circulated of vast profits to be made on the northern ranges and the intelligence propelled men, capital and cattle into the area. The northern herds increased in numbers rapidly as stockmen drove in herds from the trail towns, from ranges in the Central Plains and to some extent from the Pacific Northwest as well. Still lacking cattle in sufficient numbers, they procured additional foundation and stocker cattle from the Middle West. Between 1870 and 1880 the number of cattle in Wyoming alone rose from 11,000 to more than 500,000 head. Striking increases occurred in other parts of the Northern Plains. Increasingly midwestern farmers looked at the Plains country for the feeder cattle that they sent to slaughter after a winter of corn feeding.

Technological improvements in the packing industry also facilitated the expansion of the range cattle industry. New methods of handling meat and of cold storage widened the market for western beef as did the introduction of refrigerated railroad cars and steamships. At the same time cattlemen developed thriftier animals and improved the quality of their meat to satisfy the more discriminating tastes of easterners and Europeans. Some western stockmen purchased Hereford, Aberdeen Angus or Shorthorn bulls from importing and breeding farms in the older states to upgrade their range animals. In the early 1880's Gudgell and Simpson of Independence, Missouri, imported a young Hereford bull named Anxiety IV from England. This animal's superior qualities helped to insure that the white faces would eventually dominate western range and midwestern feed lot. Barbed wire, sometimes erected on the public lands as well as on private range, allowed cattlemen to control both breeding and grazing more effectively.

Reports of fabulous profits in the cattle industry attracted eastern as well as European capital to both northern and southern ranges. Ernest Staples Osgood wrote, "It was all so simple. The United States furnished the grass; the East, the capital; and the western stockman, the experience." Often in cooperation with western businessmen or ranchers investors organized cattle companies and in 1883, the Wyoming legislature incorporated 20 firms, capitalized in total at more than twelve million dollars. One of the largest concerns, the Swan Land and Cattle Company, valued its assets at $3,000,000.

Conservative New Englanders, flamboyant Europeans and eastern college graduates all hoped to profit from the West's new El Dorado. In studying a sample of 93 eastern investors Gene M. Gressley discovered that they were "mainly merchants, bankers, financiers and industrialists" as well as including a "small group of professional men." Often such men did not understand the practical side of the range cattle industry and some hired westerners to manage their ranches while they supervised the finances of the operation from the comfort of the Cattlemen's Club in Cheyenne or their eastern offices. Commission firms, banks and loan agencies supplied additional operating capital to the industry.

The separation of ownership and management sometimes produced conflicts between employer and employee. In their search for profits, investors often ignored their managers' advice on the problems of over-stocking, water rights, and range control. But many western managers let their desire for high returns interfere with their judgment, some were incompetent and some westerners calmly fleeced innocent eastern or foreign investors.

The failure of the federal government to develop a land policy or system of supervision for the range cattle industry, and the ineffectiveness of the territorial and state legislatures, led cattlemen to create associations to enforce the customs of the range country. The stock growers' associations which flourished in the range country during this period formulated policies and standards which regulated nearly every operational aspect of the industry. Including the most prominent ranchers and cattle corporation managers among their membership, these associations were sometimes the most powerful institution in a ranching region. Many association members sat in the western territorial and state legislatures, especially in Wyoming and Montana, giving their organizations substantial political influence. To the best of their ability, cattleman–legislators insured that territorial laws protected the best interests of the cattle industry as the large stockmen interpreted them. For a time the territorial legislature of Wyoming accepted the roundup rules and other regulations of the Wyoming Stock Growers' Association as the law of the territory. That organization was the most powerful of the associations and it did not preserve its hegemony for long, but similar groups were powerful elsewhere in the cattle country.

The members of the stock growers' associations favored law and order and their efforts to control roundups, regulate brands, investigate rustling, and inspect market consignments of cattle had a stabilizing influence on the industry. Most cattlemen complied willingly with the policies of the organizations. But despite their posture as champions of stability the leading members of the associations did constitute a power elite whose members sometimes confused law and order with their own best interests.

The struggle between "sodbusters" and ranchers has colored much of the history of the range cattle industry, and neither was blameless. The distinction between nester or small rancher and rustler was sometimes difficult to make. When farmers and less affluent cattlemen challenged the right of the large ranchers to control the range, the reaction of some stockmen and their cowboys to such presumption was violent. Assassination, rustling, poisoned water holes and fence cutting are historical fact. The Johnson County War, in which small ranchers confronted the Wyoming Stock Growers' Association in 1891, showed the willingness of both groups to take the law into their own hands to serve their own interests. Although space does not allow us to tell it here, the story of the sheepman is as interesting as that of the cattleman, and the shepherd particularly contested the cattleman's control of the more westerly ranges of the grazing empire.

By the mid-1880's experienced cattlemen believed that the ranges were becoming overstocked. As early as 1884 drought diminished the carrying capacity of the southern ranges, and President Cleveland complicated the situation still more by ordering cattlemen to remove their herds from tribal lands in Indian Territory. Northern ranchers were experiencing overcrowding on their ranges also by 1885 and some looked for new ranges in Canada or on northern Indian reservations, but their efforts did not remedy the situation. The summer of 1886 was dry and the cattle on the northern ranges entered the fall season in poor condition. An extremely severe winter followed and considerable numbers of cattle died on some ranges. The losses shocked many eastern investors and sagging meat and cattle prices during the late 1880's and early 1890's ushered in a period of severe depression in the industry, during which disenchanted investors liquidated many of the cattle corporations.

The problems of the cattlemen during the late 1880's and early 1890's stimulated far reaching adjustments in the industry. Painfully aware of the problems of the open range system, northern ranchers began to put more dependence on their own land, to fence it and to grow supplementary forage. Although the winter of 1886–1887 did not affect the southern herds, drought during the late 1880's and flagging markets prompted southwestern cattlemen to adopt similar measures. By 1900 cowboys often spent as much time riding mowing machines and pitching hay as they did on their cow ponies.

The range cattle industry united a vast area of the United States in a common economic interest. Both the ranchers of the Northern Plains and the southwestern stockmen searched for better markets, agitated for transportation facilities and tried to improve the quality of their livestock. Midwestern cattle feeders filled their feed lots in the fall with cattle drawn from the length and breadth of the western ranges. Their neighbors who maintained breeding herds sent stock westward to improve the quality of the range cattle. Although theirs was primarily a regional industry, the cattlemen supplied both national and international markets. High profits attracted eastern and European capital to the ranges, and for a time large cattle companies dominated the industry both north and south. Railroads responded to the expansion of the cattle industry and further stimulated it by extending lines farther into the range country. Towns sprang up to serve the needs of cattle raisers and cattle buyers. The cattle industry stimulated research in animal diseases, particularly Spanish fever, the development of refrigerated railroad cars, the growth of the midwestern packing industry and more scientific methods of cattle breeding. The grazing empire also left a heritage of romance, adventure and violence, and Owen Wister, Zane Gray, Max Brand and others drew upon that heritage to create a new literary genre and hero. Described in countless novels, movies and television episodes, the cowboy and the cattle business have come to symbolize the American West to many Americans.

•1•

PAUL WALLACE GATES

Cattle Kings in the Prairies

Cattle raising became a frontier industry in the colonial era and large livestock operations were to be found on the midwestern prairies during the 1830's. By the time of the Civil War a number of "Cattle Kings" dominated the cattle business there and their investments rivaled that of later cattle barons in the far West. In this selection Paul Wallace Gates discusses some of the leading prairie stockmen.

. . . Two of the earliest of the Illinois cattle kings who left notable marks on prairie development were Isaac Funk and Jacob Strawn. Funk settled in Funks Grove, southwest of Bloomington, in 1824; seven years later Strawn took up residence near Jacksonville. Buying, fattening, and driving cattle to market absorbed their attention, not farming or raising cattle. They scoured their neighborhoods for young stock which

SOURCE: Abridged from Paul Wallace Gates, "Cattle Kings in the Prairies," *Mississippi Valley Historical Review*, XXXV (December, 1948), 379-412. Reprinted by permission of the *Journal of American History* and Paul Wallace Gates.

they bought and drove to their locality for grazing and a final period of corn feeding. Keener competition for beef cattle extended Funk's and Strawn's buying trips into Missouri, the Indian country, and Texas. . . . When the cattle were ready for market Funk and Strawn set out with motley crews to drive the grazing herds overland. Funk marketed his cattle in Galena, Peoria, Chicago, and Ohio cities, while Strawn generally drove to St. Louis. . . .

Costs of cattle feeding on the prairies were low. Hired hands were employed at small wages from the floating population then flooding Illinois in search of land; cheap or free grass was available; little fencing was necessary until settlers began to push into the prairie; and taxes were few and light. . . .

Both men successfully weathered the Panic of 1837 although their operations were temporarily reduced. The prosperity of the fifties and sixties affected them favorably, their incomes rising to five and six figures in the best years. Visitors to the Funk farm during the Civil War were astonished to see fields of 2,000 to 3,000 acres in grain, and 1,600 cattle, 500 sheep, 500 hogs, and 300 horses and mules in the pastures. Funk's annual drives of livestock to the Chicago market totalled as high as 1,500 cattle and 6,000 hogs in some years. The value of his livestock in 1863 was estimated at a million dollars.

Strawn's operations were on an equally large scale and elicited as much favorable comment. On his 10,000-acre farm he had a field of 3,000 acres in corn. His "vast" herds of cattle necessitated fencing for which he spent in one year $10,000. A force of two or three hundred laborers was employed to do the work necessary for such a large business. . . .

The boom years of the fifties brought to Illinois hundreds of thousands of immigrants with little resources and hundreds of speculators with large purses, all looking for land. To protect their interests, Funk, Strawn, and other cattle kings joined in the scramble for the remaining public lands. . . . By 1856 when the public lands were gone Funk and Strawn had acquired respectively 26,000 and 20,000 acres.

Meantime, their farming operations were changing. Heavier cattle of improved breed were being produced, and increasing amounts of corn were necessary to provide for concentrated feeding. As farming became more intensive there was more labor to be performed. Miles of fences and ditches had to be constructed, new land had to be broken, and corn had to be planted in ever larger amounts. Improvements in the plow and the use of the harrow, the cultivator, the seeder, and the drill took care of some of this work but human labor was indispensable even though it was becoming less available. The high wages paid on railroad construction, industrial and building jobs in western cities, and the cheapness of land farther west absorbed much of the available labor or impelled it to move to the next frontier where government land was still to be had. When the Civil War came, the army drained the West of its remaining manpower. . . .

The shortage of labor induced Funk and Strawn to divide a part of their estates into 160-acre units on which former employees or incoming immigrants were established as tenants. The landlord built small homes for the new occupants, provided them with a team, farm implements, and credit until their first crop came in, and either paid them a stipulated sum for every bushel of corn they produced or allowed them one third of the grain. Tenants who provided their own team and farm implements and boarded themselves were permitted by Funk to retain three fifths of the grain. . . .

By 1865 the estates of the cattle kings like Funk and Strawn were no longer ranches for the pasturing of cattle but were congeries of small farms operated by tenants whose principal and too often only crop was corn. The livestock was being crowded into small enclosures or into the broken land along the streams. Tenants not only freed the landlord of responsibility for and supervision of the management of much of the land, but provided him with grain rent that sooner or later was to make him independent of the cattle business. At this point the landlord no longer needed to live on or in the vicinity of his land. . . .

John Dean Gillett's far-flung operations in land and cattle made his name almost a byword for prairie landlordism and superior quality beef in America and England. . . .

A scion of substantial Yankee stock, Gillett migrated to central Illinois in 1838 at the age of nineteen. With his partner, Robert Latham, he bought considerable Logan County land for speculation, entered land for settlers on "frontier" terms, laid out and promoted towns, improved farm lands, and by the middle fifties was selling a part of his extensive holdings. Railroads, banking, and other features of the economic life of Lincoln, the county seat with which they were intimately associated, attracted their attention and brought high returns in increasing town lot sales. It was in the development of his own prairie lands, however, that Gillett was most absorbed. . . .

Cattle attracted him as much as did land and he built his property into a ranch on which he could raise his own breeds and fatten other cattle bought from neighbors. No dilettante cattle fancier, he wasted no time or money in importing expensive bulls and cows and in building up a herd of purebred Shorthorns as did some of his neighbors. Yearling cattle bought locally combined with his own strain of Shorthorn grades and fattened for market on the prairie and blue grass and the corn he raised, constituted his business. He specialized not in purebred but in fat stock.

Gradually improvements were made on Gillett's ranch that transformed it into a modern agricultural estate. One hundred and forty-four miles of fencing were constructed, tenant houses were erected, extensive tile drainage was undertaken, and 6,500 acres were broken and put in corn. When Gillett began improving his land the pressure of incoming immigrants was such that it was easy for him to secure hired hands to do most of the work. As late as 1877 he employed 100 hands during the growing season. . . .

Gillett's livestock business was on a scale that would do credit to anything short of the cattle companies of the western plains. From 2,400 to 3,000 cattle were grazed on the estate—though never housed—and more than a thousand hogs salvaged the corn not utilized by the cattle. As many as 1,200 steers were marketed annually. The stock was pastured for three years before grain feeding began. To bring them to the best condition for market as much as 130 to 235 bushels of corn were fed each steer. It was estimated that for every steer thus fed some 500 pounds of pork was produced. . . .

Select groups of Gillett's fat cattle were shipped to Chicago and some went on to Buffalo, Albany, New York, and Montreal where they attracted excited bidding among butchers and meat packers and favorable publicity in the city papers and farm and livestock journals.

In 1875 Gillett and a New York exporter shipped some of his choicest cattle to England that took the country "by storm." The appearance of his two-thousand-pound steers—1,400 of them in three years—fattened to a high state of perfection won favorable notice from cattle dealers, quality breeders, and butchers. . . .

Despite the praise his cattle received, it became apparent to Gillett that 2,000-pound three- and four-year-olds were in less demand than lighter two-year-old steers, the feeding of which had been more carefully managed. He turned to breeding his own stock which he could bring up to 1,700 pounds in two years. In 1886 he had a thousand calves of his own breed and no longer bought feeders. At the same time he stopped shipments to England as discriminatory regulations and cattle losses made them less profitable.

Gillett found a ready market in the eighties for his yearling bulls on the western plains. Efforts by plains cattlemen to improve the size and quality of their herds led to large purchases of bulls from his

Shorthorn mixtures. In 1880 Colonel Couch of Texas bought 75 bulls at $100 each and other cattlemen in Colorado, Wyoming, Kansas, Nebraska, and Texas bought "many hundreds of young bulls and heifers" of Gillett's. In 1882 Gillett sold two carloads of bulls to "Congressman" Richard H. Whiting to stock his Kansas ranch.

From his land and cattle business Gillett accumulated an estate estimated at one and a half million dollars at the time of his death in 1883. . . .

The day of the cattle king in the prairies lasted roughly from 1850 to 1885 though the forces that were impelling a shift from cattle feeding to tenancy and grain farming were under way earlier. Every prairie county and in some places almost every township could boast, albeit rather sourly, of its big cattle farm. Rapid accumulation of wealth permitted the cattle kings to build huge rambling houses. . . . In the grand manner and with lavish expenditures they lived under conditions contrasting sharply with those of their hired hands or tenants, and of the small farmers then struggling to acquire ownership of their tracts.

Wealth amassed locally won for these cattle kings prestige and a respectful following among rural neighbors who measured success in terms of the accumulation of land and livestock. This permitted the cattle kings and other large landlords to exercise political power out of all proportion to their numbers. They were found in the inner circles of the Republican and Democratic parties in which they exerted a conservative and not altogether enlightened influence. Some, affected by the respectful attention paid them by the small farmer element, wrapped themselves in the mantle of statesmanship and were elected to the state legislature, to Congress, and to the governor's chair, not always, however, to the advantage of their state or section. . . .

The combination of cattle kings and other large landlords sought to minimize assessments upon unimproved land or land used for grazing. To that end they fought increased taxes and assessments designed to make possible improvements in roads, schools, and local government. They continually harassed local tax authorities by suits to set aside assessments, refusals to pay taxes, and efforts to compromise delinquent taxes, to evade the payment of penalties, and to recover tax titles. When they had tenants on their land, they shifted the tax burden to them and thereby secured additional support for their views on expenditures by local governments. . . .

In every pioneer community where livestock interests and small farmers were struggling to get established, friction soon appeared over the problem of fencing. The cattlemen early took advantage of the open prairies on which their cattle grazed and had no reason to advocate fencing. On the other hand, the settlers could make little progress in raising grain—their chief livelihood—until their cultivated land was protected from the depredations of livestock. . . . Since farmers were generally later comers and they were the ones needing the fences, it was easy for the cattlemen to argue that they should build them. But to fence a quarter section farm cost $500 or more, an expense that few pioneers could afford.

Fencing, therefore, became a major issue with each side trying to place the obligation on the other. Legislature after legislature in the prairie states struggled with the issue, vacillating and procrastinating and finally adopting ineffective measures that still left the obligation in the hands of farmers. In Illinois the livestock men delayed the adoption of a herd law until 1867 and it was passed then only because the cattle kings were beginning to turn their land into grain cultivation and were adopting the farmers' point of view. . . .

Cattle kings and other large landlords were the principal beneficiaries of a land system that made easy the creation of estates of many thousands of acres. They first developed their properties into ranches for the feeding of livestock, then into bonanza farms, and finally into the modern pattern of tenant-operated farms. They brought a concentration of ownership and tenancy early to the prairies and sought to perpetuate that concentration by including in their wills all the restrictions on alienation that the law allowed. The passing of a hundred years has not materially affected the ownership of these early cattle kingdoms except that a number of descendants now own parts of the whole earlier owned by the cattle kings. . . .

T. J. CAULEY

Early Business Methods in the
Texas Cattle Industry

The era of the open range and overland trailing in Texas extended from the end of the Civil War to the early 1880's and in that short time Texas stockmen greatly influenced the character of the western cattle industry. The emphasis which writers have placed upon the romantic features of the cattle business sometimes obscures the fact that Texas cattlemen, like all stockmen, were businessmen. Dollars and cents and profits and losses were of vital concern to them, and here T. J. Cauley focuses on the business and economic aspects of the Texas cattle industry.

. . . The chief method of marketing Texas cattle previous to 1860 was to send the live animals by one means or another out of the State. There were, of course, no railroads connecting Texas with other parts of the country at the time, so the cattle had to be either shipped by water or driven overland. The latter method was much cheaper under the existing conditions than the former and was more generally used.

Between 1838 and 1860 Texas cattle were driven to Louisiana, chiefly to New Orleans, in considerable numbers, although the market there was always fluctuating, uncertain, and generally inadequate. In addition to those that were driven to New Orleans, others were shipped down the Red River and the Mississippi from Shreveport and Alexandria to that point. . . .

The problem of marketing Texas cattle was not solved before the Civil War. All of the efforts mentioned above resulted after all in the movement of only a very small percentage of the merchantable cattle in the State. The need for a market was an ever present one, and the net effect of the Civil War was greatly to intensify this need.

SOURCE: Abridged from T. J. Cauley, "Early Business Methods in the Texas Cattle Industry," *Journal of Economic and Business History*, IV (May, 1932), 460–486. © 1932, Graduate School of Business Administration, Harvard University. Reprinted by permission of the *Business History Review*.

During the four years of the Civil War practically all of the able-bodied men of Texas were away in the army. Since Texas was never seriously invaded, the herds of cattle were unmolested and continued to increase at their usual rapid rate. The relatively few men and boys who had the herds in charge were, in many cases, unable to carry on the extensive branding operations necessary; and the result was that the prairies of Texas came to be inhabited by vast herds of unbranded and, in large part, unclaimed cattle. . . .

In 1866 considerable numbers of Texas cattle were driven to Baxter Springs, Kansas, the southern terminus of the Fort Scott and Gulf Railroad. Although meeting with considerable opposition from the settlers around Baxter Springs, who professed to fear the spreading of Texas fever by the Texas cattle, some of these drives were quite successful financially. The following year, J. G. McCoy established a "cattle depot" at Abilene, Kansas, on the Kansas Pacific Railroad, and most of the herds driven north from Texas went to this point. The drovers received relatively good prices for their cattle, and after 1867 trail driving to Kansas constituted a definitely established method of marketing Texas cattle. . . .

There were four important sources of demand for the Texas cattle which were driven to the markets in Kansas in the post-Civil War period. The first of these was the packing houses of Kansas City, St. Louis, and Chicago, chiefly the last-named. Although . . . cattle freshly driven out of Texas were not ordinarily well adapted to the requirements of the packers, they were marketed in that way in large numbers, particularly during the early years of the trail-driving era. . . .

A second important source of demand was to be found in the feeders of the Middle West, that is, the farmers of the Corn Belt who made a practice of buying cattle and fattening them on corn and other grain during the winter months for the butchers and packers. This came to be an industry of much importance, for the steers that came up out of Texas were not ready for the butcher's block. . . .

A third source of demand consisted in the huge purchases of beef cattle which the federal government made for its Indian wards on the reservations scattered throughout the West and the Northwest and for the troops stationed in the numerous forts and posts in the territories of the same region. . . .

The fourth, and during the later years of the era by far the most important, source of demand was furnished by the ranchmen of the vast virgin ranges of the newly opened Northwest. This region included the territories of Wyoming, Montana, the Dakotas, Idaho, Colorado, and parts of Utah, Oregon, and Washington. It had been known for many years

—since the beginning of the great migrations over the Oregon Trail, in fact—that the pasture lands of these territories produced grasses which matured in the late summer and early autumn, furnishing for cattle a subsistence comparable to grain. This approached the ideal range conditions for maturing cattle which had been bred in Texas. . . .

As the period of trail driving advanced, there was a constant shifting of trail terminals toward the west of Kansas. Beginning with Sedalia in western Missouri and Baxter Springs in the southeastern corner of Kansas, the trail shifted, as we have seen, to Abilene in 1867. From there it had shifted to Newton, to Ellsworth, and to Wichita, by 1873. After this date, there was a shift to Great Bend, a town to the west of Newton on the main line of the Santa Fé, in 1874; and in 1875, Dodge City, still further to the west on the Santa Fé, began its ascent to fame as the greatest trail town of all times. . . . Shortly after the rise of Dodge City as a market, another important cattle town appeared to the north, that of Ogallala, Nebraska, a small town on the Platte River. This market was more easily accessible to the ranchmen of the Northwest than were the Kansas towns, and thus came to be a highly important market for stock cattle and young steers. . . .

From the standpoint of the economic historian the trail-driving era presents some interesting examples of the evolution of economic practices. The changing relationship of the drover to the herd is one of these; and the methods of financing the drives is another, the two being closely allied, of course. There is also the shift from the non-capitalistic nature of the cattle industry in Texas prior to and just after the Civil War to its highly capitalistic nature after about 1870. . . .

Certain significant social aspects present themselves. Trail driving was a unique method of marketing in that it required large numbers of men to go along with the cattle to market as compared with shipping cattle by railroad. This led to a vast amount of social intercourse between the cattlemen and cowboys of Texas and the people of the North, the Northwest, and the West. The whole technique of open-range cattle-ranching was transferred from Texas to Wyoming, Montana, and adjacent areas. Along with this transfer of technique went a transfer of a sort of "bovine culture" which had arisen in the Southwest.

Trail driving in its early years was essentially a non-specialized industry. Every cattle-raiser in Texas who had enough cattle of his own to make up a herd drove them, and the small cattleman threw his marketable steers in with those of his neighbor and went along to help with the drive. This state of affairs was in marked contrast to that prevailing in the later years of the era. . . .

In keeping with the non-specialized nature of the industry in its early years, the size of the herds driven was comparatively small in the majority of cases. The herds driven to Baxter Springs and to Abilene in 1866, 1867, and 1868 included typically fewer than 1,000 head each, and some of them only a few hundred. As late as 1870, a herd of 2,000 head was considered a large herd, although some considerably larger than this had been driven in a few cases.

The number of men employed in driving these small herds was also much larger in proportion than was the working force required for the large herds driven in later years. For example, with a herd of 600 head driven to Abilene in 1868, the owner took along with him 8 cow hands and a cook. Sixteen years later, in 1884, another drover drove 15 herds of approximately 3,000 head each from south Texas to Montana with only 10 men and a cook to the herd. . . .

After 1868 there was a steady increase in the size of the herds handled, and within a few years herds of 3,000 head or more were common. In fact, cattle were seldom driven in herds of less than this number during all the later years of the era; and there are numerous cases in which as many as 4,000 and 5,000 head were moved in a single herd. The chief factor making for this increase in the size of the herds was the fact that the number of men, as has already been indicated, required to handle a herd did not increase in exact proportion to increases in the size of the herd. . . .

Prior to 1870, practically all of the herds were driven by individual drovers, many of them driving only their own cattle. During the 'seventies, partnerships, syndicates, and even corporations were developed. Trail driving, once the period of experimentation was over, was an enterprise requiring large amounts of capital; and consequently the financial resources required were usually beyond the limit of a single individual. This led to the pooling of resources and the combining of business and managerial ability. A common arrangement was for a native Texas drover to form a partnership with a northern man who had business and financial connections in the North.

Many of the partnerships, however, were made up entirely of Texans, and by about 1875 the great bulk of trail driving had gravitated into the hands of these relatively large concerns. It has been said that 75 per cent of the cattle driven out of Texas during the entire trail-driving era were driven by not more than 100 drovers. . . . This stage was superseded by one in which the drover usually raised a part of the cattle which he drove; but, in most cases, he purchased the great bulk of them from the ranchmen and made a specialty of trail driving. . . .

The final stage of development found the drover as a complete specialist, that is, he neither raised the cattle which he drove nor owned them while he was driving them. To illustrate, Ab Blocker, a typical drover, drove a herd from Colorado City, Texas, to Deadwood, South Dakota, in 1893 for a flat rate of $2.75 per head. The cattle had already been bought and paid for by the Dakota ranchmen, and Blocker was simply paid to drive them to their new home. This represents the final step in the growth of specialization in the industry. . . .

Along with this evolution in organization and very closely related to it went a change in the methods by which the drives were financed. The earliest drives were financed by what may be termed non-capitalistic methods. As was shown by an illustration already used, it was common for the community in which the herd was to be made up to contribute all that was necessary for the drive—the cattle, the men, the horses, and the food supplies. There was essentially no money outlay. . . .

A little later when the drovers began to purchase the herds which they drove, some very unusual means of doing so were employed. For example, two merchants of Gonzales, Texas, traded dry-goods to the people of the surrounding country for their cattle and then drove them to Kansas. Another would-be drover came through Bell County, Texas, in 1868, trading eight-day clocks for cattle, one clock for a matured beef. Most of the drovers who first purchased herds with money secured this cash through the sale of their own cattle in preceding years on the Kansas market; but, by the early 'seventies, banks and trust companies had entered the field of financing the cattle drives. . . In the later years of the period, some of the banks in St. Louis and Chicago extended credit for this purpose, and there were numerous banks in smaller towns which assisted in the financing of the drives. . . .

Considerable information is available concerning the costs of trail driving. The biggest item in the cost of driving a herd was the wages of the men. The cowboys employed to drive the herds usually received wages of around $30 a month and board; although in some instances higher wages were paid. . . . The cook and the horse-wrangler ordinarily received the same wages as the other hands. The boss was the highest paid member of the outfit. He commonly received $100 a month for his services. . . .

The total pay-roll for the typical herd of around 3,000 head of cattle was thus between $400 and $500 a month. In a month's time, such an outfit could move a herd between 400 and 500 miles, a herd usually making an average of about 15 miles a day. Thus it cost in wages approximately one dollar to move 3,000 head of cattle one mile, although there are instances in which the total cost per mile of moving a herd was greater than this. . . .

The percentage of losses suffered by the herds of different drovers varied considerably. In some cases it amounted to almost 100 per cent as the result of the ravages of Texas fever, but this was very rare in the case of the native longhorns. Untimely blizzards in the early spring were responsible for heavy losses in some instances, and the crossing of swollen streams frequently meant the loss of several head. Stampedes were sometimes so complete that some of the cattle were never recovered; and, in the early days, the Indians of the Territory usually exacted a toll of a few head or more, either directly or indirectly. But in the later years of the period, due to the employment of better methods, losses were reduced to not more than 2 or 3 per cent in most cases.

There were also certain methods of making up for such losses suffered along the trail. It was a poor trail driver, according to the standards of the times, who could not pick up enough strays from among the range cattle along the route, without the commission of any overt acts, to make up for the ordinary losses of the drive. This became more difficult after the practice of trail-cutting . . . at the Red River crossing and at other points was instituted by the cattlemen's associations, but it continued in some measure to the end of the period of trail driving. . . .

ERNEST S. OSGOOD

The Cattleman in the Agricultural History
of the Northwest

To a very considerable extent, northern cattlemen constructed their range empire on the public lands. Ernest S. Osgood points out that while stockmen learned to master many of the problems involved in ranching, their inability to control the use of the range contributed directly to the disastrous winter of 1886–87. In this reading Professor Osgood describes the open range system and the efforts of High Plains cattlemen to develop a more stable and less hazardous type of ranching.

. . . The chief feature of the range cattle business was, of course, the free pasturage upon the unused and unoccupied acres of the public domain. This enormous natural resource, open to all, was at once, the source of the cattleman's prosperity and strength and the cause of his ruin and weakness. The combination of cheap stock and free grass caused the northern rangeman's sudden entrance into the prosperity of the eighties;—the effort to expand the business far beyond the carrying capacity of the ranges, the speculation and booming which the earlier profits engendered caused his ruin. Most of the problems confronting the industry, and they were many, the range cattleman would have solved, the danger to his property from the cattle thief, the marauding Indian and disease. The elaborate machinery of the round-up and inspection testify to his ingenuity in meeting the problems of ownership and sale. But the one problem which he did not and could not solve was the control of the range and the prevention of overcrowding. . . .

In Wyoming where the powerful Wyoming Stock Growers' Association achieved an efficiency in organizing the range business beyond that of any group upon the High Plains, newcomers were sometimes prevented from crowding in on already occupied ranges. By the law of 1884, the

---

SOURCE: Abridged from Ernest S. Osgood, "The Cattleman in the Agricultural History of the Northwest," *Agricultural History*, III (July, 1929), 117–130. Reprinted by permission of *Agricultural History* and Ernest S. Osgood.

Association was given complete control of the stock-growing industry of the Territory. True, all stock-growers were eligible for membership in the Association, but the Association was judge of its own membership and a newcomer was not likely to crowd a range when it might result in his being denied the obvious advantages of membership. Rather than have this occur, he was likely to seek a less crowded range, if such existed. The Association, however, had no control over the expansion of the herds of its own members who during the boom period of the eighties over-bought and endangered the safety of all.

Thus where organization failed to prevent crowding, the cattleman was forced to fall back on his own efforts. To those actually in the business, it was perfectly clear by 1884 that continued prosperity depended upon the acquisition of as much land as possible. They no longer thought of themselves as temporary occupants, permitted to utilize these acres until the farmer arrived, but as natural, permanent and all important. . . .

One thing was certain, land laws made to fit the needs of the middle-western agricultural advance had broken down completely west of the hundredth meridian. Cattlemen, seeking a permanent basis for their industry, were painfully aware of this. . . . As for the rest of the country, any effort to remodel our land laws to meet the novel environment was sure to result in an outcry against land monopoly. It made little difference to a people schooled in the tradition of a farm home for everyone to point out that farm homes for poor men on the marginal land of Wyoming was a romantic absurdity. The farmer should be permitted to retain his inalienable right to fail as well as to succeed on a quarter section of free land. The agrarian discontent that was expressing itself in attacks on the railroads, the "grasping corporations" and the "money power" of Wall Street, turned upon the cattle kings along the Laramie and the Powder. . . .

The iniquity of a barbwire fence strung across the Public Domain as a possible means of range control caused a din far louder than the facts warranted. As a matter of fact, the cattlemen were not at all agreed on the wisdom of this practice. They were fully aware that such fencing limited the free movement of their herds to new grazing grounds, prevented even grazing and increased the danger of winter losses because it prevented the drifting of the cattle before the storm. The Act of 1885, declaring such fences illegal, caused no particular resentment in the cow country; indeed, it was welcomed by many large as well as small operators.

Another process of far more importance to the future of the cattle industry of the Northwest was under way. Forage, other than the range grasses, began to be of increasing importance, particularly to those with valuable herds. The early cattleman looked upon the wild hay along the streams as something to be fed off by his cattle together with the less luxuriant growth on the benches beyond. . . . The cattle boom changed all this. There was a mad scramble for ranch properties. Speculation in ranch sites became as hectic as speculation in herds. Large companies began to divert some of their capital from the buying of cattle to the purchase of land. This shift in the capital basis of the industry resulted in a tremendous increase in the disposal of land by the government under the various land laws and the appearance of frauds far more serious than those of illegal fencing.

The lands which the cattlemen were getting hold of were those along the streams, where there were natural hay lands or where there was a possibility of hay crops with a minimum of irrigation. The more valuable the herd, the greater the pressure on its owners to secure such lands. The homestead, preemption and the desert land laws were used to obtain these stream sites. . . .

In his efforts to find a practical basis for his changing industry, the cattleman turned to the purchase of railroad land. The transcontinental roads were among the first to become aware of the importance of the cattle industry of the High Plains; its capacity for expansion and its relation to the land. In 1875 the government directors of the Union Pacific were urging that the lands, "belonging to the government and to the company ought to be placed under some well devised system of pasturage. . . . whereby the growth of cattle may be fostered and the lands made immediately remunerative." . . .

But in spite of all these shifts, the northern cattleman came down to the latter years of the eighties with the open range to a large measure uncontrolled and unrestricted. Although the heart breaking winter of 1886–1887 brought disaster to the whole business, it was not an unmitigated evil. There were two beneficial effects: first, the range was cleared of those who had been operating on too narrow a basis and, second, those who did remain in the business were forced to be satisfied with small herds which would find future safety in privately owned pastures. . . .

The winter of 1886–1887 had demonstrated to large and small cattlemen alike that the grass crop of the open ranges was far too uncertain a thing and that the stock-growing industry must look to the production of hay sufficient to carry the herd through the winter at least. . . . The acreage devoted to the cultivation of hay in Wyoming and Montana increased more than tenfold during the period from 1880–1900 as the census figures for the three periods show.

These figures not only mark the decline of the range cattle industry, but also the passing of that distinctive frontier figure, the cowboy. Mowing machines, hay rakes and ditching tools became a more important part of the equipment than the chuck wagon, the lariat and the branding iron.

"Cowboys don't have as soft a time as they did," lamented one member of the fraternity.

I remember when we sat around the fire the winter through and didn't do a lick of work except to chop a little wood to build a fire to keep warm by. Now we go on general roundup, then the calf roundup, then comes haying— something that the old-time cowboy never dreamed of—then the beef roundup and the fall calf roundup and the gathering of bulls and weak cows and after all this a winter of feeding hay. I tell you times have changed. You didn't hear the sound of a mowing machine in this country ten years ago.

Some of the larger operators turned to sheep raising. In Wyoming the rise of sheep population between 1890 and 1900 is very marked. Like the cattle growers, the sheepmen began to combine the summer pastures on the open range with the winter feeding of hay, raised on privately owned land or lands leased from the state. . . .

The development of irrigation was closely associated with this shift of the stock growing industry from the open range to a ranch basis. During the early period of settlement, the raising of grain crops, wheat, oats, etc. in Montana and Wyoming had been limited to the rich bottom lands where the fertility of the soil and the greater moisture close in to the mountains made production without irrigation possible. . . . The next step in the extension of the farming area came in those spots where the contour of the land and the availability of water made irrigation comparatively easy. Miners, turned ranchmen, who had learned how to get water onto their mining claims by running ditches and flumes along the sides of the gulches began to put this knowledge to work in the narrow valley lands upon which some of them settled after the mining boom was over. . . .

By 1890, four types of holdings were distinguishable on the northern ranges. There was first the unirrigated farm which, until the appearance of the dry farmer, was limited to a few favorable localities in the mountain valleys; second, the unirrigated stock ranch, which still depended upon a combination of natural hay lands and the open range; third, the irrigated ranch, raising some crop other than forage; and fourth, the irrigated stock ranch where irrigation was carried on solely for stock raising purposes.

The first and second groups represent the older type of agriculture and stock raising. On the ranches of the third and fourth groups, irrigation was being employed either in the production of farm crops and forage or in the improvement of the natural pastures. In the third group, crop production under irrigation was being combined with stock raising; in the fourth, stock raising alone was being carried on with irrigation employed merely to increase the crop of grass found on the natural pasture. In both groups, however, stock raising and irrigation were combined and this alliance is of great importance in the process of adjustment following the range cattle days.

Even in the third group, where cereals were being raised under irrigation, the area devoted to these crops was very small compared with the acreage irrigated for forage crops or for the improvement of the natural pastures.

As for the fourth group, stock growers irrigating pasture lands, it is impossible from the available census figures to tell how many of those there were in the period following the range era or the area of land they occupied as the census does not give the figures of any group of irrigators, except those who were irrigating for other purposes than merely for increasing the grazing. They were irrigators as the term is commonly understood, but represented a transitional group who were moving over from the old range cattle group to the stock grower with forage crops raised by irrigation. . . .

SYDNEY B. SPIEGEL

Who Were the Cattle Rustlers?
A Look at the Johnson County War
in Wyoming

All too often writers present a stereotype of the struggle between the cattle barons, farmers and small ranchers in which the large stockman surrounds himself with ruthless "hired guns," and the "sodbusters" are honest yeomen who wish only to be left in peace. In this selection Sydney B. Spiegel shows that both factions in the Johnson County War resorted to violence and extralegal action to protect their interests.

. . . The main outlines of the story are not complicated. The cattle industry in Wyoming and surrounding states was built on the apparent truths that since grass was free on the public lands of the Great Plains area, and since cattle naturally multiply, all one would have to do would be to turn a few cattle loose on the public range and then sit back in a saloon and watch the money roll in. Unforeseen problems arose when too many people got the same idea and the range became overstocked; when government officials protested the appropriation of federal land which had not been purchased; when homesteaders and sheep ranchers moved in; when severe blizzards caused the death of thousands of cattle —and when some enterprising cowboys turned to cattle rustling.

Wealthy members of the Wyoming Stockgrowers Association, convinced that the orderly processes of law were not sufficient to protect their stock from rustlers, began to turn to extra-legal assassination and violence. . . .

Ranchers and farmers in Johnson county claimed that they were legitimate small operators who were being accused of thievery by the Association in order to drive them out of business and maintain a monopoly on the cattle business by Association members. . . .

SOURCE: Abridged from Sydney B. Spiegel, "Who Were the Cattle Rustlers? A Look at the Johnson County War in Wyoming," *Social Studies*, XLIX (November, 1958), 222–230. Reprinted by permission of *Social Studies* and Sydney B. Spiegel.

The conflict came to a head in the spring of 1892 when Johnson county made plans for a separate and illegal roundup. The roundup of cattle on the range was supposed to be a state-wide operation conducted by the Wyoming Stockgrowers Association, according to the law, but the small operators in Johnson county claimed their cattle were being stolen from them in these legal roundups. They decided to conduct their own illegal roundup in May.

Some of the owners of large operations hired twenty-five gunmen from Texas and moved north to Johnson county in April with the object of killing about seventy men. They succeeded in killing only two suspected rustlers, Nathan Champion and Nick Ray, when the citizens of the county became aroused over the "invasion" and surrounded the posse, besieged them in a barn, and prepared to burn down the barn and kill all the members of the group. President Harrison was aroused from his bed in the dead of night and telegraphed orders for the U. S. Army to intervene. The posse, which included some of the most prominent men in the state, including the state senator from Johnson county, surrendered to the Army and eventually were brought to Cheyenne to be tried for the murder of the two victims, Champion and Ray. . . .

The question for the history student in this conflict is: Were these men in Johnson county cattle thieves or not? For while being shot is a grievous punishment, cattle rustling is certainly a grievous fault. The claims and counter-claims of the participants in the conflict center around the "you're all a bunch of rustlers" charge and the "oh no we're not" answer. Just how much rustling was going on in Johnson county?

On March 17, 1892, the *Buffalo Bulletin* quoted the Billings, Montana, *Gazette* as saying that two-thirds of the new brands in northern Wyoming were owned by rustlers and that the *Buffalo Bulletin*

openly advocates the cause of cattle thieves. This coming spring the cattle thieves declare they will run the roundup to suit their wants. This defiance of the laws of mine and thine will certainly precipitate a conflict in which the blood of honest men will flow and commingle with that of thieves and lawless characters . . . [The *Bulletin* replied], The sentiment existing here is as strong against a thief as it is anywhere else, and the sentiment of our people against assassination is as strong as it is in most places, and apparently, stronger than in Montana . . . If a majority of our people are rustlers and thieves, we prefer their society to the murderous monsters who committed the cowardly deeds here last December. (This is a reference to the murders of the two Johnson county men, Tisdale and Jones, who were shot in the back). . . .

The reaction of the editor, Joe DeBarthe, to the charge of rustling is typical of his style. Someone accuses Johnson county of harboring rustlers and the answer is a perfunctory agreement that rustling is bad, but the big guns of the argument are turned upon the contention that illegal assassination is much worse. . . .

Perhaps the casual dismissal of charges of rustling was due to the feeling that the big cattle firms were wealthy enough anyway, and furthermore, were heavily financed by foreigners—notably English and Scotch. There is a long tradition of antipathy to wealth in America reaching back to Jackson's days—and these charges of stealing cattle from millionaire firms were being made in the days of the incipient Populist fulminations against millionaires.

The Northern Wyoming Farmers and Stockgrowers Association which was planning the threatened separate and illegal roundup in May, 1892, felt constrained to dissociate itself from extreme populistic radicalism while attacking monopoly. "In our noble association," they announced in December, 1891, "there is no communion in agrarianism. We are opposed to such spirit and management of any corporation or enterprise as tends to oppress the people and rob them of their just rights. We are not enemies to capital but we oppose the tyranny of monopoly." . . .

There was about a 700% increase in farms in Johnson County from 1880 to 1890 (from 43 to 307). The incursion of the settlers undoubtedly nettled the stockmen. . . . The Denver News said in April, 1892, about the farmers, "Their only offense is in having located upon ranges that were previously occupied by the herds of rich corporations, whose members enliven the fine society of our cities, and many of whom are foreigners living abroad and having no interest in this free country except in the dividends they draw from American free grass."

The Buffalo Bulletin on Dec. 17, 1891, tried to face the question somewhat directly but instead of condemning rustling outright took the position that the open range system had encouraged rustling; that the large cattle firms had paid their cowboys about five dollars for every maverick (unbranded motherless calf) regardless of who might have owned the maverick; or in other words, why condemn thievery when even the respectable people had condoned thievery or had begun their careers as thieves? . . .

An account of the Johnson County War which became a collector's item was Asa Mercer's The Banditti of the Plains. Mercer had been on the side of the big cattlemen and supported their policies in the livestock paper which he edited. After the invasion of Johnson county, Mercer switched sides and blasted the powerful and prominent men in the state in his book. . . .

Mercer minimized the rustling and claimed that what had really happened was that the range had become overstocked. Beef shipments fell off in quality and therefore dividends to London and Glasgow stockholders diminished. To prevent diminished profits, he said, the managers began to ship two year olds and even yearlings. But while this might bring in dividends today, it ruins the future of the herd for dividends tomorrow. Then hard winters came along, like the winter of 1886–87 which killed off large numbers of cattle unable to find shelter from the blizzards and unable to paw through the ice to the grass underneath. "It is evident," Mercer wrote,

that the general managers of cattle companies found themselves in exceedingly hot water—between the devil and the deep blue sea, so to speak. Something had to be done; their integrity and financial reputation demanded action. Dividends were passed and the shareholders demanded the reason. To explain that the herds had been systematically robbed of future beef steers in the shipment of unripe cattle would be to impeach themselves. To admit that hard winters and overstocking the range had decimated the herds would not be in harmony with official reports rendered. Some other excuse must be found. "Eureka," says one. "Thieves!" he ejaculated, and forthwith the cry echoed and re-echoed over the entire range cattle country.

About six months previous to Mercer's interpretation the *Bulletin* had similarly theorized:

The winter of 1886 sent many an outfit to the wall and small owners profited where the big ones met disaster. A thousand causes have conspired in the last decade to the disadvantage of the cattle barons, all of which the latter sum up in the term rustler. Whatever misfortune comes, wherever the responsibility belongs, it is laid to the door of the rustler, for the rustler is the cattle baron's convenient scarecrow. . . .

But to agree with the interpretation that the whole charge of rustling was absolutely baseless one would have to neglect other important evidence. Even friends of Johnson county admitted that *some* rustling was going on. E.U. Snider, the sheriff of Johnson county in 1892, when asked pointblank how many rustlers there were in Johnson county answered carefully, "Of my knowledge I know of none but I have counted twenty to twenty-five men who are reputed to be or have been designated as rustlers." . . .

It seems pretty clear that there were some rustlers there at Johnson county. The big stockmen placed the estimate as high as forty or fifty men (the posse which invaded the county had a death list of seventy-five), and friends of the rustlers spoke about twenty or twenty-five men. . . .

The *Bulletin* did not believe that any prominent men had been ter-
rorized by rustlers.

What need they fear? None of the "prominent men" of this section have been
assassinated. Only three or four poor devils who were working for a living
have laid down their lives at the call of the cattlemen's bullet or the hired
assassin's lariat. What need these "prominent people" fear? . . . . The *Bulletin*
knows there are thieves here and have been ever since the stockmen came
into this country. Go back to the time when the first maverick brand was
started in Johnson county and tell us who started it. If the conundrum is too
deep for you, we will take the trouble of reproducing it and giving the
owners' names.

It seems that the *Bulletin* could never condemn rustling and put a
period at the end of the sentence. It always qualified its condemnations
by a claim that the big cattlemen had started it, that illegal lynching
of suspected rustlers was worse than illegal appropriation of stock, etc.
Cowboy unemployment may be one clue to the development of rustlers.
After the hard winters in the 1880's some of the big firms began to lay
off their cowboy employees. The 1890 census shows that there were
1101 unemployed cowboys in the state—632 of them having been unemployed for more than six months. (There were a total of 4134 cowboys
in the state that year.) What were the unemployed cowboys doing
with their leisure time? How did they live? . . .

The big cattlemen undoubtedly suffered from rustler raids on their
herds by both professional and amateur rustlers. But public opinion,
especially in Johnson county, was against the millionaire cattle firms and
was ready and willing to close both eyes to any cattle stealing that was
going on.

History shows many examples of publicly condoned stealing or, more
euphemistically, confiscation of private property. The land reforms of
Solon, the confiscation of church estates by Henry VIII, the emancipation
of the Negro slaves, and the confiscation of Dutch property by Indo-
nesians are a few of many cases in point. These confiscations took place
because the public felt that the owners of property were guilty of many
injustices and deserved to be robbed; and those men who were leading
the demands for robbery were determined, revolutionary in spirit, with
clear-sighted goals for a new order of relationships in society.

Rustling in Johnson county was in nature, I believe, just such a type
of revolutionary, publicly condoned expropriation. But the leading men
in Johnson county, although they felt that the rich cattlemen were guilty
of many injustices, were property owners and were property conscious.
The landowners of history have never been as revolutionary as the

landless. After the French peasants were freed from serfdom and became landowners, they voted for Napoleon as emperor. Furthermore, there was no theoretical formulation of a new order of things, or a theoretical justification of robbery such as the kings had when they used the argument of heretical sects that the church should be poor, as Christ and the apostles were poor, as an excuse to rob the church. The only theory that the *professional* rustlers had was to become personally wealthy by preying on the large herds of the big stockmen, and the small rancher or farmer who rustled cattle as an *amateur* had a guilty conscience about it and, being a cattle owner himself, could subscribe to no theory that justified the stealing of cattle. . . .

The invasion of the county showed clearly that both sides were quite determined to protect their rights but accomplished little else for the invaders but a contribution to a defeat of their political leaders, mostly Republicans, at the polls a few months later. After the dust had settled, both elements continued to live in peace in the same state; some large firms cut down their operations considerably and planted hay for winter forage, and others turned to sheep. Then the Spanish-American War brought prosperity and old hates were put aside, even if not forgotten. . . .

CHAPTER XIII

The Pioneer Farmers

W ELL INTO THE TWENTIETH CENTURY, a unique opportunity remained open to the adventuresome, the dissatisfied and the landless of older American regions, as well as immigrants from foreign lands. With work and luck they could become their own masters in developing productive farms on the frontier of the United States. "The soil is as black as your hat and as mellow as a ash heep," . . . wrote a prairie pioneer, "If you John, will come on we can live like pigs in the clover." Many needed no such urging.

There were perhaps 500,000 farms and plantations in the United States in 1790. When the federal census takers of 1850 enumerated the farms of the United States for the first time, they counted approximately 1,500,000 farming units. By 1920, the number had risen to some 6,500,000. Such was the bequest of the American frontier farmer. But the proportion of Americans who lived in places of less than 2500, including most farmers, fell from 95 percent in 1790 to 80 percent in 1860 and stood at 44 percent in 1930. Although estimates vary somewhat, farmers and other farm laborers made up some 60 percent of the nation's labor force in 1860 and about 20 percent in 1930. The number of farm units rose until the 1920's but the relative capacity of the country's agriculture to provide employment had steadily declined. Such facts must be tempered somewhat; during the twentieth century agriculture continued to feed the nation well and to produce an important part of the nation's exports. An important sector of American industry used the food, feed and fiber produced on American farms. The processing of agricultural products had been the first step in the development of many of our most important industrial areas.

As the American farmers pushed westward, their industry changed in character. The original forest cover gave way to grassland, and the treeless plains yielded in turn to terrain that only irrigation could tincture with green for any length of time. Meanwhile agriculture became commercial. Horse-powered and eventually tractor-powered machinery transformed it. Improved livestock and selective breeding changed the live-stock on the range, in the field and in the feed lot. Improved domestic strains and alien crops from distant lands filled the fields and rewarded the husbandman. Such processes affected the lives of the pioneers and were in turn influenced by the westward migration in which they participated.

Most of the pioneer farmers of the early national period were highly self-sufficient. Flax or cotton or the wool of his sheep furnished fiber for the clothing of the frontier farmer and his family. Western settlers raised cattle, hogs, sheep and poultry, which provided food, rawhide, leather, feathers and down. They grew a great variety of field crops, fruit, vegetables, and herbs. But even such self-sufficing westerners needed money to pay for land for themselves and their sons, to purchase metal tools, to gratify their wives' wishes for metal utensils, and to satisfy the family appetite for salt, coffee, tea or other exotic foods. They must fulfill their family's desire for the fabrics, clothes and other goods of British and American industry or for education. Under such pressures, the western farmer spent more and more of his time producing for the market. Frontier by frontier throughout our national history his commercial orientation increased as the United States became more commercial and more industrial and the demands and offerings of its market varied increasingly.

As his commercial orientation increased, the western farmer increasingly selected for production only those crops that best suited his geographic location and markets. He stopped growing crops and raising livestock that did not reward his efforts generously. He and his family abandoned homecrafts and industries, purchasing manufactured goods or the products of other regions in their stead. We do not have indices which show the growing commercialization of the American farm during the nineteenth century, but we know that it went on. We know also that commercial agriculture increased the standard of living of farm families, but probably less rapidly than the standard of living of urban families. Such differences help to explain why workers were leaving the agriculture of the older regions during the nineteenth century and moving to industrial centers while others were opening up farms on the frontier at the same time.

While the commercialization of agriculture continued in both the East and in the West, so did mechanization, as inventors applied the technology of the Industrial Revolution to the needs of farmers. The pioneer farmer of western New York or Pennsylvania in 1800 probably owned a wagon or cart, a plow or two, a wooden harrow, some harness, a scythe, axes, forks and other hand tools. Most of his equipment was made of wood with some iron or steel fittings. He sowed his grain broadcast from a bag on his shoulder and he threshed it with a flail. How striking was the contrast with many a frontier farm of the 1870's or 1880's in Minnesota or Nebraska or in the Pacific Northwest where farmers owned farm machinery which magnified their labor at every stage of grain culture from seeding to threshing! Machinery and commercial orientation went hand in hand. The farmers bought the cast iron and steel plows, the reapers, mowers, threshing machines, seeders, cultivators and other farm machinery because the equipment helped them to increase the returns from their labor. And the purchase of machinery increased the capital cost of farming by enlarging the farmer's investment and sometimes the interest charges that he must pay on borrowed money. By allowing farmers to till more acres with the same amount of labor, mechanization also enlarged the optimum size of farm and this also increased the farmer's investment in land. The bonanza farms which men of capital developed on lands purchased from the Northern Pacific Railroad Company in the Red River valley during the 1870's and 1880's impressed contemporaries as the ultimate application of agricultural machinery to frontier farming. On these huge farms dozens of men used the most modern farm machinery in producing wheat and other small grains. But the bonanza farms were less resilient in depression years than were family farms; smaller holdings replaced them.

Although secular trends affected both the pioneer and the eastern farmer, farming on the frontier did differ from farm life in the older settlements. The western farmer and the members of his family must devote much of their time to preparing the farm for production rather than in growing crops and in the management of their livestock. Thus they must erect buildings and fences—very considerable tasks if crops were to be properly protected and harvested and livestock controlled and sheltered. On the early national frontiers, many pioneers had to slash every field from the forest. It was only partly jest when the balladeer of the Michigan Emigrants' Song called for Yankee farmers, "who've metal hearts like me, And elbow grease a plenty, To bow the forest tree . . ."

Clearing land of timber was a laborious process but the eastern farmer did not at least lack the wood for fences and buildings. It was different on the prairies and plains. There frontier farmers even tried to grow hedges to serve as fences but they were spared the labor of felling and removing forest from most of their land. Even so the sod of the grasslands was such a formidable mat of twisted roots that the settler had to use special breaking plows. Even after clearing the trees and removing the tree roots and stones on the frontiers of the older states or breaking the tough sod of the virgin grasslands, a period ensued in which the pioneer farmer could not expect to have ideal planting or harvesting conditions. In the High Plains or mountain West he often had to construct reservoirs and to dig irrigation ditches if his farm was to be productive. Most of the frontier farmers were forced, therefore, to accept the fact that they would produce small crops in their first years of developing a new farm, and there would be a time, depending in length upon the capital and labor at the disposal of each farmer, in which they could not have the proportion of land in crops that was considered appropriate on older farms. Foreign travellers and eastern farmers often criticized the western farmers as slovenly and careless and by the standards of older areas they undoubtedly were. But the tasks of development did not give them the time for "high" farming.

Distance from markets might also limit the frontier farmer in developing his holding or shape his farm enterprise significantly. If he were more than 30 or 40 miles from navigable water or a railroad station, the cost of transporting grain might encourage him to raise livestock which he could drive to market or sell to livestock dealers or drovers who would do so. On the other hand inflowing settlers might provide the first comers with a market for some grain even in relatively isolated sections of the farmer's frontier. The pioneers might feed their grain to livestock driven into the region for that very purpose by drovers or cattlemen or distill it into whiskey—a product valuable enough to warrant transportation over greater distances.

There was no particular crop which farmers emphasized on every agricultural frontier. The pioneers' ideal crop produced the largest return in cash for the smallest outlay of labor. Wheat often met this requirement on the northern frontiers but corn better supported livestock enterprises and provided meal for the mush, johnny cake, fritters and other corn recipes which ruled the menu in many pioneer cabins both north and south. Southern farmers raised the great export staples of that region as soon as possible, but seem to have been more dependent on the corn crop for food and for animal feed than were frontier farmers in the North. But the pioneers valued other crops as well. Frontier farmers searched the woods for ginseng, valuable because Asiatics believed that it fostered their virility. Other settlers of the wooded frontier pocketed their first farm income when they sold the pearl ash or potash which they had leached from the ashes of the trees burned in the process of clearing their land. Although wheat and corn were the frontiersmen's traditional grain crops, some midwestern pioneers of the late nineteenth century found flax to be a most profitable crop on their newly broken fields. Still farther westward, homesteaders gathered a harvest of buffalo bones which were shipped on the railroads to fertilizer factories in the older Middle West.

Improvements in animal husbandry and the selection of improved varieties of field crops changed the character of the agricultural enterprises during the nineteenth and the early twentieth centuries. The Hereford was a curiosity in the United States of 1850; this hardy beef animal dominated midwestern feed lots and western farms and ranches in 1910. At mid-century Turkey Red wheat was unknown in the country; by 1910 that hard winter wheat was the major variety grown in the winter wheat belt of the Central Plains. Both the Hereford and Turkey Red wheat met the environmental challenge more successfully than their rivals. Every frontier generated its own lore about the best breeds of livestock to raise and crops to grow. The pioneers of the semiarid West were forced to develop unique dry farming practices as well as irrigation agriculture. Indeed, changes in the environmental setting affected the frontier farmer in many ways, some trivial, others more important. The pioneers of the Genesee valley in western New York built log cabins, the settlers of western Kansas sought their rest in sod houses or more commonly in shacks of boards and tar paper. The easterner fenced with rails, the Kansan with wire. Obtaining adequate supplies of water was no problem to the New York settler; to the Kansan it was the difference between success and "going back to the wife's folks." As a result the experiences of each pioneer farmer differed from those of the settler in the West of the previous generation.

Although there were rich planters on the southern frontier and wealthy estate builders in the new regions of the North, there were few pioneers who could not use additional funds, and many were virtually penniless, swept westward by lack of opportunities in the East and the hope of a better day in the West. They lacked the money to buy land and the livestock and equipment necessary to farm it, let alone the means to support themselves and their families through the year or two it would take to produce crops. They must seek assistance from friends and relatives in the old settlements, from the land speculator who was willing to sell on time, from the capitalist attracted by high frontier interest rates, from the loan agent who was able to mobilize the funds of small investors and from financial institutions in the older regions. We know much more about such relationships on the frontiers of the last half of the nineteenth century than during the first 60 years of the Republic.

But we know that such obligations existed in that era as well, and they made the frontier farmer more vulnerable to depression and to the fall of agricultural prices than farmers in older settlements who had greater resources to assist them in weathering periods of economic crisis. This unique vulnerability of many frontier farmers also distinguished them from farmers in the older regions.

By 1930 the farmer's frontier had, in effect, added six million farms to the country's total. Much of the great North American grassland, or its outliers, came to production with less labor than eastern farms had required. Despite the stickiness and tough sod the grasslands yielded to the plow much more easily than did the farms of the wooded frontiers. A great part of the land in the new western farms lay in regions or subregions which were extremely productive. Not only did the frontier farmers increase the productive capacity of the United States by adding new units of production, they developed farms that had more productive capacity than did many farms east of the Appalachians. In recent years historians have begun to measure the importance of such considerations. William N. Parker and Judith L. V. Klein concluded that the movement of farmers into the West between 1839 and the end of the first decade of the twentieth century raised the national average yield per acre of wheat, oats and corn by some 25 per cent. But mechanization accounted for more of the increase in labor productivity in the culture of these crops than did soil fertility, more than 50 per cent in each case.

In the age of Jefferson few doubted that the farmer's life was an honorable and rewarding calling which satisfied man's most basic need and fostered virtue in those who followed it. By the end of the century the "hick" and the "hayseed" stereotype was well established. By this time also, as we have seen in an earlier chapter, critics of the American land disposal system were charging that it had produced both land monopolists and tenants in tragic numbers. A son of the Middle Border, Hamlin Garland poured out his disillusionment in realistic fiction that portrayed the grim, disheartening and unrewarding lives of midwestern farm people. Of the late nineteenth century farmer, Richard Hofstadter wrote, "The characteristic product of American rural society was not a yeoman or a villager, but a harrassed little country businessman who worked very hard, moved all too often, gambled with his land, and made his way alone." Had indeed industrial America perverted the true guardians of civic virtue, the farmers of the nation? Was the agricultural frontier an epic story of stalwart men or just another illustration of typical Americans in search of a "fast buck"? How could the script have been written differently?

·1·

SOLON J. BUCK

Frontier Economy in Southwestern Pennsylvania

During the late eighteenth century in the United States, the farming frontier lay for the most part in the western regions of the original states. This passage from the work of Solon J. Buck describes the era of agricultural settlement in southwestern Pennsylvania. Although farming there was subsistence in nature to a considerable degree, industrial specialization became evident very quickly.

. . . If agriculture be understood to include the making of farms and the domestic industries that were conducted on them as well as the production of crops and the raising of livestock, then the economy of southwestern Pennsylvania was almost wholly agricultural during the frontier period. . . . From an examination of tax records and descriptions of farms in newspaper advertisements it appears that farms of about three hundred acres, of which perhaps forty acres were under cultivation and a somewhat smaller amount in meadow, were common in southwestern Pennsylvania around 1790. . . .

The earliest farms were, of course, essentially self-sufficing units. Because of the isolation of the region and of the individual farms, it was more economical to produce at home the necessary commodities, makeshifts though they might be, than to transport surplus crops to a distant market and bring back the goods received in exchange; and this was true whether the transportation were done by the farmer himself or by a middleman. Moreover, in the early stages of the making of a farm, when only a few acres had been cleared and much of the energy of the farmer was devoted to clearing more, little surplus was produced. . . .

Each farm unit, therefore, was the scene of a wide variety of activities; and, since neither labor for hire nor money to pay for it was available, the work was done by the farmer and his family, with occasionally an

SOURCE: Abridged from Solon J. Buck, "Frontier Economy in Southwestern Pennsylvania," *Agricultural History*, X (January, 1936), 14-24. Reprinted by permission of *Agricultural History* and Elizabeth H. Buck.

indentured servant to help them, and everyone had to be a jack-of-all-trades. Such division of labor as there was was based on sex and on age or strength. To the men fell the tasks of hunting and fishing, clearing the land, erecting buildings and fences, plowing, cultivating, harvesting, threshing, grinding, shearing sheep, and providing firewood, together with such domestic industries as butchering, smoking meat, making maple sugar, blacksmithing, coopering, cabinet making, tanning, and shoemaking. The tasks of the women included the care of the stock, except perhaps the work animals, and of the poultry, as well as the preparation of food, the making of clothing, and the care of the house and the children. . . .

These frontier farms were never completely self-sufficing, of course. From the very beginning of settlement, iron and glass, salt and spices, and a few luxuries were brought over the mountains, at first on the backs of pack horses and later in wagons. Once a year, in the early period, an expedition from each neighborhood made the trip to the East to get the necessary supplies. . . . Cattle were sometimes driven to market, but the trip was so hard on them they could not compete successfully with eastern and southern cattle. A small local market for more bulky products was supplied by immigrants and by the military establishments, but the payments in Continental currency during the Revolution were not relished by the farmers. . . . Most of the money received for the sale of products was quickly drained out of the region in payments for land or for imported commodities. . . .

Within less than a decade after the first permanent settlements, diversification of activities began to develop within the region itself. Saw-mills, boatyards, and blacksmith shops were in operation for the benefit of traders and the army even before the advent of permanent agricultural settlers; mills for the grinding of grain soon made their appearance in every considerable neighborhood, to be followed a little later by fulling mills; weaving and distilling tended to concentrate in the hands of those who were more skillful or had better equipment than the average; and itinerant shoemakers and tinkers began to relieve the farmers of difficult tasks. Most of these industries were operated on a custom basis, and payment for the work was usually in the form of raw materials. The mills were run by water power as a rule, though occasionally horse power was used. . . .

The transformation of southwestern Pennsylvania from an isolated frontier community made up of self-sufficing agricultural units to one of specialized activities integrated with the national economy went on apace during the last decade of the eighteenth century. Several factors contributed to the acceleration of this movement. As the farmers increased their acreages of improved land, the agricultural surpluses became larger and larger. The armies of the United States operating against the Indians in the Northwest Territory from 1790 to 1794 furnished a cash market for much of this surplus, and the immigrants that poured into that territory after the Indian wars were over usually bought their equipment and supplies for the first season in southwestern Pennsylvania. . . .

[T]he removal of restrictions on the Mississippi trade effected by Pinckney's Treaty in 1795 opened the markets of the world to the farmers and merchants of the West. Flatboats and keelboats made their way to New Orleans from the upper Ohio in ever increasing numbers, and before the end of the century ocean-going ships had been built in western Pennsylvania, loaded with the produce of the region, floated down the rivers, and sailed out on the high seas. In this period also the improvement of the highway from Philadelphia to Pittsburgh, largely at the expense of the State, and the extension and improvement of local roads decreased the cost of wagon transportation and greatly facilitated the introduction and distribution of eastern commodities.

Most significant, however, of the changing economy of the region was the beginning of manufacturing as distinguished from the custom, handicraft, and domestic industries. With a market available for flour, merchant mills made their appearance in the towns and began to purchase grain with cash or with warehouse certificates, which circulated as currency. Large-scale breweries and distilleries also began to operate on a merchant basis. The first blast furnace for the manufacture of iron was blown in in Fayette County in 1790, and by the end of the decade sixteen ironworks had been established in the region. . . . A paper mill began operations at Brownsville in 1796, and two glass factories with imported workmen were established in 1797. . . . The products of the furnaces and factories not only supplied the needs of the people of the region for such commodities but also found their way down stream to the newer settlements farther west and in some cases even to New Orleans.

Southwestern Pennsylvania was still predominantly agricultural at the end of the eighteenth century, but the process of making the farms was approaching completion, commerce both internal and external was well established, and manufacturing and mining were being developed. . . . In approximately a third of a century the region had been transformed from a wilderness to the habitat of a numerous human society well supplied with capital goods in the shape of improved farms, roads, buildings, and factories, and equipped with a complex economic structure. The frontier stage in the development of the region had been completed.

ALLAN G. BOGUE

Farming in the Prairie Peninsula, 1830–1890

> When pioneer farmers reached the Middle West they had to
> begin to adapt their farming practices to prairie lands that
> lacked the heavy timber cover of southwestern Pennsylvania
> and other eastern frontiers. By this time also, American
> agriculture was becoming both more mechanized and more
> commercial. Allan G. Bogue explores some of the implications
> of these developments in this reading.

If the American pioneers had once believed that the prairies were
infertile because trees did not grow there, they were rejecting this mis-
conception by the 1820's. The smaller prairies of Ohio and the barrens of
Kentucky had already demonstrated that treeless lands could grow
abundant crops. Adjustments to the timber shortage took various forms.
In part, the claim club reflected the unique features of the prairie landscape. Where timber and prairie alternated, locations in or near wooded
areas were relatively much more attractive. This set the stage for associations, which the early comers used to engross the best locations in their
own hands for resale to later arrivals or large land speculators. If the
Midwest had been all prairie or all timber, the clubs would have been
less common. More important, as the land passed into private hands,
there developed a landholding pattern of which the timber lot was an
integral part. Settlers on the prairie purchased five or ten acres along
the stream bottoms or in the prairie groves and drove five, ten or fifteen
miles to cut building timber or to split rails during the winter months.

When he sought to fence his crops against marauding livestock, the
prairie farmer faced the timber problem at its most acute. The Virginia
worm-rail fence with stakes and riders was an efficient, although somewhat untidy fence. But it demanded timber in large amounts, and the
rails might last no more than ten to twenty years. The willow and cot-
tonwood groves of the pioneers were of no immediate help. Some
farmers tried to conserve resources by moving the division fences on

---

SOURCE: Abridged from Allan G. Bogue, "Farming in the Prairie Peninsula, 1830–
1890," *Journal of Economic History*, XXIII (March, 1963), 3–29. Reprinted by
permission of the *Journal of Economic History*.

their cropland as needed and by resorting, where possible, to the Shanghai rail fence in which several of the lower rails were omitted; such solutions were mere stopgaps.

Farmers suggested a variety of substitutes for rail fences. Early settlers had high hopes for ditch and earthen bank fence, capped perhaps by rail or hedge, but the prairie herds had discredited sod fence, on the Illinois prairies at least, by the early 1830's. Smooth iron wire fencing was popular briefly during the 1840's, but the strands stretched and sagged, inspiring only friendly contempt among western livestock.

By the 1850's, Osage orange had emerged from a host of competing hedge plants as a practicable living hedge. Despite problems in its culture and a shortage of seed during the Civil War, Osage orange hedge gained in popularity and made up a significant percentage of the fencing in prairie counties during the early 1870's. Meanwhile many prairie farmers had supported an institutional solution to the fencing problem. This was the herd law, which held the owners of livestock responsible for their confinement. . . . The invention of a practicable and cheap barbed wire solved the fencing problem. The cost of a four-strand barbed wire fence in the mid 1870's . . . was less than half that of a board fence and a third less than the cost of rail fencing, where rails were available.

Prairie farm-makers argued both about the method of breaking prairie sod and about the nature and capabilities of the soils which lay beneath it. Over time, the breakers learned that the proper time for breaking prairie extended from early May to late July. They also changed the approved technique of breaking from one in which the furrows were as deep as five inches and the overturned furrow slices lay in neatly flat, tight rows to one in which the plow pared off a thin rind of grass and roots, leaving the furrow slice broken and riffled.

The farm-makers assumed that there were important differences in the soils of the prairie regions. A writer in the *Prairie Farmer* of 1851 presented an analysis of western soils based on their suitability for wheat culture. On the uplands where the white oaks grew was a pure wheat soil; that supporting yellow and red oaks differed somewhat; and where the burr oaks and hazels grew was "perhaps the richest soil." Least adapted to wheat culture, he maintained, was the soil of the open prairie. Others suggested that wheat grew best on the soil of the timbered tracts or on the soil of the barrens, those stretches of alternating timber, hazel brush and prairie. Some believed that newly broken prairie was superior for wheat-growing to old prairie fields.

If the prairie environment perplexed the pioneer on occasion, it also rewarded his efforts. Whatever their regional variations, the prairie soils were usually highly productive, with considerable staying power. Nor was there need here for the farmer to invest a generation of family labor in removing a heavy mantle of forest. It is hard to exaggerate the importance of this fact in explaining the rapid development of mechanized agriculture in Illinois and Iowa after 1850.

A variety of factors may have influenced the pioneer farmer of the prairie triangle when he made his production plans. Markets, transportation facilities, the general price level, changes in the prices of farm products relative to each other, his cultural heritage, and his understanding of prairie soils all probably affected the farmer's calculations. On the other hand, it is sometimes suggested that pioneer agriculture was essentially subsistence agriculture or that there were typical frontier cropping sequences through which the farmers moved as their communities developed. The data of the Federal agricultural censuses from 1850 to 1890 give us considerable information about such matters. Maps based upon average county production per improved acre of the field crops, and upon numbers of farm animals per farm, show areas of high and low production on a subregional basis in Illinois and Iowa as early as 1850.

Had the farmers in newly settled areas been subsistence farmers, their counties would not ordinarily have appeared among the leading producers of wheat or corn per improved acre in Iowa or Illinois in a particular census year. Yet this was the case. Nor apparently was there any one crop-production or farm-management sequence through which most pioneer farmers of Illinois and Iowa moved. The farm-makers of northern Illinois and Iowa placed considerable emphasis upon wheat production in early years and later moved to heavier dependence on other combinations of crops and livestock; the farmers of central Illinois and southern Iowa gave a much more important place in their plans to corn and livestock from the very beginning. . . .

The farmers of the prairie triangle were never monoculturists. Even when they described themselves as wheat farmers or corn-hog farmers, their farming operations were really combinations of wheat, corn, oats, barley, hay, cattle, sheep, hogs, and other minor enterprises. Enough farmers in any particular area reacted similarly to the economic and physical environments to produce subregional production patterns. If the general farmers provided a kind of matrix of farm operators in the western community, there were also specialists living side by side with them. Usually operating larger farms than average, such men might concentrate on growing cash grain or raising hogs or on cattle feeding. . . .

Students of agricultural development in the Midwest of the nineteenth century have often suggested that cultural or ethnic influences affected the decisions of farmers. With the contention that particular cultural or ethnic groups drew upon their unique heritages to help in solving the problems of adaptation to the midwestern environment, there can be little quarrel. Writers on occasion, however, have suggested that the members of particular cultural groups consistently followed farming practices which were significantly different from those of neighbors who drew upon other cultural heritages. The Norwegians and Danes, one writer hints, may have had a particular affinity for the wet prairie in central Iowa. Contemporaries wrote that the Yankees were more apt to be orchardists than were farmers of other backgrounds. . . .

Where there is so much smoke there certainly ought to be fire. But it is quite possible that the Norwegians and Danes of Story County, Iowa, moved to the wet prairie because that was the only land which they believed they could afford. The area of Illinois which became pre-eminently a fruit region was settled for the most part by southerners, not Yankees. . . . When local conditions reinforced cultural bias, the members of a particular cultural group may have farmed somewhat differently for a time. Greater difficulty in obtaining access to capital may have accounted for differences also. Perhaps, however, cultural differences were more clearly apparent in diet, minor farm practices, and socioeconomic behavior such as the use of wives in the fields, than in significantly different combinations of enterprises, maintained over a considerable period of time.

While changes in production patterns went on, the prairie farmers worked a considerable change in the fundamental elements of production—plant strains, breeds, and techniques. In so far as they grew wheat, they changed from heavy emphasis on winter wheat in the 1840's to considerable dependence on spring wheat and by the late 1870's back, in many cases, to winter wheat. In the corn field, the northern flints, supposedly dominant in much of Illinois during the 1840's, yielded to the dent corns, so that one writer could use "western" as a synonym for "dent" in 1866. But the dents that came to rule the fields of the prairie triangle were themselves the products of hybridization with the northern flints—some of it accidental, some of it purposeful.

Under the ministrations of midwestern farmers, the American lard hog emerged in its most impressive form. For the lean, stump-sucking, mast-fed rangers of the 1830's and early 1840's, swine-raisers by the early 1870's had substituted fat hogs of gargantuan size. The nondescript prairie steer of the 1830's that might attain a top weight of 850 pounds at the age of five or six years had yielded place to animals that could reach weights in excess of 1,300 pounds in their third or fourth years by the late 1860's and early 1870's. Some zealots or publicity-conscious feeders indeed, brought the midwestern steers of this era to weights of a ton or more.

In the thirty years between 1850 and 1880 there occurred a veritable revolution in agricultural technology. In part the prairie farmer was simply the beneficiary of industrial achievements which were being applied to agriculture throughout the country. A portion of the new agricultural technology, however, bore directly on the peculiar problems of prairie agriculture. The stories of the steel plow, barbed wire and harvesting machinery are well known. Less emphasized, however, are the changes in the technology of corn culture. Here the important developments of the period were the horse-drawn corn planter and the riding and walking straddle row cultivators. A variety of practicable models of both were available by the early 1860's. Together with the steel plow, these implements increased by at least twice and perhaps three times the twenty acres of corn which a single worker could bring through satisfactorily to harvest in earlier years.

In part mechanization accounted for the changes which occurred in the draft animals of the prairie triangle between the 1840's and 1880's. As long as plowing was the major machine task in grain culture, oxen held an honored place on many farms. Mechanical harvesting equipment, however, changed the picture drastically. If the vibrating cutting bars were to operate effectively, the machines must move at a faster clip than oxen displayed. At the same time, however, the weight of such machinery emphasized the need of larger and stronger horses than the Morgan or other roadster strains that farmers had preferred until this time. The light horses, also, as one journalist put it, "were too weak in the poop" for heavy farm-to-market hauling over prairie roads or to fill the needs of the prairie towns and cities for heavy dray horses. The importation of Norman or Percheron breeding stock was a response to this situation.

Between the 1830's and the late 1870's, machinery increased the productivity of the worker in the small-grain fields by perhaps four to six times, in the hay meadow by certainly as much, and in the corn field by perhaps twice. Farmers, of course, did not spend all of their time in work on those crops or tasks which had yielded to machinery. Yet it would not be too rash probably to suggest that, over-all, the potential productivity of the individual agricultural laborer doubled during this period, most of the increase coming after 1855.

The changes in prairie agriculture sketched above did not take place with equal speed or thoroughness on every farm. In general, the operators of the larger units first adopted the cropping patterns and combinations of enterprises best adapted to the peculiar economic and physical environments of the agricultural subregions in Illinois and Iowa or led in the introduction of improved livestock. A few owners of average-sized or small farms, however, were as innovation-minded as the larger operators and gentlemen farmers were notorious experimenters. Occasionally, no doubt, landlords also assisted in the innovation process either through specific leasing terms or by retaining a larger share in management decisions than ordinary. There is reason to suspect that the innovators were somewhat better educated than the average farmer and certainly no older than the average age of farm operators in their communities. Almost certainly, too, the innovator was found among those who provided leadership in farm clubs, Grange chapters and agricultural societies. He was also apt to be a community leader in the broader sense, a township or county officeholder.

Easier access to credit would no doubt have speeded changes in farm practices and affected the combination of enterprises on many prairie farms. Complaints of plows that would not scour long after the development of the steel plow reflected the reluctance of western farmers to pay the added cost of the steel implement—almost double that of iron plows. Horses no doubt would have replaced oxen much more rapidly than they did if credit had been easier. Although available markets and transportation facilities modified the pattern, the pioneer farmer was under economic pressure to find the farming system which required the smallest capital outlay. This in many cases was cash grain farming. No doubt easier credit would have allowed some farmers to introduce livestock into their production programs to a greater extent at an earlier period than they were able to do.

The Federal census takers did not collect data on tenancy prior to the enumeration of 1880, and part of the literature on prairie tenancy is devoted simply to proving that it existed at an early date. The manuscript censuses of 1850, 1860, and 1870 do provide information from which we can calculate fairly precise maximum and minimum estimates of tenancy. Thus between 7 and 11 per cent of the farm operators in Clarion township, Bureau County, Illinois were tenants in 1850, as were between 10 and 22 per cent in Union township, Davis County, Iowa. In those sections of Illinois and Iowa which settlers occupied between 1830 and 1890, probably between 5 and 15 per cent of the farm operators were tenants at a very early stage of settlement. They became so because they did not have the funds with which to purchase a farm for themselves, or in some cases the means to develop their own small holdings rapidly enough to insure an income in their first years' residence in a new community.

We can never know the exact composition of the landlord class. Some lessors were land speculators or large holders who rented land in order to improve it or to defray the costs of taxes and supervision prior to sale. Some few planned long-term tenant operations. Others were money-lenders who met the costs of upkeep on foreclosed land by renting. The greatest number of prairie landlords, however, was probably made up of the owners of only one farm or at the most several— farm widows, local businessmen, county officers and especially farmers, both active and retired.

It is clear that the farmers of the prairie triangle in Illinois and Iowa experienced their greatest difficulties during the mid- and late 1870's. Depressed prices, bad seasons, and, in Iowa, even grasshoppers bedeviled them. In many cases, too, farm units were too small to allow the operator and his family to utilize the enhanced labor productivity which machinery had given them—they were underemployed. In three widely scattered Iowa townships the percentage of real estate mortgages which went to foreclosure proceedings between 1852 and 1896 was 3.2. But of the mortgages filed between 1870 and 1874, inclusive, and between 1875 and 1879, inclusive, the average number going to court was 5.2 per cent in both cases. By contrast the failure rate in the years 1885–1889 and 1890–1896 was 1.7 and 1.8 per cent. Somewhat less precise evidence reveals a similar picture in Illinois. Contrast these percentages with the failure rates of 40 and 50 per cent which occurred in parts of Kansas during the late·1880's and early 1890's. Here, no doubt is one reason why the farmers of Illinois and Iowa had little interest in Populism.

The more progressive farmers of the prairie triangle evidently entered the 1880's aware that their best future lay in increasing the size of their farm units to take advantage of the new technology. They had learned, too, that profit lay in judicious combinations of corn, hogs, and cattle while not discarding the small grains, particularly oats, nor ignoring tame grasses and clovers—a necessity as the prairie-grass commons disappeared.

If owner-operators were apparently solving their problems with considerable success during the 1880's and 1890's, the same was hardly true of the tenants or farm laborers who aspired to ownership. During the last half of the nineteenth century, the increased productivity of agricultural labor benefited the farm operator considerably more than it did the laborer. At the same time, the land equivalent of the monthly agricultural wage fell drastically. Land obtained for $1.25 per acre in central Illinois or eastern Iowa in the 1830's or 1840's now commanded prices of $40 to $60 and, in many cases, even more. The cost of drainage alone could add from $5 to $20 to the farmer's investment in his acres. The cost of necessary machinery had also increased during the same period, but in the face of rising land values it had become proportionately less important in the total investment of the owner-operator.

·3·

ROBERT G. DUNBAR

The Significance of the Colorado Agricultural Frontier

The settlers of the Illinois and Iowa prairies found little timber on their lands but they did receive rainfall in amounts sufficient to sustain their crops and livestock. But pioneer farmers on the High Plains and in the intermountain regions farther to the West must irrigate their crops if they were to develop an intensive agriculture. As they developed irrigation farming, they repudiated eastern water law. Robert G. Dunbar describes the institutions and procedures which Colorado settlers established for the division of irrigation waters "that influenced the institutional structure of every one of the Western states."

The "fifty-niners" who became farmers and settled in the valleys of the South Platte and its tributaries encountered problems similar to those which farmers had faced on previous frontiers—the problems of land, credit, and markets. In addition to these, they also encountered a problem peculiar to agriculture in an arid environment—that of insufficient rainfall. To supply this deficiency, they resorted to irrigation, dug ditches and developed new institutions to regulate the appropriation of the streams. Eventually, these frontier-born irrigation institutions affected those of each of the other Western states. . . .

SOURCE: Abridged from Robert G. Dunbar, "The Significance of the Colorado Agricultural Frontier," *Agricultural History*, XXXIV (July, 1960), 119–125. Reprinted by permission of *Agricultural History* and Robert G. Dunbar.

[T]he pioneer irrigators had not only to learn to dig ditches, but also to draft laws to govern the utilization of streams. They were familiar with the common-law Doctrine of Riparian Rights which had regulated their right to streams farther east, but this doctrine was unsatisfactory in desert Colorado. It restricted the use of streams to riparian owners, whereas in Colorado, both riparian and non-riparian owners needed access to the streams. It gave each user an equal right to the water of a stream, whereas the Colorado irrigator needed a less fluctuating, more stable right. It forbade a water-user to alter or diminish the stream flow, whereas Coloradoans needed not only to diminish the flow, but to exhaust it if necessary. Consequently, the farmers sought a new law.

In California, the "forty-niners" had originated new rules to govern the use of water patterned after those governing their mining claims. . . .

Many of the "fifty-niners" had been in California, and since they were acquainted with these rules, they applied them in the mining camps of Colorado. To many farmers these rules of the miners seemed preferable to the riparian rules. Consequently, the first legislature of Jefferson Territory applied these miners' rules to agriculture by the passage of "An Act Concerning Irrigation." It read as follows:

Sec. 1. Be it enacted by the General Assembly of the Provisional Government of the Territory of Jefferson, the Governor approving:—That any person or persons settling upon any stream and claiming one hundred and sixty acres or less for farming or gardening purposes, and claiming the privilege of using the water of said stream for purposes of irrigation, shall be entitled to the same as hereinafter provided.

Sec. 2. No person or persons making subsequent claims above said first claimant, shall turn out of its original channel the waters of such stream in such a manner as to deprive said first claimant of the irrigation privileges provided in section first.

Sec. 3 That nothing in section second shall be so construed as to deprive agriculturists remote from streams from applying the waters thereof to irrigation purposes. . . .

When the Territory of Colorado replaced the Territory of Jefferson, its first legislature also enacted a law which gave non-riparian as well as riparian owners right to the use of streams, although it made no mention of priority of appropriation giving the better right. However, later legislative sessions did. In fact, the new rules of the mining districts governing water became so popular in the agricultural communities that when the constitutional convention met in 1876, the farmers demanded preferential treatment as a class as well as individuals. . . . Interest in

priorities was translated into the language of the Constitution of Colorado
in these words:

The right to divert the unappropriated waters of any natural stream to
beneficial uses shall never be denied. Priority of appropriation shall give the
better right as between those using the water for the same purpose; but when
the waters of any natural stream are not sufficient for the service of all those
desiring the use of the same, those using the water for domestic purposes
shall have the preference over those claiming for any other purpose, and
those using the water for agricultural purposes shall have preference over
those using the same for manufacturing purposes.

By this action Colorado became the first Western state to incorporate
the Doctrine of Prior Appropriation into its constitutional law.

Still undecided, however, was the status of riparian rights in Colorado.
Soon a dispute among the irrigators in the St. Vrain Valley brought the
question to the attention of the Supreme Court. A group of them had
organized a mutual ditch company known as the Left Hand Ditch
Company and diverted water from the upper part of the St. Vrain Creek
to irrigate farms located in an adjacent valley. Farther down the stream
a man by the name of George W. Coffin and his neighbors who owned
lands bordering the creek had also made diversions, although somewhat
later. In 1879 when a drought was harassing these valleys, the ditch
company diverted so much water from the St. Vrain Creek that the
crops of the lower appropriators suffered. Consequently, the latter took
the law into their own hands and tore out the ditch company's dam.
Thereupon, the company sued the farmers.

When the case came before the Supreme Court of Colorado, the
farmers contended that as riparian owners they had a right to have
the water of the St. Vrain Creek flow as it was accustomed to flow,
but Justice Joseph C. Helm rejected their argument and took an unusual
position for one trained in the common law. Rejecting precedent and
stare decisis, he declared that the Doctrine of Riparian Rights had
never been the law of Colorado, that the aridity of the climate had
nullified it and necessitated the invention of another law. . . . And so
by constitutional provision, legislative enactment, and judicial decision,
the Commonweath of Colorado abrogated the Doctrine of Riparian
Rights and adopted the Doctrine of Prior Appropriation. Because of
the state's leadership, exclusive adoption of the appropriation rule
became known as the Colorado Doctrine. . . .

The right to appropriate the water of a stream and to diminish its flow
necessitated regulation. This became apparent as soon as the Union

Colony and the Chicago-Colorado Colony began to divert large quantities of water for irrigation.

The Union Colony under the leadership of Nathan C. Meeker founded the community of Greeley at the confluence of the South Platte and its Cache la Poudre tributary. As soon as the officers of the colony arrived in the spring of 1870, they began to dig first a ditch to irrigate the town lots and later a ditch to provide water for the farms. When General R. A. Cameron, the colony's vice-president, went up the Cache la Poudre and founded the Fort Collins Agricultural Colony, he and his associates took two more large canals out of the river. Consequently, when a dry season occurred in 1874 and the Fort Collins appropriators diverted so much of the stream that there was not enough water for the use of the Greeley farmers, the leaders of both communities realized the need of some regulation to protect their water rights. Meeker proposed that the Cache la Poudre be treated like an irrigation canal and be placed under the supervision of an official who would divide its water according to the prior rights of the appropriators.

Members of the Chicago-Colorado Colony at Longmont quickly came to a similar conclusion. One of them, Byron L. Carr, proposed to the constitutional convention that the state legislature be given the authority "to pass such laws as may be necessary to secure a just and equitable distribution of the water in the streams of the State. . . ." but since the convention did not heed his suggestion, the problem remained.

It was the commencement of the large Larimer and Weld Canal near Fort Collins in 1878 which brought action. With a capacity of 720 cubic feet per second, it was the largest canal in the Cache la Poudre Valley. That fall J. L. Brush of Greeley and Lorin C. Mead of Longmont were elected to the Colorado House of Representatives, and Judge Silas B. A. Haynes of Greeley was chosen to represent Weld County in the Senate. Brush was a prominent cattleman and Mead was a farmer and an officer of a ditch company. Sensing the anxiety of the farmers over the new ditch, Brush and Haynes invited their constituents to a meeting in Greeley on October 19. Those who attended concluded that a more representative assembly was advisable, and issued a call for a state-wide convention to meet in Denver.

This convention met December 5–7, 1878. More than fifty farmers attended, all of them from the valleys of the South Platte. They represented at least twenty-nine ditch companies and agricultural communities. . . . They differed, debated, compromised, and drew up a memorial to the legislature which, with modifications by the legal profession, was enacted into law by the second and third legislative assemblies in 1879 and 1881.

Having adopted a new water right, the farmers now faced the problem of inventing new methods of regulating it. . . .

By and large, the farmers in convention in Denver favored the creation of an administrative agency to provide the protection which they desired. They favored the division of the state into hydrographic districts and the appointment of a water commissioner for each district. To this official they proposed to give the duty of registering, determining and administering water rights. . . . Having assembled a registry of water rights, the stream commissioners were to divide the water among the users in accordance with these registered rights. In case a dispute arose concerning the accuracy of the registry, the farmers proposed that the commissioner take evidence and determine the priorities of the rights in controversy. Such a procedure, which was administrative adjudication of property rights, and hence ran counter to Anglo-American experience, may have been suggested to these Colorado pioneers by the practices of the United States land commissioners and their agents who often collected evidence and adjudicated controversies arising over land.

Whatever the origin of the procedure, the frontier lawyers in Colorado opposed administrative adjudication and favored adjudication by the courts. . . .

The farmers were disappointed and angry. Imperative necessity demanded not only a new water right, but also a new method of acquiring, determining, and administering that right. The new method needed to be quick and inexpensive, avoiding lengthy and costly law suits. The agrarian proposal that water rights be adjudicated by administrative officers had grown out of agrarian distrust of attorneys; in fact, it had been designed to by-pass them. . . .

In the meantime, James M. Freeman, a Greeley lawyer, had been elected State Senator from Weld County. . . . [H]e had ready for introduction three irrigation bills. Senate Bill No. 93 met the objections of the lawyers and provided for the initiation of an adjudication by a complaint in court. Senate Bill No. 124 created a new official known as a State Engineer to measure the streams and to supervise the water commissioners. A third bill provided for a registry of water rights in the offices of the county clerks. The passage of these bills completed the formulation of the Colorado System of water-right control.

To acquire an appropriative right under this system, a water user had to file a claim in the county clerk's office. Whenever a stream became over appropriated and the water scarce, the priority of rights could be determined by an adjudication suit, in which a referee appointed by a judge of a district court took testimony. After an examination of this evidence, the judge determined priorities and issued a decree. To divide the streams according to these decreed priorities, the legislation of 1879 and 1881 created water commissioners in hydrographic districts grouped in three divisions comprising the valleys of the South Platte, Arkansas, and Rio Grande. The water commissioners were supervised by a State Engineer, who also had the duty of measuring the volume of the stream flow. These were institutions new to Anglo-American experience, invented by the farmers and lawyers of the Colorado frontier in order that crops might be grown in the desert. Moreover, these institutions eventually influenced the institutional structure of every one of the Western states. . . .

·4·

JAMES C. MALIN

Kansas Population Studies

During the 1930's, Professor James C. Malin began to publish the results of an intensive study of the state and federal manuscript census rolls of Kansas. Until that time historians of the American West had done little to improve the description of the process of agricultural settlement presented by Frederick Jackson Turner. Professor Malin, however, presented a quantitative analysis of the characteristics and persistence of considerable numbers of Kansas farmers and their wives through the years 1865 to 1935. From his research he developed a new model of the settling-in process on the frontier.

. . . The present author has undertaken pioneer studies in historical demography, and the adaptation of the agricultural system to Kansas as a specific area of the central grassland. Some attention has been given to the town, to the facilities of entertainment, and to strictly social life. The most fruitful contributions thus far, both as respects methodology

Source: Abridged from James C. Malin, *The Grassland of North America: Prolegomena to its History* (Lawrence, 1947, fifth printing, by Peter Smith Publisher, Inc., 6 Lexington Ave., Magnolia, Mass., 1967), Chap. 16, 280–289. The statistics on which much of the text is based are found on pages 284–287 and on page 289. A fuller description of the research also appears in James C. Malin, "The Turnover of Farm Population in Kansas," *Kansas Historical Quarterly*, IV (November, 1935), 339–372. Reprinted by permission of James C. Malin.

and historical conclusions, have been in the first two departments, population, and agricultural studies. . . .

The sampling method is the basis of operations, using a township or community area of fixed geographical boundaries as the unit small enough that it can be manageable in the entirety of its social behavior. Several such samples can be thrown together for statistical purposes, but handled separately for narrative purposes. They can be combined as seems desirable on different kinds of classifications to emphasize community age, type-of-farming area, rainfall belts, soil types, immigrant or native populations, or other aspects that may be of interest. The sources of the data are the state and federal census records. Other records that might be used are local records of land titles, or tax lists, and probate court cases.

The procedure for studying population behavior was to list the farm operators from the agricultural schedule of the census, and then gather the data from the population schedules for each operator, his wife, and, his family, by name. As Kansas took a decennial census from 1865–1925 inclusive, the federal and state census enumerations provided lists at five year intervals to 1885, after which period the federal census records were closed to investigation. For the later period the state census was depended upon exclusively. After 1925 statistical rolls of farm operators were available in Kansas for each year, but not general population data. The census list of farm operators for the first enumeration after settlement afforded the first base for comparison, and each list thereafter was compared with the base list to determine the individual operators remaining within the census area, but not necessarily upon the same farm. In turn, each census list was used as a base list for comparison with subsequent lists. Upon the death or retirement of an original operator, a son was counted as representing the family succession in the area. Tables were then prepared showing the total number of operators at each base enumeration interval, and the number remaining at each successive enumeration; another table was prepared in terms of percentages persisting; and then graphs were constructed, plotting comparative curves for each base year.

The conclusions from these population studies are illuminating, and a few of them are summarized here. . . . In the population turnover studies, there were variations from sample to sample, but there was a general uniformity of the curves illustrating farm-operator persistence, irrespective of whether the community was settled just prior to the census of 1860 or of 1895. The rate of turnover of population (or persistence as one may choose to call it) was associated primarily with community age; very high turnover during the pioneering period, a period of relative stabilization at low levels of persistence, and lastly a period of a high degree of stabilization, especially after 1915 or later. Of course, there were limits beyond which stabilization with age could not go. New independent variables entered from time to time, such as mechanical powered farming, following which new adjustments must be made. The turnover pattern of communities of a comparable age persisted to a remarkable degree, irrespective of depressions or of drouths, and there was very little difference as respects rainfall belts of 35 inches or over and 20 inches or less. Among the most stable found were some communities in the high plains where rainfall was less than 20 inches. New settlers were always more unstable than the old residents. Thus, with every replacement by new settlers, the movers were weeded out, leaving the more permanent element. It is not safe, however, to jump at conclusions as to why some moved and others stayed, or to assume that the best stayed and the worst moved. In most samples and periods there was a tendency toward greater stability during depressions, and mobility during periods of prosperity.

A second group of conclusions has to do with the total numbers of operators in each sample. The behavior was not uniform. On the pioneering frontier, numbers usually declined during depression and drouth. As already pointed out, the rate of loss, or turnover, was not greater necessarily when a drouth, or depression, year was used as the base from which to measure, and, on the contrary was generally less. The real issue was the flow of replacement population. With a consistently high rate of loss, complete depopulation would have resulted if new settlers had not arrived promptly. An increase in the total number of farm operators meant that the flow of replacement population exceeded the losses. This usually occurred in the pioneer period, during booms. The decrease in the total numbers of farm operators meant that the flow of replacement had diminished or ceased. This occurred in the pioneer period during drouth and depression periods. The rate of turnover in either case, based on the whole number of any particular census list, fluctuated little. In other words, the frontier was not a safety valve in the sense in which that theory has been used by the Turner school of history.

No satisfactory method has been devised for tracing what became of those who moved. The local newspapers record that many returned to the East, moved to towns, went to the mines in the mountains, or worked for the railroad, during depressions, but sufficiently exact data are not available from such sources to afford reliable quantitative treatment. Significant increases in numbers occurred frequently in older samples during depressions, in part, at least, reflecting an urban-rural movement. In most respects the depression of the 1930's was no exception to the general behavior pattern. The newest settled areas suffered the highest rate of turnover and net losses, but the conspicuous characteristic was the stability regularly associated with older communities, the propaganda to the contrary notwithstanding. There were fewer farmers on the move, proportionally, than in any previous depression in Kansas. Again it should be emphasized that replacement population had ceased to flow into the region, and that, rather than instability, accounted for population losses.

A third group of conclusions relate to what proportion of the total population of a sample, at any given date, were descendants of the operators of any prior date. Allowing for wide variations in individual samples, it is clear that the high rate of turnover of operators during the pioneering phase left a very small proportion of the original settler descendants among the farmers fifty to seventy-five years later. The assumption so often made that the original settlers determined the character of a community is unsafe as a generalization. After a substantial stabilization of the community had been achieved, even though the turnover might still be relatively high, the proportionate influence of the subsequent population was much greater.

The principal foreign-born groups of farm operators in Kansas who were sufficiently concentrated to dominate the communities were Germans, Swedes, and Bohemians. On the whole, they were highly persistent, but the second and third American-born generations reflected much the American pattern of behavior. . . . With the cessation of a large replacement population from the mother countries, these communities rapidly lost much of their distinctive character. As a rule, Negroes and Jews did not appear conspicuously in farm population. Negro colonies were established during the period of the Civil War and reconstruction migrations, but the population mostly drifted to the cities. Partly, the explanation lay in inability to carry on independent farming enterprise; partly, it was failure to adapt to environment; but, more largely, the answer probably lay in the cessation of the flow of replacement population to compensate for the high turnover characteristic of all newly established enterprises.

Studies of the internal migration of the United States are handicapped by the fact that federal census enumerations recorded only the state of birth and the place of residence at the time of the enumeration. Also, all the later federal enumerations were closed to investigation, except to federal employees, so only the printed mass statistics were available.

Kansas census records, 1875–1925, recorded the additional data of the state from which the individual moved to Kansas. As the Kansas census and the early federal enumerations are open for examination of individual names, it was possible to make more satisfactory studies than have ever been made elsewhere. Even much of the migration intervening between birth and the removal to Kansas can be pieced together, for persons with families, by noting the birth states of the children. . . . The sample areas were grouped from east to west across the length of the state in seven successive frontiers. The most significant points of emphasis were that the native migration to Kansas, direct from the state of birth, increased in proportion after 1875, both 1895 and 1905 being high, and thereafter the proportion declined, and furthermore, the part of that migration that moved into Kansas from adjacent states was small in proportion to that coming from non-contiguous states. . . .

The migration was not from one frontier to the next adjacent states but from non-contiguous states, except for the farthest west frontier, which meant mostly that the settlers made the long jump from some state east of the Mississippi river to Kansas. In the case of the west tier of counties of Kansas forming the seventh group, two factors are sufficient, probably, to explain that behavior; the building of the Burlington, and Rock Island railroads into the area from Nebraska, and Iowa; and secondly, after 1895 the change in all migration was setting in, especially by 1915. The decisive aspect of the table as a whole is that, for the census dates 1875–1905, the probabilities were that very nearly three of every four, or four of every five, of the migrant operators listed on those dates had migrated from a distance to Kansas, and that the adjustments necessary to so marked a change in environment were substantial. Conspicuous also was the number of Kansas born operators in the enumerations of 1915 and 1925, a fact which contributes to an explanation of stabilization of population to its environment. Three points relative to migration need to be emphasized because of the tradition in Turner circles that one frontier supplied the population for the next. The Goodrich (1936), and Thornthwaite (1934, 1936) studies in migration employed an inadequate methodology, but made the best use possible of the mass statistics from the printed federal census enumerations. Thornthwaite's (1934, p. 10) conclusion that the trans-Mississippi states received settlers chiefly from eastern states, which had been settled forty or fifty years earlier, is so vague as to be virtually meaningless. He did not define the word "settled." Shannon (1945) followed Thornthwaite in part, concluding that only the occasional family made the long jump from non-contiguous states. The Shannon conclusions are so far out of line with the facts derived from the Kansas census data that the error must be emphasized. Whether or not studies based upon an adequate methodology would reveal different conclusions for states north or south of Kansas cannot be forecast with certainty, but the probabilities are that they would differ little from the Kansas results.

The age of the population of the frontier has been the subject of much inconsistent or contradictory treatment. One contention is that the frontier was settled by men who had made several successive removals. If so, then the frontiersman must have been anything but young. Another extreme held that the frontier was composed conspicuously of young couples who were just starting out in life. Paxson (1930, p. 29–31) defined the frontier in terms of a cycle, from the coming of the cabineer until his first born, in turn, married and set out on a new frontier. The present author, in 1936, 1940, and 1942 presented quantitative data on the subject for Kansas and for the first time removed this phase of the frontier problem from the realm of merely speculative generalization. In the samples analyzed, the young couples just beginning life were conspicuously in the minority. . . . The men were conspicuously middle-aged, and in only two . . . [rainfall belts in the year 1860] . . . did the median fall below 35. The age distribution clustered rather closely around the median. . . .

GILBERT C. FITE

Daydreams and Nightmares: The Late Nineteenth-Century Agricultural Frontiers

There was a saying of the nineteenth century in the United States that the frontier was "hell on women and oxen." Some historians have argued, however, that the tradition of pioneer hardship contained more than a little exaggeration. Gilbert C. Fite examines the "gap between anticipation and realization" that many settlers of the Plains states discovered, and concludes that it was remarkable that so many did achieve "reasonable success" there.

. . . Prospective settlers believed that the Western agricultural frontier held unlimited opportunities for the person who would work hard and manage properly. Americans had always had a love affair with the land, but their passion seemed to increase as they pushed toward the setting sun after Appomattox. The acquisition of 160 acres of land or more was the dream and ambition of thousands of young men and some young women. Settlers wanted land on which to establish a home and earn a living, or they hoped to benefit from speculation based on rising real estate values. Whatever their motives, their prime objective was to acquire land. . . .

Since promoters of economic development throughout the West believed that agriculture was the key to future growth and wealth, it is not surprising that they mixed truth and fiction liberally in presenting the West as a farming paradise. Gross exaggeration of crop yields, praise for the climate, and assurance of a happy life forever filled the pages of promotional pamphlets distributed by railroads and immigration agencies. Whether in a serious vein or with tongue in cheek, Westerners depicted agricultural opportunities in the most glowing terms. . . .

[P]ersonal letters and reports of Western settlers removed any nagging doubts about farming opportunities in the West. John Minto, who had trekked overland to Oregon in 1844 and settled in the Willamette

SOURCE: Abridged from Gilbert C. Fite, "Daydreams and Nightmares: The Late Nineteenth-Century Agricultural Frontiers," *Agricultural History*, XL (October, 1966), 285–293. Reprinted by permission of *Agricultural History* and Gilbert C. Fite.

Valley, reported in 1862 that he lived in a "roomy cottage house," cultivated forty to sixty acres of land, including seventeen acres of orchard,
and enjoyed a pleasant and happy existence. . . . The productive,
inviting soil of eastern Nebraska, unencumbered with stones or stumps,
prompted one young emigrant from Indiana to write: "Ma you can see
just as far as you please here and almost every foot in sight can be
plowed." He explained that "a man can come here with $500 and manage
properly and in a few years he can have a good comfortable home in a
beautiful looking country." Another new settler in Nebraska wrote
home to Illinois in the late 1860's that "the longer I stay in this country
the better I like it."

It is clear that the hopes and dreams of many late nineteenth-century
agricultural pioneers actually became reality. Perhaps they did not
achieve as much as they wished, but, nonetheless, they made fairly decent
homes for themselves and their families. On the other hand, there were
thousands whose expectations were forever unfulfilled and whose dreams
were shattered by the awful realities which successful farmers and the
optimistic promoters failed to mention.

The prairie-plains frontier was subjected to a series of severe and
devastating natural catastrophes in the late nineteenth century which
made life hard and, in some cases, unbearable. All the way from Texas to
Dakota, drought, grasshoppers, prairie fires, hail, blizzards, floods, and
disease intermittently took a heavy toll of crops and livestock and
sometimes even brought death to the settlers themselves. Even hardy
pioneers could not stand up under these conditions. Indeed, the poorly
financed and undercapitalized frontiersman was in the worst possible
position to deal with problems resulting from crop or livestock losses.
Poor at the beginning, any natural hazard which destroyed the crops
during the first year or two of settlement was likely to mean not only
immediate destitution, but long-run failure as well. For example, in
December 1871, following a season of hailstorms and prairie fires, a
Minnesota farmer wrote to a state official:

I have been trying to live on my place and with sickness and bad luck in
crops have well nigh run out of everything—I have been sick for months and
my wife is not well from exposure and hunger and I thought that there was
no other way than to ask you to help me—if you can let me have $25 and
some close [sic] for my wife and daughter and myself as we have not close
to cover our backs or heads—And if I can't get the money I shall lose my
place after livin' from hand to mouth for three years on the frontier.

The situation became so serious in southwestern Minnesota by the
fall of 1871 that the Governor sent his personal representative to investi-

gate conditions. The reports of Mark D. Flower would make a Scrooge weep. He reported that one family of five was "extremely destitute, nearly naked and too poor to clothe themselves." Following a bad prairie fire, one farmer had nothing left except "a good looking wife." . . .

In 1873 grasshoppers devoured the crops of many pioneer farmers in Minnesota and Iowa. With little or no financial reserves, hundreds of poor settlers became absolutely destitute. A single girl who lived with her aged father near Murray Centre, Minnesota, described their situation to Governor C. K. Davis in February 1874:

We have no money now nothing to sell to get any more clothes with as the grasshoppers destroyed all of our crops what few we had for we have not much land broke yet; as we have no team of our own we have to hire one in order to get it worked what little we have to sow, so you see it is rather hard on us to hire so much and get along. . . .

In 1874 grasshoppers devastated much of the area between Texas and Dakota, and hundreds of prairie-plains frontier farmers saw the crops which the drought had not already killed eaten by those uncontrollable and ravenous pests. A Kansas correspondent wrote that they came like a mighty cloud, blotting out the sun. Then they settled everywhere "devouring everything green; stripping the foliage, and . . . destroying every plant that is good for food or pleasant to the eyes, that man has planted. . . ."

General E. O. C. Ord, stationed at Omaha, became greatly concerned with destitution in southwestern Nebraska during the winter of 1874–1875, and he sent several officers into the region to survey conditions. One army lieutenant wrote: "It was pitiable, in most instances, upon entering the poor huts to see women and children crouched shivering around their dull fires in the midst of a cloud of pulverized snow driven in upon them by the storm." Major N. A. M. Dudley told of a boy arriving at Fort McPherson, Nebraska, with his feet wrapped in cotton bandages. The lad stated that he had left his mother and five brothers and sisters at home without any food. After the soldiers had given him some shoes and enough clothing to keep him from freezing, Major Dudley directed the supply officer to give the boy two sacks of flour and thirty pounds of bacon. . . . One little girl told an army officer that her father believed the family would starve when the present supply of flour was exhausted. But she quoted her mother as saying: "God will take care of us."

In response to the pitiful pleas for help, both private groups and state legislatures provided some relief to suffering and destitute settlers during the 1870's. A Kansas relief committee collected and distributed more than $73,000 in cash during 1874–1875, plus tons of food and clothing. In February 1875, Congress appropriated $150,000 to "prevent starvation and suffering . . . to any and all destitute and helpless persons living on the frontier who have been rendered destitute . . . by ravages of grasshoppers." The army distributed some 1,957,108 rations to 107,535 people in Minnesota, Dakota, Nebraska, Iowa, and Colorado. The United States Department of Agriculture stepped up its program of seed distribution and mailed out thousands of packages of vegetable seeds in the spring of 1875 so that farmers could plant gardens. . . .

While many farmers somehow managed to weather these natural hazards, hundreds of settlers on the frontier abandoned their land and sought opportunities elsewhere. Streams of wagons filled with broken and beaten families headed eastward. After investigating destitution in north-central Kansas, one official estimated that at least six hundred, families had forsaken a six-county area between August 1874 and January 1875.

Natural calamities intermittently struck individuals, communities, and even entire regions during the following years. Hundreds of pioneers suffered from extreme want following droughts in parts of western Kansas during 1879 and 1880. But this condition changed sharply by 1882, and during the next few years the Great Plains received an unusual amount of rainfall. Some promoters said that this proved the theory that rainfall followed the plow. In any event, there was an unprecedented rush of settlement into central Dakota, western Nebraska, western Kansas, and eastern Colorado. As one writer said at the beginning of this boom period, settlers could be seen in sod shanties and dugouts west of the 99th meridian "as contented and as happy as a preacher, as comfortable as a king." However, the boom collapsed in the late 1880's as drought returned to many sections of the agricultural frontier. A Kansas farmer wrote in his diary in July 1887: "Rained a little last night. Enough to lay the dust. Corn nearly all dried up. For the life of me I don't see how the farmers will winter. No oats, no corn, no fruit, no grass, no nothing."

Widespread drought in 1889 and 1890 left thousands of pioneers in dire want. According to Governor Arthur C. Mellette of South Dakota, some six hundred families in his state were "absolutely destitute" by December 1889. By the winter of 1890–1891, conditions had become critical for thousands of farmers on the Great Plains frontier. . . .

Again, many frontier farmers deserted their homes and returned East. Those who stayed seemed to have their faith and hope redeemed when good crops were harvested in 1891 and 1892. However, unprecedented drought, accompanied by grasshoppers, struck a vast section of the prairie-plains frontier in 1894, and thousands of farmers experienced total crop failure. . . .

The thousands of agricultural pioneers who migrated into the unsettled West after 1865 went with high hopes and confidence that they would find a new Eden. For many, however, the grim realities turned their daydreams into nightmares. Indeed, they found an unbridgeable gap between anticipation and realization. Unable to cope with conditions in the West, thousands gave up as their shattered dreams crumbled under both natural hazards and man-made handicaps. Others stayed on and settled up the country. Whether it was through luck, grit, good management, or something else, they succeeded in occupying the land and establishing homes. When all of the difficulties are considered, it is not surprising that so many pioneer farmers failed on the prairie-plains frontier. The remarkable thing is that, when judged by nineteenth-century standards, so many achieved reasonable success. The Western farmers' frontier was a great sifting process. But those who remained after the winnowing were the real conquerors of the frontier, and they laid the basis for the region's subsequent economic development.

SECTION 2

The Continuing West

CHAPTER XIV

The Politics of the West

POLITICS PLAYED an important role in all dimensions of frontier life. Earlier we have reviewed the discussion of the frontier as a "democratizing" influence in American history, and we need not introduce that debate again. On a less abstract level, however, there is little disagreement over the place of politics in western life. The hustings provided the opportunity for social gathering, religious revival and economic marketplace all at once. Perhaps the People's or Populist party of the 1890's provides the best example of western political action.

Quite early in our national history the West assumed a significant role in American politics. Coonskin caps and the increasingly significant log cabin were part of the symbolic obeisance of national politicians to the West. On a more tangible level, that of national policy, perhaps the West did not fare quite as well—witness the lengthy period of agitation prior to successful passage of the Homestead Act of 1862— yet a great deal of national political attention prior to the Civil War did focus on problems of particular moment to the West, notably those of land and transportation.

Ante-bellum national politics often displayed sharp sectional characteristics. Because eastern and southern politicians often sought distinctly different goals, western Congressmen often found themselves in the enviable position of casting the pivotal votes in Congress. Clearly the West secured the passage of the Preemption Act of 1841 partially as a result of eastern and southern battles over the tariff and the distribution of profits from land sales. The goals which the West sought to achieve were those deemed essential to a developing region: cheap land, good transportation and tariff protection for western raw materials. Western political "ideology" was of a pragmatic—often flexible—type which frequently exhibited strong antimonopoly and antibanking tendencies. These reflected western chagrin at what they believed was the economic exploitation of western settlers by "outsiders."

Despite the practical, economic bases of western political thought, the increasingly violent antislavery controversy brought East and West more closely together. The attack on Fort Sumter and the withdrawal of southerners from Congress consummated the merger of eastern and western Republicans into a position of national power.

But during the national trauma that followed, western Republicans in Congress ranged themselves against their eastern colleagues on various occasions. They charged that the West was being expected to bear an unfair share of the burden of the war. Although less important than the ideological disagreement between Radical and Moderate Republicans, western sectionalism affected the voting in Congress on such important issues as the Internal Revenue Act of 1862, the Land Grant College Law, the Pacific Railroad Act and monetary legislation.

American politics changed greatly after the Civil War. It was ironic that, in this period of greatest western expansion, national attention focused on the more dramatic reconstruction of the South and the industrialization of the East. Politically, this changing focus often resulted in policies which were unpalatable to large segments of the western population.

As the South plunged from its position of national power, the East had less reason to pacify the West in order to combat southern intransigence. After the war domestic political battles found the West pitted against the East. Old ante-bellum economic conflicts, especially those dealing with monetary, banking and land policies, flared anew. As these economic issues became salient, westerners and southerners discovered a common ground: fear of the East.

Banking and currency laws written to fulfill the needs of finance capitalism and consistent with the economic theories of eastern bankers were not always compatible with the demands of the West. The latter had specialized financial needs as agriculture became increasingly commercialized and more capital intensive. Similar frustrations developed in policy areas dealing with land, transportation and marketing.

In an economy marked by concentration of control and specialization of function the individual western farmer became more and more of an anomaly. Agriculture was an occupation marked by economic anarchy, and this at a time when American industry, American finance, and American transportation were displaying increasing organization, increasing efficiency and increasing power.

The simultaneous occurrence of greater divergence of western needs from those of the East with an apparent decrease in western ability to influence national policy portended political revolt. That the South experienced similar frustrations expanded the dimensions of this revolt.

Although the political revolution in the South equalled—if it did not exceed—that of the West, we will consider the former only when it bears directly upon the western experience.

Organized agrarian protests had some precedent in American history. Shay's Rebellion in Massachusetts and the Whiskey Revolt in Pennsylvania, directed against taxation policies, stand out as immediate examples. The first viable national farmer's organization, however, was the National Grange, or Patrons of Husbandry, founded in 1867. The Grange never organized politically—indeed, Grange charters forbade political action—but as agricultural prices dropped in the early 1870's Granger representatives began to appear in state legislatures, especially in states of the Middle West. These men, in combination with representatives of other economic interests, played a part in passing so-called "Granger laws" in several midwestern states. Sponsors of this legislation generally sought to limit the rate-fixing power of railroads, and to regulate grain elevators. The laws were generally ineffective, however, and the Grangers soon reasserted their major interest in social and educational activities.

As the Grange declined in influence during the 1880's, other organizations replaced it. Farm groups in Texas, Louisiana and Arkansas, as well as lesser bodies in the Old South, united in the mid-1880's to form the National Farmer's Alliance and Industrial Union, a group which was affiliated loosely with the Colored Farmer's National Alliance. In 1880 a Cook County, Illinois, editor, Milton George, formed agricultural alliances in states of the North and West. George's initial organizational activities coincided with a period of hard times in the West—when the prices for farm products were low, transportation rates were burdensome and the prices of manufactured goods seemed high.

Like the Grange, the Northern Alliance, as it came to be called, began ostensibly as a nonpolitical organization. From the beginning, however, there were internal pressures to utilize political means to achieve broader economic goals. Most of the early political gambits of the Alliancemen were executed within the existing two-party system, often in alliance with the state minority party.

Membership in both the Northern and Southern Alliances fluctuated with economic changes in the 1880's, but by the early 1890's the alliances had a considerable following. The Southern Alliance reported between two and three million members in 1890, while the Northern Alliance claimed over one and one-half million followers. Combination of the two organizations seemed the logical—and inevitable—next step. A meeting for this purpose in St. Louis in 1889 failed, less because of differences in objectives than because the southerners were reluctant to merge completely with the Colored Alliance and because the northerners disliked the ritualistic secrecy of the Southern Alliance.

Especially in the states of the Great Plains, Alliancemen became increasingly dissatisfied with the two established parties. Southern Alliance members were somewhat more successful than their northern counterparts in operating within the existing political structure, the Democratic party, and they were reluctant to sabotage the party that had redeemed the South.

In June 1890 at Topeka the People's Party of Kansas was formed— and this was followed shortly by the organizations of similar parties, in Nebraska, the Dakotas, Minnesota and Colorado. These political parties were not composed entirely of Alliancemen—indeed, they were a political merger of different reform groups: Greenbackers, Union Laborites, Prohibitionists, Single Taxers, Nationalists and members of Free Silver clubs.

The state parties enjoyed some startling successes in the state and local elections of 1890. Populists in the Plains states and Alliance Democrats in the South seized the balance of power in some state legislatures. The greatest prize, however, was the election of William A. Peffer of Kansas to the United States Senate. Peffer provided the Populists with national renown and some respectability. The success of 1890 provided the final catalyst for national organization. The dissidents believed that a new party was necessary because the two old parties were dominated by eastern bosses and thus were unable to articulate the needs of the West and South.

In Cincinnati in early 1891 the groundwork was laid for a national party and in St. Louis in early 1892 the political insurgents formed the People's Party. At the national convention in Omaha James B. Weaver of Iowa, Greenback presidential candidate in 1880, obtained the Populist presidential nomination, with James G. Field of Virginia receiving the vice-presidential place on the ticket. Weaver, a one-time Republican and general in the Union army, and Field, a former Democrat and Confederate general, exhibited the bipartisan and trans-sectional nature of the Populists.

The Populist ticket polled more than one million votes in 1892, seizing the electoral votes of Kansas, Colorado, Idaho, and Nevada, and electing governors in Kansas, Colorado, and North Dakota. Members of the People's Party were elated over their victories and eagerly looked ahead to 1896. The severe economic stress accompanying the panic of 1893 exacerbated the general unrest. In the off-year election of 1894 the

Populists received over a million and a half votes, at a time when the Populist official philosophy was becoming increasingly radical.

Because the People's Party was a heterogeneous collection of reform groups with different grievances and goals, a Populist "ideology" is elusive. There were four major groups in the People's Party: southern farmers, black as well as white; Great Plains farmers; western miners; and urban reform and labor groups. The immediate goals of each of these groups differed and their common denominator remained their dissatisfaction with the economic and political system of the United States during the late nineteenth century. This is not to say that the Populists were nihilist; far from it, in the period from 1890 to 1896 they developed policies and programs to deal with the problems that they perceived.

Land, the Populists argued, was the heritage of the people; therefore, they believed that vast land monopolies should be broken up and their holdings redistributed to actual settlers. As the amount of unoccupied, accessible, productive land constricted in the 1880's, this grievance and its impact—both real and imagined—on the individual farmer intensified. Specifically, the Populists proposed to end alien land ownership and to return at least the unsold and unused portions of the railroad land grants to the government for the use of settlers.

Transportation problems were very real to the western farmers of the Great Plains. Initial enthusiasm for railroad construction waned as farmers realized their vulnerability to railroad rate fluctuations. Freight rates per ton-mile west of the Missouri River were two-and-one-quarter times as high as they were east of Chicago. It cost twice as much to ship grain from the Dakotas to Minneapolis as it did from Chicago to Liverpool. The farmer failing on the Great Plains paid little heed to explanations by railroad officials which described higher fixed costs, dead-heading cars, and economies of scale. Weren't the Hills and the Goulds making their millions from the produce of the American farmer? As Mary Ellen Lease, an emotional Kansas Populist, simply put it: "If one man is a millionaire and another is a tramp, I would say that the one has something that belongs to the other."

The Populists developed a simple, if revolutionary, answer to the problems of transportation and to those of communication: government ownership of railroads and telephone and telegraph lines. Nationalization was an extreme step beyond the old Granger idea of regulation, but most Populists argued that the problem called for radical innovation.

To the Populists the problem of finance was at the root of all economic grievances. The American economy followed a sharp deflationary trend from shortly after the Civil War to the end of the nineteenth century, a trend which the government accelerated by contracting the money supply. This deflationary policy particularly harmed commodity producers and debtors. The mortgage, earlier a sign of buoyant optimism on the part of the Plains farmers, became a symbol of disaster. It often took two to four times as much wheat, for example, to repay a loan as it did at the time of borrowing. Although the Populist farmers were not the victims of a vast money-lenders conspiracy, they were heavily in debt during the late 1880's, and bad crops, low prices and currency contraction brought many of them to foreclosure.

To solve their problems of finance, the Populists believed that an inflationary monetary policy was essential. Accepting the quantity theory of money, they argued that the circulating media should be stabilized at $50 per capita, a substantial increase over the $22 current in the early 1890's. To achieve this the Populists demanded that the amount of greenbacks in circulation be increased and insisted that the federal government return immediately to free and unlimited coinage of silver at a fixed ratio with gold of 16:1. The federal government, in other words, would purchase all the silver offered to its mints at a price fixed at one-sixteenth that of gold, mint it and put it into circulation.

Because the Populist demands called for the federal government to take a more active role in the economy, it naturally followed that they insisted upon greater popular controls on the exercise of governmental power. Accordingly, they demanded the secret ballot, the initiative, the referendum and the direct election of United States Senators.

After their electoral successes in the 1890–1894 period, the Populists viewed their chances in the 1896 Presidential election optimistically. The leaders scheduled the Populist convention after the Republican and Democratic conclaves in order to pick up dissidents from the old parties. This tactic was based on the assumption that the old parties would nominate men hostile to the Populist program. The Republicans obligingly nominated William McKinley of Ohio, a conservative and an equivocating goldbug. But delegates from the South and West arrived at the Democratic National Convention in Chicago determined to alter the course of their party and stop the Populist successes in their regions. Accordingly they secured the nomination of a young Nebraska congressman, William Jennings Bryan, a skilled orator, a staunch silverite, and an articulate spokesman for the rural dissidents.

The Populists met in St. Louis and faced a severe problem. To nominate their own candidate would clearly fragment the reform vote and elect McKinley. To endorse Bryan might decimate the People's Party.

After a bitter fight the party reluctantly chose fusion with the Democratic Party. The Populists subordinated their general reform program to the immediate goal of free silver. Davis H. Waite, former Populist governor of Colorado and a longtime foe of such a policy, perhaps typified the reform Populist belief when he said that to fight silver openly would destroy Populism. By accepting Bryan's silver campaign "all remaining reform issues would naturally and rapidly drift into the controversy."

Waite proved wrong on both counts. Approval of Bryan meant the end of Populism as a viable political alternative. Other reform issues were completely subordinated to the emotional issue of silver. Bryan failed to carry a single state north of the Mason and Dixon line and east of the Mississippi River. In addition he lost Minnesota, Iowa, North Dakota, Oregon, California, Kentucky and West Virginia. Economic patterns proved a major determinant of the vote: Bryan was strongest, in the states where staple agriculture and mining predominated. He failed in the diversified farming areas of the Midwest and East, often receiving greater support from eastern industrial workers than from eastern farmers.

By the 1890's it was clear that "West" meant a specific region; no longer were "West" and "frontier" interchangeable words denoting more a frame of mind and a process than a geographic area. The successive "Wests" in American history, from the fall line of the east coast to the Rocky Mountains and on to the Pacific Ocean, were by 1896 heterogeneous and parochial areas differing economically and culturally and hence seeking distinctly different political goals. In the 1830's the new states could exercise substantial political power and forge agreement in support of the demands they made. The very success of the westward movement meant that there were now in the 1890's too many nonfrontier states. The Populist states were literally voices crying in the wilderness. The Ohio valley was more closely linked—economically, culturally, and politically—to New York than to Kansas. This process had been underway since ante-bellum days; by 1896 it was manifest to all.

The 1896 election destroyed the People's Party as an effective political force. Agrarian prosperity and inflation engendered by an increase in the gold supply blunted the party's economic appeal. Bryan's defeat had shown that sectional politics, based on the poorer, less heavily populated states, was unrewarding. Intransigent malcontents reappeared in the Socialist Party, the Progressive movement, the Non Partisan League, or, in the case of the western miners, in the Industrial Workers of the World. Many areas of Populist strength ironically became bastions of rural conservatism. The Democratic or Republican parties ultimately assimilated most Populist reforms in their own programs.

The Populist heritage in twentieth-century politics is, as we shall see, a debatable topic. But Populism was of the nineteenth century and it was the culmination of nineteenth-century patterns perhaps more than a predecessor of twentieth-century trends. Western sectionalism had been a potent political force in the period prior to the Civil War. Populism was an attempt to stop the decline in western power which had marked postwar politics. The failure of Populism and Bryan accelerated the trend. Coonskin caps became curios and log cabins became relics of an earlier day.

· 1 ·

JOHN D. HICKS

The People's Party in Minnesota

Frederick Jackson Turner suggested that the Populist uprising occurred because of the economic dislocation and psychological reaction which followed the closing of the frontier. In his classic study, *The Populist Revolt: A History of the Farmers' Alliance and the People's Party*, John D. Hicks concluded that the economic hardships of the late nineteenth century, partially caused by the end of free lands, led to the political reaction. Taken from another of his publications, this selection summarizes Professor Hicks' interpretation.

For a long time the farmer who made his home along the American frontier was the recipient of far greater favors than he knew. Here he might have land for next to nothing—virgin land, the fertility of which would not for many a year appreciably decline. Lack of capital was no great handicap. It took comparatively little to get a start, and if all went well the homesteader or the purchaser of cheap lands might hope in a

Source: Abridged from John D. Hicks, "The People's Party in Minnesota," *Minnesota History*, V (November, 1924), 531-560. Reprinted by permission of *Minnesota History* and John D. Hicks.

few years—certainly less than a lifetime—to pay off his debts and to have his farm "clear." Ceaseless labor it meant, labor which aged him while he was yet young and which, falling even more heavily upon his wife, carried her to an early grave. But the returns were good. No other farmer in all the world had such an opportunity. Foreigners realized this far better than Americans and came in an ever-increasing throng to share the bounty which providence and the American government placed before them. . . .

But the era of free lands could not last forever. Well before the close of the nineteenth century they were practically gone. The price of land had begun to climb. The landless farmer now had increasing difficulty in making a start, and the farmer who had land saw his land values appreciate without furnishing him a corresponding increase in income. The "subsidy" to agriculture had run out, and there was nothing to place in its stead. The farmer must now take his chances with the rest.

He found the competition keen enough. That spirit of ruthless conquest with which he and his progenitors had attacked the woodlands and the prairies had passed into all things American. By the end of the eighties the railways had overtaken the frontier at every point— indeed, they had appeared in time to aid materially in speeding it to an end. Their methods were the methods of the pioneer. They built with blind optimism and with prodigal expenditure wherever there seemed to be the slightest hope of gain. They relied upon and obtained the generous help of the government. They "watered" their stock well before they sold it. And they charged all the traffic would bear. Here was no mean competitor!

Nor were the railroads the only rivals the farmer had to meet. There were other corporations, usually called trusts, which with a lasting and dependable protective tariff behind them were leading the farmer a merry race. There were the trusts which furnished him with the things he wore; there were the trusts which furnished him with the machines he had to use; there were the trusts which furnished him with the fuel he had to burn; there were the trusts which furnished him with the materials of which he built his home, his barns, his fences. And worst of all, there were the trusts to which he must sell his produce—an elevator combine, a miller's ring, a packer's trust. They all played the game in true pioneer fashion. They were there to get all that they could out of a rich virgin soil. Was not this a free country? Had they not the same rights as anyone else? Who was to tell them what prices they were to charge or to give? That was for them to decide. If people didn't like their prices they knew what they could do.

And then there were the money-lenders. Ever since the Civil War the accumulation of capital, especially in the manufacturing regions of the East, had been going on apace. Here money to loan was available in large quantities, and the western lands, with their appreciating values, furnished excellent security. As for interest rates, the sky was the limit. The western farmer always wanted money badly and could rarely resist the temptation to borrow on any terms. His optimism, born of a never-faltering faith in the future, derived from generations of pioneer ancestors, made him certain that he could repay. He mortgaged his lands for all they were worth, whether it was absolutely necessary or not. As a rule, however, it was absolutely necessary. The latest improved machinery cost money even when purchased on the installment plan; and a long succession of bad years, due to drouths, grasshoppers, and hail, cost more.

These, then, were the competitors—the railroads, the trusts, and the bankers—who disputed with the farmer every step in the race for prosperity. The condition, to be sure, was not altogether new. Ever since the West began the pioneer had had to struggle with the problem of too costly transportation. He had never known a time when the price of the things he had to buy was not as much too high as the price of the things he had to sell was too low. He had had his troubles with banks and bankers. But these earlier days were the days of cheap lands and when things went wrong the disgruntled sought solace in another move to the West. Here was the chance for a new start. Broader acres, more fertile fields would surely bring the desired results. And with the restless moving ever on and on the more stable elements of society who were left behind made progress that was steady and sure. Now with the lands used up this safety valve was closed. The frontier was turned back upon itself. The restless and discontented voiced their sentiments more and fled from them less. There was a veritable chorus of denunciation directed against those individuals and those corporations who sought their own advantage without regard to the effect their actions would have upon the farmer and his interests.

Premonitions of the gathering storm had not been lacking. In the seventies the farmers protested through the Granger movement against the methods by which the railroads wrung profits from them. The movement was short-lived, however, although it did indeed establish the principle that the roads must submit to state regulation even of their rates. Perhaps its most important contribution—the lesson it taught the farmers of the necessity of coöperation—was less tangible. They learned that by combining they could get a hearing, even if they could not at first accomplish great results. This was a hard lesson to learn and was perhaps never fully mastered, for the pioneer farmer was by practice and precept an individualist. Like his ancestors before him he wished to manage his own affairs in his own way, and he asked only to be let alone. But alone he was unable to face effectively the combinations and corporations that opposed him, and clearly the only hope lay in opposing combination by combination. After the Granger movement came the Greenback movement, with its protest against the steadily mounting value of the dollar and, correspondingly, of the farmers' debts. And then came the Alliance. . . .

[T]he fundamental principle for which the original Populists fought survived and grew. They grasped the idea that the extreme individualism of the old frontier was forever a thing of the past, and that the combination of the many who were left behind in the mad race for prosperity to control the few who had forged farthest ahead was an absolute necessity if anything like equality of opportunity was to be maintained. Pioneers of an earlier age had barely tolerated government as a necessary evil, but these farmers of the last American frontier could see no other way to check the aggressive tendencies of those who opposed their interests than the interposition of the power of the state. Once they had believed in the slogan, "The less government the better," but now they saw that all ordinary men must join together in demanding an extension of governmental activity. The common people must take control of the government in order to make of it an instrument of the popular will and an adequate check on those who would otherwise make it the tool of special interests. "In brief," as Mr. Turner puts it, "the defenses of the pioneer democrat" had shifted "from free land to legislation, from the ideal of individualism to the ideal of social control through regulation by law." And that newer ideal despite setbacks both violent and recent still stands.

CHESTER McARTHUR DESTLER

Western Radicalism, 1865–1901:
Concepts and Origins

Dissatisfied with existing interpretations of western radicalism, Chester McArthur Destler examined the Populist ideology in the context of nineteenth-century American radicalism. He found in Populism a synthesis of the agrarian and urban radicalism which had characterized American reform movements throughout the century.

. . . Although students of western history have long contended for the existence of a unique agrarianism in the region after 1865, they, too, have failed to establish the existence there of a distinctive school of radical thought. Insulated by the continued influence of the frontier hypothesis from the records of contemporary or preceding urban movements within or without the region, and preoccupied largely with local sources of information, they have based the traditional story of western radicalism upon the assumption of an isolated, rural development undisturbed by external influences other than those affecting the marketing of farm surpluses. The singularly barren result, so far as knowledge of fundamental tenets or their implications is concerned, must be attributed to the conviction that radicalism in the American West was exclusively the product of repetitive sociological and economic processes at work on the frontier, which found expression in a somewhat emotional discontent or in a patchwork of remedial proposals that lacked any philosophical basis other than a desire to restore the working prosperity of a small entrepreneur, rural economy. An escape from this *cul de sac* has been suggested by the new emphasis upon the region's participation in the technological, urban, and intellectual movements of the late nineteenth century that was urged upon historians nearly a decade ago. . . .

The existence in the Upper Mississippi Valley, in 1865, of a system

SOURCE: Abridged from Chester McArthur Destler, "Western Radicalism, 1865–1901: Concepts and Origins," *Mississippi Valley Historical Review*, XXXI (December, 1944), 335–368. Reprinted by permission of the *Journal of American History* and Chester McArthur Destler.

of democratic thought derived from an earlier integration of urban radicalism with the coonskin democracy of the hardwood frontier, suggests that subsequent intercourse between urban and agrarian radicals occurred within a conceptual pattern common to both. William Trimble has shown how the working-class Locofocoism of the Jacksonian era was transplanted by the westward movement to the rich soil of the Middle West in the forties and fifties. There it fused with the similar but less well-defined conceptions of the Benton Democracy in neighboring upland southern areas of settlement. It was reproduced so completely by wheat farmers on the prairies and oak openings farther to the north that insistence upon "equal rights" and intense hostility to monopoly, chartered corporations, banks, and the "money power" are to this day frequently regarded as peculiar to the rural mind. . . .

The revival of the democratic movement in the trans-Allegheny states after the Civil War was more than the resurgence of ante-bellum quarrels provoked by exclusively western impulses. It offers the first clear illustrations in this period of the effect of intercourse and co-operation between eastern and western, urban-born and agrarian movements upon the development of western radical thought and action. This is notably true of the antimonopoly sentiment that flourished in the western states in the half dozen years before the panic of 1873. . . . Resentment against the extortions and monopolistic practices of the railroads was not peculiar to western farmers. It was shared by western merchants, eastern importers and shippers, the producers and refiners of the Pennsylvania oil region, and laboring men as well. . . .

The synchronism of the propaganda of the Cheap Freight Railway League and the Free-Trade League with the continuing antimonopoly movement in the West, is in itself highly suggestive. It is obvious that the revival of Locofoco stereotypes in the Mississippi Valley was but part of a nation-wide development that was shared by all the elements that suffered from the high tariff and the abuses of railroad and telegraph management. The central role of the tariff reformers in the Liberal Republican movement illustrates both the intersectional character of the antimonopoly revival and the role of nonagrarian elements in it. . . .

Most students of western radicalism had overlooked the dual character of the Greenback agitation that spread so rapidly after the panic of 1873. Judged by its origins Greenbackism was at once a western inflationist proposal and an eastern radical philosophy by means of which its urban working-class adherents sought to substitute a co-operative economy for the mercantile and industrial capitalism of the day. . . .

The co-operative movement is another example of the readiness with which western agrarians borrowed urban formulas ready-made in their attempts to solve agricultural problems. In this case European experience was clearly drawn upon, while the influence of organized labor in America upon the farming co-operative movements seems almost indubitable. . . .

During the same period midwestern farmers made an original and important contribution to the theory and method of democratic control over corporate enterprise. Individualistic and with no previous experience in the eastern states or Great Britain to guide them, they sought a practicable solution for the vicious practices of railroads and grain elevators. Inspired by the antimonopoly movement and by the Locofoco tradition of using the power of the democratic state to eliminate special privilege, their demands ranged from legislative rate-fixing to construction and operation of a transcontinental railroad by the national government. Eventually, they secured the adoption in a number of states of the novel method of controlling railroads and warehouses by means of independent regulatory commissions with rate-fixing powers. . . . In this case western agrarian radicalism perfected a governmental agency and an addition to democratic constitutional theory that were accepted eventually by eastern states and the national government as well. . . .

Western cities made significant contributions to the radical movements of the rural West and urban East in the seventies and eighties. The wider antimonopoly movement that was directed against industrial combinations and speculative manipulation of commodity prices received its initial impetus from Henry Demarest Lloyd. His antimonopolism was derived from a Locofoco family background. It was confirmed by four years' work as assistant secretary of the American Free-Trade League. . . . Diverted from journalism to a career of social reform, Lloyd continued the fight against monopoly by publication of his great work, *Wealth against Commonwealth,* and by participation in the Populist revolt. Until after its collapse he was regarded by the western agrarians as one of their chief inspirers.

An equally notable contribution to American radicalism came from San Francisco and Oakland, California, urban centers developing within a few hundred miles of the mining and agricultural frontier of the Far West. There Henry George, another journalist, but onetime Philadelphia printer's devil, perfected the single-tax theory in the midst of a prolonged struggle with the West Coast monopolies. An admirer of Jefferson, a Jacksonian Democrat of the Locofoco tradition, he saw in land monopoly the cause of poverty. By taxing away the unearned increment in land values, or virtually confiscating ground rents, he would break up the great speculative holdings in the West, check the dissipation of the national domain, and weaken franchise monopolies of all kinds. Abolition of all other taxes would destroy the monopolies dependent upon the protective tariff. Thus a single, decisive use of the taxing power would restore both liberty and equality of opportunity to American economic life while at the same time it would check the urban movement, revive agriculture, and enrich rural life. . . .

The examples of effective intercourse between the rural West and the urban world, whether within or outside the region, could be increased still further by reference to the agitation for reform of the nation's land policy, led by George M. Julian, and the free-silver movement. They are sufficient, however, to indicate something of the diverse origins and composite character of the western radicalism that burgeoned beyond the Alleghenies in the last third of the century. Western agrarian movements were influenced by at least five schools of reform or radical agitation originating from without the region before 1890. In at least one important field the farmers' movements of the region made a major contribution to democratic thought and action in the same period, while publicists in two western cities initiated the important antitrust and single-tax movements. Such cross-fertilization between eastern and western, urban and rural movements was but one aspect of the larger development of the West, which on intellectual, technological, business, and artistic planes was subject to similar processes of acculturation. In each field the result was a mosaic of indigenous and imported elements, all adapted in greater or lesser degree to the regional *milieu*.

This analysis suggests that in Populism may be found the system of radical thought that emerged in the West from three decades of recurring unrest, agitation, and intercourse with radical and reform movements in the urban world. Although scholars have studied it as a political movement or as the product of social and economic conditions, as a school of thought Populism has been rarely, if ever, subjected to the careful analysis that Socialism, Anarchism, or Communism have received. Yet the Populists themselves regarded Populism as a faith and a creed as well as a program. They exhibited, furthermore, a clear sense of continuity with preceding radical movements. . . .

In taking antimonopolism as its central principle Populism revealed its fundamental identity with all the varied "isms" that had agitated the West during the "Thirty Years' War," as one veteran of radical movements termed the preceding decades of agitation. Populism was laid on foundations quarried from Lockean thought and evangelical Protestantism. Upon this substratum and in the *milieu* supplied by frontier opportunities and corporate repressions Locofocoism had erected the frame of prairie radicalism and built into it an abiding hostility to monopoly. Buttressed and strengthened by the controversies of the postwar decades, the anti-monopoly spirit had attacked railroads, the protective tariff, money monopoly, and the trusts. . . .

Thus in its platform, Populism fulfilled the promise of Locofocism and successive antimonopoly movements although, unlike the earlier working-class champions of equal rights, the Populists sought relief through the extension of governmental action into economic life.

Populism was more than antimonopolism, therefore. It advocated a program of economic collectivism which it urged upon the American people as the only remedy adequate to solve the problem of mon-opoly. . . .

Collectivist though the Populist philosophy was in its demand for state intervention and ownership in the field of monopoly enterprise, it would be a mistake to conclude that it was socialistic either in purpose or spirit. The object of government ownership, as desired by the Populists, just as in the case of the independent regulatory commission championed by the Grangers two decades earlier, was the strengthening of competitive capitalism and the salvation of small enterprise. As the Populists saw it, the chief danger to the American system lay in the threatened de-struction of free enterprise by the rise of an irresponsible, unsocial monopoly system which rested in last analysis upon legislative, executive, and judicial favoritism. . . .

How radical the Populist advocacy of a democratic collectivism was in the light of the existing historical situation can be easily determined. The emotional reaction that it provoked among conservatives was so extreme that in propertied circles it made "Populists" more "a term of reproach than was 'Red' a generation later." . . . It was the obligation of democratic government, the Populists asserted, to extend its fostering care to the weak and to protect them from the strong lest the "produc-ing masses" be enslaved. Only through state intervention, control, and expropriation of the greatest economic aggregations of the day, could the problem of monopoly be solved. . . .

It is apparent that as a radical system Populism was primarily economic in character. Its contributions to political theory and constitutional prac-tice were secondary and derivative rather than of primary importance to the Populists. In order to attack monopoly, to break its hold on the government, and to apply its collectivist program, it was necessary that the government be fully and continually responsive to the public will. To accomplish this the Populists elaborated a program of direct democracy, which they offered as a corrective for the feebly functioning system of representative government. The initiative and referendum, the Australian ballot, honest elections, and the popular election of United States Senators were accepted and endorsed at Omaha in a series of supplemental resolutions that were attached to but not made an integral part of the platform. Although they were regarded undoubtedly as desirable in themselves, they were linked in Populist eyes with the larger objective of subjecting corporate capitalism to the control of the democratic state. . . .

[The] third fundamental concept in Populist economic theory, which it inherited from earlier labor and agrarian movements, was none other than the "labor-cost theory of value" as the economists term it. . . . The adherents of this theory regarded capital as the product of labor alone, possessing "no independent power of production" of its own. As such, they thought that it deserved little or no reward. . . . Loyal to this philosophy of wealth the Populists at Omaha asserted that the middleman, the financier, the railroad promoters with their watered stock and monopoly rates, the bankers and mortgage holders, and the organizers of "trusts and combines" were all nonproducers. They were profiting from bad laws and the perversion of democratic government at the expense of the producing masses who, by this process, were being so impoverished that they were "degenerating into European conditions."

Since urban labor suffered from these evils as much as the farmers, since it was denied the right to organize and, in addition, was assailed by hired bands of Pinkerton detectives, the Omaha convention urged it to join the agrarians in an independent political alliance. By means of the ballot box, they could promote a peaceful revolution in American government and economic life. . . .

The effectiveness of the Populist appeal to urban labor depended on the degree to which the labor movement still adhered to the producers' economic philosophy with its labor-cost theory and antimonopolist creed. . . . The story of the labor movement in the late eighties and early nineties centers upon the struggle between the new trades unionism and the older school of labor reform with its producers' philosophy that had united wage earner and farmer in a common faith over six decades.

It was entirely normal, therefore, for the leaders of the farmers' alliances and for agrarian advocates of a third party to confer with Terence V. Powderly rather than with Samuel Gompers between 1889 and 1892. Unfortunately for the Populists, the swift decline of the Knights of Labor, champions of the older philosophy of American wage earners, made them an insufficient recruiting ground. The trades union leaders, on the other hand, apart from their job-conscious, autonomous outlook, were hardly conciliated by Populist preference for the leaders of the rival labor movement. . . . The success of the Populists in recruiting a following from the ranks of organized labor depended, therefore, upon whether the wage earners' attachment for the older and more distinctively American philosophy of labor reform was greater than its loyalty to the newer, imported trades unionism. In 1892 the hold of the latter seems to have been stronger. . . .

The depression years . . . [of the 1890's, however,], tended to force organized labor back into the older philosophy and justified making one more attempt to form a common front with the agrarian movement. This presented the Populists with their long-sought opportunity to recruit heavily from urban labor. It furnished the acid test of a radical creed based upon antimonopolism, the labor-cost theory of wealth, and belief in the common interests of all producers, which offered a limited but clearly defined economic collectivism as the goal of the farmer-labor alliance.

Perhaps because they have been preoccupied with interpretations derived from the older Turnerism, historians are just beginning to inquire into this neglected aspect of the Populist movement. When it is given full attention it will be found that the greatest problem of ideological conflict and adaptation produced by the attempted coalition did not develop out of a clash between Populism and the half-formulated philosophy of a shattered trades unionism. It occurred, instead, between the indigenous radicalism that Populism had inherited from decades of cross-fertilization between urban and agrarian radical movements, and an imported, proletarian Socialism which made its first great appeal to English-speaking wage earners in America in the depression-ridden nineties. At least some of the zeal with which the Populist national headquarters and Congressional delegation turned to free silver in 1895–1896 was the result of this far more irreconcilable conflict. The tendency of the strong antimonopoly bloc within the party to come to provisional terms with the Socialists on the basis of government ownership of all monopolies, which Henry D. Lloyd and the Nationalists supported, motivated some of the steamroller tactics with which Herman E. Taubeneck and Senator William V. Allen deprived the powerful antimonopolist-Nationalist-labor-and-Socialist element at the St. Louis convention of effective expression in 1896 and delivered the People's Party into the hands of the free-silver Democracy. This precipitated the withdrawal of the labor and left wing elements from all association with the Populists.

Leaderless, lacking a separate party organization after the turn of the century, the antimonopolist radicalism of the West survived as a vital force in American thought and politics. . . . Populist antimonopolist collectivism was re-enforced in the new century in America by the social awakening of the middle class and continued as the central feature of the neo-democratic movement. Essentially American still, somewhat less extreme in the devices that it advocated as the means of governing the economic forces of the day, it produced nevertheless a new crop of "American radicals." . . . Led by Robert M. LaFollette, Hiram Johnson, George W. Norris, and the Bryan brothers, they continued the old fight against the railroads, tariff, trusts, "Wall Street," and corporate exploitation of the public domain. Less extreme in their collectivism than the Populists had been, they borrowed the agrarian conception of the democratic welfare state and employed the independent regulatory commission as their chief agency in subjecting American capitalism to a system of government regulation and control that has expanded with each revival of the democratic movement. Thus the alleged radicalism with which the "New Deal" has multiplied the number of regulatory agencies and commissions and ventured upon public ownership in the electric power industry, as well as its confused and contradictory banking and monetary policies, can be traced to "the general philosophy and specific ideas" of the Greenback, Granger, and Populist movements of the late nineteenth-century West. . . .

VICTOR C. FERKISS

Populist Influences on American Fascism

In response to the hysteria of the McCarthy period during
the early 1950's, some concerned scholars searched for the
genesis of what they conceived to be an American fascism.
Most identified the Populist movement of the 1890's as the
prototype of political irrationalism. In this selection Victor C.
Ferkiss discusses the Populist roots of twentieth-century reaction.

. . . Populism is used herein as a generic term to denote not merely
the People's Party, or Populism properly so-called, but such closely allied
movements as the Greenback party, the Bryan free silver crusades,
La Follette Progressivism, and similar manifestations of primarily agrarian revolt against domination by Eastern financial and industrial interests.

The Populist economic program was, of course, tailored to the needs
of the farmers of the prairies. The class struggle throughout American
history has traditionally been waged not by laborers against employers,
but by debtors against creditors. Agrarian discontent had a long history
prior to the Civil War. Following that conflict the West was opened to
settlers under the Homestead Act. These settlers needed money for
capital and were dependent upon the railroads to sell their goods. The
value of money appreciated so greatly that they had difficulty in paying
their debts. The railroads, controlled by Eastern financial interests, were
able to exploit them. The local governments and press were to a considerable extent the creatures of Eastern money, as were most of the
local banks. A struggle began for a government which would regulate
credit and control the railroads so that the settlers might prosper as
middle-class landowners. This struggle reached its climax in Bryan's
campaign of 1896 and abated thereafter as a result of the increasing
amount of gold in circulation.

Economic Program. The motives of these Populists were similar to

SOURCE: Abridged from Victor C. Ferkiss, "Populist Influences on American
Facism," *Western Political Quarterly*, X (June, 1957), 350–373. Reprinted by permission of the University of Utah, copyright owners, and Victor C. Ferkiss.

those which produced the rank-and-file twentieth-century American fascist. The Populists' aim was not the destruction of capitalism as they knew it, but was rather its preservation and extension. They were interested in protecting capitalism and the small entrepreneur from abuse at the hands of the monopolist and the banker. Populism was a middle-class movement; the Populists saw in Eastern finance capitalism a force which, unless controlled, would destroy their status and reduce them to proletarians.

The Populist economic program centered about the need for public control of credit. Senator Peffer of Kansas described the Populist economic creed in the following words:

If there is any part of the Populist's creed which he regards as more important than another, and which, therefore, may be taken as leading, it is that which demands the issue and circulation of national money, made by authority of the people for their use, money that they will at any and all times be responsible for, money that persons in business can procure on good security at cost, money handled only by public agencies, thus doing away with all back issues of paper to be used as money.

The extent of Bryan's faith in cheap credit as a panacea is reminiscent of the Chartist faith in universal suffrage as the sovereign remedy for social ills: ". . . When we have restored the money of the Constitution all other necessary reforms will be possible; but . . . until this is done there is no other reform that can be accomplished."

This, then, was the most important plank in the Populist economic platform—the restoration to the people of their "sovereign power" to control money; private control is held to be a violation of the Constitution and a usurpation of a governmental function. In addition, the railroads and similar interests must also be controlled by a strong, central government capable of crushing the selfish few in the interests of the nation as a whole.

Populists believe in the exercise of national authority in any and every case where the general welfare will be promoted thereby. . . .

Populism teaches the doctrine that the rights and interests of the whole body of the people are superior, and, therefore, paramount to those of individuals. The Populist believes in calling in the power of the people in every case where the public interest requires it or will be promoted.

Public power will protect the national interest against the selfish few.

Though the People's party flirted with the labor theory of value their inferences from it resembled those of Locke rather than those of Marx. Populism was no attack on private property or the wage system. It was the attempt of its adherents to retain the former and avoid becoming subject to the latter; hence Populism's lack of sympathy for and appeal to urban labor. Despite some concessions during the 1896 campaign, Bryan's appeal to the voters, even the Eastern workers, was to put their trust in free silver as the basic solution to all of their difficulties.

Nationalism and Anti-Semitism. Nationalism was to be found in Populism principally in the form of a suspicious isolationism which regarded foreign involvements as inimical to the national interest and as existing solely to promote the interests of Eastern capitalists. Economic nationalism was reflected in Peter Cooper's proposal for protective tariffs, and Populists often advocated severe restrictions on immigration.

The protest against financial interests was frequently associated with a hatred of cities as centers of exploitation and of moral as well as political corruption. Nationalistic impulses cloaked themselves in the garb of sectionalism and Bryan referred to the East as "the enemy's country." Dwight MacDonald has noted that because of the varied national origins of its population, its geographic isolation, and its relatively higher standard of living, the venom of American nationalism will ever be directed against New York City, "which is properly and correctly considered an outpost of Europe on this continent." Populist and, later, fascist nationalism confirms this judgment.

The final ingredient of Populist nationalism was the anti-Semitism endemic throughout the rural West. The correlation between hatred of Jews (though in a mild form and wholly without dialectical formulation) with sentiment for Bryan has been noted by Professor Oscar Handlin. The prairie farmer associated the Jew with the merchant, the financier, and the corrupt and domineering Eastern city.

Populist racial hostility was directed against those believed capable of destroying the small farmer's economic status and way of life. To the Midwesterner, the Negro presented no problem since he was not physically present and since he (unlike the Jew) could hardly be pictured as scheming to undermine the position of Midwestern farmers and shopkeepers from afar.

Plebiscitary Democracy. Populism's predisposition to anti-Semitism and to nationalism and its suspicion of the corruption of urban life are all tendencies opposed to those trends which issue in democratic socialism in the humanist tradition; these proclivities more closely coincide with the patterns of conservative or fascist social beliefs. There is a tendency on the part of observers to overlook the true import of these propensities because of the role played by Populist and Progressive movements in the development of American democracy. To these movements America largely owes, for better or for worse, the direct primary, popular election of senators, the initiative, the referendum and recall, and the Wisconsin tradition of clean, efficient government, conducted with the assistance of experts.

Yet some qualifications must be made of the popular conception of Populism as a democratic or liberal force. First, the agrarian trend toward political reform was rarely based upon any broad ideas about human freedom or the fuller human life. Populist-inspired reforms were instrumental. The farmer wanted particular political changes because he felt they were needed to effect the defeat of the "money power" and to gain for farmers certain direct economic benefits. From their support of these measures we can not infer a willingness on the part of the Populists to support egalitarian measures which would conduce to the benefit of others with different substantive aims.

Secondly, all these reforms serve to strengthen not liberalism but direct, plebiscitary democracy. They are designed to make the will of the majority immediately effective and to sweep away intervening institutions such as the legislatures, the older political parties, and the courts, which have all been corrupted by the money power. . . .

If the existing parties are controlled by a gigantic conspiracy and the nation is at the mercy of an "international gold trust" then the trust's opponents cannot be expected to treat these conspirators in quite the fashion one would treat honest dissenters. The rhetoric of "Bloody Bridles" Waite and Mary Ellen Lease is strong even for their times. It bespeaks an unwillingness to compromise, a crusading zeal, and an inability to conceive of a sincerely motivated opposition that ill befits any group participating in parliamentary democracy. So, too, the oft-repeated charge that the press is controlled by special interests, whether true or not, leaves the way open for insuring "true" freedom of the press through the enactment of measures which might endanger freedom of speech as it has traditionally been understood in Anglo-Saxon law.

William Jennings Bryan many years later was to shed light on the devotion of the Populist crusade to liberal institutions when he held that the people in prosecuting Scopes were simply asserting their right "to have what they want in government, including the kind of education they want." The people are the rulers and "a man cannot demand a salary for saying what his employers do not want said."

In short, Populist political thought is compatible in spirit with the plebiscitary democracy of a Huey Long or a Hitler. This is not to say that Populists and Progressives universally opposed free speech as such or that Weaver, Lindbergh, Sr., or the elder La Follette would ever have seized power and then denied to the opposition an opportunity to regain power through constitutional means. They did believe that the opposition, including the press, was corrupt and antisocial; but they still believed that an aroused people could regain control of the government from the selfish few who had usurped it. It is only with the passing of time that Populism degenerates into fascism and comes to believe that the power of the enemy and his ability to corrupt the people is so great that constitutitonal institutions are a useless sham and that the people can only effectuate their will by modifying these institutions in form or spirit in such a manner as to deny their use to the conspiratorial enemy. . . .

· 4 ·

NORMAN POLLACK

Fear of Man:
Populism, Authoritarianism,
and the Historian

In recent debate on the place of the Populist movement in American political history, Norman Pollack has emerged as an enthusiastic champion of the Populists. Rejecting the contention that the Populists were irrational and reactionary, Dr. Pollack instead places them in the mainstream of the radical tradition in American politics. In this selection he summarizes the nature of Populism.

Populists sought the establishment of a just social order founded on a democratized industrial system and a transformation of social values, each reinforcing the other in the direction of greater concern for the welfare of all. They rejected unbridled individualism and the competitive mentality, maintaining instead that neither a few nor a class should enjoy the benefits of civilization. The quality of life of the masses was

SOURCE: Abridged from Norman Pollack, "Fear of Man: Populism, Authoritarianism, and the Historian," *Agricultural History*, 39 (April, 1965), 59-67. Reprinted by permission of *Agricultural History* and Norman Pollack.

the index by which to measure social improvement. There was little of the self-conscious in the Populist enshrinement of the common man: Society must be attuned to *his* needs, or it ceases to be democratic. Yet in place of a society suffused with an equalitarian spirit, a society which is responsive to the growth of all and oppresses none, Populists pointed to the mortgage-ridden farmer, the unemployed worker, and the so-called "tramp" moving from one town to the next in search of work. In place of the free citizen, deriving benefit from his labor on the farm or in the factory, determining the policies under which he is to be governed, and enjoying a sense of dignity in his daily life, Populists found man to be impoverished, voiceless and degraded. Thus their critique of existing arrangements went beyond economic conditions to embrace the question of the individual's plight, his dehumanization, his loss of autonomy in a society which rapidly reduced him to a dependent state.

Their protest was a consequence of the times, not only of the 1890's but of the preceding two decades, where the rule was all-pervasive hardship: declining crop prices; increased tenantry and share-cropping; an appreciating dollar; the ever-present mortgage in the West, and even more pressing, the crop-lien in the South; business combinations, tariffs and artificially high prices in the manufacturing sector; a railroad system which practiced discrimination against the farmer, gave preferential treatment to favored shippers, dominated state legislatures, blackmailed towns into issuing bonds, held large tracts of land off the market, refused to assume a proper share of the tax burden, and contributed to the creation of a closed system for the distribution of goods. Populists recognized that the industrial worker confronted similar conditions: subsistence wages, company towns, frequent unemployment, and the use of coercion in the form of Pinkertons, militias and imported strikebreakers to prevent him from rectifying the situation by forming unions. Finally, Populists confronted a political framework where grievances were never aired, and if anything, were obscured by the raising of all manner of diversions from the "bloody shirt" to the cry of tariff. Populists addressed themselves to each of these issues, as well as to others of a like character. Theirs was indeed a response to the times, but it was also something more; it was an attempt to transcend those times, and in the act of transcending the existing social context, to pose an alternative conception for the development of America.

Populism was not a retrogressive social force. It did not seek to restore a lost world of yeomen farmers and village artisans. The reverse was true. Of course Populists borrowed from the past, but they borrowed selectively. What they took was not a petrified pre-industrialism but a set of political principles, principles which they believed could be applied at any point, present and future as well as past. From Jefferson and Jackson came the recurring theme of "equal rights to all, and special privileges to none," from these and other sources came the labor theory of value, and from the Constitution came the commerce clause and other passages sanctioning government regulation in the general interest. Beyond this Populists did not go, for their gaze was directed to what lay ahead rather than to what lay behind.

In seeking to democratize rather than abolish industrialism, Populism was a progressive social force. Yet its orientation was progressive not only because it based its remedies on an accommodation to social change, but also because in pursuing these policies it adopted a highly affirmative stance. The two are difficult to separate. For to be forward-looking while not at the same time possessing confidence that men do have the power to remake their institutions and values is to be as helpless, as escapist, as the one who rests content with a restoration of the past. To acquiesce in social change does not, by itself, insure a progressive outlook. A more positive frame of mind is required, and this Populists had. Woven into the texture of their thought was the insistence that men *could* consciously make their future. Populists contended that there is nothing inevitable about misery and squalor, nothing irreversible about the tendencies toward the concentration of wealth and the legitimation of corporate power. Not the impersonal tendency but men themselves are responsible for the contemporary society, and for this reason men can—according to Populists, must—alter the course of that society in a humanistic direction. What stands out, then, about the Populist mind is an affirmation of man, a faith in man's capability to shape his own history.

This positive aspect of Populist thought is not exhausted by the fact that numerous concrete proposals were offered to attack existing problems. More important was the attitude behind their formulation, and ultimately, the attitude toward the relation beween the individual and his government. In keeping with the emphasis on men as the wielders of power and the source of legislation, Populists held that there was nothing sacred about the status quo, or for that matter, about the institutions which safeguarded that status quo. They did not repudiate the notion of law and order but they did assert that *existing* law was class law, intended to protect the rich at the expense of the poor, and that order meant in the contemporary context the imposition of legalized repression to prevent the broadening of that law. Thus Populist reforms stemmed from an attitude of healthy skepticism concerning the sacrosanct nature of government. Since government was no more than an instrument to be used for good or ill by the groups which controlled it, then let the farmers and workers organize to secure that control, and prevent further encroachments on the general welfare.

Yet Populists found even this to be entirely too negative. Government should be more than a neutral observer. It was created to *serve* man, and must be a dynamic force in bringing about equality. Thus, Populists contended, government must be a responsive tool, one which can actively intervene in the economy to regulate matters affecting the public interest, and when necessary own outright monopolies of this character, and can just as actively aid the underprivileged and work for a more equitable distribution of wealth. . . .

·5·

WALTER T. K. NUGENT

Some Parameters of Populism

In his studies of the Kansas Populists Walter T. K. Nugent has taken issue with those who believe that the Populists were antisemitic and chauvinistic nativists as well as with the idea that the Populists were "walking ideologues." Rather, Professor Nugent maintains that Populism was simply an agrarian "response to economic distress." Other attributes of the movement were incidental to this central theme.

Why did people become Populists? Was it chiefly for the reasons that the Populists themselves gave—that they were a victimized economic class? Did Populist rhetoric about money, land, and transportation have any correspondence to actual economic conditions and events? Or were the Populists agitated because of status problems and, hence, liable to be criticized (as they since have been) as neurotic, stubbornly disdainful of reality, and a mucker group recklessly trying to upset the homely but happy applecart of American politics and society?

According to some historians, the Populists overdrew their problems.

SOURCE: Abridged from Walter T. K. Nugent, "Some Parameters of Populism," *Agricultural History*, XL (October, 1966), 255–270. Reprinted by permission of *Agricultural History* and Walter T. K. Nugent.

Things were grim indeed, but the violent protest reflected in Populist rhetoric had no firm base in reality. Populism was an aberration, rather than a chapter, in American liberal reform. However, other writers have maintained that there were sufficient economic grounds for Populist political protest. This study confirms the latter view and refines it at a number of points. . . .

What follows, then, is an attempt to answer the following questions. Did Populists and non-Populists, in the same time and place, differ significantly, and if so to what degree, and to what degree of certainty, in their social, economic, and cultural characteristics and conditions? If differences did exist, were they the differences implied in the political rhetoric of the time? More succinctly: were the Populists' calamity howls justified by actual conditions? If they were, then presumably these conditions related somehow to the serious shift in political behavior undertaken by most of the people who became Populists around 1890. If conditions did not support rhetoric, then some very different sort of hypothesis about why people became Populists (for example, a sociopsychological one) would be justified. . . .

I selected for comparison political groups in one Great Plains state in which Populists abounded, namely, Kansas. Two pairs of groups lent themselves to this. The first pair were Republican and Populist state legislators, members of the Kansas House elected in 1890 and the Senate elected in 1892. The second pair were candidates on the Republican, Democratic, and Populist tickets for county offices in nine Kansas counties from 1889 through 1892. These groups represented the best compromise between the typical but anonymous rank-and-file voter, on the one hand, and the thoroughly documented but atypical high official (Governor, Congressman), on the other. . . .

In all of . . . [the] comparisons of Republican and Populist state legislators, one difference stands out markedly—rural-urban cleavage. Populists and Republicans were much alike: they were about the same age; many from each party had served the Union cause; they differed in some (but not many) respects as to their birthplaces; they went to much the same churches; they had attended or avoided schools about equally; and they shared a common culture. What distinguished them was that Populists had held political office much less often, and the great majority of them were active farmers. Whether the same social and cultural characteristics obtained among the rank-and-file mass of Populist and Republican voters, the sources do not say. It seems sensible to assume that they did.

Comparisons of Populist and non-Populist county office candidates concerned not only socio-cultural characteristics, which paralleled those just described, but also the mortgage question, about which the Populists complained mightily. Here the differences between the groups outran the similarities. . . .

The Populist was apparently a man of lower capital and of lower speculative energy than a Republican. Although the Populists and Republicans mortgaged land about equally often, the Populist did so far more often than the Republican did, in terms of his total participation in the real estate market. Mortgage distress was not only real, but particularly severe, for the Populists. . . .

Populist mortgages occurred more often in prosperous times, and they were probably entered into to a large extent for purposes of improvement, rather than to alleviate distress. This suggests that a lack of capital beset the Populists, both before the bust when borrowing seemed the best way to get ahead and after the bust when they were probably considered poor credit risks. . . .

The Populist was less able or less willing to speculate—probably both. His real property involvement was probably with a single or a very few pieces of land, constituting his principal or sole real assets. He fought with considerable success to maintain these assets, although he was very hard pressed to do so. His economic enterprise was noticeably more precarious than the Republicans', but he did not sell or mortgage his assets until absolutely necessary, with the exception that he did some mortgaging, probably for improvement or expansion, whenever the pre-1889 money market permitted. . . .

Occupational comparisons for . . . [county office candidates] revealed the same very decided rural-urban cleavage as the legislators did. Republicans included a far greater number of merchants, manufacturers, bankers, loan agents, surveyors, and skilled laborers than did Populists. Republicans outnumbered Populists also, but less decisively, in the categories of medicine, law, and journalism. The two groups were about equally favored with ministers. Again, however, farming was the main occupation of Populists, while Republican farmers were much more scarce. . . .

Among the county office candidates, Republicans edged Populists in Middle Atlantic and Old Northwest nativity. Populists, on the other hand, more frequently were natives of the upper Mississippi Valley or Missouri Valley and the Old Southwest. In these comparisons, therefore, Populists seem to have come more often from recently settled states, Republicans from older ones. As with the legislators, immigrants occurred more frequently among the Populists. The Populist tendency to include the foreign-born, less pronounced among these people than among the legislators, approached but did not quite reach statistical significance. The Republicans in this group were foreign-born in 10.9 percent of the cases, the Populists in 17.9 percent; the federal census of 1890 gave the percentage of foreign-born residents of Kansas as about 10.4 percent.

Again, the Populists do not seem to have been a party of old men; they seem to have been about as active in the Civil War as Republicans had been; they were very heavily rural in contrast to the usually urban-based Republicans; their places of birth and previous out-of-state residence varied, but not according to a systematic pattern; and immigrants were more common among them.

The census included no educational or political data, but it was a unique source of comparative property-holding and land use information. Rural-urban cleavage was extremely significant statistically, confirming observations already noted. The most important fact, in the context of everything that has already been said, is that the size and value of a residential farm did not differ greatly according to the political affiliation of the man who operated it. The average acreage of a Republican farm, either mean or median, was only slightly larger than that of a Populist. The assessed valuation of these farms did not vary significantly according to party affiliation, nor did the value of the equipment on them. These were the farms of residence; for Populists one would guess that they were probably their main or only properties.

If this is so, it would indicate that Populists were probably not as well capitalized as the Republicans, in terms of total net worth, but it would support a contention that the farms they operated and from which they derived the bulk of their income were competitive commercial enterprises. The safe conclusion seems to be this: the Populists may have been generally less wealthy and more sensitive to hard times, but to call them a "have-not" group in relation to their neighbors would be a gross oversimplification. . . .

Before undertaking this study, it seemed to me anomalous that the Populists seemed in so many ways to resemble their Republican neighbors, yet behaved so differently as political animals. Were they like the Republicans (which would suggest that their behavior was not very rational), or were they unlike the Republicans? The only hypothesis that seemed to fit was that they were like and unlike the Republicans at the same time, but this answer obviously raised many other questions requiring somewhat refined answers. The analyses of quantitative data just described seem to support not only the idea of simultaneous similarity and dissimilarity, but to indicate where these lay.

To put it very crudely, the Populists seem to have resembled the Republicans in most major discoverable sociological ways and in some economic ways, but their economic situation was more precarious. The generalization is very rough and slurs many qualifications already indicated. Finally and generally, however, the conclusion must be that there was a realistic economic basis to the Populist land issue and, by extension, to money and transportation too, since people already harder pressed would have greater difficulty with the high freight rates and scarce currency and credit that afflicted the section at large. Populists were harder pressed. Tight conditions with regard to mortgages, farm income, and freight costs were more severely felt by those whose capital was less extensive and whose enterprise was more marginal to begin with.

Another conclusion, though a more tentative one, is this. If one defines "yeoman-like" farming as a kind that reflects a desire to own, operate, and remain on a given parcel, and commercially oriented farming as characterized by greater transiency and speculativeness, then the Populists actually did lean more to the "yeoman" type. Their "yeoman myth" rhetoric was by no means self-delusive or unthinking. The Populist self-image as a yeoman farmer, to the extent that it did exist, derived from a real mirror of events, though one often cloudy and distorted, and not solely from imagination and folk tales. Perhaps it is also well to remember that "yeoman" and "commercial" agrarianism have a polarity that exists only in logic. Tension and aggression would have resulted only if the two were in psychic conflict. But the Populists were not aware of the distinction, nor subject to the psychic stress that might have resulted. To the degree that the polarity applies at all, the Populists themselves were situated at some point on a continuum between the two, nearer the yeoman end than the Republicans, and there they perched harmoniously.

Populists, then, resembled Republicans sociologically, differed from them economically, and were more "yeoman-like"; in short, they were scratching where they itched. These are the main conclusions. It should be remembered that Populist political rhetoric did not correspond perfectly, sometimes not even approximately, to economic, social, or political realities. It is impossible to measure the difference precisely; these data establish no "coefficient of inaccuracy" or "standard deviation" of rhetoric from reality. That rhetoric came from many pens and many throats. Some of it was mild, some sharp and pungent, some of it reeked. It should also be remembered that, while variations in economic conditions and to a lesser extent in social background did in fact exist, very few were black and white. Enough exceptions have already appeared to forbid one from concluding that Populists were wholly unlike Republicans economically, or wholly like them socially, or that, therefore, Populism attracted its membership entirely as a result of economic distresses affecting them in particular. Populist behavior was a chosen response to economic distress. It was not determined by this distress.

One can support with more confidence the interpretation that Populism was primarily a political response to economic trouble, both real and felt. It was not a case study in class struggle, nor a group (one hundred thousand-plus strong) of walking ideologues, nor a group of one-gallus mudsills fighting established society and the progressive trends within it, nor a group of neurotic malcontents trying to throttle their equally hard-pressed but saner neighbors. It was, instead, a momentarily very large and diverse group of people, seeking by a handy means to preserve themselves against such inimical forces in their society as were threatening, in very concrete ways, their personal arrangements and, therefore, their view of life.

CHAPTER XV

The West and American Religion

I

In his essay, "The Mission as a Frontier Institution in the Spanish-American Colonies," Herbert E. Bolton described the way in which Spanish missionaries of the great Roman Catholic religious orders helped to advance the Spanish-American frontiers during the colonial period. With the encouragement of the government, the churchmen developed mission communities among the Indians of the frontier where they taught them the rudiments of agriculture, manual arts and Christianity. Although many Indians failed to survive the impact of Spanish civilization, life in the missions prepared the remainder for existence in settled communities under the government of Spanish officials and the administration of pastoral clergy. To the Spanish monarch and his ministers, Bolton maintained, the missionaries were instruments of the state in expanding its colonial territory: they explored new regions and described them in the journals of their expeditions, they helped to establish Spanish claims to new regions and they rendered the Indians docile. Shortly before they were dissolved in 1834, 21 missions of Mexican California served some 31,000 Indians who assisted in tending almost 400,000 cattle, more than 300,000 smaller animals and some 60,000 horses. The harvest fields of these establishments produced in excess of 100,000 bushels of grain and orchard, garden, loom, shop and forge added still more to their production.

On the Anglo-American frontier, the Indian mission was less important than in Spanish-America. In 1819 the Superintendent of the Indian Trade reported that he knew of only a few schools for Indian children which religious organizations maintained in the Indian country. There were also three which were located in the older settlements. In all, this was an unimpressive showing in comparison to the Spanish missions in California. Professor Bolton suggested that the Spanish lacked the manpower and resources to settle an empire and in default used the native peoples to achieve that purpose. The British colonists and the

Americans of the early national period were largely Protestant in religion and had no organizations corresponding to the Roman Catholic orders. But more important than this consideration, Anglo-Americans were mainly interested in their own economic and religious welfare and were eager to develop the lands of North America themselves. Their abundant numbers, their cultural values, and their belief that the Indians were of an inferior civilization all prepared the Anglo-Americans to put their major dependence on military force in dealing with the Indians.

Some Americans did believe that organized religion should play a role in the Indian policy of the United States. The first Secretary of War, Henry Knox, suggested that missionaries be selected to live among the Indians, and help them to become farmers. But in a nation committed to the separation of church and state, few believed that the government should subsidize Indian missions as religious institutions. The churchman in the role of secular educator was less offensive to American politicians and during the first half of the nineteenth century the missionaries of a number of denominations or religious societies received education funds, provided in Indian treaties or from the "Civilization Fund" established by Congress in 1819. Such aid stimulated a small efflorescence of church-sponsored educational activity among the Indians. Thirty-eight schools among the Indians reported 281 teachers and 1,159 students in 1826.

Organized religion challenged the Indian policy of the United States most dramatically in the South during the 1820's and 1830's. Missionaries of the American Board of Commissioners for Foreign Missions and other agencies worked industriously among the southern tribes in this era, reinforcing the Cherokees' desire to retain their remaining tribal lands east of the Mississippi River, encouraging them to learn Sequoya's alphabet, helping them to draft a constitution and a code of laws, and assisting them in establishing and running their newspaper, the *Cherokee Phoenix.* The state of Georgia imprisoned the most famous of these missionaries, Samuel A. Worcester, and a companion, when he refused to obey the laws in which the Georgia legislators proclaimed their authority over Cherokee lands in their state. John Marshall sustained the missionary's position in *Worcester* v. *Georgia,* but the efforts of the missionary band failed to avert the Cherokee "Trail of Tears." The work of Isaac McCoy and a little band of Baptist missionaries among the tribes of the Old Northwest during the same years was energetic but less spectacular than the labors of the Cherokee missionaries. Like many churchmen, McCoy hoped that the Indians might be gathered together and so elevated in status that they could have their own territory and eventually an Indian state.

American missionaries made their greatest contributions to national objectives in the Pacific Northwest. That story began when several Indians of that distant region journeyed to St. Louis in 1831 to visit the legendary William Clark and to learn more of the black-robed priests whom Iroquois trappers had described to them. A Methodist journal portrayed them as poor heathen in search of the white man's religion and plans materialized for a Methodist mission to the Flatheads during the stirring of interest which the story provoked. When Jason Lee, his nephew Daniel, and several lay assistants went to the Pacific Northwest in 1834, they did not, curiously enough, settle among the Flatheads, but selected a mission site in the fertile Willamette valley to the south of Fort Vancouver, the Hudson's Bay Company establishment on the lower Columbia River. In soliciting aid to maintain their western enterprise, the Methodist missionaries advertised the Oregon country and their mission in the Willamette valley became a magnet for American settlers, some of whom in turn became outspoken advocates of annexing the Pacific Northwest. Although the Lee mission served the national interest, it did rather less for the Indians of the region. Other Methodist missionaries came to assist the Lees but the churchmen disagreed among themselves as to whether they were helping the scattered and dying Indians of the Willamette. The Whitmans and other missionaries of the American Board also established themselves in the Pacific Northwest, but the Roman Catholics, including the indefatigable Father De Smet, subsequently inherited the Indian mission fields there to a considerable extent.

Seventy-seven missionaries were serving among the Indians in the United States in 1861 of whom 19 were Roman Catholics. Church schools often supported by government funds, were of great importance in the acculturation of many Indians after the Civil War. In that era also, as we have seen, President Grant began the policy of allowing the church denominations to nominate Indian agents. But in retrospect, the religious energy marshalled in behalf of the Indian was a rather small part of the American missionary impulse.

II

Although even pious immigrants might dream of the wealth and social status that could, perhaps, be theirs in the New World, the statements, behavior and traditions of the original settlers in New England and Pennsylvania show that religious considerations had been a powerful stimulus to emigration. Religious dissenters from the Massachusetts Bay Colony contributed to the early settlement of Rhode Island, New Hampshire and Connecticut. But religious motivation was not the major incentive that carried pioneers to the late colonial and national frontiers. There are exceptions to this generalization in the history of the United States; some settlers did move to the frontier to escape the dominant religions of older settlements or to establish religious communities in the West. In size and dramatic impact the migration of the members of the Church of Jesus Christ of Latter Day Saints eclipsed all others of this sort. Although the basic motivation of most western emigrants was economic in nature, religious concern often affected the details of western settlement. The tendency of New England Congregationalists or Pennsylvania Presbyterians to cluster together in western settlements, for instance, sometimes reflected their desire to maintain congenial religious institutions.

Students of American religious history disagree about the impact of the frontier on American religion and for that matter American religion on frontier society. We can, however, offer some generalizations that most scholars will accept. The Revolutionary Era disorganized most American churches, some already shocked by the Great Awakening of the 1740's. The division of the colonists into Patriots and Tories rent congregations; neighbors came to fear and distrust one another; some church members fled or were driven into exile; others left their communities to serve in state or continental forces. Military campaigns diverted the minds of men from religious concerns. Some national leaders professed themselves to be deists. In those states where the Anglican Church had been the state church, Americans ended its established status. The first amendment of the federal Constitution endorsed the separation of church and state. Such was the situation when Americans began to move westward during the early national period in numbers which had never been approached during the colonial period. This tremendous flow of people into the great valley of the Mississippi posed religious problems both to the migrants and to the residents of the seaboard states.

If he was devout, the settler was indeed challenged by the frontier. How was he to reinforce his faith, to worship under the guidance of the clergy of his preference, to implant religious ideals in his children, and to insure that his church helped provide social decorum and community stability in the West? Such questions must have concerned many western settlers. The western migration challenged the church laity and leaders of the older areas as well. How could they help the westerners? How could they prevent their friends and relatives in the West from becoming unchurched, their children ignorant of God and His commandments? More than simple altruism was at stake. Westerners bought eastern goods on credit, and they borrowed eastern money to buy western land or to improve it. Western representatives joined easterners in Congress to amend and supplement the laws of the nation. Not too far in the future western men might be a majority in Congress. If religious sentiment fosters business and civic virtue, as many residents of the older regions believed, easterners would derive practical benefit from supporting western religious institutions.

But how devout was the westerner of the early national period? Of some 3,500,000 Americans in 1790, some 20,000 were Roman Catholics and about 6,000 were Jews. Nominally the remainder were Protestants. But one recent writer argues bluntly that the United States was a heathen nation—"One of the most needy mission fields in the world." Eastern churchmen, as for example, Presbyterians, Congregationalists, Baptists, Dutch Reformed and Quakers would hardly have accepted this as a description of their own region. The problem of the West, however, was very real to them and they feared that westerners were lapsing into infidelity and barbarism.

Some church historians distinguish between the response of churchmen to the frontier in the northern United States and their reaction in the southern states. Northeastern Congregationalists, Presbyterians and Baptists, as well as some smaller Protestant groups, considered the West to be a mission field, which they must aid to the best of their ability. In a Plan of Union of 1801 the Presbyterians and Congregationalists agreed to cooperate in serving their western communicants, and specified that either Congregational or Presbyterian pastors might serve congregations of either denomination. Since the major distinctions between Congregationalists and Presbyterians were organizational rather than doctrinal, the arrangement worked well for many years and contributed to the most efficient use of the resources of these church groups.

Easterners were concerned that adequate numbers of well-trained clergymen serve the West. During the early years of the Republic, individual congregations, synods or other regional church bodies sent missionaries to the frontier. The system was inefficient and eastern churchmen developed organizations to manage the home mission effort of one or more denominations. Drawing support from the Presbyterians, the Congregationalists and some smaller church bodies, the American Home Missionary Society dispatched missionaries westward and aided them after they had selected a mission field. The organization also sent books, clothes, and other aid to resident western clergymen whose charges could not support them adequately. The Methodists and Baptists developed somewhat similar organizations. Indeed the major Protestant denominations developed a veritable squadron of voluntary associations to fight religious ignorance in the West. The American Education Society supported religious auxiliaries and helped to found and maintain seminaries. The American Sunday School Union, the American Bible Society and the American Tract Society all played important roles in the struggle to redeem the West. During the late 1820's the societies mounted a great "Valley Campaign" to insure that there was a Bible in every home, a Sunday School in every district and a pastor for every thousand souls beyond the Appalachians.

The response of northern Protestants to the challenge of the frontier was impressive. It is also true that the Presbyterians and the Congregationalists were the largest American denominations at the end of the colonial period and that they did not acquire western followings to the extent that this fact would suggest. When these groups terminated the Plan of Union at mid century, Congregationalists accused the Presbyterians of milking Congregational cows but making only Presbyterian cheese. Such recrimination over division of the souls was beside the point. Both denominations had proven to be less popular in the West than other church groups. Particularly in the trans-Appalachian South but in the northwestern states to some extent as well, the Methodists and Baptists had grown in numbers with amazing rapidity. We can seek the explanation for these developments in the doctrinal messages, or the administrative organizations of the church bodies or perhaps in a combination of the two.

In the search for western souls, the denomination which best adapted its organization to the special needs of the new western communities gained an advantage over less flexible groups. Struggling to survive the first few years of farm making, pioneers were often too few, too busy and too impoverished to raise a church building or to call a pastor to serve them. They might not even realize that eastern churchmen would perhaps send them a minister or other spiritual aid if asked. Ideal in such situations was the Methodist system in which enthusiastic circuit riders ministered to a number of "classes" and a presiding elder supervised a number of circuits. Sometimes the chinking was still wet between the logs of frontier cabins when the circuit rider appeared and volunteered to hold service. The Baptists also had a flexible and econonomical organization well adapted to the frontier, for they raised members of their congregations to the pulpit who continued to support themselves in their accustomed occupations, while serving as ministers.

Most of the American Protestants of the early national period subscribed to an evangelical doctrine. They believed that man's condition normally was one of sin, that God had revealed his grace by giving

Christ to mankind, and that man must be redeemed by his faith in God and in His word. Such redemption occurred when the sinner experienced conversion. Calvinist doctrine as generally held by Presbyterians and Congregationalists presumed that an elect was predestined to be saved and that the individual's efforts or his conviction that he had obtained grace would not necessarily bring him among the elect. God was all powerful and inscrutable, and his justice was not to be questioned. The degree of emphasis which American Protestant groups placed upon the various elements in this presentation varied as did supplementary doctrine and detail. Countering the Calvinist emphasis upon predestination and election was the Arminian doctrine that men could of their own free will choose the way of Christ and that good works could contribute to eternal happiness if they were the sincere expression of Christian love.

There were also differences in the style with which churchmen approached doctrine. The Presbyterians and the Congregationalists believed that conversion was a rational experience, reached by the application of logic to man's religious condition. In contrast was "heart religion" in which conversion was largely an emotional experience, induced by the penitent's overwhelming consciousness of sin and his sense that God's claim upon him was just. Revivalism was a method which American ministers had used during the colonial period to induce the conversion experience, and it was found in all evangelical churches, but the degree to which ministers allowed emotionalism to color their efforts varied greatly. So powerfully did some divines exhort their listeners that conversion might involve physical manifestations in which the limbs of converts jerked uncontrollably or they fell in paroxysms to the ground.

When religious excitement developed in Kentucky during the late 1790's and a great series of emotional, outdoor revivals were held there, Presbyterian, Methodist and Baptist ministers all participated. But the Presbyterians distrusted the conversions effected under such circumstances and soon moderated their revivalism. The Methodists, on the other hand, made the camp meeting revival uniquely their own during the early national period. Simple, powerful and emotional in style and stressing free grace, Methodist divines used it as the setting in which thousands of westerners experienced conversion. Peter Cartwright and other "sons of thunder" who warned their audiences that they were hair-hung and breeze-blown over Hell became frontier legends. A historian of the camp meeting, Charles Johnson, argues that the sensational features of the camp meeting have been exaggerated. By no means all Methodist clergymen were "sons of thunder," he maintains, and in older western communities particularly, the camp meeting became a rather sedate affair. Whatever its true nature the camp meeting apparently helped to make the Methodists the largest American Protestant denomination in 1850. Next in numbers were the Baptists who also used an emotional revivalistic message in which the harsher Calvinist tenets were muted. And indeed by the 1830's Presbyterian and Congregationalist revivalists were preaching a more popular message also.

During the course of these developments westerners questioned the importance which eastern churchmen placed upon the training of clergymen. Educational levels were lower on the frontier, particularly in the South, than in the seaboard regions. Presbyterians and Congregationalists believed that their clergy should undergo considerable formal training. The ability to read the Bible, to apply its precepts to the problems of life and to expound these lessons with some fluency and conviction was all that many westerners believed necessary in their clergymen. Some Baptists became particularly hostile to a trained clergy and most Methodist circuit riders of the early century were informally trained in "Brush College," the lonely reaches of western wood and prairie. Yet they apparently communicated with western congregations more easily than did the eastern seminarians who came to the frontier. To a considerable extent western impatience with eastern standards of training produced the Cumberland Presbyterian schism. But in the interest of both eastern and western churchmen in the training of western clergy one finds the source of many western seminaries and colleges and church influences were also important in fostering elementary education both in the western public schools and through the parochial schools of some immigrant groups.

In the western setting the determined rebel within older denominations could easily win a hearing and support for schismatic doctrine. Thus former Methodists, Baptists and Presbyterians were able to develop a new denomination, the Disciples of Christ, demanding a return to New Testament practices and the rejection of creeds that fallible humans had superimposed upon its tenets. Although there was sometimes cooperation in the great task of saving the West, fierce competition between the denominations developed as well. Its echoes still sound in the Methodist song of the camp-meeting era:

> We've searched the law of heaven,
> Throughout the sacred code;
> Of baptism there, by dipping
> We've never found a word

and in the Baptist rejoinder,

Not *at* the river Jordan,
But *in* the flowing stream
Stood John the Baptist preacher
When he baptized him.

To some church historians the impact of the frontier on American religion was obvious. In their view the denominations that met the frontier challenge most successfully became the largest Protestant bodies in the United States. Protestant church government, they believed, came to reflect the democracy and individualism of the West. Some recent scholars question this position. After all the most popular denominations found new converts in both the West and the East. Nor was Methodist church organization, headed by a bishop, the most democratic system among the Protestant bodies. Students of church history have been less concerned with the reciprocal influence of the church on the frontiersmen. But our frontier experience would have been far different had not benevolent and religious impulses fed the voluntary associations and spurred the circuit rider over lonely western trails.

The historians of American religion have shown less interest in the frontier experience after 1850. By this time, they believe, the basic Protestant denominational structure had been established and the task of absorbing the immigrants, adapting to urbanization, and accommodating to the growth of Roman Catholicism were the great challenges confronting American Protestants. But the story of religion on the settler's frontier was by no means over. The far western chapter of the Mormon story was largely written after mid-century. A Roman Catholic bishop established ten settlements in western Minnesota between 1876 and 1881. Recently Franklin H. Littell has maintained that "religious voluntaryism and pluralism have been most readily accepted and are becoming institutionalized in various ways," on the Great Plains, the American farmer's "last frontier." The relation of organized religion to the settlement process still requires study.

FRANCIS I. MOATS

The Rise of Methodism in the Middle West

Some historians have maintained that the Methodist Episcopal Church increased in membership phenomenally between 1790 and 1850 because that denomination's organization and doctrinal message was uniquely appropriate to the social conditions in newly settled regions. Francis I. Moats published a classic statement of that position in 1928.

. . . The Methodist Episcopal Church was founded at the time the great westward movement was getting into full swing—a movement of people that has no parallel in history. Even before the rupture with England that resulted in the Revolution, restless and energetic leaders were establishing settlements beyond the mountains and the movement, checked by war, quickly began again with the close of hostilities. . . .

The new West was to become the melting-pot for the earlier sectionalism. Social distinction was scarcely known and here also "The freedom to worship God, which the Pilgrims 'sought afar' was found in the 'New England of the West' as Ohio was called. Religious liberty ran riot and was not distinguished, in some cases, from license." It was in this new West that democracy was born, and it was here that Methodism was to have that phenomenal growth that, in less than half a century, was to make of it the most numerous religious sect in the United States and give it a membership in the Mississippi Valley equal to, or greater than all other Protestant denominations combined. . . .

Both the Baptists and the Presbyterians were on the field in force in the West before the Methodists were fully ready for their great work. . . .

Methodism progressed rapidly in the new territory after 1800. By 1803 the Ohio circuits had been formed into a district and in 1808 another district was added in Ohio from new circuits. A circuit was formed in Indiana Territory in 1806, and by 1811 there were five circuits in that territory. A district was formed in the territory of Mississippi in 1805

SOURCE: Abridged from Francis I. Moats, "The Rise of Methodism in the Middle West," *Mississippi Valley Historical Review*, XV (June, 1928), 69–88. Reprinted by permission of the *Journal of American History.*

comprising four circuits. . . . [T]he great stronghold of Methodism in 1783 was south of the Mason and Dixon Line. The Revolution had cut off New York from contact with the other colonies for several years and New England was hostile to the doctrines of Methodism. Furthermore, preachers were plentiful in New England and Congregationalism was supported by law. . . .

The enthusiasm with which Methodism was received in the newer sections contrasted sharply with the cool reception accorded it in New England. Moving westward from Virginia and the Carolinas, it gained rapidly in Kentucky and Tennessee and after 1800 kept pace with the rapidly expanding population. From a total membership of less than 15,000 when the church was organized in 1784, it grew to almost 65,000 in 1800, and to 174,560 in 1810. The organization had now become highly efficient and the increase even more rapid. In 1830 the sect had grown to 476,000 members, of whom 190,000 were in the Mississippi Valley, and when the Schism came in the church in 1844 the total was 1,171,356, of whom fully one-half were west of the mountains. . . .

It is probable that from 1840 to 1845 the Methodist denomination in the Mississippi Valley equaled or exceeded in membership all other Protestant denominations combined. The Methodists had made this remarkable record in the face of competition with the older and well-established denominations. . . .

Disorganization, discord, lack of adaptability, lack of organization, and emphasis of doctrines ill-suited to the frontier—all these had served to limit the effectiveness of the older denominations in the newer and more democratic sections of the growing nation. It was the greater degree of adaptability of men, methods, and doctrine, that contributed to the greater success of Methodism in the back country of the seaboard states and on the new western frontier.

As the westward movement continued, Methodism kept pace with it in this democratic uncultured West, where society knew little social distinction and where the political philosophy of Jackson was declaring the political equality of all men. The superior organization of Methodism was peculiarly adapted to the sparsely settled areas and to the more densely populated areas of the settled districts as well, for money was scarce and though all of the older denominations and creeds could claim a following, none had adherents in sufficient number to support regular religious establishments in the new communities. The circuits, districts, and conferences of the Methodists, on the other hand, were all moulded into one harmonious whole. As the circuit rider advanced into new territory he left behind him a chain of stations to be formed into a circuit; circuits were joined into districts over which was the presiding elder. The elder was an important link in the system. It was his duty to travel over his district comprising a number of circuits and embracing a vast territory. . . .

But it is to the circuit rider that Methodism owes most for its success in the new settlements. Organization alone could not reach out to the great masses. It was the itinerating ministry that reached out and carried the gospel to the remote hamlets and to the scattered rural population. . . .

The preachers were largely frontiersmen and well adapted to the tasks that confronted them. Their appeal was direct and went straight to the hearts of the great masses of the less cultured rural sections. . . .

Few of these preachers had been schooled in the classics which represented the greater part of the college course of the period. No theological schools were to be found among the Methodists. Whatever of book knowledge they possessed came from a small stock of books prescribed by the various conferences as a prerequisite for admission to the traveling ranks. . . . While the unlettered preachers were winning whole communities to Christianity on the frontier, college-trained Presbyterians found themselves seriously handicapped in these sections. . . .

If the Methodist circuit riders lacked in education and culture they did not lack in zeal and devotion to their cause, and if this limitation placed a barrier between them and the more intellectual and cultured classes it served to give them that contact with the great masses of less cultured western pioneers out of which has come the Methodist church of today. The great zeal of Methodism was directed to the saving of souls. It mattered not to them just what means should be used to bring men into the Kingdom. The important consideration was to reach them. From the beginning of their work in America emotion had played an important part in Methodist evangelical preaching. . . .

The camp meeting revivals which were begun in Kentucky and reached such tremendous proportions in the neighborhood of Cane Ridge meeting-house, in 1800, probably have no parallel in history. Begun largely by the Presbyterians, the meetings quickly drew in other denominations—in particular the Methodists, who had already become accustomed to this method of appeal. For years these meetings were continued and were attended by thousands. . . .

All denominations joined in the remarkable manifestations of religious enthusiasm for a few years in which the Presbyterians and Methodists permitted greater freedom for emotion than the Baptists. Gradually the Presbyterians, with few exceptions, came to frown upon them and those who persisted in allowing a free rein to the emotions were suspended. The Baptists, always holding aloof from the other denominations for reasons of doctrine, had not joined as heartily in the great meetings as had the Methodists and Presbyterians. But the Methodists, says one writer, "had long been accustomed to regard extreme religious enthusiasm as indispensable." Not all Methodists, however, joined in the use of excessive emotion as a means of appeal. It would appear, rather, that most of them did not permit extremes but some came to regard the exercises as an indication of successful preaching and by the proper appeal could depend upon certain members of their congregations to respond by "falling" or "jerking." . . .

Among the factors that contributed to Methodist success in the West and in the back country, none was greater than the doctrine preached by the itinerants. While the Presbyterians were holding to the stern doctrines of election and predestination with a limited salvation and the Baptists were insisting on immersion as essential to salvation, with only a little less emphasis on the Calvinistic doctrines, the Methodists were proclaiming the doctrine of a full and free salvation for all and the freedom of the individual to determine for himself what doctrines he should accept or whether he should accept any of them. Doctrinal controversy formed the basis for much of the preaching during the early part of the nineteenth century, and in a society of scant social distinction and extreme individualism the democratic doctrines of Methodism were far more adaptable. The Methodist itinerant showed equal concern for the soul of the most lowly as for the soul of the man in a higher social station. Religion for him knew no class distinction and no one was beyond the reach of salvation. . . .

The remarkable adaptation of the Methodists to frontier conditions had thus brought into the Methodist ranks great numbers of the plain, sturdy rural settlers who were laying the foundations of the great West. It is evident that they possessed but little of the intellectual leadership even in a territory where this quality of civilization was limited. But their sturdy qualities of industry and their willingness to endure hardships in their devotion to duty made of them the great moral force in the new and uncultured settlements. It was on this foundation that Methodism was to build and it was out of such material that it must develop a cultural program. The great masses of the denomination were indifferent to anything but the very rudiments of education and many of its leaders were openly hostile to anything pertaining to higher learning. The mission of the Methodists, thus far, had been to evangelize the masses; the saving of souls was their chief concern. A new leadership was necessary before a cultural and educational program could make much progress within the Methodist Church.

The qualities of leadership common to the itinerant preachers were well suited to a frontier society. Themselves the product of a society with but scant culture, they were received with enthusiasm by the simple western farming population. But with the passing of the frontier the unlettered preachers were ill adapted to the changed conditions. . . . The old system had its place for a time on the new frontier but it had done its work and had built up a powerful church group. This success had resulted from superior organization, a self-sacrificing and zealous ministry, adaptable men and adaptable methods, and, finally, from a democratic doctrine well suited to a democratic society. The future success of the denomination depended on its ability to adapt itself to the changing conditions.

·2·

WILLIAM W. SWEET

The Churches as Moral Courts of the Frontier

William W. Sweet was the most eminent American church historian of his generation and the author of many books and articles on the history of Protestantism in the United States. Here he explains the ways in which the Protestant denomination served as an agency of social control in pioneer communities. Going further, he also argues that intemperance was the underlying cause of the basic moral problems found in the new settlements.

We Americans have been inclined to over-idealize the frontier period of our history, and have been perhaps too ready to resent any implication of unwonted moral laxity among the pioneers. It is now universally known that the great majority of the people who colonized the Atlantic seaboard came from the lower stratum of European society, and only a comparatively few represented the best in education and culture.

SOURCE: Abridged from William W. Sweet, "The Churches as Moral Courts of the Frontier," *Church History*, II (March, 1933), 3-21. Reprinted by permission of *Church History*.

Throughout the entire colonial period, at least until the colonial Awaken-
ings, the great mass of the lower classes were little influenced by organized religion, and only a very small proportion of the total population
of the thirteen colonies were members of the colonial churches. At the
end of the colonial period there were undoubtedly more unchurched
people in North America, in proportion to the population, than were
to be found in any other land in Christendom.

It is also well known that the Revolution, together with the two
decades following, was a period of religious and moral deadness throughout the United States. Never was religion at such low ebb. . . .

It was during these post-revolutionary years, when the general moral
and religious conditions in the nation were especially deplorable, that
population began to push westward in ever increasing streams; this era
also saw the admission of the first western states into the Union. If
morals and religion were at low ebb in the older settled seaboard
regions, what could be expected in the newer, ruder sections? Cut off
from the restraints and softening influences of the old home and the
old home community with its church and school and the observance
of the Sabbath, a vast majority of the early pioneer communities west
of the Alleghenies soon became notorious for lawlessness, rowdyism,
Sabbath breaking, gambling, swearing, drinking, and fighting. . . .

In the rough frontier communities the amount of liquor consumed
was incredible. Everyone, with few exceptions, seems to have indulged,
including women and children and even the preachers. Those who objected to the use of liquor as a common beverage often took it as a
tonic or as a preventive of the diseases common to the frontier, such as
ague and fever, and large quantities were consumed avowedly for these
purposes. . . . The offer of a dram from a bottle or jug was the first
gesture of welcome to almost every cabin, and to refuse to drink was an
"unpardonable incivility." Whisky was considered with meat and bread
as one of the necessities. In almost every store there was a whisky pail
or barrel with cups attached and all comers were at liberty to help
themselves.

Under such conditions much excessive drinking was to be expected
and drunkenness led to quarrelling and fighting. When Lincoln clerked
in Offut's store in New Salem, Illinois, on the Sangamon, "everybody
came on Saturdays to trade, gossip, wrestle, raffle, pitch horseshoes,
run races, get drunk, maul one another with their fists,' and indulge
generally, in frontier happiness, as a relief from the week's monotonous
drudgery on the raw and difficult farms."

When John Mason Peck, the first Baptist home missionary, arrived in
St. Louis in the year 1817, he found an astonishing mixture of population,

many of whom were of the most degraded character, spending their spare time in gambling and drinking. Some of the blasphemous infidels boasted to him that "the Sabbath shall never cross the Mississippi." The people in southwestern Missouri he describes as "stupid, listless, and apparently indifferent to everything. Few could read and fewer families had Bibles."

There is considerable evidence also that in the matter of sexual morality the frontier presented a lower standard than that prevailing in the older sections of the country. Here women were of course in the minority and for that reason were in much greater demand. The comparatively large number of cases recorded in the early county court records of rape, divorce, bigamy, and adultery would indicate that social relations were loose and undisciplined. . . .

That every frontier was in pressing need of moral restraint and guidance there can be no reasonable doubt, and in most instances the only guardians of the morals of these communities were the little frontier churches. From the standpoint of numbers and effectiveness on the frontier the most important churches were the Baptist, the Presbyterian, and the Methodist bodies. In Kentucky, for instance, in the year 1820 the total population was 563,317, while the churched population was but 46,730, or one person in about every twelve. The great western revival had resulted in sweeping thousands into the churches, more than ten thousand having been added to the Baptist churches alone between 1800 and 1803, and about an equal number to the Methodists. In 1820 the Methodists and Baptists had about 21,000 members each in the state of Kentucky; the Presbyterians, both Cumberland and regular, had about 3,700, while all other religious organizations combined had less than 1,000 members. These proportions will hold good, I think, for most of the frontier communities at this period.

In the Baptist Church the congregation is the governing body. Most of the frontier churches held their regular congregational meeting at least once each month, most frequently on Saturdays, and one of the obligations of church membership was attendance upon these meetings. Discipline occupied much, if not most, of the attention of these business meetings. . . .

A random turning of the pages of any of the old record books of the early Baptist churches west of the Alleghenies will soon convince one that the church was of tremendous importance in the preservation of order and the maintenance of decency. Discipline was meted out for adultery; betting; fraudulent business dealings; calling another a liar; deceiving and defrauding; destroying corner trees; disobeying the call of the church; false accusation of lying; fighting; frolicking and dancing; gambling; immoral conduct; improper conduct in time of worship; intoxication; lies of hypocrisy; tale-bearing; making unrighteous landmarks; misusing of a wife; non-attendance at church; playing carnal plays; quarrelling; running an incorrect line; selling an unsound mare; stealing; swearing; refusing to obey the call of the church; shooting for liquor; swapping horses; talking improperly; threatening a slave; treating the church with contempt; use of hard and censorious expressions; villainy; and withdrawing from the church in a disorderly manner.

The church not only guarded the private morals of its members, it likewise assumed the responsibility of looking into and regulating business dealings. . . .

In the Methodist Societies the quarterly conferences were the courts where members were brought to trial, while the preachers were subject to the annual conference. Part of the business of each quarterly conference was to hear complaints and to receive and try appeals, while one of the most important functions of the annual conferences was to pass on the character of ministers.

Wesley's original rule regulating the use of spirituous liquors had forbidden "drunkenness, or buying or selling spirituous liquors, or drinking them, unless in cases of extreme necessity." But this stern prohibition was soon abandoned by the American Methodists. . . .

With this relaxation from the original rule, numerous local preachers as well as many members had taken up the practice of both distilling and selling liquors. Soon the prevalence of such practices was causing scandal throughout the church and stricter rules to control the situation were soon being agitated. The frontier preachers were particularly concerned, and none more than James Axley who at each succeeding General Conference presented resolutions to that effect. Finally in 1836 Wesley's original rule was restored by an almost unanimous vote.

While the question was being agitated in the church, many of the frontier preachers especially became rabid anti-liquor advocates. Some took heroic measures against it. . . . The following is a summary of some of the experiences of the famous Methodist circuit-rider, Peter Cartwright, in attempting to preserve order and decency at camp-meetings.

The camp-meetings were almost always infested by rowdies, who often organized under a captain and did all in their power to break up the religious exercise by noise personal violence, liquor selling and drinking, riotous conduct, stealing horses and wagons and all manner of annoyances. On one occasion Cartwright blocked their game by appointing their captain himself to the business of preserving order. On another occasion the captain of the rowdies was "struck down" among the penitents just as he was about to quietly hang a string of frogs around the preacher's neck. Once he knocked the rowdy chief from his horse with a club and having captured him, saw that he was fined the sum of fifty dollars. Again he captured the whisky the rowdies were drinking, and when they came at night to stone the preacher's tent, Cartwright was among them in disguise, learned their plans and drove them off single handed with a sharp volley of pebbles. . . .

Turning now to the Presbyterian-Congregational churches in the west, we note a somewhat different condition as well as different methods of administering discipline. The members of these churches represented perhaps a somewhat higher educational level than the average among Baptists and Methodists, though an examination of their frontier documents would show that this difference was not as great as many have supposed. As a whole their administration does not seem quite so stern, nor as frequent. We also must note the general pronouncements on moral questions of their presbyteries, synods, and general assemblies, as well as the administration of discipline by the sessions of the individual churches. . . .

Comparing Presbyterians and Congregationalists on the frontier with Baptists and Methodists in regard to their attitude toward the problem of intoxicating liquor, the documents indicate that there was little difference between them. . . .

Some of the offences tried before the Presbyterian church at Franklin, Ohio, in the Western Reserve, between the years 1819 and 1839, were as follows: consenting to an illegal and unchristian marriage; departing from the church; dealing unjustly in the sale of dried fruit; publishing faults before the first and second steps were taken; refusing to commune because of difficulties with another man; attending places of vain amusement and allowing their children to attend; refusing to walk with the church in regard to the use of intoxicating liquors; obstinate refusal to hear the church; dancing; being destitute of piety; and imprudent and unchristian conduct. . . .

It is true that the number of church members in the average frontier community was proportionately small. But these little frontier churches undoubtedly exercised an influence far larger than their number or membership would indicate.

Undoubtedly the basic moral problems which confronted the average frontier community grew directly or indirectly out of the abundant supply of intoxicating liquor which was to be found on every new and raw frontier. Here we have the answer to the question which many people have been asking in recent years, why Baptists, Methodists and to a somewhat lesser degree perhaps Presbyterians, Congregationalists and Disciples are so vehement in their denunciation of liquor and all it stands for. On every frontier from the Alleghenies to the Pacific these were the people who fought the battle for decency and order, and to a large degree saved the west from semi-barbarism, and the attitudes created by these bitter struggles remain to this day.

·3·

WILLIAM MULDER

The Mormons in American History

The Mormon faith has been called one of the few truly indigenous American religions. The westward migration of the Mormons, the members of the Church of Jesus Christ of Latter Day Saints, during the nineteenth century, was the most spectacular illustration of religious migration in the national period of the country's history. In the following passage, a scholar member of that church reflects upon the meaning of the Mormon experience during the nineteenth century.

. . . The formal separation of church and state, so dear to the American tradition, has not meant a separation of church and society, religion divorced from our national life. The story of religion in America is in many respects synonymous with the history of our country. From the Bible Commonwealth of colonial New England to the Bible Belt still with us both as a state of mind and as a region, the religious background of American culture deserves equal attention with the political, the social, and the economic. They are, in fact, inseparable. . . .

Mormonism seen in this perspective assumes an unusual identity with American history, all the more because it is as native to the United

---

SOURCE: Abridged from William Mulder, "The Mormons in American History," *Utah Historical Quarterly*, XXVII (January, 1959), 58–77. Reprinted by permission of the *Utah Historical Quarterly* and William Mulder.

States as Indian corn and the buffalo nickel. We have to specify an American Judaism or an American Catholicism, but Mormonism is American by birth, although the United States was long reluctant to accept the honor. In its New England origins, its utopian experiments and reforms, its westward drive, and its early expansion to Europe resulting in a great program of immigration and settlement, nineteenth-century Mormonism expressed prominent traits and tendencies that were already shaping American society. It was not simply a colorful reflection of the times; it was a dynamic reworking of the diverse elements of American culture. Mormonism is unique primarily in the way it combined these elements, in what it added or neglected, making it now a perfect epitome of its time and place, and now a puzzling contradiction.

In early Mormon theology, for example, we get a fairly complete cross section of the American mind in the early nineteenth century. In the current argument among scholars over the degree and nature of the nineteenth century's optimism and stress on progress, Mormon eschatology is especially pertinent. It embraced both the belief in progress and the underlying sense of doom and destruction in an era we have too simply thought of as a romantic Age of Jackson. . . .

Again, the Order of Enoch, or the first United Order, tried briefly in Missouri from 1831 to 1833, was Mormonism's version of economic equality. Through its law of consecration and stewardship it hoped to preserve initiative and avoid the pitfalls of common stock that were ruining communal societies living like big families. In principle it tried to bring together the advantages of both private enterprise and co-operation. In the same way the blueprint for the ideal city of Zion tried to combine the advantages of town and country living, an anticipation of the garden cities of our own time. And in the same way Mormonism combined the advantages of lay leadership and central authority in giving the priesthood to every man subject to the direction of revelation from the president and prophet.

Again, polygamy was the Mormon version of the daring attempts by contemporaries to modify the basic structure of the family, attempts which ran from the celibacy of the Shakers at one extreme to the free love of the Oneida Community at the other. . . . Sooner or later an expansive America had to produce its cult of fertility to match its own teeming natural abundance. But polygamy was not a pagan indulgence: a Puritan asceticism disciplined it in practice and an Old Testament sociology exalted it. Only the image of Mormon clerks and farmers seeing themselves as Abrahams and girding themselves for godhood in the eternities to come can fully explain this most imaginative of all doctrines.

In its sociology Mormonism expressed the bold, experimental spirit of the times, on occasion moving far ahead of them. In its theology, however, it reacted strongly against the progressive religious liberalism of the day which made the mind its own church. Mormonism returned to the Puritan tradition which made church covenants as important as civil covenants. Again the Mormons combined elements: they combined dissent with authority; they restored the one true authoritative church, as they supposed, with a divinely ordained prophet to lead it but reserved to the membership at large the right of common consent to the nominations from on high. . . .

Besides these topical connections, the Mormons had dramatic connections with American history in time and space. In their westward movement they were like the fine filament preceding the thread as it seeks the eye of the needle. They were part of the vanguard of settlement that was already making the Oregon and California Trail a dusty highway. The first company of Mormon pioneers, by the way, was not a ragged band of refugees but the best prepared of all western overlanders in terms of purpose, knowledge of the country, organization, and equipment. . . .

Mormonism was a movement in a very real sense. In their efforts to plant Zion the restless Mormons were constantly in motion. In less than a generation they crossed the continent in one tragic uprooting after another, leaving their houses unsold and their crops unharvested in a dozen communities hopefully begun in Ohio, Missouri, Illinois, and Iowa, until the final removal to the West. Mormon names still dot the map from Mormon Hill in New York to Mormon Island in California, with historic Mormon roads and trails and ferries in between. In the process the Mormons became a genuine people, a covenant folk like ancient Israel with a shared history and at last a homeland. They moved within a magnificent metaphor, the image of themselves as Latter-day Israel. The parallel sustained them, and events sustained the parallel. Persecution and martyrdom deepened the image. Their exodus under Brigham Young, an American Moses, and their chronicles in early Deseret, the new Land of Promise—with its Dead Sea and River Jordan, and with its patriarchal order of marriage and the ensuing struggle with the Philistines, or Gentiles—completed the Old Testament likeness. Emerson, visiting Brigham Young in 1871, noted this Biblical imagination and called the Mormons "an afterclap of Puritanism." . . .

America as a land of promise and destiny, where the ancient dream of a more abundant life could be realized, is a major theme in Mormon as in American history. It finds eloquent expression in "the gathering," long the heart of the whole Mormon movement. The gathering, not polygamy, is Mormonism's oldest and most influential doctrine. It looked back to the promises made to ancient Israel and forward to the Second Coming. It was Mormonism's way of channeling what the nineteenth century called the religious affections; it disciplined into action the fervor that in revival faiths was dissipated in an aimless love affair with Christ.

Mormonism, like other adventist faiths, was a millennial proclamation, a warning that a final judgment was at hand. But it was also a program designed to prepare for this eventuality. The gathering involved more than a trip to the sinner's bench. It was to be a roll call of Saints without halos, an assembling of a people not already saved but eager to create conditions under which salvation might be achieved. This determination was the mainspring of Mormon social reform, whether it was a United Order or a Deseret Alphabet. . . .

While other millennialists set a time, the Mormons appointed a place. America was the preordained site of this stupendous homecoming of the Lord's scattered hosts. On this continental stage the last great dramas foretold in the Old and New Testaments would be enacted: Daniel's stone would roll forth, St. John's heavenly city come to earth, and Rachel would weep no more for her children. For this, all history had been mere prologue. The discovery of America by Columbus, the Reformation in Europe, the coming of the Pilgrim Fathers, the founding of the Republic, and the raising of "that glorious standard" as the Mormons called the Constitution, were all preliminary to this grand design. "The happiness of America," as George Washington himself believed, was in turn to be but "the first link in a series of universal victories."

The Mormons made this common Protestant view of Providence controlling America's destiny peculiarly their own. In Mormon sermons, the American eagle spread broad wings. . . . Zion was to be model for America as America was to be model for the world.

Once more Mormon belief reflected a contemporary idea and went beyond it: America as the Garden of the World, an Arcadia of civilizations, was just then pleasing America's poets and painters, whose imaginations were being fired by a bountiful and still virgin land extending from the Hudson to the Columbia. The *Book of Mormon* was part of that literature, as moral as it was romantic. With its grand refrain of the continent as a favored land providentially preserved for the gathering of a righteous people, it provided the American dream its own scripture and endowed it with sacred legend. Whatever else the *Book of Mormon* may be, it is America's oldest immigration story, chronicling several folk wanderings. . . .

What for other millennial faiths marked the end, for the Mormons was just the beginning. Their expectation of the Second Coming was momentary, but they planned for mansions on earth rather than in the sky. The Advent itself would bring no more than a change in administration, so to speak—the benevolent monarchy of the King of Kings. The Kingdom, already established, would go right on, and its yeomanry would keep their inheritances, tilling their fields and tending their shops as they had done the day before. If in America every man was king, in the Mormon Zion every man was to be king and priest. This breathtaking vision of Zion was Biblical, its ardor and materialism characteristically American. It could have been conceived only in the heady atmopshere of Jacksonian democracy, when, as Lowell put it, every man carried a blueprint for utopia in his pocket. . . .

Zion, with the great heart of the gathering pumping converts and their resources into it, made history in two directions—in the west and in Europe. The Mormons planted approximations of the ideal on the frontier and took Zion's image abroad, where Mormonism became an influential American "ism" leading thousands of northern Europeans to try America's promise on Mormon terms. The ideal was tried briefly in its purest form in Jackson County, Missouri, in the early 1830's; in the city-state of Nauvoo in the 1840's; and in Deseret's theocracy, quickly modified after the arrival of the first federal officials in 1852 but a very lively and visible ghost for years afterward.

America rejected each of these attempts, and for the traditional American reason that the Mormons united the civil and religious order to an uncomfortable degree and posed a political threat. The Mormons interpreted the Biblical Kingdom all too realistically. Americans insisted that God must not dare unite what man and the Constitution had sundered. . . .

The longest trial of Mormon social and political nonconformity growing out of its religious collectivism came in Utah after an exodus from Nauvoo which rivaled the trek of the Boers in South Africa and the flight of Longfellow's Evangeline and her fellow Acadians from Nova Scotia. At the outset Zion in the West was the provisional State of Deseret, a regional empire bounded by the Rocky Mountains and the Sierras, the Oregon country and Mexico, with a corridor opening to San Diego on the Pacific as an eventual port of entry for immigrants expected to come the water route around the Horn. . . .

Colonizing the drought-ridden, scattered valleys of Zion demanded co-operation both far-flung and intimate, with every new settlement part of the larger design and every settler a responsive part of the community in a life at once determined by desert conditions and overcoming them.

The Mormon farm-village at the same time expressed an ideal—it was the Kingdom in small, patterned after Joseph Smith's blueprint for the City of Zion. Isolation, Indians, irrigation, and a New England town tradition were merely immediate causes of what already had a final cause in the heavenly model.

As pioneers the Mormons differed little, perhaps, from Americans pioneering other frontiers. But as yeomen developing Zion they were significantly different. Desperate private struggle and life-saving co-operation were common enough on the American frontier, but on the Mormon frontier the idea of the Kingdom encouraged survival when lesser hopes failed, and the conditions of life "under the ditch" promoted co-operation not merely occasional like a house-raising or a harvesting bee but daily and endemic to the society. . . .

A closed society like Zion, where every social and civil difference amounted to a religious difference, could not brook dissenters. There was no room for what the British Parliament calls a loyal opposition. Who was not for the Kingdom was against it. The archetype lay in heaven itself, which had cast out the rebel angels.

The world outside, unaware of Zion's unique workings, saw in all this only an oppressive society made up largely of the ignorant and the super-stitious. The cathedral builders of medieval Europe would have under-stood Zion's unity and devotion, but not a Protestant America, more at home among warring and freespoken sects and splinters. . . .

Extremists called for cannon of the biggest bore to thunder the seventh commandment into the Mormons; they wanted to dissolve the legislature and govern Utah by commission; they clamored for enforceable legisla-tion that would disfranchise polygamists and prohibit Mormon im-migration. On a rising tide of public feeling against the Mormons, one congressional bill after another and one presidential message after another sought the formula that would at last throttle Utah's unortho-doxies. Against a background of bitter enmity between the Mormon People's party and the Gentile Liberal party in Utah, Governor Eli Murray in 1883 warned the country that Utah beset them with "another irrepressible conflict." The Edmunds Act that year sent the cohabs, as polygamists were called, underground; and in 1887 the Edmunds-Tucker Act finally brought the Mormons to their knees: it disincorporated the church itself, disfranchised the women, dissolved the Perpetual Emigrat-ing Fund, and led to the Manifesto of 1890 abandoning polygamy. The next year the United States added polygamists to the excluded classes in the Immigration Act, along with paupers and imbeciles.

But it was anticlimax. The legislation merely hastened what changing social and economic conditions were already accomplishing. By 1896 Utah was considered unspotted enough to be admitted to the Union. The conflict and crusade gave way to an era of good feeling, and the Mormons became in time eminently respected.

Zion, once preached with so much intensity and conviction, and expressed in the great program of gathering into utopian communities on the frontier, was no longer a closed society. As the price of survival it had to accommodate itself to the times. . . .

· 4 ·

T. SCOTT MIYAKAWA

The Heritage of the Popular Denominations

The sociologist T. Scott Miyakawa argues that the Protestant frontiersmen who were church members should be considered "members of disciplined groups and an increasingly organized society," rather than "lone individuals in an atomistic society." More strikingly he suggests that those American religious denominations that had originated as dissenting sects in the Old World and in colonial America, such as the Baptists and Methodists, "helped to infuse secular society in the American West with certain traits now regarded as typically western." In other words those traits that Turner believed to be products of the frontier were really characteristics of the dissenters so common in the West.

In the first decades of the nineteenth century, the small struggling Dissenting sects grew rapidly to become the largest Protestant denominations in the West and in the United States as a whole. As it happened in the Old World, so too on the seaboard, the established churches and educated upper classes modified Dissent in the East. In the West, Dissent was freer to realize its potentialities.

SOURCE: Reprinted from T. Scott Miyakawa, *Protestants and Pioneers: Individualism and Conformity on the American Frontier* (Chicago, 1964), 213–240 by permission of the University of Chicago Press and T. Scott Miyakawa. Copyright 1964 by The University of Chicago.

Contrary to popular tendency today to correlate the frontier with dissociated individuals, many western Dissenters were in fact conforming members of society and disciplined formal organizations with definite personal and social standards. . . . Dissent expected its members, however humble their circumstances, to assume responsibility for its activities and thus trained many in organizational leadership. The Dissenters then extended their experience with religious associations to secular organizations and to politics to realize additional objectives and to influence the government.

A concrete social contribution made by Dissent, as the result of a basic organizational purpose—the formation of a vital fellowship—was to provide a means for hitherto complete strangers, migrants on the frontier, to establish close personal relations quickly. Its discipline was avowedly aimed at encouraging its members and their families to maintain high standards of personal and social behavior and at preserving group unity. . . .

Besides fulfilling latent functions for individual migrants, Dissent also carried out many latent group functions. Settlers in early frontier society, lacking many traditional informal and formal legal agencies of control, had to take deliberate steps to maintain order and unity. The Dissenting fellowship, discipline, and church courts were well-suited to confront such a situation. The community could count on a solid core of disciplined citizens organized for religious purposes, it is true, but also latently able to wield collective as well as individual influence for peace and order. . . .

The second main thesis of this study involves the more specific institutional and cultural traits of Dissent and their impact on western society: the popular denominations strengthened or were the source of many institutions and qualities, secular as well as religious, regarded as typically western and sometimes as characteristically American. In addition to its voluntary organizational features, equalitarianism, and faith in the common man, Dissent popularized the once peculiarly aristocratic Calvinistic system of calling, a heritage which the larger society later secularized into the idealization of the successful self-made man and his worldly achievements. The more controversial attitude of earlier Dissent included its suspicion of scholarship and art and its opposition to professionalism. With some notable exceptions, western popular denominations accepted or were ambivalent toward racism and slavery and, partly under revivalistic influence, long retained what some churchmen regarded as sectarian provincialism. . . .

Within their organization, Dissenting denominations eliminated nearly all invidious distinctions, other than race, arising from accidents of birth and condition. They sought members among the humbler people and encouraged leadership from their ranks. Long before the Jacksonian movement, they opened all denominational offices to the many and infused their organizational life with new vigor. . . .

Since both Calvinism and Dissent emphasized the calling, it is difficult to distinguish their respective influences in implanting this system in western life. Initially in the West, even the Presbyterians had an almost sectarian attitude toward many cultural interests and defined the calling more narrowly than did the more urbane Old World Calvinists. Dissent was even narrower in its outlook and tended to restrict the calling, aside from the ministry, to economic or political activities. . . .

Devotion to this-worldly duties, we should remember, originally expressed a religious ethic for other-worldly ends and was not a mundane preoccupation with materialism. Greed as such was always sinful. Strange as it may seem to us today, sectarian Dissent feared intellectual and cultural pursuits as potentially more dangerous distractions from the path to salvation than it feared business. . . .

The western Dissenting stress on the calling would seem to contradict its persistent suspicion of scholarship and art. Opposition to cultural pursuits was originally a feature of the sectarian efforts to "withdraw" from the world, while the system of calling came from the Calvinistic ethic to enter, conquer, and transform the same world. . . . Yet, the popular denominations continued to oppose most efforts to establish professional standards, partly because they interpreted such attempts as undemocratic plots to prevent able but formally unschooled persons from realizing their potentialities. . . .

The popular denominational outlook was essentially what we would today consider middle class and not that of a traditional peasantry or radical revolutionaries. The Dissenters soon learned to appreciate elementary education and practical training as valuable for their callings. Before 1850, however, the majority could scarcely be expected to understand the extent to which religion and practical knowledge depended upon the Western (that is, Occidental) cultural heritage and its continuing development. While criticizing scholars and artists, Dissent unconsciously assumed their existence outside its membership and pragmatically utilized their contributions whenever convenient. Early western Dissent was more apt to understand democracy as eliminating intellectual standards than as providing better educational and cultural facilities open to all to train religious and civic leadership and to enrich the common life. . . .

At this point, perhaps we should consider briefly some implications that our findings may have for studies in American history and its frontier heritage. The present inquiry did not attempt to survey the pioneer West as such or to analyze the various frontier theories, but examining Dissenting life has raised some questions concerning the Frederick Jackson Turner thesis and other accounts of the frontier. . . .

At the outset, it is perhaps appropriate to observe that the individualistic interpretations of the pioneer West pay little attention to popular denominational organization, discipline, life, and attitudes—for which there is a significant volume of empirical data; or, if they mention these factors, they do not fully incorporate them into their views on western life. . . .

If we turn from Turner's broad generalizations about the unbounded individualism to consider his more specific observations on frontier individualism, equality, and democracy, we find them generally applicable to pioneer Dissenters. The individualistic qualities which he finds in the backwoodsmen have obvious associations with the Dissenters resolutely engaged in their calling. To a degree, the buoyant frontier optimism and the restless energy reflected the drive idealized for the faithful in their calling, confident of ultimate success even as they were overcoming obstacles. . . . The fierce equalitarianism, the faith in the common man, and the impatience with the niceties and professionalism which Turner admired, we have already noted in the Dissenters, even to the Methodist bishops in their shirtsleeves and the Baptists calling a fellow farmer or artisan or shopkeeper to the ministry. . . .

Turner, departing from his previous stress on individualism, strongly emphasized the nationalizing influence of the frontier. This view combined some previously mentioned concepts concerning the West with assumptions which were essentially sociological, economic, and political in nature. . . . [A]s far as the western Dissenters were concerned, we have already noticed their enthusiastic participation in the Jacksonian movement and the importance that they and other settlers attached to democratizing and extending governmental functions. . . . The Dissenters were experienced in relating their local church activities to the denominational regional and national programs, and they applied their religious group training to civic and political movements. . . .

The previous comments on the collectivistic and co-operative features of the frontier society did not negate its individualistic aspects. . . . To reiterate, then, while frontier life had strongly individualistic qualities, both historical data and theoretical analyses would broaden the individualistic interpretations to include the pioneer society, its voluntary associations, and its religious and cultural heritage. In any case, the issue was not individual versus society. Man as a social being cannot realize his potentialities outside society, and society does not exist outside its constituent individuals. While the relation of any particular individual to society is never entirely harmonious, some societies encourage initiative and in them individuals and private groups do many things without governmental intervention. . . .

Turner felt that the West rejected much of the seaboard and Old World culture. . . . Instead of discarding their seaboard heritage, the Dissenters and other settlers clung to whatever cultural background they esteemed or their religion encouraged them to value, even to their prejudices. . . .

In its beginnings in the colonies, Dissent appealed primarily to the humbler, less-educated classes. Consequently, when the first Dissenters moved westward, they carried with them the early sectarian hostility to scholarly and artistic activities rather than the culture of the eastern elite or of the total seaboard society. That is, the Dissenting migrants had rejected or had been opposed to many cultural interests for religious reasons while they were still living on the seaboard and before they thought of migrating. . . . In the West, the popular denominations exerted a far greater influence than they did on the seaboard where the educated classes had their own standards and the Dissenting suspicion of learning persisted longer, particularly in the rural areas, than on the coast. In many early western communities, no cultural elite existed to challenge them. . . . Several eastern Baptist churches had instrumental music in the eighteenth century. Western sectarian hostility to many aspects of the seaboard heritage seems to have led some frontier theorists to conclude that it was the frontier rather than the Dissenting sectarianism which had induced many westerners to turn away from the old culture.

The data reviewed in the present study would suggest that in advancing his more sweeping generalizations, Turner was at times on shaky ground. He did not fully utilize certain historical material and sociological principles known in his day, which would have strengthened his basic data and might have modified his conclusions. Thus, he did not theoretically reconcile his frontier individualism, nationalism, sectionalism, and innovating power. Each concept had supporting data, but partly because he misunderstood the sociological and anthropological approaches, these emphases were not subsumed under a more inclusive interpretation. On the other hand, his vivid description of the pioneers often fit the Dissenters. His colorful comments on their activism and equalitarianism bring them to life and are consistent with the independent data on the Dissenters and other settlers. Obviously, many backwoodsmen whom Turner was discussing were Dissenters or were influenced by Dissent, and, conversely, Dissenters shared many traits with other frontiersmen.

More fundamentally, it is apparent that actual experience, social background, and traditions of the settlers, among whom the Dissenters were both numerous and influential, were among the major forces shaping western society. Dissenting democracy, equalitarianism, system of calling, and organization did not spring from the wilderness. Instead, they moved in the opposite direction: Pioneer Dissenters carried these qualities into the forests and propagated them among their neighbors—"stark and strong and full of life." The frontier provided the physical setting and the limits but did not determine the pioneer social organization and culture. The frontier West was the stage, as it were, but the settlers under the influence of their cultural heritage selected the plays and their roles. Siberian wilderness, South American forests, and even French Quebec woods did not create those dynamic, aggressive, and buoyant qualities and that democracy and equalitarianism which stirred Turner's imagination. The very traits which he admired indicate the great part the Dissenting denominations had in the West, a role roughly similar to, even if more limited than, that of Puritanism in New England. They helped to mold our cherished institutions and our ways of feeling, thinking, and acting. The Dissenters left a permanent impress on the West and on modern American life as a whole.

CHAPTER XVI

The West and the
Character of Americans

I

To the frontier the American intellect owes its most striking char-, acteristics," wrote Frederick Jackson Turner in one of the most striking passages of his essay on the significance of the frontier in American history. He continued,

That coarseness and strength combined with acuteness and inquisitiveness; that practical, inventive turn of mind, quick to find expedients; that masterful grasp of material things, lacking in the artistic but powerful to effect great ends; that restless, nervous energy; that dominant individualism, working for good and for evil, and withal that buoyancy and exuberance which comes with freedom—these are traits of the frontier. . . .

We know that the opportunities of the frontier drew generations of native Americans and foreign-born immigrants westward. We know that many of them stayed in the West and fashioned new lives for themselves there. It is less clear that these experiences changed the personalties of the westering folk.

Foreign writers of the frontier era loved to describe the Americans. There was both fun and profit in it and generations of travellers from abroad, particularly the British, dissected the Americans and collected literary royalties for doing so. They were usually quite sure that the residents of the United States were very different from themselves. They found Americans dedicated one and all to pursuit of the dollar and they ⊬ populated the American West with bragging brawlers. Historians have mined the travellers' accounts industriously and repeated their stories, sometimes as unvarnished fact, sometimes with tongue-in-cheek. But the travel literature is treacherous because the authors differed greatly in intelligence, sophistication, and literary ability. They often lumped the fundamental and the trivial together without discrimination. If the historian is to do more than repeat the observations of the travellers he must venture into the realm of psychological interpretation and few have had the appetite for that. But without turning ourselves into psychiatrists we can hazard a few questions and answers about the social processes of the frontier and their impact on the character of Americans.

Was the way of life of Americans on the frontier indeed different from that in older regions in the United States? In varying degrees the trader, miner, lumberman, cattleman and farmer enjoyed free use of the frontier resources for a time. The trappers gathered nature's bounty, thousands of miners sifted the placers in the public lands of the West without charge. Pioneer lumbermen often neglected to purchase the lands which they logged. Western grazers pastured their herds on the public lands and pioneer farmers improved their claims prior to the federal land sales. Almost all frontiersmen faced problems in marketing their products which were very different from those experienced in older settlements. Their need for capital was of a special sort and required special solutions. Even so the frontiers were chronically short of capital and were highly vulnerable as a result to business fluctuations. To solve the peculiar problems of frontier industry westerners developed the codes of the mining districts, the associations of the stock growers, the log driving and river improvement associations of the lumbermen, the claim clubs and anti-horse thief associations of the farmers' frontier, and the vigilante bands of frontier city and mining camp. Among the fur men a unique subculture developed—a strange half-way culture, part Indian and part Anglo-American.

The frontiersmen did more than exploit the natural resources of the West; in the process they built communities—some fleeting, others which have served as the foundation for the towns and cities of today. But when we examine the institutions of even those pioneer communities with a future, the schools, the churches and the institutions of local government, we discover that they were weak or inadequate by the standards of older regions in the United States. New settlements lacked capital and this fact explains the fragility of the community structure to some extent; schools and government cost money, churches required contributions from their members. But the characteristics of frontier populations also helped to explain the nature of western institutions. Sometimes preponderantly male and usually young or young middle-aged adults, the westerners were mobile, sometimes thinly spread over broad territories, and often mixed in background. Most westerners were experiencing the anxieties of starting new enterprises and the problems involved in fitting themselves into new social structures, unsettling experiences, as college freshmen can testify. Such were the men and women who established and shaped the new western communities. Government officers, local men of substance and the agents of capital provided leadership, but they were usually new to each other and to the people of their settlements and often untested by problems of the sort they faced in the West. Very seldom was the power of such leaders enhanced by the degree of social status or economic power which the leaders in some older American communities or in foreign lands enjoyed. The westerner, therefore, lived in a new physical environment from which he must extract a living and he lived for a time at least in a different kind of social environment than he had known in older America.

Of course westerners were linked to the older settlements by personal and economic bonds, they experienced economic pressures similar to those of residents in the East and the economic processes of the nineteenth century affected the frontier industries as well as those in the longer settled regions. We observe the concentration of capital and an increase in the size of business units in the West as well as in the East, illustrated by the growth of the American Fur Company, the mining corporations that replaced simple placer operations, the great western cattle enterprises, the large lumber companies, the bonanza farms in the Northern Plains and the western railroad empires. But it is clear that the westerners lived in a society that was different from those of the older regions.

II

To some historians it has seemed clear that the differences in physical and social environment in the West, *must* have produced new ways of doing and thinking. Here was economic opportunity, here was release from the bondage of older social structures, here was the challenge to innovate and to adapt to the unexpected, here would be attitudes which reflected thousands of success stories. And from the writings of the frontier travellers the industrious historian can build a veritable mountain of references that attest that this was so. The more careful work of this sort must be treated with respect.

But how were differences in the social and economic environment of the West converted into new ways of thinking and behaving? The westerners moved out to develop natural resources which by their standards were under-used and which promised wealth or a congenial occupation. Moreover, the technology of the Industrial Revolution enabled them to exploit the continent's resources at a rate that was undreamed of a century earlier. David Potter has pointed out that this helped to make the United States a land of abundance and Americans a "people of plenty." Abundance, Potter suggested, may have affected child-rearing practices in various ways, even to the point of causing a fundamental change in the personality of Americans. In other words, the frontier helped to make the United States a land of abundance and that condition may have modified the character of its people, changing what some psychologists have called the nation's "basic personality structure." Westerners obviously shared in the process if it occurred. But if the circumstances of frontier living either intensified or diminished the impact of abundance, we might expect a somewhat different personality in the children raised there. And perhaps there were other characteristics of western life which affected child-rearing as well.

Some social scientists argue that social stress or tension may influence the behavior of adults significantly. Did the frontier environment place the individual in situations which produced unusual stress? Durkheim argued that people often experienced *anomie* or normlessness after leaving their accustomed life ways and social relationships in the provinces and moving to Paris. The behavioral patterns of such individuals might change drastically and sometimes they experienced depression so deep that they committed suicide. Sorokin maintained that mobile individuals suffer unusual stress, manifesting their tensions in patterns of behavior somewhat similar to those that Turner attributed to the influence of the frontier. Many westerners were indeed highly mobile. Could the experience of working and dealing with new people, of facing new problems, of living in an unstable economic environment have created sufficient stress to change the behavior of adults on the frontier and this in turn also have affected child-rearing patterns?

Some students of human behavior prefer to picture it in dramaturgical terms and study the various social roles which the individual plays in his relations with his friends and acquaintances. Such roles they believe are shaped both by the actor's own ambitions and by his understanding of the ways in which others view the requirements of a particular role. The personal imprint that an individual gives to such a role is called his style. Did the frontiersman's style of role-playing differ from that of residents in the longer settled regions? Thomas C. Cochran has suggested that some conflicts between eastern financiers and western businessmen during the nineteenth century occurred because westerner and easterner misunderstood the basic assumptions which the other brought to his role as a businessman. In this illustration, the western style of role-playing collided with the eastern and as usual in such cases both were probably altered as a result. Can we assume that there were enough collisions of the sort to affect the national style of role-playing—the national character—in a significant way?

Like others who applied a common sense approach to the frontier experience, Frederick Jackson Turner was somewhat vague as to the precise ways in which the frontier might change the individual's thought processes. Clearly, modified Freudianism or the dramaturgical approach allow us, theoretically at least, to analyze frontier differences more precisely and suggest ways in which frontier adaptations might have been internalized and transmitted. This method of transfer is important both because the frontier experience in any area was relatively brief and because of the suggestion sometimes encountered that frontier influences affected older regions as well as the frontier. Robert F. Berkhofer Jr. introduces the concept of culture as a normative system in Chapter I and this approach also can be used to shed some light on the transmission of ways of doing and thinking.

Professor Berkhofer argued that the cultural values of the pioneers dictated the ways in which they used the resources of the frontier. This region represented opportunity to the Anglo-American settlers because they believed in working hard and in improving their personal status; the possession of land contributed to both objectives. Approvingly he referred to Richard H. Shryock's study of the Pennsylvania Germans during the colonial period. This scholar suggested that these industrious and careful livestock and grain farmers would have created much the same kind of economy in colonial Virginia and Maryland had they settled there, as they had actually developed in Pennsylvania, in contrast to the tidewater tobacco plantations which money-seeking British settlers actually developed in the colonies of the upper South. More recent research suggests that the Pennsylvania Germans farmed less differently from their neighbors of other cultural backgrounds than Shryock assumed. Such findings may only prove, however, that Professor Shryock went too far in assuming that cultural values dictated specific farming methods. For few deny that cultural values are indeed powerful regulators of human behavior. The pioneers of every generation have held deep convictions as to what was right and proper, how they should meet opportunity and adversity, and the proper place in life of work, play, God and their fellow men.

After studying a community which homesteaders developed on America's southwestern farming frontier during the 1920's and 1930's, the anthropologist, Evon Z. Vogt, concluded in the early 1950's that the commitment of the settlers to certain value orientations was leading to the disintegration of the community. A pattern of widely scattered small ranches was replacing the original farming village. Such value orientations, defined by Vogt as "patterned clusters of certain associated values around important foci in the life situation of a cultural group," included among others: "A strong stress upon *individualism*," an "accent upon . . . *hopeful mastery over nature*," and "an emphasis upon the *future*." These or other value orientations obviously might retard or reinforce the individual settler's response to environmental pressures, depending on the particular situation. Such values can be transmitted in home, church and school from the members of one generation to those of another, or by the migration of individuals to other segments of a population.

What changes cultural values? They change through time apparently in response to basic changes in the economic and social environments. Stanley Elkins inspired a storm of protest when he drew an analogy between the Nazi concentration camps and Southern slave plantations and suggested that slavery may have significantly modified the personalities of the black people in bondage. But the insight was a powerful one and the western historian must ask himself if the frontier experience could have generated sufficient cultural shock to alter the value systems of those participating in it or if, over time, the experience of exploiting new natural resources could have eroded or reinforced the value systems of the frontier population. If so, was the frontier subculture sufficiently powerful to effect a significant alteration in the national matrix of cultural values?

Ray A. Billington has recently summarized the thinking of social scientists as follows:

. . . Americans stand apart because of the strength of their drive toward success and the resulting social mobility, their dependence on the opinions of their contemporaries, their preoccupation with the individual as opposed to the social group, and the inner tensions that result from inevitable failure in a highly competitive society.

How if at all did the frontier contribute to this result? The approaches that we have discussed may allow us to answer the question eventually. It is clear, however, that the frontier did not of itself produce the new man. The heritage of the Protestant denominations, the industrialization of the nation, the mixing of ethnic groups and many other factors have all made a contribution as well in producing the modern American.

III

During the last generation the analysis of the literature dealing with the West has contributed considerably to our understanding of the impact of that region upon American life and thought. Symbols or myths, literary analysts argue, accumulate in the public consciousness.

These are emotion-charged conceptions, or, as Henry Nash Smith has put it, intellectual constructions that fuse "concept and emotion into an image." The historian Mario S. DePillis argues that "time, place, beliefs and the unconscious" are all implied in the most satisfactory definition of myth. Myths may persist, passing from generation to generation, if the conditions which produced them remain or if they fill some popular need. The outstanding illustration of mythic analysis as applied to western materials is the book, *Virgin Land: The American West as Symbol and Myth* by Henry Nash Smith. Since the publication of this study, historians have become much more concerned with the symbolic images of the West and western phenomena which Americans have shared in our history.

A number of such myths have existed including: that of the Noble Savage; that of Leatherstocking, the primitive white hunter; that of the West as the route to the Orient; that of the West as the Great American Desert; that of the West as the Garden of the World; and that of the Cowboy and the Gunfighter. Such mythic constructs have conditioned the thinking of Americans to a surprising degree. Many thoughtful and humane Americans dismissed the problem of the Indians as insoluble because the myth of the Noble Savage was an unchallenged element in their thinking. In how many difficult decisions was General Eisenhower fortified by his belief in the code of the West, which he invoked publicly in the quotation given by Professor Dykstra (Chapter VIII) and which has been an integral part of the myth of the Gunfighter? How else can we explain the enthusiasm of eastern workingmen for the Homestead Law but in terms of their belief that the Agricultural Garden could ease the painful pressures of industrialism? Common sense should have told them that free homesteads would not greatly increase the safety-valve effect of the agricultural frontier but minds otherwise conditioned did not perceive such truth. The number of western myths and the frequency with which they appeared in the literature by the nineteenth century are convincing proof of the important place that the frontier filled in the American consciousness. Defenders of the western myths faced the derision of social critics late in the century and the competition of the myths of industrialism, but some such myths, at least, still live in the public consciousness.

Why was the western story such a favorite during the first 60 years of the twentieth century? Avid readers devoured cowboy story after cowboy story, although the plots in this genre have long been stereotyped to a considerable degree. Some have suggested that addicts of popular fiction, whether committed to westerns or detective stories or science fiction, do not read for novelty but rather because they find comforting ideas repeated in them. After analyzing a considerable sample of westerns which had appeared in book form between 1900 and 1955, John Clifford was impressed by the fact that most so-called cowboy stories presented heroes who were the sons of substantial ranchers or other high status individuals, although perhaps temporarily down on their luck. The plots typically involved threats to property. The heroes solved the central problem against heavy odds and usually by fortitude, personal skill and luck. With this done, they married the heroine and lived happily ever after on a ranch in the Superstitions or some other appropriate locale. This writer suggested that the reading public, as members of a nation of property owners, identified with the hero in such stories, found the central problem vaguely analogous to their own and were reinforced by the outcome in their conviction that hard work and a little luck would bring a person through his troubles.

Less common but sometimes highly successful was the plot in which the super gunman restored order to a paralyzed community, renounced the heroine and rode off into the sunset. Some analysts have suggested that the appeal of this variant of the western was to the beleagured or alienated side of the reader's character, striking a particularly strong response in the minds of those who consciously or unconsciously longed for a superman who could set all things right. Latent totalitarianism accounted for the popularity of such books. John G. Cawelti's conclusions in the third reading of this chapter differ somewhat from these suggestions.

Although it rests on assumptions derived from Freudian psychology, a recent article by Alan C. Beckman deserves mention here because the analysis is essentially literary rather than scientific. Professor Beckman assumed that the critics of Frederick Jackson Turner's thesis were essentially correct. Why, if this be true, he inquired, should the frontier hypothesis have remained popular? Suppose, he suggested, that the Turner thesis be considered a myth in which the major actors were the frontier or West, the frontiersman, and the East or government. After analyzing Turner's description of the *dramatis personae* and their interaction he concluded that the

frontier thesis is a symbolic re-enactment of a universal wish drama of childhood, the Oedipus conflict. . . . The West, or frontier, is the mother who had once been the source of early gratifications, but who now becomes the object of those first, primitive, but nevertheless masculine stirrings and strivings of her young son, our frontiersman.

The reader will wish perhaps to review the excerpt from Turner's writing in Chapter I and decide whether he agrees with Professor Beckman. Historians have not found this example of mythic analysis to be completely convincing, but we can be sure that it is not the last attempt to explain the meaning of the frontier and its relation to the American mind.

·1·

ARTHUR M. SCHLESINGER

"What Then Is the American, This New Man?"

Arthur M. Schlesinger was one of the scholars most responsible for the increasing interest in social history among historians during the years since 1930. The concept of national character both fascinates and frustrates historians and, from time to time, Professor Schlesinger wrote on aspects of that difficult subject. In this extract from one of his best known essays, he discusses the agrarian origins of the American character.

What elements of the national character are attributable to this long-time agrarian environment? First and foremost is the habit of work. For the colonial farmer ceaseless striving constituted the price of survival; every member of the community must be up and doing. . . .

The tradition of toil so begun found new sustenance as settlers opened up the boundless stretches of the interior. "In the free States," wrote Harriet Martineau in 1837, "labour is more really and heartily honoured than, perhaps, in any other part of the civilised world." Alonzo Potter voiced the general opinion of the American people when he asserted a few years later, "Without a definite pursuit, a man is an excrescence on society. . . . In isolating himself from the cares and employments of other men, he forfeits much of their sympathy, and can neither give nor

SOURCE: Abridged from Arthur M. Schlesinger, *Paths to the Present* (New York: The Macmillan Company, 1949), 1–22. Reprinted by permission of Elizabeth B. Schlesinger.

receive great benefit." Even when the usual motives for work did not exist, the social compulsion remained. As William Ellery Channing put it, "The rich man has no more right to repose than the poor," for nobody should so live as to "throw all toil on another class of society."

One source of Northern antagonism to the system of human bondage was the fear that it was jeopardizing this basic tenet of the American creed. . . .

Probably no legacy from our farmer forebears has entered more deeply into the national psychology. If an American has no purposeful work on hand, the fever in his blood impels him nevertheless to some visible form of activity. When seated he keeps moving in a rocking chair. . . . This worship of work has made it difficult for Americans to learn how to play. . . .

Into it goes all the fierce energy that once felled the forests and broke the prairies. Americans play games not for fun but to win. They attend social gatherings grimly determined to have a "good time." Maxim Gorky said of Coney Island, "What an unhappy people it must be that turns for happiness here." The "rich gift of extemporizing pleasures," of taking leisure leisurely, seems alien to the national temper. It is significant that the English *Who's Who* includes the recreations of the notables listed, while the American does not.

The importance attached to useful work had the further effect of helping to make "this new man" indifferent to aesthetic considerations. To the farmer a tree was not a thing of beauty and a joy forever, but an obstacle to be replaced as quickly as possible with a patch of corn. In the words of an eighteenth-century American, "The Plow-man that raiseth Grain is more serviceable to Mankind, than the Painter who draws only to please the Eye. The Carpenter who builds a good House to defend us from the Wind and Weather, is more serviceable than the curious Carver, who employs his Art to please the Fancy." The cult of beauty, in other words, had nothing to contribute to the stern business of living; it wasn't "practical." The bias thus given to the national mentality lasted well into America's urban age. One result has been the architectural monotony and ugliness which have invariably offended travelers used to the picturesque charm of Old World cities. . . .

On the other hand, the complicated nature of the farmer's job, especially during the first two and a half centuries, afforded an unexcelled training in mechanical ingenuity. These ex-Europeans and their descendants became a race of whittlers and tinkers, daily engaged in devising, improving and repairing tools and other utensils until, as Emerson said, they had "the power and habit of invention in their brain." "Would any one but an American," asked one of Emerson's contemporaries, "have ever invented a milking machine? or a machine to beat eggs? or machines to black boots, scour knives, pare apples, and do a hundred things that all other peoples have done with their ten fingers from time immemorial?" . . .

The farmer's success in coping with his multitudinous tasks aroused a pride of accomplishment that made him scorn the specialist or expert. As a Jack-of-all-trades he was content to be master of none, choosing to do many things well enough rather than anything supremely well. Accordingly, versatility became another outstanding American attribute. . . .

Even in his principal occupation of growing food, the farmer encountered harsh criticism from foreign observers because of the way he wore out the land, neglected livestock and destroyed forest resources. But Old World agriculture rested on a ratio of man to land which in the New World was the reverse. It was as logical for the American farmer to "mine" the soil and move on to a virgin tract as it was for the European peasant to husband his few acres in the interest of generations unborn. Not till the opening years of the twentieth century, when the pressure of population dramatized the evils of past misuse, did the conservation of natural resources become a set national policy.

Meanwhile the tradition of wasteful living, bred by an evironment of plenty, had fastened itself upon the American character, disposing men to condone extravagance in public as well as in private life. Even governmental corruption could be winked at on the ground that a wealthy country like the United States could afford it. In their daily living, Americans were improvident of riches that another people would have carefully preserved. . . .

Toward women the American male early acquired an attitude which sharply distinguished him from his brother in the Old World. As in every new country, women had a high scarcity value, both in the colonies and later in the pioneer West. They were in demand not only as sweethearts and wives, but also because of their economic importance, for they performed the endless work about the house and helped with the heavy farm labor. "The cry is everywhere for girls; girls, and more girls!" wrote a traveler in 1866. He noted that men outnumbered women in thirty-eight of the forty-five states and territories. In California the proportion was three to one; in Colorado, twenty to one. "Guess my husband's got to look after me, and make himself agreeable to me, if he can," a pretty Western girl remarked, "if he don't, there's plenty will." In the circumstances men paid women a deference and accorded them a status unknown in older societies. European observers attributed the high standard of sex morals largely to this fact, and it is significant that the most rapid strides toward equal suffrage took place in those commonwealths whose rural characteristics were strongest. . . .

Since the agriculturalist regarded his farm as only a temporary abode —an investment rather than a home—he soon contracted the habit of being "permanently transitory." Distances that would have daunted the stoutest-hearted European deterred "this new man" not at all. Many an Atlantic Coast family migrated from place to place across the continent until the second or third generation reached the rim of the Pacific, then the next one began the journey back. "In no State of the Union," wrote James Bryce in 1888, "is the bulk of the population so fixed in its residence as everywhere in Europe; in many it is almost nomadic." . . .

Geographic or horizontal mobility, however, has been a less fundamental aspect of American life than social or vertical mobility, though the two are not unrelated. The European conception of a graded society, with each class everlastingly performing its allotted function, vanished quickly amidst primitive surroundings that invited the humblest to move upward as well as outward. Instead of everybody being nobody, they found that anybody might become somebody. . . .

Accordingly, there arose the ingrained belief in equality of opportunity, the right of all men to a free and fair start—a view which in one of its most significant ramifications led to the establishment of free tax-supported schools. This was far from being a dogma of enforced equality. To benefit from equality of opportunity a man must be equal to his opportunities, with the government serving principally as an umpire to supervise the game with a minimum of rules. The upshot was a conception of democracy rigorously qualified by individualism.

This individualistic bias sometimes assumed forms that defied government. The colonists in their relations with the mother country evaded unwelcome regulations and, prompted by their theologians and lawyers, insisted that acts of Parliament contrary to their "unalienable rights" were void. . . . As a substitute for constituted authority the settlers sometimes created their own unofficial tribunals, which adjudicated property titles and punished offenders against the public peace. In other instances they resorted to the swifter retribution of individual gunplay, or of mob action and lynch law, for from taking the law into one's hands when it could not function it was but a step to taking the law into one's hands when it did not function as one wanted it to.

The tendency to violence so generated has continued to condition the national mentality to the present time. Thoreau, the great philosopher of individualism, knew of no reason why a citizen should "ever for a moment, or in the least degree, resign his conscience to the legislator," declaring that "we should be men first, and subjects afterward." A similar conviction undoubtedly inspired William H. Seward's flaming declaration to the proslavery Senators in 1850 that "there is a higher law than the Constitution," just as it actuated the thousands of churchgoing Northerners who secretly banded together to violate the Fugitive Slave Act. But generally it has been self-interest or convenience, rather than conscience, that has provided the incentive to lawbreaking, as in the case of the businessman chafing against legislative restrictions or of the motorist disobeying traffic regulations. Sometimes the attitude has paraded under such high-sounding names as states' rights and nullification. This lawless streak in the American character has often been directed to wrong purposes, but it has also served as a check on the abuse of governmental powers and as a safeguard of minority rights.

In still another aspect, the individualism of the pioneer farmer does much to explain the intense cultivation of the acquisitive spirit. In the absence of hereditary distinctions of birth and rank the piling up of wealth constituted the most obvious badge of social superiority, and once the process was begun, the inbred urge to keep on working made it difficult to stop. "The poor struggle to be rich, the rich to be richer," remarked an onlooker in the mid-nineteenth century. Thanks to equality of opportunity with plenty for all, the class struggle in America has consisted in the struggle to climb out of one class into a higher one. The zest of competition frequently led to sharp trading, fraud and chicanery, but in the popular mind guilt attached less to the practices than to being caught at them. Financial success was accepted as the highest success, and not till the twentieth century did a religious leader venture to advance the un-American doctrine that ill-gotten wealth was "tainted money," even when devoted to benevolent uses. . . .

The fact is that, for a people who recalled how hungry and oppressed their ancestors had been through long centuries in the Old World, the chance to make money was like the sunlight at the end of a tunnel. It was the means of living a life of human dignity. It was a symbol of idealism rather than materialism. Hence "this new man" had an instinctive sympathy for the underdog, and even persons of moderate substance freely shared it with the less fortunate, helping to endow charities, schools, hospitals and art galleries and to nourish humanitarian undertakings which might otherwise have died a-borning.

The energy that entered into many of these causes was heightened by another national attitude: optimism. It was this quality that sustained the European men and women who with heavy hearts left ancestral homes to try their fortunes in a wild and far-off continent. The same trait animated the pioneer farmers confronted by the hardships, loneliness and terrors of the primeval forest, and served also to spur their successors who, though facing less dire conditions, were constantly pitted against both the uncertainties of the weather and the unpredictable demands of the market. . . . This quality of optimism sometimes soared to dizzy heights, inpelling men to strive for earthly perfection in communistic societies or to prepare to greet the imminent return of Christ.

It attained its most blatant expression, however, in the national addiction to bragging. At bottom, this habit sprang from pride in a country of vast distances and huge elevations plus an illimitable faith in its possibilities of being great as well as big. The American glorified the future in much the same spirit as the European glorified the past, both tending to exalt what they had the most of. And by a simple transition the American went on to speak of expected events as though they had already happened, being prompted perhaps by an urge to compensate for an inner sense of inferiority. . . .

The national character, as we at present know it, is thus a mixture of long-persisting traits tempered by some newly acquired ones. Based upon the solid qualities of those Europeans who planted the colonies, it assumed distinctive form under pressure of adaptation to the radically different situation. "Our ancestors sought a new continent," said James Russell Lowell. "What they found was a new condition of mind." The protracted tutelage to the soil acted as the chief formative influence, dispelling ancient inhibitions, freeing dormant energies, revamping mental attitudes. The rise of the city confirmed or strengthened many of the earlier characteristics while reshaping others. Probably no one of the traits is peculiar to the American people; some occasion apology rather than pride; but the aggregate represents a way of life unlike that of any other nation. . . .

•2•

ALLAN G. BOGUE

Social Theory and the Pioneer

To ease the plight of residents in marginal farming areas
of the United States during the depression of the 1930's,
agencies of the United States government sponsored the development of a number of new agricultural communities.
Social scientists studied the social processes at work in some
of these communities or comparable settlements and Allan
G. Bogue has tried tentatively to generalize from the findings and develop a model of settlement behavior on the
midwestern frontier of the late nineteenth century.

Most settlers moved to the new lands of the Middle West in the expectation that they would improve their economic and social positions. The
two are closely related and any considerable improvement in one is
almost invariably accompanied by improvement in the other. Economic
position is the most important determinant of social status in America
today, and this was all the more the case on the frontier where no
community tradition of deference to particular families existed to cloud
the relationship.

By the act of migration the new settlers had broken those social
relationships which had assisted them in patterning their lives in their
former homes. Of course the severance was not necessarily absolute.
The young bachelor making a start in life might journey to the west
alone, but he might well be accompanied by friend or brother. If the
migrant were married he was accompanied by his family or soon
brought out the other members of his family circle to join him. A number of related families might well move together and old neighborhood
friends might be discovered by accident or design in the new settlements.
Colonization companies were organized in older communities occasionally for the purpose of migration. But unquestionably the move west
shattered the social structure of which most pioneers had been a part

SOURCE: Abridged from Allan G. Bogue, "Social Theory and the Pioneer," *Agricultural History*, XXXIV (January, 1960), 21-34. Reprinted by permission of
Agricultural History.

and they had to fit themselves into a new one. The unity of the family and those other intimate social relations which are called primary relationships were often broken, and much more completely shattered were the bonds of less intimate acquaintance which the resident of any locality builds up over time and which are sometimes called secondary relationships.

We must, of course, qualify our position to some extent. Although the practice was uncommon, a closely knit social group might move to the frontier in a body. The removal of the Ebenezer Society from western New York to the Amana settlements in eastern Iowa illustrated such migration. At Amana the social structure was maintained and the members of the group faced only the task of re-establishing their means of livelihood in a new environment. The cohesion of such groups stemmed from the loyalty of the members to their peculiar social and religious beliefs. On the other hand, the community of interest shared by the members of a foreign language group might assist its members to build new social structures but certainly did not eliminate the need to do so.

Frequently, the pioneers settled among neighbors who differed from them in cultural background. The foreign born, the Yankee stock and the members of the southern migration, which moved out of the southern border states in the years after 1800, constituted the major groups that participated in the settlement of the Middle West. But within these groups the social origins were varied. This was particularly so among the foreign born, but the settler of Yankee persuasion who was born and spent his early years in central New York differed somewhat in his standard of values and life training from one who had been born in New England or Ohio. Members of the major cultural groups tended to settle in the same areas, but there was usually some intermingling with other cultural groups, particularly in those regions where the dominance of one major group shaded into the dominance of another.

But if the pioneer had neighbors, they were often distant at first. Isolation was frequently the lot of the settler. Such isolation might be physical, it might be social and often it was both. The frontier farmer could expect to go through a period when neighbors were few or scattered, and the tendency of the farm unit to increase in size as the frontier moved west through the prairies similarly worked to increase the isolation of the individual farm family. Socially, the pioneer was isolated until he could build up a net of primary and secondary relationships. Social isolation of this sort could be accentuated by language barriers or less striking but still important, cultural differences. The "Nobscotter" members of New England settlements in Iowa might seem uncongenial neighbors indeed to nearby farmers of southern stock. . . .

The members of most social groups do not participate on a basis of complete equality, but rather, informally or formally, ascribe varying degrees of leadership and status to each other. In a period when groups are being formed, competition exists among potential leaders to a considerable extent, creating a situation which is much more unstable than is ultimately the case when the group has shaken down and the members have come to know the virtues and deficiencies of their fellows more thoroughly. An important function of the leaders is to regulate the membership of the group. Acceptance of new members depends to a considerable extent upon the decisions of the leaders. The absence of a well-established leadership hierarchy duly recognized by a majority of the local residents was an important characteristic of frontier society. New residents, as a result, lacked authoritative guidance in fitting themselves into the social structure of the new communities.

The new settlers faced a strange and untamed physical environment on the frontier. The farmer in the older settlements who moved to a new neighborhood also moved into a strange environment, but at least the resources upon which he expended his labor had yielded in large part to the ministrations of his predecessors. Although the pioneer might inherit a few improvements from a squatter or a previous owner, he still must face in some measure the rudimentary tasks of farm making— clearing, breaking, fencing, draining and well digging in addition to the construction of farm buildings.

Settlers faced the challenge of the physical environment with differing degrees of preparation. The internal migration patterns of the nineteenth century show that the pioneers of American stock had themselves often been reared in frontier communities and where such was the case they had a good understanding of the problems which they faced. At the other extreme, of course, stood the European immigrant coming from communities where the agricultural resources had been in use for unremembered generations. But even the immigrants were usually rural in background and the agriculture of nineteenth century America required few skills that were difficult for anyone reared in agriculture to acquire. The tendency of migrants to move along isothermal lines assisted them to some extent in acclimatization and removed the necessity of learning how to cultivate new plants. But the prairies and particularly the plains would present problems unknown on earlier American frontiers.

Migrants to the West seldom found themselves completely outside a formal institutional framework, although the wagon trains moving through the plains country constituted something of an exception. The land distribution agencies of the federal government served the pioneer and on occasion federal troops or officers assisted in maintenance of order. A system of territorial government provided laws for the settlers although settlement might be extremely scanty. Both in the territories and in the subsequent frontier states, local county government moved with the settler. The churches, the major private agencies of social control, were never far behind the settlers, the denominations to greater or lesser extent modifying their doctrines and organization to meet the special problems of the frontier.

But if a formal institutional framework did exist on the frontier of the agricultural settler and his town and village counterpart in the Middle West, it was often rudimentary or even sadly defective in its operation. The story of the agricultural frontier is interspersed with conflicts over land titles, and even the normal operation of the land laws in the Middle West operated in such a way that extralegal claim clubs developed or at best uncertainty over titles existed. In the early years of any agricultural community the revenues which could be raised by taxation might be inadequate to insure the satisfactory performance of community services by the local government or its agencies. In so far as the churches were concerned, the means to support a full-time clergy could seldom be found within the community.

Finally, in generalizing upon the frontier community of the prairies, we can say that the economic foundations were infirm, for it was highly dependent upon a continued flow of new personnel and additional capital and thus extremely vulnerable to fluctuations in business conditions. The nineteenth century pioneer farmer cannot be regarded as purely a subsistence farmer. Prior to the passage of the Homestead Act, and afterwards to a considerable extent as well, he must meet the costs of his land as well as other expenses involved in the farm making process. Particularly if communications with the older settlements were poor, an important part of the settler's market was provided by incoming migrants who were forced to buy much of their own food as well as various services from the "old settlers" until their own acres came to bearing. Capital flowed into the frontier community in a variety of ways—as savings brought by the newcomers, in the form of loans made by residents of older areas, in the shape of goods sold to the frontier merchants on credit, and through the medium of speculative land purchases which were in turn sold to the pioneer settlers on credit or in some cases rented to them. Such movement was closely related to the business cycle throughout the nineteenth century. Both settlers and capital ceased to move to the frontier settlements in time of depression.

At this point we can make explicit a number of assumptions about the social behavior of the individual, which may perhaps be relevant in explaining some characteristics of society on the prairie frontier. In the first place, the individual finds primary and secondary relationships essential to satisfactory living. Few individuals are really content to be hermits. Taken from their accustomed web of social relationships they may suffer from what is termed *anomie* or normlessness. The leading exponent of sociometry, J. L. Moreno, has carried this idea to the point of arguing that group relationships may actually serve as therapy for the maladjusted.

On such basis we can at least argue that most individuals who moved to the frontier were highly interested in reestablishing a satisfying system of social relations. We can safely assume as well that the skills and aptitudes of individuals in a particular social setting vary in the degree to which they are appropriate for solving the economic and social problems which confront them. Some individuals could, then, adapt themselves to frontier conditions more successfully than others.

Again, we can generalize that communication problems are an important source of conflict situations. If it was possible for individuals to explain their point of view perfectly there would be much less misunderstanding and argument. The greater the difference in the cultural backgrounds of individuals thrown into a common social setting the greater, it would seem, the danger of difficulties in communication. We can also suggest that the individual experiences deprivation when he fails to achieve a level of satisfaction which he considers minimal in the light of his experiences and future expectations. For the individual on the frontier undoubtedly the point at which deprivation set in was established, whether he realized it or not, prior to his movement to the new settlements.

Finally, deprivation often prompts the individual to indulge in forms of substitute behavior. Failing to achieve adequate gratification by working in the recognized social channels he goes beyond them, and resorts on the one hand, perhaps, to crime, or at the other extreme, retreats into fantasy. Emotional religion is sometimes considered to be an illustration of substitute behavior and undoubtedly a greater degree of horizontal mobility than ordinary can be justly considered in the same light.

On the basis of such postulates and the general characteristics of frontier communities we can draw certain generalizations or hypotheses. Since individuals on the frontier lacked both the well-established institutions and the social customs which had assisted them in patterning their behavior in the communities from which they came, since a hetero-geneous population engendered difficulties in communication, and since the economic resources were temporarily inadequate or might become so in short order, they were involved in a greater number of conflict situations than before migration. Since the economic environment pre-sented problems that the individual found impossible, or extremely difficult, to solve for himself, there was a greater amount of informal co-operation when conflict was absent on the frontier than in older com-munities. Conflict situations, the failure to re-establish satisfactory social relationships, the absence of clearly defined social norms, and the failure of the new environment to meet the expectations of betterment originally held by some migrants produced considerable deprivation. This was reflected in: high crime rates, resort to emotional religion, heavy inci-dence of mental disease, and continued mobility. Finally, there was a greater degree of political participation on the frontier than in older communities. This resulted from the efforts of individuals to gain status through leadership in a relatively unstructured society, from the effort to establish group ties, and from the greater relative significance of the economic rewards of politics in the frontier community.

Value orientations undoubtedly modified frontier social processes, holding the pioneers firm against environmental pressures at some points —predisposing them to yield at others. But each western settler was a unique individual and if many in a pioneer neighborhood reacted sim-ilarly and made similar decisions some did not. Knowing that this was so, we cannot be too rigorously deterministic in explaining the behavior of the pioneers.

JOHN G. CAWELTI

Cowboys, Indians, Outlaws

A great many themes are intertwined in the common body of tradition and values that Americans share. Few of us can deny that mention of the western "hero" brings to mind a variety of mental images and associated values, of brave, self-reliant men for instance, or on the other hand perhaps, inadequately policed communities in which rationality had been sacrificed on the altar of violence. In the popularity and durability of the western hero lies a key to the understanding of at least part of what is American. John G. Cawelti traces the history of the myth.

On December 16, 1872, as their city was recovering from the disastrous fire of the preceding year, a sellout crowd of Chicagoans was waiting for the curtain to rise on a play entitled *The Scouts of the Plains*. The play turned out to be something less than a masterpiece. The playwright, a redoutable character whose career had included everything from bigamy to temperance lectures, was a writer of dime novels who called himself Ned Buntline, though his real name was Edward Zane Carroll Judson. . . .

The cast of *The Scouts of the Plains* also left something to be desired. The only member who could charitably be called a trained professional was an Italian actress named Mademoiselle Morlacchi who played the part of Dove-Eye, an Indian maiden. The three male leads not only had little previous theatrical experience, but two of them completely forgot their lines. The cast was rounded out by ten down-and-out extras rather unconvincingly made up as Indians. The performance with which this distinguished company favored its audience was unbelievable. In summing up his reaction to it, the critic of the Chicago *Times* wrote:

On the whole, it is not probable that Chicago will ever look upon the like again. Such a combination of incongruous drama, execrable acting, renowned

SOURCE: Abridged from John G. Cawelti, "Cowboys, Indians, Outlaws," *American West*, I (Spring, 1964), 28-35, 77-79. Reprinted by permission of *American West* and John G Cawelti.

performers, mixed audience, intolerable stench, scalping, blood and thunder, is not likely to be vouchsafed to a city for a second time,—even Chicago.

Judging from other reports of the performance, one can readily sympathize with this long-suffering critic. Nonetheless, *The Scouts of the Plains* was an early and crude version of one of America's most distinctive contributions to world culture, the Western, which some critics have called one of the few authentic modern folk-epics or myths. Furthermore, *The Scouts of the Plains* was the theatrical debut of the individual who probably did most to impose the image of the Wild West on the world's imagination, William F. Cody or Buffalo Bill.

The Western, as we know it today in novels, movies, and television, is essentially the elaboration of the image of the West created by the Wild West Show of Buffalo Bill and the dime novels of the later nineteenth century. Indeed, one of the fascinating questions which awaits the definitive historian of the Western is why the myth of the West became fixed on what was actually a very minor part of the actual history of the West, the struggles of cowboys, Indians, and outlaws on the Great Plains. . . . Out of a frontier history of almost three hundred years, Americans have selected a twenty-year period and made it eternal in myth as *the* West.

If Buffalo Bill's Wild West and the popular adventure stories of the dime novels . . . were largely responsible for fixing the shape of the Western, they can hardly be called creators of the mythology of the West. To a considerable extent their contribution was rather one of adapting, simplifying, dramatizing—one might almost say jazzing up— an already existing mythic pattern which went back at least as far as the early nineteenth century and had already been given an important literary embodiment long before anyone had ever heard of cowboys.

Until the end of the nineteenth century the existence of a western frontier was part of the American experience. As early as 1682 there appeared an extremely popular work of literature which was, in a sense, a western story, Mrs. Mary Rowlandson's narrative of her life as a captive among the Indians. However, Mrs. Rowlandson's story was more or less an actual narrative based on her own experiences. . . . Throughout the eighteenth and nineteenth centuries, western travelers and actual settlers attempted to set down their experience of the West. In the twentieth century this tradition of eyewitness accounts has been continued in the work of serious historical novelists such as A. B. Guthrie, Walter Van Tilburg Clark, and H. L. Davis, who, with the help of careful research, have attempted to recreate in fiction the reality of various phases of frontier life. . . . Nevertheless, the tradition of serious historical writing, whether factual or fictional, should be differentiated from the Western. In fact, one distinguishing mark of the serious historical novelist of the West is his tendency to eschew the cowboys, injuns, and outlaws who dominate the popular myth in order to deal with the life of the farmers and other settlers whose life was, after all, more representative of the typical western experience.

Another literary tradition connected with the West was also quite distinct from the Western myth: the great tradition of western humor, satire, and tall tale which reached its zenith in the early work of Mark Twain. The great hero of this tradition was not the noble frontiersman or cowboy of the epic but the picaresque rogue. . . . The great classic of western humor, Mark Twain's *Roughing It*, was the antithesis in attitude and treatment of Buffalo Bill's Wild West, while even the more sentimental and picturesque stories of Bret Harte had little to do with the West of the mythic tradition. Perhaps the major influence of western humor on the growth of *the* Western lay in its development of the comic westerner, who as a sidekick of the hero, became a *sine qua non* of the Hollywood B Western. Those rather boring buffoons played by Andy Devine were probably the debilitated grandchildren of Mark Twain's great comic creations.

There was always an interplay between the three strands of eyewitness and historical narrative, western humor, and the myth of the West, but they remained essentially separate cultural traditions. The first two were the work of actual westerners and, in their different ways, reflected western experience and attitudes. The mythology of the West, however, was primarily the creation of men who any self-respecting cowboy would have called dudes. . . . To see the western legend in proper perspective, we must realize that it has always been more expressive of the values and needs of a highly complex eastern society than of the actual experience of the advancing frontier.

This was true from the inception of the legendary West. America's first important western hero was the great frontiersman Daniel Boone. Boone's exploits were first celebrated in an appendix to the *Discovery, Settlement, and Present State of Kentucke* published in 1784 by John Filson, one of the pioneer settlers of the state. His material was evidently gathered directly from Boone and was written as if it were an autobiography of the hero. However, it seems unlikely that the unlettered frontiersman would have described his experience in the language and ideas Filson ascribed to him. . . . In fact, though substantially accurate as to the events of Boone's life, Filson's account tended to interpret these events in terms of European literary and philosophical ideas. This influence became even more intense in Timothy Flint's *Biographical Memoir of Daniel Boone* (1833). Flint . . . was a Harvard-educated New Englander who moved to Cincinnati for his health. Flint's Daniel Boone was born of Chateaubriand, Rousseau and Parson Weems. . . .

Thus, the real-life Daniel Boone was soon transformed by his literary eulogists into the mythical figure of the natural genius free from the artificial restrictions and false pomp of civilization and in direct communion with the Divine Being and His creation. However, Flint's version of this romantic ideal was that of a tenderfoot literary poseur compared with the far more virile creation of his contemporary James Fenimore Cooper. Cooper's "Leatherstocking Series," published between 1823 and 1841, remains the greatest literary monument to the legendary West. Unlike the shallow romanticism of Timothy Flint and other American apostles of a sophisticated primitivism, Cooper's philosophy was deeply felt and embodied a complex cultural criticism. Leatherstocking was by no means the stock figure of the noble savage, though, as Mark Twain later pointed out in his scathing attack in "James Fenimore Cooper's Literary Offenses," Cooper was not untouched by the romantic ideal. Actually, Leatherstocking was part of a complex myth in which Cooper expressed his view of the progress of civilization, a process which he felt had gone off the track in the acquisitive, speculating spirit of his own day. Leatherstocking symbolically embodied the innocent and simple virtues which Cooper felt Americans had lost. However, Cooper had no desire to stave off the progress of civilization. On the contrary, his real hero was not the primitive frontiersman but the cultivated gentleman. Yet he shared the belief of many of his contemporaries that there was great danger in the too rapid pre-emption of the wilderness and in the dominantly acquisitive and materialistic attitude with which Americans pursued their Manifest Destiny. Thus, Cooper's myth of the West expressed the ambiguity and anxiety which many early nineteenth-century Americans felt toward the mobile, dynamically changing society which they were creating, a new social order which threatened many of their traditional moral, religious, and social values. . . .

After the Civil War the Western in dime novel, Wild West Show, and finally in the movies, lost much of its earlier complexity as it became a form of popular entertainment. Spectacle and action were more strongly emphasized than philosophical or political content. Building on the myth of the West as elaborated in the work of Cooper, the dime novelists created an action-filled formula which, with minor changes in event and character, could be duplicated over and over again. Most importantly, they gradually transformed the setting and the cast of characters of the

Western. Increasingly, writers of popular Westerns turned to the Great Plains and the 1850's and 1860's for the locale of their stories, and they developed the cowboy hero. . . . Certainly, there was no single reason why the cowboy of the Great Plains became *the* mythical archetype of the West. In part, it was probably a matter of unique historical circumstance such as the tremendous popularity of Buffalo Bill's Wild West. . . .

But there were doubtless other reasons why the cowboy was such a successful mythic figure. There were, for example, what might loosely be called artistic reasons. A popular myth requires clear conflicts and the potential for spectacle. The cowboy in his struggle with Indians and badmen provided simple but exciting conflicts of heroes and villains. Perhaps even more important was the horse. The earlier frontiersman had been a walker, but the horse transformed the spectacle of action and brought about that image of rapid movement across a vast space which became at once the most characteristic and most thrilling aspect of the Western. . . .

Finally, Leatherstocking's replacement by the cowboy doubtless reflected some shift in the general cultural attitudes of Americans, though with our present knowledge it is difficult to say definitely just how. Henry Nash Smith has argued that the earlier Leatherstocking figure was usually subordinate in Cooper's plots to the traditional upper-class hero and heroine because the cult of aristocratic gentility made it impossible for Americans to imagine a crude frontiersman as a romantic hero. The coming of the cowboy, who occupied the center of the story, reflected a decline of this aristocratic prejudice. . . .

Smith is certainly correct that after the Civil War the western myth evolved into a form of popular entertainment which lacked the philosophical and artistic breadth of its progenitor. From a certain point of view this could be called a progressive deterioration. I am not sure Smith's analysis is correct in saying that the genre lost its social significance, however. The cowboy was, as he was developed in the later nineteenth century, not simply the child of nature whose simple virtues were opposed to the complexity of civilization. Nor was he, in Cooper's fashion, the thesis in a complex, quasi-Hegelian dialectic of progress. In the later nineteenth-century Western, a stage in the development of the frontier was removed from the processes of time and progress by focusing the action not on the coming of civilization but on the immediate conflicts arising out of the march of civilization. Where Leatherstocking's primary struggle was with those who sought to destroy his wilderness, the cowboy hero fought those who, like Indians and rustlers,

sought to break the peace and transgress the code by which he lived. . . .
Owen Wister in *The Virginian* (1902), the fountainhead of the twentieth-
century Western, gave this new moral dimension its classic formulation.
Wister's hero, who made his appearance with the classic Westernism
"smile when you say that, podner," on his lips, was far less the incarnation
of nature than the symbol of a heroic code. The central theme of the
book was not the conflict between nature and civilization but the struggle
between the values of eastern middle-class respectability as represented
by the heroine and the heroic code of the hero. . . .

The conflict between the eastern ideal of the respectable, law-abiding
nonviolent citizen and the western code of honor and individual justice
which Wister built into *The Virginian* has become a basic theme of the
Western myth, appearing most typically in the situation where the
hero discovers that the legal and political structure of the community
is paralyzed and that he must resort to extra-legal violence to bring
justice and restore the peace. The great duel on the main street with
which Wister resolved his story has become an almost ritualistic observance commemorating the ultimate breakdown and violent restoration of
the political and legal process. It is this thematic aspect of the contemporary Western which has most fascinated critical analysts because it
seems to reflect profound ambiguities of value in American culture. . . .
I am inclined to think that the conflict between the code of the West
and the middle-class values of the East is a projection into fantasy of a
reaction against the dominant middle-class values of our culture, a
collective imagining of a way of life in which the individual is freed from
the frustrating pressures of domesticity, steady employment, civic responsibility, and the other public virtues of modern middle-class life.
In my view, the cowboy is an antihero to the successful law-abiding
citizen, projected back into an eternalized moment of the past so that
his essentially subversive message cannot seriously challenge our accepted
values. . . .

In the twentieth century the dime-novel tradition continued to develop
in pulps and pocketbooks, while the more sophisticated tradition of Owen
Wister went through such writers as Zane Grey and Harold Bell Wright
into the present day. The movies and television have, of course, had a
considerable influence on the form and have brought it to even wider
audiences than before. On the whole, however, the movies seem to have
depended to a surprising extent on the established tradition. . . . Television too has depended to a considerable extent on existing materials,
but in a few cases such programs as "Gunsmoke" and "Have Gun, Will
Travel"—the so-called adult Westerns—television has found a formula

of its own. The extent to which these television Westerns constitute a departure from the basic tradition of the myth comparable to the evolution of the cowboy hero after the Civil War is debatable, but the sophisticated treatment of stock Western themes has always been a part of the tradition. For all its importance as cultural myth, one should never forget that one basic reason why the Western has survived and prospered is that, for all its tendency to slip into stock formulas and stereotype situations, it has always been varied and flexible enough to engage, from time to time, the efforts of major creative imaginations. . . .

•4•

LAURENCE R. VEYSEY

Myth and Reality in Approaching American Regionalism

Although the student of American character may find literary analysis to be very rewarding, the concept of myth and its use do involve some dangers. In this reading Laurence R. Veysey points out some of the problems involved in the employment of myth and symbol in the book by Henry Nash Smith, *Virgin Land: The American West as Symbol and Myth.* He suggests that, in some instances at least, we may find the study of regional stereotypes to be more rewarding than the elaboration of myth and symbol.

. . . The flavor of localities often lies captured within their legends. Inexorably the would-be regional historian finds himself drawn toward the pungent stereotypes which comprise the mythology of his terrain. What is the West without Daniel Boone and "Buffalo Bill" and the Mountain Men? New England instantly conjures the shrewd, thrifty trader and the stern, righteous Puritan. Can the South come alive with less than the vision of a stately mansion painted in white? . . .

SOURCE: Abridged from Laurence R. Veysey, "Myth and Reality in Approaching American Regionalism," *American Quarterly,* XII (Spring, 1960), 31-43. © 1960, Trustees of the University of Pennsylvania. Reprinted by permission of *American Quarterly* and Laurence R. Veysey.

Yet the legend cannot be approached with simple trust. It cannot be swallowed whole, for the rather obvious reason that it is not the total fact, and the historian must ultimately come to terms with fact. Davy Crockett, however homespun, was a Whig. The Puritans had an eager, optimistic zest for life, politics and literature. Only a tiny fraction of antebellum Southerners owned large numbers of slaves. The myth, in short, often appears to be at wide variance with the reality. Can myths then be safely used?

Two widely divergent approaches to this problem of myth and reality— in the broader context of the American experience as a whole—have developed. . . . On the one hand, the intellectual and literary historian tended to exult over the potency of the myths he had discovered, and to call upon empirical reality only for fitful and sporadic documentation as to the force of these ideas. On the other, the social and economic historian tended to rejoice in the distinction because he comprehended in it a wedge by which he could pry loose a "false" ideological super-structure, and, in an iconoclastic release from such encumbrance, reveal a "new truth" about "how things really were." . . .

In a period when appreciation for intellectual history has become a dominant fashion, it is much easier to grasp and berate the deficiencies of the "realist" who gleefully shatters myth than it is to comprehend the more subtle and profound difficulties of the scholar who lets myths and patterns of ideas run too freely and independently at large. For this very reason, it becomes especially pertinent now to re-examine the work of Henry Nash Smith, whose broad and deep penetration of the literature of nineteenth-century America has justifiably become the major landmark of this whole latter approach. Any attempt to seek out a new synthesis beyond the resting-place of his assumptions must acknowledge enormous debt to his prowess in having advanced the argument so far, and the vital successes of his *Virgin Land* in so many directions them-selves comprise the indispensable foundation of any critique.

Seeking a means for analyzing the role of ideas in the development of the American West, Smith attached special definitions to the terms "myth" and "symbol":

I use the words to designate larger or smaller units of the same kind of thing, namely an intellectual construction that fuses concept and emotion into an image. The myths and symbols with which I deal have the further characteristic of being collective representations rather than the work of a single mind. I do not mean to raise the question whether such products of the imagination accurately reflect empirical fact. They exist on a different plane. But as I have tried to show, they sometimes exert a decided influence on practical affairs.

That is, Smith was concerned with commonly held ideas that may have moved men to move across mountains, even though these myths were quite likely "untrue." The Westerner would often behave according to rigidly fixed, artificial preconceptions, rather than in response to the logic of his own interests. Thus pervasive ideas, or "myths," might and did alter the "actual" course of events. . . .

It is the relation of "myth" to "fact" that becomes a chief stumbling block in Smith's approach. . . . If the myth exerts influence upon reality, it is no less true that the myth springs from psychological reality, and further, that there is much diverse and continuous traffic along this two-way street. But too often Smith rests content far short of this comprehensive picture; his myths become great "given" entities, which, like Jungian archetypes, are the only constants. The myths which silhouette a society are, on the other hand, closely correlated with the plodding activities of changing human beings and with the functioning of social institutions.

Throughout Smith's analysis of the Western hero in fiction, he persistently concerned himself with the "class" status of the protagonist and heroine. In great detail he pointed out the difficulties which James Fenimore Cooper underwent in retaining the social clichés of the "sentimental novel" when writing about "the rough equality" of the West. . . . Again, central for Smith was the difficulty over "the class status of the Western farmer."

How much concerned was the Western farmer over his "class status" in actual fact? And who were these novelists? What kind of lives were *they* leading? Smith asserted that the forces at work within Cooper "closely reproduced the patterns of thought and feeling that prevailed in the society at large." But then, immediately, Smith admitted that Cooper "was at once more strongly devoted to the principle of social order and more vividly responsive to the ideas of nature and freedom in the Western forest than . . . were [his contemporaries]." These statements, appearing within what is a masterful essay in *literary* history, leave a trail of doubt behind them. Can a study of internal evidence in novels—when deliberately divorced from a comprehensive analysis of the society at large—produce trustworthy evidence for an assertion that *here* lie the basic ideas, or myths, which shaped the development of that society? Indeed, were not most litterateurs pathetically shielded from the dominant currents of nineteenth-century American life? After all, it was this problem which Emerson addressed in "The American Scholar."

There is a danger in singling out any one group to speak for a society as a whole; the result, in this instance, may be far more of a commentary upon the *novelists* than upon America. The danger is compounded when the limited group is made to speak in an area as universal in import as social status, and in a book which avowedly abstains from the "empirical" level of analysis. The themes and heroes of literature certainly offer major avenues of approach to the understanding of civilizations and their regional variants, but if, at every step, such themes are not correlated to the non-fictional experiences of the population, the result may easily fail to comprehend the history of ideas in general and instead fasten only upon the ideas of a few self-conscious and isolated literary individuals. It is as if a handful of "black belt" plantation owners could—on their own recommendation—be entrusted to speak for the entire South.

In his long final section devoted to "The Garden of the World," Smith betrays weaknesses of a somewhat different order. Here he developed in full his concept of the "myth of the garden"—the agrarian, utopian ideal which sought its fulfillment in the West. The words "sought its fulfillment" form the key to Smith's basic assumption. The myth was named, and all too soon it became an abstraction dictating as if it were a vast person. The myth moved actively; it was the subject of many verbs. "The myth of the garden affirmed that the dominant force in the future society of the Mississippi Valley would be agriculture." Again:

During the crisis that preceded the Civil War the ideal of a yeoman society in the West exerted a powerful, perhaps even a decisive influence on the course of American history by shaping the policy of the Republican party.

But in its westward course the myth stumbled across a rival "beastie" of large dimensions.

In order to establish itself in the vast new areas of the plains . . . the myth of the garden had to confront and overcome another myth of exactly opposed meaning, although of inferior strength—the myth of the Great American Desert.

These interacting myths even assumed a chemical quality:

The final merging of the notion of an American continental empire and the myth of the garden yields a single image of great imaginative force. But in the process the idea of empire has lost its transitive reference. It no longer beckons toward the Pacific and Far East, but becomes, like the myth of the garden, an introspective, even narcissistic symbol. . . .

The myth of the garden was destined to receive its death blow in the economic distress of Populism, presumably around the year 1892. This cataclysmic event might be expected logically to have ended such a long and busy lifespan for the myth. But no; a funeral oration would not yet be appropriate (although Smith inserts one). For we are told that the same myth (phoenix-like?) was also the "core" if not the cause of isolationism, which certainly reached its peak some thirty years after 1892 and persisted until Pearl Harbor. In plain fact, the vital statistics of this myth, which was engaging in intercourse with its fellows, begetting all sorts of profound movements, and strangely dying in midstream, do become a bit muddled.

Are we not in danger here of what Whitehead called the fallacy of "misplaced concreteness"? A point is soon reached at which the label— be it "myth," "democracy" or "nationalism"—becomes a shield, cloaking crucial distinctions between men and between decades behind a bland facade of sameness. When all happenings in American history have been rechristened in mythological terminology, the end result is apt to be an exotic *Jurgen* world, more elusive and synthetic than clarifying. . . .

Smith . . . assumed a wide and rather continuous gulf between legend and "reality." Such a dualistic conceptual scheme is severely limiting. It divides the stuff of society into two uneasy categories. "Myth," in this view, enjoys such an uncertain relationship to empirical fact that Smith deliberately sought to avoid the issue. "Reality," in turn, may be defined, after all, as anything from social class structure to the titles of little Ina Coolbraith's poems. Further, the bleak dualism thus involved leaves unanswered a most basic question: why certain "myths" and not others should arise in a particular social or physical climate.

Myth, when it exists in more than the historian's imagination, is in fact merely another order of reality. The legendary and empirical planes deserve genuine integration. The nature of such a fusion, which incidentally involves the further merging of much that has been considered "social," "intellectual," and "literary" history, must often vary, simply because the American subcultures, and the useful myths or legends accompanying each, are not all alike.

On the simplest level, there are two distinct kinds of regions in the United States. The first depends for its character upon *continuing* qualities, upon traditions preserved over a long period of time. In this group naturally fall New England, Tidewater Virginia, the Hudson Valley, the Appalachian, and the New Orleans Creole cultures among others. The second type, especially, indigenous to America, derives its character precisely from its social impermanence, from its shifting (which is, in the broad sense, to say *frontier*) characteristics. . . .

The stable subculture obviously possesses its important, hallowed legends, which may serve as keys to the understanding of its group experience, when examined in close conjunction with the records of everyday activity. In the instance of Southern California and other frontier sub-cultures, the myths and images are apt to be rather recent and artificial, as [Carey] McWilliams pointed out concerning Ramona. . . . Yet, even in the case of such regions, stereotypes do appear. They are more diffused, more generalized than in the subcultures which possess tradi-tional orientation, but, in myriad forms, in literature in the widest sense, they may be caught. Texan self-awareness involves vastness of physical possessions. And, in Southern California, a similar starting-point is El Dorado, combined with bizarre escape—architectural, religious or fune-real—from traditional American institutions, whether two-story house, Protestant denomination or certain rituals of death.

Such stereotypes are "myths" of a sort, but they have the virtue of leading back into concrete social experience, which may be tested by documents. . . . They become Geiger counters, sensitively measuring specific actions and institutions. And if a gulf between belief and actual structure appears, such becomes a particular fact, a discrepancy to be accounted for in concrete terms, rather than an "inevitable" consequence of a rigidly preconceived dichotomy. The stereotyped generalization immediately opens a wide range of significant further questions, com-mencing, basically, with: what people sought to behave in such and such a way; how did they go about it; why should this—rather than some differing—patterns of behavior emerge into the life and the legend of the region; and what factors in the society aided or dragged upon the result? Answers to these questions will come from novelists, poets, sociologists and orthodox historians, including the purely local chroniclers of former decades.

The result may be a line of regional distinction which, besides being neither too thick nor too thin, will take its color more from the social landscape and less from the historian's paint box.

CHAPTER XVII

The Indian in the Twentieth Century

U NFORTUNATELY FOR HISTORIANS past events seldom fit neatly into chronological compartments. The Dawes Act of 1887 did not terminate the military phase of relations between the Indians and the Anglo-Americans, although Geronimo had surrendered in the previous year. The end came rather on Wounded Knee Creek in South Dakota during the year 1890. In this sorry affair, we find a number of elements typical of the armed clashes between the two societies and this last gasp of the warrior culture of the Northern Plains deserves a retrospective glance for this reason if no other. Periodically the Indians of particular tribes or regions had thrilled to the message of a prophet who exhorted them to renounce the white man's role and return to the old beliefs and life ways. Although the prophets might only promise renewed prosperity and more satisfying lives, some of their converts usually concluded that they would be able to drive the white man from their old hunting grounds if they faithfully obeyed the teaching of the holy men. The Delaware Prophet of Pontiac's time, and Tecumseh's brother, The Prophet, both illustrate the type. Cultures in chaos, deprivation and frustration prepared the ground for such revivalism, particularly among the conservative tribal elements most hostile to the penetration of white influence.

In Nevada, an obscure Paiute medicine man, Jack Wilson, known also as Wovoka, came to believe that he had consulted the Great Spirit while seriously ill during the year 1888. Once recovered, he spread the word that the buffalo would throng the plains once more, that the white man would vanish, and that Indians could hasten these happy events if they performed the ceremonials of the ghost dance. Word of the prophecy filtered through the Indian lines of communication and stirred the proud but dejected warriors of other years like old Sitting Bull, now chafing at the Indian agencies of the Northern Plains. Ironically the white man's boarding schools for Indian youth helped to spread the intelligence because children from various tribes mingled there. The new hope, the excitement and the rituals of the Indians aroused by Wovoka's message disturbed the officers of the Bureau of Indian Affairs; troops were concentrated near reservations where revivalist fervor pulsed.

Only among the Sioux did the ghost dance end in violence. Diminished rations for the Indians at the Pine Ridge Agency, a panicky new agent who could not control the conservative faction among his charges, extremists among the Indians who demanded resistance to the Army forces, soldiers of the Seventh Cavalry who were more eager to use the Hotchkiss gun and the rifle than to wait out the Indians—these were the elements. Three hundred tribal members died, a third of them women and children. So ended the Indian wars in December 1890 and January 1891. A deranged white messiah told Red Cloud's Oglalas that the new era would still come when the star pansies bloomed during the next spring. But the old chief reasoned that there would be no Indian renaissance in that hopeful season and he was right.

Unfortunately the reformers who supported the Dawes Severalty Act of 1887 read the future less well than the great leader of the Dakotas. Many of them were sure that the new law and programs to educate the next generation of Indians would solve the "Indian problem." They relaxed their vigilant watch over Indian affairs or lost interest in the problems of the Indians altogether. Some supporters of the Dawes Act had been more interested in removing Indian title from western lands, or in divesting the Indian of the protection which was his as a ward of the government than in the welfare of the first Americans. Time proved that the Severalty Act helped men of this stamp more than the Indian. Human jackals in the predatory fringe of Anglo-American society agitated for the allotment and sale of Indian reservations, jostled to fleece the allottees of their lands, and competed to administer Indian estates and serve as the guardians of minor Indians who were surrendered to the probate machinery of the states under the allotment policy.

Statistics tell a stark and brutal story. In 1887, Indian lands numbered 138 million acres, but by 1933, the acreage had fallen to some 48 million acres and perhaps 20 million of these were so arid as to be almost worthless. Some scholars believe that the value of the Indian lands of 1934 was only 15 per cent of those of 1887. Had such statistics of Indian land-holding and value reflected the migration of well-trained workers from the reservations to remunerative jobs in industrial America, they would have been gratifying to those who wished to prepare the Indian to fend for himself in American society. But actually the statistics merely showed that the resource base which supported most American Indians had shrunk drastically. Nor did the figures reveal the hopelessness, the infant mortality, the tuberculosis and trachoma, the inadequate diets and other dimensions of the incredible poverty in which most Indians lived during the early twentieth century. Anthropologists urged their graduate students to do their field work as soon as possible; the North American Indians were a dying race.

Generalizations do not reveal the diversity of the Indian community in the United States during the early twentieth century. Despite war, disease, alcohol and identity-threatening removals, dozens of the aboriginal languages were still spoken. Tribal lists showed between 200 and 300 different tribes or major tribal bands and some of these were still further subdivided by regional location. Acculturative influences had played upon the ancestors of these Indians with varying degrees of intensity through varying lengths of time. Some had in effect met the ships of the colonists during the seventeenth century. The white invasion had affected other tribesmen only indirectly until the nineteenth century was well advanced. The size of the tribes, their regional location, the policies of particular chiefs or headmen and many other factors all affected cultural contact and its results. But most Anglo-Americans were little aware of such differences or had little interest in them.

Allotment procedures under the Dawes Act created other distinctions among the Indians of the United States. The law provided that adult tribesmen should receive 160-acre holdings and that women and minors be given lesser acreages. A 25-year period of federal trusteeship must elapse, however, before the allottees enjoyed fee simple title. The Act did not apply to the Cherokees and the other major tribes from the lower South, and there were other exceptions as well. But special legislation later applied the allotment policy to the great southern tribes; individual ownership of land had been accepted as a universal cultural solvent.

By the 1920's we can distinguish several kinds of land tenure status among the Indians. The ancestors of some tribesmen, particularly in the Pacific coast states, had never received a reservation or annuity payments from the United States government. If such Indians held land, they had acquired it by purchase in the open market. Others occupied reservations that had not yet been allotted in severalty. Some of these Indians, like the Navajos, lived a more or less nomadic life on their lands; others, as for instance, the Pueblos, had divided their land among themselves, although they did not have deeds or patents in the Anglo-American sense. More or less, the allotment policy had touched most of the remaining tribesmen. In some cases, the federal government had allotted a tribal reservation but not yet sold the lands in excess of the acreage needed for allotments nor had the government yet granted fee simple title to any of the allottees. At the other extreme were reservations where government officers had sold the surplus lands and given full ownership to the Indian landholders—titles which in many cases were already slipping into the hands of Anglo-Americans. The children of allottees, born after the allotment process was applied to their parents' reservation, constituted another class. These young Indians might obtain reservation land by inheritance or purchase but they had no claim to the old tribal holdings in their own right. Officers of the Bureau of Indian Affairs sometimes sold the land of Indian allottees who had died to provide money for the support of minor heirs or to simplify the settlement of estates. In other cases, numerous heirs received driblets of rental income from the allotment of a deceased Indian. No matter their landholding status, tribal members might share in government annuity payments and have vested rights in moneys which the government had derived from selling tribal lands or in other ways and held in trust for them.

Some of the allotted reservations lay in regions where even the most diligent and lucky of Anglo-American farmers could not have supported himself on 160 acres, but perhaps the fate of the Indians whose allotments lay above southwestern oil fields was no less disheartening. If used constructively this wealth might have helped a great number of Indians, and considerable sums did pass through the hands of some tribesmen. But a generation of sharpers plundered them. Unfortunately too the Indian who sold his land for a song or surrendered it in satisfaction of some dubious debt did not then feel obliged to compete in Anglo-American society for a living as the reformers of the 1880's had hoped. Usually he withdrew to the lands of relatives or became a hopeless squatter on some tract of wasteland.

Until the passage of the Burke Act in 1906, Indians who accepted allotments automatically became American citizens. Thereafter, allottees obtained citizenship only after they had obtained the full title to their lands at the expiration of the trust period, sometimes shortened from the 25 years prescribed in the Dawes Act by the competency procedures of the law of 1906. On the other hand, Congress actually lengthened the prescribed trust period of some allottees. Finally the members of Congress terminated such discrimination against a people who had contributed its share of soldiers in the first World War and granted citizenship to all of the descendants of the original Americans in 1924.

Many Indians did retain their land, but observers complained that they were smothered by the all-pervasive paternalism of the Bureau of Indian Affairs. Government farmers told the tribesmen what to produce and often sold the harvests for them. When Indians leased their land, government officers arranged the business details. The Indian could not even govern his personal relations with the supernatural. He must, decreed the administrators in the Bureau of Indian Affairs, think Christian. As late as 1926 the Bureau of Indian Affairs was warring on the Indian religions that survived on some reservations. How, asked some critics, could tribal members regain their lost self-respect or develop a sense of responsibility under such conditions? Franklin Delano Roosevelt referred to the "system of autocracy" under which some 200,000 Indians lived and later critics, hardly objective perhaps, stigmatized the Bureau of Indian Affairs, "and its empire of wards" as a "totalitarian state within a state."

Although American Indian policy was less than successful during the early twentieth century, a significant development was under way by the 1920's. The Indian population had begun to increase in numbers. The vanishing American was not to disappear after all. Reform that ignored the growing numbers of Indians would be unsatisfactory—the inadequate reservations and allotments would be rendered even more so by population increase.

Franklin Delano Roosevelt's Commissioner of Indian Affairs, John Collier, and the men who assisted him in shaping the Indian's New Deal believed that they were inaugurating an era of "creative self-determination" for the American Indian. Almost 200 of some 266 eligible tribes or bands accepted the Indian Reorganization Act of 1934, and it led to many encouraging developments. Tribesmen organized tribal governments and began to participate in managing their own affairs. They used government loans to improve their herds of livestock and to purchase new lands. Soil conservation experts assisted them in checking soil erosion and in developing efficient systems of land use. The Indian Bureau ceased its war upon the native religions, even encouraging Indians to recapture the lore of their past and to revive old rituals, on the assumption that such effort would help the Indian find a sense of identity and a new strength in facing an alien culture. An Indian Arts and Crafts Board worked to stimulate the production and sale of Indian rugs, jewelry, pottery and painting. Indians entered the service of the Indian Bureau in greater numbers than ever before. More and more Indian youths went to college. Other encouraging developments occurred also. States that had denied the vote to Indians dropped their restrictions and, officially at least, state legislators eliminated discrimination against the Indians in their laws governing assistance to the elderly, to the blind and to dependent children. Congress and the Supreme Court continued to strengthen the position of these Americans. Between 1934 and 1950 the land holdings of the Indians increased, their income rose and they increased considerably in numbers. Some scholars believe that these years were a brief golden age of American Indian policy.

Yet the members of Congress never appropriated funds as generously under the Indian Reorganization Act as they might have. During the 1940's Congressmen groused more and more about the cost of Indian administration. The striking increase in the population of some tribes increased their need for land, but their Anglo-American neighbors were highly suspicious of programs to enlarge Indian acreage. The law, establishing the Indian Claims Commission in 1946, revealed a commendable desire to render justice to the Indians, but it also reflected the impatience of many Americans with a stubbornly persistent problem. In the past, Congress had allowed Indian tribes to sue the United States in special circumstances only. Now the legislators threw open the Court of Claims allowing the Indian tribes to present long-standing claims against the government for damages or inadequate compensation. To some lawmakers the act was merely fair play, but others hoped that it would be a major step in the process of withdrawing the government from Indian administration. Under this law many tribesmen have received additional compensation for lands surrendered long ago to the federal government.

Many members of Congress were soon ready to carry "emancipation" a step farther. During the first Eisenhower administration, Congress approved a House resolution declaring it

the policy of Congress as rapidly as possible to make the Indians . . . subject to the same laws and entitled to the same privileges and responsibilities as are applicable to other citizens of the United States, to end their status as wards of the United States, and to grant them all of the rights and prerogatives pertaining to American citizenship. . . .

The resolution provided that a number of designated tribes were to be "freed from Federal supervision" as rapidly as possible. So began the termination policy, described by the "Commission on the Rights, Liberties and Responsibilities of the American Indian" later in this chapter. The announcement shocked most of the Indians under the protection of the Bureau of Indian Affairs, as did the first examples of termination. Many of them believed that the United States government was repudiating commitments and preparing to surrender the remaining Indian resources to rapacious white men. "Terminated" Indians have found the cost of "freedom" to be high indeed.

With the return of the Democrats to power in 1960, the Bureau of

Indian Affairs began to stress programs designed to improve the vocational education opportunities for Indians, to transfer Indians to urban areas where jobs were available, to attract industry to the reservations or their vicinity and to develop the resources of the reservations more intensively. Critics, however, maintained that these policies were ineffectual or inadequate to solve the problems of our Indian minority.

During the last generation, the Indians have begun to defend their own interests more aggressively. In 1944 Indian employees in the Bureau of Indian Affairs organized the National Congress of Indians and this group allowed Indian leaders to reinforce each other, assisted them in articulating an Indian point of view, and helped them to lobby more effectively. Indian veterans returned to the reservations after the second World War prepared to resent a second class citizenship and to voice their grievances. Anthropologists began to describe Pan-Indianism, the increasing tendency of Indians to think and act as Indians rather than as the members of a particular Indian tribe.

In 1960 young college-trained Indians organized the National Indian Youth Council and began to sound a militant note. Spokesmen of the group, like Clyde Warrior of the Poncas and Mel Thom of the Paiutes, denied the desirability of complete assimilation. Indian culture, they maintained, is in some respects based on values which are superior to that of Anglo-American society. These must not be lost and the representatives of Indian culture must be supported in their efforts to maintain it. The angry young people of the National Indian Youth Council sharply criticized the Indian employees of the Bureau of Indian Affairs who numbered almost half of the employees of this agency during the late 1960's, as well as older tribal leaders. Such Indians, they charged, had sold out their people by accepting the leadership and direction of the Bureau of Indian Affairs without complaint; they were "Uncle Tomahawks."

The Youth Council fought the erosion of Indian rights, as for instance, loss of their privilege of hunting during all seasons on tribal lands or fishing at locations, sanctified by ancestral custom, in any way they saw fit. Council members provided much of the leadership in the fish-ins in the state of Washington during 1964, when Indians defied the fish and game laws there. They believed that the reservations must serve as focal points of Indian culture, and so they fought the termination policy or suggestions that Congress allow tribal lands or other assets to be mortgaged in order to raise capital to attract industry or to stimulate the economic development of the reservations. But they were also critical of the paternalism of the Bureau of Indian Affairs and argued that its administrators did not adapt programs to the realities of Indian culture. They argued for self-determination; and they demanded that federal lawmakers take the advice of Indians seriously when drafting legislation; they asked that Indians be given complete control of reservations affairs and developmental programs; and they urged increased support for Indian education and massive social and economic aid to the reservations, similar to that extended to underdeveloped nations abroad. They pointed to the example of the Cheyenne River Sioux as an illustration of Indian potential. In 1940 members of this tribe began a land consolidation program when only some 40,000 acres of land remained in their hands. By 1968 they owned more than a million acres of land and tribal enterprises dotted the region. Tribal assets were valued at more than $15,000,000. The tribesmen had achieved these results by buying into the small business and service industries of the region and funneling the profits into the tribal treasury.

Sometimes the young people of the Youth Council sounded radical indeed. During a confrontation between Cherokees and the Oklahoma state game authorities, Clyde Warrior predicted "an uprising that will make Kenyatta's Mau Mau movement look like a Sunday-School picnic." Some scoffed at the rhetoric of the Red Power Movement but the young leaders had done much to make older tribal leaders more militant and aggressive. By the late 1960's the Indians were registering to vote as never before in western states where they live in substantial numbers. Indian representatives had begun to appear in western state legislatures, a development unthought of in 1940 or even 1950. In May 1968, the Commissioner of Indian Affairs, an Indian, Robert L. Bennett, prophesied that a new era was beginning in the history of the American Indian, in which he would attain equality of economic and social opportunity at last. This was greatly to be desired, but the supporters of the Dawes Act and the Indian Reorganization Act of 1934 had believed the same thing. By this time black Americans had succeeded in stirring the conscience of a substantial number of their fellow citizens. Although red joined black in the "Poor Peoples' Campaign" of 1968, the North American Indians had not yet succeeded in forcing Americans to consider the obligations which a rich and humane society owes to the descendants of the country's first inhabitants.

·1·

RANDOLPH C. DOWNES

A Crusade for Indian Reform, 1922–1934

During the 1870's and 1880's a squadron of altruists mobilized to reform American Indian policy and the Dawes
Act was the culmination of their labors. Time proved that
their formula was more poison than cure. During the 1920's,
the members of a revitalized reform movement once again
demanded a fundamental revision in our programs of Indian
administration. In this reading, Randolph C. Downes describes some of the villains, reformers and measures of the
new crusade and the Indian's New Deal which followed.

The 8th of February, 1887 "may be called the Indian emancipation
day." Thus spoke the reform-minded, government-sponsored Board of
Indian Commissioners in 1887 in reporting to the Secretary of the Interior on the passage of the Dawes Act for the allotment of tribal land
in individual farms to the American Indians. Forty-seven years later,
on June 18, 1934, President Franklin D. Roosevelt signed the Wheeler-
Howard Act which had for its aim the restoration and revival of Indian
tribal life, and the stoppage of all further individual allotting of land.
Said John Collier concerning this event: "Whether that date shall be
known hereafter as the Independence Day of Indian history will be determined by the Indians themselves. . . . The Allotment law—the agony
and ruin of the Indians—has been repealed." Thus spoke the reform-
minded, government-sponsored Commissioner of Indian Affairs as he
set about the job of inaugurating a typically twentieth-century collectivistic reform to replace a typically nineteenth-century individualistic
one. . . .

"The allotment act," said Commissioner Collier in submitting his draft
of the reform bill to the Indian Affairs committees of Senator Burton K.
Wheeler and Representative Edgar Howard, "contemplates total land-
lessness for the Indians of the third generation of each allotted tribe."
He pointed out that since 1887 the total Indian land holdings had de-

SOURCE: Abridged from Randolph C. Downes, "A Crusade for Indian Reform,
1922–1934," *Mississippi Valley Historical Review*, XXXII (December, 1945), 331–354.
Reprinted by permission of the *Journal of American History* and Randolph C. Downes.

creased from 138,000,000 acres to 48,000,000 acres, 20,000,000 of which were arid or semi-arid. Three kinds of sales had accounted for this diminution: sales of "surplus" lands left over on a reservation after the members of the tribe had received their allotments; sales by Indians after they had received full title to their allotments; and sales of allotments divided into small pieces by parents who never increased the size of their holdings, but who either divided the land in their wills evenly among their children or who died intestate. The continuation of these sales, especially of the third type, for two more generations "mathematically insures and practically requires that the remaining Indian allotted lands shall pass to whites." This means that there was a gradually accelerating fragmentation of the Indian lands especially by division among the heirs of the original allottees and this fragmentation was reducing the size of the holdings to unworkable dimensions. . . .

Before the administrators of Indian affairs could take hold of the job of reform, the problem had to go through the muckraking stage. Conditions had to be played up, even exaggerated, by those who could focus public attention on the problem through the publicity of episodes seemingly illustrative of particularly outrageous treatment of the Indians. And it would have been unusual if the scandal-ridden years of the early 1920's had not provided grist for reformers of Indian affairs. It is not surprising then that in 1922–1924 the fight against the so-called Bursum Pueblo Land bill provided an appropriate episode, and that the principal villain should be the ill-starred Secretary of Interior Albert B. Fall of Teapot Dome fame. It was this affair which gave birth to the dynamic, crusading American Indian Defense Association, and it was this association, through its indefatigable executive secretary, John Collier, which sparked the reform movement that reached its climax in the adoption of the Wheeler-Howard Act.

In 1922 Senator Holm O. Bursum of New Mexico introduced a measure known as "An Act to quiet the title to lands within Pueblo Indian land grants. . . ." This bill, growing out of an ancient feud in New Mexico between the whites and the Pueblos, sought to restore the white man's advantage, lost in 1913, when the United States Supreme Court in the case of *United States* vs *Sandoval* brought the Pueblo Indians under Federal jurisdiction in such a way that squatters who had been gradually encroaching on Pueblo lands for years found the burden of proof forced upon them when the Indians challenged squatter rights in Federal courts. The ensuing suits were so embarrassing to the whites that Senator Bursum sought to remedy the situation by obliging the Indians to produce proof of title from the hopelessly confused and vague evidences lost in the maze of over two centuries of Spanish, Mexican, and American land transactions. In the lack of evidence satisfactory to the Federal courts, a scale of periods and types of residence by the whites was set up which would be deemed necessary to qualify the occupier to receive a title deed. It offended the Indians because it would accelerate white encroachments and encourage dissident Indians, mixed bloods, and unfriendly white or Mexican neighbors to settle land disputes outside the traditional and more or less informal and friendly auspices of the tribal councils.

The Pueblo protest quickly reached national proportions. On November 5, 1922, there met at the Pueblo of Santo Domingo a special council, widely advertised as the first all-Pueblo union since the anti-Spanish revolt of 1680. This council adopted "a memorial to the American people" denouncing the change in judicial procedure and appealing for fair play and the preservation of "our Pueblo life." Friends of the Indians quickly joined in the outcry. . . . While Fall and Bursum defended their bill and called its critics propagandists, philanthropists like Herbert Welsh, president of the Indian Rights Association, rallied supporters of the Indians to the cause; anthropologists like Herbert J. Spinden of the Peabody Museum at Harvard extolled the beauty of Pueblo community life, their songs, their crafts, their ancient traditions; and the gallant editor of the New York *Times* pleaded for the defense of "minority rights at home." Led by Collier, ten Pueblos took to the road, turning up in Washington, Chicago, and New York City to denounce the land grabbers before clubs and town meetings where they raised over $6,000 for the Pueblo Indian Defense Fund. The House Indian Affairs Committee, however, denounced the propaganda as "insidious, untruthful, and malicious." Nevertheless, the Bursum bill was killed, and in 1924 an impartial and competent Pueblo Lands Board was created to untangle the land claims.

The Indian reform movement was now under way. The summer of 1923 saw the issuance by the newly-formed American Indian Defense Association of a statement of general principles drawn up by Dr. Spinden in collaboration with the Indian Welfare Committee of the General Federation of Women's Clubs. The program emphasized the need of developing Indian " 'group loyalties and communal responsibilities'," including tribal landholding, self-government, and religious freedom, the creation of an organization to promote the sale of genuine products of Indian arts and craftsmanship, and a complete reorganization of the education, health, and irrigation services. Not to be outdone, the 42-year-old Indian Rights Association revamped its services with the aid of a grant from John D. Rockefeller, Jr., and in February, 1924 began to issue a monthly bulletin known as *Indian Truth*. The two associations collaborated in an exposé of the exploitation of Oklahoma's Indians, but eventually found themselves at variance because of the more radical aims and less quietistic policies of the Indian Defense Association of which the militant Collier was executive secretary. . . .

An orgy of muckraking ensued. Alleged government maladministration in tribe after tribe was set before the public. Loudest and longest in the attack, though not first was *Sunset*, "the West's Great National Magazine," which, from November, 1922 until June, 1924, had only six issues without at least one leading article denouncing the Indian Bureau. . . .

The climax came early in 1924 with the publication by the Indian Rights Association of a pamphlet entitled "Oklahoma's Poor Rich Indians," and subtitled "An Orgy of Graft and Exploitation of the Five Civilized Tribes—Legalized Robbery." It was written by Gertrude Bonnin, Research Agent of the Indian Welfare Committee of the General Federation of Women's Clubs, Charles H. Fabens of the American Indian Defense Association, and Matthew K. Sniffen of the Indian Rights Association. It asserted that, as the result of the transfer in 1908 to the county probate courts in Oklahoma of all jurisdiction over the estates of Indian minors and incompetents, the Indians were being "shamelessly and openly robbed in a scientific and ruthless manner." It was claimed that in many counties the Indians were virtually at the mercy of groups or rings of judges, guardians, attorneys, bankers, merchants, and undertakers, all of whom regarded the Indian estates as "legitimate game." . . .

The Pueblo Lands Board Act of 1924 and the Osage Guardianship Act of 1925 were signs of a new day. It was not long before administrators began to see that, in order to avoid the embarrassment of these pinprick reforms, a general review of the entire Indian service would be a good thing. The occasion for this was the accession in 1923 of Hubert Work as Secretary of Interior in the place of Fall. With the air full of slurs on the quality of the Indian Service, Work sought to clarify the situation by inviting one hundred leaders in the field of Indian welfare to constitute a National Advisory Committee on Indian Affairs. A heterogeneous collection of seventy-five advisers thereupon assembled in Washington on December 11 and 12, 1923, and, after two days of futile wrangling and parliamentary ineptitude, passed a series of innocuous resolutions in which, save for a health proposal, "not one fundamental proposition . . . was put across," to use John Collier's words. . . .

Secretary Work was no radical reformer, but he could see, as Collier saw, the amateur quality of the report of the Advisory Committee. Therefore, on June 23, 1925, ignoring temporarily Collier's proposal to engage the fact-finding services of the Institute for Government Research, he called upon the 55-year-old advisory Board of Indian Commissioners to investigate and make recommendations. . . .

The Board's unpublished report of January 26, 1926 was a whitewash. It said that all charges against Commissioner Burke were "puerile," and that those against Superintendent Wallen of the Five Civilized Tribes in Oklahoma were "politics." It recommended that the office of Superintendent of the Five Civilized Tribes be put under the Civil Service and that all Indians having annual incomes of over $5,000 be segregated for special aid in the administration of their estates. . . .

Even before the official submission of this report Work had made up his mind, and, on June 12, 1926, had requested W. F. Willoughby, director of the Institute for Government Research, to make a survey of the economic and social conditions of the American Indians. Members of the staff of the Institute headed by Lewis Meriam, aided by nine specially selected experts, at once applied themselves to the job, and, after seven months intensive field work, prepared the monumental report which Willoughby submitted to Work on February 21, 1928.

The Meriam Report was a masterpiece of reform propaganda in the best sense of the word. It's high-minded scientific accuracy was never seriously questioned. Its non-controversial tone commanded the respect of both supporters and critics of the Indian Bureau. Although highly critical of American Indian policy, it avoided personalities. Indeed, it won friends from the very Bureau which it criticized. . . .

But these investigations had very little effect on the Indian Service during the years of Secretary Work's incumbency. The Commissioner of Indian Affairs from 1921 to 1929 was Charles H. Burke, formerly Congressman from South Dakota, and author of the so-called Burke Act of 1906 speeding up the individual distribution of Indian land under the allotment system. Burke was an avowed rugged individualist. In 1923 he was quoted as saying: "'I believe in making the Indian take his chance, just the same as white folks do. . . . Don't fool yourself. The Indian makes good when he has the chance.'" This attitude led the New York *Times* to say editorially that prior to 1929 the administration of the Bureau of Indian Affairs "never quite overcame the frontiersman's attitude" toward the Indians. This last of the "frontier" Commissioners was quite contemptuous of reformers of the Collier type. . . .

The pre-New Deal phase of the Indian reform movement really got under way in 1929 when President Hoover appointed Ray Lyman

Wilbur, educator, social worker, and president of Leland Stanford University to be Secretary of the Interior. That Wilbur's appointment presaged progressive measures in the Indian Bureau was seen in the replacement of Burke and Meritt, the last of the "frontier" administrators, by two Quaker humanitarians, Charles J. Rhoads, wealthy Philadelphia banker, and president of the Indian Rights Association, and J. Henry Scattergood, treasurer of Haverford and Bryn Mawr Colleges, Pennsylvania Working Home for the Blind, and Christiansburg Industrial Institute. Reformers rejoiced. . . .

[T]he Meriam Survey concluded that the measure of the failure of past Indian policies was the lack of a sound educational program. Secretary Wilbur now made educational reform the keystone of the new era for the Indians. In nominating Rhoads for Commissioner, he stated:

The Indian shall no longer be viewed as a ward of the nation, but shall be considered a potential citizen. As rapidly as possible he is to have the full responsibility for himself. . . . In order to bring this about it will be necessary to revise our educational program into one of a practical and vocational character, and to mature plans for the absorption of the Indian into the industrial and agricultural life of the nation.

Aided by the vigorous insistence of President Hoover in December, 1929, on a Congressional educational equipment appropriation of $3,100,000 and by subsequent annual expenditures which advanced from $10,324,654 in 1930 to $12,336,900 in 1932, Rhoads was able to translate these high-sounding pronouncements into some form and degree of practical application. He selected as the Bureau's Director of Education, Dr. W. Carson Ryan, Jr., president of the National Vocational Guidance Association, and member of the executive council of the National Education Association. Since Ryan had been a member of the staff of the Meriam Survey, it is obvious that the educational recommendations of the Survey were at the basis of the reforms of the Rhoads administration. . . .

Annual regional conferences of superintendents of Indian schools and agencies were inaugurated in 1931 to improve and unify the teaching programs. A pattern was set for the solution of the boarding school problem by shifting the weight of enrollment from the lower to the upper grades, making the training more practically vocational in character, and eliminating, or converting to day-schools, those institutions whose value as boarding schools could no longer be justified. The worst evils of the remaining boarding schools were corrected—over-crowding, inadequate food, and child labor. Whenever it was feasible, Indian students were encouraged to attend public schools. Ryan fostered, wherever possible, closer cooperation between the states and the Bureau, as, for example, when he requested his teachers to use as their guide state courses of study and to enrich them with material suitable to Indian needs. Greater means were provided for qualified Indians to obtain professional education in state or private colleges. There was created a new Guidance and Placement Division to help bridge the gap between school and employment. And finally, to cap the structure of vocational usefulness, extension work among the Indians was improved by increased appropriations, and by the creation of a new Division of Agricultural Extension and Industries, headed by Agricultural Specialist A. C. Cooley and counselled by the services, for one year, of Dr. Erl Bates of Cornell University. . . .

How much farther along the road to reform Rhoads would have gone if he had not been replaced by Collier in 1933 is, of course, impossible to say. . . .

[F]rom 1933 on, as Collier groomed himself to strike down what Rhoads feared to attack, the Rhoads achievements in education, health, and other lines were carried on and supplemented. The transfer of Indian children from boarding schools to day schools near their homes was speeded up as boarding school enrollment dropped from 22,000 in 1933 to 17,500 in 1934, and plans were made for a decrease to 13,000 in 1935. In the meantime the remaining boarding schools were being transformed into institutions for the care of special classes of children: orphans, those with poor home environments, those without local school facilities, and high school pupils needing vocational training not offered locally. A new spirit came into the Indian Service as Collier issued an order based on the most progressive educational and psychological foundations:

No interference with Indian religious life or expression will hereafter be tolerated. The cultural history of Indians is in all respects to be considered equal to that of any non-Indian group. And it is desirable that Indians be bilingual. . . . The Indian arts are to be prized, nourished, and honored. . . .

The story is quickly told. The time of timorous testing was over, and Commissioner Collier was determined to give the new Indian policy a charter basis. Accordingly the Bureau drafted its own bill with great care and, in February, 1934, submitted it to the tender mercies of Senate and House consideration. . . .

Although assailed as communistic, pagan, and Bureau-bought, the measure became law with little difficulty. The title itself is an adequate summary:

An Act to conserve and develop Indian lands and resources; to extend to Indians the right to form business and other organizations; to establish a credit system for Indians; to grant certain rights of home rule to Indians; to provide for vocational education for Indians; and for other purposes.

Thus allotment in severalty was explicitly forbidden and any surplus lands still remaining were to be restored to tribal ownership. Sales of lands to, and inheritance by, non-Indians were most drastically restricted. The Secretary of the Interior was enabled to acquire land for incorporation into tribal estates and the expenditure of not over $2,000,-000 a year for this purpose was authorized. The sum of $250,000 a year might be spent to defray the expenses of organizing Indian chartered corporations. A revolving fund of $10,000,000 was authorized to make loans to such corporations "for the purpose of promoting the economic development" of the tribes. Another sum of $250,000 a year was to be spent for tuition loans to Indians attending "recognized vocational and trade schools." Exemption of Indians from civil service rules was granted to promote an increase in the number of tribesmen in the staff of the Indian Service. Tribal constitutions were authorized to be created and ratified by the Indians themselves to give them extensive rights of political home rule. The act itself was not to apply to any tribe which should vote not to accept it. . . .

·2·

THOMAS LE DUC

The Work of the Indian Claims Commission
Under the Act of 1946

Although the government of the United States has protected
the Indian in various ways during the twentieth century,
it has also limited his freedom of action in some respects.
For many years after the establishment of the United States
Court of Claims, Indian groups were not allowed to bring
suit against the government unless Congress approved the
action. But in 1946 the federal lawmakers established the
Indian Claims Commission to hear and rule on Indian claims
against the government, its decisions to be subject to appeal
in the Court of Claims. Writing in 1957, Thomas Le Duc
discusses the work of the Commission.

All through American history the Congress and the federal courts have
recognized that, notwithstanding the guarantees of the Fifth Amendment, actions of the national government sometimes operate to deprive
persons of property without just compensation. The courts have regularly
held that the United States, as a sovereign, is immune to suit, and until
about a century ago the principal remedy available to aggrieved parties
was petition to Congress for an act of indemnity. The property guarantees
of the Fifth Amendment are in themselves empty. Without statutory
provisions to enforce them, private rights do not exist. A *fortiori*, claims
grounded on mere law or equity do not run against the sovereign. The
government must acknowledge liability and provide for determination
of the judgment. In the strict sense there is no such thing as liability;
every act of Congress in respect to private claims is an act of grace.

Over the years Congress grew weary of considering the increasingly
numerous petitions for private acts of indemnity and now has largely
surrendered the judicial function that it at first performed. A number
of general acts have authorized suits against the United States in respect

SOURCE: Abridged from Thomas Le Duc, "The Work of the Indian Claims Commission Under the Act of 1946." © 1957 by the Pacific Coast Branch, American
Historical Association. Reprinted from *Pacific Historical Review*, Vol. XXVI, 1–16.
by permission of the Branch and Thomas Le Duc.

to claims in specified categories, a larger number of special acts have authorized named persons to sue on particular complaints, and Congress has created jurisdictions to hear the petitions. A century ago the Court of Claims was established, and to it has flowed a steadily expanding volume of litigation. But until 1946 Indian tribes were by statute denied access to the Court except under special acts permitting a named tribe to sue on a specified cause.

While denying the permission available to white citizens under the general acts, Congress, beginning in 1881, many times authorized the Court of Claims to adjudicate particular complaints brought by Indian tribes against the government. Prior to the enactment of the Indian Claims Act of 1946 there was, therefore, a good deal of experience with tribal suits, and the writers of the 1946 law had the benefit of that experience. The act created a broad jurisdiction to determine the claims of all recognized tribes and "indentifiable groups." In view of the large number of old claims, an independent three-man commission was created to hear claims originating before the date of the act, and the Court of Claims was given appellate jurisdiction. In respect to claims accruing after the date of the act, original jurisdiction, much narrower in scope, goes to the Court of Claims. In all cases appeal from the Court of Claims lies directly with the Supreme Court. . . .

Indian claims are enormously expensive to maintain. As most of the tribes are without funds, and as the Bureau of Indian Affairs is unwilling to permit tribal trust funds in federal custody to be spent for litigation until the courts have adjudged the government liable, the attorneys must risk their own money as well as their own time. . . .

All contracts between tribes and attorneys are subject to the approval of the Office of Indian Affairs. Normally, and almost universally, the Office will approve only contracts that provide for compensation and reimbursement on a contingent basis, that is, if the claim results in a final award. This policy is designed, first, to protect the tribe against total loss if the claim is denied and, secondly, to provide sufficient incentive to the attorney to maintain aggressive prosecution of just claims. . . . Jurisdictional acts usually establish a maximum fee of 10 per cent of the recovery, together with repayment of expenses, but the actual fee is subject not only to that ceiling but to court approval. Even on such terms many Indian claims have fallen into the hands of attorneys who cannot stage a competent case because they lack either the ability or the funds. On the other hand a high percentage of the claims are in the hands of distinguished metropolitan counsel with access to the funds necessary to assemble the necessary evidence. Government attorneys are generally competent, informed, and resourceful in resisting the claims. . . .

The 1946 law extends a jurisdiction of unparalleled sweep and creates causes of action and liability hitherto unknown. The boundaries are not yet fully established by judicial construction, but it is hard to think of a claim that cannot be heard under its provisions. Many earlier tribal suits had been dismissed for want of jurisdiction because the law permitting suit had limited recovery to claims resting on law or equity. The 1946 act recognized government liability not only under the usual principles of law and equity but also under obligations of "fair and honorable dealings that are not recognized by any existing rule of law or equity." . . .

Reservations created by treaty or other Congressional action are fully compensable. It is true that tribal title even to lands purchased and patented is inalienable without federal consent. But while the quality of the title is less perfect than that of a fee simple, the courts have generally held that its monetary value is equivalent to that of the fee. This holding rests on the theory that the United States stands in the relationship of guardian and that restrictions on alienability were imposed for the benefit of the tribe and not the guardian. . . .

The most exciting question of title that has arisen is the responsibility of the federal government to compensate tribes for cessions of their aboriginal domains. In most instances the government made some agreement at the time of cession to pay for these lands. If it is proven that the contemporary value of the land exceeded the consideration, is the government now liable for the balance? The government contends that the original payment was an act of grace and that the 1946 act creates no liability. The government's theory is that it acquired the fee along with the sovereignty and that the tribal right of occupancy was not a right but a privilege, that, in other words, the Indians, like squatters, were only tenants-at-will. . . .

In establishing "exclusive use and occupancy" of a definable area the burden of proof is on the claimant tribe. It is customary to offer voluminous documentary evidence and to present an ethnologist or historian to interpret it. The absence of written tribal records normally means that reliance must be put on contemporary accounts by explorers, missionaries, traders, and government officials. The fact that the tribes were often in a long-term dynamic relation as a result of migration or aggression sometimes makes it extremely difficult to establish the bounds of their domains at a specific date. From the rule of use and occupancy it follows that abandonment operates to effect lapse of title. . . .

After determining title to the land the Commission is faced with the perplexing task of fixing its value at the time of taking. Mr. Justice Holmes once said that an appraisal of real property is, at best, an informed guess. Remote retrospective appraisal is not, and cannot be, an exact science. Every parcel of land is unique and so is every moment in time. If the identical parcel had been sold at the identical moment of cession by a willing seller to a willing buyer, there would be no need of an appraisal.

The appraiser deals therefore in hypothetical situations. His object is to establish the probable terms of a sale that never took place. To help him he has a large body of law and a substantial body of economic thought arising from eminent-domain proceedings. But most of this experience deals with properties whose values can be more readily ascertained than those involved in Indian claims. The law and practice of condemnation has grown up around tracts relatively small compared to those claimed by the Indians; they are generally much more highly developed; and the valuation dates are less remote.

The traditional definition of value in eminent-domain proceedings is market value, wherever it is ascertainable. But it is not necessary to prove the existence of a market, or even of a person able and willing to buy. Where a market does not exist and where fair market value cannot be determined, the courts have based their awards on actual, or intrinsic, value. . . .

One approach to valuation taken by witnesses for the Attorney General was to assign as the value of the land the capital sum whose income at 5 per cent would produce the cash value of contemporary army rations for the number of Indians known to have occupied the land at the time of cession. This procedure the Commission implicitly and the Court of Claims explicitly and scornfully rejected. The Attorney General has discontinued using this method.

Another procedure was to use government sales of the subject land as an index to demand at stated prices. The Attorney General seems to view this kind of analysis with great esteem and frequently uses it. It is easy to show that government sales of public land for cash are usually small for many years after the opening of land to entry. It is not the practice of the Attorney General to tell the Commission how many acres were conveyed under forms of entry other than cash sale: inchoate titles passed by homestead and pre-emption entry, timber filings, and withdrawals for railroad grants. Not reflected in the cash figure were the grants to the states and the entries in which veterans' warrants and other kinds of land paper were used for payment. The Attorney General does not tell the Commission about these enormous transfers. In one hearing the government presented a spectacular colored map purporting to show by township for all of eastern Kansas the amount of land open for acquisition as of July, 1865. Anyone familiar with the history of the public lands in that area could see at once how deceptive the map was. It omitted from the count all lands granted to the state or to railroads and all pre-emption filings, even those inchoate titles so valuable that they would normally ripen by proof and payment into absolute titles. Above all, it omitted the absolute conveyances made in exchange for veterans' land paper and agricultural-college scrip. The discrepancies between the map and the facts were as great in some townships as 75 per cent. The plaintiff in the case was able to demonstrate how false the map was and how meaningless are land entry figures confined only to cash transactions. The Attorney General has probably exhausted the possibilities of misrepresentation in using them, for the Commission has become educated to the fundamentals of the public land system.

Still another approach is to derive values by discounting back to the date of [cession] taking subsequent sales prices of the subject land. The attitude of the courts to this method varies, but it may be safely said that the evidence has some probative value. Discounting has the merit of ana-lyzing sales data for the subject lands, but for several reasons it is not wholly acceptable. It violates the principle that information not avail-able at the time of sale is inadmissible. Apart from this legal objec-tion, it offers practical difficulties. In using later sales prices it is neces-sary to determine and subtract the value of any improvements to the land. Conveyances do not supply this information, nor do the census returns. . . .

Undoubtedly the most acceptable appraisal is one that uses contem-porary sales of comparable unimproved lands. But one could argue that the United States, by virtue of its vast operations in the land market in the nineteenth century, held a monopolistic power over land prices throughout the country, and that the price of private land was substan-tially a function of public policy. After 1840, certainly, federal policy affected adversely the value of private land in the United States. Is the United States, defendant in these Indian claims, now to reap the advan-tage of market values depressed by its own monopolistic power? To say this is to say that the defendant can fix the damages. But that is what the courts have recently said in similar circumstances. . . .

The appraiser must, therefore, calculate values as they prevailed within the orbit of prices determined by government dumping of land at low prices. If the subject was relatively small and surrounded by private land for which there was an active market, there is little difficulty in estimating its value with some precision. Data on resources, commodity markets, transportation facilities, and the going price for land are not only abundant but easily recoverable. With large aboriginal domains there is more trouble in determining value. It is not easy to discover what was known of the land's resources, or how they were estimated, or what value was attached to them, or how they were thought to compare with other lands for which value data have survived. By their very nature, as Indian lands up to the moment of cession, they were not only closed to white occupation, but were usually remote from areas of settlement. In some cases, of course, they lay athwart established routes of travel and their features were widely known. In one sense the tribes did themselves a favor by granting travel easements along such familiar routes as the Santa Fe and Oregon trails, and across Iowa. For less-traveled areas the records of traders, missionaries, and the Army supply information concerning the climate, the soil, the timber and other vegetation, the mineral resources at or near the surface, and the game and fish. Other sources add to our knowledge of the transportation and marketing facilities for potential produce. . . .

After ten years what has been accomplished under the Indian Claims Act? The intent of Congress was clearly to give the Indians their day in court for a hearing of all accumulated grievances. The object was to liquidate claims resting on moral as well as legal and equitable grounds. A number of ill-founded claims have been dismissed and a few of the seemingly worthy major claims have been concluded. But hundreds of claims are still on the docket. The Attorney General has moved at a leisurely pace. The task force of the Hoover Commission reported in 1955 that:

One of the worst examples of delay that the task force study reveals occurs in the Indian Claims Commission, where in five case dockets . . . petitions have been filed and proceedings have been pending since at least August 10, 1951, without any answer by the Government more than three years later.

The Justice Department not only resorts to delaying tactics in its fight against the Indians, but refuses to settle out of court even the most meritorious claims. In all other civil proceedings the government habitually relies on out-of-court settlements, but in Indian claims cases it requires the tribe to engage costly counsel and investigators to establish even the most elementary and undeniable facts. In the premises one could say that official chicanery at the expense of the Indians has merely been transferred from the Indian Bureau and the Army to the Justice Department.

Harold Ickes prophesied this course of events when he urged that the Claims Commission operate its own division of investigation as a check on the Attorney General. The Claims Commission, however, has failed to make full use of its powers to investigate claims independently. The Commissioners, all attorneys by profession and hitherto without experience in an administrative agency, seem to prefer to view their function as strictly judicial in proceedings that are purely adversary. . . .

·3·

EVON Z. VOGT

The Acculturation of American Indians

Most of the Americans who have interested themselves in American Indian policy have believed that the problems of the Indians would be solved when they became completely assimilated in the dominant American culture. But Indian culture has shown a surprising resiliency and persistence even among the members of groups who have been most exposed to white culture. An anthropologist, Evon Z. Vogt, discusses the reasons why this has been true, and suggests that "our persisting Anglo-American 'racial attitudes'" have been particularly important in slowing Indian acculturation.

By the mid-twentieth century it has become apparent to social scientists studying the American Indian that the Indian population of the United States is markedly increasing and that the rate of basic acculturation to white American ways of life is incredibly slower than our earlier assumptions led us to believe. During the latter part of the nineteenth century and the early part of this century, the American Indians were prevailingly thought of in American public opinion as a "vanishing race." . . .

We were led to these comfortable assumptions about the vanishing American Indian by the fact that there *were* important population declines earlier in our history—many Indian tribes, in fact, became extinct—

SOURCE: Abridged from Evon Z. Vogt, "The Acculturation of American Indians," *Annals of the American Academy of Political and Social Science*, CCCXI (May, 1957), 137–146. Reprinted by permission of the American Academy of Political and Social Science and Evon Z. Vogt.

and by the observation that the Indians *had* undergone impressive changes in certain aspects of their cultures. It was anticipated that the population decline would continue and that the acculturative changes would proceed apace with all tribes and in all aspects of their culture as white American institutions impinged upon them. . . .

It has also been felt strongly that just as European immigrant groups are becoming Americanized within a few generations in the great American "melting pot" so, too, will the American Indians become assimilated. However, students did not stop to raise seriously enough the question of the vast difference between the American Indian and the Europeans. European immigrants all came from the same general stream of Western culture and they, by and large, were motivated toward assimilation when they migrated to the United States. Not only were the Indians linguistically and culturally completely different from the peoples of Europe, but they also had little choice in the matter. European culture came to them in their native habitat and proceeded by force to overrun the continent.

The acculturative changes which formed the basis for our earlier observations involved several different kinds of processes. These processes have been in operation in varying degrees since 1540 when Coronado arrived at Zuni and established the first contact between Europeans and American Indians within what are now the continental borders of the United States. In the first place there has been an important "drifting out" process from almost all American Indian populations over the centuries in which individuals and families have left their native settlements to take up residence in American communities. In some cases, this rate of migration has been great enough to involve almost all of the Indian population; but in many other cases, it has had the effect of "draining off" the most acculturated segment of the population each generation and of leaving a conservative reservoir of more traditional culture carriers intact to carry on their Indian way of life. We now also perceive clearly that we must differentiate between acculturative changes taking place in these individuals and families that are drifting away from the traditional ways of life and the Indian sociocultural system which may be undergoing quite a different type of change and at a much slower rate. This difference between *individual* change and *system* change in acculturation situations is fundamental, and it means that we should not jump to the conclusion that full acculturation will soon take place simply because we observe a certain segment of the population leaving Indian country to take up residence in the white world.

A second widespread and continuing process has been the replacement of Indian material culture with goods, techniques, and technological equipment of the white American way of life. There is no American Indian tribe today who is living close to the aboriginal level in its patterns of food, clothing, and shelter. But it is now clear that just because Zuni Indians, for example, build more modern type houses with running water and electric lights, invest in radios and refrigerators, and drive new automobiles, it does not mean that they necessarily abandon their kinship obligations or give up dancing in Katchina dances. Indeed, it has been startling to many of us to observe how completely the inventories of material culture in Indian households are composed of items derived from white American culture, and, yet, how relatively slow the rate of change is in social organization and religion in the same community.

All American Indian populations have also been undergoing a process of increasing involvement with our white American sociocultural system: in economic relationships to our market economy; in crucial adjustments to our state and national political systems, which now hold the ultimate control of force, and to our educational system, which now provides schools for almost all Indian children; in important connections with Christian missionary movements that now touch every Indian population. . . .

But what is interesting to the close observer is that, despite all these pressures for change, there are still basically Indian systems of social structure and culture persisting with variable vigor within conservative nuclei of American Indian populations. It would be rash indeed to predict now that these cultural features will completely disappear in the course of acculturation in one, two, or even several generations. . . .

A number of hypotheses have been advanced to account for the persistence of Indian culture ·in the face of increasing pressure from white American society toward full acculturation and the complete assimilation of Indian populations. To mention only a few of the common hypotheses, there is, in the first place, the argument, often advanced by the lay public, that isolation of the Indian populations on remote reservations administered by the Indian Bureau has insulated them from proper exposure to educational facilities, mass communications, and so forth and has prevented them from obtaining the means for assimilation. This hypothesis has undoubted merit, but it certainly fails to account for the many cases of Indian groups which have been subjected to a great deal of contact, yet who continue to maintain many of their old patterns. . . .

A more interesting hypothesis, also emphasizing contact conditions, has been advanced by Dozier and others to the effect that "forced" acculturation, if not so extreme as to lead to early absorption of the subordinate group, will result in a high degree of resistance to change in indigenous cultural patterns. This formulation appears to work well for cases like the Southwestern Pueblo where the aboriginal sociocultural systems were highly enough organized to develop patterns of resistance when "forced" acculturation occurred. It applies less well to tribes with a low level of aboriginal sociocultural integration, and, of course, does not apply at all to cases where the acculturation process was relatively "permissive" and the groups still maintain their old patterns.

A third type of hypothesis, involving a theory about the nature of culture, has been the thesis that while the material aspects of a culture can change readily, family and kinship institutions are more persistent; that the aspects of a way of life which have been labeled as core culture, implicit values, cultural orientations, and personality type, are still more persistent. . . . But the formulation in its present form will not account for all the variability we observe in rates of change in different aspects of American Indian culture. It also does not answer the basic question as to why *any* Indian patterns should be preserved at all considering the kind and degree of pressure for change many Indian tribes have experienced.

Still a fourth hypothesis stresses the importance of an organized communal structure. Eric Wolf has recently characterized this structure as a "corporate" community that maintains a bounded social system with clear-cut limits, in relation to both outsiders and insiders, and has structural identity over time. His thesis is that in Latin America the persistence of Indian-culture content seems to have depended primarily on maintenance of this structure and that where the structure collapsed, traditional cultural forms quickly gave way. This formulation has not been systematically explored with United States–Indian data; but it strikes me as an attractive hypothesis, especially in accounting for the high degree of persistence we observe among still very conservative tribes living in compact communities, like the Southwestern Pueblos. It is also crucial in explaining many of the differences between the acculturation of the American Negroes and the slower acculturation of the American Indians. But what concerns us more in this attempt to understand the limiting factors to full acculturation is why some important Indian patterns continue to persist among groups whose corporate structure has been shattered.

In all of these hypotheses, and others which cannot be discussed for lack of space, it is my impression that we have tended to de-emphasize recently, in our analyses of United States–Indian data, what is perhaps the most important factor of all: our persisting Anglo-American "racial" attitudes, derived historically from Puritan Colonialism, which strongly devaluate other physical types bearing different cultural traditions. These inflexible attitudes are of course directly related to the superordinate-subordinate structural character of Indian-white relationships in the United States. They are also related to the lack of a large mixed Indian–white population which would provide cultural models and reference groups along the continuum of acculturation for the conservative nuclei still living in the native-oriented Indian communities.

We pay lip service to the idea of Indians being the "First Americans," we now manifest considerable interest in their customs, and we decorate our homes with Indian rugs and pottery and dress our women in fashionable "squaw dresses" derived from Indian styles; but the barriers to full acceptance measured by such an index as the rate of intermarriage are still formidable in most areas of the United States.

The contrast with Mexico is sharp and illuminating. In Mexico inter-breeding between Spanish and Indian began almost immediately after the Spanish conquest. Even though miscegenation was prohibited during the late Colonial period, the total process has moved far enough to produce a profoundly "mestizo" nation. There are still relatively unac-culturated and unassimilated Indians remaining in various parts of the nation; but when Indian groups enter a transitional stage and begin to move in the direction of integration, there are cultural models and refer-ence groups for them all along the continuum of acculturation, from the most native-oriented Indian communities to the sophisticated urban life in Mexico City. The sociocultural system is also open for the ambitious and talented Indian individual like Benito Juarez who began his career in an isolated Zapotec Indian village and went on to become one of Mexico's greatest presidents. But, even more important, the system is relatively open for transitional Indian groups as they proceed generation by generation along the continuum to fuller integration and acculturation. There is now a conscious and conspicuous positive valuation of the Indian heritage on the part of Mexico's political and intellectual leaders.

In the United States, on the other hand, the path to full acculturation is confusing and frustrating, and an ultimate ceiling is still firmly clamped down by our persisting Anglo-American "racial" attitudes. Instead of proceeding generation by generation along a continuum to full accultura-tion, it is as if an American-Indian group must at some point leap across a spark gap to achieve a fully integrated position in white American society.

I do not mean to imply that biological interbreeding per se affects the process, but that biological miscegenation leads to profoundly different self-conceptions and evaluations; to the kinds of reference groups that seem to provide a kind of natural "ladder of acculturation" in many areas of Mexico that is so conspicuously lacking in the United States; and to a much more permeable barrier at the extreme end of the acculturation continuum.

Since a kind of ultimate lid or ceiling has been placed upon full acculturation and assimilation in the United States, it is now pertinent to raise the question as to what is happening to Indian groups who become reasonably well educated by our standards and move a great distance from their aboriginal ways of life without becoming fully integrated in the larger United States society. One way of looking at the problem is that we shall continue with a type of cultural pluralism for some generations to come. But in a vast number of cases, the process has moved too far for Indian groups to continue to find much meaning in their own particular aboriginal cultures, and what appears to be emerging is an interesting type of "Pan-Indianism."

This Pan-Indianism is assuming a form in which increasing numbers of American Indians are participating in customs and institutions that are describable only as Indian. These customs and institutions are being synthesized from elements derived from diverse Indian cultures and to some extent from white American culture. There exists also in many regions, and especially in Oklahoma, a loosely knit, informally organized grouping of Indians who have joined forces to participate in these Pan-Indian activities.

Historically, the beginnings of this type of Pan-Indianism are found in many of the nativistic movements which followed in the wake of conquest, the spread of the Ghost Dances being a classic type of example. The later emergence of the Peyote Cult, which involved not only the exchange of customs and ideas among Indian tribes and the incorporation of Christian concepts, but also intertribal participation in the same ceremonies, carried the process much further and continues to be one of the focal points in Pan-Indianism.

Conspicuous more recent developments are the various powwows and intertribal ceremonial gatherings. Some are organized by the Indians themselves, especially in Oklahoma and the Middle West; others, like the annual Gallup Inter-Tribal Indian Ceremonial, are managed by white businessmen to promote local business interests. . . .

Although the cultural elements found in this emerging Pan-Indian movement are derived from diverse Indian sources, it is highly significant that a high proportion of these elements are drawn from Plains culture: the war bonnet, the Plains-type war dance, and so forth. These elements have become symbols of Indianism to the Indians themselves to a degree that bears little relationship to the aboriginal facts. And it is probable that their importance as symbols derives in part from the fact that these elements are central features of the prevailing white-American stereotype of the American Indian. They are the features of Indian culture which white tourists expect to find when they attend intertribal ceremonials and Indians are rewarded by the whites for behaving in conformity to the stereotype. . . .

Other features of Pan-Indianism include intertribal visiting and inter-marriage, which are also of crucial importance, and the national Indian organizations such as the National Congress of American Indians which, to date, are less important than the powwows.

The significance of this Pan-Indianism in general terms is that it provides a social and cultural framework within which acculturating Indian groups can maintain their sense of identity and integrity as Indians as long as the dominant larger society assigns them to subordinate status. In the future, it is probable that this Pan-Indianism will develop greater political significance than it has at present, and that organizations like the National Congress of American Indians will speak more effectively for a more highly organized American-Indian minority which will begin to take the franchise more seriously and be more carefully listened to in the halls of the United States Congress in Washington.

THE COMMISSION ON THE RIGHTS, LIBERTIES
AND RESPONSIBILITIES OF THE AMERICAN INDIAN

Policies Which Impede Indian Assimilation

The implications and early results of the "termination resolution" which the members of Congress adopted in 1953 were
profoundly unsettling to some Americans. In 1957 The Fund
for the Republic, Inc., established a commission to appraise
the status of the Indian in American society. From the report
of this group we reproduce an assessment of the termination
policy. Significantly enough the chapter of the report which
deals almost solely with termination and from which this
reading was drawn was given the title which we have used
here.

The realization that conformity cannot be legislated changed the
national policy toward Indians. The conviction that men and cultures
differing from us and our culture must, nevertheless, be respected led
to the Indian Reorganization Act of 1934, which shifted the initiative
in relation to Indian problems from the B. I. A. to the Indian tribes
themselves. However, before the efficacy of the act could be adequately
demonstrated, World War II broke out; and after the war the old
attitude of trying to assimilate Indians by legislation reasserted itself,
culminating in the "termination resolution" (House Concurrent Resolution Number 108, of August 1, 1953, and Public Law 280, of August
15, 1953), which has been proved capable of disrupting Indian life by
depriving Indians of powers in their tribal governments and which
concentrates, not on the best interests of the Indians, but on easing
the burden on the federal government. The effect has been to deprive
Indians of both their property and the public services for which the
federal government has long been obligated. . . .

Between 1950 and 1960 the major controversy in Indian affairs was
over whether the United States should follow a program of pressing
for prompt termination of tribes without the consent of their members.

Source: From *The Indian: America's Unfinished Business*, 179–191 by William A.
Brophy and Sophie D. Aberle. © 1966, University of Oklahoma Press.

Policies were confused, the secretary seeming to espouse one kind and the B. I. A. another. But mandatory termination appeared to be the goal until September 18, 1958, when Secretary of the Interior Fred A. Seaton, broadcasting over radio station KCLS, Flagstaff, Arizona, surprised everyone by stating that no tribe would be involuntarily terminated. Since its adoption in 1953, House Concurrent Resolution No. 108, which states that the policy of Congress is to terminate as soon as practicable, has been in effect. However, since the publication of "A Program for Indian Citizens" in January, 1961, the mimeographed report of President Kennedy's Task Force in July, 1961, the declaration by various groups in Chicago under the aegis of Professor Sol Tax, and Secretary Udall's elucidation of Indian policy, the administration has emphasized the development of Indian resources. . . .

Nobody knows exactly what termination really means—neither the Indians nor anyone else. Termination can mean, for example, that one branch of the federal government surrenders a function, as in the transfer to the United States Public Health Service of the B. I. A.'s Division of Health. It may refer to a contract made by the B. I. A. with a state or local government for special services, such as the education of Indians in public schools. It may signify the relinquishing by the B. I. A. of part of its control of property, such as is involved when Indians are allowed to negotiate their own leases for allotted land or when B. I. A. transfers a function to the tribal government, as in the transfer of irrigation works and their operation to the Navaho tribe. (These works then do not become subject to state law.) It may even mean the withdrawal from a tribe of certain services usually rendered by the B. I. A., as, for example, the Bureau's removal of a superintendent capable of advising the inexperienced Umatillas in retaining their land and replacing him with ·a man whose previous experience had been chiefly in *selling* federal land. It may mean that a state is given Congressional authorization to extend its criminal and civil laws to Indian reservations, thereby depriving the tribes of substantial powers of local self-government (Public Law 280). It may also mean the passing of laws by Congress severing the historic relationship between the federal government and the tribes, abolishing their long-existing governments, and placing their affairs and resources under control of a state. It is in the sense of the last two meanings that the word "termination" is used in this report. Termination not only is not assimilation; it is not even assured integration. Integration comes only as a race is dispersed within the general population. If Indians so choose, they can now effect such dispersal, but it must be voluntary. . . .

Unlike many of the earlier federal statutes which granted only judicial jurisdiction to states, Public Law 280 conveys legislative authority, thus giving states the right to enact measures that could vitally change the character of the communities in which the Indians live without any option on their part. A state could wipe out most tribal customs, reduce or destroy the family's traditional control, abolish customary or undocumented marriages and so make children illegitimate, change the inheritance laws, and apply a complicated criminal code to a simple people. . . .

In 1962 Public Law 280 was in all stages of adoption. Nevada, North Dakota and South Dakota have acted to extend their jurisdictions. The Nevada statute allows counties to petition to be excepted from its provisions. It is reported that every county but one has followed the tribes' wishes, even though the law does not require tribal consent. North Dakota in 1958 amended its state constitution to enable the legislature to accept jurisdiction on its own terms, but the lawmakers have yet to take action. The South Dakota law, calling for tribal referendums, authorizes counties to assume the responsibility only on the impossible condition that the United States defray the cost, which federal law does not permit. . . .

The Senate Subcommittee on Constitutional Rights has since 1961 conducted an extensive investigation into the Constitutional rights of the Indian, the first such study ever made by Congress. On the basis of their findings, Senate Bill 966 was introduced into Congress. It would repeal Public Law 280 and provide a feasible and equitable method of state civil and criminal jurisdiction over Indian country for those tribesmen who might elect to come under state law. Judge Lewis in a recent opinion said:

The legal history of the status of Indian tribes under State and Federal law presents a complex and ever-changing concept of an artificial entity progressing from independent but helpless sovereignty toward a status of complete integration in the legal, economic and moral life of the people of the United States. . . .

Integration of Indian tribes under state law is moving forward at an accelerated rate. . . .

From 1954 through 1960 many laws and amendments were passed abolishing tribes as political entities—to "get the United States out of the Indian business"—and shifting responsibility for Indian affairs from the federal government to the states. During these years sixty-one tribes, groups, communities, *rancherías,* or allotments were terminated. . . .

The policy of termination and the legislation implementing it are characterized by several glaring weaknesses. (1) The basic assumption of assimilation-by-legislation is invalid. (2) Action has been taken precipitately. (3) Indians were given inadequate information and explanation regarding all probable effects of the policy, were rushed into the situation, and were permitted no true voice in the matter. (4) Although several tribes have been abolished as governmental units, ambiguities have been written into individual termination acts, which leave many highly important jurisdictional areas unclear. (5) The remaining obligations of the federal government to the Indians must yet be defined, probably by court action. For example, a terminated tribe does not know whether a state or a tribal tax should be levied on tribesmen and on persons doing business on its land. In case of a conflict, what is the proper federal action? (6) The traditional rights of a tribe to determine —in the absence of federal law—its own membership and to possess as a unit its assets in perpetuity have been transferred to federal jurisdiction. (7) The policy resulted, during the years when House Concurrent Resolution 108 was the guideline, in Congressional and B. I. A. concentration upon the withdrawal of federal services, instead of upon improving the Indian situation. It brought, in this connection, the appointment of private trustees to take over some of the federal functions (such as handling tribal resources) and the selection by the secretary of the interior (instead of by the tribes concerned) of management specialists to handle—under the secretary's instructions—whatever economic resources a "terminated tribe" may have had. (8) The legislation prohibits a tribe from spending before the termination date any tribal funds in the Treasury unless approved by the secretary.

There are other inequities wrought by the legislation, other potentially disastrous situations caused by the policy. To say the least, termination has been ill considered and weak; to say more, it has proved genuinely destructive of its own announced aim. House Concurrent Resolution 108, which the Indians believed had the force of a statute, effected some of the above far-reaching changes immediately, even regarding tribes not actually terminated by law. Once more, acquisitive white men looked toward Indian land. Once more, confusion increased regarding the status of the Indians. And the Indians themselves were seized with fear, made additionally insecure, and forced to rely for strength upon their own cultural conventions, thereby automatically accentuating every ethnic trait separating them from the dominant society.

The termination policy emphasized the housekeeping activities of trusteeship. The result was that many B. I. A. administrators became indifferent to basic Indian needs. The shortsighted policy of forcing Indians into the white man's pattern took precedence over any need to understand the effects of such a policy upon the individual. Mass transfers of students were made from federal to public schools to implement the policy, without taking into account the quality of teaching or the readiness or unreadiness of a child for the change.

The B. I. A. extension service was transferred to the Extension Division of the Department of Agriculture with the sole aim of getting rid of the Indian Service. The additional expenses involved and the compounding of administrative problems went unheeded. Land was made available for sale, with little or no thought given to the Indian's future after he had lost his land.

The historic connections between the tribes and the United States were severed by the termination acts, without a clear understanding on either side of what was involved. Special services the United States had rendered were stopped without any assurance that they would or could thereafter be provided willingly, by the states or their local units. For example, the United States, as well as the B. I. A., builds roads on Indian tribal land with federal money. The western states, in obtaining their share of funds from the Bureau of Public Roads, include Indian reservations in the total land area, which is a basis for allocations. The B. I. A. also performs maintenance work. Some states or local units undoubtedly would not have money for such programs if federal support were withdrawn. . . .

If there had been more time for the Indians to understand and consider these termination bills, and had they then been given the opportunity to amend or reject them without the immediate inducement of cash resulting from a division of tribal funds, the Klamath and Menominee bills at least would probably never have taken the form in which they were enacted. Some states, especially those with large Indian populations, have declined to assume the responsibility to Indians without extra federal compensation. If local governments are willing but financially unable to render such services, the United States should make financial arrangements with them. If the cost of service is less than taxes, adjustments should be made to forestall the realization of local profits from the transaction. There should never be any termination without federally enforcible assurances that adequate services will be continued. Court injunctions are no substitutes for schools, roads, or police protection.

If termination is so patently unfair to Indians, why—one might well ask—have some tribes accepted it? Many diverse factors have pushed tribes into such "acceptance." Near the top of the list one must place the inducement of the funds to be distributed among individual tribesmen. Perhaps the most persuasive factor, however, has been the fact that Indians have grown weary of too much supervision and resentful of what they feel to be the "father-knows-best" attitude of the B. I. A. Yet, despite their discontent, most existing tribes oppose termination because they are accustomed to a dependent relationship with the federal government and because they know they are unprepared for a clean break.

Some tribal members favor termination because they want to buy tribal land or use the reservation, but the strongest proponents are members no longer living on reservations. In some instances they presently receive nothing from tribal land, but would get their share of the proceeds if the property were divided and sold. Also, there are the selfishly interested whites—ranchers, farmers, stockmen, and speculators in oil, minerals, timber, or real estate—who are totally unconcerned with the welfare of the Indians or the moral and legal obligations of the federal government, wanting only to get their hands upon reservation acres. . . .

CHAPTER XVIII

The Conservation Movement

ALTHOUGH FRONTIERSMEN or capitalists might try to amend the land code of the United States in their own interests during the mid-nineteenth century, they and most Americans of the time expected that the government would transfer the resources of the public domain as rapidly as possible to individuals who were prepared to use them. Development of such resources they believed, could safely be left to the initiative of American farmers and businessmen. The officers of the United States government who administered the public domain believed themselves responsible only for applying the land laws and in no way obligated to suggest major changes of policy or to shape public opinion in support of them.

How different were the years of the Theodore Roosevelt administration! The amateur pugilist, sometime cavalry leader and walrus-tusked outdoorsman in the White House bombarded the nation with pleas to save or more effectively utilize the soil, forests, water and mineral resources of the nation. He asked Congress for legislation to these ends and Congress frequently acquiesced. In the bureaus and departments at Washington, a cadre of hard-working and imaginative public officers prepared conservation propaganda, mapped legislative strategy, and suggested ways of circumventing Congress by administrative action when the legislators were balky. Thus began the conservation age; Theodore Roosevelt was its political prophet and the chief forester of the United States, Gifford Pinchot, so the President said, was the "keeper of his conscience."

The first major achievement in reshaping American resource policy was the Revision Act of 1891 which ended the sale of agricultural land except under an amended Desert Land Act, and the Homestead Law and its amendments. A clause in the legislation of 1891 allowed the President to establish Forest Reserves—a most important provision, as time would show. The Roosevelt administration confirmed and amplified the revisionary tendencies in a most striking way and William Howard Taft and Woodrow Wilson also developed significant policies and legislation for the nation's public resources. Conservationists fought to preserve the remaining agricultural lands in the public domain from fraudulent entry and supported successful efforts to alter the homestead laws by increasing the acreage first to 320 acres and later to 640 acres for stock raisers, as well as by reducing the residency requirement to three years. These were changes dictated by the aridity of the western regions in which most of the unoccupied lands lay. By the end of the year 1900, homesteaders had patented some 80,000,000 acres of land; after that date they acquired title to approximately 190,000,000 acres within the contiguous territories and states. But the reformers were particularly interested in applying conservation policies to the forests, mineral lands, western rivers, water power sites and unassigned grazing lands.

Of all America's natural resources, none was more important to conservationists than the Forest Reserves or National Forests as they were ultimately called. Many of the undeveloped mineral lands and water power sites in the nation lay within them. The sources or major tributaries of important western rivers rose there or at least flowed through them and management of the forest watersheds directly affected the supplies of water which irrigationists or other residents needed at lower levels. Great stretches of grazing land were within the forests also and lessons learned in their administration might perhaps be applied to similar terrain, still untaken by settlers, in the public domain outside the forests. Conservationists were jubilant therefore when Roosevelt transferred administration of the forests from the Department of the Interior, the "give-away" agency, to the Division of Forestry in the Department of Agriculture, headed by Gifford Pinchot.

Before Congress terminated the President's authority to create and enlarge forest reserves, Theodore Roosevelt increased the extent of the nation's reserved timberlands to some 150 million acres in 159 separate locations. Meanwhile the Forest Service had begun sustained yield practices and developed a system of livestock quotas, grazing fees, and range improvement procedures on the forest ranges. During the Taft administration Congress passed the Weeks Act which allowed the government to purchase land in watersheds where the forest cover affected run-off and the utilization of streams. The conservationists ultimately used this legislation in developing our present National Forests in the eastern United States.

Meanwhile government administrators and legislators initiated policies for the development of the water resources on the public lands. Their first step during the Roosevelt administration was to reserve many of the promising water power sites on the public domain from entry under the land laws of the United States on the pretext that ranger stations were to be located there. In the later days of the Wilson administration, Congress approved a lease and permit system that allowed private corporations to develop such locations under the supervision of the Federal Electric Power Commission. In the meantime western power companies and other major economic interests of the region fought the plans and policies of the conservationists. But the Supreme Court validated major federal procedures and scotched the efforts of state authorities to use the right of eminent domain to open reserved water-power sites. The reservation policy was only one aspect of the national government's interest in the management of the water resources of the West. The Newland's Act of 1902 created the Bureau of Reclamation, authorized to build dams and distribute irrigation water from the reservoirs so as to allow intensive agriculture on hitherto arid lands. In the irrigation projects of the Bureau settlers purchased land on long-term contract. But reclamation dams obviously could be used to produce electric power, and conservationists urged the multiple use of western water resources. In the Power Act of 1920, Congress authorized the government to generate electric power at federal dams and sell it.

During the first 20 years of the twentieth century, conservationists also managed to apply the reservation policy to considerable acreages of mineral lands. The Roosevelt administration had withdrawn coal lands from entry, ostensibly for reclassification. Legislation of 1910 endorsed that action and also applied the policy to oil, gas and phosphate lands as well. President Taft later obtained Congressional approval to extend the policy to lands which contained subsurface deposits of copper and iron. The General Leasing Act of 1920 established guidelines for the development of such resources under lease from the government, and provided that the states would share the income with the federal government. For the most part the latter's share was to be used in financing western irrigation projects.

Their western opponents charged that the conservationists were trying to lock up the resources of the West and prevent that region from developing a healthy and prosperous economy. The reformers heartily denied the accusation. They wished only to guarantee, they maintained, that the resources of the public domain would be developed wisely, scientifically, and in the interests of all Americans. Nor could the westerners maintain a united front against the reformers. Many who lived beyond the one-hundredth meridian realized that the reclamation programs would diversify and strengthen the agriculture of their region. The officers of large lumber firms recognized that the forest reserve policy enhanced the value of their timberlands and protected them against the uncontrolled cutting and cut-throat marketing practices that might have developed in the lumber industry if all of the nation's forests had been sold to private parties. Lumbermen who owned efficient mills on large holdings near the reserves knew that they could profitably bid higher for stumpage on the reserves than could the independent logger or mill man of small means. Thus it was the small lumberman who criticized the Forest Reserve policy most bitterly. Although stockmen were initially suspicious of the Forest Service, many of them came to appreciate the stability which its lease and quota system established on ranges that had been racked by feuds between cattlemen and sheepmen and disagreements between resident stockmen and the owners of tramp herds.

There were, of course, differences among the conservationists themselves. Subscribing to the doctrine of executive stewardship, Roosevelt's dynamic Secretary of the Interior, James R. Garfield, believed in using every iota of power over natural resources that Congress had given to the executive branch of government and supplementing it by executive action when the needs of conservation dictated. Although a committed conservationist, William Howard Taft assumed that the initiative in such matters rested in Congress. Administrative officers could recommend legislation to the Congress, but in performing their duties they must follow the word of the statutes rather than their own interpretation of what was best for the nation. As much as anything perhaps, this difference in style underlay the Pinchot-Ballinger controversy during President Taft's administration. When Gifford Pinchot concluded that the Secretary of the Interior, Richard A. Ballinger, was helping western mining interests to plunder Alaskan coal reserves and refused to temper his criticism, President Taft dismissed him. The evidence of witnesses at the Congressional hearings which followed was profoundly embarrassing to the administration and convinced many conservationists, including Theodore Roosevelt, that Taft was a traitor to the conservation cause.

The conservationist of the Roosevelt or Pinchot breed believed in the controlled use of America's natural resources. In this same era, groups were gaining strength whose members wished mainly to preserve unspoiled portions of the nation's wilderness for the enjoyment and the inspiration of their generation and those to come. Symbolized best by John Muir and his friends of the Sierra Club, the preservationists demonstrated their strength when they mobilized opposition against the plans of San Francisco's municipal officials to build a reservoir in the wild and beautiful Hetch-Hetchy valley of Yosemite National Park. The pragmatic nature of the "orthodox" conservationists is well illustrated in the fact that Pinchot opposed the preservationists in this contest. Although the "esthetic" conservationists failed at Hetch-Hetchy, their growing influence is also reflected in the legislation of the early twentieth century. Congress had created Yellowstone National Park in 1872; laws authorizing the Sequoya, Yosemite, and Mt. Rainier National Parks followed before 1900. Now sentiment grew for the development of additional parks. In appropriate legislation Congress provided for the naming and care of national antiquities and established a unified system for administering the National Parks in 1916. Significantly, the park system remained under the supervision of the Department of the Interior despite the aspirations of the Forest Service to control it. The memory of Hetch-Hetchy was fresh and bitter in the minds of the preservationists and they were determined that the Forest Service should not enlarge its province.

During the Republican administrations of the 1920's the conservationists were less successful in advancing their cause than in the earlier years of the century. The Teapot Dome affair spectacularly illustrated the new era; Albert B. Fall, Secretary of the Interior, was shown to have accepted payment from the executives of oil companies in return for leases on oil lands hitherto reserved. Even so, conservationists in the United States Senate brought the robbers to justice and Teapot Dome is not an appropriate symbol of Republican natural resource policy. Although President Harding and President Coolidge showed little interest in expanding federal authority over natural resources and stressed federal cooperation with the states instead, dedicated leaders within the conservation agencies were able to point to some achievements. The members of Congress authorized increased forest management research and fire protection measures. They approved the Boulder Canyon project, the first great federal river basin development which illustrated multiple use concepts. Federal officers created a system of migratory bird sanctuaries and the National Parks prospered. Fundamental research and basic knowledge accumulated in various agencies, awaiting more receptive administrations. A sincere conservationist, in his rather limited way, Herbert Hoover appointed a Committee on the Conservation and Administration of the Public Domain which reported in 1931. The members recommended that the national government should surrender the remaining public lands to the states in which they lay.

But they did not suggest releasing federal rights to minerals in those lands nor did they recommend that the central government should surrender lands which were already reserved for other uses. So limited a concession was of little interest to the opponents of conservation in the West. Even the business-oriented Republican administrations were, they discovered, prepared to preserve many of the achievements of the conservation movement.

Depression and the New Deal threw open the gates of reform once more. During the traumatic 1930's, Americans accepted the use of public programs to stimulate the economy and also reassessed the significance of the nation's resources. Projects designed to provide employment for the unemployed fostered the conservation cause. The young men of the Civilian Conservation Corps labored mightily in the National Forests, building fire trails and reseeding or planting seedlings in burned-over areas; in the National Parks they developed access roads and campsites. Reclamation and power dams rose on western rivers as never before. Under the provisions of the Taylor Grazing Act of 1934, employees of the Department of the Interior placed most of the unreserved public domain in grazing districts to be supervised by the grazing service of that department. After three-quarters of a century, Americans had decided that the free homestead was no longer an appropriate use of the nation's western resources.

Not all Americans have been willing to accept the policies of the 1930's as definitive statements of resource policy. Western stockmen bitterly criticized the management of the Grazing Districts and their representatives in Congress reflected their views. During the 1940's and early 1950's Senator Patrick A. McCarran of Nevada harried the Grazing Service of the Department of the Interior unmercifully. Under his chairmanship, the Senate Public Lands Committee refused to allow the Service to increase grazing fees, while the House Appropriations Committee, at the same time, declined to increase allocations to the agency from the general fund until the grazing charges were increased. During this contest a substantial number of employees of the Grazing Service resigned or had to be released, it lost its status as an independent bureau, and the public ranges unquestionably suffered. Utility companies have also fought the concepts and agencies of public power, less spectacularly but no less energetically, and miners, oil men and some lumbermen have all been critical of the natural resource policies of the United States government.

During the 1960's there still remained some 350 million acres of the original public domain in the United States in addition to the untapped resources of Alaska. Some 170 million acres of the public lands within the contiguous states lay in federal grazing districts; the National Forests included another 150 million acres; and almost 15 million acres were in the National Parks and National Monuments. In addition there were various mineral land reserves, reclamation development lands unpatented as yet to settlers, and various lands of special status, like the famous O. and C. lands of Oregon, which the Oregon and California Railroad received originally as a land grant but which were revested in the United States because the railroad corporation failed to fulfill its charter obligations. The federal government still owned some 85 per cent of Nevada. The Bureau of Land Management and other agencies of the Interior Department and the Forest Service of the Department of Agriculture administered most of the public lands, although the Defense Department controlled some of them.

During the 1960's the management of the public lands was still of great interest to many Americans. Cattlemen and sheepmen who used the Grazing Districts and the ranges of the National Forests were deeply concerned about the administration of these grasslands. The grazing quotas of the stockmen had actually become capitalized in the value of their ranches. Mining corporations desired that their prospectors should have easy access to the public lands and that there be generous leasing procedures under which they might develop their discoveries in the National Forests and within the mineral land reserves. They were displeased because their activities were restricted in the National Parks. Oil companies wished to obtain drilling privileges on oil land reserves and access to oil shale deposits. Lumbermen wanted to purchase timber from National Forests or from the Grazing Districts as cheaply and as simply as possible. Although the power companies were somewhat less interested in the acquisition of power sites than in an earlier era, they were keenly interested in the way in which the government developed and sold electric power at federal dams. Public power competed with private power. In unparalleled numbers sportsmen and nature lovers wished to hunt, fish, hike and camp on the public lands. These were "user groups," represented in every case by regional or national organizations whose spokesmen lobbied skillfully in Congress and carried their pleas to key members of the executive branch. Other groups as well were often deeply interested in the administration of the public lands, particularly when local businessmen in the West requested that reserved lands be released for industrial development or when the decision of a federal agency would affect the tourist industry. The decisions in such cases might affect the tax revenues of a local government or the long range economic development of a region.

Natural resource policies in the United States have produced much controversy and will continue to do so. What has the impact of this great national treasure trove been on American life and economic development? Have we been prodigals or misers? What rules should have prevailed when competing interest groups demanded the right to develop or control the same resources? What concessions are owed to the local residents of regions which the citizens of the whole nation wish to use as their campground? To what degree should the private citizen be allowed to exploit the commercial possibilities of scenic and recreational areas? How wise have we been in developing western irrigable lands while eastern farmers complained of inadequate markets? Is public power the unfair competitor that the private utility corporations maintain? Would the national welfare be fostered if the government surrendered the Grazing Districts to the local stockmen or the miners and oil men were given unrestricted access to the public lands? And what of the national resources of Alaska? Will the hard-won wisdom that several generations of conservationists have accumulated in the older states be repudiated there? Uncle Sam's acres are still broad but they are not limitless; his resources are great but they are not infinite. The decisions of the future may be more important even than those that have been made in the past.

W J McGEE

The Conservation of Natural Resources

Less well known than some of the other leading conservationists, W J McGee was a gifted and versatile scientist who held responsible posts in various government agencies during the late nineteenth and early twentieth centuries. In this reading McGee presents a conservationist's interpretation of the history of resource utilization in the United States. But his approach is more than a sober account of the progressive exhaustion of resources; it is suffused with moral fervor-and we should ask why this should have been so.

. . . Now the line between East and West is a shifting one. When the Nation was young, New York and Pennsylvania were western States; then Ohio became the Far West and Indiana an Ultima Thule, while the Empire and Keystone commonwealths became Middle States. Now the Mississippi is an eastern river; Kansas and Nebraska and the Dakotas are the actual Middle States; and the Pacific States are the West—with a new Far West away beyond in Hawaii and the Philippines. In every stage of settlement from the eastern flanks of the Appalachians to the western face of the Rockies and the foot-slopes of the Sierra the geographic and climatal means tended toward extremes, and thus toward more stressful experiences among the settlers; and so the West, drawing its blood and bone and brawn from the East, has repaid in brain and in brain-wrought Conquest over Nature. . . .

The widening division between East and West has kept pace with our history; and in each generation the West of the time was the more stressful and dynamic in that it was the seat of pioneering and in that the extremes were wider. When Independence was declared and the Constitution was framed, no resources were reckoned except the Men who made the nation and the Land on which they lived. The very munitions of war, like the tools and utensils of peace, were mainly imported. Some iron was indeed wrought expensively with charcoal, but a half-century passed before coal mining and effective smelting began.

SOURCE: Abridged from W J McGee, "The Conservation of Natural Resources," Mississippi Valley Historical Association, *Proceedings*, III (1909–1910), 361–379.

Meantime the trees of centuries-old forests were deemed obstructions to settlement rather than values in themselves; and the most strenuous work of any people in any country in all the world's history up to the middle of the nineteenth century was that performed by the pioneers in destroying the magnificent forests of the western frontier in Ohio and neighboring States—a work that bent the backs, though it could not break the spirits, of eastern-born men and women as they felled trees, burned logs, and grubbed stumps in clearing homesteads worth less to-day than would be the timber had it been left standing!

Now because the Fathers saw Land as the sole natural resource of the country, so the succeeding generations remained indifferent to the values residing in the minerals below and the forests above, and parted with all together as acres or "sections" of land. Herein lay what now seems the most serious error in the world's greatest Republic. Monarchs are accustomed to retaining royal or imperial rights in the forests and minerals, and these eventually inure to the benefit of their people; ecclesiastic institutions allied with monarchial rule have commonly held rein over rarer resources until they were reclaimed by the growing generations of men; but through a lamentable lack of foresight our Republic hasted to give away, under the guise of land to live on, values far greater than the land itself—and this policy continued for generations. Men still living remember when the finest coal fields of the then western States of Pennsylvania and Virginia were sold as mere lands, with no added price for the coal beneath or the wood above; their sons remember when the iron ranges of the newer West in the Lake Superior region and in Alabama were transferred at the lowest government figures for land, with no added rates for the vast mineral wealth; and even younglings well recall the sale of fine woodlands at the conventional farm-land price of $1.25 per acre—and that, too, when each tree of the hundred or two standing on each acre was worth more than the acre-price! . . .

In the material aspect, our individual liberty became collective license, and our legislative and administrative prodigality grew . to national profligacy; the balance between impulse and responsibi.cy was lost, the future of the People and Nation was forgotten, and the very name of posterity was made a by-word by men in high places; and worst of all the very profligacies came to be venerated as law and even crystallized foolishly in decisions or more questionably in enactments—and for long there were none to stand in the way of the growing avalanche of extravagance. The waste was always wildest in the West, for as settlement followed the sun new resources were discovered or came into being through natural growth; yet at last even the vigorous West was awakened, and that largely through the reckless alienation of land—as noted later. . . .

The free gift of minerals and forests opened for foresighted men ways to wealth and power beyond all historical precedent; and so America became a manufacturing nation, rich and powerful among the world's nations, with unexampled rapidity. At the same time the free gift of these resources—having no value in themselves apart from that given them by the growth of the People—opened the way to monopoly, and the resources passed under monopolistic control with a rapidity never before seen in all the world's history; and it is hardly too much to say that the Nation has become one of the Captains of Industry first, and one of the People and their chosen representatives only second. . . .

An incidental result of the free gift of resources was habitual failure to appreciate their worth; and they were wasted recklessly. Up to the middle of the last century, when coal fields were sold as land and coal was appraised only at the labor of extracting it, operators were content to take out but a quarter or third of the natural fuel, leaving the rest as waste. Even up to date, coal mining operations have left forever inaccessible in the ground about as much coal as that taken out; and incredible as it may sound, even today hardly five per cent of the thermal energy of the hundreds of millions of tons of coal consumed each year is utilized for heat or power—and much less than one per cent for light from the abounding electric arc! In the metals the waste is less, since tailings may be, and often are, reworked. In timber the case is worse. While settlement spread, forest fires spread more rapidly; and up to date the destruction by fire has been far beyond that by the axe. So, too, wastes in logging and lumbering and milling have exceeded the utilization of timber; even during the past decade the wood actually used was hardly a third of that standing in the forest as the cutting began. Nor are other wastes less appalling. The losses due to preventable conflagration run into the hundreds of millions yearly; America's loss of life through carelessness in mining exceeds her losses of life in war, and the toll continues at the rate of more than a full regiment yearly; while the loss of life and limb in reckless railroading is still more ghastly. Perhaps the gravest single item is the loss through erosion of the soil due to careless farming, which is estimated at $500,000,000 per year— the heaviest tax borne by the American farmer. The spirit of prodigality begotten of the policy of free gift has come to pervade thought and deaden sensibility—such lavish and foolish waste as that of this country during recent decades the world never saw before! . . .

As time passed the People grew, and with them other values opening opportunities less to People than to Privilege; and wealth beyond the visions of avarice and power above the dreams of tyranny have come to the few—at vast cost to the just patrimony of the multitude—while much of the substance of the Nation has been wasted and many of the People have passed under the domination of the beneficiaries of Privilege. Ample resources indeed remain—enough to insure the perpetuity of the People—but the question also remains whether these shall be held and used by the People, whose travail gave them value and whose rights therein are inalienable and indefeasible under the Declaration of Independence and the Constitution, or whether they shall go chiefly into the hands of the self-chosen and self-annointed few, largely to forge new shackles for the wrists and ankles of the many! . . .

When the Nation was young its area was small; but successive additions of territory were made on the West—the ever-growing new West —afforded new frontiers for pioneering and final conquest, until the area of mainland United States came to approximate two billion acres. A third of this area is arid; and a quarter-century ago John Wesley Powell—soldier, scientist, philosopher, a western man in breeding and spirit—saw that the public lands available for individual settlement under the original plan were nearly exhausted, and conceived the idea of virtually extending the public domain by making the arid lands available for settlement through irrigation; and, as Director of the Geological Survey, he initiated practical work in that direction. It was characteristically a task of the West! Meantime the forests were still passing under the destructive fire and wasteful axe, until a practical Prophet of the Forest appeared in the person of Gifford Pinchot—born and bred in the East but receptive of the spirit of the West; one styled a "brilliant dreamer," though better described as a modern Ajax—who boldly conceived the patriotic plan of protecting the country's forests for the country's benefit. Several statesmen were hospitable to the plans of Powell and Pinchot for extending the habitable lands and conserving the woods, and the work went forward slowly. Powell was soon succeeded in the reclamation work by Frederick Haynes Newell, who opened a new chapter in the engineering history of the world by the magnitude and long foresight of his reclamation projects; while Pinchot's forest policy became no less epoch-marking. In good time came Theodore Roosevelt—in whom East and West met in ceaseless struggle for supremacy, making him the typical American of his generation—and as President he not only sustained the Forest and Reclamation Services, but pushed on toward the reclamation of the rivers for navigation and other uses, an effort in which his hands were held up by many—

notably James Rudolph Garfield, first as Commissioner of Corporations and later as Secretary of the Interior. Now as Pinchot and Newell and Garfield traversed the West in their work, they were impressed by the broad areas of public land transferred nominally to actual settlers—that is, to the landed citizenry foreshadowed in the visions of the Fathers of the Republic—yet in such wise that it actually passed into the owner-ship of great corporations, who were so mightily enriched and strength-ened thereby as to become a power in legislative halls of the States, if not of the Nation. . . .

Pinchot and Garfield especially, and Roosevelt in his turn, sought to counteract the tendency toward wholesale alienation of the public lands for the benefit of the corporation and the oppression or suppression of the settler; and in the end their efforts resulted in what is now known as the Conservation Movement: a movement leading through a Water-ways Commission, a Conference of Governors in the White House, a Conservation Commission, and a dozen congresses and conventions—though none the less the offspring of a few far-seeing minds, and a gift of the dynamic West to the waiting East.

The National Conservation Commission made an inventory of the country's resources, the most comprehensive ever prepared in any land. The figures are preliminary, and will be modified by fuller data; yet they may be relied on to guide current thought and action. At the current increasing rates of consumption and waste, our forests would last twenty-five years, or, allowing for growth, thirty-three years, a single generation; our high grade iron ores (of which we mine annually some 1300 pounds for each man and woman and child of our population) would be gone by the middle of the century and the low grade ores by its end; our coal (of which we consume some five tons per capita yearly) would last well toward the end of the next century. . . . Of our two billion acres of land, about one-third is virtually unproductive by reason of aridity, while in another third the rainfall is less than is required for full productivity in the present state of agriculture; some two-fifths of the whole is occupied by farms, and about one-fifth is actually farmed. Meantime, our waters are not only ill-utilized, but wantonly wasted, allowed to run off in destructive floods, to become contaminated at appalling cost of life, to erode the soil and carry away its richest part, and thus to limit navigation and other uses. All our national extravagances are shocking to sensibilities once awakened; none are more so than our waste of water—the last to be realized, partly because the supply is permanent although limited, partly because of a short-sighted ancestral custom of treating the life-giving liquid as a mere appurtenance of the land, a custom unhappily fastened on us by decisions as a common law doctrine without constitutional warrant. . . .

On its face the Conservation Movement is material—ultra-material. At first blush the moral and the social in which cults arise and from which doctrines draw inspiration may not appear. Yet in truth there has never been in all human history a popular movement more firmly grounded in ethics, in the eternal equities, in the divinity of human rights! Whether we rise into the spiritual empyrean or cling more closely to the essence of humanity, we find our loftiest ideals made real in the Cult of Conservation. . . .

What *right* has any citizen of a free country, whatever his foresight and shrewdness, to seize on sources of life for his own behoof that are the common heritage of all; what *right* has legislature or court to help in the seizure; and striking still more deeply, what *right* has any generation to wholly consume, much less to waste, those sources of life without which the children or the children's children must starve or freeze? These are among the questions arising among intelligent minds in every part of this country, and giving form to a national feeling which is gradually rising to a new plane of equity. . . .

J. LEONARD BATES

Fulfilling American Democracy: The Conservation Movement, 1907-1921

The origins of reform are usually complex. Here J. Leonard Bates explores the ideas of the conservationists, their place in the Progressive Movement and the influence which the give-and-take of American politics and the impact of external events exerted in the formulation of conservation legislation.

"Conservation," as related to an evolving government policy in the twentieth century, has not been a clearly defined term. For average citizens it has meant in a general way the prevention of waste. For scholars and government administrators it has frequently meant a little more definitely the careful management of natural resources. . . . The acceptance of conservation in a broad sense represents a considerable advance from the nineteenth century when with a few notable exceptions squandering of public and private resources went on recklessly and often cynically. Moreover, its acceptance was a tribute to a group of men whose concept of official responsibility for conservation was not a loose, vague theory, nor a matter of efficiency as such, but a fighting, democratic faith. . . .

The usual interpretation today is that the Progressive Movement was essentially an uprising of the middle class, protesting against monopoly and boss control of politics, stressing heavily the virtues of competition, freedom, and morality. With respect to conservation this view leads to the criticism that there existed a fundamental inconsistency between the ideas of protecting natural resources and the dominant beliefs in individualism and competition with the resultant low prices, heavy consumption, and waste.

There was another side to the Progressive Movement—perhaps the most significant side: the decline of laissez faire, the development of a

SOURCE: Abridged from J. Leonard Bates, "Fulfilling American Democracy: The Conservation Movement, 1907–1921," *Mississippi Valley Historical Review*, XLIV (June, 1957), 29-57. Reprinted by permission of the *Journal of American History* and J. Leonard Bates.

social conscience, the repudiation of Social Darwinism. Most leaders of progressivism believed in a positive state. Some came to believe in the sort of factory and social legislation, welfare action, utility regulation, and limited government ownership that is associated with the New Deal. A few wished to go farther than the New Deal ever went. While the conservationists, like others progressively inclined, differed among themselves, nevertheless they had a program which may be described as limited socialism in the public interest. Influenced by Henry George, Edward Bellamy, Lester Ward, William James, Arthur Twining Hadley, Thorstein Veblen, Charles A. Beard, and others, these protectors of the public lands were far removed from classical economics.

The organized conservationists were concerned more with economic justice and democracy in the handling of resources than with mere prevention of waste. One aspect of the matter was the price and income situation, the actual monetary rewards from the marvelous wealth of this land. Conservationists believed that somehow the common heritage, the socially created resources and institutions, had passed into the hands of vested interests and that the benefits were siphoned into the hands of a few. There were several ways in which this situation might be remedied, as they saw it: first, to hold on to the remaining public lands, at least temporarily, preventing further monopolization; second, to attempt to give the people a fuller share of opportunities and profits; and finally, in that period of low income to keep prices proportionately low. The monopolists who jacked up prices were anathema, even though their methods might contribute to conservation by reducing consumption. Conservation through penalizing the public was something which democratically motivated leaders were not prepared to accept. . . .

In a sense the conservation movement was a nonpartisan, statesmanlike cause, winning support from scientists, politicians, and others all over the country. But a fact of long-range significance was its Republican origin; Republicans led by Pinchot and Roosevelt were the main inspiration of this program. These men were proud of their work, many of them almost fanatically devoted to Roosevelt. They did not easily dissociate the Republican party or the "Republican Roosevelt," who had first given them their chance, from the body of their accomplishments. Politics and personalities help appreciably to explain the conservation fight from 1907 to 1921. . . .

The developing rationale of the conservationists is of the utmost importance in explaining their conduct and influence. By no means were they all alike, but people such as Roosevelt, Pinchot, and La Follette believed that a larger amount of governmental interference and regulation in the public interest was required. They were especially concerned about the remaining public lands, which, according to principles grounded in the Homestead and other acts, belonged to all. Millions of acres had been given away or sold to corporate interests for a trifling price or had been actually stolen. This record of carelessness and exploitation could not be expunged. However, to conserve and use wisely that which remained, to show that civilized man could profit from mistakes of the past, to democratize the handling of a common heritage, would be a genuine consolation. A crisis, they felt, existed. Such an attitude was a compound of idealism, passion, and sober analysis. These men realized that American society in the twentieth century must be increasingly one of co-operative and collective gains.

As progressives they agreed passionately on the need for honesty and a social conscience in the administration of resources. Declared Pinchot in 1910: "There is no hunger like land hunger, and no object for which men are more ready to use unfair and desperate means than the acquisition of land." Americans had to make up their minds whether their political system was to be devoted to "unclean money or free men." It was fortunate, he believed, that special interests were afflicted with a "blindness" because of their "wholly commercialized point of view." Conservationists were convinced that hostility toward materialism and toward money men and special interests usually was warranted, that history afforded ample justification for suspicion. If nothing else united the conservationists, there was this hatred of the boodler, the rank materialist, the exploiter.

Intellectually there was much that drew these men together. McGee, whom Pinchot called "the scientific brains" of the conservation movement, provided a rationale for action. "Every revolution," said McGee, "whatever its material manifestations . . . is first and foremost a revolution in thought and spirit." Believing that Americans had largely lost their rights in the land, McGee felt that knowledge of how this had occurred might yet insure the "perpetuity" of the people. . . .

Pinchot and his group . . . believed in using the authority of federal and state government to compel conservation practices ("socialization of management"), even aiming to do this on *private* forest lands. With respect to the alternatives of federal or state action Pinchot once remarked:

I have very little interest in the abstract question whether the nation is encroaching upon the rights of the states or the states upon the nation. Power falls naturally to that person or agency which can and does use it, and . . . the nation acts . . . [while] the states do not.

The influence of these ideas and the impact of the Pinchot organization cannot be minimized. Nevertheless, Pinchot and his friends did not constitute the entire conservation movement. There were issues which inevitably divided the conservationists as a whole: the clashing of personalities and ambitions, disagreement over methods if not over goals, disputes between Democrats and Republicans, and economic sectionalism especially as it arose between the West and the East. Any issue or event could impinge upon conservation with divisive results or with diverse and complicating effects—for example World War I. In general, one accepting the designation of "conservationist" was a progressive, believing in the necessity of strong executive leadership and federal action. He might be a radical or an outright socialist. Frequently, on the other hand, he emphasized as heavily as did President Taft the authority of Congress, the statutory system that must be erected, the quieting of any doubts as to constitutionality. And it was not strange for a conservationist to consider himself a conservative; one who believed in honest government and orderly processes, who hated boodling, who watched vigilantly for the sly steals that special interests might perpetrate. . . .

There was one charge endlessly repeated against the conservationist with the effect of creating cleavages in the ranks. Time and again their foes, or those who called themselves moderate and reasonable conservationists, asserted that the Pinchot policy resolved itself into keeping resources in cold storage, or under lock and key, or hermetically sealed up. They implied or even declared that Pinchot and his adherents had no interest in jobs and opportunities for the people of the West; that they cared nothing for necessary development. . . .

[I]t was true that the Roosevelt-Pinchot-Taft withdrawals of land, the study for purposes of classification, and the shaping of new laws meant some delay. How much of this delay was to be charged to them and how much was to be charged to their enemies among state righters and special interests remained an open question.

From 1910 to 1912 two dramatic events had the effect of both quickening the conservation movement and causing its reorientation; and World War I, following shortly, added complications. First, there was the famous Ballinger-Pinchot controversy, in which Pinchot, becoming a critic of the Secretary of the Interior, was fired from his job as chief United States forester. Pinchot and the progressives convinced themselves that President Taft had been a traitor to their cause; that the Secretary of the Interior, Richard A. Ballinger of Seattle, had yielded to the big interests; and that the majority report, after a congressional investigation, was a "whitewash." . . . Whatever the exact meaning of this affair, many progressives never forgave Taft; nor doubted that Ballinger was in league with the Guggenheims; nor forgot that such a man as Edwin Denby (later secretary of the navy under Harding) had been among the "whitewashers" in Congress. And on the other side, Taft was reported as believing that Pinchot was "a socialist and a spiritualist . . . capable of any extreme act."

All of this helped to precipitate the second event, the revolt of Republican progressives, and the formation of the Roosevelt "Bull Moose" party in 1912. As a result of this schism Woodrow Wilson came to the White House, and for the first time a Democratic administration had to cope with twentieth-century problems, including conservation. The relations between Republicans who had inaugurated this policy and the polyglot Democrats who tried more or less to carry it out were well-nigh predictable. Prospects of mutual satisfaction were scant. . . .

The coming of a Democratic administration in 1913 produced a reorientation affecting everyone in the fight for conservation. This was due partly to the status of the withdrawal question; nonmetallic mineral lands and water power sites no longer were being sold or given away and had to be made available under some scheme for development. Prior to 1913, Republicans had argued mostly among themselves; they could now sit back and watch the Democrats undertake the direction of policy, and could wait for an appropriate occasion to assail and expose them. Wilson believed in conservation, and the policy of his administration was directed toward formulation of a leasing system. But on the question of how this should be done his own advisers were often in sharp disagreement, thereby giving the Republicans their opportunity for criticism. In the beginning, La Follette, Pinchot, and many Republicans of a progressive mind were sympathetic to Wilson's program. A few turned against him by 1916; many others by 1918; and by 1920 their abandonment was almost complete.

World War I and industrial mobilization were largely responsible for this time of trouble. Of deepest concern to the organized conservationists was this question: How disinterested, how patriotic, were the businessmen who came streaming into Wilson's government for the purpose of preparing the nation for war? In the attitude of conservationists toward dollar-a-year men one finds new evidence that their aims went far beyond the mere prevention of waste. They were concerned with problems of men against money, with profiteering, with economic justice, with maintaining democracy. By these standards Wilson qualified, at the least, as a moderate conservationist. He believed that leasing laws opening western lands to development must be passed; that the war (creating new demands for petroleum and other resources) made a solution most urgent; and that a compromise doing justice to all parties could be effected. Wilson was cautious and showed a wariness about the possibility of profiteering and corruption under cloak of war. . . .

One effect of the southern leadership in the Wilson administration was to stimulate sectional rivalries, with some important effects upon conservation. The western states resisted at first a federal program for the public lands while eastern and southern leaders were forcing the issue. . . .

The organized conservationists from the start had resisted as best they could the regional prejudices that might reduce their influence on policy or disrupt their plans in Congress. Nevertheless, as advocates of a withdrawal policy they had to face intrenched hostility from many western interests. The conservationists were of course convinced that their policies benefited the western people, as distinguished from the big interests. They were correct in asserting, as Pinchot did, that "monopolistic control was infinitely more potent in the West . . . than in the East." It was in this region of the enterprising pioneer and the free individual that the special interests attained their most ruthless power. . . .

The West, however, was always divided. Men like Representative William Kent and Governor George C. Pardee of California, Judge Ben Lindsey of Colorado, Senator John B. Kendrick of Wyoming, and Governor Joseph M. Dixon of Montana were in the conservationist camp. The trend in the Progressive Era was conservationist. Roosevelt's dramatic flair was combined with Pinchot's incessant labors for the cause. It was formidable propaganda for the justice, wisdom, and democracy of the federal government's program. Western senators and representatives, who had been almost unanimous against the land withdrawals, who favored the old policy of gift and sale, slowly had to recognize the handwriting on the wall. Public sentiment had come to favor the forest reserves, the government retention of mineral areas and water power sites, and an active federal policy. . . .

The Northeast and the Southeast, in effect, were able at last to force a leasing system upon the West. The passage of the Water Power Act and the Mineral Leasing Act of 1920 inaugurated a new policy of continuing public ownership and federal trusteeship in which conservation and the national interest seemed to be the winners. . . . The leasing laws of 1920 grew, however, from a long struggle, involving many people who remembered clearly the controversies of the recent past. To separate this and other conservation issues from the pall of suspicions and hatreds in 1918–1921 is impossible. . . .

Conservation had arrived at a crisis in 1920–1921 more serious than its adherents suspected. Their achievements were not quite so momentous nor so unshakeable as they liked to believe. Political partisanship had become intensified; co-operation between northerners and southerners in behalf of conservation had been rendered more difficult. Albert B. Fall and others who shared his views were moving into positions of responsibility. Many honest men during the 1920's declared for a watered-down version of conservation almost synonymous with business efficiency or gave serious consideration to plans for turning public lands over to the states. Business organizations appropriated, with more or less sincerity, the word "conservation." If ever an opportunity afforded itself for the rejection of Pinchot's ideals concerning democracy in resource use, this was the time.

Conservation not only survived the 1920's; it emerged in some respects stronger than ever. William Kent had observed in 1919 that the conservation principles were gaining acceptance all over the West and that, moreover, many of the ideals growing out of this movement were affecting sentiment in all directions. His own work in conservation had been of all his efforts the most satisfying and constructive. In 1923 Governor Joseph M. Dixon of Montana, the old "Bull Mooser" then engaged in a bitter struggle against the Anaconda Copper Company, remarked on the growing popularity of the conservation policy. Even its enemies in the West were being converted, he wrote to Pinchot. .   .

RICHARD POLENBERG

Conservation and Reorganization: The Forest Service Lobby, 1937-1938

Political ideology, public opinion, the activity of pressure groups, the personal element ·and the bureaucrat all play a part in policy formation and legislative outcomes in Washington. Here Richard Polenberg describes the effort made during the New Deal to transform the Department of the Interior into a Department of Conservation and to transfer the Forest Service from the Department of Agriculture to the new agency. The historical antecedents and the variety of interests involved in the controversy over transfer make the story a classic illustration of conservation lobbying.

The controversy over the Forest Service was one of the most difficult administrative problems which confronted President Franklin D. Roosevelt. The Forest Service had been placed in the Department of Agriculture in 1905, but shortly after Harold Ickes entered the Cabinet he hoped to restore it to the Department of the Interior. Ickes appears to have been motivated by an ambition to increase his power and prestige, by a sincere belief that he could succor the cause of conservation, and by a desire to build up public confidence in his department. Ickes' efforts, however, met with stiff opposition from Secretary of Agriculture Henry A. Wallace and many conservation organizations. The interdepartmental rivalry sometimes flared into the open; in 1935 and 1936 spokesmen for the Department of Agriculture denounced Ickes' stratagems for acquiring the Forest Service and tried to stir up Congressional opposition to them.

The clash was intensified in January 1937 when Roosevelt proposed an extensive reorganization of executive agencies. His plan was based upon a report by the President's Committee on Administrative Management, headed by Louis Brownlow. The committee, in recommending far-reaching changes in government administration, urged that the De-

SOURCE: Abridged from Richard Polenberg, "Conservation and Reorganization: The Forest Service Lobby, 1937–1938," *Agricultural History*, XXXIX (October, 1965), 230–239. Reprinted by permission of *Agricultural History* and Richard Polenberg.

partment of the Interior become a Department of Conservation and that the President be given broad authority to transfer agencies from one department to another. Both Ickes and Wallace recognized that the Brownlow plan would inevitably mean transfer of the Forest Service. Ickes noted that if reorganization went through, the Forest Service would be placed in his new department. "That will prevent overlapping and clashing and jealousies in the future," he added. When Wallace learned of the Brownlow report he warned the President that any reorganization plan which removed Forestry from Agriculture would "excite the serious opposition of the agricultural, wild life, forest conservation, and other organizations which have been and are now so vitally interested in this question."

Wallace proved to be prophetic. The proposed transfer had encountered resistance in the past, but never was the Forest Service lobby so active and well-organized as in 1937 and 1938. Mustering support throughout the country, especially in the West, it inspired an avalanche of angry resolutions and letters which brought unremitting pressure on Congress. . . .

The Forest Service lobby was composed of disparate elements that wanted to preserve the status quo for various, even conflicting reasons. Five distinct groups united to form the lobby: professional foresters in the Forest Service, the Society of American Foresters, and the Association of State Foresters; lay conservation groups such as the American Forestry Association and the Izaak Walton League; farm organizations such as the National Grange and the American Farm Bureau Federation; the lumber industry through the National Lumber Manufacturer's Association and the West Coast Lumberman's Association; and the grazing interests through the National Livestock Association and the National Woolgrowers' Association. Diverse aims dictated their action, but these groups stood together against transfer of the Forest Service. . . .

Several common assumptions linked the friends of the Forest Service. They believed that, as a crop, trees logically belonged in the Department of Agriculture. "A forest is a crop, and forestry is uniformly classed as a branch of agriculture," said Pinchot in 1911, and his disciples never deviated from the faith. They argued that all organic resources—things that grew—should be in Agriculture; only inorganic resources—coal, gas, oil and minerals—should be in Interior. To divide the forests on the basis of ownership, by giving commercial forests to Agriculture and national forests to Interior, would create an "artificial distinction which has no existence in nature," and do untold damage. More pragmatic arguments also were brought forth. The Forest Service seemed to be functioning well. "Why rock the boat?" asked Pinchot. Then again, reorganization might open the Forest Service to political appointments, and undermine the professional esprit de corps built up by strict adherence to the merit system. Moreover, separating the science of forestry from the technical research facilities of the Department of Agriculture would be disastrous. Creating a department of "conservation," argued Henry Wallace, made no more sense than creating a department of "integrity." . . .

The antagonism of those conservationists who backed the Forest Service stemmed, in part, from a nearly pathological distrust of the Interior Department. The memory of Richard Ballinger still lingered, and they recalled all too clearly Albert Fall's pursuit of the Forest Service under President Harding. . . .

Professional foresters also vigorously attempted to thwart the transfer. In part, their opposition represented normal bureaucratic resistance to change. One observer asserted that "the present anti-transfer fight smacks too much of bureaucratic self interest." Foresters had established close bonds with their associates in Agriculture. To Pinchot, the Interior Department under the "Chicago lawyer" Ickes, seemed citified and effete. Pinchot believed that he remembered how Interior Department foresters had behaved; one, "a tenderfoot of tenderfeet, utterly ignorant of the West, wore a white tie and shawl, and was afraid to go farther into the Forest . . . than the end of the stage line." Some intensely disliked Ickes. One West Coast forester wanted "to be in on the kill if . . . our friend Ickes has exposed the right part of his anatomy for punishment." The Forest Service feared that its traditional autonomy would be lost in Interior. Pinchot believed that Interior "is the most centralized Department in the Government, and Ickes is the worst centralizer among all the Secretaries of the Interior in the last forty years." It seemed unlikely that Ickes would sanction the independence to which foresters had been accustomed since 1905.

In addition, the Forest Service and Interior held conflicting philosophies of land management; the former stressed use and renewal, the latter stressed enjoyment and removal. Pinchot and his disciples believed in cutting trees scientifically, so that new trees would, in time, replace them. To them, conservation meant rational planning to promote the use and development of natural resources. They did not want to withdraw resources from use, but to ensure that they were used wisely. The Interior Department, as administrator of the national parks, leaned to the view that forests should be preserved for aesthetic enjoyment and recreation. Ickes' department did not, of course, reject the use of natural resources; but it was much more reluctant to cut down trees hundreds of years old to obtain timber than was the Forest Service. . . . The conflict between Interior and Agriculture was but one phase of a struggle between aesthetic and utilitarian conservationists which had existed since the time of Theodore Roosevelt. . . .

The arguments against transfer appear to be shot through with contradictions. Many conservationists, with an eye to the past, objected to giving the national forests to Interior because they feared renewed spoliation; yet the foresters opposed the transfer precisely because Interior might carve more parks out of existing national forests and restrict economic utilization. Indeed, the line between the two groups sometimes seemed indistinct, and men like Pinchot employed both arguments. Still, the controversy helps to account for the support tendered the Forest Service by the lumbering and grazing interests.

Over the years, lumber operators had developed a high regard for the Forest Service. Once initial suspicion vanished, the industry recognized that foresters were not inimical, but sympathetic. . . . Progressive lumbermen saw eye to eye with the Forest Service view of resource utilization. Both resisted the extension of national parks. . . . Also, the decentralization of the Forest Service proved conducive to good relations. National forest officials were usually men of long acquaintance, who identified with local interests and were subject to local pressures. The lumber industry knew where it stood with the Forest Service.

Similar bonds united the Forest Service with the grazing interests. . . . Fear that Interior would introduce a sweeping program of resource withdrawal also obsessed the grazing industry. The position of the National Woolgrowers' Association reflected this apprehension:

Mining, grazing, and sportsmen interests alike are fearful of the proposed transfer of the National Forests because they know that such a move would remove once and for all the main barriers to unlimited expansion of the National Parks, which in turn would automatically eliminate future use of national-forest lands for prospecting, grazing use, and hunting.

The industry opposed reorganization because it suspected that "an immediate extension of National Parks would result from the transfer of the Forest Service to the Interior Department."

The partiality of lumbermen and stockmen toward the Forest Service naturally gave rise to charges of collusion. "The exploiters of our forests," snorted Ickes, "want to choose the policemen to protect the forests." But to picture the Forest Service as toadying to these interests would be erroneous. Ferdinand A. Silcox, appointed Chief of the Forest Service in 1933, supported use rather than removal, but antagonized the industry by advocating strict federal control of timber cutting. . . .

Professional foresters, the timber and grazing industries, and many conservationists opposed transfer of the Forest Service for a variety of reasons. The opposition of farm groups is more difficult to explain. Their stance may have reflected the interlocking leadership of farm and forestry associations; it may have represented a natural loyalty to the Department of Agriculture. Moreover, the practical autonomy enjoyed by the Forest Service tended to enhance the influence of special interest groups, such as the National Grange. Still, the position of farm groups seemed puzzling. "Just why the American Farm Bureau Federation should take such an interest in the matter of the reorganization of the Government is a mystery to me," wrote Senator Josiah Bailey of North Carolina. He suggested to the president of the Federation that it might "be much better for the cause you represent if you would concentrate upon farm legislation."

Nevertheless, leaders of the major farm organizations joined with spokesmen for forestry and conservation groups to create a powerful lobby. The Forest Service lobby performed a dual function: to build up local sentiment against the transfer, and to mobilize this sentiment in the form of petitions and personal appeals to Congressmen. Moreover, the lobby served as a "catalytic pressure group"; it coordinated the activities of the various factions opposing the transfer and charted in broad outline their strategy. It enlisted the aid of Gifford Pinchot and, for a time, of the Department of Agriculture itself; a professional lobbyist named Charles Dunwoody directed daily operations. The lobby concentrated most of its efforts on 11 western states with large national forests. . . .

Dunwoody received the fervid support of the General Federation of Women's Clubs. Counting two million members, the Federation was a potent force and Emily G. Bogert, its conservation chairman, backed the Forest Service to the hilt. . . .

Gifford Pinchot also swung into action. His reputation gave him access to many legislators, and he used it to full advantage. . . .

Pinchot, Dunwoody, and the women's clubs were joined by the Department of Agriculture itself. Wallace's department, as part of the executive branch, could not openly attack the Chief Executive's program. Torn between duty and desire, it followed a checkered course. . . .

All this opposition brought to life the minority of conservationists who endorsed reorganization. On November 4, 1937, Richard Lieber, president of the National Conference of State Parks, confided: "I am at this time engaged in a quiet manner to win over a number of my editor friends and strengthen the attitude of others respecting the Reorganization bill." . . . They wished to combat the propaganda issued by the Forest Service lobby; more specifically, they hoped "to set up an effective organization" to promote a Department of Conservation. They conferred with the President in December, and then set about publicizing their view. But their efforts did not convince many.

The effectiveness of the Forest Service lobby could be measured in the mailrooms of the House and Senate office buildings. Congressmen from the South and West were bombarded. . . .

When Congress returned in January 1938, Dunwoody stepped up his activity. He asked that volunteers come to Washington to help influence Congressmen, and warned his supporters to "be prepared to meet any *surprise move* for the Department of Conservation plan." On February 12 the surprise move occurred: the Senate Reorganization Committee voted to strike out the Department of Conservation. Rather than hailing this as a victory, the forestry lobby chose to go on with the struggle. . . . As the Senate moved toward a vote, Dunwoody remained confident: "We are heading into the last round-up and things look exceedingly good."

Dunwoody's euphoria was soon shattered. On March 22 the Senate rejected an amendment designed to exempt the Forest Service from transfer by a vote of 50-33. Even worse, only 10 Senators from the 11 Western states supported the amendment; 10 voted against it, and 2 were absent. What had gone wrong? The elimination of the Department of Conservation had undermined the lobbyists in two ways. First, it allowed the Administration to make verbal promises not to transfer Forestry, which satisfied many Senators. . . . Second, it permitted Henry Wallace to come out for the bill, since no transfer was necessarily implied. Wallace seemed willing to take his chances if the bill passed without a Department of Conservation. . . .

Although the Senate passed the modified reorganization bill, it went down to defeat in the House on April 8 by the narrow margin of 204–196. . . . Western Republicans would have voted against the measure in any event; of the Democrats from Western states, 25 voted for the bill and only 9 voted against it. Still, the Forest Service lobby had played a crucial role in the conflict over reorganization. Given the closeness of the vote, Dunwoody could have determined the outcome by swinging only four doubtful votes. Also, the lobby had been instrumental in killing the proposed Department of Conservation. Moreover the Administration's promise not to transfer the Forest Service meant that the lobby had been successful.

During the 1930's few observers managed to view the transfer issue in proper perspective. Conservation societies devoted so much effort to denouncing Roosevelt's plan of reorganization that they often lost sight of—or took for granted—the Administration's many contributions to their cause. Moreover, in their zeal to protect the position of one administrative agency, the groups which comprised the Forest Service lobby blocked the creation of an executive department which, in the long run, could have provided leadership and coherence for the conservation movement.

·4·

SAMUEL P. HAYS

Conservation and the Structure of American Politics: The Progressive Era

In 1959, Samuel P. Hays published *Conservation and the Gospel of Efficiency: The Progressive Conservation Movement, 1890–1920,* in which he emphasized the importance of technical experts in the leadership of the Conservation Movement during the early twentieth century, the commitment of these men to the principle of efficiency and their emphasis on developing rational methods of resource utilization. In this selection he summarizes his position and suggests also that conservation politics must be understood as an illustration of fundamental developments in American political life, particularly the "tension between centralizing and decentralizing tendencies."

The conservation movement has long provided grist for the historian's mill as a prime example of "progressivism." "Progressivism," so the argument goes, consisted of a public reaction in the early 20th century against the domination of public affairs by an alliance of greedy businessmen and selfish politicians. In many facets of public life, the coalition of politicians and businessmen had distorted public values, thwarted public impulses and created an arena of politics that was removed from public control. The reaction against this state of affairs came on an equally

SOURCE: © 1969, Samuel P. Hays. Reprinted by permission of Samuel P. Hays.

broad variety of fronts: reforms in municipal government, federal regulation of private business, laws to improve the conditions of workingmen. Through such innovations the public exercised control over private business affairs, thereby assuring that they be conducted in the "public interest."

The exploitation of natural resources was a major example of the misdeeds of private enterprise. Lumbermen cut timber with no thought for the morrow; private power companies developed rivers for their own benefit; cattlemen on the public range drove out the honest homesteader; mining companies plundered the reserves of ore without thought of the long-run public interest. The movement to preserve natural resources, which came to be called the conservation movement, therefore, constituted a means of public control of undesirable private enterprise. A whole range of public actions—executive orders and congressional legislation—were the accomplishments of the movement: establishment of the national forests and the U.S. Forest Service, development of the national park system, establishment of federal irrigation works, the public regulation of private hydroelectric power production, the retention of the public lands in public ownership and their controlled development under the Department of the Interior. An equally wide range of colorful battles and personalities enlivened the movement: the dramatic executive orders of President Theodore Roosevelt in establishing a host of national forests before Congress could act to prevent it; the colorful battle between ex-U.S. Forester Gifford Pinchot and Secretary of the Interior Richard Ballinger; the quiet lease of oil lands to private companies which led to the celebrated Teapot Dome scandal of the 1920's.

This interpretation of the conservation movement has been transferred directly from the movement's ideology to the historical literature. It constituted the movement's self-conception, and liberal historians— those who interpret history as a long struggle between business and its opponents—have taken it over as an accurate description of the past. But the ideologies of social movements, geared to combat in the arena of public opinion and public action, cannot be taken so readily as an accurate description of the times. Those ideologies, though crucial elements of social movements, without which they cannot be understood, describe reality only through a limited angle of vision. History requires a broader perspective. Liberal historians, in fact, have become a captive of "progressive" ideology in their treatment of the "progressive" movement, and of conservation ideology in their treatment of the conservation movement. We must move beyond the ideological perspective of conservation before it can be understood.

Let us first shift from the logical content of the laws, the statements of public policy, the administrative decisions and the judicial interpretations, and the publicly debated ideas to the people in the movement. Let us root a drive for political change in the situation and circumstances of those who spearheaded change. For history is the story of people and not of policies or ideas abstracted from human beings and human circumstance. If this be done, the most striking characteristic of the conservation leaders was their commitment to the efficiency, the rationality, and system of modern technological life. Despite their preachments against waste, they were not Malthusian prophets of doom and gloom, but were swayed by the vision of the possibilities of applying science to modern life, and, in this instance, to the care and development of natural resources. They were highly optimistic about the future; they were committed to the physical development of the material base of American society; and they had found the key in science, technology and efficiency. They spoke their faith in efficiency as a gospel heralding the new day for America.

The conservation movement, therefore, must be understood as a phase of the impulse in modern science and technology for precision, efficiency, order and system. One must trace conservation leaders not to a mass public from which they hopefully sought political support, but to the scientific societies, the technical training, the evolving administrative systems and the practice of efficient management which constituted the climate within which these leaders lived and from which they brought the spirit of efficiency to the field of resource management. From this background arose ideas about sustained-yield forest management, multiple-purpose river development, classification of lands and scientific land use, the wisdom of resource development within "preserved" park lands. From the same sources came ideas about how decisions should be made and who should make them, certainly not by means of inefficient log-rolling in Congress, the give and take of competing political demands, but by the systematic adjustment of rival uses to create the most efficient development of water, land and minerals. Scientists and technicians who knew what was best as measured by a standard of efficiency should prevail over politicians who thought primarily of the limited and selfish private interests among their constituents.

The forward thrust of the conservation movement was rooted not in the public at large, not in a mass base, but in a relatively small number of articulate public leaders. There is considerable evidence, for example, that an organized conservation movement was an utter failure in enrolling large numbers of members, despite the efforts of such leaders as

Gifford Pinchot to do so. Time and again, in fact, those leaders sought the refuge of executive action, freed from the limitations of Congressional influence or public opinion, realizing that their best bet lay in a sympathetic President rather than a relatively unsympathetic Congress or an indifferent public. From their political philosophy emerges not a faith in mass involvement in decision-making, but a fear of it and the desire to insulate efficiency from political impulses in the wider society. "Democracy" and the "public" to them, in fact, referred far more to equality in the benefits of the economic and political system than to equality of involvement in making public decisions.

If the forward thrust of the conservation movement was the establishment of efficiency and system in the rational use of resources, what of the opposition? For many years that opposition has been described simply as "selfish" private enterprise. But this is far too simple a notion. It seems clear, for example, that segments of the large private corporate systems of business enterprise shared with conservationists their zeal for large-scale centralized efficient management. But it seems clear also that the opposition is best described as a wide range of particularistic resource users who preferred that use conform to their immediate concerns rather than to the demands of an overall system. Standing at the opposite pole of the political spectrum to the conservationists were irrigators and shippers on the inland waterways; homesteaders, sheepmen and cattlemen; big game hunters and park and recreation enthusiasts; landowners whose property would be inundated by reservoirs and landowners who sought protection from floods. Each of these resource users was concerned with a particular resource problem to which he sought a particular and separate solution. And he wished to influence that decision, rather than simply permit an efficiency expert in Washington to make it.

A striking example of the tension between competing users occurred on the public lands. For decades the public range had been fought over by cattlemen, sheepmen and homesteaders. Now cattlemen sought to stabilize the range and balance the annual forage growth and the number of cattle, thereby preserving an adequate and continuous supply of feed. But this required controlled use to make sure that the range was not overstocked. In cooperation with resource planners in Washington cattlemen worked out a system of range management which would guarantee a sustained yield of forage based upon control of the number of animals using it. But sheepmen, often migratory and moving across wide areas of range land, complained that this favored the resident cattleman who had staked out a prior-use claim to the land. Homesteaders also objected since they wished to move into former grazing lands to carve out permanent homesteads. But that was not all. Game hunters felt entitled to their share as well; they wished large areas of the public lands to be reserved from other uses—sheep, and cattle grazing and homesteading—and for their particular use. How to decide amid these competing users? Conservationists would do it by some precise calculus of maximum benefit determined by scientists and technicians. But to range users this would shift the location of decision-making beyond their capacity to influence it. They preferred the more open process of legislative combat and log-rolling so as to gain as large a share for their type of use as possible.

Controversy over the range indicates dramatically how inadequate the liberal interpretation of the conservation movement has been. It was the large cattle owners in the West, organized in state associations who worked closely with range management experts—conservationists—to establish a system of controlled range land use. They had a sympathetic ear in the old Bureau of Forestry and its successor, the U.S. Forest Service; after working out the details of range management for lands within the national forests, they proposed a similar system to cover all the remaining public lands, then under the jurisdiction of the Department of the Interior. But the opposition was too great; when it was presented to Congress the plan received short shrift. The demands of competing users as expressed through elected representatives overcame the combination of cattlemen and conservationists. In this case it seems clear that the small property owner succeeded in blunting the thrust of systematization, efficiency and centralization.

A similar tension between planners and users arose in the treatment of river development. The vision of multiple-purpose river development was highly attractive. For the most part the waters in the nation's rivers flowed to the sea unused by man. They were not harnessed for navigation, for hydroelectric power, for irrigation; moreover, uncontrolled they wreaked havoc in periodic floods across the country. But modern engineering could change all this. The construction of large works, dams, locks, floodwalls and ditches would bring about the means to control the flow of rivers, store the water in months of heavy rainfall and release it according to plan throughout the remainder of the year. From a wide variety of sources, from engineering societies and electric power companies, from the U.S. Army Corps of Engineers and irrigation developers in the West, from shippers in cities on the inland waterways to owners of riparian lands came the demand that large-scale river development be undertaken. By the first decade of the 20th century these demands had converged upon the federal government; they added up to one of the most influential political forces in federal resource policy.

But how to develop rivers? Here, again, resource planners were convinced that one overall viewpoint should dominate, that river development involved the reconciliation of competing uses by means of precise, expert, calculations, that the river and its tributaries comprised one unit which should be subject to one system for maximum, efficient development. Competition in water use was a severe problem. Those most concerned with floods wished public works to be built so as to provide maximum benefit for them. The irrigator wished water to be released for his needs, the user of hydroelectric power for his, and the navigator for his. If any one use dominated, so the resource planner argued, the maximum use for all would be compromised; multiple-use became the watchword, an overall plan of balanced use which added up to the maximum possible utilization, taking all needs into account. The concept of multiple-purpose river development, with its centralized direction and reconcilation of competing uses by experts was increasingly thrust forward in the first decade of the 20th century. Few of these proposals reached the conceptual perfection desired by the most ardent planners.

Multiple-purpose river development ran aground the same kinds of political forces as did scientific land management. Particular kinds of users sought to influence public policy in their direction. The first to succeed were those interested in irrigation who had secured a law as early as 1902, the Newlands Act, to provide federal funds for irrigation development in the West. Next were the shippers on the inland waterways of the Ohio and the Mississippi. Thwarted in the first decade of the century they began to secure a more sympathetic hearing in Congress after 1910 and a number of river development projects emphasizing navigation ensued. Those concerned with flood control on the lower Mississippi secured their demands in 1917. But an overall program of river development, with elements of multiple-purpose planning, a measure pushed for years by Senator Newlands of Nevada, failed when the Water Power Act of 1920 preempted the field for single-purpose development.

Such are some of the details of conflicts over conservation policy. How are we to understand them? Do they reflect simply issues of public control of private enterprise as liberal historians have argued? To this writer, the answer is clearly that they do not. In fact, one must scrap entirely the framework, the mode of thinking, the ideological categories of traditional liberal history and reassemble the past in entirely new patterns of thought. It is customary in liberal historiography to focus heavily on the public nature of federal regulation of private business. Their very assertion of the public will, the public interest, stamped such measures as part of the movement which ran counter to private enterprise. Yet there were forces far more fundamental at work in American society than this. To grasp them we must shift attention from conservation as simply a public policy and see it as a significant element in the evolution of the political structure of modern America. Behind the substance of programs, of sustained-yield forestry, multiple-purpose river development and efficient land management, behind the drama of events and decisions in Congress and the executive branch lay an unfolding pattern of political relationships. We should be concerned not just with those events and decisions, not with the way in which political forces generated a given result, but with the way in which those events and decisions can provide an opportunity to establish the patterns of forces which constitute the larger system.

Looked at this way, conservation, with its interplay between the centralizing tendencies of systematization and expertise on the one hand and decentralization and localism on the other, provides considerable insight into the larger processes of centralization and decentralization of which it is typical. One can conceive of these forces as poles of a continuum. On the one hand many aspects of human endeavor were bound up with the daily routines of job, home, religion, recreation and education which focus on inter-personal relationships within relatively small geographical, local, areas. These contexts of experience involve personal interaction, personal communication, a sense of consciousness and experience limited by specific locality, the desire to remain separate from the larger forces of society, and preference for a political system which provides considerable autonomy and influence for geographically organized sub-groups. On the other hand, modernization gives rise to larger patterns of human interaction, to ties extending over wide geographical areas, to corporate systems which integrate far-flung activities, to impersonal means of communication and impersonal forms of understanding, to the use of expertise and to centralization in the process of decision-making.

The dominant trend was toward centralization. In the early 20th century many were drawn to the manifest characteristics of this process—efficiency, expertise, order—and called it "progressivism." Looking back the political historian emphasizes two major forms of this process, systematization and functional organization. Systematization refers to the dovetailing of human relationships into interdependent activities, into more tightly knit and often centrally directed patterns. In some cases this process took place in consciously directed ventures, corporate systems—both public and private—planned efforts to bring together many resources into one venture for pre-conceived ends. But system developed in other ways as well, especially out of the daily choices of millions of people who wished to participate in the conditions of life brought about by greater system which they considered beneficial: patronage at large-scale supermarkets rather than neighborhood grocery stores; subscription to the metropolitan newspaper and listening to the large-city radio rather than local media with their emphasis on life of the small community. But no matter from what source, efficiency, expertise, system infused the entire order.

Functional organizations constituted an equally important aspect of the reordering of human relationships in modern society. They grew out of the ever-increasing specialization of the occupational structure, and the equally significant focus on the acquisition of specialized skills, especially white collar technical and professional skills, as preparation. for specialized occupations. These functional specializations cut many ways: farmers who produced different commodities, merchants who bought and sold different goods, manufacturers who produced different products, workers with different skills, professionals with different types of highly developed expertise. These specialized functions generated a vast network of new human relationships, of ties with others on the basis of common functions and common outlooks. A host of contacts developed which gave rise to organizations called trade associations, trade unions and commodity organizations. As the network of their economic affairs extended to ever wider circles so did their organizations and the conditions they sought to influence.

As a result of these new patterns of organization the location of decision-making shifted steadily away from the smaller levels of human interaction to the larger networks of life. A wide variety of developments in the late nineteenth and early twentieth centuries display this tendency: the shift from ward to city-wide representation in urban government and the concomitant increase in executive power; a similar upward shift from the rural township to the county and from the county to the state in matters of school and road administration; the growth of federal regulation, such as in railroad affairs, which increasingly overshadowed state regulation. At each level of governmental life the thrust toward an upward shift in affairs transformed decision-making institutions. These changes did not arise out of political theory or the inherent rightness of proper public policies or constitutional arrangements. They stemmed directly from the fact that those involved in the new corporate and functional systems of social organization and thereby in an increasingly broad network of human relationships, sought formal governmental systems which were in scope and applicability as broad as the scope of affairs they wished to influence and control. The upward movement of the location of decision-making in formal governmental institutions reflected directly the more general upward movement in the level of human affairs.

Not all segments of society participated to the same degree in this process of social change. Many segments, often most clearly identified as distinct geographical areas, were relatively uninvolved in the major thrust of change. Often they were reluctant participants, at times attracted by the benefits of modern development, ever hopeful of economic growth and prosperity, yet at the same time fearful of social change and of the potential dependence upon larger outside forces which they could not control. Thus, the more undeveloped sections of the nation, some in the rural areas of the East, but others consisting of entire sections of the nation such as the South and the West, reached out for the advantages of modern life but also resisted the external influences over their affairs which it entailed.

The forces of modernization and the resulting tension between centralizing and decentralizing tendencies occurred in a wide variety of contexts. Natural resource—conservation—policies constituted one of these. They involved both the extension of the new techniques of modernization —system, expertise, centralized direction and manipulation—and the activation of opposing forces at the more decentralized level. Conservation leaders sought to advance the spirit of "rational" use in resource development; they stressed efficiency, planning, the application of precise, technical knowledge to national problems. An integral part of this outlook was the preferable system of decision-making, consistent with the spirit of efficiency, a process by which the expert, not the elected representative, would make decisions in terms of the least wasteful dovetailing of all competing uses according to "objective," "rational," criteria. They sought to advance one system of making decisions, that inherent in the spirit of modern science and technology, for another, that inherent in the give-and-take among smaller contexts of life freely competing within the larger system.

Struggles over conservation policy brought into particularly sharp focus one aspect of this tension in the processes of decision-making— the conflict between federal and state authority. From one point of view the "state's rights" protest from the West against federal resource policy was simply a matter of political theory, another version of the struggle over federalism. But behind the debate over constitutional theory lay the tension between the underdeveloped West and the developed East. The West, an economically dependent region, faced particularly severe limitations of climate and transportation on its economic growth. Desperately requiring external sources of capital, both private and public, it courted federal assistance in development. At the same time, however, it bitterly resisted the resulting controls, the federal involvements in adjusting competing resource uses, the insistence that loans for irrigation works be repaid on schedule, and that the cost of land use management be paid for by user fees. In these controversies the states took the part of resource users in the West; the federal government spoke for the conservationists. But all this was merely a variant on the general tension which recurred in many forms throughout American society between divergent tendencies toward centralization and decentralization.

Conservation political struggles bring into focus two competing political systems in twentieth century America. On the one hand is the spirit of science and technology, of system and organization, of the specialization of management and the creation of a social structure separating out those who make decisions from those who have decisions made about them. This tendency shifted the location of decision-making continually upward so as to reduce drastically the range of impulses impinging upon the point of decision-making and to guide that process by means of large, cosmopolitan considerations, technical expertise, and the objectives implicit in the wider networks of modern life. These forces tended toward a more closed system of decision-making. On the other hand, however, were a host of political impulses, diffuse and often struggling against each other, often separate and conflicting, each striving for a larger share of influence within the political order. This welter of impulses sustained a more open political system, a wider range of alternatives open for choice, in which complex and difficult to understand expert knowledge possessed by only a few did not dominate the process of decision-making and the satisfaction of more limited impulses remained a constantly live characteristic of the political order.

The history of the conservation movement in the Progressive Era, therefore, sheds light not so much on the content of public policy but on the political structure of systematization, one of the most far reaching aspects of modern American history.

INDEX

Currency, Continental, 428
Currency laws, 456; see also Free silver,
 Greenbacks
Curtis, Benjamin R., 164, 167
Curtis, Edward J., 170
Curtis, Major General Samuel R., 131
Custer, George Armstrong, 115, 134

Daily Rocky Mountain News (Denver,
 Colorado), 132
Dairies, 53
Dakotas, 73, 81, 112, 139, 151, 169, 172,
 209, 394, 405, 449-51, 458-59, 593,
 see also North Dakota, South Dakota.
Dakota Indians, 102-07, 550, see also
 Sioux.
Dalmatian coast, 310
Daly, Marcus, 366
Dane, Nathan, 153, 158, 160
Danes, 433
Danhof, Clarence, 305
Daniel, Peter V., 166
Darwin, Charles, 72
Davenport, Iowa, 248
Davis, Benjamin O., Jr., 143
Davis, C. K., 450
Davis, H. L., 538
Davis, Jefferson, 59
Dawes, Severalty Act, 82-83, 549-52,
 556-57
Dead Sea, 507
Deadwood, South Dakota, 408
DeBarthe, Joe, 416
DeBow's Commercial Review, 59
Debtors, in class struggle, 474
Decentralization, as force in politics,
 618-21
Decision-making, 29, 620-21; in politics,
 619
Declaration of Independence, 153, 596
Deflation, in U.S. economy, 459-60
Deists, 490
Delaware, 175
Delaware Prophet, 549
Delaware River, 38
Democracy, 9-10, 20, 24, 26-30, 514,
 528, 600; in Europe, 9; in Australia,
 16; defined, 26
Democratic Party, 59, 170, 402, 462,
 602-03, 611; in Congress, 169, 172;
 convention, 1896, 251, 460
Democratic Review, 354
Denby, Edwin, 603
Denig, Edwin T., 343

Denver, 128, 131-32, 362, 367, 384-85,
 387, 441
Denver News, 417
DePillis, Mario S., 523
Depreciation Tracts, 191
Depressions, economic, 444, 457; 1819,
 183; 1837, 290, 399; in prairie agri-
 culture, 436; late nineteenth century,
 449-52; 1890's, 472; 1870's, 479;
 1930's, 590
Deprivation, of individuals on frontier,
 535-36; cultural, 549
Deseret, 507, 509
Desert Land laws, 185, 187, 412, 585
De Smet, Father Peter John, 489
Destler, Chester McArthur, 466-73
Detroit, 23, 240, 263, 330-32, 336
Devine, Andy, 539
DeVoto, Bernard, 117-21
Diggers, 20
Dillon, Montana, 119
Disciples of Christ, 494, 505
*Discovery, Settlement, and Present State
 of Kentucke,* 539
Disease, 449, 551
Dissenting religious sects, 511-16
Distilling, 428-29
District of Columbia, 162
Ditching, 399; tools, 413
Dixon, Joseph M., 118, 604-05
Dodge, William E., 68
Dodge City, Kansas, 393, 406
Domestic industries, 428
Donnel, William M., 199
Dowd, Douglas F., 298-301
Downes, Randolph C., 557-64
Dozier, Edward P., 573
Drainage, of farm land, 401, 437, 533
Dred Scott v. Sandford, 164-67
Drewyer (Drouillard), George, 118
Droughts, 444, 449, 451, 464
Drought resistant crops, 20
Dry farmers, 413
Dubuque, Iowa, 248
Du Chaiilu, Paul Belloni, 72
Dudley, Major N. A. M., 450
Dugouts, 451
Dulles, Foster Rhea, 57
Duluth, Minnesota, 240
Dunbar, Robert G., 437-42
Dunbar, William, 72
Dunwoody, Charles, 610, 611
Durkheim, Émile, 520
Dust bowl, 22

THE BOOK MANUFACTURE

The West of the American People was typeset by Kopecky Typesetting, Inc., offset printing and binding was by Kingsport Press. The paper is Perkins & Squier's Wove Antique. John Goetz designed the internal and cover design. The type in this book is Caledonia with Bodoni Bold display.